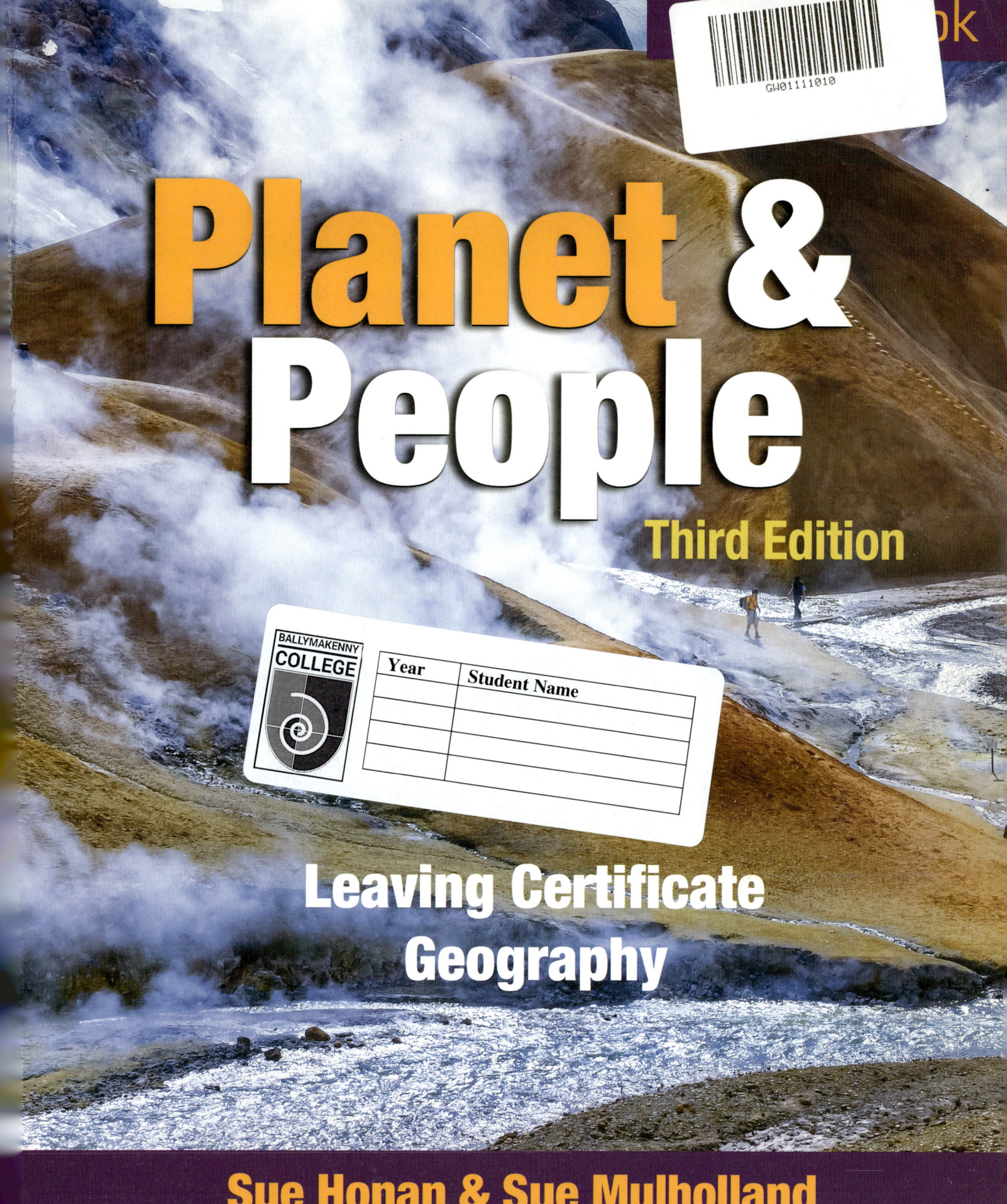

MENTOR BOOKS
43 Furze Road
Sandyford Industrial Estate
Dublin 18
Tel: 01-295 2112
Fax: 01-295 2114
Website: www.mentorbooks.ie
email: admin@mentorbooks.ie

All rights reserved

Edited by:	Treasa O'Mahony
Subject Editor:	Dr Tom Hunt
Typesetting:	Kathryn O'Sullivan
Cover photograph:	Thinkstock Photos
Cover Design:	Kathryn O'Sullivan
Illustrations:	Michael Phillips
	Christine Warner

The Publishers have made every effort to trace and acknowledge the holders of copyright for material used in this book. In the event of any copyright holder having been omitted, the Publishers will come to a suitable arrangement at the first opportunity.

ISBN: 978-1–909417-58-8
© Sue Honan, Sue Mulholland 2016

Contents

CORE UNIT: Patterns and Processes in the Physical Environment

Chapter 1	Plate Tectonics	7
Chapter 2	Earthquakes	26
Chapter 3	Volcanoes	40
Chapter 4	Folding and Faulting in the Earth's Crust	57
Chapter 5	Rock Types and their Formation	67
Chapter 6	Weathering and Erosion	84
Chapter 7	Rock Types and Landscapes	95
Chapter 8	Fluvial Processes, Patterns and Landforms	109
Chapter 9	Glacial Processes, Patterns and Landforms	143
Chapter 10	Coastal Processes, Patterns and Landforms	165
Chapter 11	Mass Movement Processes, Patterns and Landforms	192
Chapter 12	Isostacy and Eustacy (Higher Level)	206

CORE UNIT: Geographical Investigation and Skills

| Chapter 13 | OS Maps and Aerial Photos | 216 |
| Chapter 14 | Weather Maps, Satellite Images and Graphical Skills | 255 |

CORE UNIT: Regional Geography

Chapter 15	Physical, Administative and Cultural Regions	275
Chapter 16	Socio-Economic Regions	301
Chapter 17	An Irish Peripheral Region	316
Chapter 18	An Irish Core Region and an Irish City Region	337
Chapter 19	A European Peripheral Region	362
Chapter 20	A European Core and City Region	381
Chapter 21	Brazil – A Continental Region	399
Chapter 22	The Complexity of Regions	428

Dedication

This book is dedicated to:

Chris, Eleanor and Maedhbh Honan and
Gerard, Patricia and Eoghan Mulholland

Acknowledgements

The authors wish to thank Danny McCarthy, Kathryn O'Sullivan and Treasa O'Mahony of Mentor Books.

Arctic Refuge; Arigna Mining Experience; Ballymun Regeneration Project; Bear Mountaineering, Canada; Olga Beegan; Boliden Tara Mines; Bord Gáis; Bord Iascaigh Mhara; Brazilian Embassy, London; Bull Island Nature Reserve; Phil Callery; Jean Cantwell; John Carter; Central Statistics Office; Chuck de Mets; Karl Cikste; Clare County Council and Library; Ann Cleary; Clonmel Corporation; Coillte; Tony Collinson; Joanne Connolly; Cork City Council; Matt Corbett; Mary Coveney; Crag Caves; Daniel Deery; David Daly; Department of Agriculture; Department of Community, Rural and Gaeltacht Affairs; Discover Ireland; John Donnelly of Largo Foods; Mike Doukas, USGS; Dave Drew; Dublin Port Tunnel / Siobhan Maher; Dublin Regional Authority; Dublin Transportation Office; Jean Duffy; Dundalk County Council; Tony Dunne; EC/ECHO/Olivier Brouant; EC/ECHO/Nick Bridger; EC/ECHO South Asia Office; John and Maureen Enright; eriding.net; ESB; European Photo Services; European Commission; examvillage.com; Fáilte Ireland; Fingal County Council; German Embassy; Geokem.com; Guggenheim Museum, Bilbao; Greenpeace; Pat Hayes; Chris Honan; Heritage Council; IDA; *Irish Examiner*; JPL-Caltech; Junglephotos.com; Karst Working Group; Peter and Angela Kelly; John Lambe, Wexford County Council; Landau Forte College, UK; Peter W Lipman, USGS; Vincent McAlinden; Dermot McCarthy; Con McGinley; Billy and Mimi McNabb; Kevin, Paul and Will McNabb; Katriona Mahon; Tom Marmion; mayang.com; Met Éireann; Mid-East Regional Authority; Chris Miley; Frank Milling; Bruce F Molnia, USGS; Anne Marie Morgan; Gerry Morgan; Rory Mulholland; Anne Mulligan; Lisa Murphy; Brigid Murray; NASA; NOAA; Graham Neilan of the Department of Agriculture, Fisheries and Food; Olive O'Brien, Fáilte Ireland; Fiona O'Connor; Páraic Ó Náraigh; Office of the NDP; Ó Ingólfsson; Ordnance Survey Ireland; Joe O'Shaughnessy; Lisa O'Shaughnessy; Photos.com; Kevin Poe; Polishroots.org; Port of Bilbao; Gearoid Quinn, Merit Medical Ireland Ltd.; Red Bull Storm Chase; Readers Digest; Michael Redmond; Val Redmond; Brother Fred Rech; rpg.ie; Ian Sanders; Mike Simms; ski-dondiego.com; Oliver and Conor Seery; Ciara Spain; Staff and students at St Laurence College, Loughlinstown; Staff and students at St Mary's College, Dundalk; State Examination Commission; Gregory Takats, AusAID; *The Irish Times*; Teagasc; Trócaire; United States Geological Survey (USGS); UpTheDeise.com; USGS Cascades Volcano Observatory/Lyn Topinka; Oisín Van Gelderen; Sooz Wallace; Clare Walsh; Wexford County Council; Anita White; wicklowtoday.com

Introduction

In this third edition of the *Planet & People* **Core Book** we have:

Supplied **Digital Resources** for Teachers and Students using it as their class textbook. These resources reinforce the material in the textbook and provide helpful classroom materials for each chapter. They contain specific learning targets for each topic, Powerpoints, case studies, weblinks and worksheets for classroom, homework or revision use.

Used the **updated edition of the OSI's 1:50,000 maps** throughout the book to ensure students encounter the same maps in their textbook as they will on their Leaving Certificate Exam Paper.

Extensively modified the **Regional Geography** section focusing on and interlinking **factors** affecting the physical and human processes within and between dynamic regions, using **new icons** to indicate text which relates specifically to human or physical factors.

Updated the section on local government to ensure the **new division of regional authorities** is clearly explained (e.g. the **Northern and Western region** has replaced large parts of the **BMW region**).

Highlighted important **key terms, concepts and processes** throughout the text. These terms are designed to focus teaching, learning and literacy in the classroom and to **support students' self-directed learning** at home. A **glossary** of these terms is provided in our Digital Resources. The font and colour used to highlight the key terms were chosen to help students with visual disabilities to read them with greater ease.

Carefully updated statistics, photographs and aerial photographs and provided **exam-oriented** case studies. They provide important **significant relevant point (SRP)** material required in the Leaving Certificate exam. All case studies from previous editions of *Planet & People* are still available and can be found in the Digital Resources for each chapter @ mentorbooks.ie/resources.

Provided additional well-researched **weblinks** for each chapter. These helpful links give clear and relevant information on topics studied when and where necessary. They contain an **engaging variety** of animations, diagrams, photographs, maps, articles, PowerPoint presentations, and video clips to **support a range of learning styles**. They also provide an avenue for further research/investigation and **self-directed learning** increasing students' geographical awareness in a globalised world. The links can be accessed by clicking directly on the link when viewing the ebook or by going to the Weblinks document for each chapter in the **Digital Resources**.

A useful list of **skills** and **learning targets** is presented at the beginning of each chapter. **Higher Level only material** is clearly shown where relevant.

In the section on landform development, the syllabus requires students to choose one topic (rivers, ice, sea or mass movement) to study in detail. The extra material they need to cover is clearly marked in boxes labelled **In Depth**.

Important diagrams that students may be expected to draw in the Leaving Cert exam have helpful **Exam Diagram** labels. They are designed to be easily reproduced by students. **Geographical skills exercises** appear throughout the book, particularly in Chapter 14.

Chapter revision questions that test students' knowledge of the text are provided at the end of each chapter to reinforce literacy and numeracy. Higher and Ordinary Level questions are clearly marked. **Official State Exams Commission (SEC) questions** provide students with familiarity of terminology and experience in completing Leaving Cert exam questions.

This core book is carefully designed to **link closely** with the two Electives and the Optional Units. As a result, students will see the interaction between physical and human processes which will reinforce their knowledge of any topic they study.

Plate Tectonics

Key Theme

Forces within the earth create, alter and destroy landforms on the earth's surface.

Learning Outcomes

At the end of this chapter you will be able to:
- Describe and draw the internal structure of the earth.
- Explain the structure of the earth's crust.
- Describe and explain the tectonic cycle.
- Explain the theory of plate tectonics.
- Understand the formation of landforms associated with plate margins.

Contents

1.1	Introduction: The world beneath our feet	8
1.2	The internal structure of the earth	8
1.3	The theory of plate tectonics	10
1.4	Plate boundaries and their associated landforms	15
	Case Study 1: Sea-floor spreading in Iceland	16
	Case Study 2: The Hawaiian hotspot	20

Revision Space

Chapter Revision Questions – LC Exam Questions – Key Word List 23

CORE UNIT: PATTERNS AND PROCESSES IN THE PHYSICAL ENVIRONMENT

1.1 Introduction: The world beneath our feet

The surface of planet Earth is constantly changing. These changes may be due to **surface** (exogenic) forces such as weathering and erosion or **internal** (endogenic) forces such as moving magma. Internal and external forces combine constantly to produce the world we live in.

Fig. 1 Lava, a product of the earth's internal heat

Fig. 2 Cracks in a road following an earthquake

weblink
Tectonics of Planet Earth

1.2 The internal structure of the earth

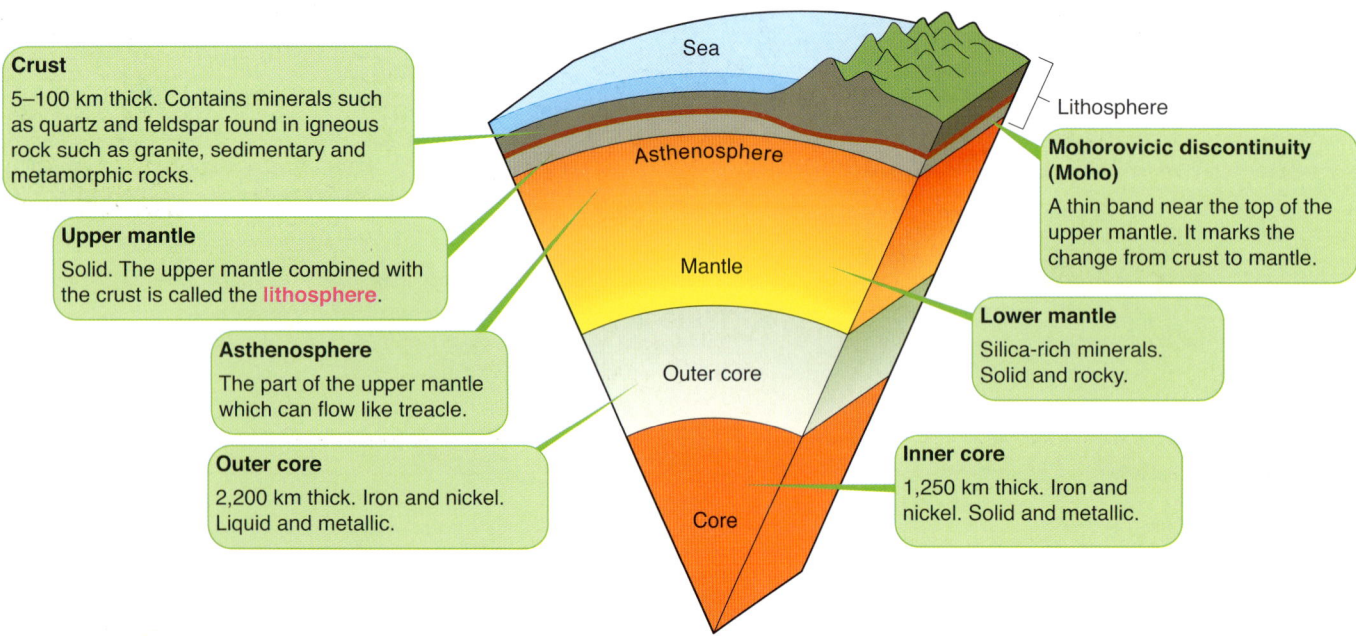

Crust
5–100 km thick. Contains minerals such as quartz and feldspar found in igneous rock such as granite, sedimentary and metamorphic rocks.

Upper mantle
Solid. The upper mantle combined with the crust is called the lithosphere.

Asthenosphere
The part of the upper mantle which can flow like treacle.

Outer core
2,200 km thick. Iron and nickel. Liquid and metallic.

Mohorovicic discontinuity (Moho)
A thin band near the top of the upper mantle. It marks the change from crust to mantle.

Lower mantle
Silica-rich minerals. Solid and rocky.

Inner core
1,250 km thick. Iron and nickel. Solid and metallic.

Fig. 3 View of the earth's layered structure. The distance from the surface to the centre of the earth is 6,378 km.

8

The earth's crust

The earth's solid crust is made of **continental crust** and **oceanic crust**, both of which 'float' on the mantle below. These two types of crust are carried about by huge convection currents which occur in a region of the upper part of the mantle called the **asthenosphere**, a hot zone where molten rock flows. Within the asthenosphere, heat is transferred upwards from the core by convection currents. These currents create the **tectonic cycle** where the crust moves and is split into large slabs of rock called **plates**.

These plates have oceans and continents on them, but some plates have both, e.g. North American and Eurasian plates. The zone where continental crust changes to oceanic crust on the same plate is called a **passive plate margin**. No earthquake or volcanic activity occurs at passive margins (see Fig. 4).

Oceanic crust
6–12 km thick. Dense, heavy rock, e.g. basalt. Younger than continental crust. Made of silicon- and magnesium-rich rocks.
Short name: SIMA

Continental crust
40–60 km thick. Less dense, light rocks, e.g. granite. Older than oceanic crust. Made of silicon- and aluminium-rich rocks.
Short name: SIAL

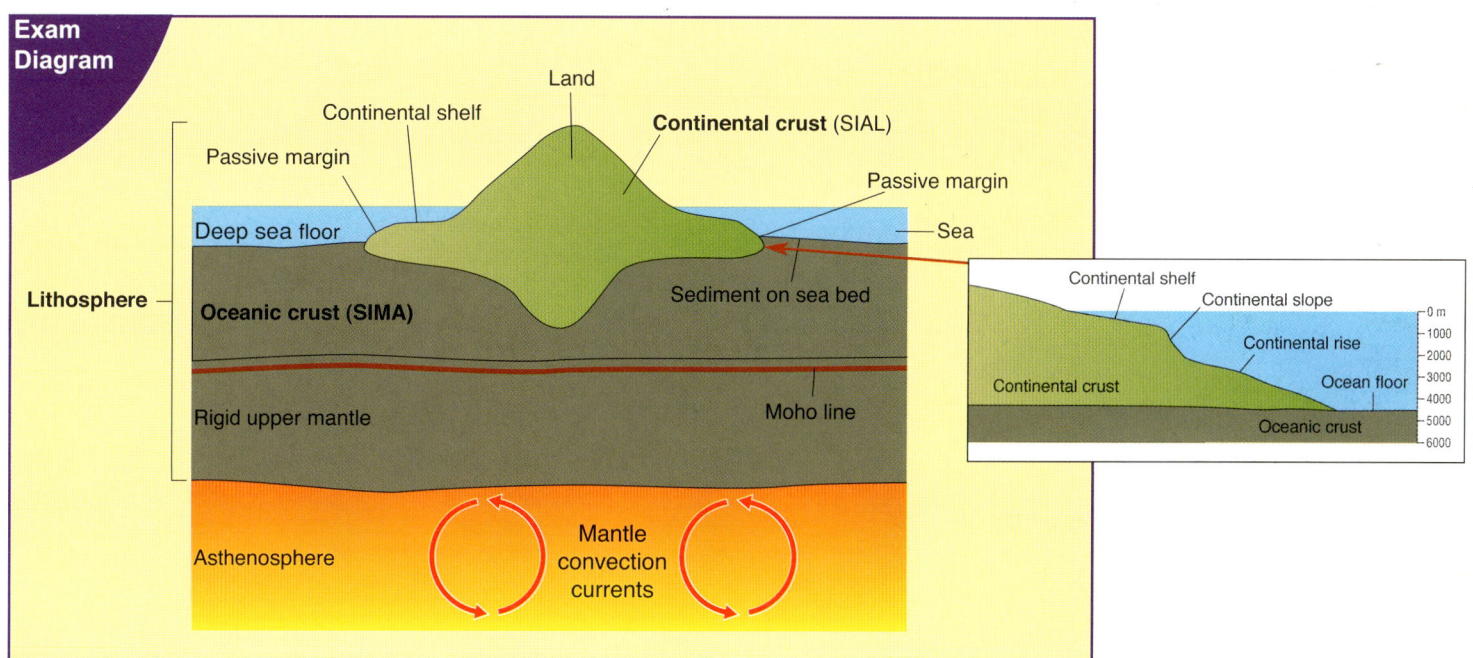

Fig. 4 The earth's crust

weblink
Convection currents

CORE UNIT: PATTERNS AND PROCESSES IN THE PHYSICAL ENVIRONMENT

1.3 The theory of plate tectonics

What is plate tectonics?

- **Plate tectonics** is the study of the processes that cause the movement of the earth's plates and the landforms that result.
- The theory of plate tectonics states that the earth's crust is broken into a dozen or more slabs of rock called plates.
- These plates carry the oceans and continents.
- The plates are in continual slow motion around the globe.
- Massive convection currents within the asthenosphere drive this motion.
- The convection currents drag the plates along as they circulate causing them to collide and separate. This is known as the tectonic cycle.

Fig. 5 The major crustal plates of the world

The theory of plate tectonics explains why earthquakes, volcanoes, fault lines and fold mountains occur in specific places in the world.

The plates collide, separate and slide past each other, all the while destroying, creating and modifying the crust. This is all part of the tectonic cycle.

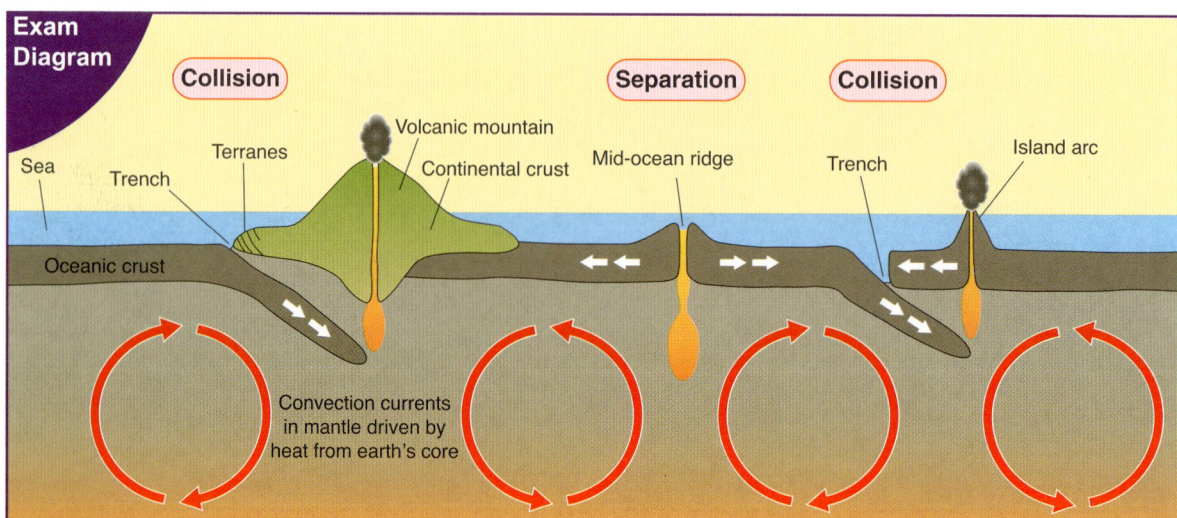

Fig. 6 The tectonic cycle: the continuous destruction and formation of the earth's crust at plate boundaries.

Development of the theory of plate tectonics

Continental drift – Wegener 1912

The basis for modern plate tectonic theory was proposed by Alfred Wegener in 1912. Wegener believed the earth was once one large landmass which he called **Pangaea** (all land). He stated that Pangaea split into two large continents called **Gondwanaland** and **Laurasia**. With time these then split into the landmasses and oceans we see today. He called this **continental drift**.

Wegener based his theory on the evidence listed below:
1. The distribution of identical fossils around the world.
2. Matching mountain trends and rock types on continents separated by thousands of miles of sea (Scandinavia and the Appalachians in the USA).
3. Matching coastline shape (Africa and South America).

weblink
Continental drift

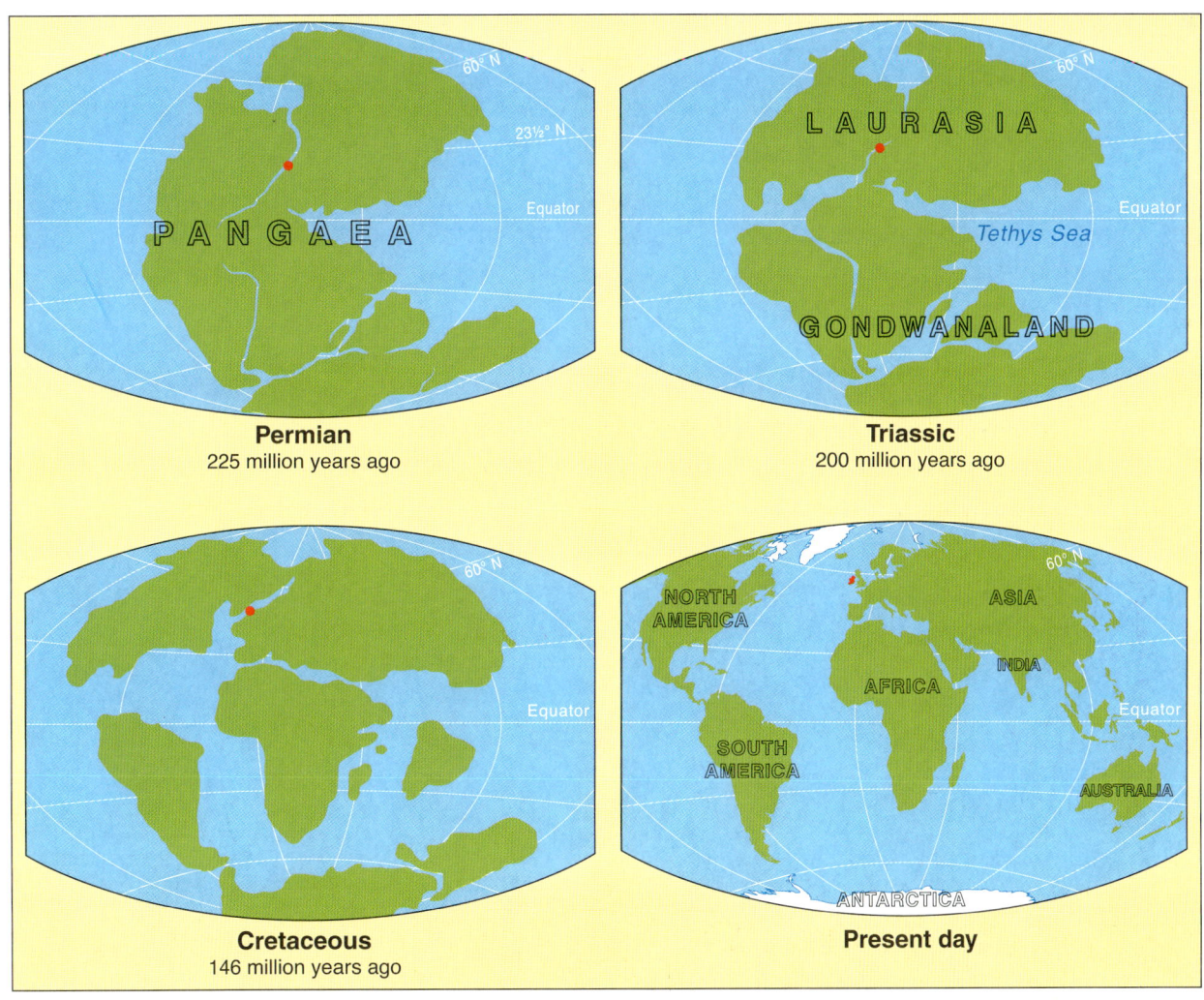

Fig. 7 The movement of the continents by continental drift over the last 225 million years. The red dot indicates the position of Ireland.

At first most scientists did not accept Wegener's theory because he could not explain how the continents moved. However he was convinced, and continued to collect data in support of his ideas. He died while on expedition in Greenland trying to prove his theory. Today the idea of continents moving around is widely accepted.

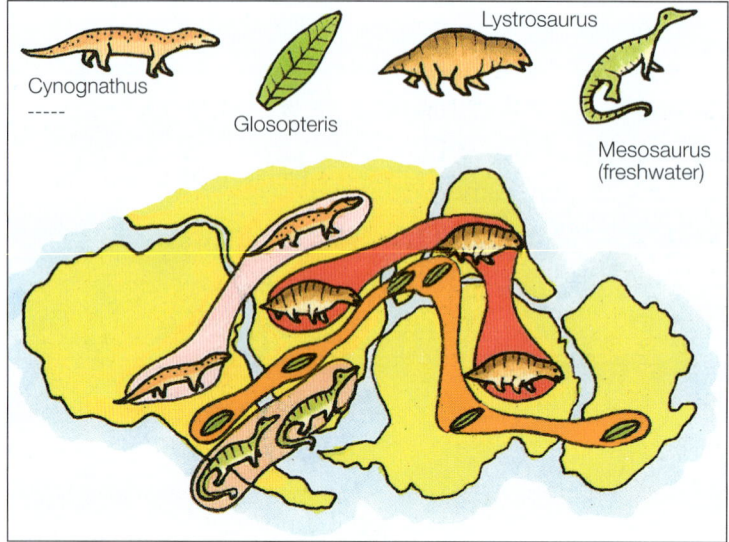

Fig. 8 Distribution of fossils across the southern continents of Pangaea. Also note the shape of the coastline.

Ireland has also moved over the planet during the last 500 million years. This is because the continents have been moved around by mantle convection currents beneath the crust. In later chapters you will learn more about how these movements helped to create the rocks and landscapes we see today.

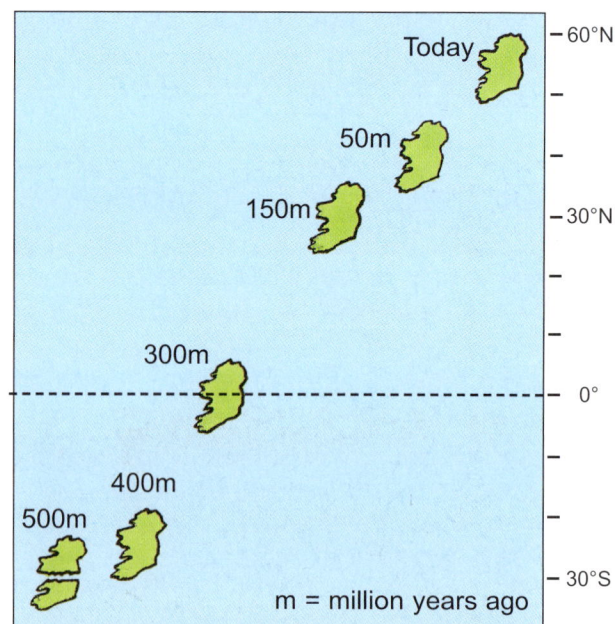

Fig. 9 The geographical position of Ireland over the last 500 million years

Sea-floor spreading – Hess, 1960s

In the mid-twentieth century American geologist Harry Hess mapped and viewed the sea floor while on naval patrol. He saw volcanoes erupting from the sea floor, making long submarine mountain ridges. He realised that new crust was being created here and he called this process **sea-floor spreading**.

Proof that sea-floor spreading occurs

1. The different magnetisms locked into the rocks either side of the mid-ocean ridge match up. Magnetism locked into rocks as they cool is proof of sea-floor spreading. Lava contains grains of iron that point toward the magnetic pole as the lava solidifies. The grains are a permanent record of the earth's magnetic field. The earth's magnetic poles have reversed many times in the past. Scientists have matched the magnetic bands in the rock either side of the Mid-Atlantic Ridge and used them as proof that sea-floor spreading occurs.
2. The age of the sea floor is youngest at the mid-ocean ridges and older further away from it. Young volcanic islands are found near the ridge; older volcanic islands are found further away from it.

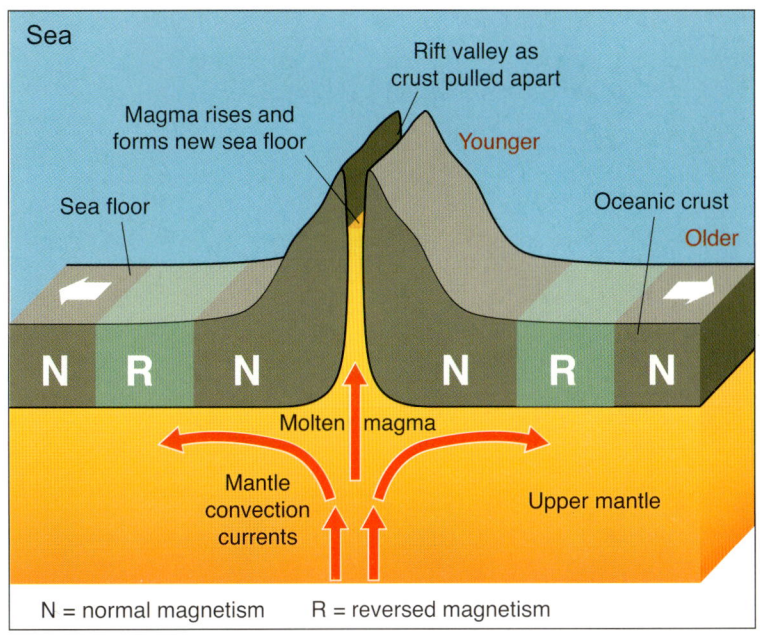

Fig. 10 Matching magnetic strips on sea floor either side of a mid-ocean ridge

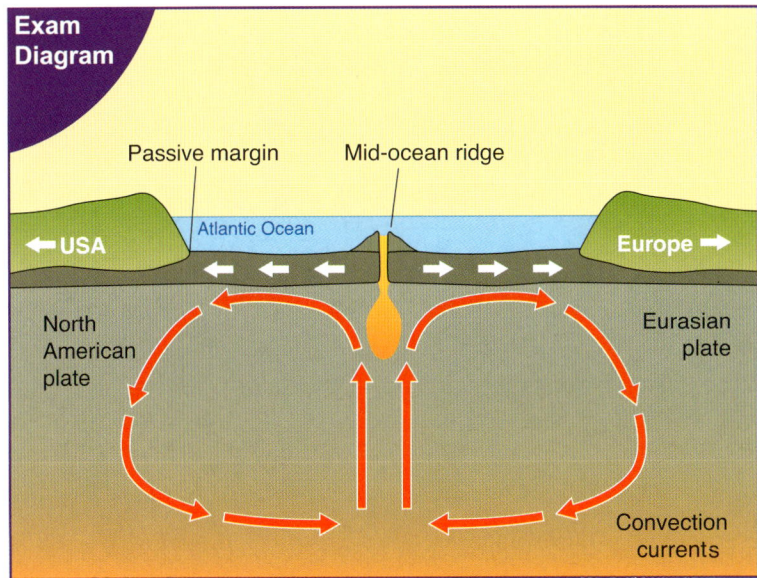

Fig. 11 Sea-floor spreading is making the Atlantic Ocean wider. Note the passive margin. This is where continental crust and oceanic crust share the same plate. The junction of the two types of crust is not an active plate margin.

weblink
Magnetic polarity

The Atlantic Ocean is getting wider at the same speed that your fingernails grow.

CORE UNIT: PATTERNS AND PROCESSES IN THE PHYSICAL ENVIRONMENT

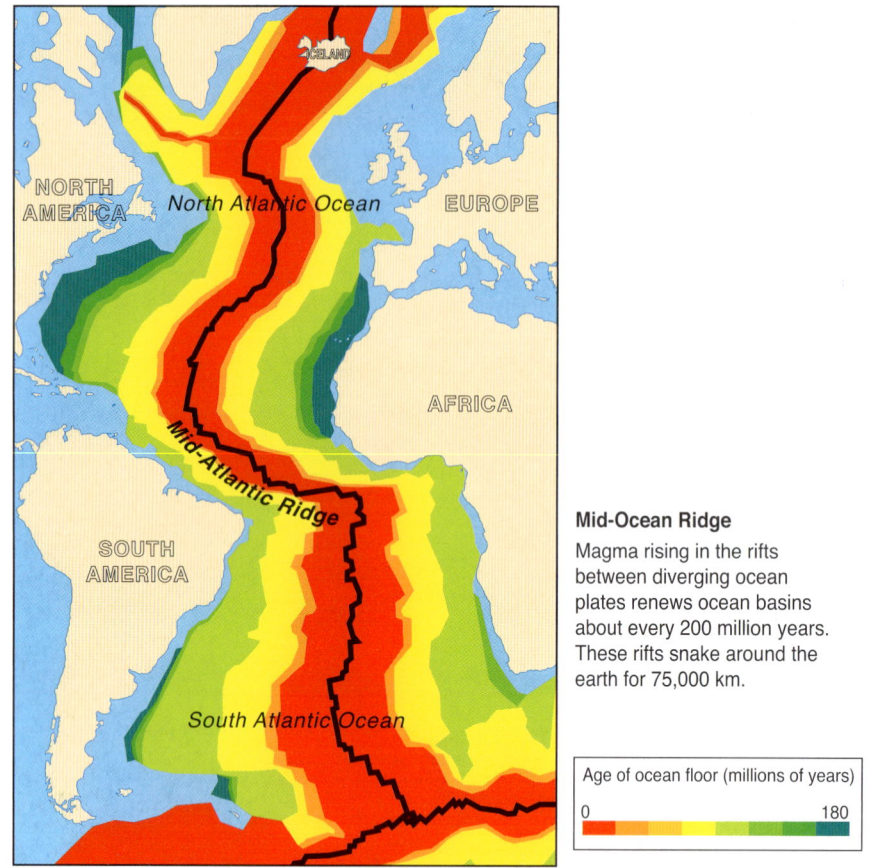

Fig. 12 The location of the Mid-Atlantic Ridge

Plate tectonic theory – Vine and Matthews (late 1960s)

Vine and Matthews put together the earlier ideas of continental drift (Wegener) and sea-floor spreading (Hess) to form the basis of the plate tectonic theory we know today. They mapped the distribution of earthquakes and volcanoes across the world. These maps revealed how the crust is broken up into large and small plates. They identified the movement of convection currents of molten magma in the mantle as the mechanism for moving these plates.

Note the relationship between plate boundaries and the location of earthquakes and volcanoes. See Fig. 5 and Fig. 12.

Fig. 13 Map showing the distribution of earthquakes and volcanoes

1.4 Plate boundaries and their associated landforms

Plate tectonic theory identifies three types of plate boundary.
1. Constructive (divergent)
2. Destructive (convergent)
3. Conservative (transform or transverse)

weblink Boundary types

1. Constructive (divergent) plate boundaries – mid-ocean ridges

These boundaries occur where plates are pulled apart by the convection currents in the mantle below. As the crust splits, a **rift valley** is formed allowing magma to rise and fill the gap making new crust. Shallow earthquakes and volcanoes also occur, e.g. Iceland 2010 and 2014. As magma solidifies, it forces the plates apart even further, allowing more magma to rise. Over millions of years repeated separations and eruptions have formed the ocean floors. This process is known as sea-floor spreading. The crack where plates separate is marked by a line of volcanic mountains known as a **mid-ocean ridge**.

An example of this is the Mid-Atlantic Ridge. This submerged mountain chain stretches over 40,000 km from the North Pole to the South Pole.

The crust is moving apart at a rate of about five cm per year. This works out at about 25 km per million years. This may seem slow to us, but it took 200 million years to create the Atlantic Ocean.

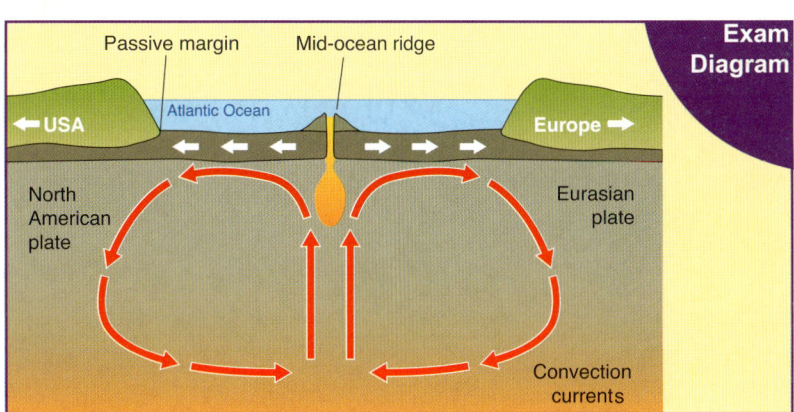

Fig. 14 The formation of new crust at a constructive/divergent plate boundary caused by sea-floor spreading

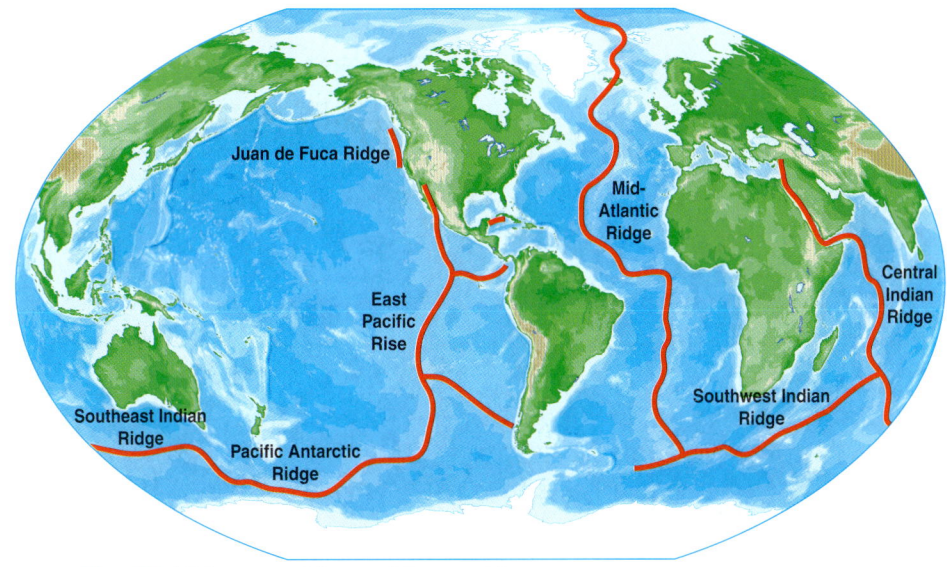

Fig. 15 Mid-ocean ridges of the world

weblink Earthquakes and volcanoes

15

CORE UNIT: PATTERNS AND PROCESSES IN THE PHYSICAL ENVIRONMENT

CHAPTER 1

Case Study 1

Sea-floor spreading in Iceland

Iceland has formed where the Mid-Atlantic Ridge appears above the sea. Iceland is getting wider due to the process of sea-floor spreading. One side of the country is on the North American plate, the other on the Eurasian plate.

Iceland has over 200 active and dormant volcanoes. There are also many long cracks, or fissures, which form as the crust is split. Magma erupts through these. Submarine eruptions are common in the south west. Earthquakes are frequent but rarely dangerous.

The Eyjafjallajokull volcano erupted throughout 2010, disrupting transatlantic and European flights.

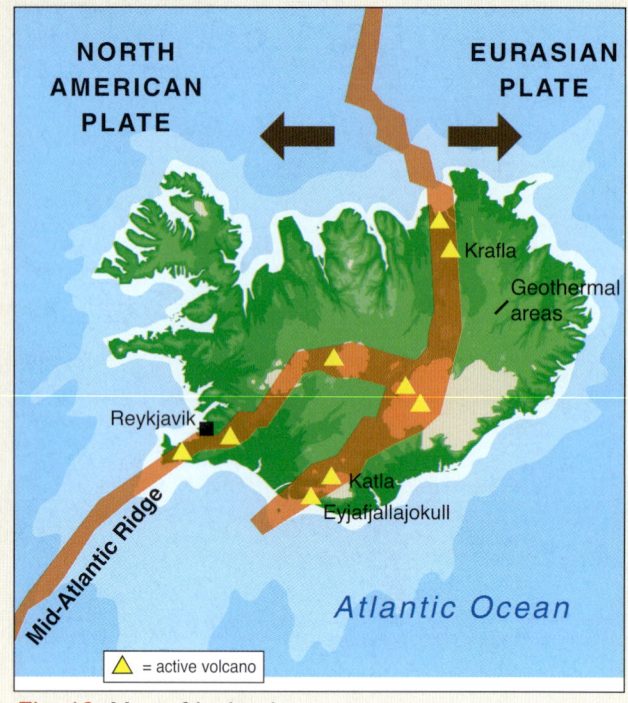

Fig. 16 Map of Iceland

2. Destructive (convergent) plate boundaries

Here plates move together and collide, destroying the crust. There are three situations where this happens.

(a) Collision between two continental plates.
(b) Collision between oceanic and continental plates.
(c) Collision between two oceanic plates.

(a) Continental–continental plate collision – fold mountains

When two continental plates collide **fold mountains** are created. Mountain ranges such as the Himalayas and Alps have been folded up by the massive power of plate collision. Fifty million years ago the Indian plate began its slow collision with the Eurasian plate. This caused the Eurasian plate to crumple and rise creating the Tibetan Plateau and the Himalayas. When two continental plates collide, neither of them tends to sink into the mantle. They resist sinking much like two icebergs colliding at sea. Colliding continental plates tend to move upwards or sideways, sometimes causing devastating shallow earthquakes such as the one that occurred in Pakistan in 2005 in which

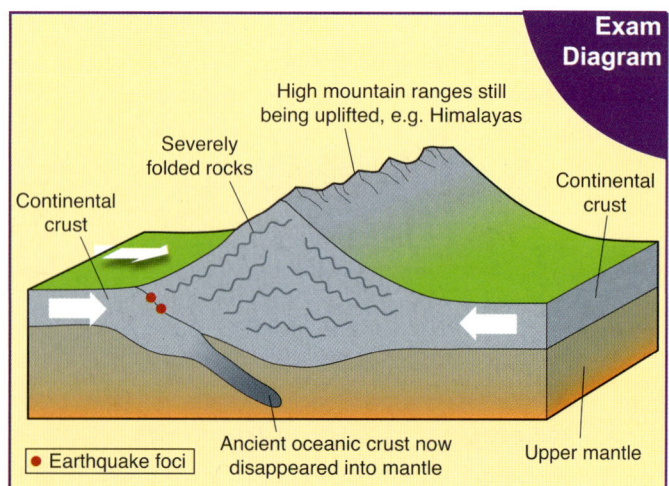

Fig. 17 Two continental plates collide to form fold mountains.

16

over 89,000 people died, and the quake that occurred in Nepal in 2015 in which over 8,000 people died and more than 1.5 million people were displaced.

Fold mountains are often composed of sedimentary rocks such as limestone that formed beneath the sea. Climbers and trekkers in Nepal frequently see marine fossils thousands of kilometres inland and several thousand metres above sea level, high in the Himalayas.

(b) Oceanic–continental plate collision – subduction zones

In this case heavier oceanic crust collides with and slides beneath the lighter continental crust. As it slides into the mantle it melts and is recycled. This process is called **subduction** and it is an important part of the tectonic cycle.

The melted crust turns to magma and moves up through the continental crust above to create some of the most explosive volcanoes in the world, e.g. Mount St Helens in the United States. Deep earthquakes are also common in these areas.

At the junction of the two colliding plates a massively deep **trench** is created. Such trenches mark all subduction zones (see Fig. 18). Many are thousands of kilometres long and up to 8–11 km deep, e.g. the Peru-Chile trench.

Sediments that are carried on the sea bed of the sinking oceanic plate are scraped off and pile up against the edge of the continent, forming **fold mountains**. These sediments form unique geological areas known as **terranes**, e.g. the Andes in Peru.

The **Pacific Ring of Fire** is so named because many active volcanoes created at subduction zones mark the edge of the Pacific plate. Mount Pinatubo in the Philippines and Mount Fuji in Japan are classic examples.

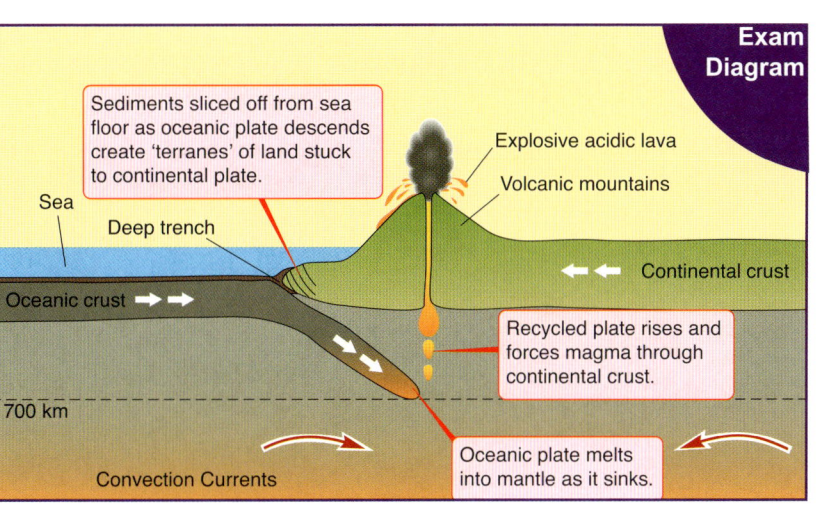

Fig. 18 Oceanic–continental plate collision

(c) Oceanic–oceanic plate collision – trenches and island arcs

When two oceanic plates collide, one is usually subducted beneath the other. Where one plate sinks beneath the other, deep trenches form. These are the deepest parts of the ocean. The Mariana Trench in the western Pacific Ocean marks the place where the fast-moving Pacific plate collides with and subducts under the slower-moving Philippine plate. Strong deep earthquakes occur at trenches due to the huge stresses that are released as the plates slide into the asthenosphere, e.g. Japan 2011.

CORE UNIT: PATTERNS AND PROCESSES IN THE PHYSICAL ENVIRONMENT

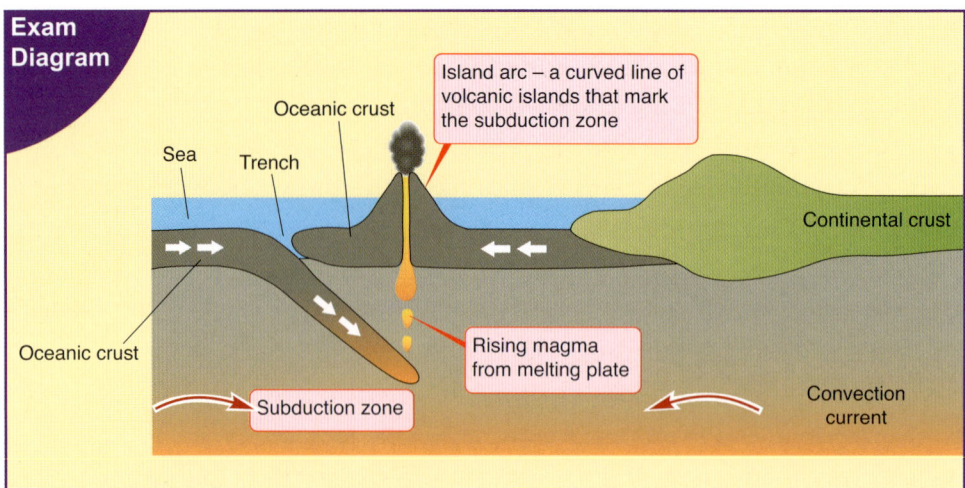

Fig. 19 Oceanic–oceanic plate collision

Oceanic-oceanic plate collision zones are also marked by curved lines of volcanic islands known as **island arcs**. These volcanoes form when the subducted plate sinks and melts, creating rising bubbles (**plumes**) of magma that break through the crust above. These active volcanoes have built up on the sea floor over millions of years until they appear above the surface of the water. The Aleutian Islands, the Philippine Islands and Japanese islands have all been formed in this way.

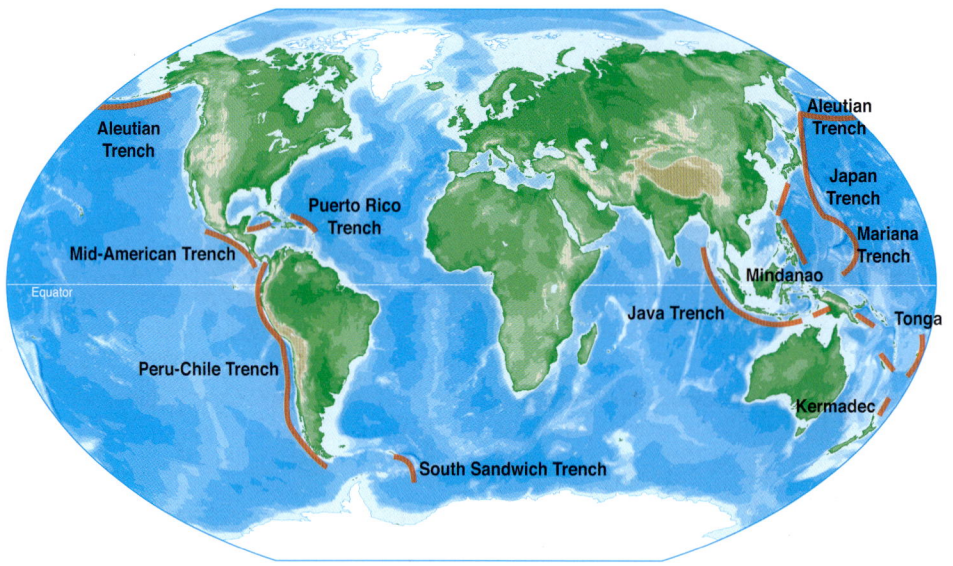

Fig. 20 Oceanic trenches of the world

3. Conservative (transverse or transform) plate boundaries – fault lines

A **conservative plate boundary** is where two plates slide past each other. Land is neither created nor destroyed at these boundaries. These boundaries are marked by **fault lines**; they are thousands of kilometres long and up to eight kilometres deep. They are associated with shallow earthquakes. Most occur under the sea.

A few conservative boundaries occur on land. The best known is the San Andreas Fault in California. This fault is 1,300 kilometeres long and tens of kilometres wide in places.

18

CHAPTER 1: PLATE TECTONICS

At this fault the Pacific plate and the North American plate are both moving in a north-westerly direction. The Pacific plate, however, is moving faster at a rate of about five cm per year. The slippage is not smooth and the plates may stick for many decades. This leads to the build-up of enormous pressure between the two plates until they suddenly lurch past each other causing an earthquake. In the 1906 San Francisco earthquake the Pacific plate moved over six metres in one minute.

Los Angeles will eventually arrive beside San Francisco if the Pacific plate keeps moving northwards, but it will take 16 million years. The Haiti 2010 earthquake also occurred on a transform boundary between the Caribbean and North American plates.

Fig. 21 Aerial photograph of the San Andreas Fault

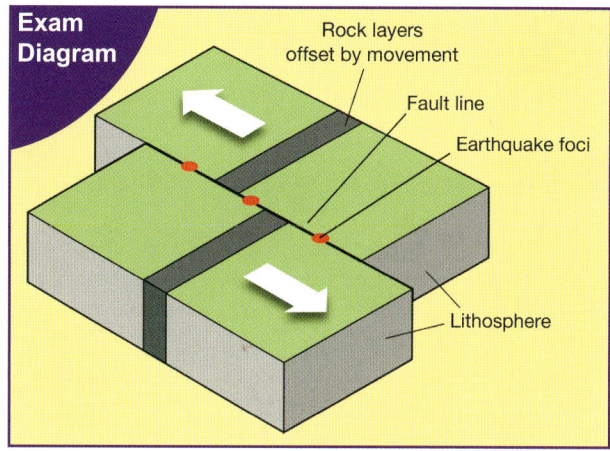

Fig. 22 A conservative plate boundary

Activity

Look at the map to the right and answer the questions which follow.

(a) What type of plate boundary is shown in this diagram?
(b) Name the two plates involved.
(c) What type of tectonic activity occurs along the plate boundary shown?

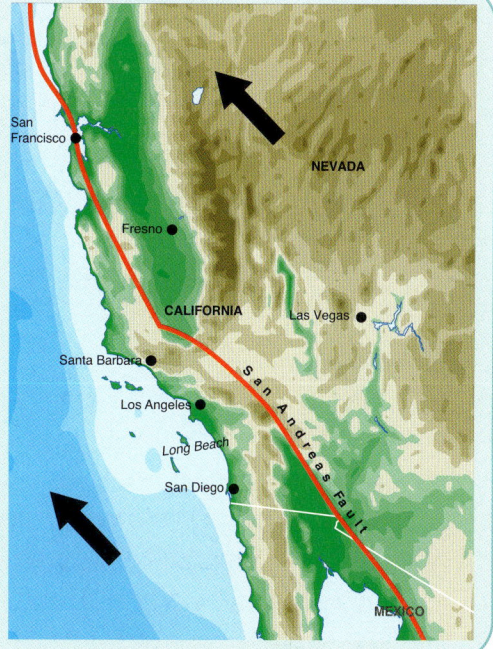

19

Tectonic activity in the middle of plates – hotspots

Sometimes volcanoes are found thousands of kilometres from the edges of plates. They occur in areas where high temperatures in the mantle produce a rising fountain (**plume**) of molten rock known as a **hotspot**. Hotspots are extremely hot areas deep in the upper mantle (asthenosphere). A column of magma rises from the hotspot and pushes to the surface erupting through the plate above. It is thought that these fountains are stationary inside the asthenosphere and the plates move over them. As the plate moves the magma erupts through fissures or other weaknesses in the bulging crust, forming volcanoes. The Hawaiian Islands were formed as the Pacific plate moved over one such hotspot. Some hotspots stretch and split the crust causing rift valleys, e.g. the East African Rift Valley, (see Chapter 4, page 63).

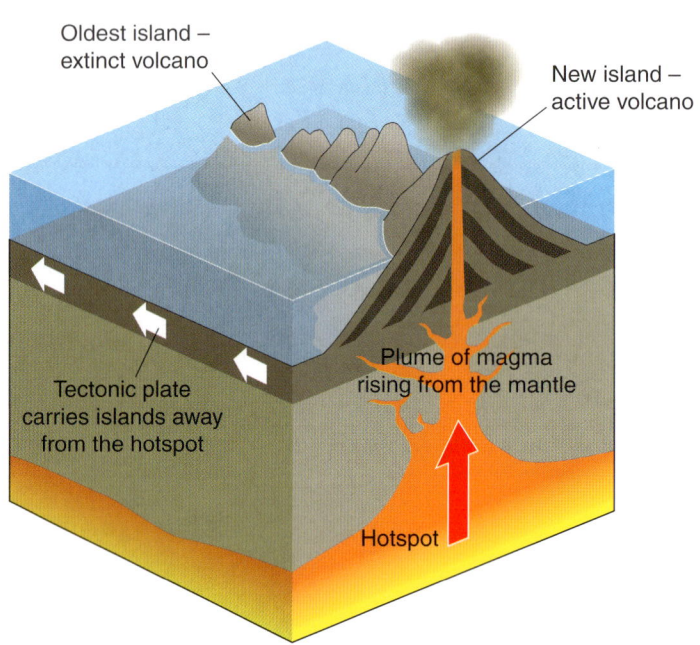

Fig. 23 The Hawaiian hotspot volcanoes

The Hawaiian hotspot

1. The Hawaiian hotspot is responsible for the formation of the Hawaiian Islands. The Hawaiian Islands are a chain of volcanic islands in the middle of the Pacific plate located over 3,200 km from the nearest plate boundary. As the Pacific plate passes over the hotspot, volcanoes burst through in succession, producing the islands.

Fig. 24 Kauai Island, one of the Hawaiian Islands

2. As the Pacific plate moves over the hotspot, volcanoes grow, become dormant and eventually become extinct over a period of 500,000 years. The Pacific plate moves north-west over the hotspot at a rate of about 10 cm per year.

3. The Hawaiian hotspot is about 500 – 600 km wide and lies about 100 km below the surface. The hotspot is approximately 86 million years old. The Hawaiian Islands are the most recent volcanoes to grow over it.

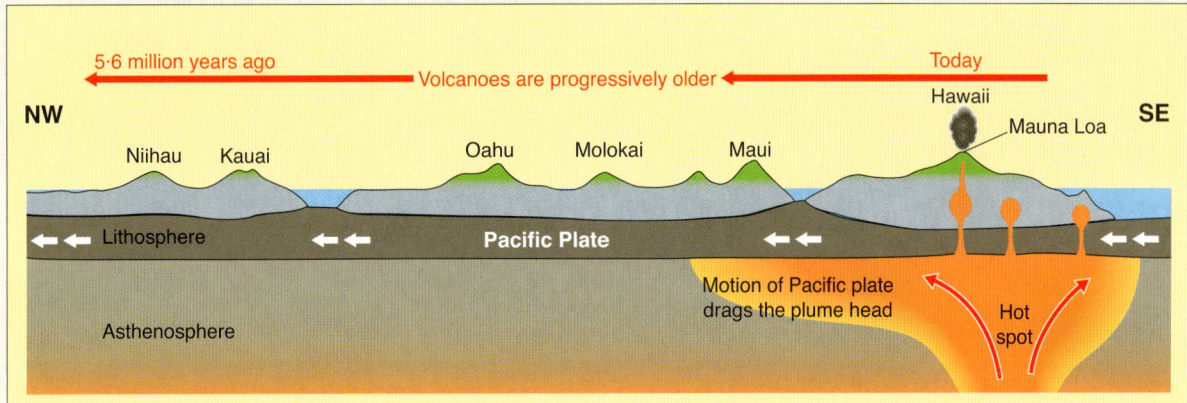

Fig. 25 The Hawaiian hotspot

4. The tallest volcanic mountain in Hawaii is Mauna Kea (4,205 m above sea level). If measured from the seabed, this volcano is 10,203 m high – nearly 1.3 km higher than Mount Everest.

Fig. 26 Map of Hawaii

CORE UNIT: PATTERNS AND PROCESSES IN THE PHYSICAL ENVIRONMENT

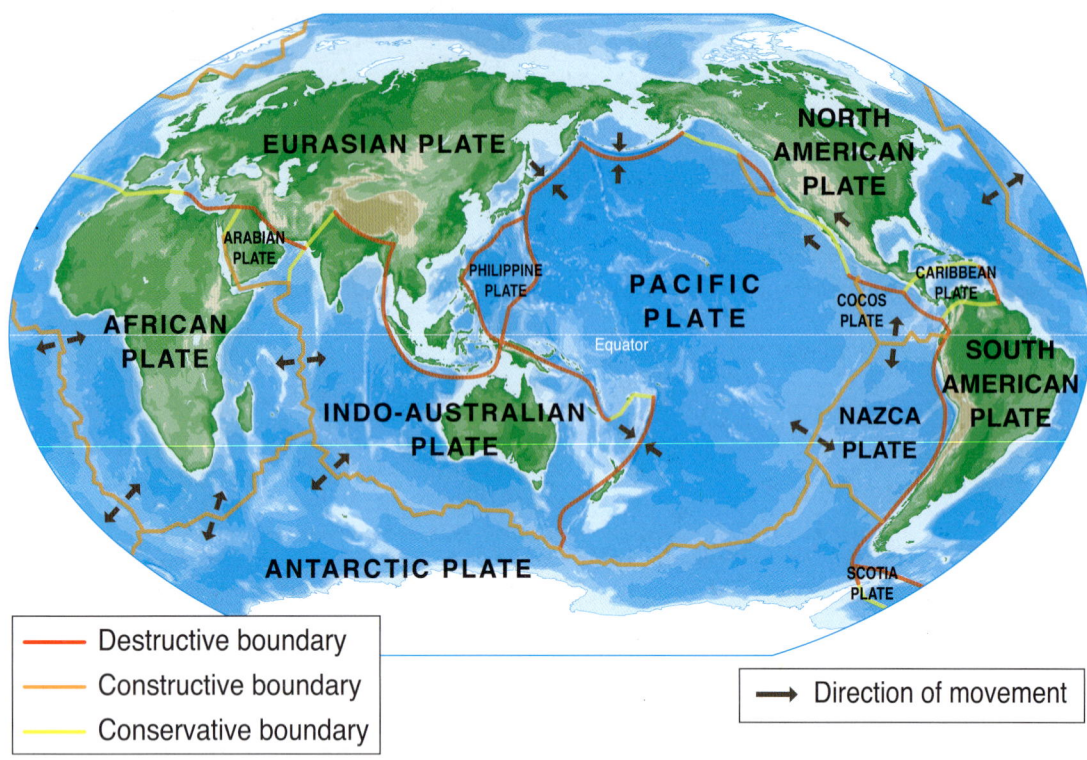

Fig. 27 Map to show plate boundaries and direction of plate movement

SUMMARY OF PLATE BOUNDARIES			
Type of boundary	Processes involved (cause)	Resulting landforms	Examples
Constructive (Divergent)	Separation Rift valley formation Upwelling of magma	Mid-ocean ridges New ocean floor Shallow earthquakes Volcanic islands	Iceland East Pacific Rise Tristan da Cunha
Destructive (Convergent) (a) Continental–continental crust (b) Oceanic–continental crust (c) Oceanic–oceanic crust	Folding of ocean sediments Uplift Collision Subduction Melting Rising magma	Fold mountains Shallow earthquakes Volcanic mountains Deep earthquakes Trenches Island arcs Terrances	Himalayas, Alps Andes Mariana Trench Japan
Conservative (Transverse or Transform)	Plates slide horizontally past each other	Transform faults Shallow earthquakes	San Andreas Fault

CHAPTER 1: PLATE TECTONICS

Chapter Revision Questions

1. Explain the following terms: (a) surface (exogenic) forces and (b) internal (endogenic) forces.
2. Draw a labelled diagram showing the internal structure of the earth.
3. What is the lithosphere? Draw a well-labelled diagram of it.
4. What are tectonic plates? Give **two** examples.
5. What are convection currents? What is their importance to plate tectonic theory?
6. What is the tectonic cycle?
7. Explain the terms sea-floor spreading, subduction zone and hotspots.
8. Explain what plate tectonic theory is and how it was developed.
9. Briefly explain why earthquakes and volcanoes only occur in certain areas of the world.
10. What are island arcs and ocean trenches? How do they form? Give examples.
11. Explain with the aid of a diagram how the Himalayas were formed.
12. Describe with the aid of diagrams **three** ways in which plates can collide.
13. 'Mid-ocean ridges form at constructive plate boundaries.' Explain this statement.
14. Copy the diagram below of the tectonic cycle into your copybook and label the parts A–G shown.

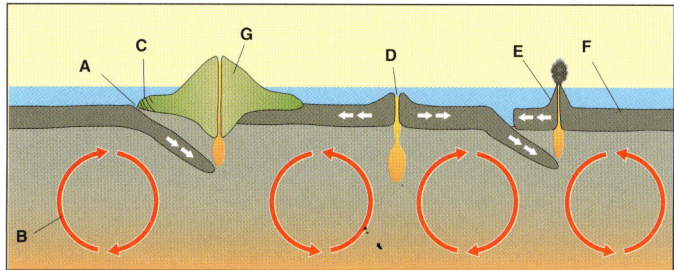

15. Link each of the features 1–7 with its matching process (a)–(g).

Feature	Process	Number	Letter
(1) Iceland	(a) Subduction zone	(1)	
(2) Himalayas	(b) Hotspot	(2)	
(3) Hawaii	(c) Conservative plate boundary	(3)	
(4) Philippine Islands	(d) Sea-floor spreading	(4)	
(5) Terranes	(e) Continental-continental collision	(5)	
(6) Mariana Trench	(f) Island Arc	(6)	
(7) San Andreas Fault	(g) Oceanic-continental collision	(7)	

23

CORE UNIT: PATTERNS AND PROCESSES IN THE PHYSICAL ENVIRONMENT

LC Exam Questions

Higher Level students must be able to answer Ordinary and Higher Level questions.

■ OL Questions

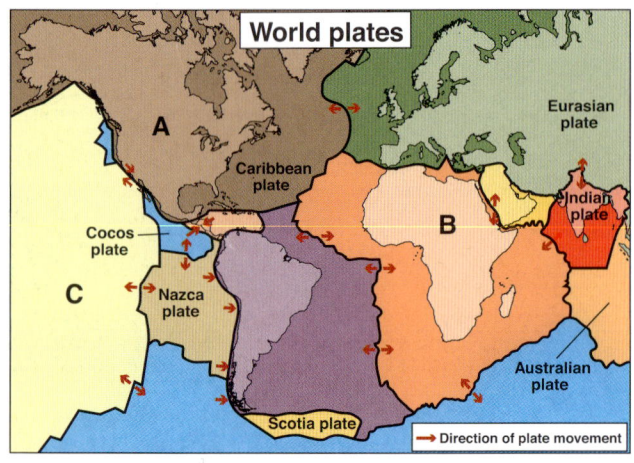

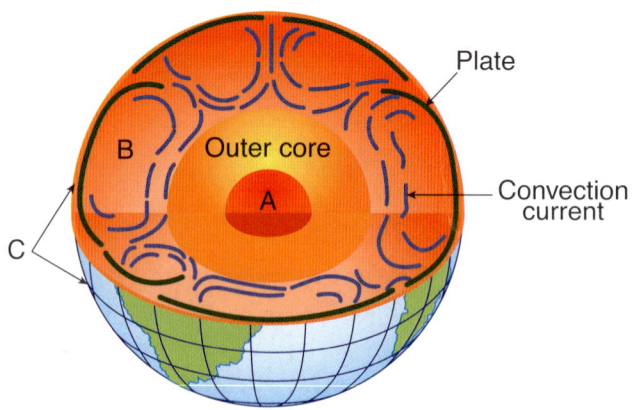

16. Examine the map above and answer each of the following questions.
    (i) Match each of the letters A, B and C on the map with the correct tectonic plate in the table below.

Tectonic Plate	Letter
African Plate	
North American Plate	
Pacific Plate	

    (ii) Name two plates that are colliding together.
    (iii) Name the plate on which Ireland lies.

17. Describe and explain what happens at plate boundaries.

18. Examine the diagram of the structure of the earth above and answer each of the questions which follow.
    (i) Name each of the layers of the earth labelled A, B and C.
    (ii) Explain briefly what is meant by the term 'plate'.
    (iii) Explain briefly what causes plates to move.

19. Examine the map below and answer the following questions.

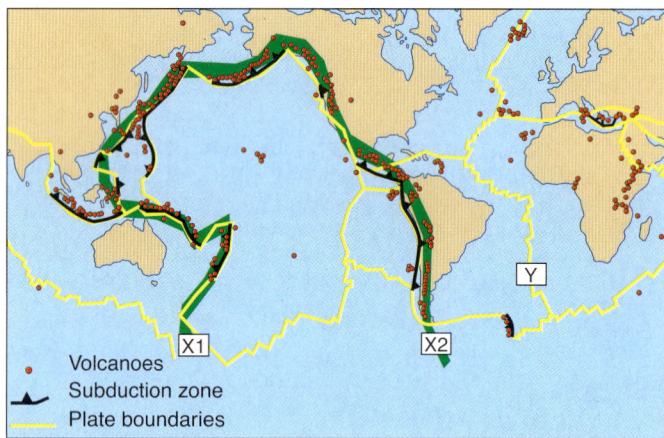

   (i) What is the name given to the region from X1, along the shaded line, to X2?
   (ii) Name the ridge running north from Y.
   (iii) Name any two volcanoes.
   (iv) Name any two crustal plates.
   (v) Briefly explain what is meant by subduction.

CHAPTER 1: PLATE TECTONICS

LC Exam Questions

■ **HL Questions**

20. Examine the diagram below showing a plate boundary and answer the following questions.

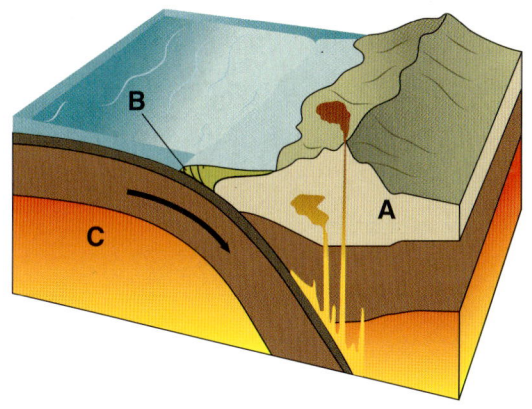

(i) Name the type of plate boundary shown above.
(ii) Name the type of plate at A.
(iii) Name the process taking place at B.
(iv) Name the part of the mantle at C.

21. Examine the map below showing the major crustal plates of the earth and answer the following questions:
(i) Name the plates A, B, C and D.
(ii) Name the plate boundary at X.

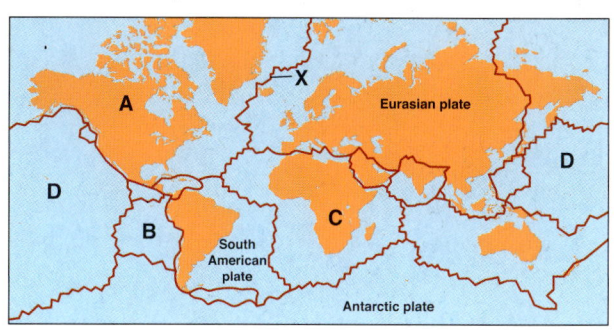

22. Describe and explain destructive plate boundaries.
23. 'Plate boundaries are zones where crust is both created and destroyed.'
Examine the above statement with reference to examples you have studied.

Key Words

You should be able to explain both verbally and in writing each of the key words listed below.

asthenosphere
conservative (transform/transverse) plate boundary
constructive (divergent) plate boundary
continental crust
continental drift
destructive (convergent) plate boundary
endogenic
exogenic
fault lines
fold mountains
Gondwanaland
hotspot
island arcs
Laurasia

lithosphere
mid-ocean ridge
oceanic crust
Pacific Ring of Fire
Pangaea
passive plate margin
plates
plate tectonics
plumes
rift valley
sea-floor spreading
subduction
tectonic cycle
terranes
trench

Key Words Chapter 1

 Digital Resources are available for this chapter at mentorbooks.ie/resources

CHAPTER 2

Earthquakes

Key Theme

Earthquakes are created by forces within the earth.

Learning Outcomes

At the end of this chapter you will be able to:
- Explain the terms focus, tremor, epicentre.
- Name and explain the methods used to measure earthquakes.
- Briefly describe the different types of earthquake waves.
- Describe the effects of earthquakes using the case studies provided.
- Outline methods used to predict and prevent earthquake damage.

Contents

2.1.	Earthquakes	27
2.2.	Location and depth of earthquakes	27
2.3.	Earthquake waves	28
2.4.	The effects of earthquakes	31
	Case Study: The Great Japan earthquake and tsunami, March 2011	32
2.5.	Predicting earthquakes and preventing earthquake damage	35

Revision Space

Chapter Revision Questions – LC Exam Questions – Key Word List 37

Chapter 2: Earthquakes

2.1 Earthquakes

Earthquakes occur at all plate boundaries (see Chapter 1). They are vibrations or **tremors** in the earth's crust, and are caused by the movement of plates over the mantle which makes the crust stretch and tear. The stress and pressure becomes greater than the strength of the rocks which can suddenly give way along a fault line in the crust.

Shock waves or tremors travel out from the origin or **focus** of the earthquake just as ripples travel across the surface of water when a stone is thrown. The site directly above the focus on the surface of the earth is known as the **epicentre**. Most damage is done here. There are thousands of earthquakes that are strong enough to be felt by people each year but there are over one million other earthquakes that are detected only by instruments.

As the plates settle back to their normal positions after the earthquake (**elastic rebound**) more earthquakes, or **aftershocks**, can occur. These can do more damage to already weakened buildings and send panic through affected populations.

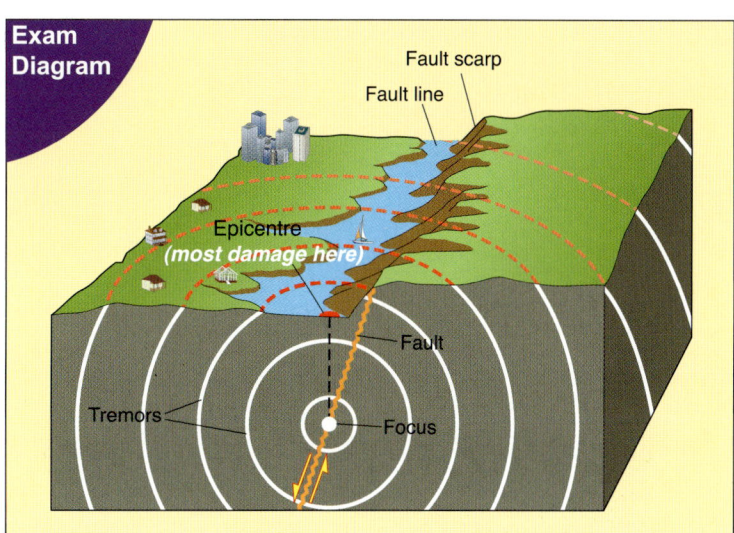

Fig. 1 Focus and epicentre of an earthquake

weblink
Earthquakes and plate tectonics

2.2 Location and depth of earthquakes

Earthquakes occur at all types of plate boundaries and at different depths in the crust.

Shallow earthquakes: Less than 70 km below the surface; associated with mid-ocean ridges, continental–continental plate collision and conservative plate boundaries

Intermediate earthquakes: 70 – 300 km below the surface; associated with oceanic–continental plate collision

Deep earthquakes: Greater than 300 km below the surface; associated with oceanic–oceanic plate collision

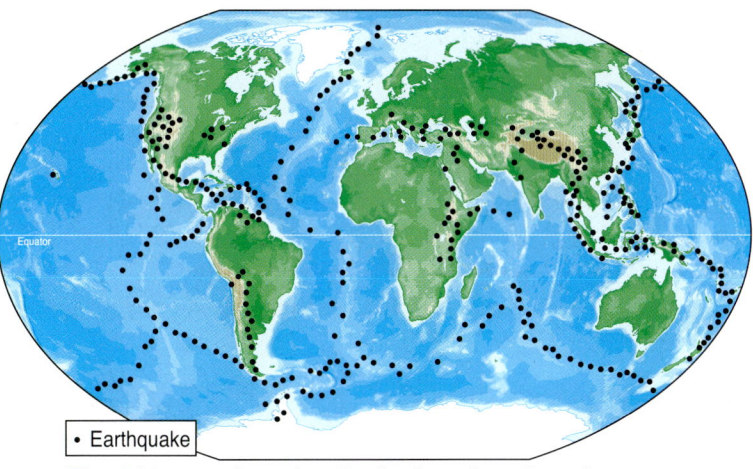

Fig. 2 Map to show the distribution of earthquakes

27

2.3 Earthquake waves

Earthquake tremors/**seismic** waves travel inside the earth and along the earth's surface at great speed. There are three main types:

1. **P waves**, or **primary waves**, arrive first. They push and shake the ground back and forth in the same direction as the wave is moving. These are very fast but do little damage; they can pass through a building in less than a second.

2. An **S wave**, or **secondary wave**, shakes the ground back and forth perpendicular to the direction in which the wave is moving. They arrive after the P waves as they travel more slowly (8 km per second); they can damage buildings.

3. **Surface waves** travel slowly along the earth's surface. They move the surface of the earth up and down as well as from side to side. They are extremely devastating because they travel slowly (up to 3.5 km per second).

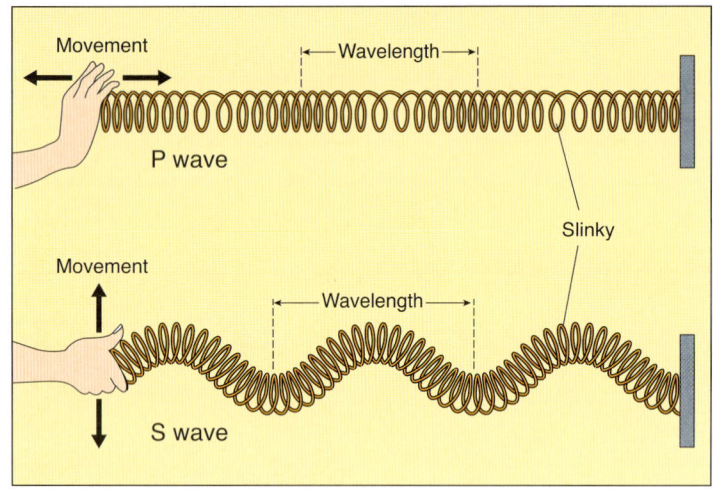

Fig. 3 The different types of earthquake waves = P and S

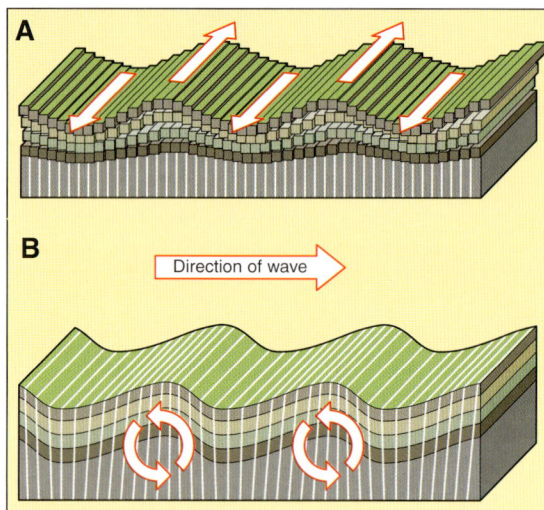

Fig. 4 Surface waves

Recording and measuring earthquakes

1. Seismographs/seismometers
2. The Richter scale
3. The Modified Mercalli scale

1. Seismographs

Sensitive instruments called **seismographs/seismometers** detect and record earthquake waves. These detect earthquakes and help monitor nuclear tests. The Global Seismic Network (GSN) is a web of 128 recording stations across the world.

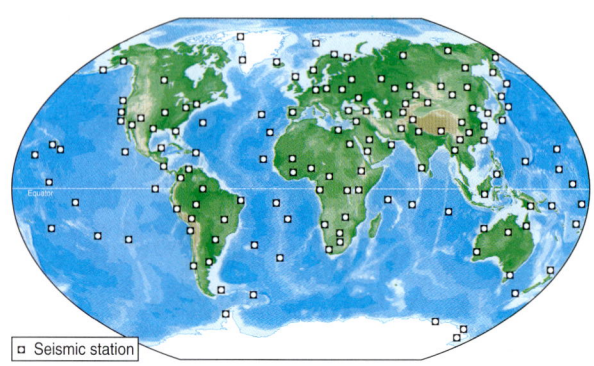

Fig. 5 The global seismic network

CHAPTER 2: EARTHQUAKES

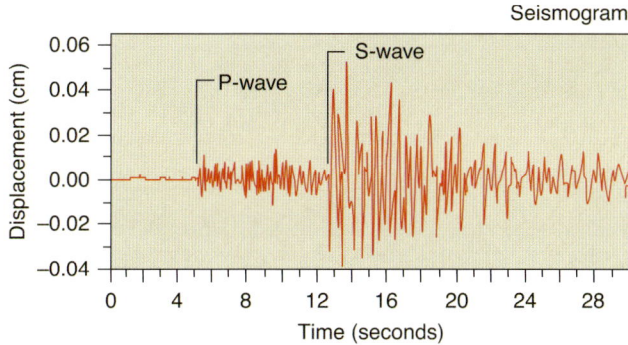

Fig. 6 A seismograph is used to calculate the magnitude of an earthquake.

2. The Richter scale

The **energy** released by an earthquake is called its **magnitude** and is measured using the **Richter scale**. This is an open-ended scale which was devised by Charles F. Richter. It is a measure of the amount of energy released by an earthquake as the rock breaks. An earthquake of magnitude 6 (M6) is ten times as powerful as one of M5 on the scale. The Richter scale is usually quoted on TV and news bulletins when an earthquake happens.

Typical effects of some earthquake magnitudes are shown in Fig. 7.

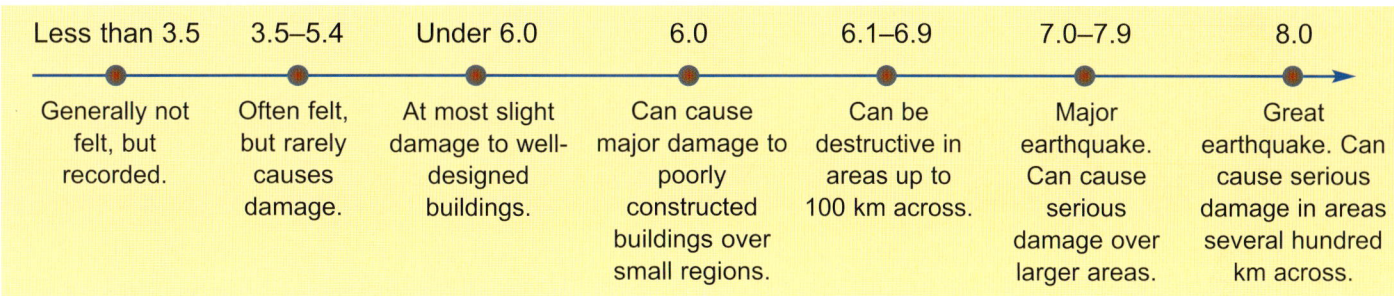

Fig. 7 Some Richter magnitudes and their effects

3. The Modified Mercalli scale

Earthquake **intensity** is a measure of the **effects** experienced and observed by people during an earthquake and is recorded using the **Modified Mercalli scale**.

The Modified Mercalli scale is commonly used in the United States by seismologists seeking information from people on the severity of earthquake effects.

The effects of any one earthquake vary greatly from place to place, being severe at the epicentre and less so further away. There may be many intensity values (denoted by the Roman numerals i to xii) measured during an earthquake depending on where people were when the earthquake happened.

Measuring the intensity of an earthquake's effects does not require any instruments. Seismologists can use newspaper accounts, diaries and other historical records to give intensity ratings for past earthquakes. Such research helps promote our understanding of earthquake history in a region and helps estimate future hazards.

> **weblink**
> Modified Mercalli scale in action.

CORE UNIT: PATTERNS AND PROCESSES IN THE PHYSICAL ENVIRONMENT

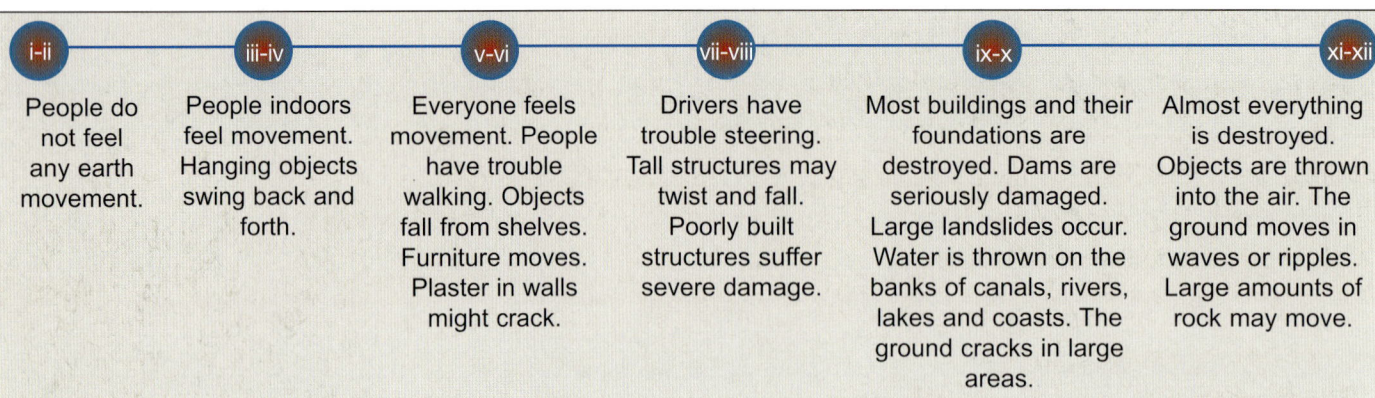

i-ii	iii-iv	v-vi	vii-viii	ix-x	xi-xii
People do not feel any earth movement.	People indoors feel movement. Hanging objects swing back and forth.	Everyone feels movement. People have trouble walking. Objects fall from shelves. Furniture moves. Plaster in walls might crack.	Drivers have trouble steering. Tall structures may twist and fall. Poorly built structures suffer severe damage.	Most buildings and their foundations are destroyed. Dams are seriously damaged. Large landslides occur. Water is thrown on the banks of canals, rivers, lakes and coasts. The ground cracks in large areas.	Almost everything is destroyed. Objects are thrown into the air. The ground moves in waves or ripples. Large amounts of rock may move.

Fig. 8 Modified Mercalli scale

Fig. 9 Seismologists use newspaper accounts, diaries, photos and other historical records to give intensity ratings for past earthquakes.

Richter Scale	Modified Mercalli Scale
Measures the energy released (its magnitude) by an earthquake.	Measures the intensity (what people feel/see) of an earthquake.
Uses instruments called seismometers / seismographs.	Uses peoples' accounts and observations of what they see, hear and feel happening during a quake.
Seismographs record the strength of the P, S and Surface waves released during a quake.	No instruments are used.
The readings on a seismograph are converted to a single magnitude on the Richter Scale.	Peoples' accounts are fitted into a scale of damage and effects. A quake can have many intensity readings depending on where people are during the quake.
The Richter Scale is open-ended.	The Modified Mercalli scale goes from I to XII
Each number on the scale represents a quake ten times stronger than the one below it.	Each number on the Modified Mercalli scale is a separate description of the increasing damage observed.
Quakes with a magnitude less than 3.5 are not usually felt. Quakes measuring over 7 may cause major damage.	Quakes measuring I are rarely felt, a quake measuring XII results in complete devastation.
An advantage of using this scale is that each quake has one magnitude that is internationally accepted.	An advantage of this scale is that historical accounts of quakes that occurred centuries ago can be used to assign an intensity reading to the quake.
The Richter Scale was invented by Charles Richter in 1935.	The original Mercalli Scale (I to X) was invented by Guiseppe Mercalli in 1902. It was later expanded (I to XII) and is now called the Modified Mercalli Scale.

Fig. 10 Summary of Richter Scale and Modified Mercalli Scale

CHAPTER 2: EARTHQUAKES

2.4 The effects of earthquakes

Earthquakes are traumatic events for the people who experience them. The social and economic effects are devastating. It may take years to rebuild damaged buildings and some people never recover from the psychological distress. Whole economies suffer as industrial capability is reduced and generations of people disappear.

Immediate effects:

1. Death and destruction, **tsunamis**, gas explosions, fire, loss of fresh water supplies, homelessness.
2. **Liquefaction** occurs where settlements are built on deep, loosely-consolidated soils or reclaimed land rather than on solid bedrock. The ground turns to liquid due to intense shaking during an earthquake. Buildings sink into the ground, e.g. Mexico City; Los Angeles.

Longer-term effects:

1. Migration – thousands are displaced while damaged buildings are cleared and rebuilt.
2. Disease – water and sewerage pipes burst and take time to repair.
3. Economic slowdown – shops close, industry is destroyed and government spending is diverted from other projects.

Tsunamis

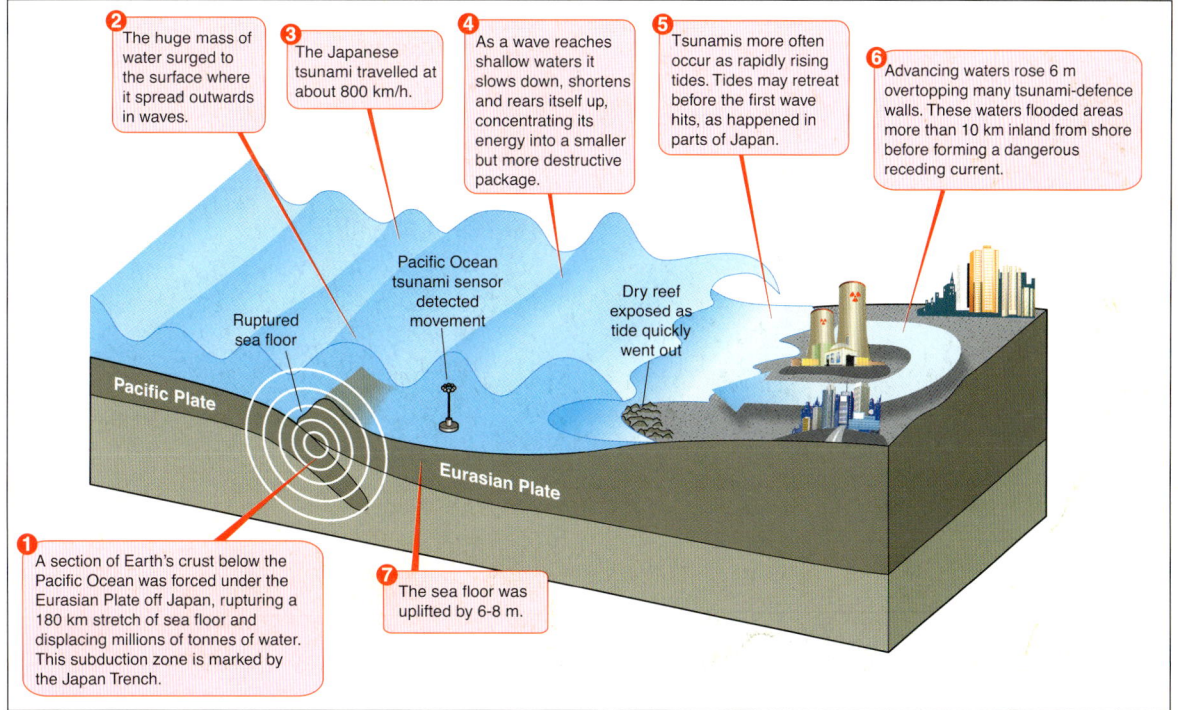

Fig. 11 How the 2011 Japanese tsunami was caused

31

CORE UNIT: PATTERNS AND PROCESSES IN THE PHYSICAL ENVIRONMENT

The Great Japan earthquake and tsunami, March 2011

CHAPTER 2 Case Study

On March 11, 2011 one of Japan's deadliest natural disasters occurred. A powerful earthquake occurred about 130 km off the coast of Japan's most populated island, Honshu. It was the strongest earthquake to occur in Japan since records began.

Several large foreshocks were felt before the main earthquake. The main shock was felt in Russia, Taiwan and Beijing in China. The earthquake triggered tsunami warnings throughout the whole Pacific region from California to the Aleutian islands, and from Hawaii to Antarctica.

Cause

1. The magnitude 9 earthquake was caused by the collision of the Pacific plate with the Eurasian plate. At this destructive boundary the oceanic Pacific plate slides under (is subducted beneath) the continental Eurasian Plate. The plate boundary is marked by the 10 km-deep Japan Trench. The earthquake focus was 30 km below the sea floor.
2. The epicentre was located about 130 km east of the city of Sendai.
3. The tsunami was triggered by the 8 m upthrust of 180 km of seabed.

Short-term effects

Tsunami

1. The earthquake triggered a series of large and deadly tsunami waves that quickly devastated low-lying north-eastern coastal areas of the country. Many waves were up to 6 metres (3 storeys) high and reached as far as 10 km inland in places.
2. Whole towns were washed away by the powerful surge of water.
3. Debris-laden water rapidly flooded coastal towns. Huge areas of farmland and low-lying land were left submerged under seawater.
4. Hundreds of aftershocks, many up to magnitude 6.0 or greater, followed in the days and weeks after the main quake.

Fig. 13 Airmen fly over the Sendai Airport in Japan to survey the tsunami aftermath.

Fig. 12 The earthquake in 2011 triggered a tsunami that destroyed many low-lying coastal parts in the north-east of Japan.

weblink Video of tsunami

Death and destruction

1. The death toll was over 20,000.
2. The tsunami walls were overtopped by the wave which meant that many coastal buildings were destroyed.
3. Infrastructure was heavily damaged, e.g. roads and rail lines. Electric power was knocked out, and water and sewerage systems were disrupted.
4. The tsunami caused a cooling system failure at a nuclear power plant which led to a level 7 nuclear meltdown and the release of radioactive materials.

Long-term effects

1. The economic destruction of the 'Triple Disaster' (earthquake, tsunami, nuclear meltdown) was massive: 138,000 buildings were destroyed and €254 billion in economic losses were incurred. This was the most expensive disaster in human history.
2. Since the earthquake only two nuclear reactors have reopened. As a result, the Japanese government has had to import large amounts of fossil fuels to make the electricity it needs. Consequently, Japan has experienced record trade deficits of around €70 billion per year since the disaster.
3. Residents in Japan are still recovering from the disaster. More than 450,000 people are still living in temporary housing after losing their homes in the tsunami.
4. About 300 tonnes of radioactive water continues to leak from the plant every day into the Pacific Ocean, affecting fish and other marine life.
5. The fishing and tourist industry is affected with people refusing to buy produce or visit the region in case of radioactive contamination.

Fig. 14 Fukushima power plant after the earthquake

Global effects

1. The earthquake upset the axis of rotation of the earth slightly. This shock shortened the length of day by about a microsecond and broke icebergs off ice shelves in Antarctica.
2. The tsunami raced across the Pacific, reaching Alaska, Hawaii and Chile. In Chile the tsunami was 2 metres high when it reached the shore.
3. Many countries, including Ireland, donated over €4 billion to help the recovery of the region.

Fig. 15 Aftermath of tsunami in Japan 2011

CORE UNIT: PATTERNS AND PROCESSES IN THE PHYSICAL ENVIRONMENT

Early warning saved lives

- Thanks to Japan's earthquake early warning system, residents of Tokyo received a minute of warning before the strong shaking hit the city.
- The country's early warning system and strict seismic building codes prevented many deaths from the earthquake. High-speed trains were stopped and factory automated assembly lines halted.
- People in Japan also received text alerts on their mobile phones warning them about the earthquake. But the size of the tsunami wave was far higher than was prepared for or expected.

Activity

Read the report on the earthquake in Japan which occurred in March 2011 and answer each of the following questions.

EARTHQUAKE ROCKS JAPAN. This was one of the most powerful earthquakes recorded in Japanese history, 8.9 magnitude. The tremors were the result of a violent uplift of the sea floor, 130 kilometres off the coast of the city of Sendai. The earthquake happened at a depth of 24 kilometres below the sea floor. This was the sixth largest earthquake in the world since 1900, when seismological records began. The tsunami moved across the Pacific Ocean at a speed of 800 km/h. The largest waves measured 7 metres high in the north-east of Japan.
Adapted from www.guardian.co.uk

(i) What was the magnitude of the earthquake?
(ii) Name the city close to the earthquake.
(iii) At what depth did the earthquake occur?
(iv) What speed did the tsunami reach as it moved across the Pacific Ocean?
(v) Briefly explain how a tsunami occurs.

2.5 Predicting earthquakes and preventing earthquake damage

Being able to predict earthquakes reliably and successfully would save thousands of lives and billions of dollars. Also, knowing when and where earthquakes might occur is very useful when making decisions on building structures such as bridges, dams, tall buildings and nuclear and other power stations.

At present we know which **regions** of the earth are most likely to experience earthquakes but we cannot determine when, within a short time frame, a major earthquake will occur. This makes evacuation almost impossible.

Methods used to try to predict earthquakes

1. Looking at patterns of **seismograph activity** on maps to see which areas might be next.
2. Measuring **crustal stress levels** with instruments placed in holes that are 1.5 km deep to map what is happening in the crust.
3. Measuring **ground tilting** with lasers to see which areas are moving.
4. Measuring **radon gas emissions** from wells and rocks which often increase when rocks are under stress.
5. Observing changes in **levels of oil and water** in wells. Rising levels mean the ground is under pressure.
6. Computer models are developed and used to predict the possible locations and times of future earthquakes.
7. Observing **unusual animal behaviour**. There have been reports of snakes coming out of hibernation early, farm animals refusing to enter buildings and restless pets. However, there are many reasons why animals may be restless so this is not very helpful.

> Few wild animals were killed by the Southeast Asian tsunami in 2004; they had sensed something and moved away from the coast.

Methods used to prevent earthquake damage

1. Since it is so difficult to successfully predict when an earthquake will occur, most governments invest millions of dollars in protecting their cities from structural damage.
2. Governments also prepare rescue and recovery plans to deal with the aftermath of an earthquake.
3. Many towns in earthquake-prone areas have public awareness programmes and 'earthquake drills' for their civil defence teams. Many schools have earthquake drills in the same way that Irish schools practise fire drills.
4. Earthquake-proof buildings help to prevent damage and death. Most people are killed by falling furniture and other unsecured items in buildings. Imagine all the cupboards in your home suddenly opening and the contents falling on you or the contents of the attic suddenly falling on top of you as you sleep. The simple measures shown in the table on the next page are very effective in reducing death and injury in the home during an earthquake.

CORE UNIT: PATTERNS AND PROCESSES IN THE PHYSICAL ENVIRONMENT

TO MAKE BUILDINGS EARTHQUAKE-PROOF

1. All kitchen items should be secured to the wall, e.g. fridges, cookers, cupboards, washing machines.
2. A bar should be placed across the front of cupboards to stop jars and tins sliding out.
3. Open-fronted shelving should not be used in sitting rooms or bedrooms. They should be fixed to the wall and cupboards locked.
4. In offices filing cabinets, photocopiers, desks and chairs should be fixed so they can't move around in an earthquake.
5. All windows should be shatterproof.
6. Building foundations should have 'seismic isolators' which absorb the force of the quake and reduce movement of the building.
7. Flexible material that can sway with and absorb the movement of the ground should be used.
8. Extra supports are attached to the corners on each floor to support the building as it shakes. These supports are cheap but effective.

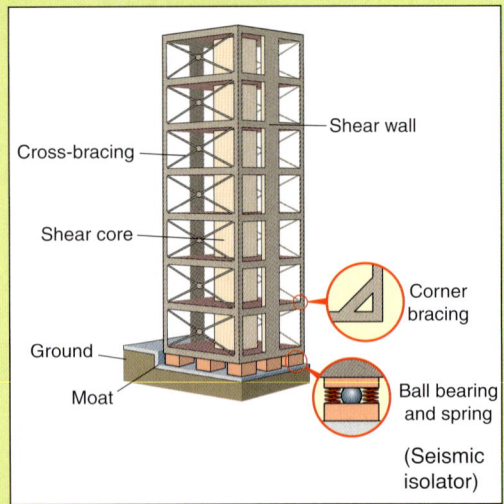

Fig. 16 How to make a building earthquake-proof

weblink Earthquake-resistant structures

Activity

Study the table and answer the questions.

1. Copy out the table below and write the names of the plates involved in causing the earthquakes. Some have been done for you.

Location	Year	Richter	Deaths	Plates
Nepal	2015	9.2	8,000+	Eurasian & Indian
Japan	2011	8.9	20,000	Eurasian & Pacific
Chile	2010	8.8	507	South American & Nazca
Haiti	2010	7.0	230,000	Caribbean & North American
Italy	2009	6.8	290	
China	2008	7.8	9,000	
Pakistan	2005	7.6	89,000	
Indonesia (tsunami)	2004	9.0	230,000	
Japan	2001	6.9	1 person	
Turkey	1999	7.2	18,000	
India	1993	6.6	100,000	
San Francisco	1989	6.9	64	

2. Research the cause and effects of any earthquake that you have studied.

Chapter Revision Questions

1. Explain the terms (a) focus, (b) epicentre, (c) aftershock, (d) tremor, (e) earthquake.
2. Name and describe **three** types of earthquake wave.
3. (a) What instrument is used to record earthquake activity?
   (b) What scale is used to measure the magnitude of an earthquake?
   (c) What scale is used to measure the intensity of an earthquake?
   (d) How do the scales you named in (b) and (c) above differ?
4. What is a tsunami? Why are they so devastating?
5. How are people in Japan warned of a tsunami in the Pacific Ocean region?
6. Describe **four** of the methods used in earthquake prediction.
7. Describe the cause and effects of the 2011 Japanese tsunami.
8. Examine the methods used to reduce the destructive effects of earthquakes.
9. Research the cause and effects of any earthquake that you have studied.
10. Using the diagram, choose the correct answer in each of the sentences listed below.
    (a) **B** is the point where the actual earthquake occurred. It is known as the: epicentre / focus / Richter point.
    (b) **A** is the point on the earth's surface directly above where the earthquake occurred. It is known as the: epicentre / focus / hot point.
    (c) Earthquakes are measured using an instrument called a: seismograph / thermograph / cardiogram.
    (d) Earthquake magnitude is classified according to the: Mercalli scale / Beaufort scale / Richter scale.

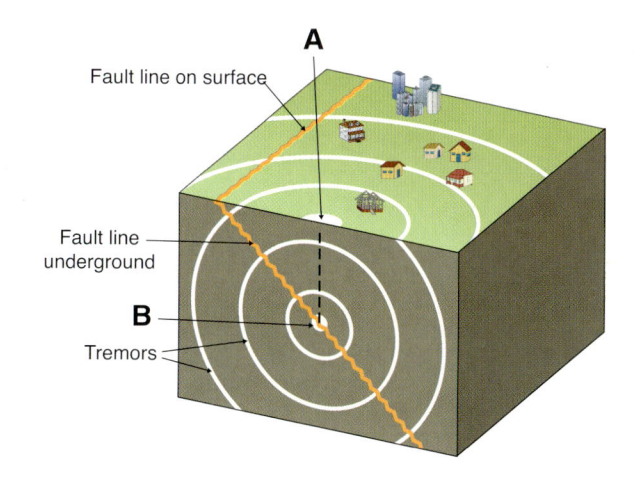

CORE UNIT: PATTERNS AND PROCESSES IN THE PHYSICAL ENVIRONMENT

LC Exam Questions

Higher Level students must be able to answer Ordinary and Higher Level questions.

■ OL Questions

11. (i) Match each of the letters **A**, **B** and **C** in the diagram with the correct feature in the table below.

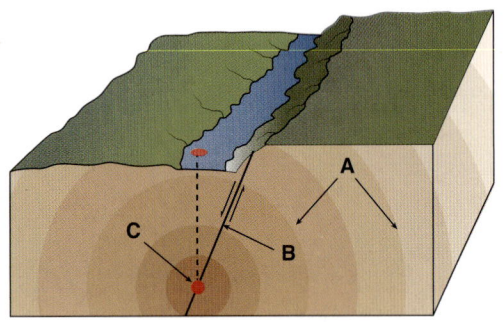

Feature	Letter
Focus	
Shockwaves	
Faultline	

    (ii) Name a scale used to measure earthquakes.

    (iii) What is the name given to a large wave caused by an earthquake under the water in the ocean?

12. (i) Name **one** location where an earthquake has occurred.

    (ii) Name a scale used to measure the force of an earthquake.

    (iii) Describe how earthquakes occur and describe their main effects.

13. Read the newspaper article and answer each of the questions that follow.

    EARTHQUAKE IN THE IRISH SEA

    A 3.8 magnitude earthquake struck this morning. The epicentre was located approximately 2 km off the coast of the Lleyn Peninsula in Wales and was 97 km southeast of Dublin. The quake was followed four minutes later by a smaller 1.7 magnitude tremor. Moderate shaking was felt in Carlow, Kildare, Wicklow, Wexford and Dublin. Earthquake stations as far away as Valentia, Donegal and Galway also recorded the earthquake.

    Adapted from the *Irish Independent*, June 28, 2013

    (i) What direction from Dublin was the epicentre of the earthquake and how far, in kilometres, was the epicentre from Dublin?

    (ii) Name **two** locations in Ireland where the earthquake was felt.

    (iii) What is the term given to the smaller tremors which follow the main earthquake?

    (iv) State **two** effects of earthquakes.

    (v) Explain briefly why Ireland has not experienced major earthquakes.

14. Explain with reference to examples that you have studied how the theory of plate tectonics helps explain the distribution of earthquakes around the world.

■ HL Questions

15. Examine the map below and answer the following questions.

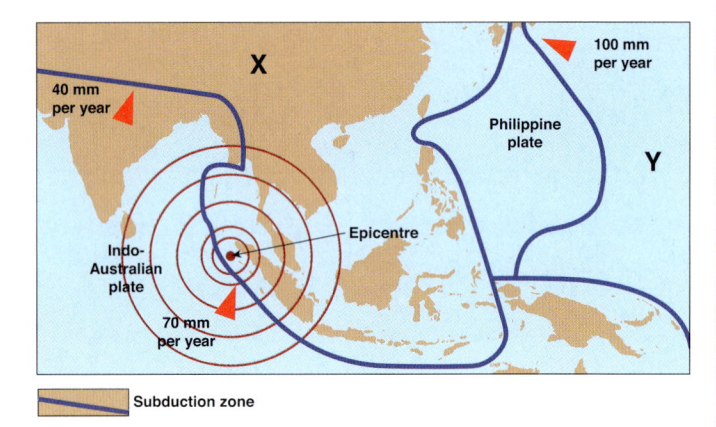

    (i) Name the plates marked X and Y.

    (ii) What is the average annual movement of the Indo-Australian Plate?

    (iii) Explain what is meant by the term 'epicentre'.

    (iv) Given that the epicentre of the earthquake shown above is off shore, name and briefly explain the main effect of this earthquake on the sea.

    (v) Name **two** scales that measure the magnitude/intensity of an earthquake.

16. Explain how the occurrence of earthquakes and volcanic eruptions can be monitored and predicted.

CHAPTER 2: EARTHQUAKES

Key Words

You should be able to explain both verbally and in writing each of the key words listed below.

- aftershock
- elastic rebound
- epicentre
- focus
- intensity
- liquefaction
- magnitude
- Modified Mercalli Scale
- P (primary) waves
- Richter scale
- S (secondary) waves
- seismic
- seismograph
- shock waves
- surface waves
- tremor
- tsunami

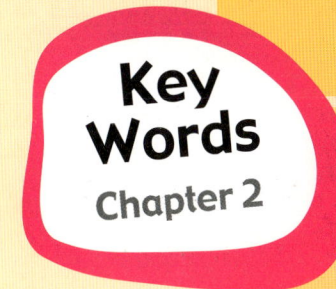

Digital Resources are available for this chapter at mentorbooks.ie/resources

CHAPTER 3

Volcanoes

Key Theme

Volcanoes and their associated landforms are created by forces within the earth.

Learning Outcomes

At the end of this chapter you will be able to:
- Explain why volcanoes occur where they do in the world.
- Name and describe the formation of volcanic landforms.
- Describe the effects of volcanoes on people using the case studies provided.
- Outline methods used to measure and predict volcanoes.

Contents

3.1	Volcanoes	41
3.2	The distribution of volcanic activity	41
3.3	The life cycle of volcanoes	41
3.4	Products of volcanic eruptions	42
3.5	External/extrusive volcanic landforms	44
3.6	Internal/intrusive plutonic landforms	48
3.7	Positive and negative effects of volcanoes	50
3.8	Predicting volcanic eruptions	51
	Case Study: Mount St Helens, USA	52

Revision Space

Chapter Revision Questions – LC Exam Questions – Key Word List 54

3.1 Volcanoes

A volcano occurs when molten magma forces its way up to the earth's surface either through a **vent** (hole) or through a **fissure** (large cracks). As magma rises, gas bubbles expand and help force it up to the earth's surface through the crust. Once the magma reaches the surface the sudden release of pressure causes a volcanic eruption. A vent eruption leads to the formation of the typical cone-shaped mountain. Fissure eruptions lead to the formation of a wider and flatter **plateau**. Upon reaching the surface the magma is called **lava**. Depending on the type of lava being ejected, eruptions may be extremely violent or gentle.

Fig. 1 Stromboli volcano erupting in Italy

weblink
Summary of volcano shapes and lava type

3.2 The distribution of volcanic activity

Volcanoes occur in three types of locations:
1. Mid-ocean ridges (at constructive plate margins).
2. Subduction zones (at destructive plate margins, i.e. oceanic–oceanic and oceanic–continental plate collision zones).
3. Hotspots in the middle of plates.

The reasons for these locations have been explained in Chapter 1.

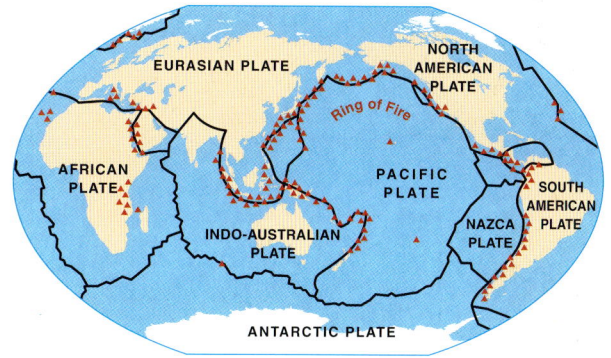

Fig. 2 Global distribution of volcanoes

3.3 The life cycle of volcanoes

weblink
Volcanism at subduction zone

A volcano may fall into one of three categories:

Active volcano: Continuously erupting, e.g. Stromboli, Italy; Mount Etna, Italy.

Dormant volcano: This is a volcano which has not erupted for many hundreds of years. Mount St Helens in the US was dormant for 123 years until its spectacular but predicted eruption in 1980, and Mount Pinatubo in the Philippines had not erupted for 600 years before its 1995 eruption.

Extinct volcano: This is a volcano that has not erupted in recorded history, e.g. Slemish in County Antrim.

Over time, the magma beneath the earth's surface may cool down or move away. This can reduce volcanic activity on the surface, leaving areas with hot springs and geysers. Yellowstone National Park in the United States and Bath in England are such areas.

CORE UNIT: PATTERNS AND PROCESSES IN THE PHYSICAL ENVIRONMENT

3.4 Products of volcanic eruptions

Volcanic eruptions produce the following substances:

1. Lava
2. Pyroclasts and pyroclastic flows
3. Poisonous gases
4. Ash, pumice and dust (**tephra**)
5. Water vapour.

weblink Erupted materials

Fig. 3 Erupting volcano at Kamchatka, Russia

1. Lava

There are two types of lava.

Acid lava
Basic lava

They each have different compositions based on the amount of silica they contain. The lavas are produced at different locations, form different volcanic landforms and have different volcanic eruption types (see table below).

weblink Scientists getting lava sample

Fig. 4 Lava at Kilauea in Hawaii

TABLE TO SUMMARISE THE CHARACTERISTICS OF ACID AND BASIC LAVA

Properties	Acid lava	Basic lava
Silica content	70% or more	Less than 55%
Trapped gases	Lots of trapped gases due to high silica content which makes lava highly viscous (sticky). Gases cannot escape.	Few trapped gases due to low silica content. Lava is very fluid and runny allowing gases to escape easily.
Type of eruption	Very explosive, violent, destructive, e.g. Mount St Helens, USA.	Non-explosive, gentle lava eruptions. Lava fountains, e.g. Mauna Loa, Hawaii.
Volcanic cone shape	Dome	Shield Volcano
Typical location	Subduction zones. Destructive plate boundaries involving oceanic crust.	(a) Constructive plate boundaries – mid-ocean ridges. (b) Hotspots
Examples	Destructive boundary between Nazca plate and South American plate.	(a) Mid-Atlantic Ridge (Iceland), Mount Hekla (b) Hawaii, e.g. Mauna Loa.

2. Pyroclasts and pyroclastic flows
Pyroclasts are hot ash, lava and rock fragments that are thrown out of the volcano. These are sometimes called **volcanic bombs**.

Pyroclastic flows are boiling clouds of ash and rock which travel at great speeds (up to 600 km/h) down the sides of the volcano. They smother and destroy everything in their path. These flows are also called *nuée ardentes*. Examples include Mount Pinatubo in the Philippines and Mount Vesuvius in Italy. In AD 79, Mount Vesuvius erupted during which the pyroclastic flow covered the town of Pompeii in southern Italy.

Fig. 5 A pyroclastic flow on Mount Etna

weblink
Documentary on Lake Nyos

3. Poisonous gases
Volcanoes release several dangerous gases. Carbon dioxide suffocates people and animals when it bubbles from crater lakes as has happened several times in Lake Nyos, Cameroon. Chlorine and sulfur dioxide are also released. The amount of sulfur dioxide gas released increases rapidly close to the time of eruption, e.g. Mount St Helens in 1980.

4. Ash, pumice and dust (tephra)
In explosive volcanoes the power of the eruption pulverises rock into a fine ash inside the vent and cone. The ash is thrown many kilometres into the sky and may be carried by winds across the world and can disrupt air travel e.g. Iceland 2010. The height to which an ash cloud rises is used to measure the force of a volcanic eruption on the **volcanic explosivity index (VEI)**.

When lava is thrown from the volcano it is whipped up and becomes full of air bubbles. If it cools quickly enough these bubbles are trapped in the rock and it is now called **pumice**. Some pieces contain so much air that they float in water.

5. Water vapour
Many volcanoes along subduction zones release huge amounts of water vapour (from the sea water carried into the mantle by the sinking oceanic plates). As this vapour rises into the air it cools rapidly creating torrential rain during the eruption. The intense rainfall can trigger **lahars**, e.g. Mount St Helens, 1980; Colombia, 1985.

CORE UNIT: PATTERNS AND PROCESSES IN THE PHYSICAL ENVIRONMENT

> **IN DEPTH: Lahars**
>
> - Lahar is an Indonesian word that describes a mixture of water and rock fragments flowing down the slopes of a volcano.
> - Volcanic eruptions may trigger one or more lahars by quickly melting snow and ice on a volcano.
> - Usually lahars are formed by intense rainfall during or after an eruption – rainwater can easily erode loose volcanic rock and soil on hillsides. Some of the largest lahars begin as landslides of saturated rock on the sides of a volcano.
> - When moving, a lahar looks like a mass of wet concrete that can carry rock debris up to 10 m in diameter.
> - Lahars vary in size and speed. Small lahars less than a few metres wide and several centimetres deep may flow at speeds of a few metres per second. Large lahars, hundreds of metres wide and tens of metres deep, can flow at over 80 km/h – much too fast for people to outrun, e.g. Nevado del Ruiz, Colombia which killed 25,000 people.
>
> Fig. 6 A lahar flows from Mount St Helens' crater.

weblink
Lahar on Mount Ruapehu, New Zealand

3.5 External/extrusive volcanic landforms

Volcanic features found on the earth's surface include:

1. **Lava plateaux**, e.g. the Antrim Plateau in Northern Ireland and the Deccan Plateau in India.
2. **Volcanic cones**, e.g. Mount Etna. These can be of varying shapes, sizes and composition depending upon the type of lava and/or ash ejected. Examples include a dome volcano, shield volcano, ash/cinder cone, composite volcano.
3. **Craters and calderas**, e.g. Crater Lake, Oregon, USA; Lake Taal, Philippines.
4. **Volcanic plugs** – the remains of magma that solidified in the vent. The volcano has since eroded away. Examples include Le Puy, France and the location of Edinburgh Castle, Scotland.

This section will focus on volcanic cones and lava plateaux.

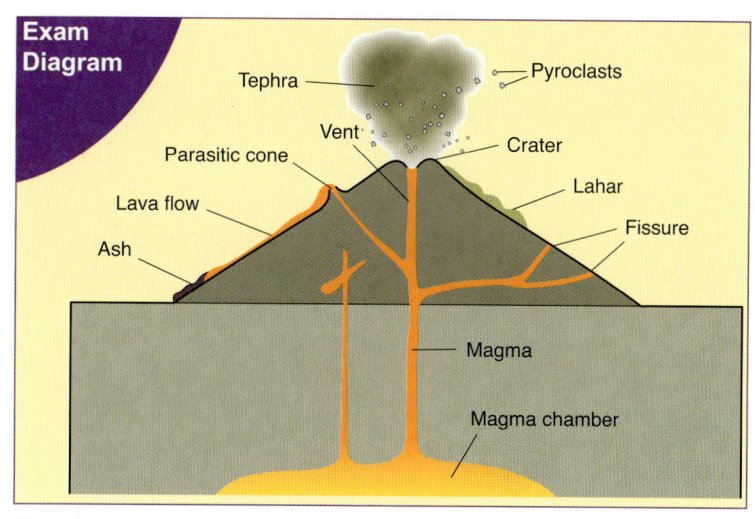

Fig. 7 Parts and products of a typical volcano

Volcanic cones

Volcanic cones are extrusive volcanic landforms. Volcanic cones form when magma rises from the mantle and forces its way to the surface through a weakness (vent) in the crust. As the magma rises gas bubbles expand within it, helping to force it through cracks in the rock above. Once the magma reaches the surface, a volcanic eruption occurs gradually forming a volcanic cone. There are many types of volcanic cones depending on the type of eruption. We shall focus on two types – shield volcanoes and volcanic domes.

(a) Shield volcanoes

Shield volcanoes are volcanic cones with broad, gentle, concave slopes, e.g. Mauna Loa, Hawaii. They are associated with hotspots where large amounts of highly fluid, basic (less than 55% silica) lava erupts to the surface. Basic lava tends to build enormous low angle cones because it flows so easily over the ground for many kilometres before it solidifies into basalt rock.

Over time thousands of lava flows build up and cool, one above the other to form some of the largest volcanoes in the world. Mauna Loa in Hawaii rises over 4,160 m above sea level but when measured from its base on the sea floor it is just over 10,000 m high, almost 2 km taller than Mount Everest.

Fig. 8 Mauna Loa, Hawaii – a shield volcano

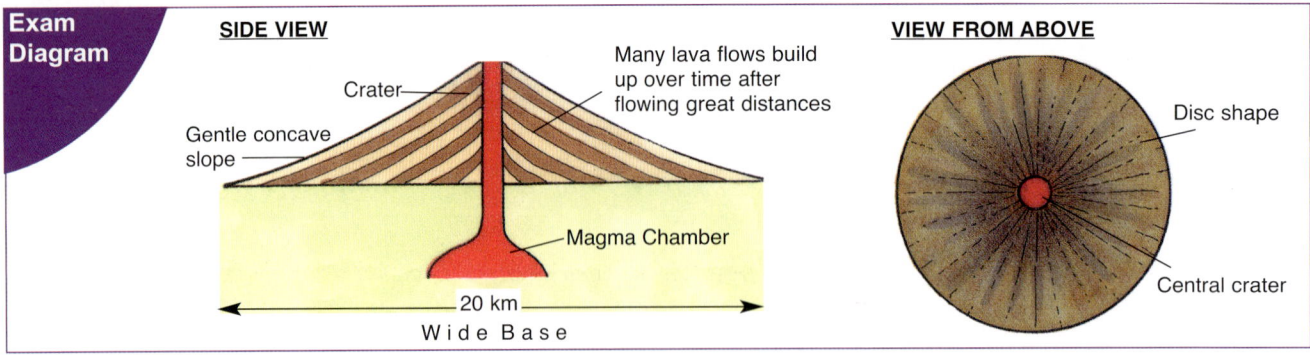

CORE UNIT: PATTERNS AND PROCESSES IN THE PHYSICAL ENVIRONMENT

Fig. 9 A shield volcano

Fig. 10 Looking down into the crater in Mount Vesuvius

(b) Volcanic domes

Volcanic domes are mounds that form when viscous acidic (greater than 70% silica) lava is erupted slowly and piles up covering the vent, rather than flowing away down the mountain. Volcanic domes are common at subduction zones where they may grow inside **strato volcanoes** (volcanic cones made of layers of ash, lava and dust). Volcanic domes have steep-sided convex slopes that are very unstable and may collapse causing massive landslides. This happened at Mount St Helens during the eruption in 1980.

Volcanic domes can grow in two ways: (i) magma from the magma chamber rises into the volcano causing it to bulge, (ii) magma can rise through the vent to the volcanic crater and form a dome structure in the crater. Both of these types of doming can occur in the same volcano, e.g. Mount St Helens, USA.

Fig. 11 The dome of Merapi volcano in Indonesia

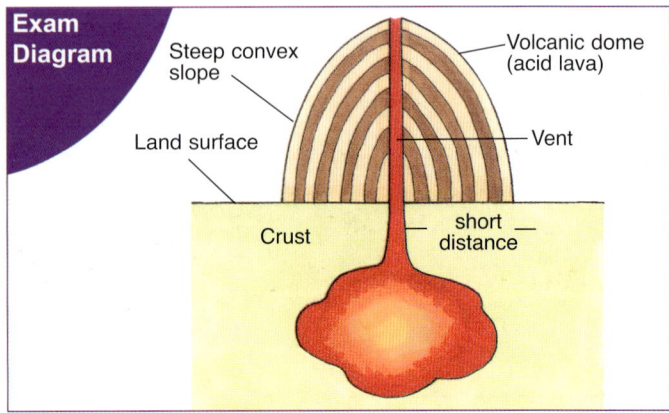

Fig. 12 A dome volcano

Lava plateaux

Lava plateaux are steep-sided flat-topped uplands of basalt that cover large areas.

They are formed by the large but less explosive eruptions of highly fluid basic lava that pours from long narrow openings or fissures in the crust. During each eruption, the lava flows out from these openings, solidifies and builds up layer upon layer each time.

The eruptions are less explosive because the basic lava does not contain trapped gases.

Examples include the Antrim Plateau in County Antrim, Northern Ireland and the Deccan Plateau, India.

All lava plateaux have the same characteristics:
- They cover very large areas of land.
- They have a layered structure due to basalt flows solidifying one above the other.
- Each lava flow eruption makes the plateau higher.

In Ireland the Antrim Plateau was formed when a constructive plate boundary formed about 60 million years ago. When the plates started to move apart, the landscape of north-east Ireland would have resembled that of present-day Iceland. The crust of the earth was stretched and huge cracks or fissures were formed out of which poured enormous flows of basic lava that covered the land. These lava flows continued for nearly 2 million years producing a plateau almost 1,800 m high. The lava flows cooled to form basalt, a dark fine-grained rock characteristic of fissure eruptions.

As the thick lava flows cooled and contracted, the basalt formed unique polygonal (many-sided) columns. At the Giant's Causeway in County Antrim the columns are hexagonal and are an important tourist attraction.

Fig. 13 Lava plateau at the Giant's Causeway, County Antrim

weblink
Tectonic settings

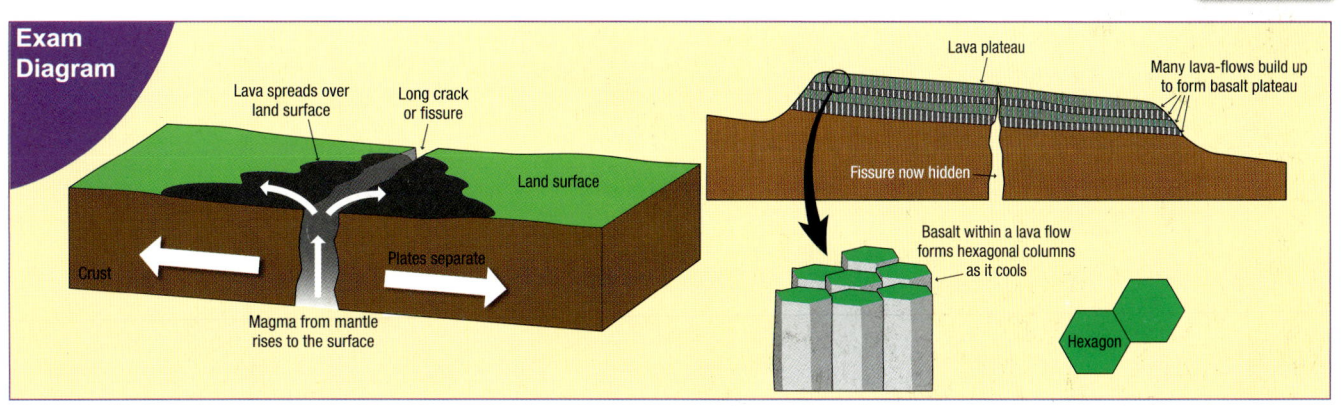

Fig. 14 The formation of a lava plateau

CORE UNIT: PATTERNS AND PROCESSES IN THE PHYSICAL ENVIRONMENT

3.6 Internal/intrusive plutonic landforms

Plutonic landforms occur beneath the earth's surface when magma cooled and hardened into rock but they are visible today because weathering and erosion have removed the overlying rocks.

1. Batholiths

A **batholith** is a large mass of igneous rock (granite) that formed as magma from the mantle pushed (intruded) into the crust above and slowly, over thousands of years, cooled down and solidified.

In Ireland, a granite batholith formed 400 million years ago during the Caledonian fold mountain building period. Magma was injected into and cooled inside the folded rocks. Heat from the magma metamorphosed the overlying rock forming a **metamorphic aureole** around the batholith. Weathering and erosion removed the rocks above so that today we see the exposed batholiths as low, rounded, granite mountains, e.g. the Wicklow mountain range and the Mourne mountains in County Down.

weblink
Summary of intrusive landforms

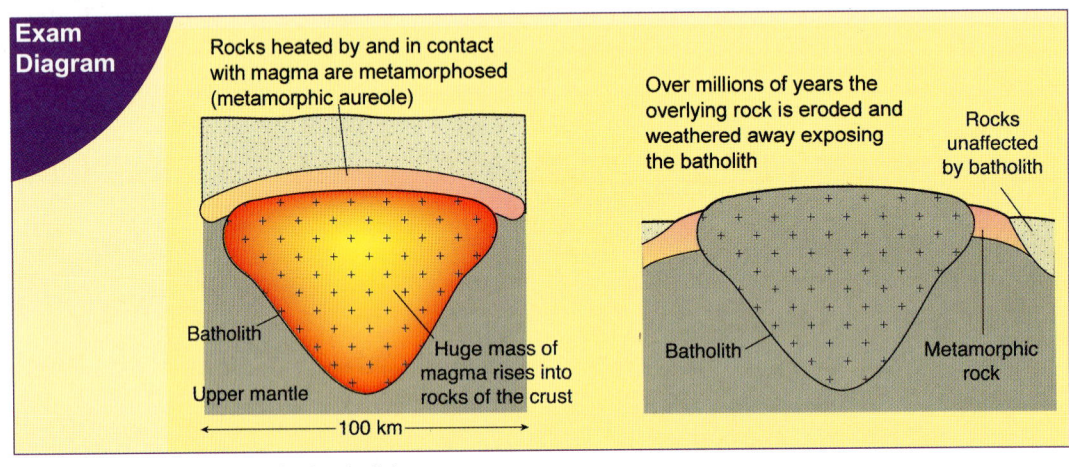

Fig. 15 The formation of a batholith

2. Sills

Sills form as magma pushes its way between layers of rock, then cools and solidifies as large flat areas of igneous rock, e.g. Fair Head, County Antrim.

3. Dykes

Dykes form as magma forces its way across rock layers, cools and solidifies. Dykes are walls of basalt or granite running perpendicular to the rock layers. They are very common in volcanoes where magma forces its way through fissures in the cone and then cools. They add strength and support to the cone, acting like a ribcage for the volcano.

Fig. 16 Basalt dyke, County Down

4. Laccoliths

Laccoliths form when magma seeps between rock layers pushing them upwards and cools to form dome-like structures. If the laccolith occurs very close to the surface, doming may occur. Dome mountains are the result of a great amount of melted rock pushing its way up under the earth. The crust is heaved upward, without folding or faulting, into a rounded dome. Weathering and erosion attack the upland areas formed by the dome, often exposing the igneous rock at the heart of the dome mountains. Dome mountains are common in North America, e.g. the Black Mountains of South Dakota.

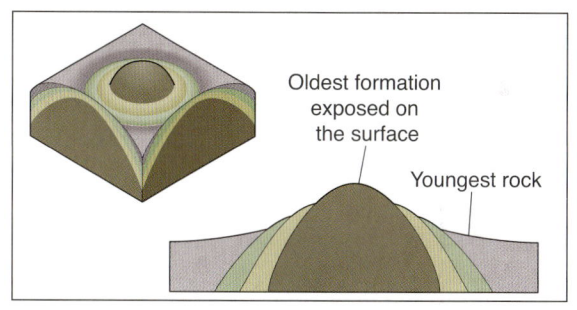

Fig. 17 Doming

5. Lopoliths

Lopoliths form in a similar way to laccoliths except the weight of magma causes the rock layers to sag downwards.

Fig. 18 Laccolith in Montana, USA

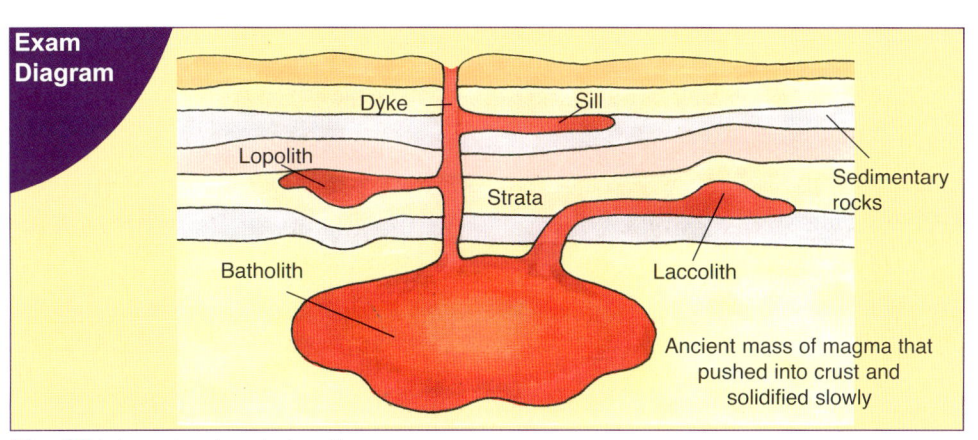

Fig. 19 Internal volcanic landforms

SUMMARY OF LANDFORMS

	Name	Example
Extrusive volcanic landforms	lava plateau volcanic cones caldera volcanic plug	Giant's Causeway, County Antrim Mount St Helens, USA (dome, composite) Mauna Loa, Hawaii (shield) Crater Lake, Oregon, USA Le Puy, France
Intrusive volcanic landforms	batholith lopolith sill dyke laccolith	Wicklow Mountains, County Wicklow Montana, USA Fair Head, County Antrim Newry, County Down Black Mountains, South Dakota, USA

49

3.7 Positive and negative effects of volcanoes

Positive effects

1. New land created: Surtsey Island, Iceland and Hawaii, a physical and economic benefit.
2. Geothermal energy: New Zealand and Iceland, an economic benefit.
3. Fertile soil after lava has been weathered and eroded: Terra Rossa soils in the Canary Islands and Brazil, a physical, economic and social benefit.
4. Minerals: sulfur rock outcrops in Malaysia, an economic benefit.
5. Tourism: geysers, Old Faithful Geyser in Yellowstone National Park and Iceland, Pompeii in Italy, economic and social benefit.

Fig. 20 Geothermal energy provides economic benefits.

Fig. 21 Tourists travel to Iceland to watch geysers spectacularly erupt.

Negative effects

1. Lava flows: basic lava destroys land as it flows long distances, e.g. Hawaii.
2. Volcanic ash blown into the atmosphere can disrupt air travel, e.g. Iceland 2010.
3. Lahars: hot rivers of mud that flow down the slopes of volcanoes and travel many kilometres often at great speeds. In 1985 the Nevado del Ruiz lahar in Colombia killed 22,000 people in the town of Armero as the eruption melted the snow cap.
4. Pyroclastic flows: hot clouds of ash and rock flow down valleys – Mount Pinatubo in the Philippines in 1991.
5. Poisonous gases: chlorine, sulfur, carbon dioxide. In 1986 carbon dioxide burst out of Lake Nyos in Cameroon killing over 2,000 people.

Fig. 22 Lava can cause great destruction to an area.

Fig. 23 Volcanic ash can disrupt air travel.

3.8 Predicting volcanic eruptions

The prediction of volcanic eruptions is generally more reliable than that of earthquakes. Most active volcanoes are well known, monitored and mapped by vulcanologists. Twenty per cent of the world's volcanoes are watched 24 hours a day.

Dormant volcanoes are also well known and those likely to erupt near large populations are constantly monitored and evacuation plans are already in place, e.g. Mount Vesuvius in Italy.

Methods of predicting volcanic eruptions

1. Ground deformation

Swelling of a volcano signals that magma is rising within it. Scientists monitoring an active volcano will measure the tilt of the slope and track changes in the rate of swelling. The Mount St Helens' dome swelled by 1.5 m per day in the month before it erupted in May 1980 due to magma rising into the volcanic cone. When the land around a volcano is deformed by magma underground, the water level in nearby wells may rise or fall. If the volcano is near the coast, the shoreline may rise or be submerged. An increased rate of swelling, especially if accompanied by an increase in sulfur dioxide emissions and earthquakes, is almost a sure sign of an impending eruption.

2. History of volcanic eruptions

Checking historic records can identify the pattern of eruptions. For example, Mount Katla in Iceland erupts every 80 years on average. It last erupted in 1918.

weblink
Eruption at Mount St Helens

3. Gas emissions

Before an eruption, gas emissions can increase by more than 5-10 their normal levels. As magma nears the surface, gases escape more easily. This process is much like what happens when you open a bottle of soda and carbon dioxide escapes. Sulfur dioxide is one of the main volcanic gases, and increasing amounts of it usually means the arrival of more and more magma near the surface. For example, on 13 May 1991, 500 tonnes of sulfur dioxide per day was released from Mount Pinatubo in the Philippines. On 28 May, just two weeks later, sulfur dioxide emissions had increased to 5,000 tonnes per day, ten times the earlier amount. Mount Pinatubo erupted on 12 June 1991.

weblink
Volcanic info

4. Seismic patterns

Volcanoes trigger earthquakes before they erupt. These quakes have a pattern that can help predict when the volcano will erupt.

All of these methods were combined to help avert major loss of life before the Mount St Helens (USA) eruption in 1980 and the Mount Pinatubo (Philippines) eruption in 1995. They were also used to predict the 2010 eruption of Mount Merapi in Indonesia.

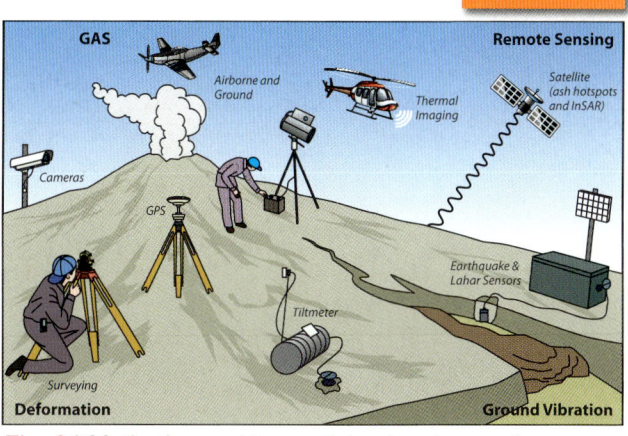

Fig. 24 Methods used to predict volcanic eruptions

CORE UNIT: PATTERNS AND PROCESSES IN THE PHYSICAL ENVIRONMENT

CHAPTER 3
Case Study

Mount St Helens, USA
A predicted volcanic eruption in 1980

weblink
Sudden eruption of Mount St Helens

1. Mount St Helens is an active stratovolcano (volcanic cone is composed of layers of ash and lava) located on the west coast of North America in Washington State.
2. Mount St Helens is located along the Pacific Ring of Fire at the destructive plate boundary between the Oceanic Juan de Fuca plate and the Continental North American plate. It is one of a chain of volcanoes called the Cascades.
3. Mount St Helens lay dormant for 123 years until 1980. Today Mount St Helens is the most active of all the Cascades volcanoes.

Predicting the eruption

Geologists had set up a network of monitoring equipment on the volcano:
- Laser measurements monitored the shape of the cone.
- Heat sensors took the ground temperature.
- Seismometers measured the vibrations caused by moving magma.
- Gas sensors measured sulfur dioxide, carbon dioxide and radon emissions.

4. During March 1980, there were many small earthquakes and steam-venting episodes as magma moved below the volcano, indicating a renewal of activity.
5. Slowly a huge bulge (volcanic dome) and a fracture system formed on the north slope of the volcano. Deep underground, huge volumes of magma were being pushed up into the volcano. The dome in the crater grew by up to 1.8 m per day.

Fig. 25 Geologists measure the shape of the volcanic dome to help predict when it will erupt.

6. The earthquake activity continued and caused avalanches of snow and ice. People were evacuated from their homes. The side of the volcano was pushed upwards and outwards by over 135 m.
7. Geologists warned that sliding/movement of the bulge could cause a landslide which might trigger volcanic eruptions.

The eruption

8. On 18 May, a 5.1 earthquake beneath the mountain triggered the sudden collapse of one side/flank of the volcano. This caused a massive landslide on the north slope of the volcano. This landslide, the largest in recorded history, relieved pressure from within the volcano and allowed thousands of cubic metres of snow and meltwater to flow in. As the cold water came into contact with the hot lava dome, it vaporised and caused a huge lateral explosion. This blast, travelling at 483 km/h, swept out of the north side of the mountain. It blasted out a mixture of rock pieces, ash and steam destroying everything in its path. A 60 km^2 fan-shaped area was completely destroyed.
9. The massive ash cloud rose 24 km into the atmosphere in just 15 minutes and reached the east coast of America in 3 days. Most of the ash fell within 500 km

CHAPTER 3: VOLCANOES

of the mountain; finer ash circled the earth in 15 days. The eruption measured 4 on the volcanic explosivity index.

10. Mudflows/lahars of melted snow and ice travelled down the valleys destroying everything in its path.

11. Pyroclastic flows with temperatures of 700°C rolled out of the crater. These flows covered 10 km² and killed 57 people.

Effects of the eruption
On infrastructure

12. The eruption destroyed 27 bridges, 24 km of railway and 300 km of roads. The mudflows and flooding affected sewage and water treatment. Flights were cancelled due to the ash. Electricity transformers were shortcircuited by the ash causing major blackouts.

On wildlife

13. Twenty-four thousand hectares of forest were damaged/destroyed, crops were ruined and animals and fish were wiped out.

On the economy

14. The eruption cost €1 billion in terms of lost timber, repair works and agricultural losses.

On the volcano

15. The top 400 m of the volcano was blown away by the eruption.

Since 1980

16. Mount St Helens remains active. It is expected to continue erupting but no one knows for how long. The volcano is being carefully monitored by a volcano observatory 5 km away. Seismic disturbances, gas emissions, temperature, changes in height, water levels, sediment flow rates and even magma movement are all carefully measured and evaluated for risk. A new dome continues to grow slowly in the crater.

weblink Living beside a volcano

weblink Monitoring Mount St Helens

Fig. 26 Mount St Helens before and after the eruption. In the 'after' photo note the steaming dome growing within the crater.

Activity

Examine the map and legend to the right showing the extent of the materials deposited as a result of the eruption of the Mount St Helens volcano and answer the following questions.

(i) What were the most extensive deposits as a result of the eruption?
(ii) What was the direction of the pyroclastic flow deposits?
(iii) What distance did the pyroclastic flow deposits extend to?
(iv) Name two examples of pyroclastic materials.
(v) Explain briefly why some volcanoes erupt violently.

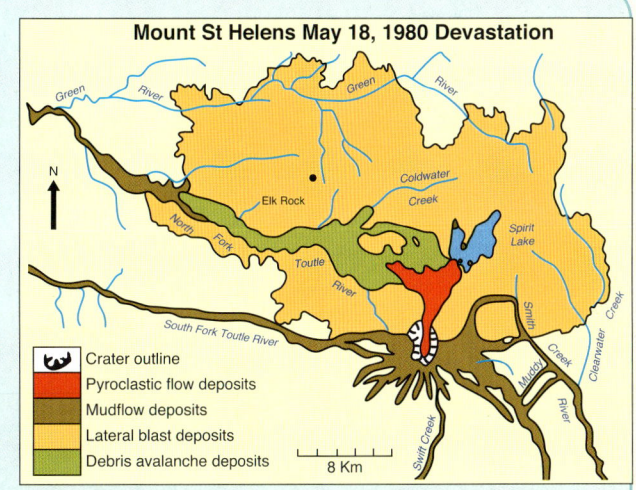

Fig. 27 Materials deposited as a result of eruption

CORE UNIT: PATTERNS AND PROCESSES IN THE PHYSICAL ENVIRONMENT

Chapter Revision Questions

1. Draw a labelled diagram showing the main parts of a typical volcano.

2. Name and describe the **three** stages in the life cycle of a volcano and give an example of each.

3. Name and describe **three** products of volcanic eruptions. Give an example of each.

4. Explain the differences between acidic and basic lava. Why do some volcanoes erupt violently?

5. Explain each of the following terms: (a) pyroclastic flow, (b) lahar, (c) magma chamber.

6. Name, describe and give an example of **two** external and **two** internal volcanic landforms. Draw a diagram to illustrate your answer.

7. Explain **three** methods used to predict volcanic eruptions, and **three** methods used to monitor eruptions. Name and briefly explain **one** way of measuring volcanic eruptions.

8. Volcanoes can have both negative and positive effects on the landscape and on people. Explain one negative and one positive effect of volcanoes.

9. Outline the consequences of the eruption of the volcano on Mount St Helens. Describe how the volcano is monitored and the methods used to predict further volcanic activity.

10. Using the diagram below, match each of the intrusive volcanic landforms with the letters A-E in the diagram: sill; laccolith; dyke; batholith; lopolith.

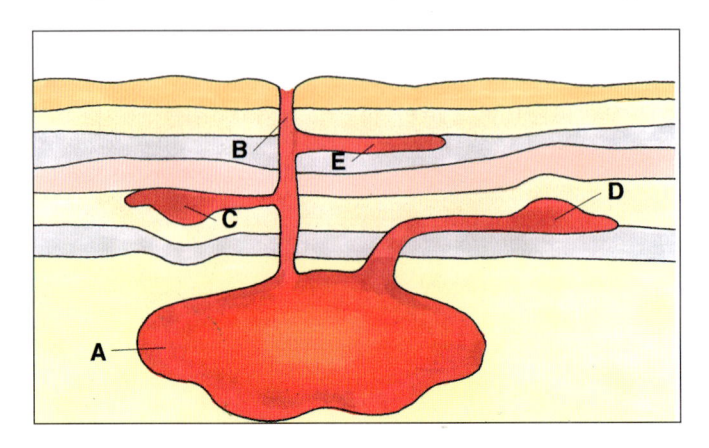

CHAPTER 3: VOLCANOES

LC Exam Questions

Higher Level students must be able to answer Ordinary and Higher Level questions.

OL Questions

11. Examine the diagram of a volcano below. Match the letters A–E with the following features: vent; secondary cone; ash cloud; crater; magma chamber.

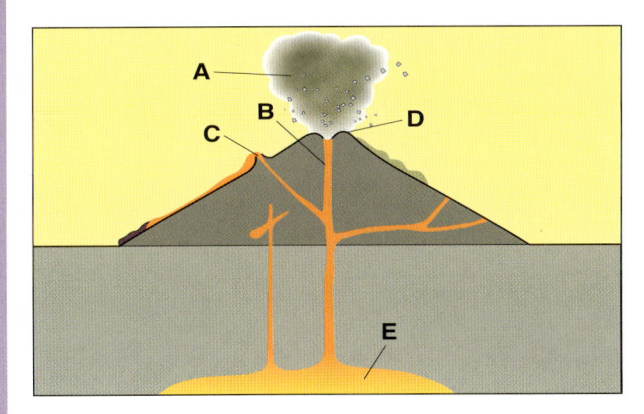

A	
B	
C	
D	
E	

12. Explain in detail how volcanoes occur.
13. Explain with the aid of an example which you have studied why volcanic activity happens at plate margins.

HL Questions

14. Examine the diagram below and answer each of the following questions.

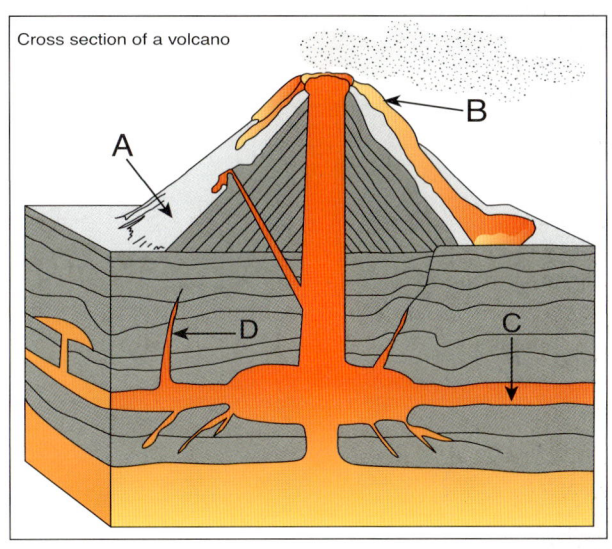

    Cross section of a volcano

    (i) Match each of the letters A, B, C and D with the feature that best matches it in the table below.

    (ii) Indicate whether plutonic processes or volcanic processes are most associated with each of the features by ticking the correct box in the table.

Feature	(i) Letter	(ii) Plutonic	(iii) Volcanic
Sill			
Pyroclastic sediment			
Dyke			
Lava flow			

15. Explain how the study of plate tectonics has helped us to understand the global distribution of volcanoes.
16. Examine the processes that have led to the formation of any **two** volcanic landforms.

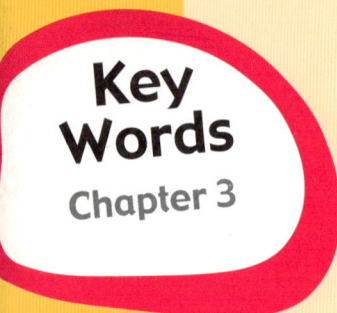

CORE UNIT: PATTERNS AND PROCESSES IN THE PHYSICAL ENVIRONMENT

Key Words — Chapter 3

Key Words

You should be able to explain both verbally and in writing each of the key words listed below.

acidic lava	metamorphic aureole
active volcano	plateau
basic lava	plutonic landforms
batholith	pumice
caldera	pyroclastic flows
crater	pyroclasts
dormant volcano	shield volcanoes
dykes	sills
extinct volcano	strato volcano
extrusive	tephra
fissure	vent
intrusive	volcanic bombs
laccolith	volcanic cone
lahar	volcanic domes
lava	volcanic explosivity index (VEI)
lava plateau	volcanic plugs
lopolith	

Digital Resources are available for this chapter at mentorbooks.ie/resources

CHAPTER 4

Folding and Faulting in the Earth's Crust

Key Theme

Rocks of the earth's crust are folded and faulted by forces within the earth.

Learning Outcomes

At the end of this chapter you should be able to:
- Name the parts of a fold and draw the main types of folds.
- Name and describe the three phases of fold mountain building.
- Explain what a fault is and describe the main types of faults.
- Describe the formation of fold mountains in southern Ireland.
- Describe the landforms created by faulting of the earth's crust.

Contents

4.1	Folding	58
4.2	Fold mountains in Ireland	60
	Case Study 1: The Munster Ridge and Valley Province	
4.3	Faulting and associated landscapes	61
	Case Study 2: The Great African Rift Valley	63

Revision Space

Chapter Revision Questions – LC Exam Questions – Key Word List 64

4.1 Folding

When tectonic plates collide, they place huge pressure (plate **compression**) on the rocks of the earth's surface. When rock layers are crumpled up by these forces, they **fold** up into ridges called **anticlines** and valleys called **synclines**.

Folds can be seen very easily in sedimentary rocks, e.g. Loughshinny in north County Dublin and the Rock of Cashel in County Tipperary. Rocks can be folded because at depth they are subjected to great heat and pressure which allows the rock to bend without breaking. Different types of fold are formed depending on the strength and direction of the pressure put on the rock. These are shown in Figs. 2 and 3.

Fig. 1 Folded limestone rock at Loughshinny, North County Dublin

Types of folding
Symmetric/simple folds

Symmetric folds are formed when pressure is applied gently and equally from both sides of the rock layers. They have nearly vertical axial planes and the limbs dip at a similar angle to each other. Symmetrical folds are found near the edges of mountain ranges where tectonic activity is relatively quiet.

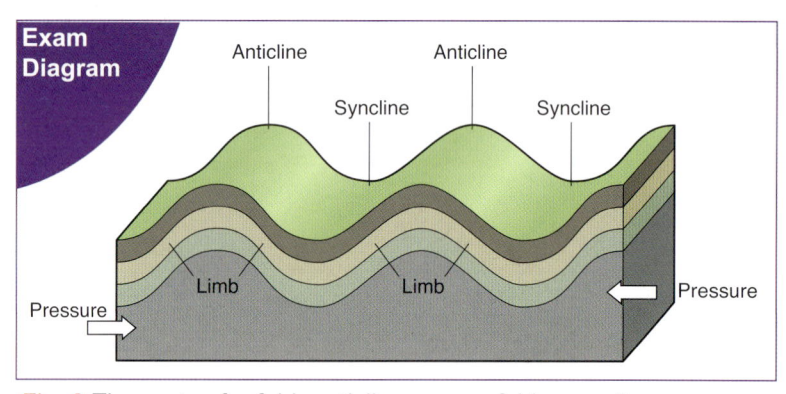

Fig. 2 The parts of a fold: anticlines are upfolds, synclines are downfolds.

Asymmetrical folds

Asymmetrical folds are formed when the pressure applied to the rock layer is greater on one side than the other. In asymmetrical folds the fold axis is tilted relative to the surface and fold limbs may be of unequal steepness.

Overfold/recumbent fold

An **overfold** is formed when larger amounts of pressure are applied to one side of a rock layer. The rock fold is turned over on itself so that one or both limbs dip in the same direction. If the axial plane is nearly horizontal the fold is called a **recumbent** fold.

Overthrust fold

When the compression of rock layers is very great, a crack or fault occurs in the fold. One limb is then pushed over the other limb forming an **overthrust** fold, e.g. the Rocky Mountains, USA.

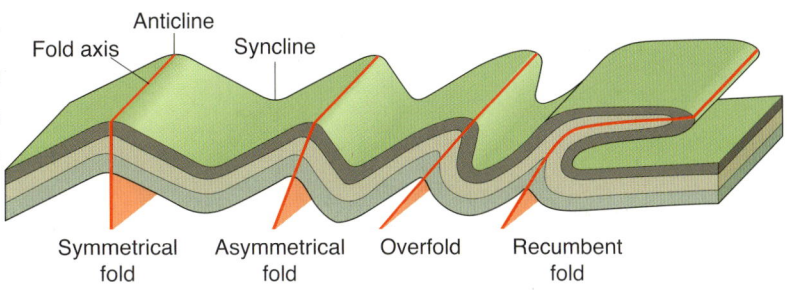

Fig. 3 Types of fold

Fold mountain building

The formation of fold mountains is also called **orogeny**. Over the last 500 million years there have been several fold mountain building phases across the world.

1. **Caledonian folding** occurred around 400 million years ago. The mountain ridges run or **trend** from north-east to south-west, e.g. the Leinster mountains and the mountains of north-west Ireland and Scotland. As these are extremely old mountains, they have been worn down and today are rounded in shape.

2. **Armorican folding** occurred around 300 million years ago. The mountain ridges trend from east to west, e.g. the Munster ridge and valley province, Paris Basin in France. These are higher and more rugged than the Caledonian mountains because they are younger.

Fig. 4 Recumbent fold in the Swiss Alps

3. **Alpine folding** occurred 50 million years ago. This is not found in Ireland. Mountain ridges trend from east to west, e.g. Alps and Himalayas. These are the highest and most jagged mountains in the world because they are so young.

Activity

In your copybook, draw the map on the right and mark the following fold mountain ranges on it:

(a) Derryveagh Mountains
(b) Wicklow Mountains
(c) Macgillycuddy's Reeks Mountains
(d) Comeragh Mountains.

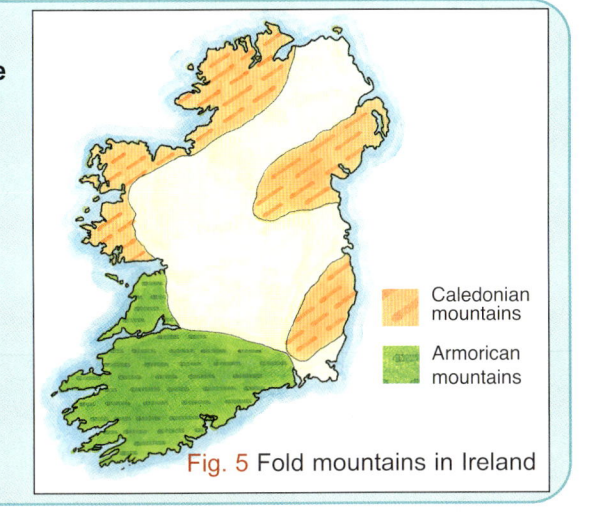

Fig. 5 Fold mountains in Ireland

CORE UNIT: PATTERNS AND PROCESSES IN THE PHYSICAL ENVIRONMENT

CHAPTER 4
Case Study 1

4.2 Fold mountains in Ireland

The Munster Ridge and Valley Province

1. Between 350 and 400 million years ago Ireland lay closer to the equator and experienced a dry desert climate. Huge amounts of sand were deposited in an enormous hollow called a **geosyncline** that is now the south and south-west of Ireland. Today this is known as **Old Red Sandstone**. Later, a warm shallow sea covered the area and limestone was laid down on top of the sandstone.

2. About 300 million years ago, during the Armorican orogeny, the rocks of Ireland were squeezed by plate collision, forming **fold mountains**.

3. These fold mountains stretch from Waterford to Kerry. Their east-west trending anticlines, or ridges, are responsible for mountains such as the Comeraghs, Silvermines and Galtee Mountains (see Fig. 7). These ridges are made of resistant sandstone rock. During folding, rocks in the anticlines were stretched and cracks formed, weakening the overlying limestone. Over time, weathering and erosion removed the limestone from the anticlines exposing the sandstone beneath.

4. Today the fold synclines are still covered with this limestone and form wide valleys. The Golden Vale and the Blackwater Valley are examples.

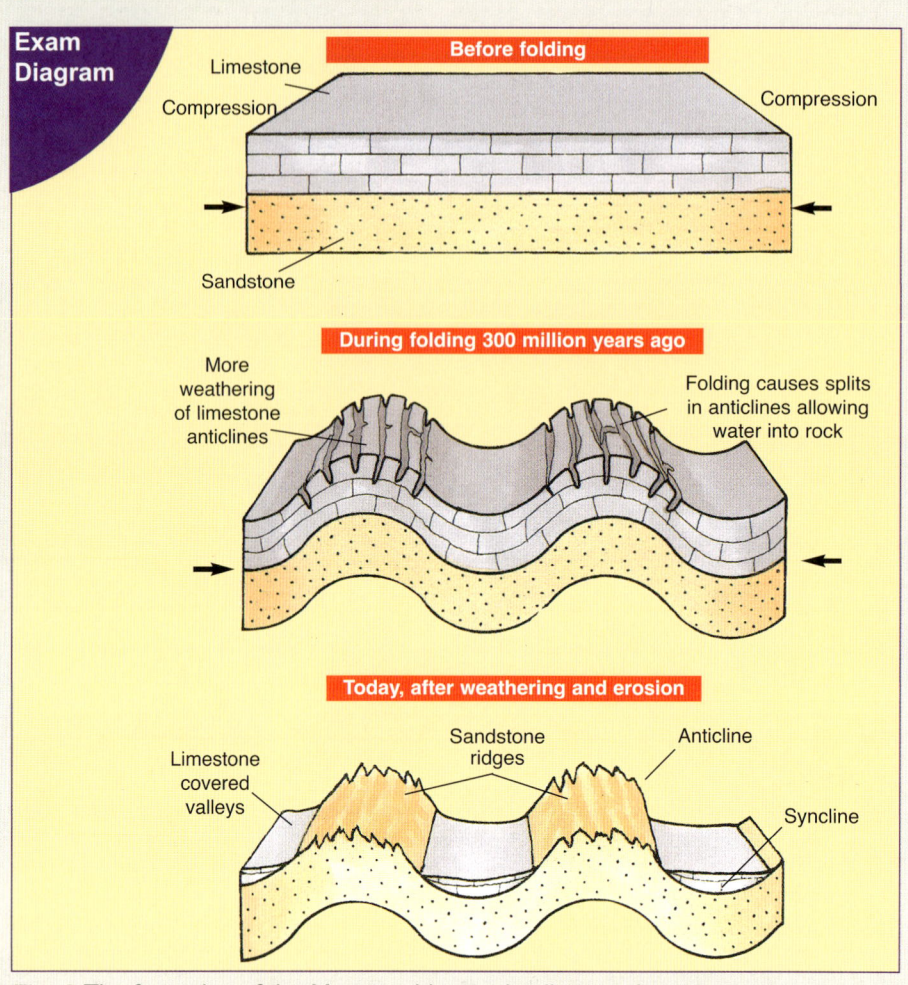

Fig. 6 The formation of the Munster ridge and valley province

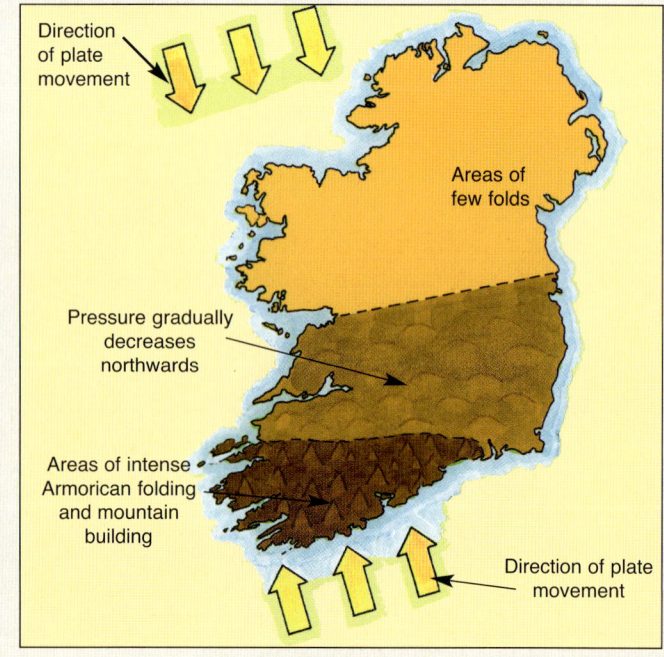

Fig. 7 Location map of Munster ridge and valley province

CHAPTER 4: FOLDING AND FAULTING IN THE EARTH'S CRUST

4.3 Faulting and associated landscapes

Near the surface of the earth, rock is brittle and will crack or fracture when placed under great stress by earth movements. Rocks contain many small fractures or joints. When movement happens along a rock fracture, it is called a **fault**.

Faults often occur in parallel sets because the stress that produces them operates over a large area. Pressure and **tension** make the land either side of the fault move up, down or sideways.

Normal faults

When a sloping fault is created and land slips down along one side of it, a **normal fault** is formed. These are caused by the land being pulled apart (tension), sometimes making a rift valley. The exposed face of the fault is called the **fault scarp**.

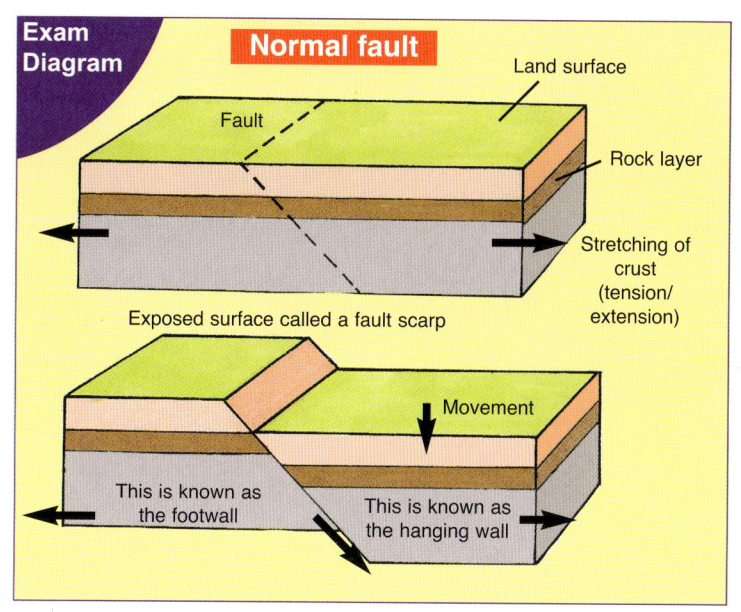

Fig. 8 A normal fault

Landform made by normal faulting

A **rift valley**, or **graben**, is formed when a block of land slips down between sets of parallel normal faults. This is due to stretching of the crust. Lough Neagh and the lower Bann valley occupy such a rift valley.

Larger rift valleys occur in Germany, such as the Rhine Rift Valley between the Vosges and Black Forest Mountains. The Midland Valley of Scotland is another example. (See the case study on the Great African Rift Valley on page 63.)

Fig. 9 A normal fault in sedimentary rock in El Salvador

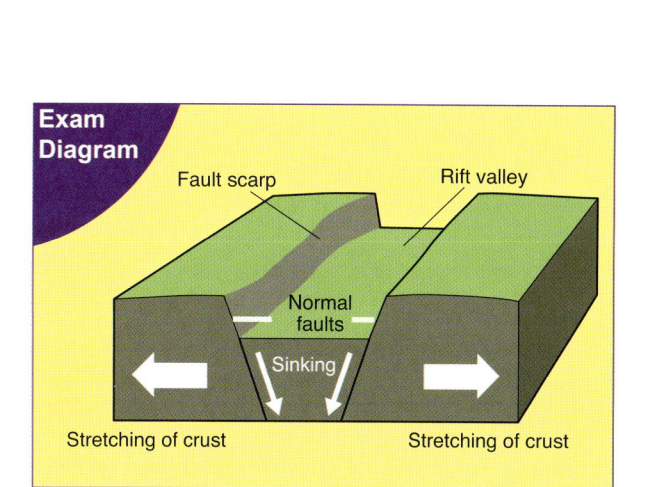

Fig. 10 Rift valleys

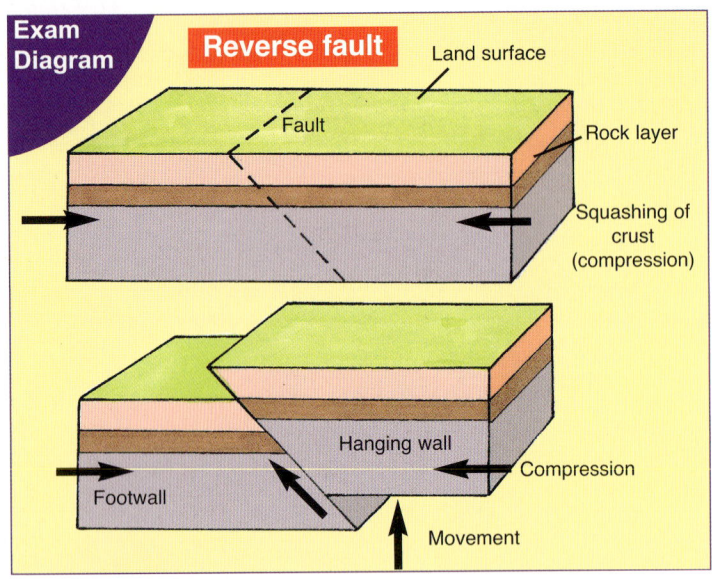

CORE UNIT: PATTERNS AND PROCESSES IN THE PHYSICAL ENVIRONMENT

Fig. 11 A reverse fault

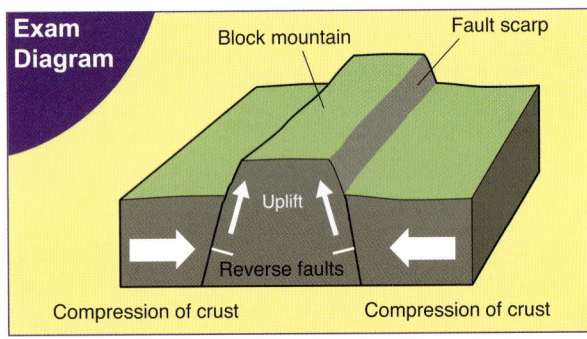

Fig. 12 Block mountains

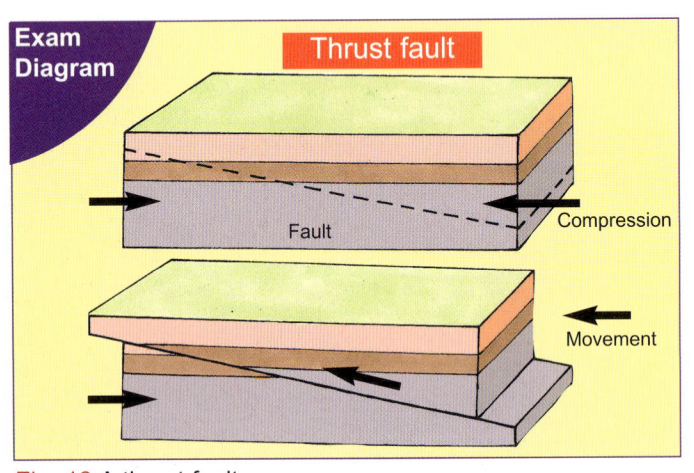

Fig. 13 A thrust fault

weblink Fault motion

Reverse faults

If pressure from earth movements (compression) causes land to move up along a sloping fault line a *reverse fault* is formed, sometimes making block mountains, for example the Ox Mountains of County Sligo.

Landform made at a reverse fault

A *block mountain* (*horst*) is a block of land left standing between two reverse faults, e.g. Vosges and Black Forest mountains. The Ox Mountains of Sligo were formed in this way. Here a block of gneiss was pushed up between reverse faults in limestone and conglomerate rocks.

Thrust faults

A *thrust fault* is a type of reverse fault where the angle of the fault plane is very low, < 20° (i.e. less than 20°).

Tear faults

Tear faults (*transform faults*) occur when there is a vertical fault in the landscape but movement has been horizontal. This is similar to the movement along the San Andreas fault in California.

The long east to west anticlines of Cork and Waterford are crossed by many tear faults. Geological maps show that a movement of 2 km occurred along tear faults close to Slieve Gullion in County Armagh.

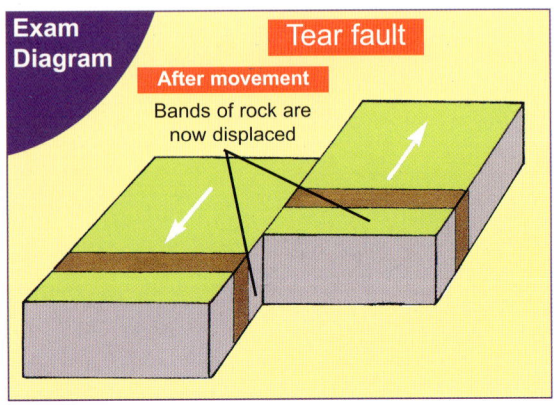

Fig. 14 A tear fault

The Great African Rift Valley – A landscape formed by faulting

1. The African Rift Valley is a landform made by faulting. This huge rift valley is visible from space as it is the world's largest surface fracture. It extends more than 6,000 kilometres from the Red Sea in the north to Mozambique in the south.

2. The African Rift Valley formed during the last 20 million years due to the presence of a hotspot beneath the crust. The hotspot is causing the African continent to bulge, stretch and split. As the crust is pulled apart, long parallel cracks called normal faults are formed.

3. Huge blocks of crust are sinking between the normal faults forming a large flat-floored rift valley or graben.

4. The land has subsided so much in places that it lies more than 153 m below sea level. The fault lines are marked by high fault scarps or escarpments rising steeply several thousand metres from the valley floor.

5. At the same time magma is forced up to the surface in places and erupts, forming volcanoes, e.g. Mount Kilimanjaro and Mount Kenya.

6. The African Rift Valley varies in width from 40 to 100 km and is widening at a rate of up to 4 mm per year.

7. Many lakes have also formed in the floor of the rift valley. The deepest is Lake Tanganyika which is nearly 1,420 m deep.

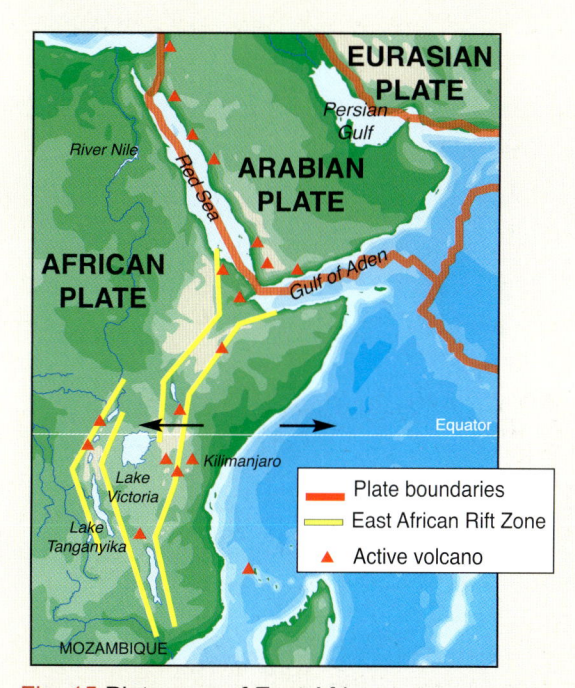

Fig. 15 Plate map of East Africa

Fig. 16 Fault scarp in the African Rift Valley

CORE UNIT: PATTERNS AND PROCESSES IN THE PHYSICAL ENVIRONMENT

Chapter Revision Questions

1. Draw and label a symmetric fold. In your diagram show the limb, anticline, syncline and fold axes.

2. Explain the difference between the formation of a symmetric fold and an overfold.

3. Explain the terms (a) compression and (b) tension.

4. Name and briefly describe the three orogenies you have studied. Give an example of each.

5. Describe the formation of the Munster ridge and valley province.

6. What is a fault?

7. Draw labelled diagrams of normal, reverse and thrust faults.

8. Using examples and diagrams, describe the formation of a block mountain and rift valley.

9. Describe the formation of the Great African Rift Valley.

10. Copy the diagram below into your copybook. Using the words provided, label the diagram.

    - Fault scarp
    - Rift valley
    - Stretching of crust/tension
    - Normal fault

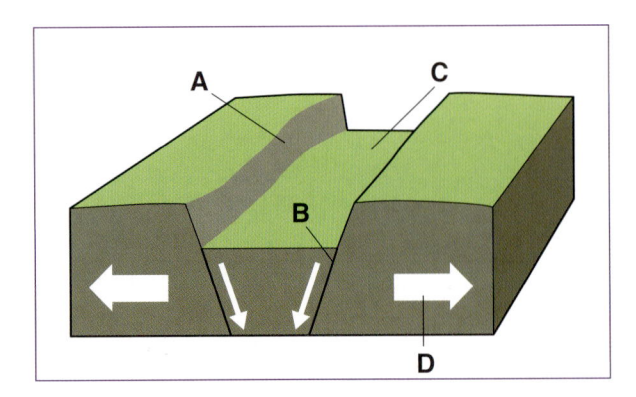

CHAPTER 4: FOLDING AND FAULTING IN THE EARTH'S CRUST

LC Exam Questions

Higher Level students must be able to answer Ordinary and Higher Level questions.

■ OL Questions

11. (i) Name **one** example of fold mountains.
    (ii) With the aid of a diagram(s) explain how fold mountains are formed.

■ HL Questions

12. Examine the diagram below. Match each of the letters A - H with the feature or process that best matches it in the table below.

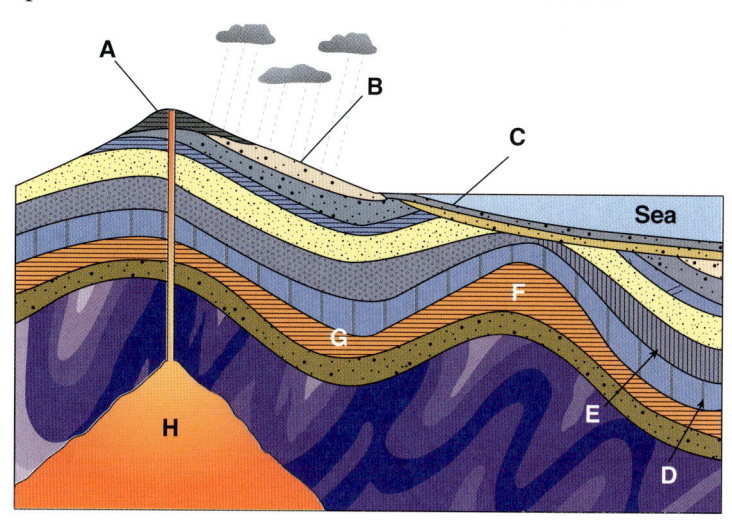

Feature / Process	Letter
Joint	
Syncline	
Volcano	
Coastal deposits	
Bedding plane	
Magma chamber	
Weathering	
Anticline	

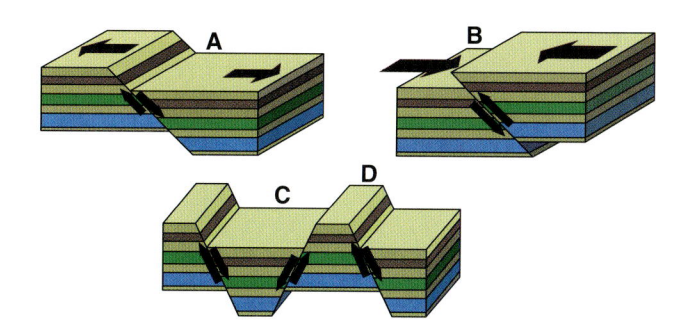

13. Examine the diagrams above and answer the following questions.
    (i) Name the type of fault at A and the type of fault at B.
    (ii) Explain briefly what causes the type of faulting at A or at B.
    (iii) Name the landform at C and the landform at D that result from faulting.

14. Explain how the study of plate tectonics has helped us to understand the global distribution of fold mountains.

15. Explain how **one** of the following influences the development of landforms:
    • Folding
    • Faulting.

65

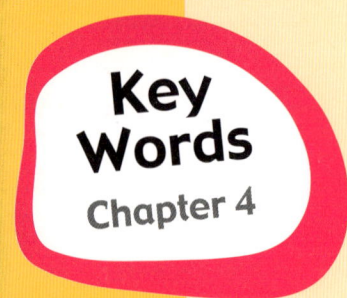

CORE UNIT: PATTERNS AND PROCESSES IN THE PHYSICAL ENVIRONMENT

Key Words Chapter 4

Key Words

You should be able to explain both verbally and in writing each of the key words listed below.

Alpine folding
anticline
Armorican folding
asymmetric fold
block mountain/horst
Caledonian folding
fault
fault scarp
fold
geosyncline
normal fault
Old Red Sandstone

orogeny
overfold/recumbent fold
overthrust fold
plate compression
reverse fault
rift valley/graben
symmetric fold
syncline
tear/transform fault
tension
thrust fault
trend

Digital Resources are available for this chapter at mentorbooks.ie/resources

CHAPTER 5

Rock Types and their Formation

Key Theme

Rocks are continually formed, changed, destroyed and reconstructed as part of the rock cycle. They are formed and changed by forces within the earth. They are destroyed by forces at work on the earth's surface such as weathering and erosion. Rocks are reconstructed by the deposition of sediments.

Learning Outcomes

At the end of this chapter you will be able to:
- Explain the formation of igneous, sedimentary and metamorphic rocks.
- Name and give examples of three different rock types found in Ireland.
- Describe how sediment is turned into rock (lithification).
- Explain how the rock cycle works.
- Discuss human interaction with the rock cycle.

Contents

5.1	Igneous rocks	68
5.2	Sedimentary rocks	69
5.3	Metamorphic rocks	72
5.4	The rock cycle	75
5.5	Human interaction with the rock cycle	76
	Case Study 1: Tara lead and zinc mines, County Meath	77
	Case Study 2: Geothermal energy in Iceland	79

Revision Space

Chapter Revision Questions – LC Exam Questions – Key Word List 81

Rock Types

There are many different rock types in the earth's crust. They can be divided into three main groups.
1. **Igneous**
2. **Sedimentary**
3. **Metamorphic**

5.1 Igneous rocks

Igneous rocks are formed from magma which cools and solidifies slowly below ground, forming **intrusive** igneous rock. Magma that reaches the surface is called lava which cools and solidifies quickly on the earth's surface, forming **volcanic** (**extrusive**) igneous rock. These igneous rocks are made of crystals, which may be large or small depending on how fast the magma cools.

Intrusive igneous rock

Intrusive igneous rock can be divided into two groups:
- Plutonic rocks
- Intermediate rocks.

1. **Plutonic** rocks form as magma cools very slowly (taking thousands of years) deep inside the earth's crust. They have large crystals of quartz, felspar and mica. **Granite** is a common example. It is often grey in colour. When very large masses of magma are injected into the crust they slowly cool to form large granite structures called **batholiths**. Weathering and erosion can remove the rock above these structures so that today we can see the batholiths in places such as the Wicklow Mountains.

Fig. 1 Granite is composed of three minerals: feldspar, quartz and mica. The white crystals are feldspar, the black ones are mica and the grey crystals are quartz.

weblink
How do igneous rocks form?

2. **Intermediate** (**hypabyssal**) rocks form when magma makes its way closer to the earth's surface and cools more quickly than plutonic rock so that the crystals are smaller. **Dolerite** is a common example. It is a dull grey colour and is found in the Fair Head Sill, County Antrim. Both granite and dolerite are acidic igneous rocks as they contain more than 55% silica.

Volcanic/extrusive rock

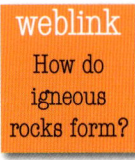

Volcanic (extrusive) igneous rock, e.g. **basalt**, forms when magma reaches the earth's surface, at which point it is called lava. Basalt is a basic igneous rock if it contains less than 55% silica. It cools quickly out in the open or under water. It is a dull brown or black colour with microscopic crystals. In Ireland basalt formed in the Giant's Causeway 90 to 65 million years ago when the crust split apart and the Atlantic Ocean began to form. This rifting allowed basic magma to reach the surface and pour over the land, forming the Antrim Plateau. Basalt is a hard rock, resistant to weathering and erosion.

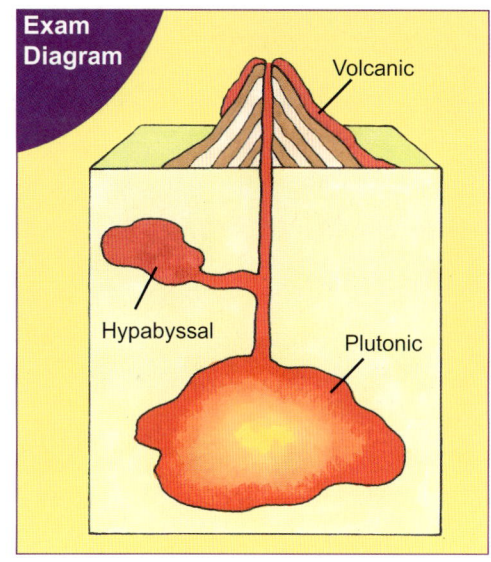

Fig. 2 The formation of igneous rocks

5.2 Sedimentary rocks

Sedimentary rocks are made from the build-up (**accumulation**) of layers of inorganic or organic sediments. Each layer (**strata**) is deposited on a lower layer, squashing out water, minerals and air. As the sediment layers are buried they become **compacted** and eventually cemented together by silica or calcite to form solid rock.
This process of turning sediment into stone is known as **lithification**.
Horizontal joints called **bedding planes** separate the layers.

Near the surface a loose pile of sediment which is saturated with water is squashed (compacted) by the weight of overlying sediment.

The spaces between the grains (pore spaces) are reduced and any water is pushed out of them.

The grains are cemented together at depth by substances such as calcite and silica which are deposited around the grains as they are pressed together (compacted). If silica is deposited around the grains the rock is usually hard and resistant to weathering.

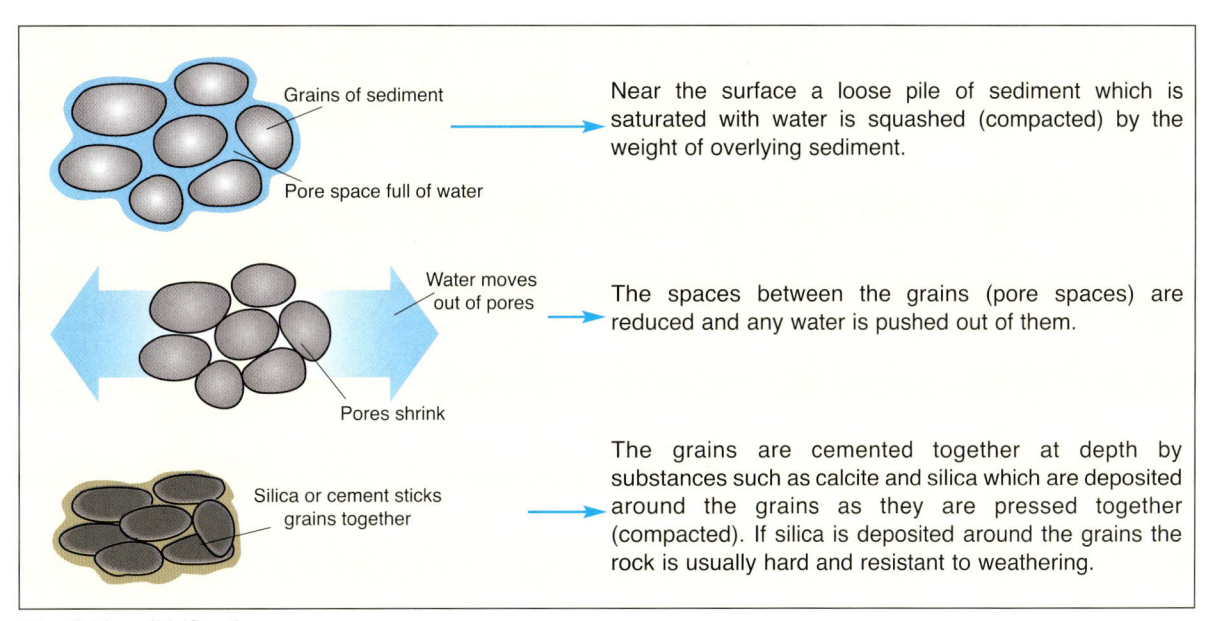

Fig. 3 How lithification occurs

Sedimentary rocks are classified according to how they were formed:
1. **Organically formed**
2. **Inorganically or mechanically formed**
3. **Chemically formed.**

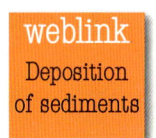

weblink
Deposition of sediments

69

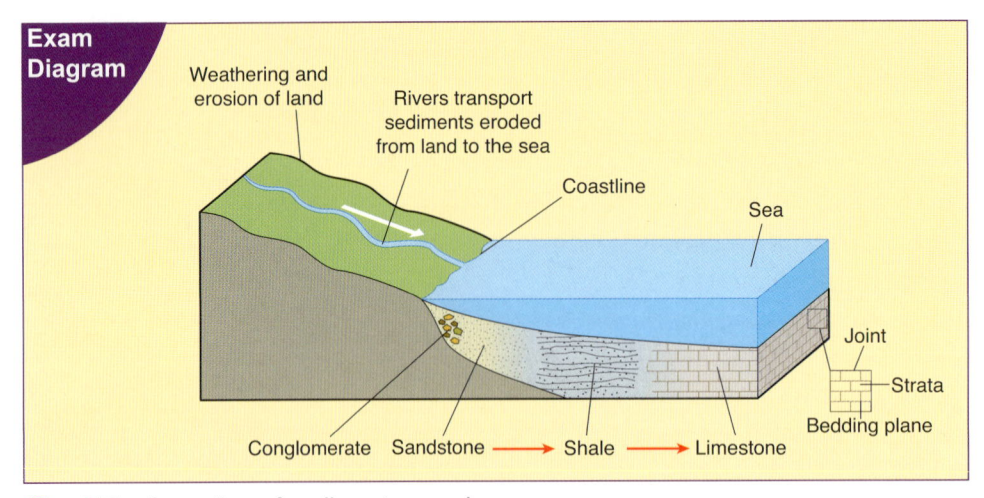

CORE UNIT: PATTERNS AND PROCESSES IN THE PHYSICAL ENVIRONMENT

Fig. 4 The formation of sedimentary rocks

1. Organically formed sedimentary rocks

These are rocks made up of layers of dead organisms (fish, shells, vegetation). During lithification, **calcite cement** is squeezed from shells in the sediment. This glues the organic particles together, forming distinctive sedimentary rocks.

Limestone is the most common rock in Ireland. Most Irish limestone formed 350 to 300 million years ago when Ireland lay close to the equator and was covered by a warm shallow sea, similar to that found in the Caribbean today. The grains were cemented with calcium carbonate (calcite) which came from shells. Sometimes the remains of living things are well preserved as **fossils** in the rock e.g. the Burren, County Clare. Limestone is pervious, meaning that water can pass through the joints and bedding planes.

Chalk is a pure white form of limestone. Much of the chalk deposited in Ireland has been eroded but some is still preserved under the basalt of the Giant's Causeway, County Antrim.

Coal is a hard black/brown rock. It forms from the compression of peat deposits, e.g. Arigna, County Roscommon.

Fig. 5 Strata and bedding planes of sedimentary rock

Fig. 6 Ammonite fossils in limestone

2. Inorganically/mechanically formed sedimentary rocks

These rocks form from the lithification of rock fragments.

Sandstone is formed when particles of eroded igneous, metamorphic and other sedimentary rocks are carried by rivers and build up on the seabed or on lake floors. During lithification **silica** from sand grains glues the sediments together. Sandstone is a **porous**, **permeable** rock. The spaces between sand grains are called pores. These pores may be filled with air, water, oil or gas. Liquids and gases pass easily through the pores, making sandstone a permeable rock. Irish sandstone formed 400 to 350 million years ago when Ireland lay 30° south of the equator. At this time and latitude, Ireland experienced very dry desert conditions. Huge rivers flowed across this dry landscape carrying the sediments that eventually formed the Old Red Sandstone which is now found in the Cork and Kerry mountains.

Shale or **mudstone** form when layers of fine particles of silt and mud build up in deep river or sea water. Lithification turns them into a dark grey or black rock. Shale is found in south County Clare.

Conglomerates form when a mix of sand grains and pebbles stick together. The pebbles may be rounded or angular and have many different colours, e.g. Skerries and Rush in north County Dublin.

Fig. 7 Sandstone rock

Fig. 8 Shale rock

3. Chemically formed sedimentary rocks (evaporites)

Gypsum and **salt** are rocks formed from the evaporation of sea water from enclosed lakes or seas in hot climates.

Many times in the geological past, areas of salt water were cut off from the open sea, where they formed lakes that slowly evaporated and dried up leaving thick layers of salt, e.g. Salt Lake City, USA.

Fig. 9 Conglomerate rock

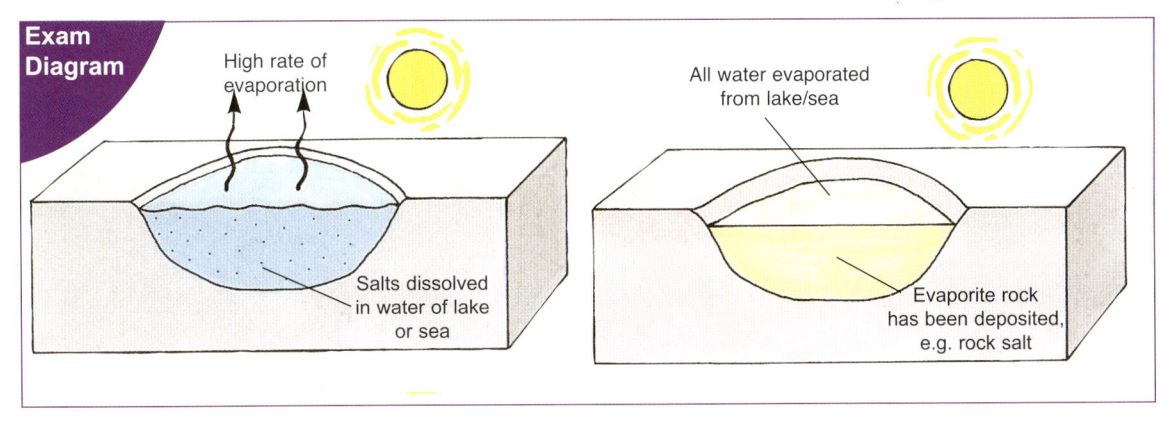

Fig. 10 Formation of evaporites

When sea water evaporates, the least soluble salt is deposited first and the most soluble last. Chemically formed rocks are thus deposited in a definite order:
- gypsum is deposited when 37% of the water has evaporated,
- rock salt is deposited when 93% of the water has evaporated.

Often in the past only one of these rocks would be formed. Gypsum alone is deposited in a thick layer near Kingscourt in County Cavan. Rock salt and gypsum occur in Carrickfergus, County Antrim – 20% of the rock salt from this mine is used in road gritting in Ireland. The rest is exported.

5.3 Metamorphic rocks

Metamorphic rocks are igneous or sedimentary rocks which change their form either chemically or physically due to intense heat and/or pressure caused by plate movements. Earthquakes, folding, faulting and vulcanicity can cause metamorphism (changes) in the rock. Some of Ireland's metamorphic rocks were formed around 400 million years ago when the American and European plates collided and formed the Caledonian fold mountains.

Types of metamorphism
Metamorphic rocks are classified into three types:
1. Thermal
2. Dynamic
3. Regional

1. Thermal metamorphism
In this case rocks are changed by intense heat. Molten magma and lava come into contact with a rock (often along the edges of dykes, batholiths and sills) and bake it causing recrystallisation of the rock minerals.

Quartzite is a pale-looking rock formed by the thermal metamorphism of sandstone, e.g. Mount Errigal, County Donegal.

Marble is formed from the thermal metamorphism of limestone. Unlike limestone, marble is sparkly and has a variety of colours from green to red according to the mineral content, e.g. Connemara marble is green. The white marble of Rathlin Island, County Antrim is often used by sculptors.

Fig. 11 Quartzite

Fig. 12 Marble

weblink: Classic sedimentary rocks forming

2. Dynamic metamorphism

In this case plate movement causes great pressure to be placed on rocks. This pressure converts them into much harder rock types and also causes banding/**foliation** of rock minerals.

Slate forms from the dynamic metamorphism of shale. The great pressure applied during metamorphism compresses the shale, hardening it into a purple-grey foliated rock (banded rock) with very fine layers in it. Slate can be split very easily along the layers, making it a useful building material, e.g. Valentia Island, County Kerry.

Plate movement causes intense pressure especially along fault lines within rocks. At these faults the rock is ground into a fine sticky powder called **fault gouge**.

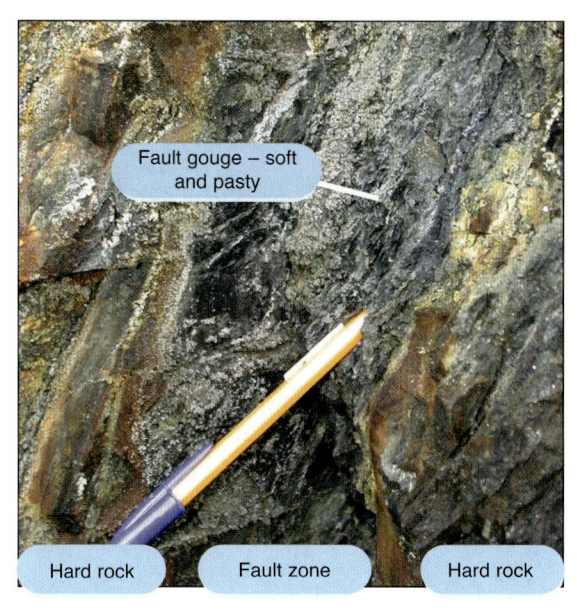

3. Regional metamorphism

In this case large areas of rock covering thousands of square kilometres are metamorphosed.

Plate movement puts pressure on rocks, deforming them and forcing them deep into the earth's crust where they may be heated to temperatures of up to 1,000°C. This combination of heat and pressure changes the rocks. Much of north-west Scotland, north-west Ireland and Canada were affected in this way during the Caledonian folding 400 million years ago.

Gneiss (**pronounced: nice**) is a metamorphic rock.

It was originally granite. Many of the original granite minerals are still present but they have become segregated into pale and dark wavy bands, e.g. the Belmullet peninsula in County Mayo.

The effect of metamorphism on rock

Metamorphism changes the colour, hardness, mineral alignment and chemical composition of rocks.

Hardness: All metamorphic rocks are harder than their original rock type.

Colour: Metamorphism may change the colour of rocks due to the effect of heat, e.g. limestone is grey but when metamorphosed the resulting marble may be green, yellow or white.

Foliation: Foliation happens when the pressure is greater from one side causing the mineral crystals in the rock to line up in parallel bands, e.g. gneiss. Some rocks have their sediments flattened and hardened into very thin layers, e.g. slate.

Chemical composition: Heat and pressure may cause the rock minerals to recombine to form different minerals in the metamorphic rock.

Fig. 13 Fault gouge. The pen is pushed into the soft, ground-up rock in the fault between the two hard rock layers either side of the fault.

Fig. 14 Slate is used to make roof tiles.

Fig. 15 This gneiss has been polished for use as a kitchen worktop. Notice the bands of black and pink crystals typical of gneiss.

weblink
Metamorphic rocks

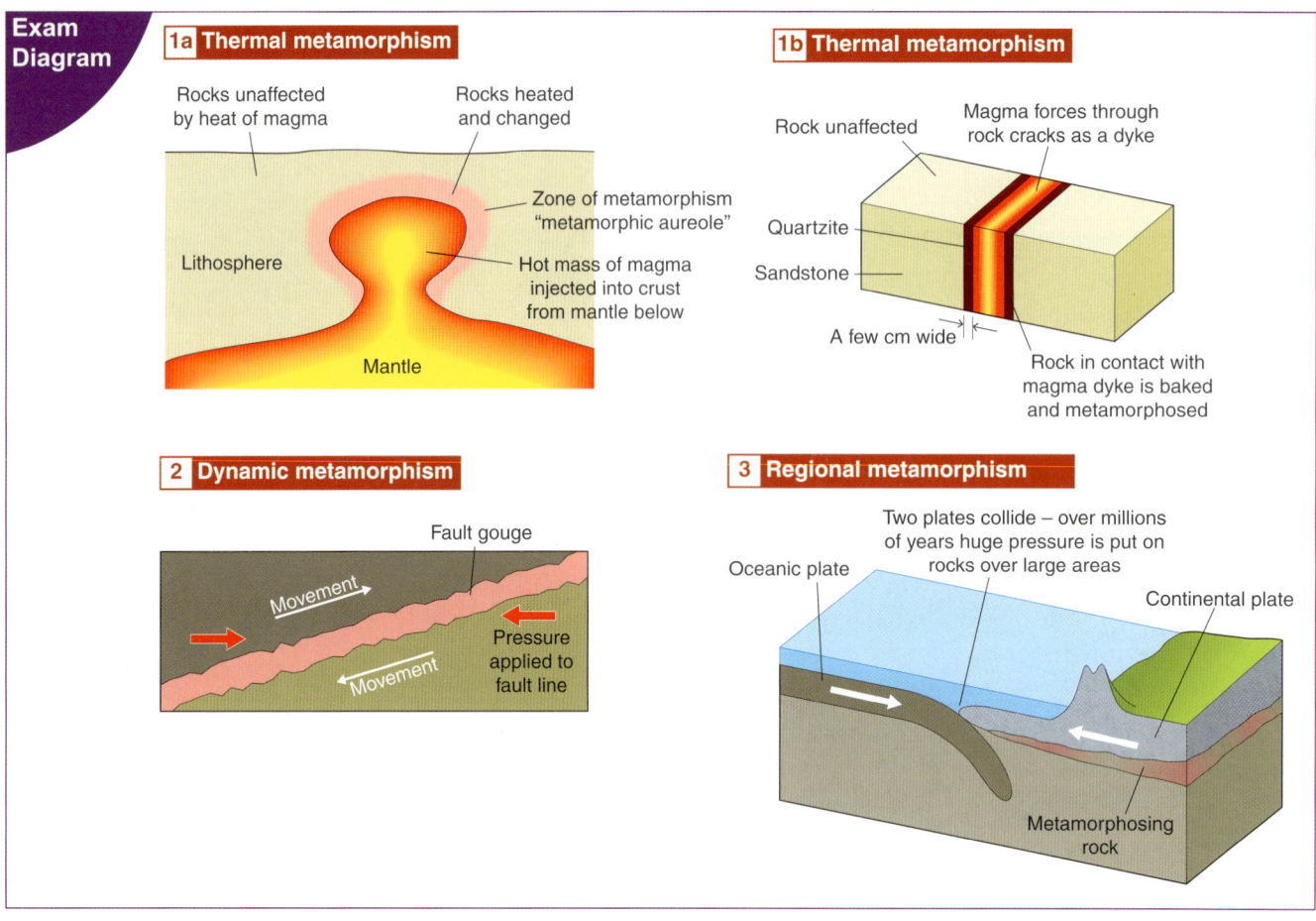

CORE UNIT: PATTERNS AND PROCESSES IN THE PHYSICAL ENVIRONMENT

Exam Diagram

1a Thermal metamorphism
- Rocks unaffected by heat of magma
- Rocks heated and changed
- Zone of metamorphism "metamorphic aureole"
- Lithosphere
- Hot mass of magma injected into crust from mantle below
- Mantle

1b Thermal metamorphism
- Rock unaffected
- Magma forces through rock cracks as a dyke
- Quartzite
- Sandstone
- A few cm wide
- Rock in contact with magma dyke is baked and metamorphosed

2 Dynamic metamorphism
- Fault gouge
- Movement
- Pressure applied to fault line

3 Regional metamorphism
- Two plates collide – over millions of years huge pressure is put on rocks over large areas
- Oceanic plate
- Continental plate
- Metamorphosing rock

Fig. 16 The formation of metamorphic rocks

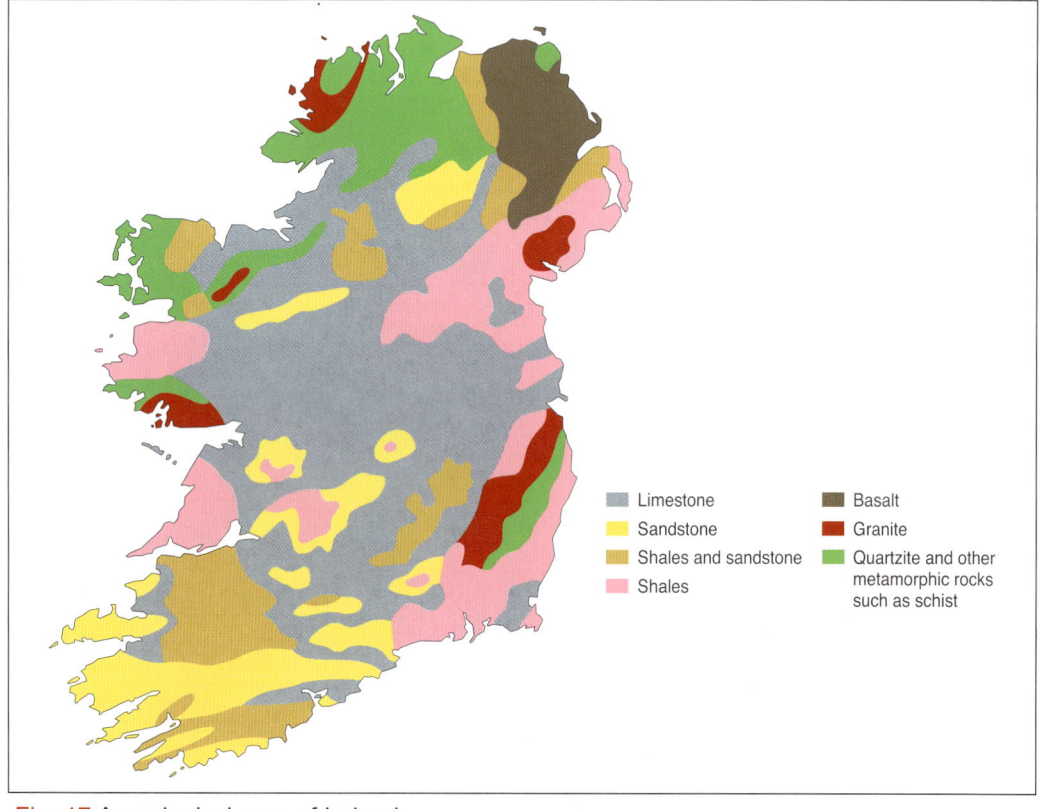

- Limestone
- Sandstone
- Shales and sandstone
- Shales
- Basalt
- Granite
- Quartzite and other metamorphic rocks such as schist

Fig. 17 A geological map of Ireland

5.4 The rock cycle

The **rock cycle** is the process by which each rock type can be changed into another. Rocks can be transformed into one another by melting, weathering and erosion and by great heat and pressure.

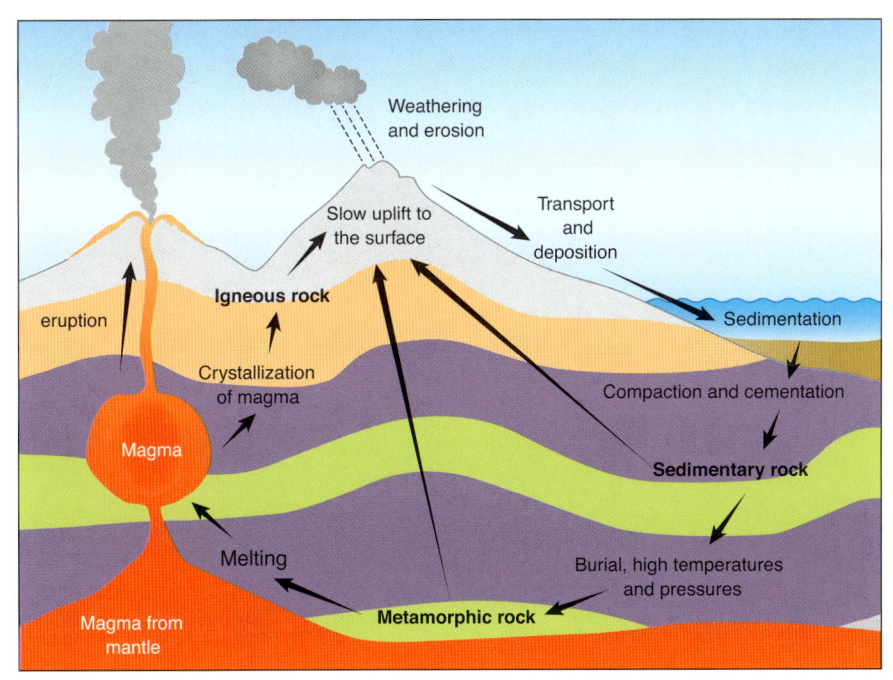

Fig. 18 The rock cycle

Activity

The rock cycle always begins with the formation of magma. Look carefully at the diagram of the rock cycle and answer the questions which follow.

1. What processes change sedimentary rock into metamorphic rock?
2. What processes change igneous rock to metamorphic rock?
3. How is sediment converted to sedimentary rock?
4. How is metamorphic rock converted to sedimentary rock?
5. How does magma change to igneous rock?
6. How is sedimentary rock changed back into sediment?
7. How is metamorphic rock converted into magma?

How the rock cycle works

The rock cycle begins when magma is made from melted minerals in the mantle. Igneous rock forms when magma cools. It can form underground, where magma cools slowly, or it can form above ground, where lava cools quickly.

On the earth's surface, the processes of weathering and erosion then break rock into smaller pieces. Wind and water transport these rock pieces to other places. Usually, the rock pieces, called sediments, are deposited in layers under water.

The layers are buried under other layers of sediment. After a long time the sediments can be cemented together to make sedimentary rock. In this way, igneous rock has become sedimentary rock.

Inside our planet the weight of the earth creates intense heat at great depths. Heat is also made by friction generated by moving plates and by the radioactive decay of certain elements. Heat inside the earth bakes the rock. Baked rock does not melt, but it does change. It forms crystals. If it is crystalline already, it forms even larger crystals. Rocks changed by heat and pressure are called metamorphic rock.

Internal and external forces drive the rock cycle. Melting, heating, pressure, weathering and erosion may again change the rocks into another rock group.

5.5 Human interaction with the rock cycle

We get many resources from rocks and use them for a variety of business and leisure activities as shown in Fig. 19.

Recreation
Rock climbing, hill walking

Carrantuohil, County Kerry

Metals
Iron, copper, tin, lead, zinc, gold, silver

Construction materials
Sand, gravel, limestone, quarries

Toonagh Quarry, County Clare

Beauty products

Kaolin clay is used in mudpacks

Tourism
Karst landscapes (Burren)

Burren, County Clare

Decorative pieces
Statues, work-tops, fireplaces, headstones, shop fronts

Energy Source
Coal, oil, gas, geothermal

Geothermal plant and volcanic rocks on the Reykjanes Peninsula in Iceland

Fig. 19 The value of rocks to people

[Note: Choose Option 1 OR 2]

Option 1: Tara lead and zinc mine, County Meath

Case Study 1

The Tara lead and zinc mine in Navan, County Meath is the largest lead and zinc mine in Europe and the fifth largest in the world. It produces over 2.7 million tonnes (Mt) of zinc and lead concentrate each year.

Formation of lead and zinc

Rock containing metal is referred to as **ore**. At Tara Mines, lead and zinc is found in the sedimentary bedding planes of carboniferous limestone and dolomite rocks.

The origin of the lead and zinc ores is linked to the movement of groundwater through the rock. Sea water seeped down many kilometres into the rock under the seabed and was heated up by geothermal energy from deep inside the earth. As the hot sea water (**brine**) moved down through the fault planes, joints and bedding planes in the rock, it dissolved small amounts of lead and zinc out of the rock.

This brine containing the dissolved lead and zinc then began to rise through the cracks and fissures in the newly-formed limestone. As the brine rose, it cooled causing tiny crystals of lead and zinc sulphide to form. Over millions of years the metal sulphides built up into metal rich layers called **veins** within the rock. These veins are mined for their metal.

Fig. 20 Aerial photo of Tara Mines at Navan

Mining operations

Tara Mines is an underground **shaft mine** that operates 24 hours a day 52 weeks a year. To extract the metals from the rock, vertical and horizontal mine shafts are cut to a depth of 50-900 m below the surface. A process called **stope and pillar** extraction is used.

Stopes are the massive caverns left when huge areas of rock are blasted out and removed. Pillars are the sections of rock that are left behind to act as supports to the mine tunnels.

While underground the huge blasted chunks of ore are crushed. They are then brought to the surface for chemical treatment. On the surface the rock is crushed again and mixed with water and chemicals.

Fig. 21 Mechanical scaling underground at Tara Mines

The chemicals separate the metal from the rock. This mixture is then filtered and a metal rich powder obtained. This is dried to form a **concentrate**.

The concentrate is sent by rail to Dublin Port where it is exported to European smelters in Finland and Norway where lead and zinc metal is produced from the concentrate.

The waste sediment (**tailings**) from the concentration process is deposited in large ponds called tailings ponds. The tailings settle and are eventually mixed with concrete and pumped back into the mine to refill the stopes in order to provide support.

Fig. 22 The Concentrator at Tara Mines, where a metal-rich powder is obtained from a mixture of chemicals and crushed rocks.

The Environmental Protection Agency (EPA) monitors surface and underground operations. It checks air, water, noise and visual pollution levels. The mine is extensively landscaped to reduce its visual impact.

Uses of lead and zinc

Lead and zinc are very useful metals.

Lead: Used in batteries (60% of lead mined is used for batteries), lead solder, plumbing, soundproofing, X-Ray gowns. Lead is added to glass screens in order to block harmful radiation from TV and PC monitors.

Zinc: Used to rustproof (galvanise) steel, cosmetics, food supplements, sun creams, soaps, paint, ink and many other uses.

Spin-off effects of the mine operations

Employment by the mine has an important multiplier or spin-off effect on the local and national economy. All mining and quarrying in Ireland generates just under €1 billion per annum to the Irish economy.

It is estimated that for every one job at Tara Mines, an additional three indirect jobs are supported. The mine employs over 600 people in a variety of different jobs, e.g. chemists, environmental scientists, miners, geologists. Many indirect jobs are created by the mining operations such as caterers, accountants, truck drivers, safety consultants and metallurgists.

CHAPTER 5: ROCK TYPES AND THEIR FORMATION

Option 2: Geothermal energy in Iceland

Case Study 2

Geothermal energy is heat energy captured from hot rocks in the earth's crust. Iceland is a major producer of geothermal energy.

1. Iceland is located on the Mid-Atlantic ridge. This is the constructive plate boundary between the North American and Eurasian tectonic plates. The two plates are moving apart at a rate of about 2 cm per year. This allows magma to reach the surface of the earth forming hot igneous rock that is used to make geothermal energy.
2. In Iceland the active volcanic zone stretches through the country from the south-west to the north-east and contains more than 200 volcanoes. This volcanic zone is used to generate geothermal energy.

How is geothermal energy captured?

3. Magma rising from the mantle heats the ground to over 200°C just 1 km below the surface.
4. Precipitation (rain and snow) falling on the highland seeps (**percolates**) three kilometres into the bedrock where it is heated by the hot rocks beneath the surface. In some areas the water is heated to more than 380°C. The hot water then rises towards the surface often forming hot springs and steam vents.
5. The rocks are drilled (**boreholes**) to capture the hot water. As the hot water reaches the surface, the pressure drops causing it to turn into steam. The steam is used to turn a turbine to make electricity. After this the steam cools and condenses into cold water which is returned to the ground through a different borehole where it is reheated and the cycle starts again.

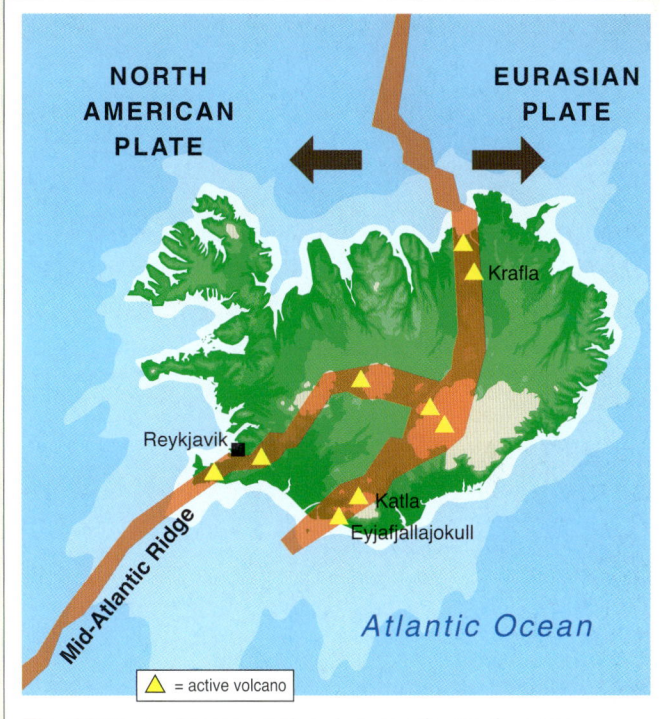

Fig. 23 Map of Iceland showing geothermal zones

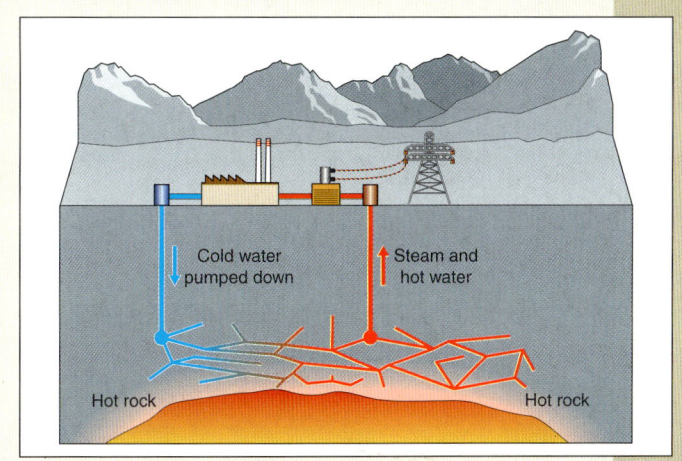

Fig. 24 Capturing geothermal energy in Iceland

Uses of geothermal energy

6. Iceland has used geothermal energy since the 1930s. Today five major and many other smaller geothermal power plants exist in Iceland. These produce over 30% of the nation's energy.
7. Geothermal energy plants provide heating and hot water for approximately 87% of all buildings in Iceland. Water usage is metered and people pay for the water they use.

CORE UNIT: PATTERNS AND PROCESSES IN THE PHYSICAL ENVIRONMENT

8. In Iceland's two largest cities, the capital Reykjavík and Akureyri, pavements and car parks are kept ice-free during winter by underground heating systems.

9. One of Iceland's most important uses of geothermal energy is for heating greenhouses. For years, the naturally warm soil has been used for growing potatoes and other vegetables. Horticulture has benefited considerably from geothermal resources, as the heating of greenhouses has increased production, lengthened the growing season and reduced the cost of importing heating oil for growers.

Fig. 25 A geothermal energy plant in Iceland

Benefits of geothermal energy

10. There is potential to generate 40% of Icelandic energy requirements from geothermal sources. This reduces the need to import expensive fossil fuels. The use of geothermal energy has also benefited the environment due to lower CO_2 emissions compared to fossil fuel power plants.

11. The availability of cheap electricity has made Iceland an attractive location for the **energy-intensive** [energy hungry] metal-smelting industries. Aluminium smelting is worth one-seventh of Iceland's GDP. For example, one American smelting company, Century Aluminium, produces 300,000 tonnes of aluminium per year in Iceland.

12. There are plans to lay 1,300 kilometres of submarine electricity cables from Iceland to Scotland so that geothermal energy can be exported to Europe.

13. Geothermal activity is important to the Icelandic tourist industry, e.g. geysers, hot pools and the Blue Lagoon (geothermal swimming pool).

weblinks
Cable between Iceland and Britain

Powering Scotland from Icelandic volcanoes

Fig. 26 The Blue Lagoon tourist attraction

CHAPTER 5: ROCK TYPES AND THEIR FORMATION

Chapter Revision Questions

1. Explain the terms: igneous rock, plutonic rock, intermediate (hypabyssal) rock and volcanic rock. Give an example of each rock type.
2. Explain with the aid of a labelled diagram the process by which sediment is turned to stone (lithification).
3. Contrast organic and inorganic sedimentary rock types. Give an example of each and state where it is found in Ireland.
4. How are chemically formed sedimentary rocks made?
5. Match the description of the rock with the name of the rock by writing the correct letter in the table provided.

Letter	Description of Rock
A	Contains grains of sand which were cemented together.
B	Was formed from the fossils of many sea creatures and contains calcium carbonate.
C	Contains tiny crystals and was formed on or near the surface of the earth; is found in the Giant's Causeway.
D	Was once limestone or chalk but changed due to heat or pressure.
E	Contains large crystals and was formed within the crust; is found in the Wicklow mountains.

Name of Rock	Letter
Granite	
Marble	
Limestone	
Sandstone	
Basalt	

6. (a) Name **one** type of igneous rock.
   (b) Name **one** Irish location for this type of rock.
   (c) Explain in detail how this rock was formed.
7. (a) Name **one** type of sedimentary rock.
   (b) Name **one** Irish location of this type of rock.
   (c) Explain in detail how this rock was formed.
8. (a) Name **one** type of metamorphic rock.
   (b) Give a specific location in Ireland where this metamorphic rock can be found.
   (c) Describe how metamorphic rock is formed.
9. Limestone, basalt, marble, sandstone, slate, granite: place each of these rocks into the category of igneous, sedimentary or metamorphic.
10. Draw a sketch map of Ireland to show the location of each of the following rock types: marble, limestone, basalt, sandstone, granite, quartzite.
11. Explain how man interacts with the rock cycle in **one** of the following: (a) the production of geothermal energy in Iceland or (b) the mining of lead and zinc at Tara Mines in Navan, County Meath.

LC Exam Questions

Higher Level students must be able to answer Ordinary and Higher Level questions.

■ OL Questions

12. (a) Name any **two** examples of sedimentary rock.
    (b) Name any **two** uses of the sedimentary rocks named above.
    (c) Describe how sedimentary rock is formed.

13. (a) Name any **two** examples of igneous rock.
    (b) Name any **two** uses of the igneous rocks named above.
    (c) Describe how igneous rock is formed.

14. (a) Name any **two** examples of metamorphic rock.
    (b) Name any **two** uses of the metamorphic rocks named above.
    (c) Describe how metamorphic rock is formed.

15. Examine the diagram of the rock cycle and answer each of the following questions:
    (i) Name the category of rock formed at X.
    (ii) Give an example of the category of rock formed at X.
    (iii) Name the category of rock formed at Y.
    (iv) Give an example of the category of rock formed at Y.
    (v) Name any **two** ways rocks are used.

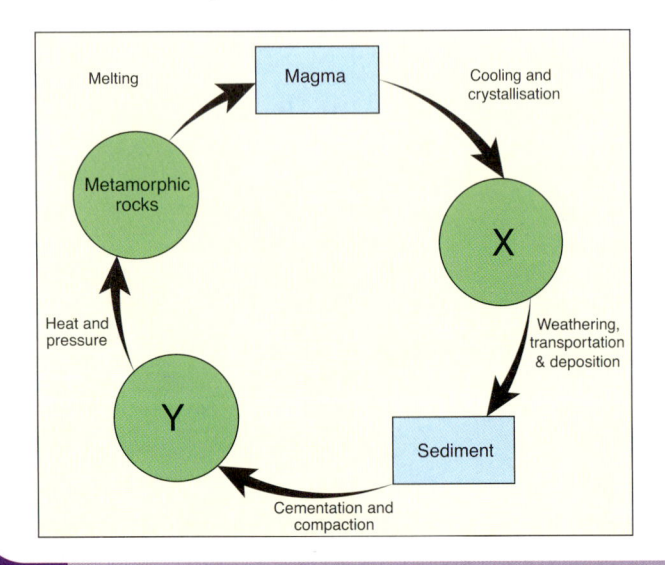

16. The diagram shows the origin of igneous, sedimentary and metamorphic rocks.

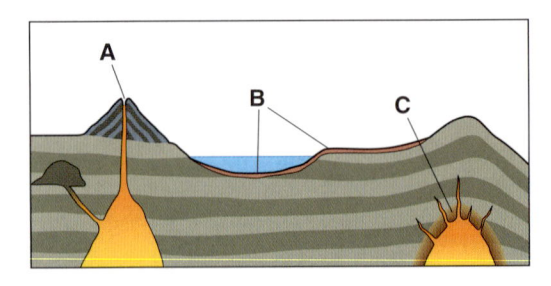

    (a) Identify the rock types that form at A, B and C.
    (b) Name a specific type of rock formed in area C that is widely used across the world.
    (c) Name a specific type of rock formed in area B that is used as a source of energy.

17. Describe any **one** of the following examples of how humans interact with the rock cycle:
    • Quarrying
    • Mining
    • Oil/Gas exploration
    • Geothermal energy production.

■ HL Questions

18. Examine how humans interact with the rock cycle, with reference to **one** of the following:
    • Mining
    • Extraction of building materials
    • Oil/gas exploration
    • Geothermal energy production.

19. Explain the formation of igneous rocks with reference to Irish examples.

20. Explain the formation of sedimentary rocks with reference to Irish examples.

21. Explain the formation of metamorphic rocks with reference to Irish examples.

CHAPTER 5: ROCK TYPES AND THEIR FORMATION

Key Words

You should be able to explain both verbally and in writing each of the key words listed below.

accumulation
basalt
batholiths
bedding planes
calcite cement
chalk
chemically formed
coal
compacted
conglomerate
dolerite
dynamic metamorphism
fault gouge
foliation
fossils
gneiss
granite
gypsum
igneous
inorganic/mechanically formed
intermediate/hypabyssal
intrusive

limestone
lithification
marble
metamorphic
mudstone
organically formed
permeable
plutonic
porous
quartzite
regional metamorphism
rock cycle
salt
sandstone
sedimentary
shale
silica
strata
slate
thermal metamorphism
volcanic/extrusive

Key Words Chapter 5

Digital Resources are available for this chapter at mentorbooks.ie/resources

CHAPTER 6

Weathering and Erosion

Key Theme

Rocks are broken down by mechanical and chemical means. The weathered particles are transported elsewhere by the agents of erosion.

Learning Outcomes

At the end of this chapter you will be able to:
- Explain the terms weathering and erosion.
- Explain the difference between these terms.
- Name and describe the processes of chemical and mechanical weathering.
- Name the agents of erosion.

Contents

6.1	Weathering and erosion	85
6.2	Types of weathering	85
6.3	Erosion	91

Revision Space

Chapter Revision Questions – LC Exam Questions – Key Word List 92

CHAPTER 6: WEATHERING AND EROSION

6.1 Weathering and erosion

The wearing down of the earth's surface is called **denudation**. Both weathering and erosion are called **agents of denudation** as they wear away the landscape and gradually change its surface.

Weathering and **erosion** are both exogenic (external) forces. This means that weathering and erosion operate on the surface of the earth as opposed to inside it.

Weathering is the **process** (series of changes) that breaks down rocks into smaller pieces. Weathering does not transport material; instead it is transported by the agents of erosion or by the action of gravity (mass movement) and later deposited.

Weathering agents include frost, extreme changes of temperature and chemical reactions between rocks, oxygen, carbon dioxide and water.

Erosion is the process by which the earth's rocks are broken down, transported and deposited elsewhere. Erosion agents are rivers, ice, sea and wind.

6.2 Types of weathering

There are three types of weathering.

1. **Mechanical weathering**: This breaks down rocks into smaller pieces. It is a physical disintegration (falling apart) of rock.
2. **Chemical weathering**: This happens when a chemical reaction occurs in the rock causing it to decompose and rot away. New chemical substances are formed.
3. **Biological weathering**: This is the disintegration of rocks due to the physical and/or chemical actions of living things such as plants, animals and humans.

Mechanical (rocks disintegrate)	Chemical (rocks dissolve or rot)	Biological
Freeze-thaw Onion weathering Crystallisation of salts	Carbonation Hydration Oxidation Hydrolysis	Plants Animals Humans

1. Mechanical weathering

In this case local pressure is put on rocks causing them to crack and split apart. This may occur as a result of temperature change or crystallisation of salts, so that rock layers eventually split and fall away. No new substances are formed as the chemical composition of the rock does not change. There are three ways in which mechanical weathering can occur.

(a) **Freeze-thaw action**
(b) **Onion weathering (exfoliation)**
(c) **Crystallisation of salts**

Fig. 1 This sandstone rock has been weathered into an unusual shape at the Garden of the Gods, Colorado Springs, USA.

85

(a) Freeze-thaw action

When water gathers in cracks in rocks and the temperature becomes colder at night (or any time the temperature drops below 0°C), the water freezes and expands by about 10%. This expansion places great pressure on a rock face. When daytime comes the ice melts. Repeated freezing and thawing of the water eventually splits the rock fragments off the exposed rock surfaces and they fall as angular blocks of rock called **scree** (**talus**).

The presence of scree is an indicator that freeze-thaw action has occurred. An accumulation of scree can protect the lower slopes of a hill from further weathering.

Freeze-thaw action occurs:
- Where temperatures vary above and below freezing and water is present.
- In arctic as well as temperate zones such as Ireland.
- On mountain tops in equatorial areas such as Kilimanjaro.

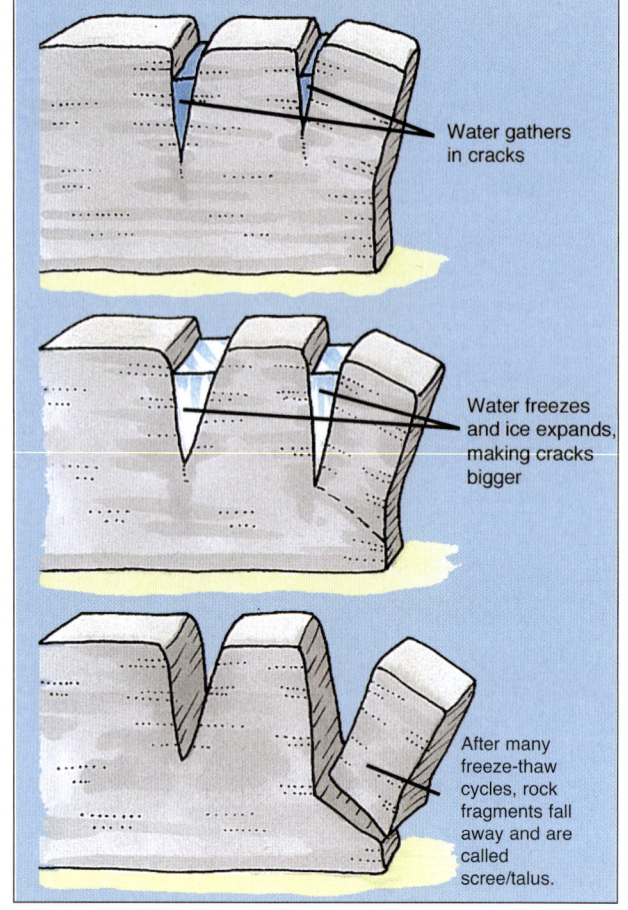

Fig. 2 How freeze-thaw action occurs

Fig. 3 Freeze-thaw action happening in the Swiss Alps

Fig. 4 Scree slope in the Comeragh Mountains, County Waterford.

weblink
Erosion - landscape formation

(b) Onion weathering (exfoliation)

This is when the surface of the rock peels away layer by layer. The peeled fragments drop to the ground and are themselves weathered.

Extreme heat during the day causes the outer rock layers to **expand**. At night as the rock cools it shrinks (**contracts**) slightly. If this is repeated many times the rock is weakened and surface layers peel away. The presence of even tiny amounts of water can speed up this exfoliation process. Exfoliation is also increased if the rock is composed of many different minerals which can expand and contract at different speeds.

Onion weathering occurs in hot dry climates where the temperature difference between day and night (**diurnal range**) is high (40°C), e.g. desert areas such as Arizona.

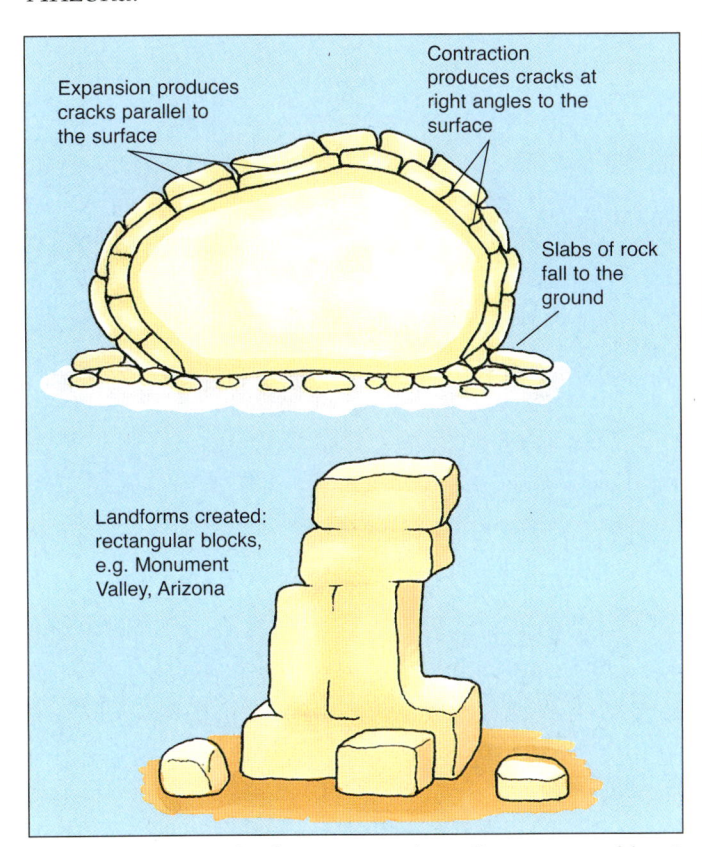

Fig. 6 Onion weathering of rock

Fig. 5 Onion weathering occurs where there are sudden temperature changes.

(c) Crystallisation of salts

This type of mechanical weathering is due to pressure caused by the growth of salts in a rock, which then splits it apart.

When water evaporates, any dissolved salts in it are re-crystallised. You may have carried out an experiment in science class to show this. In nature, salts such as calcium sulfate and sodium carbonate are present in water. As water evaporates from rock surfaces, the salt crystals grow inside any cracks that are present. This growth places great pressure on the rock, causing it to crumble or peel away in slices. This has happened in buildings such as Christ Church Cathedral and the National Museum in Dublin.

> **weblink**
> Weathering and erosion basics

> A 'salt' is a combination of a metal and non-metal. Table salt is a combination of sodium (a metal) and chlorine (a gas).

CORE UNIT: PATTERNS AND PROCESSES IN THE PHYSICAL ENVIRONMENT

2. Chemical weathering

Chemical weathering happens because water contains many dissolved substances, such as carbon dioxide from the air, that can chemically attack rock. Chemical weathering causes the rock to rot away (**decompose**).

Sedimentary rocks have grains bonded together during lithification with cementing agents such as silica and calcite. These cementing agents are easily chemically weathered so that some sedimentary rocks such as limestone weather quickly. Chemical weathering is important for the formation of soils across the world.

Quartz and mica (the glassy and silvery minerals common in granite) are the only minerals resistant to chemical weathering.

There are four processes of chemical weathering.
(a) **Carbonation**
(b) **Hydration**
(c) **Oxidation**
(d) **Hydrolysis**

(a) Carbonation

Carbonation is the chemical reaction between rock minerals and rain water. When rainwater absorbs carbon dioxide from the air it becomes a weak **carbonic acid**. As the rainwater seeps through the soil it may also absorb humic acids created by rotting plant and animal remains. By the time the rainwater has reached the rock below the soil, it is quite acidic and dissolves the rock, especially limestone. This occurs when the acid reacts with the calcium carbonate in the limestone to form soluble calcium bicarbonate.

> rain + carbon dioxide = weak carbonic acid
> weak carbonic acid + limestone (insoluble calcium carbonate) = calcium bicarbonate (soluble)

Limestone regions found in Ireland and elsewhere are weathered by carbonation, producing unusual and beautiful surface and underground landscapes called karst landscapes, e.g. the Burren, County Clare.

Fig. 7 Weathered limestone

CHAPTER 6: WEATHERING AND EROSION

Fig. 8 Bubbles of carbon dioxide gas being released from the reaction of hydrochloric acid on limestone.

> **Class Demonstration**
> Place a piece of chalk into some dilute hydrochloric acid. The chalk dissolves, and bubbles of carbon dioxide gas are released. This is similar to what happens to limestone in rain, only it happens much faster in acid. Carry out the same experiment with a sample of limestone.

(b) Hydration

This is the chemical combination of rock minerals with water. As these minerals are hydrated they expand, causing stress and strain within a rock causing it to crumble.

This may seem similar to the mechanical process of crystallisation of salts; however hydration is a chemical reaction and hydrated minerals are different to their unhydrated parents. Hydration affects shale.

> **Hydration in everyday life**
> Hydration is used to provide nappies with their water-absorbing properties. The liquid-absorbing substance in nappies undergoes hydration. Water-holding gels for houseplants also work by using hydration. Pour some water onto a nappy or water-holding gel and watch it slowly expand.

(c) Oxidation

Oxidation happens when a rock mineral chemically combines with oxygen in water or air. The rusting of iron is an oxidation process. Rocks that contain iron are easily weathered by oxidation. Iron oxides in rock appear as reddish, orange-yellow streaks seeping out of a rock. Oxidised soils may also appear reddish in colour, e.g. latosols and terra rossa soils.

Fig. 9 Iron oxide being leached from rock layers in cliffs at Ballybunion, County Kerry

(d) Hydrolysis

Hydrolysis is the action of acidic water on rock-forming minerals such as feldspar. **Feldspar** in granite is converted into **kaolin** (china clay) by hydrolysis. This causes the other minerals in granite, such as quartz (which is resistant to hydrolysis), to fall out of the rock. As a result, hydrolysis causes granite to slowly fall apart.

Hydrolysis is one of the most important weathering agents. It occurs in the top few metres of the earth's crust and plays a major role in soil formation because hydrolysis leads to the formation of clay.

The rate of hydrolysis, like most chemical reactions, is affected by temperature. For every 10°C rise in temperature, the rate of hydrolysis doubles. Thus it is most effective in hot, wet regions of the world such as the tropics, which have deep soils as a result. Brazilian latosol soils are over 20 m deep in places.

> **China clay (kaolin)** is formed by the hydrolysis of the mineral feldspar in granite rocks. Kaolin deposits in Belleek in County Fermanagh are used to make porcelain objects. Kaolin is also used for many cosmetic skin preparations. As a powder it is used as a pest control in orchards.

Fig. 10 This Irish granite rock is being weathered by hydrolysis.

3. Biological weathering

The action of plants, animals and man can speed up both mechanical and chemical weathering. Burrowing animals, the growth of plant roots in cracks in rocks, quarrying, road building and deforestation expose rock and soil to weathering processes.

Fig. 11 Tree roots causing biological weathering of a wall in Wexford Town

Fig. 12 Plants growing in a brick wall

6.3 Erosion

A **process** is anything that happens to change the earth's surface. Erosion is the process by which the earth's surface is broken down, transported from one place to another and deposited.

The main **agents of erosion** are:
1. Rivers
2. Moving ice
3. The sea
4. Wind.

	Rivers	**Ice**	**Sea**
Erosion	Hydraulic action Abrasion Solution Attrition	Plucking Abrasion	Hydraulic action Abrasion Air compression Solution Attrition
Transportation	Solution Suspension Saltation Traction	Sliding (basal flow) Plastic flow Moraine: debris is transported at the sides, in front of, within and under the ice	Longshore drift
Deposition	Reduced energy – slows down – load increases – reduction in volume	Melting – unsorted (till) – sorted (fluvioglacial deposits)	Change in coastline shape Constructive waves – sheltered bays – calm seas

SURFACE PROCESSES OF EROSION, TRANSPORTATION AND DEPOSITION

Fig. 13 Look carefully to identify where ice, river and sea processes are at work.

CORE UNIT: PATTERNS AND PROCESSES IN THE PHYSICAL ENVIRONMENT

Chapter Revision Questions

1. Match the photographs A–D with the different weathering processes:

   (i) carbonation   (ii) freeze-thaw action
   (iii) hydrolysis   (iv) oxidation

   A

   B

   C

   D

2. Explain the terms: chemical, mechanical and biological weathering.

3. Give **three** examples of each type of weathering.

4. With the aid of diagrams describe how freeze-thaw action and exfoliation occur.

5. Carbonation, oxidation, hydration, hydrolysis.
   Choose any **three** of these processes and explain how they weather rock.

6. Weathering may be classified into three groups. Name these groups and give an example of **two** types of weathering processes in each group you have named.

7. Explain the term erosion. List the main agents of erosion.

LC Exam Questions

Higher Level students must be able to answer Ordinary and Higher Level questions.

■ OL Questions

8. Examine this diagram of a weathering process.

   (a) Name the process shown.
   (b) Name **one** location in Ireland where this process occurs.
   (c) Name **one** other type of weathering.

9. Describe and explain any **one** of the following weathering processes that you have studied:
   - freeze-thaw action
   - carbonation.

10. Choose **one** example of each type of weathering process listed in the table below and explain how it occurs.

Weathering Process		
Mechanical	**Chemical**	**Biological**
freeze-thaw	carbonation	plants
exfoliation	hydration	animals
salt crystallisation	hydrolysis	human activity

■ HL Questions

11. Examine the photograph.
    (a) Identify the type of weathering which shaped this rock.
    (b) Where is this type of weathering most likely to occur?

12. Examine the impact of mechanical and chemical weathering on the landscape.

13. Explain the process(es) of physical weathering or the process(es) of chemical weathering.

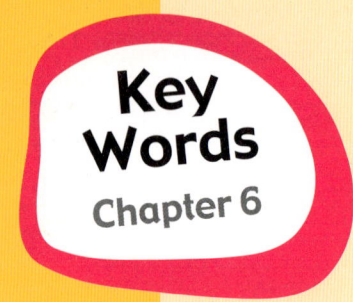

CORE UNIT: PATTERNS AND PROCESSES IN THE PHYSICAL ENVIRONMENT

Key Words Chapter 6

Key Words

You should be able to explain both verbally and in writing each of the key words listed below.

agent of denudation	freeze-thaw action
agent of erosion	hydration
biological weathering	hydrolysis
carbonation	mechanical weathering
carbonic acid	onion weathering/exfoliation
chemical weathering	oxidation
crystallisation of salt	process
denudation	scree/talus
diurnal range	weathering
erosion	

Digital Resources are available for this chapter at mentorbooks.ie/resources

CHAPTER 7

Rock Types and Landscapes

Key Theme

The development of a landscape is influenced by the rocks that lie beneath it.

Learning Outcomes

At the end of this chapter you will be able to:
- Name and give examples of landscapes associated with different rock types.
- Explain how limestone landscapes are formed.

Contents

7.1	Introduction	96
7.2	Limestone landscapes	97
7.3	Surface and underground landforms in karst areas	99

Revision Space

Chapter Revision Questions – LC Exam Questions – Key Word List 104

7.1 Introduction

There is a great variety of rock types in Ireland. The landscapes of some parts of the country are unusual because they are associated with a certain rock. Look at Fig. 1 below to see how different rock types can form different landscapes.

There are two reasons why rock type influences the landscape:

1. Certain rocks are formed or weathered in unique ways producing landforms found in no other rock, e.g. the Burren in County Clare (limestone), the Giant's Causeway in County Antrim (basalt) and the Wicklow Mountains (granite).

2. Earth movements have folded and uplifted some rocks to produce mountains and valleys in certain regions, e.g. the Munster Ridge and Valley landscape.

The Burren, County Clare (limestone)

Giant's Causeway, County Antrim (basalt)

Cliffs of Moher, County Clare (limestone, sandstone and shale)

Mount Errigal, County Donegal (quartzite)

Benbulben, County Sligo (shale and limestone)

Fig. 1 Famous landscapes around Ireland

7.2 Limestone landscapes

The unusual landscapes formed by the chemical weathering and erosion of limestone are known as **karst** or karstic landscapes.

All karst regions share the same characteristics. These are:
1. A lack of surface water because rainwater and rivers are swallowed up by the cracks and fissures in the rock and flow underground very quickly.
2. The presence of swallow holes.
3. The presence of enclosed hollows called dolines.
4. The presence of underground water.

> The word 'karst' comes from the Slovenian word *kras* meaning bare, stony ground. Some of the best karstic landforms can be seen in Slovenia, Serbia and Croatia.

Fig. 2 Limestone terraces in the Burren, County Clare

Fig. 3 Inishmore, Aran Islands, County Galway

Fig. 4 The Burren, County Clare

Fig. 5 Ringfort near Fanore, the Burren, County Clare

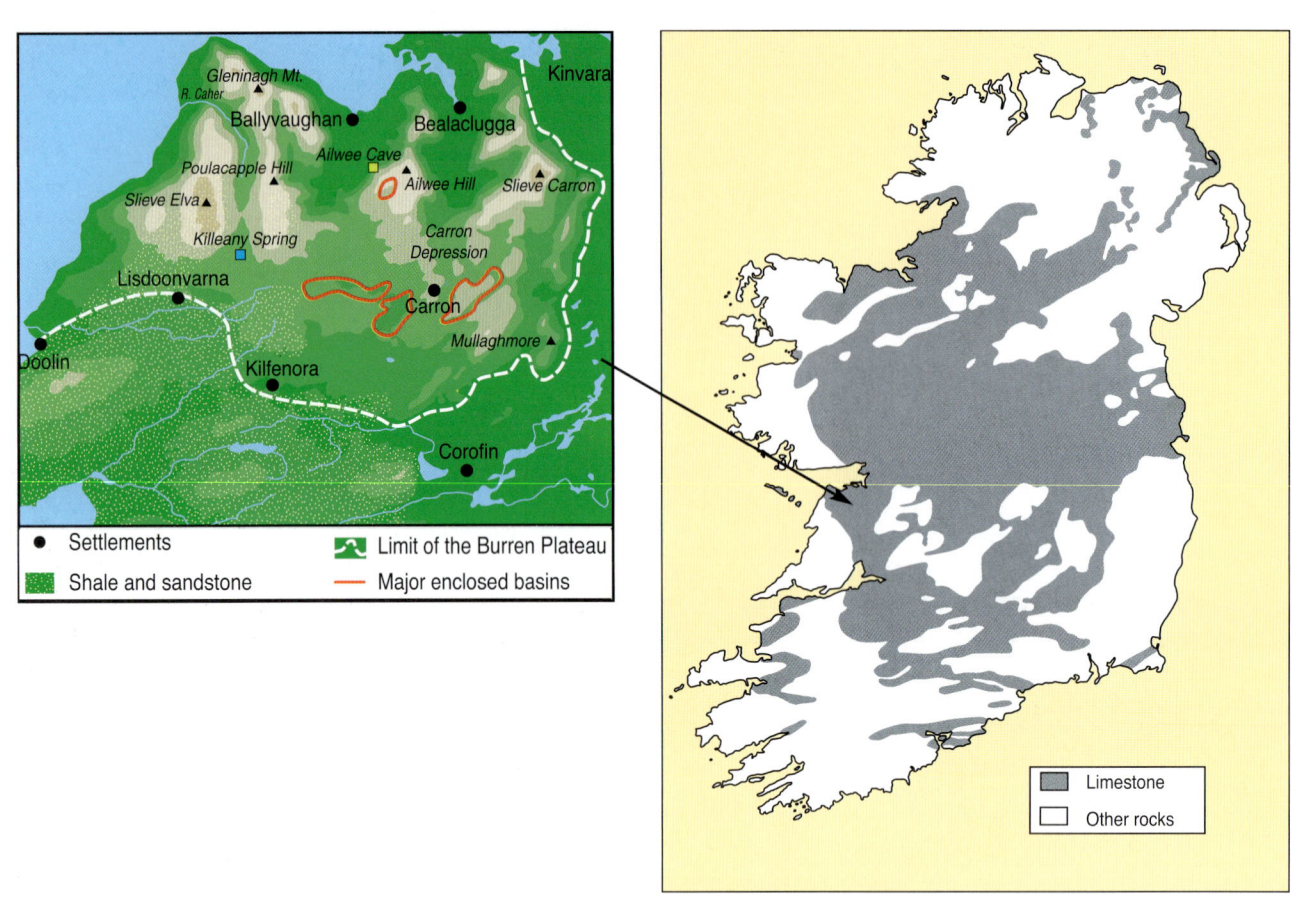

CORE UNIT: PATTERNS AND PROCESSES IN THE PHYSICAL ENVIRONMENT

Fig. 6 Limestone deposits in Ireland

Limestone is easily chemically weathered and produces unique karst landscapes for the following reasons:
1. Limestone contains many vertical cracks called **joints** and horizontal cracks called **bedding planes**.
2. Limestone is **permeable** and **pervious** – it allows water to pass through the joints and bedding planes.
3. Limestone contains **calcium carbonate** from the shells of marine creatures. It is chemically weathered by the **carbonation** process.
4. Rainwater is slightly acidic because it has absorbed carbon dioxide from the air as it falls. This acid (carbonic acid) reacts with the calcium carbonate in limestone forming soluble **calcium bicarbonate**. This is then carried away in **solution** (dissolved in water) by the rainwater.
5. The acidified rainwater trickles down through the cracks and bedding planes enlarging them by the carbonation process, so that even more water can pass through the rock. Eventually the fissures are so large that most of the rain that falls goes underground within minutes.

weblink
Animation: water going underground

CHAPTER 7: ROCK TYPES AND LANDSCAPES

7.3 Surface and underground landforms in karst areas

Surface landforms
Limestone pavement
Dolines
Swallow holes
Turloughs

Underground landforms
Caves
Stalactites
Stalagmites
Pillars

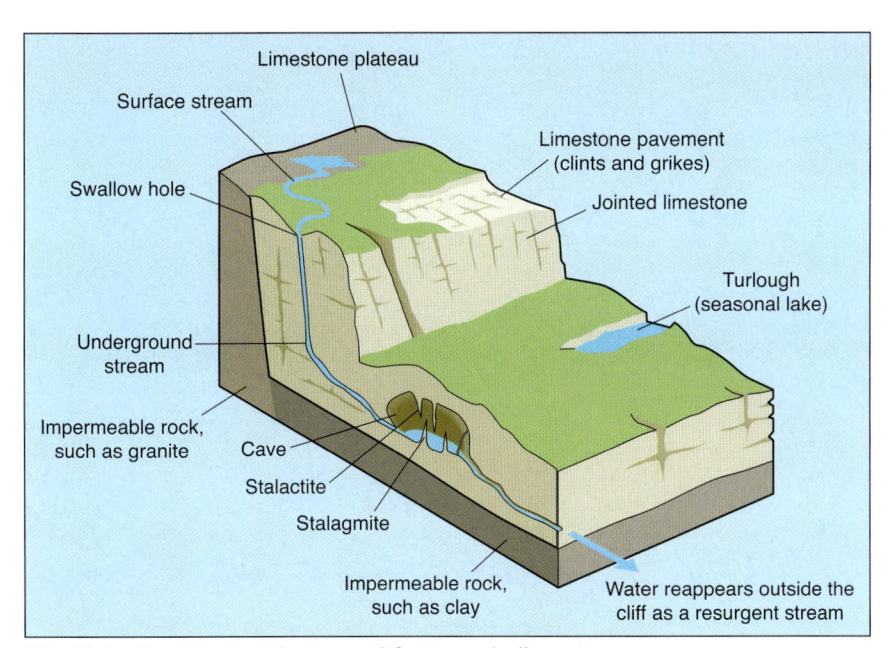

Fig. 7 Surface and underground features in limestone areas

Fig. 8 Limestone pavement in the Burren, County Clare

Fig. 9 Resurgent streams in the Burren, County Clare

Fig. 10 Limestone terraces at Mullaghmore, County Sligo

Surface landforms

Limestone pavement

A **limestone pavement** is a landform of chemical weathering formed by **carbonation**. It is a flat surface of bare limestone rock, e.g. the Burren, County Clare.

The formation of Irish limestone pavements began with the scouring of the limestone by thick glaciers during the last Ice Age. The ice removed the soil that lay over the limestone, leaving level platforms of exposed limestone. Then a thick layer of boulder clay (glacial till) was deposited as the glaciers melted.

Acidic rainwater seeped through the boulder clay soil becoming more acidic as it absorbed humic acids from decaying vegetation. When this acidic water reached the limestone below carbonation began. It easily dissolved vertical lines of weakness (**joints**) in the rock, widening and deepening them to become **grikes**. The flat surfaces of rock left between the grikes are called **clints**.

Sometimes the surface of the clints is also slowly dissolved by carbonation. Smaller hollows and sharp-edged grooves form on the surface of the clints. These are called **karren**.

Gradually the soil on top of the limestone pavement was washed away, falling deep underground through the grikes.

The entire rock surface of the pavement looks like crazy paving slabs.

In the Burren, the soil was washed away sometime in the late Bronze Age, roughly 3,000 years ago when the climate became wetter. The people cleared the forest and farmed the land. Without plant roots to bind the soil together it was easily removed by the rain.

Fig. 11 Clints and grikes on limestone pavement

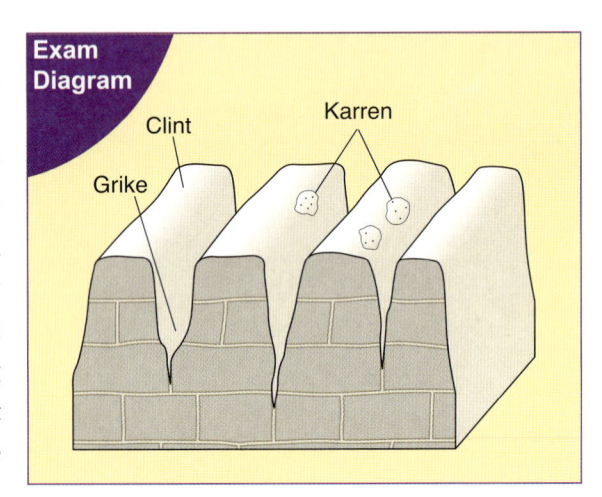

Fig. 12 Limestone pavement

Fig. 13 Karren hollows on a clint

Dolines/sinkholes

Enclosed hollows found on the limestone surface are called **dolines**. They are also known as sinkholes, e.g. Dunmore Cave, County Kilkenny. Dolines are conical-shaped depressions. These hollows form when the roofs in underground caves collapse. They may be anything from a few metres up to a kilometre wide, and a few metres to 150 m deep.

Human activity can lead to the formation of sinkholes when people remove the groundwater for home or industrial use. Caves which were previously flooded with water are emptied causing them to collapse, forming a sinkhole, e.g. Florida, USA.

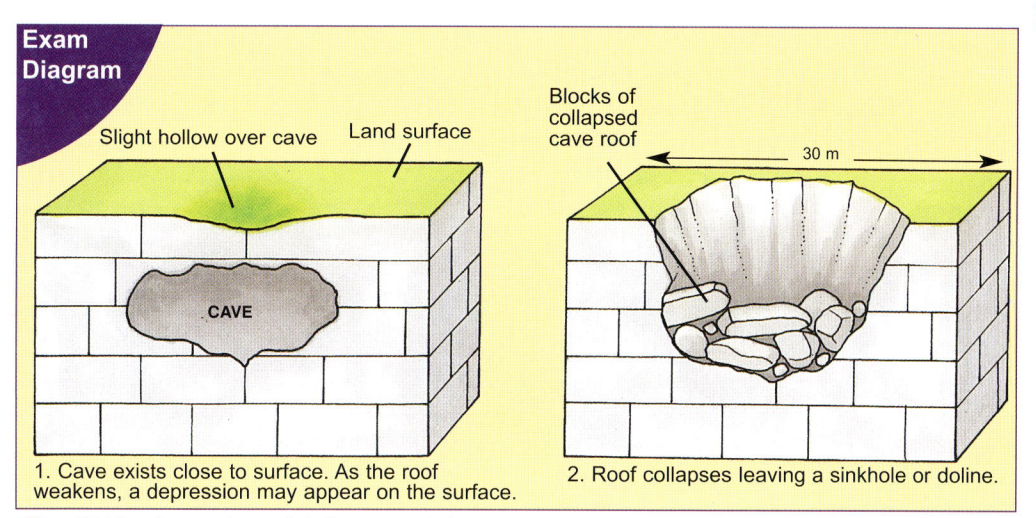

Fig. 14 A doline in a karst region

Exam Diagram

1. Cave exists close to surface. As the roof weakens, a depression may appear on the surface.
2. Roof collapses leaving a sinkhole or doline.

Fig. 15 The formation of dolines or sinkholes

Swallow holes

The place where a river disappears underground is called a **swallow hole**. Rivers erode limestone by the processes of solution, hydraulic action and abrasion. A river, which may begin in a non-limestone area, often disappears underground when it reaches a limestone surface. Swallow holes may be small or large depending on the size of the river. Pollnagollum swallow hole in the Burren is over 6 m wide and 16 m deep.

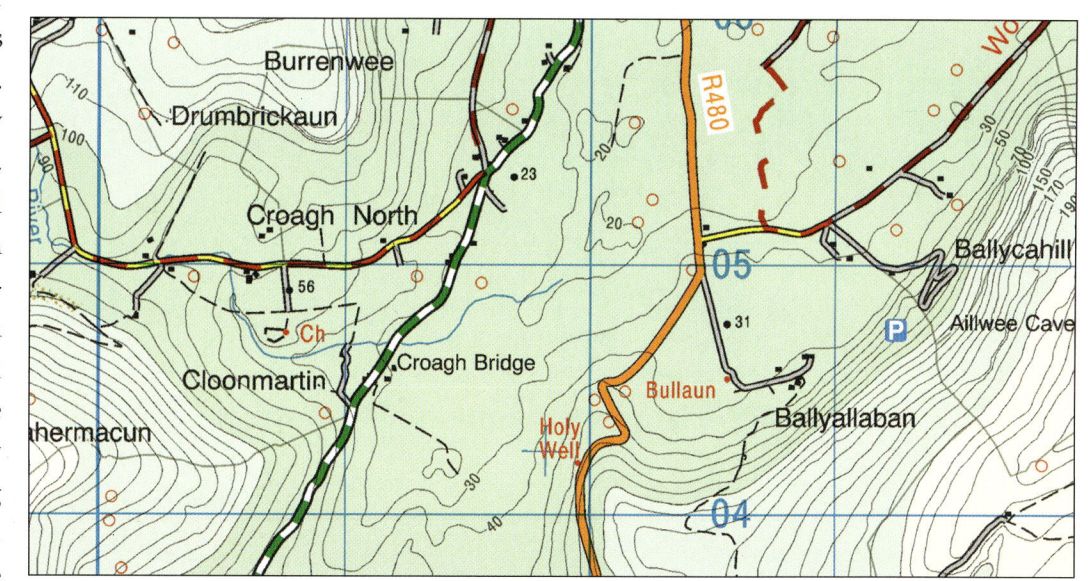

Fig. 16 Map showing a disappearing stream in the Burren. (See the blue line suddenly disappear between Croagh Bridge and the R480.)

Turloughs

Turloughs are temporary lakes that appear in winter. In winter and other times of heavy rain all the caves' fissures in limestone fill with water. If this happens the **water table** rises in the rocks and turloughs form. These are common in the lowland regions of Galway. In summer they dry up as the water table drops when the water sinks underground. Turloughs are often called **seasonal** or **disappearing lakes**, e.g. Gort, County Galway. Filling of the turloughs contributes to regular floods in County Galway.

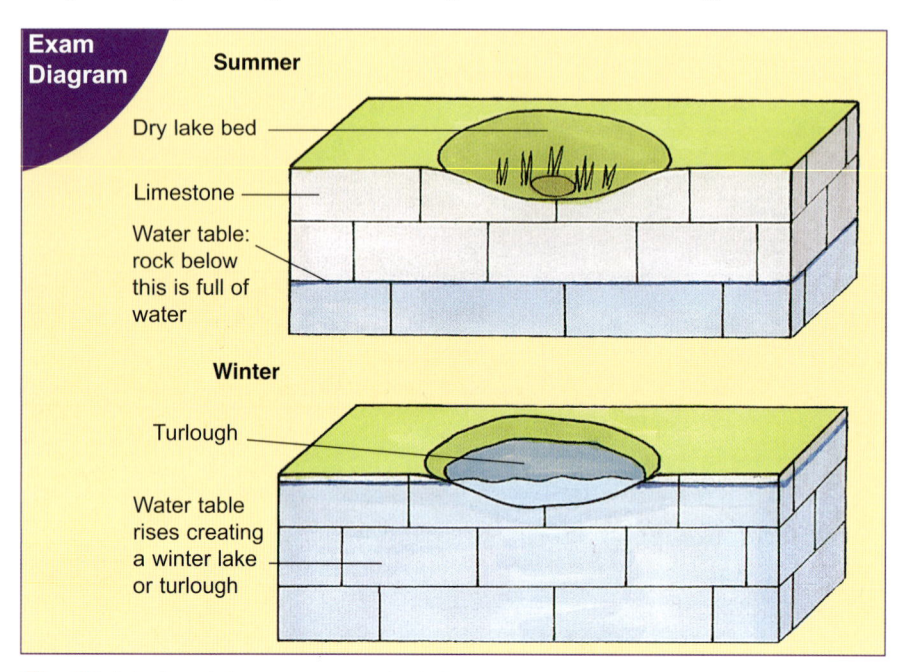

Fig. 17 A turlough in summer and winter

Fig. 18 Carron Turlough, County Clare

Underground limestone landforms

Caves/caverns

Caves are underground chambers. Large caves are called **caverns**. The water in underground rivers and streams uses the processes of erosion and carbonation to enlarge the bedding planes in the limestone, making caves and caverns, e.g. Crag Cave, County Kerry. Underground rivers often reappear out of hillsides as **resurgent streams**.

Chapter 7: Rock Types and Landscapes

Stalactites, stalagmites and pillars [dripstones]

As rainwater seeps underground through the joints and bedding planes of limestone it dissolves the rock by carbonation. The rainwater carries the calcium bicarbonate away in solution deep underground.

When the rainwater reaches the roof of a cave it forms droplets of water which drip constantly from the roof.

Each droplet evaporates slightly leaving a tiny ring-like deposit of **calcite** on the roof (reversing the carbonation process). This calcite gradually builds up to form a straw-like tube that hangs from the ceiling. If a tiny fragment of rock blocks the tube, the calcite is deposited on the outside of the straw to form a carrot-shaped formation called a **stalactite** (e.g. Ailwee Cave, County Clare; Crag Cave, County Kerry).

If the water drips from a narrow crack in the cave ceiling, a curtain-like formation of calcite is deposited called a curtain stalactite.

At the same time the water droplets splash onto the floor beneath the stalactite and evaporate on the ground, leaving an irregular-shaped mound of calcite known as a **stalagmite**. Sometimes the mounds may cover a large area and are called **flowstone** as they appear to be 'flowing' over the ground but are in fact solid rock.

Eventually a stalactite grows down and meets a stalagmite growing upwards. When this happens a single **column** or **pillar** structure is formed in the cave.

> **Memory Aid**
> Tites hang on tight to the ceiling, and mites might reach the ceiling!

Fig. 19 Stalactites, stalagmites and pillars in a cave

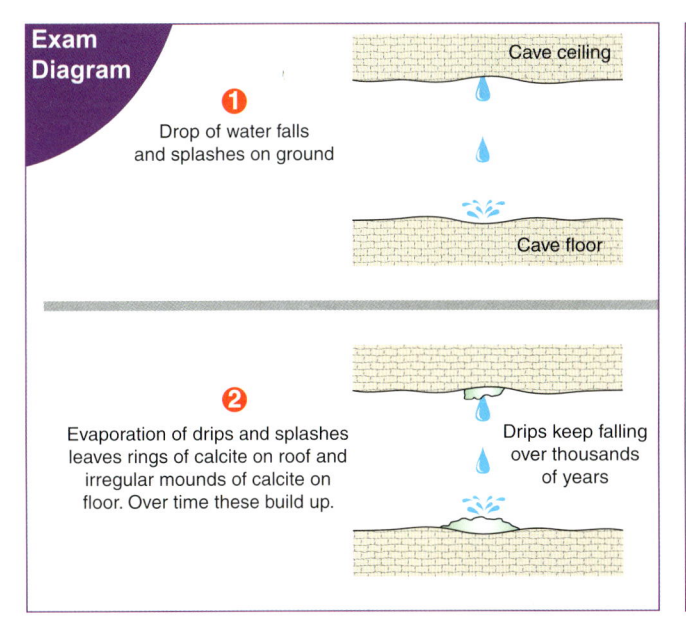

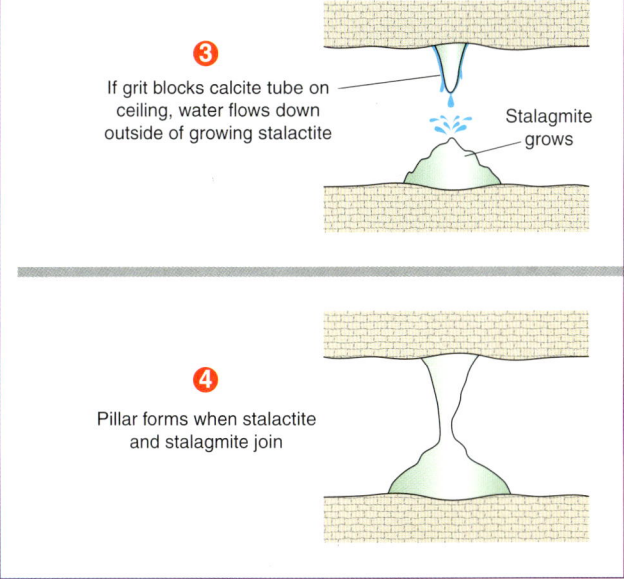

Exam Diagram

① Drop of water falls and splashes on ground

② Evaporation of drips and splashes leaves rings of calcite on roof and irregular mounds of calcite on floor. Over time these build up. Drips keep falling over thousands of years

③ If grit blocks calcite tube on ceiling, water flows down outside of growing stalactite. Stalagmite grows

④ Pillar forms when stalactite and stalagmite join

Fig. 20 The formation of stalactites, stalagmites and pillars

103

CORE UNIT: PATTERNS AND PROCESSES IN THE PHYSICAL ENVIRONMENT

Chapter Revision Questions

1. Explain **two** reasons why limestone forms unique landscapes.
2. Explain the term karst.
3. Explain how the process of carbonation weathers limestone.
4. Link the landform (letter) with the correct location (number) in the table provided. One is completed for you.

Landform	Location
A Clints/Grikes	1 Underground
B Cave	2 Surface
C Stalactite	3 Surface
D Limestone pavement	4 Underground

Letter	No
D	3

5. Explain the terms clint, grike, karren, dripstone, swallow hole, cave, resurgent stream.
6. Name and explain the formation of **two** surface features found in a karst landscape and give an example.
7. Name and explain the formation of **two** underground features found in a karst landscape and give an example.
8. Match the term in Table X with the definition in Table Y.

X	
A	Doline
B	Pillar
C	Spring
D	Turlough
E	Cavern
F	Dripstone

Y	
1.	Disappearing lake
2.	Enlarged underground cave
3.	Large hollows on karst landscape
4.	Stalagmite
5.	Landform made by stalagmite and stalactite growing together.
6.	Resurgent stream

A	
B	
C	
D	
E	
F	

CHAPTER 7: ROCK TYPES AND LANDSCAPES

LC Exam Questions

Higher Level students must be able to answer Ordinary and Higher Level questions.

■ OL Questions

9. Study the diagram of a karst landscape and answer the following questions.

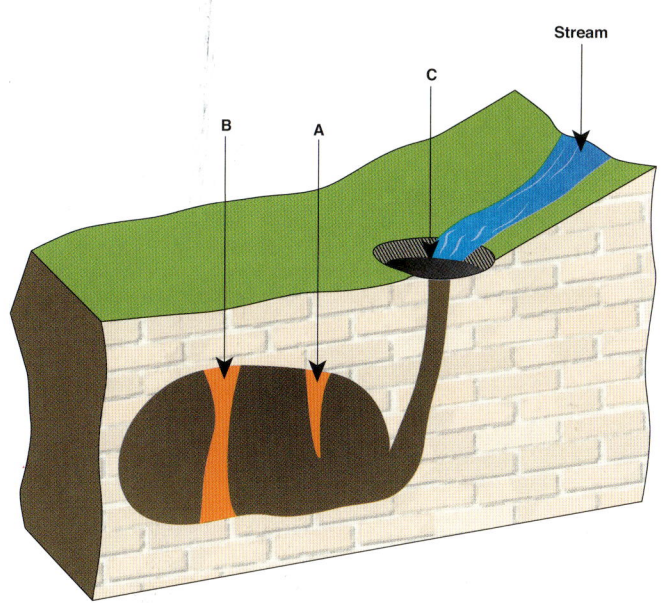

    (i) Name the three features marked A, B and C.
    (ii) Name **one** other feature found in karst landscapes.
    (iii) Explain, with the aid of a diagram, how any **one** feature in a karst region is formed.

10. Examine the photograph below showing a section of a limestone pavement and answer the following questions.
    (i) Name the limestone features A and B.
    (ii) Name **one** location in Ireland where features like these are found.

11. (i) Name **one** example of a karst landscape that you have studied.
    (ii) Explain, with the aid of a diagram, how **one** surface feature in a karst landscape is formed.
    (iii) Explain, with the aid of a diagram, how **one** underground feature in a karst landscape is formed.

12. Describe how any **two** surface landforms in karst regions are formed.

■ HL Questions

13. (a) Examine this photo of underground karst features. Name **two** features visible in the photograph. Name the type of weathering responsible for the formation of these features.
    (b) Give **one** example in County Clare and **one** example in County Fermanagh where these features can be found.

14. With the aid of a diagram(s), explain how chemical weathering has shaped the limestone pavement in a karst region.

15. Examine how different rock types produce distinctive landscapes, with reference to examples that you have studied.

105

CORE UNIT: PATTERNS AND PROCESSES IN THE PHYSICAL ENVIRONMENT

LC Exam Questions

16. Examine the photograph below and answer the following questions.

    (i) What is the name of the feature marked A?
    (ii) What is the name of the feature marked B?
    (iii) What is the name of the overall feature in the photograph?
    (iv) Name **one** process which helped to form these features.
    (v) Name the type of rock most associated with these features.

17. With reference to the Irish landscape, examine how the processes of weathering have influenced the development of any **one** limestone feature.

18. Examine how sedimentary structures, such as bedding planes and joints, influence the development of landforms.

19. Examine the diagram and answer each of the following questions.
    (i) Name each of the landforms A, B, C, D, E and F.
    (ii) Name any **two** processes of chemical weathering.
    (iii) State what is meant by the term permeable rock and name an example of a permeable rock.

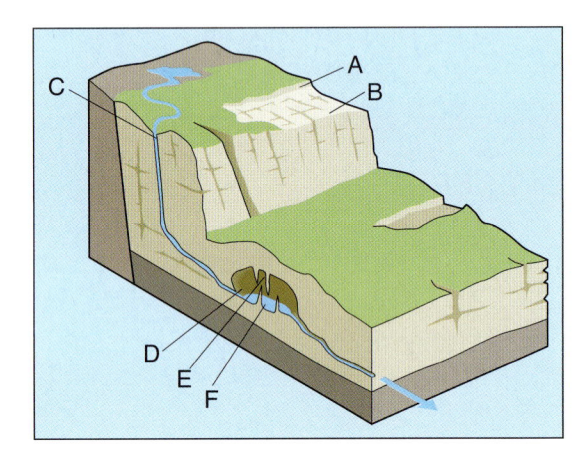

CHAPTER 7: ROCK TYPES AND LANDSCAPES

Key Words

You should be able to explain both verbally and in writing each of the key words listed below.

Key Words Chapter 7

bedding planes
calcite
calcium bicarbonate
calcium carbonate
caverns
caves
clints
column
dolines/sinkholes
flowstone
grikes
joints
karren

karst
limestone pavement
permeable
pervious
pillar
resurgent stream
stalactite
stalagmite
solution
swallow hole/disappearing stream
turloughs/seasonal lake
water table

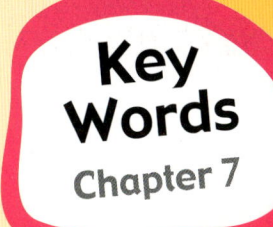

Digital Resources are available for this chapter at mentorbooks.ie/resources

Landform Development

Key Theme

Surface processes (weathering and erosion) can change in their strength and frequency, influencing the development of landforms. These processes also change over time and place (temporally and spatially). Human activities can impact on the operation of surface processes.

Contents

Chapter 8. Fluvial Processes, Patterns and Landforms 109
Chapter 9. Glacial Processes, Patterns and Landforms 143
Chapter 10. Coastal Processes, Patterns and Landforms 165
Chapter 11. Mass Movement Processes, Patterns and Landforms . . 192

Exam Note

You are expected to have a general knowledge of *all* surface processes named in Chapters 8, 9, 10 and 11. This means that on diagrams, maps and photos, you must be able to *name and describe all the processes and identify the landforms created*.

You must focus on one chapter (8 or 9 or 10 or 11) of your choice and be able to *describe in detail the formation* of the landforms.

You must also study human interaction with river processes OR coastal processes OR mass movement processes.

Higher Level students should study how landforms represent a balance between internal and surface forces in Chapter 12.

CHAPTER 8

Landform Development:
Fluvial Processes, Patterns and Landforms

Learning Outcomes

At the end of this chapter you will be able to:
- Name and explain the processes of river erosion, transport and deposition.
- Identify river landforms on diagrams, maps and photographs.
- Describe the formation of river landforms.
- Identify the river processes at work on maps and photographs.
- Identify, describe and explain river drainage patterns.
- Describe using case studies how people interact with rivers.

Contents

8.1	A river's course	110
8.2	River/fluvial processes	114
8.3	The life cycle of a river	118
8.4	Landforms found along a river's course	119
8.5	Human interaction with river processes	134
	Case Study 1: The impact of canals: The River Rhine	134
	Case Study 2: The impact of dam building: The Three Gorges Dam, China	136
	Case Study 3: Flood control on an Irish river: The River Suir, Clonmel	137

Exam Note: If you are studying this chapter in detail, you must be able to explain **river** processes and how the landforms are made. You must be able to identify them on diagrams, maps and photos. The extra material you need to know is indicated by a yellow arrow. If you are not studying this chapter in detail, then you should be able to identify the landforms on diagrams, maps and photos and briefly explain the processes that made them.

Revision Space

Chapter Revision Questions – LC Exam Questions – Key Word List 139

CORE UNIT: PATTERNS AND PROCESSES IN THE PHYSICAL ENVIRONMENT

8.1 A river's course

- Rivers flow from their **source** high in the mountains down along their **course** until they reach their **mouth** at the sea or lakes.
- The area drained by one river and its **tributaries** is called the **drainage basin area**.
- Hills and mountains, known as **watersheds**, separate different drainage basin areas from each other, e.g. the River Slaney and the River Barrow are separated by the watershed of the Blackstairs Mountains.
- Different river patterns may be seen in each drainage basin area.
- The point where rivers meet each other is called a **confluence**.
- The tidal part of a river, close to where it reaches the sea, is called an **estuary**.

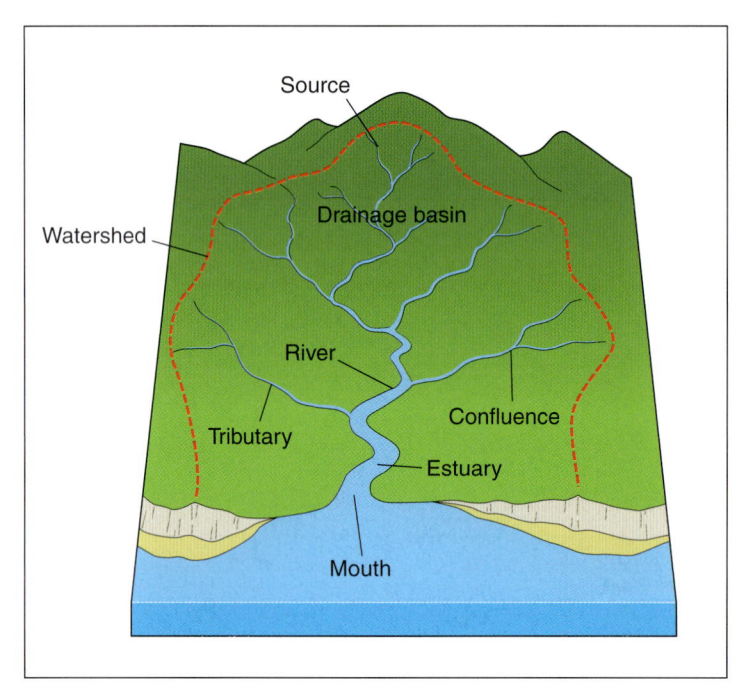

Fig. 1 A river's course

Fig. 2 Aasleagh Waterfall, County Mayo

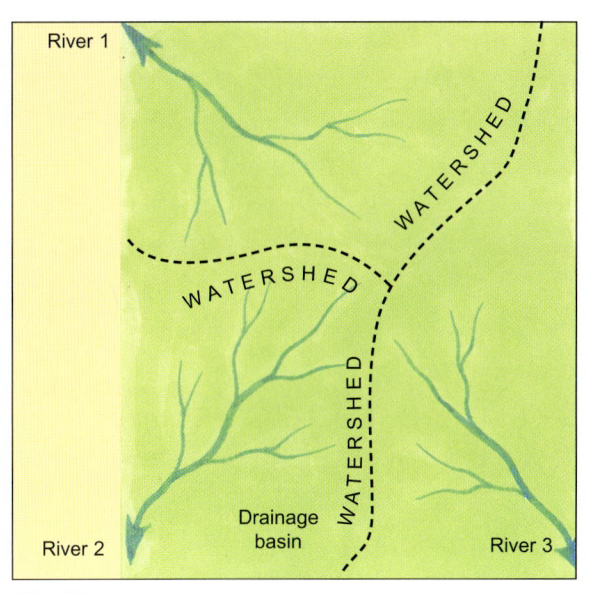

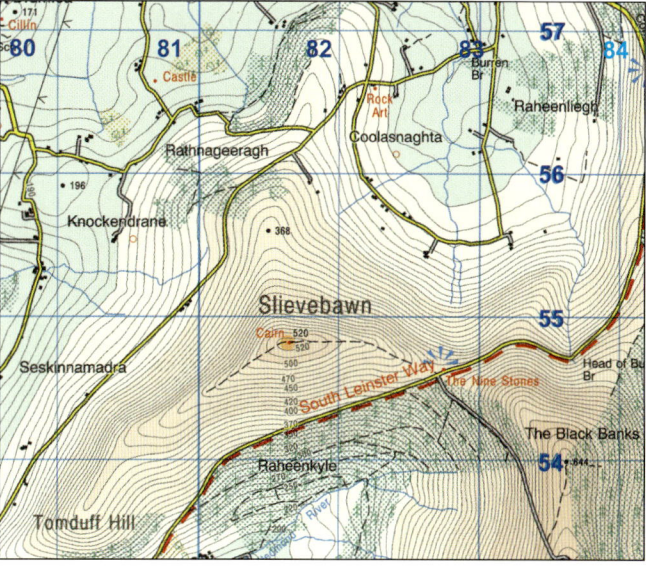

CHAPTER 8: FLUVIAL PROCESSES, PATTERNS AND LANDFORMS

Fig. 3 Watershed and drainage basin

Fig. 4 Draw a line along the watershed on this map.

A river's profile is a graph of its course (Fig. 5). As the river moves along its course it tries to reach a balance between **erosion** and **deposition**. This balance creates a smooth graded profile, but because of the varied rock types over which rivers flow, they rarely achieve a graded profile. The slope of a river's course is instead called its **long profile**. The lowest point reached by a river in its course is called its base level of erosion. The base level may change due to changes in sea level (HL – see Chapter 12).

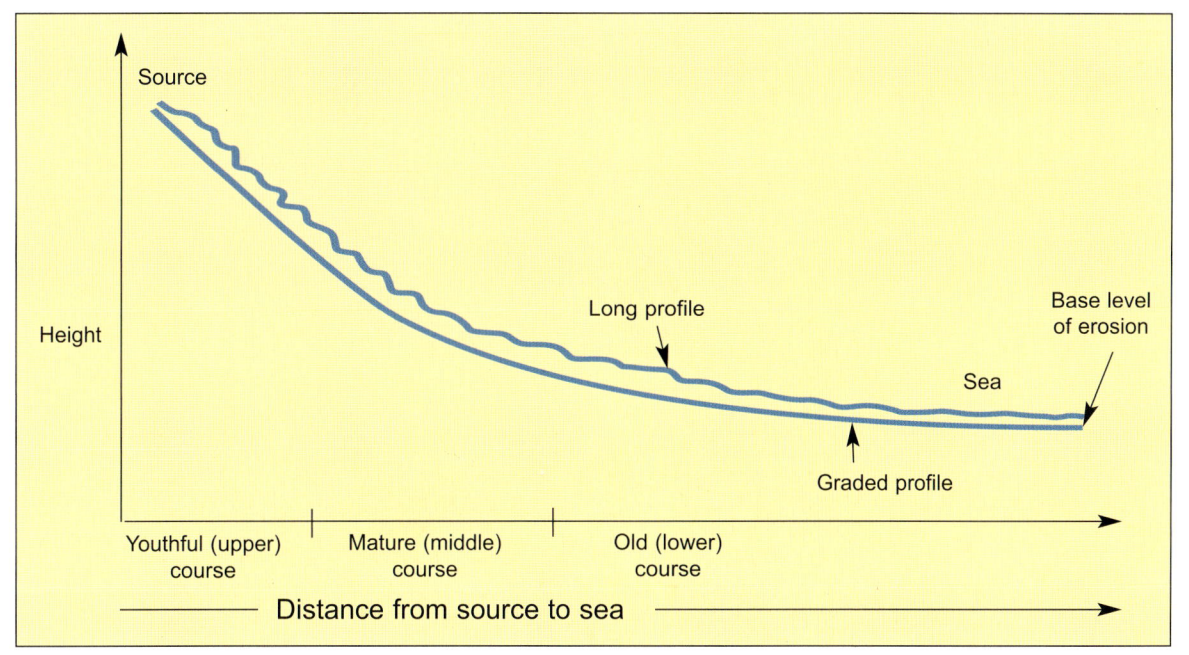

Fig. 5 Long and graded profiles of a river

111

CORE UNIT: PATTERNS AND PROCESSES IN THE PHYSICAL ENVIRONMENT

Drainage patterns

Drainage patterns are the shapes made by a river and its tributaries as they flow over the landscape. There are three main patterns visible in the Irish landscape.

1. **Dendritic drainage pattern**
2. **Trellis drainage pattern**
3. **Radial drainage pattern**

1. Dendritic pattern

This pattern is like the branching shape of a tree. Each river consists of a main 'trunk' which is fed by its tributaries (the branches). These patterns form where the slope of the land is fairly even and the rock type is similar (uniform) across the drainage basin.

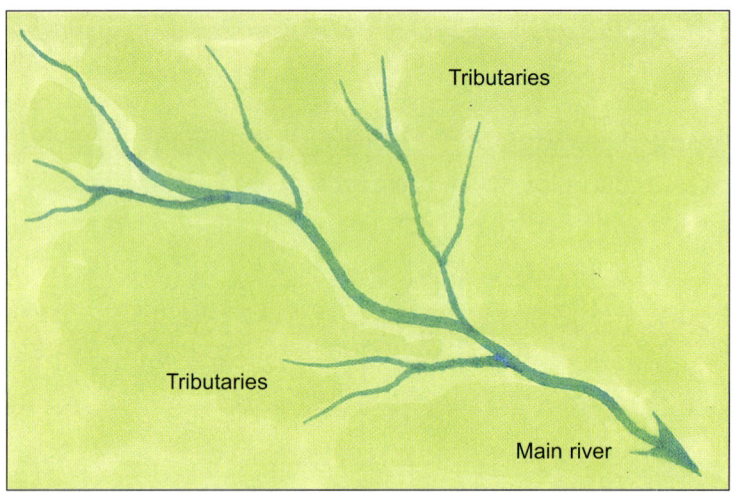

Fig. 6 Dendritic drainage patterns resemble the branching shape of a tree.

Fig. 7 Close-up of a dendritic drainage pattern

CHAPTER 8: FLUVIAL PROCESSES, PATTERNS AND LANDFORMS

2. Trellis pattern

In this pattern tributaries join the main river at right angles, forming a pattern similar to a garden-wall trellis.

These patterns form when the main stream flows across landscapes made of bands of hard and soft rock. Smaller tributaries cut their valleys in the bands of soft rock. They then join the main river at right angles.

Many glaciated valleys also have this pattern. Streams flow down steep valley sides from hanging valleys into the main valley with little space to meander across before reaching the main river, so their confluences are at right angles to each other.

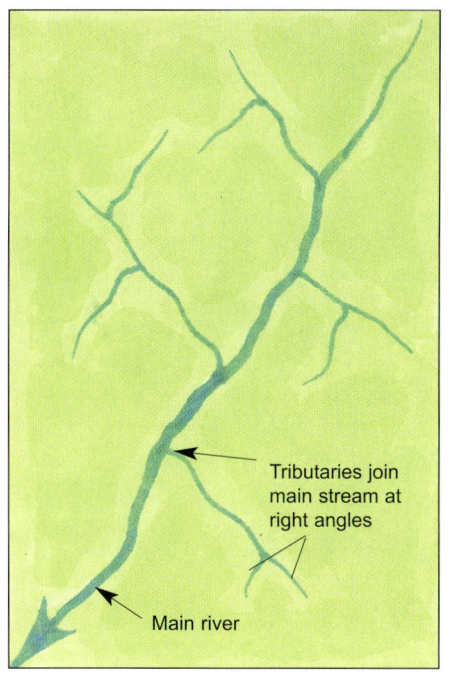

Fig. 8 Trellis drainage pattern shows tributaries joining the main river at right angles.

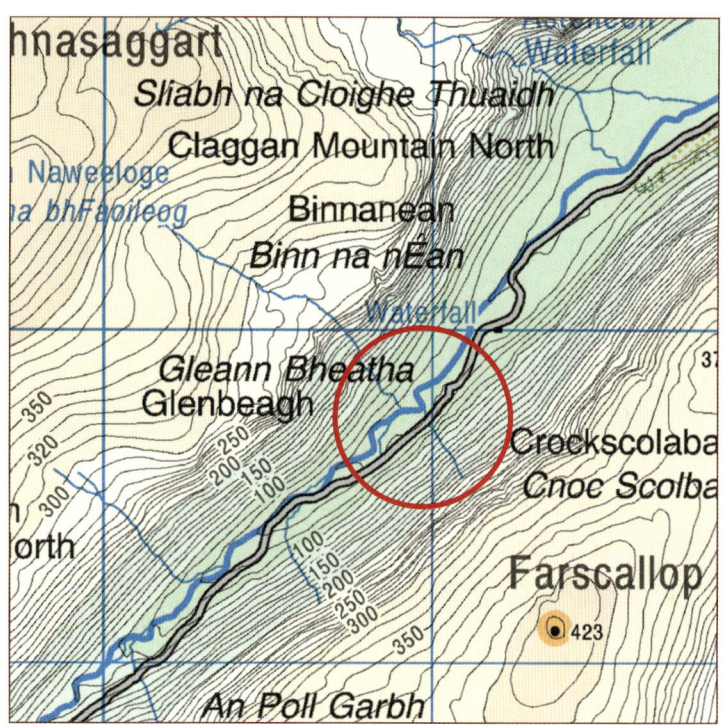

Fig. 9 Trellis drainage pattern. Note right-angled confluences circled on map.

3. Radial pattern

This pattern forms when rivers flow in many directions away from an upland area, much like water flowing off an umbrella. The rivers radiate out from a central upland area. Round or oval-shaped hills show this best, e.g. Brandon Hill, County Kilkenny. The rivers flowing off the upland region may also have their own individual drainage patterns (see Fig. 7).

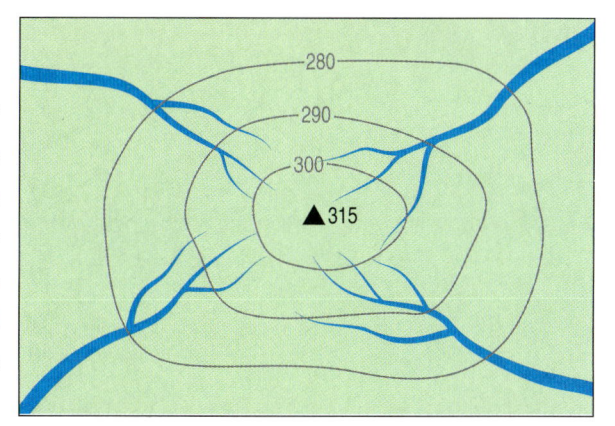

Fig. 10 Radial drainage pattern: rivers flow from a central upland area.

weblink
Rivers

113

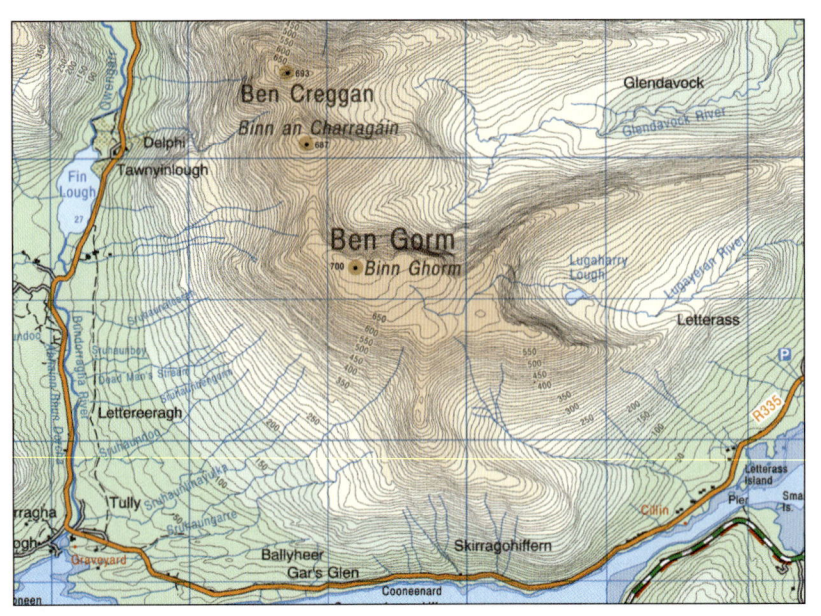

CORE UNIT: PATTERNS AND PROCESSES IN THE PHYSICAL ENVIRONMENT

Fig. 11 Radial drainage pattern in County Mayo. Note dendritic and trellis pattern of individual rivers.

8.2 River/fluvial processes

A process is anything that happens to change the earth's surface. There are three river processes: **erosion**, **transport** and **deposition**. River processes are also known as *fluvial processes*. The sediment carried by a river is called its *load*. The load is formed by erosion and the addition of sediment by mass movement (soil moved downhill by rain and gravity) from the valley sides. Much of the river's **energy** is used in transporting the load. These processes of erosion, transport and deposition continually reshape the landscape over which the river flows.

Factors affecting fluvial processes

The ability of a river to erode, transport and deposit its load depends upon the following factors:
- River volume
- River speed/velocity
- Load
- Slope/gradient
- Channel width and depth.

Each of these factors influence the river's energy (its ability to do its work) and the river's **efficiency**. The more energy a river has, the more erosion it is capable of doing and the greater the load it can carry.

An efficient river has a smooth channel (bed and banks). Its energy is used mainly in transporting its load. An inefficient river has a rough river bed and banks with boulders which cause friction. This means that the river's energy is used overcoming these obstacles.

CHAPTER 8: FLUVIAL PROCESSES, PATTERNS AND LANDFORMS

River volume, speed/velocity and load

The energy of a river depends on the volume of water and speed of flow (velocity). Large fast-flowing rivers are very powerful. Rivers in flood do so much damage because they are faster and larger than normal and have immense energy. They can cut deeply into the river channel (**vertical erosion**) and carry huge quantities of sediment, e.g. the Mississippi River carries one million tonnes of sediment into the sea each day.

River gradient and channel width and depth

The speed of a river is affected by the steepness of the slope (**gradient**) down which it flows, by the depth of the water and by the width of the river channel. It is also affected by the roughness of the river bed. Youthful rivers with large boulders in their channel flow more slowly than older rivers with smoother channel beds.

Deep rivers flowing down sloping land are very powerful with lots of energy. Shallow rivers flowing over flatter ground are less powerful. This is because of the drag (**friction**) between the river with its bed and banks. Wide and deep rivers flow faster than narrow, shallow rivers.

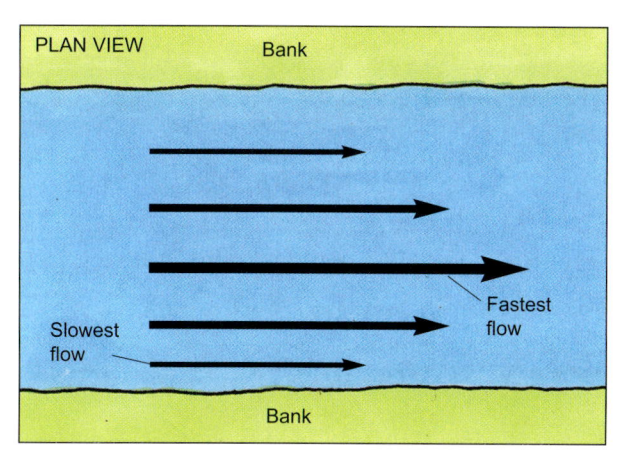

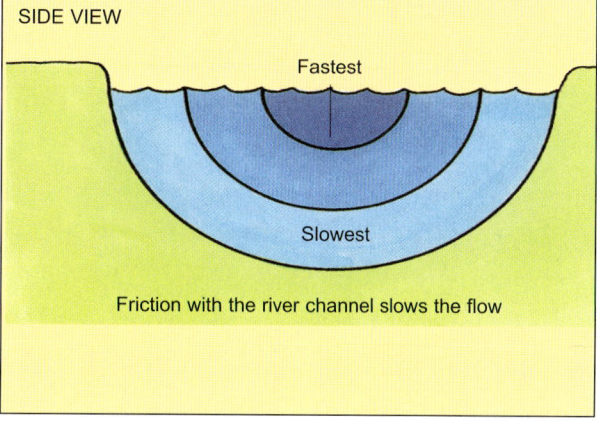

Fig. 12 The effect of friction on a river's flow: the speed of a river changes as you cross from one bank to another.

Fig. 13 The River Inagh in Ennistymon, County Clare

115

CORE UNIT: PATTERNS AND PROCESSES IN THE PHYSICAL ENVIRONMENT

Processes of river erosion

River erosion processes are (a) **hydraulic action**, (b) **abrasion**, (c) **attrition** and (d) **solution**. Erosion can occur at the river banks (**lateral erosion**) and at the riverbed (**vertical erosion**), causing a widening and deepening of the river channel.

(a) Hydraulic action (the force of moving water)

This is the force of fast-moving water. Fast-moving water forces out loose rock and earth from the riverbed and banks. Banks collapse as the turbulent water undercuts the river bank, a process known as **bank caving**. Also, bubbles of air in this turbulent water burst (**cavitation**) and their tiny shockwaves loosen the rocks and soil on the bed and banks making it easier to wash away.

Fig. 14 Hydraulic action in the Spring River, USA

(b) Abrasion (corrosion)

This is the wearing away of the riverbed and banks by its load. The load scrapes and smoothes the channel as it whirls and rolls along in the moving water.

(c) Attrition

This is when pieces of rock, carried by the river, hit off each other as they move along. This process gradually wears away the stones to make them smooth and round.

(d) Solution

In this process river water chemically dissolves the soft rock over which it flows. This process is very effective in limestone regions where soluble minerals are dissolved and transported away in solution. Discoloured river water is evidence of solution, e.g. rivers draining peat bogs.

Processes of river transport

The load formed by river erosion is **transported** by the river to a new location. Any material carried along the riverbed is called its **bedload**.

River transport processes are:

(1) solution
(2) suspension
(3) saltation
(4) traction

(1) Solution

In this case the load is carried along dissolved in the water. This load is invisible but may discolour the river water.

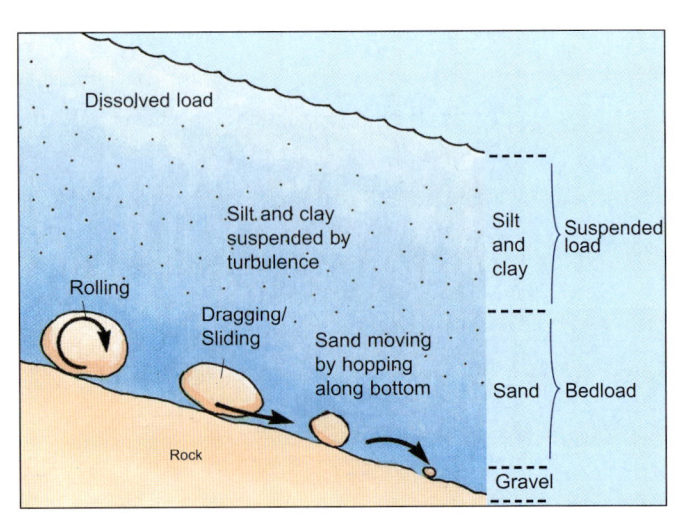

Fig. 15 The processes of river transport

weblink
Sediment transportation

(2) Suspension

In this case fine sediment is carried within the flowing water. Most of the river's load is carried this way. This process gives the water a muddy brown appearance. Fast-moving water keeps the sediment mixed up in it.

(3) Saltation

In this case the load bounces and hops along the riverbed. This process helps to make the pebbles and stones smooth and more rounded.

Fig. 16 River deposition in the Glendasan River, County Wicklow

(4) Traction

During times of flood the larger bedload (rocks and boulders) is rolled and dragged along the riverbed by the fast-flowing river.

Processes of river deposition

Eventually the load is deposited. **Deposition** processes can shape the land by leaving sediment in new places, making new land or adding to existing land.

There are several reasons why a river deposits its load.

(a) Reduction in the river's velocity

If a river slows down, deposition will occur. Rivers slow down when:
- they enter a lake or the sea.
- they shrink in times of low rainfall or high temperatures.
- their slope/gradient decreases.
- they meet an obstruction to their flow, for example, a dam.

In each case deposition will occur.

(b) Increases in the size of the load

When the load increases, the river may not have enough energy to carry it and so deposition will occur. A river's load may increase due to:
- mass movement, for example, a landslide into the river.
- heavy rainfall causing the river to erode its banks adding more load.
- tributaries adding their load to the amount of sediment already in the river.

(c) Reduction in the volume of the river

Reducing the volume of water in the river reduces its energy, causing deposition.
A river's water volume may be reduced due to:
- evaporation as the river flows through a hot area.
- the ending of the rainy season.
- taking water for urban use and irrigation schemes.
- drought.

weblink
River processes

CORE UNIT: PATTERNS AND PROCESSES IN THE PHYSICAL ENVIRONMENT

8.3 The life cycle of a river

Depending on the river's energy, different processes will occur in different parts of the river along its course. These different processes (erosion, transport and deposition) create distinct landforms along the river valley which enable us to divide the river's long profile into **youthful**, **mature** and **old age** stages. These can also be called the upper course, middle course and lower course.

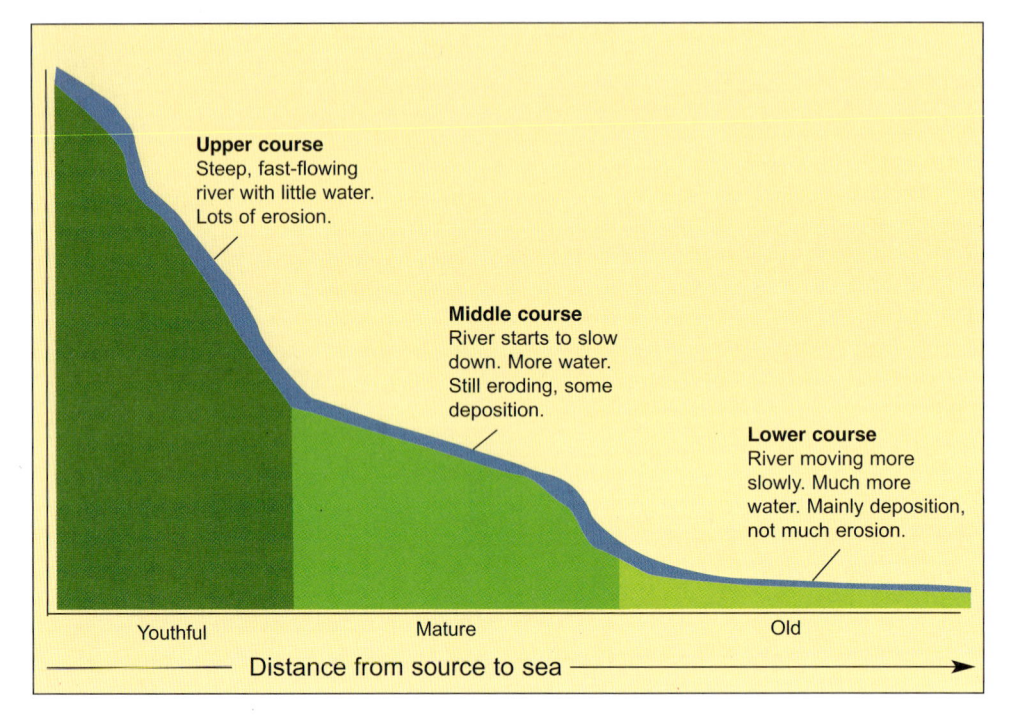

Upper course
Steep, fast-flowing river with little water. Lots of erosion.

Middle course
River starts to slow down. More water. Still eroding, some deposition.

Lower course
River moving more slowly. Much more water. Mainly deposition, not much erosion.

Youthful — Mature — Old
Distance from source to sea

Fig. 17 The processes that occur along the course of a river

Exam Note: When describing the formation of a landform you must name, describe and link the river processes to that feature.

Fig. 18 The life cycle of rivers: Youthful, mature and old age stages

CHAPTER 8: FLUVIAL PROCESSES, PATTERNS AND LANDFORMS

8.4 Landforms found along a river's course

The table below lists river landforms and their locations along the river's course.

RIVER LANDFORMS / FEATURES		
Stage	**Landforms**	**Examples**
Youthful stage (vertical erosion is dominant)	V-shaped valleys Interlocking spurs Waterfalls and gorges	Upper course of River Barrow Upper Glencullen River, County Wicklow Torc Waterfall, County Kerry
Mature stage (lateral erosion and deposition are dominant)	Meanders Oxbow lakes Floodplains	River Boyne River Moy, County Mayo River Slaney
Old stage (lateral erosion and deposition are dominant)	Wider floodplains Levees Wider, flatter valleys Larger meanders Oxbow lakes and meander scars Deltas	River Shannon The Rivers Moy, Shannon and Barrow River Liffey River Barrow River Moy, County Mayo Estuarine delta in River Shannon

Youthful stage landforms

1. **V-shaped valleys**
2. **Interlocking spurs**
3. **Waterfalls and gorges**

These three landforms are made by river **erosion**.

1. V-shaped valleys

V-shaped valleys are landforms of river/fluvial erosion found in the youthful stage of a river.
Main processes: vertical erosion, hydraulic action, abrasion, mass movement, weathering.
Example: River Moy, County Mayo.

A V-shaped valley is a narrow valley that has a **cross section** (side view) in the shape of the letter V.

V-shaped valleys form in highland areas where streams are flowing down steep slopes. They are formed by the river cutting downwards into its bed. This is known as **vertical** erosion.

The floor of a V-shaped valley is very narrow and there is little or no flat land beside the stream. The stream channel is often very narrow and shallow.

Exam Diagram

Vertical erosion
Weathering weakens sides of valley
Mass movement of material downhill into the river
Mass movement occurs on valley sides creating distinctive V-shaped valley

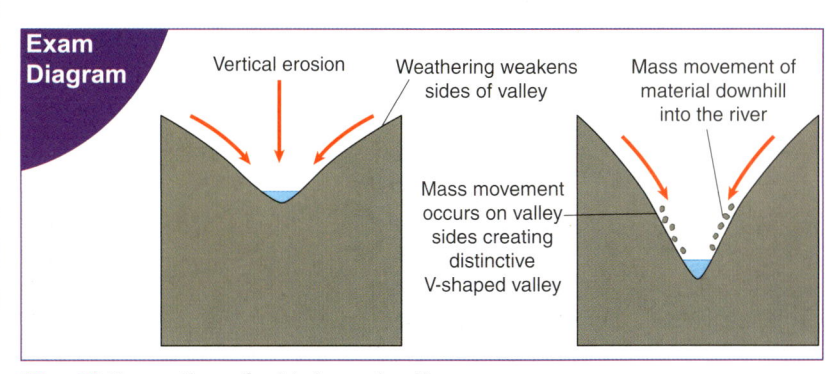

Fig. 19 Formation of a V-shaped valley

CORE UNIT: PATTERNS AND PROCESSES IN THE PHYSICAL ENVIRONMENT

All IN DEPTH sections contain material you need to know if you are studying this chapter in detail.

IN DEPTH: V-shaped valley

- The volume and speed of flow in a young river is often low due to the lack of tributaries feeding the river in its upper stages. Energy is also used up overcoming the friction between the water and the rough, stony bed causing inefficient flow. Where the gradient is steeper and the channel bed is less rough, the river velocity can increase. Vertical erosion will then occur, especially following heavy rainfall or melting of winter snow.
- **Hydraulic action** is the erosion process caused by the physical force of flowing water which loosens and carries away the bedrock and soil of the river channel.
- **Abrasion:** The erosion caused by the river's load will wear down bedrock as the load hits the sides and bed of the river channel. This will deepen the riverbed by forming potholes which are circular hollows formed by swirling stones.
- The valley sides will also be exposed to **weathering** and **mass movement**. Mechanical and chemical weathering weaken the rock and soil on the valley sides.
- The depth of the V is controlled by a combination of factors:
  - The **speed of vertical erosion**: in general fast rates of erosion lead to deeper valleys.
  - The **type of bedrock**: hard rocks such as granite resist erosion, making more shallow valleys.
  - **Weathering and mass movement** on the sides of the valley: These processes weaken and loosen the stones and soil on the sides of the valley. Scree and soil move downhill under the force of gravity and add to the river's load, increasing its ability to erode and deepen its channel by abrasion.

Fig. 20 A V-shaped valley in Asia

weblink
V-shaped valley and interlocking spur formation

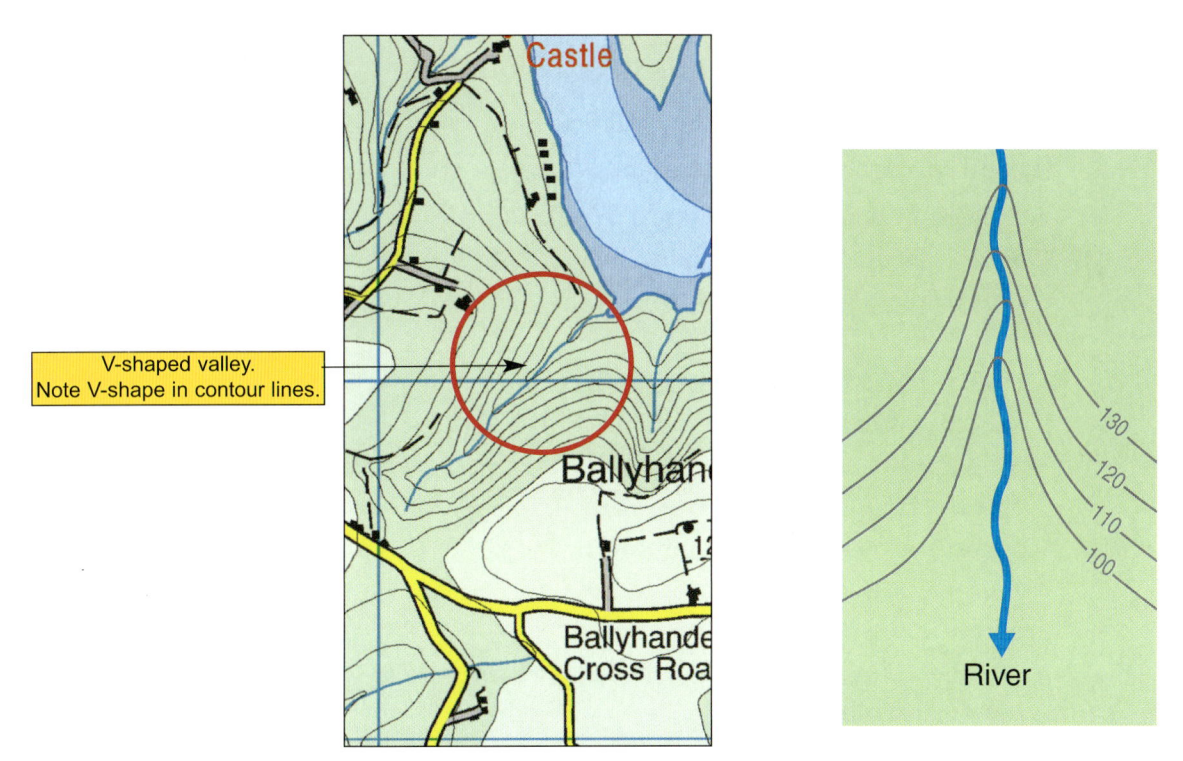

CHAPTER 8: FLUVIAL PROCESSES, PATTERNS AND LANDFORMS

Fig. 21 A V-shaped valley near Kinsale, County Cork and contour pattern of a V-shaped valley

2. Interlocking spurs

Interlocking spurs are landforms of river erosion found in the youthful stage of a river.

Main processes: vertical erosion, hydraulic action, abrasion, solution, winding streams.

Example: Upper stage of the River Barrow

Interlocking spurs are hills or ridges of land (**spurs**) around which the river winds. If you look up a river valley, these spurs or hills seem to overlap across each other (**interlock**) blocking the view of the river. Viewed from above you can clearly see the river winding around these hills/spurs.

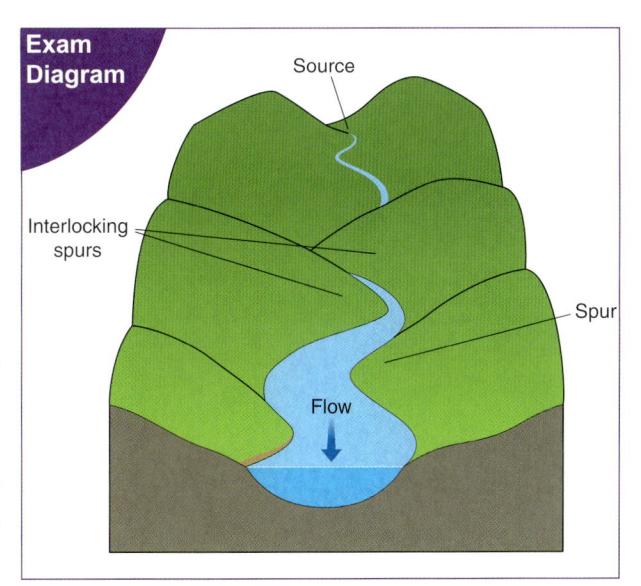

Fig. 22 Interlocking spurs

121

CORE UNIT: PATTERNS AND PROCESSES IN THE PHYSICAL ENVIRONMENT

IN DEPTH: Interlocking spurs

- Rivers have a natural tendency to flow in a winding manner. As youthful rivers are small they do not have the energy to remove large obstacles in their path. Young rivers do not carry a large load so **abrasion** is limited.
- **Hydraulic action** is the main erosion process. As the river flows, it winds around the hard patches of rock found along its course. These obstacles in the channel further deflect the river from side to side, so that it changes from a relatively straight to a winding course.
- The current is stronger on the outside of a bend. Therefore, hydraulic action and abrasion are concentrated here and the bends become more developed. This erosion of the river valley leaves parts of the valley sides projecting as small hills or spurs into the bends in the river channel.
- Eventually in the middle and lower stages the river becomes larger and more powerful by the addition of water from tributaries and removes the interlocking spurs completely.

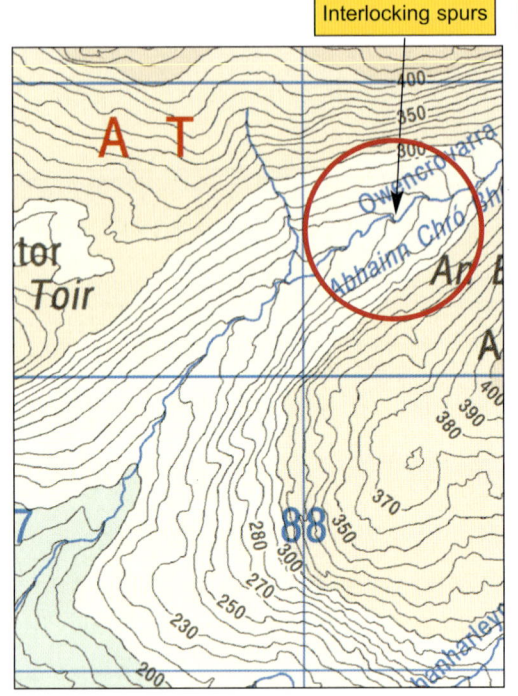

Fig. 23 Map showing interlocking spurs

Fig. 24 A V-shaped valley and interlocking spurs in a Scottish river. Note evidence of mass movement.

CHAPTER 8: FLUVIAL PROCESSES, PATTERNS AND LANDFORMS

3. Waterfalls

Waterfalls are landforms of river erosion found in the youthful stage of a river.
Main processes: abrasion, hydraulic action, solution, vertical erosion.
Example: Powerscourt, County Wicklow; Torc, County Kerry.

A waterfall is a vertical fall of water.

IN DEPTH: Waterfalls

- When a river meets a band of hard rock lying across its path it will have difficulty eroding it. Any soft rock on the downstream end will be eroded more quickly. This is called **differential erosion**. Now the river falls over the hard rock. The **hydraulic** force of the falling water rushing into cracks in the soft rock causes it to break up. This broken rock then causes **abrasion** to widen and deepen the foot of the waterfall, making a *plunge pool*. The plunge pool under the Niagara Falls is 35 m deep.
- The falling water splashes against the back wall of the waterfall, dissolving some of it away by the process of **solution**. This *splashback* soon creates a cave behind the waterfall leaving an overhang of hard rock at the top of the waterfall. This eventually collapses making the waterfall retreat upstream. This process of retreat is called *headward erosion*.
- As the waterfall erodes back upstream, a steep-sided valley called a *gorge* is formed downstream from the waterfall.

Fig. 25 Mahon Falls, County Waterford

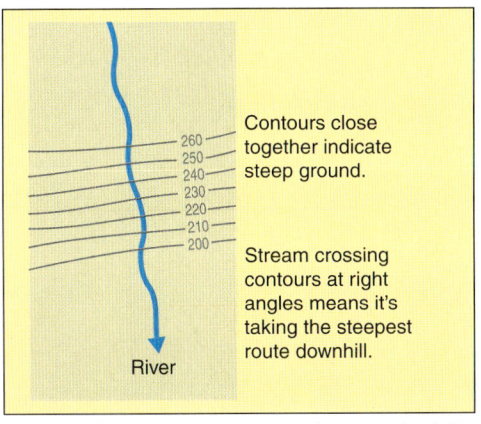

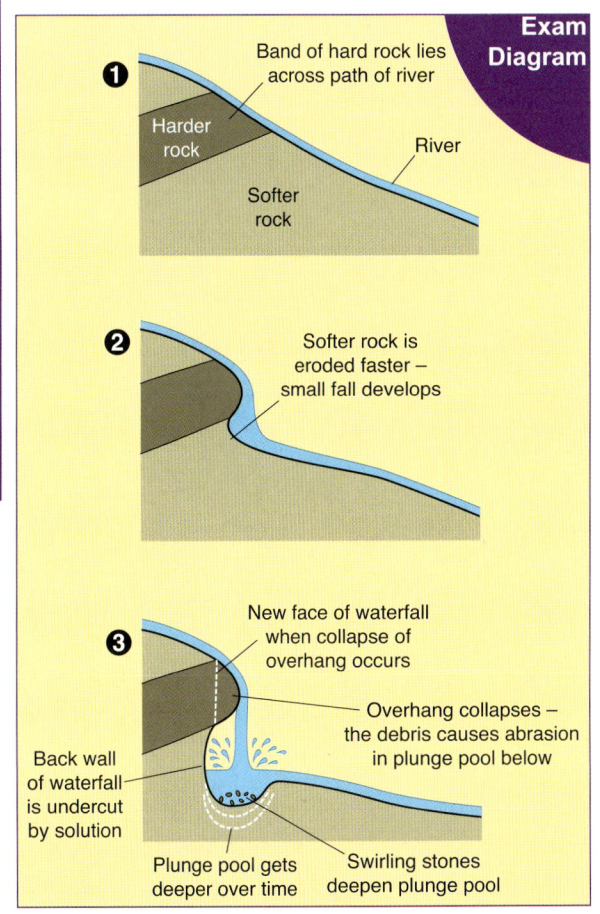

Fig. 26 Contour pattern to show waterfalls

Fig. 27 The development of a waterfall

weblink
River erosion

123

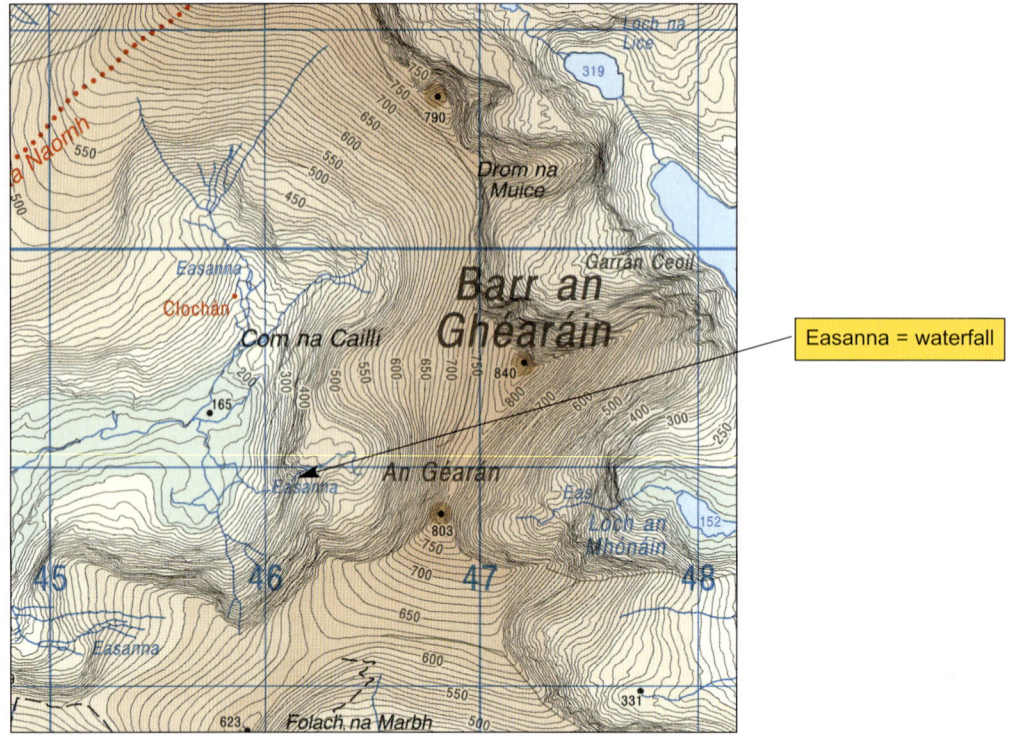

CORE UNIT: PATTERNS AND PROCESSES IN THE PHYSICAL ENVIRONMENT

Easanna = waterfall

Fig. 28 Waterfalls and possible sites of waterfalls in County Kerry. Look for mountain rivers crossing contour lines at right angles and the word 'waterfall' or 'easanna'.

Mature stage landforms

Three mature stage landforms are:

1. **Meanders**
2. **Oxbow lakes and meander scars/mortlakes**
3. **Floodplains**.

1. Meanders

Meanders are landforms of river/fluvial erosion and deposition found in the mature and old stages of a river. Meanders are s-shaped bends in a river.
Main processes: lateral erosion, hydraulic action, abrasion, cavitation, deposition.
Example: River Boyne, County Meath.

Rivers naturally flow in a winding manner. This makes the water swing from side to side, eroding an S-shaped channel into the landscape. They are found in the mature stage of a river and enlarged in the old stage.

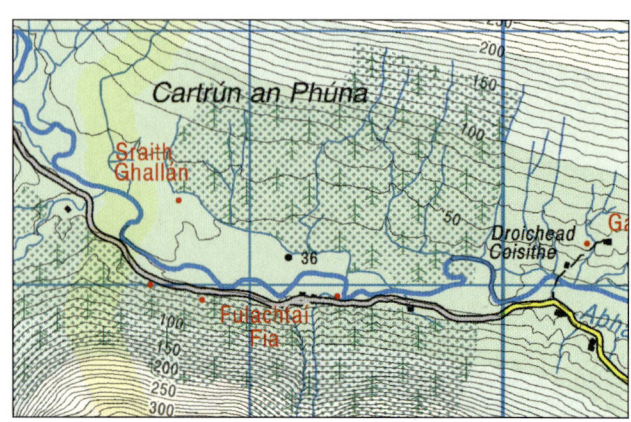

Fig. 29 Map to show meanders on a river near Poundcarton, County Donegal

CHAPTER 8: FLUVIAL PROCESSES, PATTERNS AND LANDFORMS

IN DEPTH: Meanders

- Water flows fastest on the outside bend of the meander, causing lateral erosion by **hydraulic action** and **abrasion**. (It is similar to being thrown to one side of a car as it goes around a corner.) Because the flow is faster and has more energy at this point, it erodes the outer bend with more force. Hydraulic action and abrasion can cause undercutting, creating a steep river cliff which is cut into the bank. Hydraulic action also forces bubbles of air into the river bank, creating shock waves inside the bank. This is called **cavitation**. This further loosens the bank and some falls away. The continued undercutting of the bank leads to its collapse (**bank caving**) and a widening of the river channel (lateral erosion).
- The speed of flow is much slower on the inside bend causing deposition. A small beach called a point bar is deposited on the inside bend. This point bar further deflects the fast-moving water to the outer bend, increasing lateral erosion there.
- Gradually, the river wanders over its floodplain in a series of sweeping meanders. The continuous erosion and deposition makes the meanders move across the landscape a bit like a snake. These are called migrating meanders.

Exam Diagram

Flow is fast. Causes undercutting of river bank and formation of river cliff

Point bar

Flow is slow at inner bank. Leads to deposition and formation of point bar

River cliff

CROSS SECTION

River cliff
Point bar
Undercutting
Slow upward current deposits material
Strong, fast, downward current scrapes at the river bank

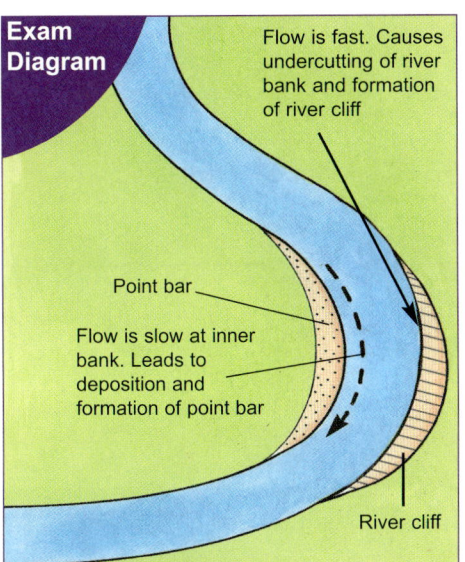

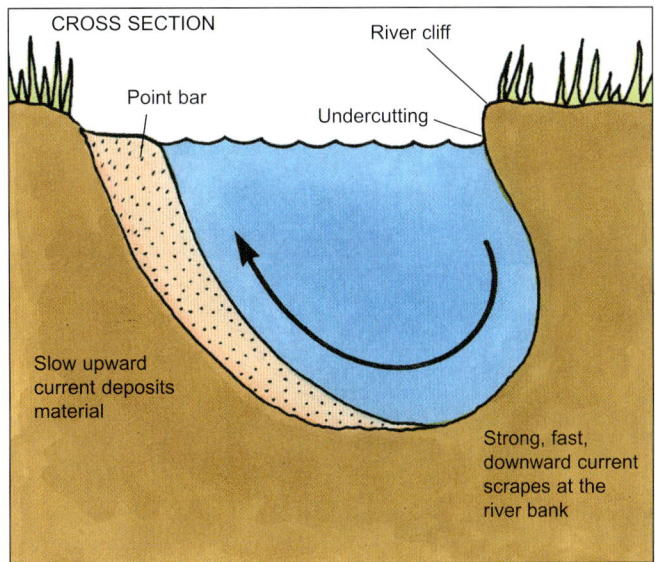

Fig. 30 The development of meanders

Fig. 31 Meanders on a river in County Galway

weblink
Meander formation

Activity

Look at the photograph.
Identify a point bar and a river cliff.

125

CORE UNIT: PATTERNS AND PROCESSES IN THE PHYSICAL ENVIRONMENT

2. Oxbow lakes

Oxbow lakes are landforms formed by fluvial erosion. They are found in the mature and old stages of a river.
Main processes: flooding, erosion, deposition.
Example: River Moy, County Mayo.
Oxbow lakes are the remains of meanders that have been cut off from the river's course. They are often called cut-offs for this reason.

IN DEPTH: Oxbow lakes

- Oxbow lakes form when meanders become so developed that the bend is very tight and there is only a narrow neck of land separating the two sides of the meander bend. In times of flood the water flows across the neck of land rather than going around the bend. By doing this, **hydraulic action** and **abrasion** erode a new path for the river, straightening it in the process.
- Because the river is not confined between its banks as it flows across the meander loop, it slows down and loses energy. This leads to **deposition** which, over time, seals off the old meander bend. The old meander loop is now cut off from the new course leaving an oxbow lake behind. Slowly it dries out because of evaporation and seepage through the ground and becomes a dead lake or a **mortlake**. Mortlakes are also known as **meander scars**.

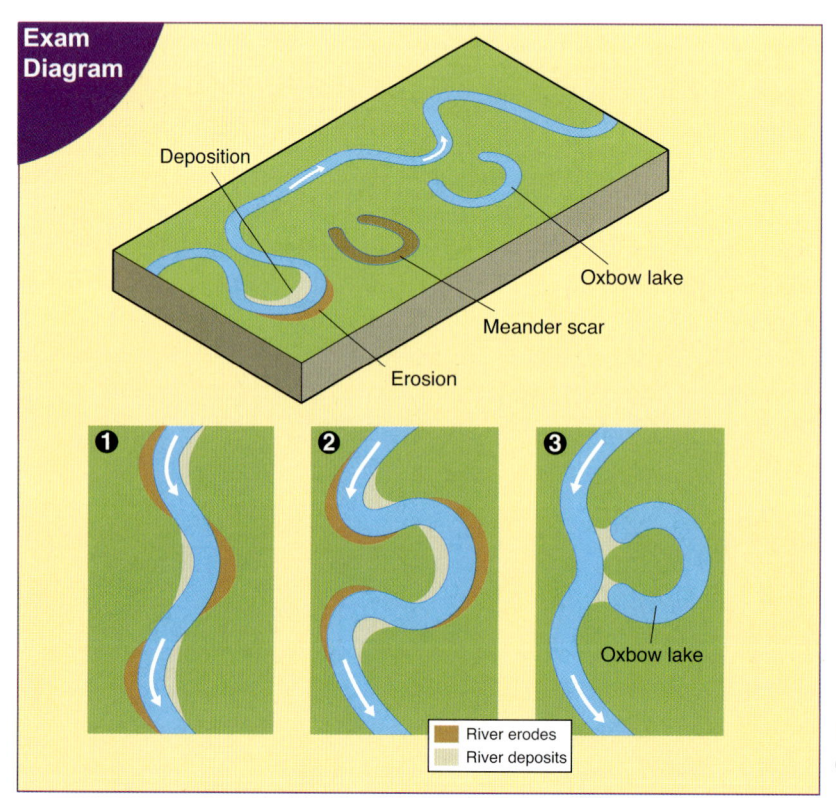

Fig. 32 The development of oxbow lakes

126

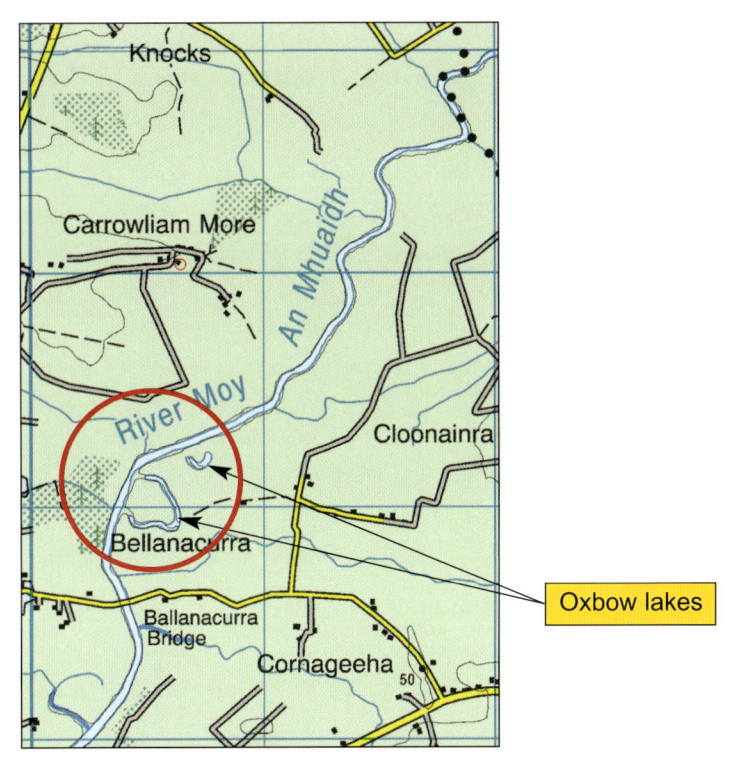

CHAPTER 8: FLUVIAL PROCESSES, PATTERNS AND LANDFORMS

Fig. 33 Meanders and oxbow lakes on the River Moy, County Mayo

Fig. 34 Meanders on a mature stage river in Russia

127

CORE UNIT: PATTERNS AND PROCESSES IN THE PHYSICAL ENVIRONMENT

3. Floodplains

Floodplains are landforms formed by river deposition. They are found in the mature and old stages of a river.

Main processes: flooding, deposition.

Example: River Suir, County Waterford.

A floodplain is a flat area of land either side of the river.

> **IN DEPTH: Floodplains**
>
> - Meanders swinging across the valley floor remove interlocking spurs as they migrate downstream. Doing this, they create a flat area in the centre of the valley. This is the floodplain.
> - During a flood the river **overspills** its banks and the flood water flows across the floodplain. As the river spreads out across the floodplain it loses some of its energy. This causes the river to slow down. Some of the flood water gradually soaks (**percolates**) into the ground, **depositing** a thin layer of sediment known as **alluvium** onto the floodplain. This is very fertile. These sediments may be many metres deep representing centuries of repeated flooding.
> - The edges of floodplains are known as **river bluffs**.
> - Floodplains are a river's safety valve. In times of heavy rain the river has to overflow its banks onto its floodplain. The flat ground slows the river down and encourages deposition. This reduces the damage caused by erosion.
> - Because of their flat and fertile nature, floodplains are heavily populated.

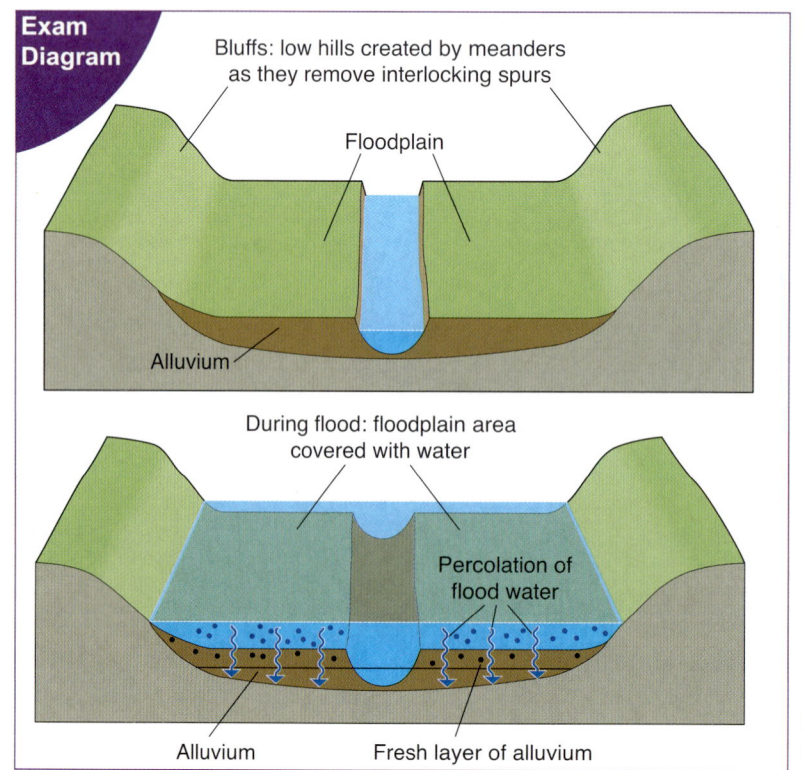

Fig. 35 The formation of a floodplain

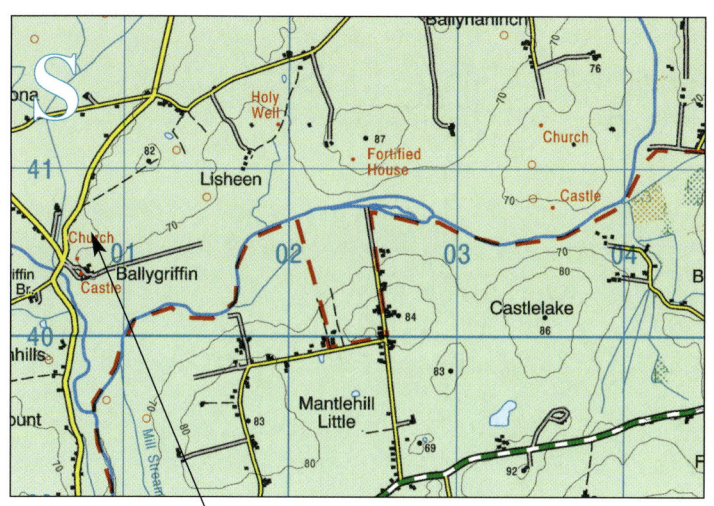

CHAPTER 8: FLUVIAL PROCESSES, PATTERNS AND LANDFORMS

Fig. 36 A floodplain near Cashel, County Tipperary. Note the lack of settlement below the 70 m contour line in some grid squares.

Fig. 37 The River Shannon in flood

Old stage landforms

The landforms made in the old stage are similar to those of the mature stage but are larger. Meanders swing in wide sweeps across the very wide, flat floodplain of the river valley. There may also be many oxbow lakes and meander scars.

Other characteristic landforms found in the old stage are **levees** and **deltas**, both depositional features.

1. Levees

Levees are landforms of fluvial/river deposition. They are found in the old stage of a river's course.
Main processes: flooding, deposition.
Example: River Moy, south of Ballina in County Mayo.

A levee is a wide low ridge of sediment deposited on riverbanks.

IN DEPTH: Levees

- On its floodplain an old river flows over very flat land (**low gradient**). It is carrying a large load of sand and silt.
- During a flood, the river spills over its banks and across its floodplain. As the river **floods** over its banks, the water spreads out, slows down and deposits its load of sediment. The largest/coarsest particles of gravel and sand are deposited closest to the banks due to the sudden decrease in the river's energy. These deposits are called **levees**.
- Finer sediments (**alluvium**) are carried by the flood water further out over the floodplain. The alluvium is then deposited over the floodplain as the water seeps (**percolates**) into the ground after the flood has finished.
- After many flood events the levee is enlarged. At the same time, during normal flow the river will **deposit** material on the riverbed. This will raise the level of the riverbed and the river itself.

CORE UNIT: PATTERNS AND PROCESSES IN THE PHYSICAL ENVIRONMENT

> **IN DEPTH: Levees**
>
> - The combination of levee growth and deposition on a riverbed often leads to a situation where the entire river is confined between the levees in a channel that is higher than its floodplain. This would cause flooding unless the levees are strong enough to prevent flood water reaching the floodplain. Levees are often built and strengthened by humans to protect valuable farm land and urban settlements built on the floodplain, e.g. along the Mississippi River in the USA. Levees may be built up using sediment dredged from the riverbed, e.g. the River Barrow in County Wexford.

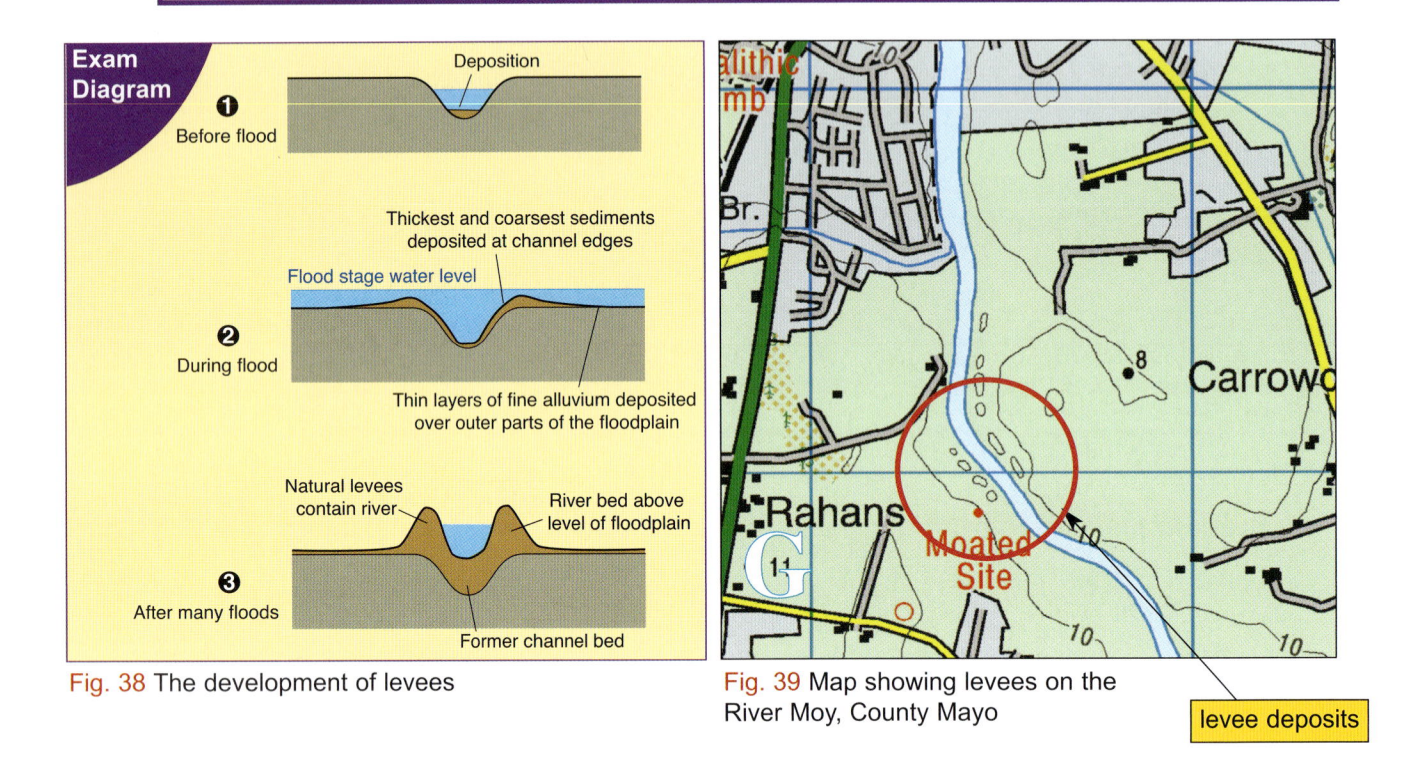

Fig. 38 The development of levees

Fig. 39 Map showing levees on the River Moy, County Mayo

2. Deltas

Deltas are landforms of river deposition. Deltas are found in the old stage of a river.

Main process: deposition.

Examples: Lough Tay, County Wicklow – a lacustrine delta; Shannon Estuary, County Limerick – an estuarine delta.

Deltas are areas of land at the mouth of a river made from deposits of alluvium, sand and gravel. Deltas occur where tidal currents and longshore drift (see Chapter 10) are not powerful enough to remove the river deposits. Deltas can form in a lake and are called **lacustrine deltas**; those that occur at the coast are called **marine deltas**. For marine deltas to form, a river has to flow out into a low energy coastline where the power of the waves is weak. As the Irish coastline is so indented (jagged) this does not occur. However, delta deposits have built up along some Irish estuaries, e.g. the Shannon Estuary.

CHAPTER 8: FLUVIAL PROCESSES, PATTERNS AND LANDFORMS

IN DEPTH: Deltas

- Rivers transport huge amounts of sediment (load) from their source to the sea. When the river enters a sea, lake or reservoir, the river speed is suddenly forced to slow down. This causes a rapid loss of energy so **deposition** occurs.
- As the fresh river water meets the salty sea water, a small electric charge is created which makes the sand, silt and clay particles clump together and sink to the sea floor. Gradually layers of deposited sediment build up at the river mouth. These layers of sediment are called **beds**. Deltas contain different types of bed.

    - **Foreset beds**

      The heaviest and coarser silt and sand sediments are deposited first due to the sudden decrease in river velocity upon meeting the sea. These sediments settle on the sea floor at the river mouth. They are called **foreset beds**. The river is like a conveyor belt constantly adding foreset beds to the sea. The sediment rolls down the front of the delta and builds up in sloping layers covering the sea bed. This makes the delta grow out to sea. Foreset beds make up the majority of the delta.

    - **Bottomset beds**

      At the same time the finest clay sediments are carried in suspension a little further out to sea and slowly settle in front of this main delta. They are laid down in horizontal layers which are called **bottomset beds**.

      The bottomset beds will eventually be covered over by the foreset bed sediments as they roll down the front of the delta face.

    - **Topset beds**

      Lastly, the **topset beds** are deposited by the river in horizontal layers on top of the foreset beds of the advancing delta. These are generally smaller gravelly sediments deposited after the larger foreset material.

      As the delta sediments build up close to the surface of the water, they are exposed at low tide. The river sometimes splits into smaller streams called **distributaries** as it flows over the exposed sediments. Distributaries occur in larger rivers.

      Over many years the delta deposits are stabilised by plants, and people can live on them, e.g. the Nile delta and Bangladesh on the delta of the River Ganges. Flooding is very common in low-lying Bangladesh, as only one quarter of the land is more than three metres in height. Catastrophic floods cause thousands of deaths each year during monsoon season.

Exam Diagram

1. Fine sand and silt
2. Coarse sand
3. Gravel

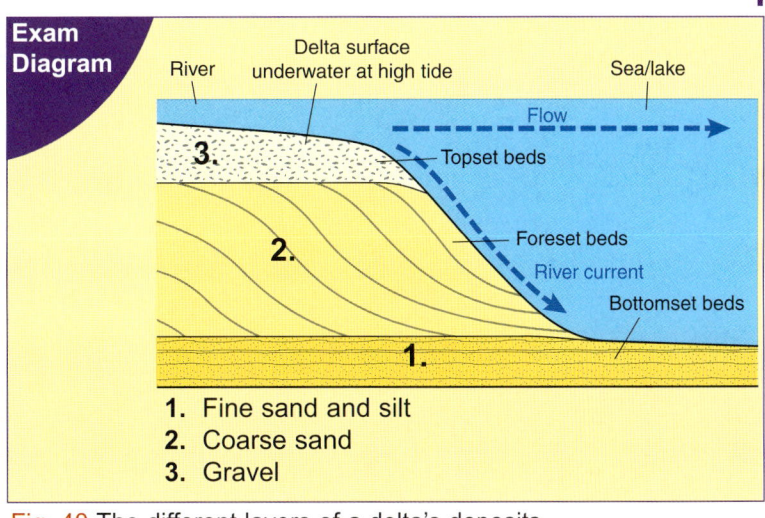

Fig. 40 The different layers of a delta's deposits

weblink
Delta formation

131

CORE UNIT: PATTERNS AND PROCESSES IN THE PHYSICAL ENVIRONMENT

> **IN DEPTH**
>
> **Delta shapes**
> Deltas have many shapes and sizes. They are named delta after the Greek symbol Δ (letter D).
>
> 1. **Arcuate delta (arc-shaped)**
>   This delta has a triangular shape and the apex of the triangle points upstream. It is named after the shape of the Nile delta in Egypt.
>   These deltas are made of bigger (coarse) **sand** and **gravel sediments** which are very porous so there are many distributaries which rarely meet.
>   **Examples:** The Po in Italy, which extends at a rate of 12 m per year. The River Flesk has a small arcuate delta where it enters Lough Leane in County Kerry (see Fig. 41). The Nile delta in Egypt (see Fig. 43).
>
> 2. **Bird's foot delta**
>   These deltas form when rivers carry large amounts of fine sediment. There are very few distributaries. Levees are deposited along any distributaries that form, causing long finger-like projections to extend into the sea forming a delta with a shape similar to that of a bird's foot.
>   **Example:** The Mississippi River, which extends at a rate of 75 m per year (see Fig. 44).
>
> 3. **Estuarine delta**
>   This type of delta forms when deposits are dropped in long, narrow lines, like strips, on both sides of the estuary.
>   **Example:** The Shannon Estuary.

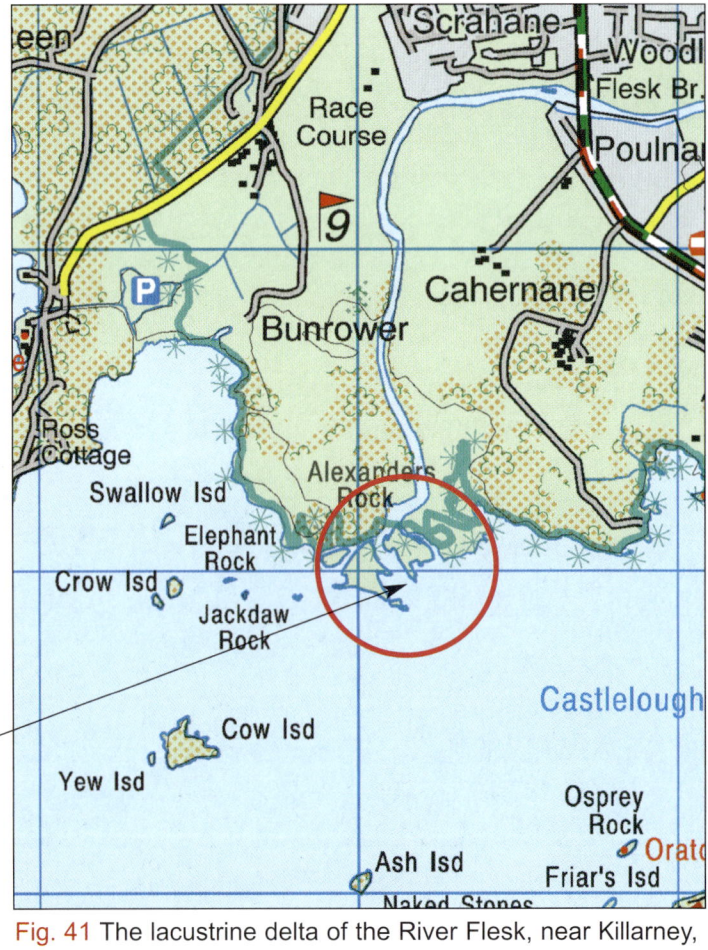

Fig. 41 The lacustrine delta of the River Flesk, near Killarney, County Kerry

CHAPTER 8: FLUVIAL PROCESSES, PATTERNS AND LANDFORMS

Fig. 42 River delta in Honduras, Central America

Fig. 43 The Nile delta forms where the River Nile enters the Mediterranean Sea.

Fig. 44 The Mississippi delta from space. River water spills out into the Gulf of Mexico where its suspended load is deposited to form the Mississippi River delta. Marshes and mudflats grow between the shipping channels that have been cut into the delta.

133

CORE UNIT: PATTERNS AND PROCESSES IN THE PHYSICAL ENVIRONMENT

8.5 Human interaction with river processes

Human activities (processes) can impact on the operation of surface processes. Rivers are important resources for humanity. They have been used, controlled and misused by people for centuries. Most major towns and cities in the world were built beside rivers because they provided:

- Water supply and fish
- A fertile floodplain
- Transport and trade artery
- Defence
- Bridging points.

> **Exam Note**: You must study human interaction with river processes OR coastal processes OR mass movement processes

Controlling rivers

Humans manage the flow of rivers by:
1. Building **dams** and **reservoirs** to hold back floods and generate power, e.g. the Three Gorges Dam, China.
2. Changing the course of rivers. We straighten and bypass their meanders with canals to allow ships travel more quickly, e.g. River Rhine, Germany.
3. Strengthening and **raising levees** so that we can settle on once uninhabitable floodplains, e.g. River Rhine, Germany and the Mississippi River, USA.

In Ireland controlling floods is an important issue for rural and urban areas, e.g. Clonmel, County Tipperary.

> **Exam Note**: You may be asked to discuss a single case study or a combination of three case studies provided on pages 134–138.

CHAPTER 8
Case Study 1

The impact of canals: The River Rhine

1. The River Rhine is a major artery for transporting goods and people through Europe. Its mouth in Rotterdam, Holland is regarded as the 'Gateway to Europe'. The Rhine flows through or links with canals, nine European countries. This river flows through some of the most highly-industrialised and densely-populated urban areas of Europe.

2. The need to reduce costs and save time has led to the development of this river. For example, constructing canals and bypassing meander bends has shortened the river by 50 km. This has affected all of the river processes. The river velocity is increased because the river is now flowing higher inside the confined canals and levees.

3. Canals also increase the erosive power of the river by confining it. Because flooding is controlled, deposition cannot occur on the surrounding floodplain. Some deposition occurs on the riverbed, also raising the level of the river within the levees.

CHAPTER 8: FLUVIAL PROCESSES, PATTERNS AND LANDFORMS

4. Continued urban sprawl and reduction in farmland has meant run-off from rain reaches streams and rivers more quickly than in the past. Instead of rainwater seeping through the ground and taking many days to reach the river, it now reaches it quickly in a matter of hours through pipes and drains. It used to take up to five days for a flood surge to pass downstream but today, due to man's control of the river's natural processes, it takes three days. This has led to increased flooding during heavy rains. Flood water puts great pressure on the polders/reclaimed land and levees along the river. Holland has spent more than €1.3 billion on flood control measures. Its polderlands are now protected by levees which are 10 m high.

5. During floods, the authorities pump flood water into retention basins outside the levees. These basins reduce the flood water height by 60 cm for 10–12 hours. When the flood has receded the water is pumped back into the river. These retention basins are then left as nature reserves or grazing land.

Fig. 45 Meander in the Rhine Valley near Boppard, Germany

Fig. 46 The River Rhine

Fig. 47 Location of Rhine floods

CORE UNIT: PATTERNS AND PROCESSES IN THE PHYSICAL ENVIRONMENT

CHAPTER 8 Case Study 2

The impact of dam building: The Three Gorges Dam, China

Dams are large walls built across river valleys to trap river water, creating reservoirs behind the dam wall. They can be used to control floods, generate hydro electric power (HEP) and provide water for irrigation and for domestic and industrial uses.

One of the world's largest schemes to control a river and manage its flow is at the Three Gorges Dam in China. It is the biggest and most powerful dam ever built in the world. It is often called the Second Great Wall of China. Devastating floods in 1931 killed 250,000 people living along the Yangtze and Whang Ho rivers. Annual floods on these rivers would still kill thousands but for the dam.

Hydro Electric Power Station at the Three Gorges Dam, China

The Three Gorges dam is 185 m high and 2.3 km wide. The reservoir is 560 km long and 160 m deep. From Malin Head to Mizen Head, Ireland would fit into the reservoir's length. It generates electricity and cost €48 billion to build.

The flooding of the land behind the Yangtze dam to make the reservoir led to the displacement of over two million people as their land, homes, cities and industries were flooded.

Impact on river erosion processes

1. Dams usually reduce the size and frequency of flood events.
2. As water is trapped behind the dam and then released to generate electricity, the flow of the water downstream is interrupted, creating surges in velocity and thereby increasing hydraulic action and increasing vertical erosion.
3. Downstream of the dam, the controlled river is often smaller and carries less load; this can increase hydraulic action which can further deepen and widen the river channel resulting in river channels that are much lower than the floodplain.
4. On occasions when heavy rains occur, it may be necessary to release excess water from the reservoir due to dangerous water pressure on the dam wall.

Impact on river deposition processes

1. Dam walls trap river sediment behind them. This sediment would, before the dam's construction, have been transported downstream and deposited as alluvium onto floodplains. Because of dams, the middle and lower stages of the river's lifecycle are deprived of fertile alluvium. Soil fertility is lost as floodplain sediments are not replaced.

weblink The largest dam in the world

Fig. 48 Location of the Three Gorges Dam project

CHAPTER 8: FLUVIAL PROCESSES, PATTERNS AND LANDFORMS

2. The Yangtze carries 37.6 kg of silt per cubic metre of river water which builds up behind the dam. In older dams across the world, such accumulation of silt would put increased pressure on the dam wall, but at the Three Gorges engineers have built the dam system so that finer grains of silt pass through.
3. Dams reduce the volume of water in the river. This affects the delta area. Salt water is then able to seep back into the delta lands and poison freshwater ecosystems. This can turn fertile land into waterlogged salt marsh. The Shanghai Delta is being carefully monitored to ensure this does not happen.

Impact on river transport processes

1. Dams interrupt the natural flow of a river and reduce its ability to carry sediment from source to sea.
2. Some sediments carried by the river are trapped in the reservoir behind the dam. Deltas downstream of dams often shrink as a result of dam building because deltas at river mouths are deprived of their coarse foreset bed material and are now more easily eroded by the sea. The Yangtze delta at Shanghai is at risk.
3. Changes in the size of the load being carried means that the type of transport process occurring such as solution, suspension, saltation and traction also change.

Fig. 49 The Three Gorges Dam showing the power of the flow of water through the dam.

4. River flooding is stopped by the dam so the people living downstream are protected, thereby preventing loss of life and damage to farmland.

CHAPTER 8 Case Study 3

Flood control on an Irish river: The River Suir, Clonmel, County Tipperary

The regular flooding process is a result of the interaction between natural and man-made factors.

Man-made factors that contributed to flooding in Clonmel

1. The Old Bridge was too narrow for flood water to pass through easily.
2. A weir (small dam) prevented flood water moving downstream quickly.
3. Construction of the New Quay restricted the river flow.

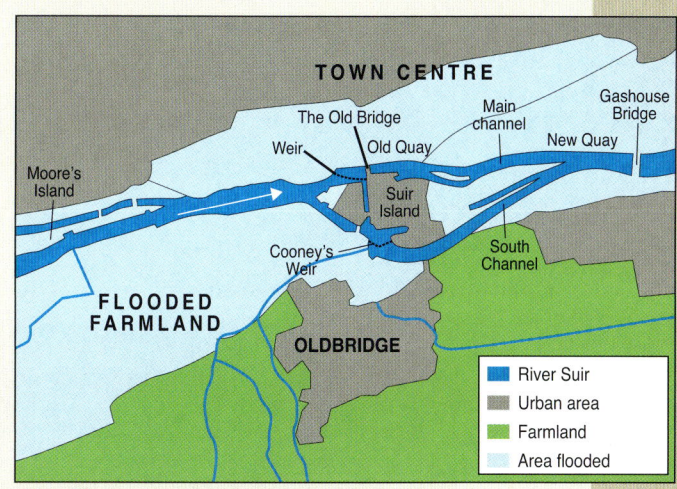

Fig. 50 Flooding in Clonmel

137

In times of normal flow, the Suir passes under the Old Bridge. In times of flood, water could not get through it quickly enough, leading to a back-up of water upstream. This caused flooding (much like too many people trying to get through a narrow doorway).

The weir also caused a back-up of flow adding to the flood problem.

Natural factors leading to flooding in Clonmel

1. The Suir valley is very flat. The gradient falls only 15 m in a 23 km-stretch between Clonmel and Carrick-on-Suir. This gentle gradient slows down the river's flow.
2. Climate change has led to increased rainfall which triggers more floods.
3. The volume of water is increased due to the meeting (confluence) of the south channel and the main river channel at the town.

The combined flow of water from the two channels is funnelled through the Gashouse Bridge. This increased volume leads to flooding of the town centre, Suir Island and South Channel as the water squeezes under the bridge. When the soil and bedrock are saturated, heavy rainfall has nowhere to go except over the land and into rivers.

Fig. 51 Extent of flooding in Clonmel town centre

How flooding has been reduced in Clonmel

1. **Reduced blockage points on the river**

    Moveable glass sidewalls were fitted to the historically important Old Bridge. In times of flood, the bridge is sealed off at each end, and the glass walls are lowered. This allows the river to flow over and under the bridge allowing flood water to pass quickly through the town. Cooney's Weir has also been modified to allow more water to flow over it.

Fig. 52 A simple but effective flood defence measure

2. **Improved flood defences**

    Flood defence walls were built along the river where it flows through the town. Earthen levees/berms were also built and have been successful in protecting Clonmel.

    Since these flood works were built, Clonmel has avoided severe flooding.

weblink
Plans for flood defence

Chapter Revision Questions

1. (a) Explain **four** ways in which a river can erode the landscape.
   (b) Briefly examine the factors that influence a river's ability to erode the landscape.
2. Name and describe the processes of river transport.
3. Name and explain the factors influencing river deposition.
4. With the aid of diagrams, discuss the formation of **two** landforms found in the youthful stage of a river.
5. With the aid of diagrams, discuss the formation of **two** landforms found in the mature stage of a river.
6. With the aid of diagrams, discuss the formation of **two** landforms found in the old stage of a river.
7. (a) Explain the term drainage pattern.
   (b) Name and briefly account for the occurrence of any **two** drainage patterns.
8. With reference to a river you have studied, describe how humans have managed river processes.
9. Give an overview of the human and natural causes of flooding in an area you have studied.
10. Copy and complete the table below using **two** landforms from each stage. The first one has been done for you.
11. Look carefully at the map below. Give a six-figure grid reference for each of the following landforms you can identify on the map.
    1. V-shaped valley
    2. Dendritic drainage pattern
    3. Tributary
    4. Watershed
    5. Mature stage
    6. Radial drainage pattern
    7. Young stage
    8. Waterfall

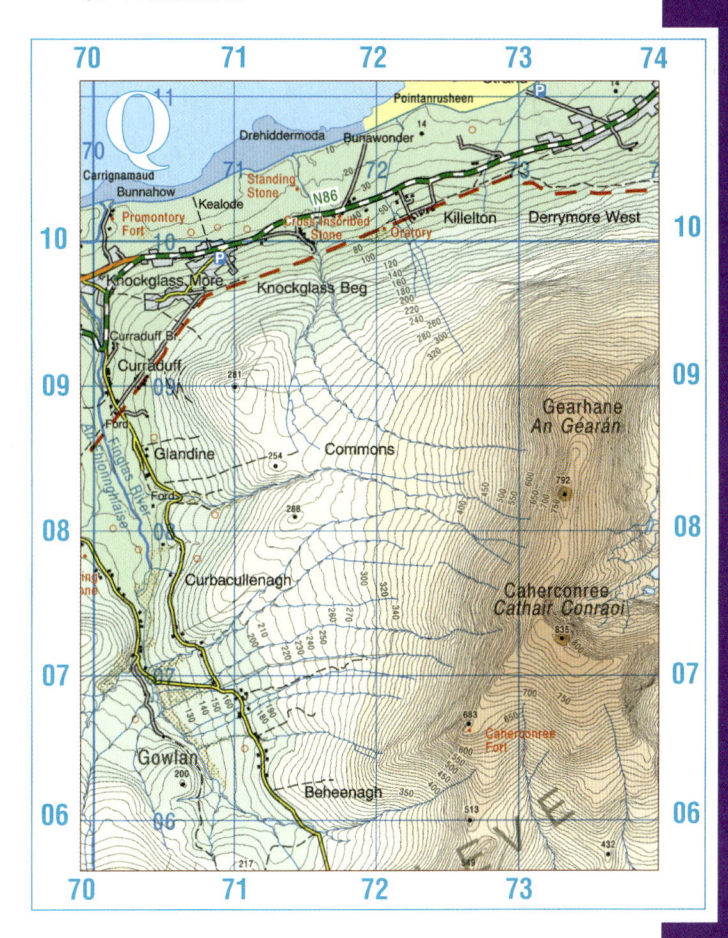

Stage	Landform	Process	Irish Example
Upper / Youthful stage	V-shaped valley	Erosion	River Suir
Middle / Mature stage			
Lower / Old stage			

CORE UNIT: PATTERNS AND PROCESSES IN THE PHYSICAL ENVIRONMENT

LC Exam Questions

Higher Level students must be able to answer Ordinary and Higher Level questions.

■ OL Questions

12. Describe and explain how humans attempt to control **one** of the following surface processes:
    - River processes
    - Sea processes
    - Mass movement.

13. Examine the diagrams A, B and C. Name each of the three river drainage patterns.

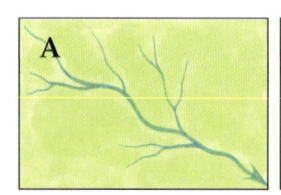

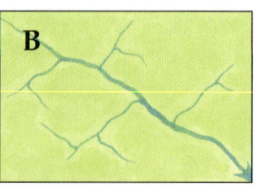

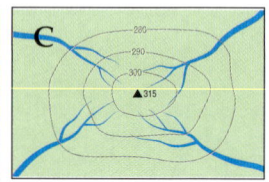

14. Explain with the aid of diagrams the formation of any **two** landforms that you have studied.

15. Select any **one** of the following surface processes: (a) sea/marine action; (b) river action; (c) glacial action; (d) mass movement.
    Explain the formation of any **two** Irish landforms caused by your selected process with the aid of diagrams.

16. The OS map extract below shows a river valley.
    (a) Is the River Argideen in its upper or middle or lower course?
    (b) What name is given to the feature marked X on the map?

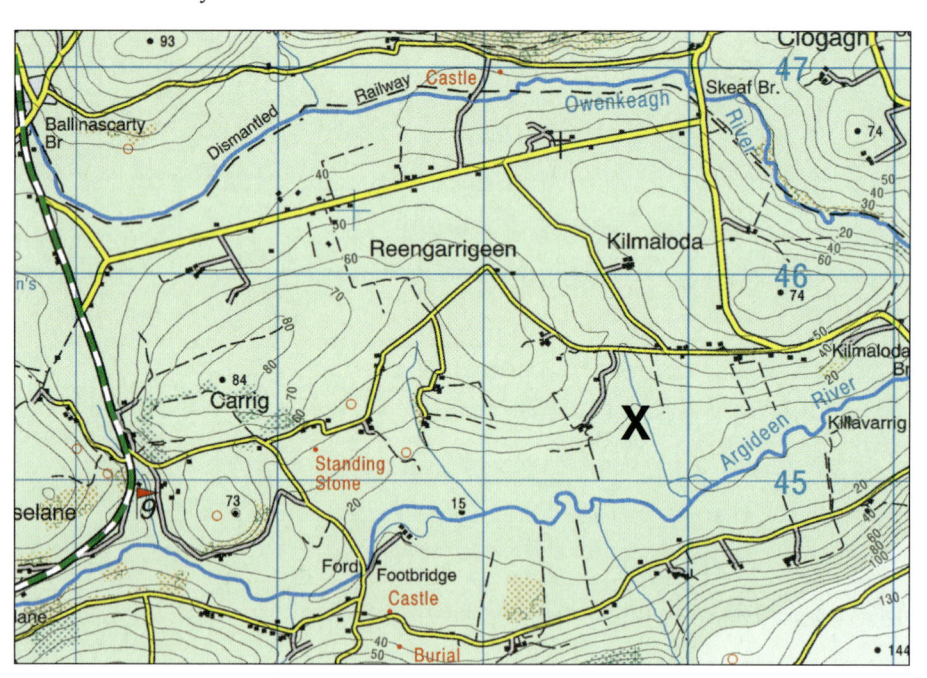

■ HL Questions

17. Explain with the aid of a labelled diagram(s) the formation of **one** landform of deposition that you have studied.

18. Explain with the aid of a labelled diagram(s) the formation of **one** landform of erosion that you have studied.

19. Explain the formation of **one** landform of erosion and **one** landform of deposition that you have studied.

CHAPTER 8: FLUVIAL PROCESSES, PATTERNS AND LANDFORMS

LC Exam Questions

20. The area shown on the 1:50000 Ordnance Survey map below has been shaped by fluvial processes.

    (i) Name **one** landform on the Ordnance Survey map that was formed by fluvial processes and give a six figure grid reference for its location.

    (ii) Describe and explain with the aid of diagram(s) the processes involved in the formation of this landform.

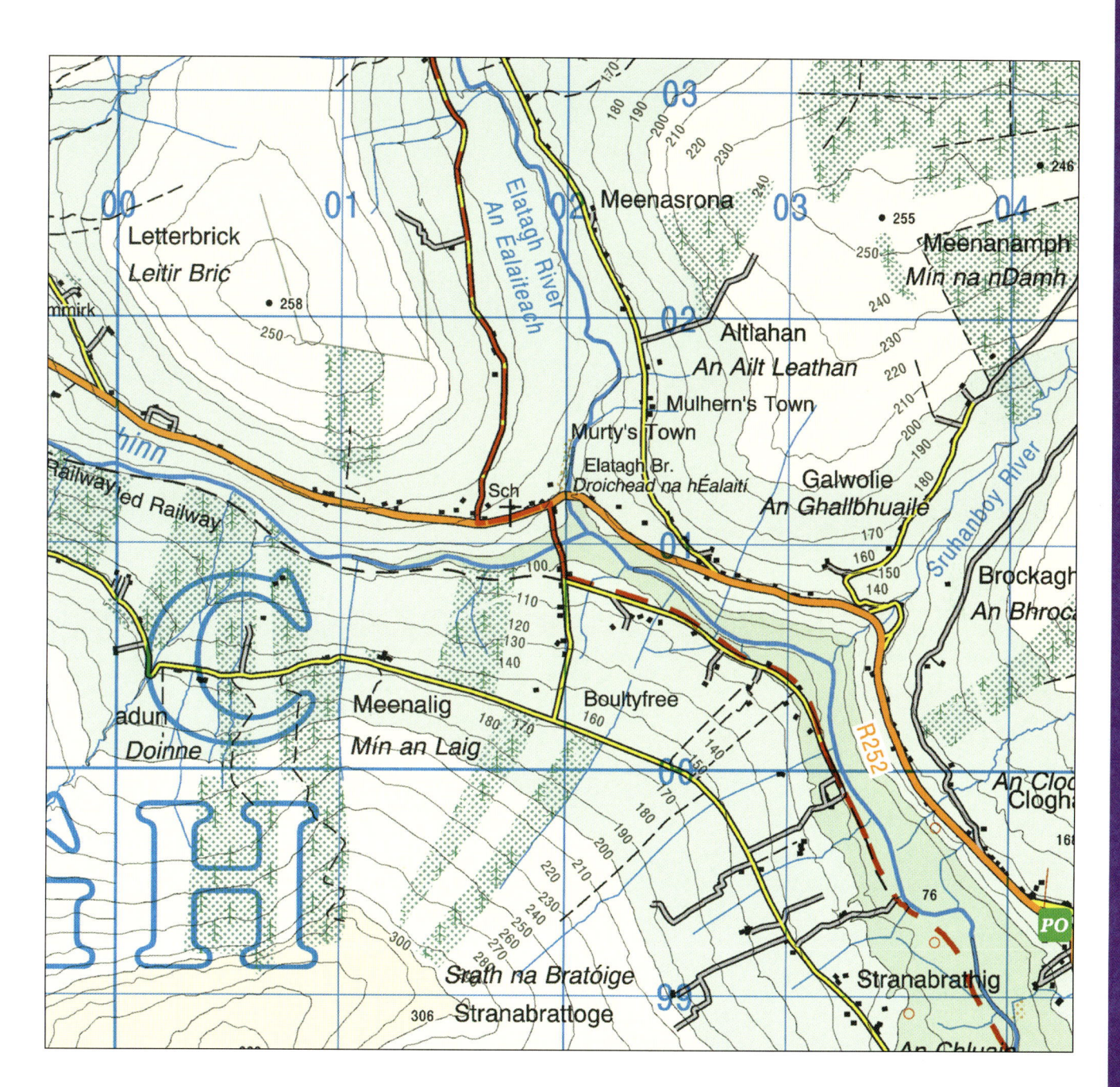

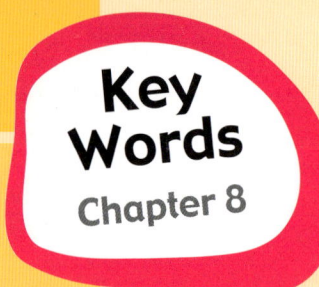

CORE UNIT: PATTERNS AND PROCESSES IN THE PHYSICAL ENVIRONMENT

Key Words
Key Words Chapter 8

You should be able to explain both verbally and in writing each of the key words listed below.

abrasion	marine delta
alluvium	mature stage/middle course
arcuate delta	meander
attrition	meander scar
bank caving	migrating meanders
base level of erosion	mortlake
bird's foot delta	mouth
cavitation	plunge pool
confluence	point bar
course	old age stage/lower course
delta	oxbow lake
dendritic pattern	radial pattern
deposition	river bluff
distributaries	river cliff
drainage basin area	saltation
estuarine delta	solution
estuary	source
floodplain	splashback
fluvial process	suspension
gorge	topset, foreset and bottomset beds
graded profile	traction
headward erosion	trellis pattern
hydraulic action	tributary
interlocking spur	V-shaped valley
lacustrine delta	vertical erosion
lateral erosion	waterfall
levee	watershed
load	youthful stage/upper course

Digital Resources are available for this chapter at mentorbooks.ie/resources

CHAPTER 9

Glacial Processes, Patterns and Landforms

Learning Outcomes

At the end of this chapter you will be able to:
- Understand how glacier ice is formed.
- Name and explain the processes of glacial erosion, transport and deposition.
- Identify glacial landforms on diagrams, maps and photographs.
- Describe the formation of glacial landforms.
- Identify locations around Ireland and the world where glacial landforms exist.

Contents

9.1	Glaciation 144	**9.4**	Glacial processes 146
9.2	The formation of glacier ice . 144	**9.5**	Glacial landforms 148
9.3	Types of glaciers 145	**9.6**	The glaciation of Ireland 159

Exam Note: If you are studying this chapter in detail, you must be able to explain **glacial** processes and how the landforms are made. You must be able to identify them on diagrams, maps and photos. The extra material you need to know is indicated by a yellow arrow. If you are not studying this chapter in detail, then you should be able to identify the landforms on diagrams, maps and photos and briefly explain the processes that made them.

Revision Space

Chapter Revision Questions – LC Exam Questions – Key Word List 161

CORE UNIT: PATTERNS AND PROCESSES IN THE PHYSICAL ENVIRONMENT

9.1 Glaciation

Glaciation refers to the spread of great masses of ice across large areas of land and sea. There have been many ice ages (**glacials**) in the past. The warmer time between ice ages is known as an **interglacial**. We are now in an interglacial period that began about 10,000 years ago.

During the last ice age, which ended 10,000 years ago, 30% of the world was covered in ice. Today, just 10% of the world is covered in ice and this is shrinking fast as global warming continues.

Today, most permanent ice cover is found in Antarctica, Greenland, the Arctic Ocean and on high mountains such as the Alps, the Himalayas and the Andes.

Fig. 1 Glacier Bay in Alaska

9.2 The formation of glacier ice

A glacier can be thought of as a river of ice but, unlike rivers, glaciers are solid, much deeper and move more slowly. Glacier ice is formed when the build-up (**accumulation**) of snow is greater than melting (**ablation**).

As snow falls, the ice crystals are compressed (like squashing soft snow in your hand to make an icy snowball), pushing air out and creating a type of ice called **firn** or **neve**.

weblink
Glacial advance and retreat

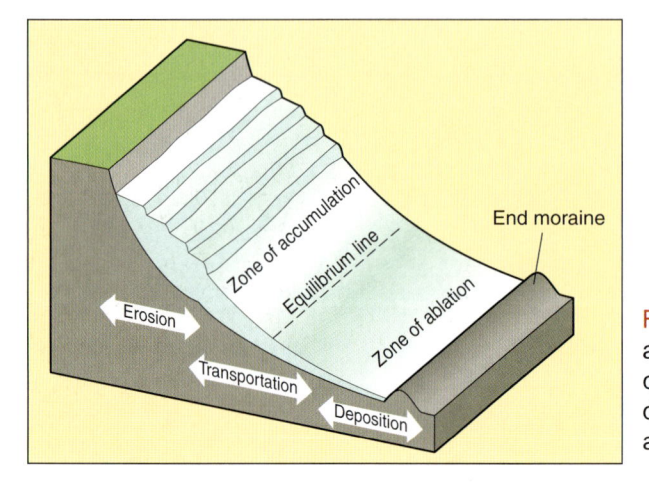

Fig. 2 The balance between accumulation and ablation (also called wastage) of ice in a glacier determines whether the glacier advances or retreats.

CHAPTER 9: GLACIAL PROCESSES, PATTERNS AND LANDFORMS

Over time, after a great weight of ice has accumulated (about 30 m), so much air has been squeezed out by compression that the ice turns hard and blue. It takes 30 to 40 years for snow to form this dense blue glacier ice. Blue glacier ice is so hard that when carrying rock fragments, it can bulldoze through rock and soil, completely reshaping the landscape.

Whether a glacier moves forward or retreats back up the valley depends on the balance between accumulation and melting. If more snow is added than is lost through melting, the glacier will move forward.

Glaciers slide downhill because of the force of gravity. They will mould or wrap themselves around obstacles in their path. Their movement may pause and when this happens glaciers freeze to the rocks below.

As the ice moves downhill it may move at different speeds over the landscape, causing huge cracks called **crevasses** to open and close on the surface of the ice. Imagine bending a chocolate-covered caramel bar slowly; the base stays connected but the chocolate surface cracks.

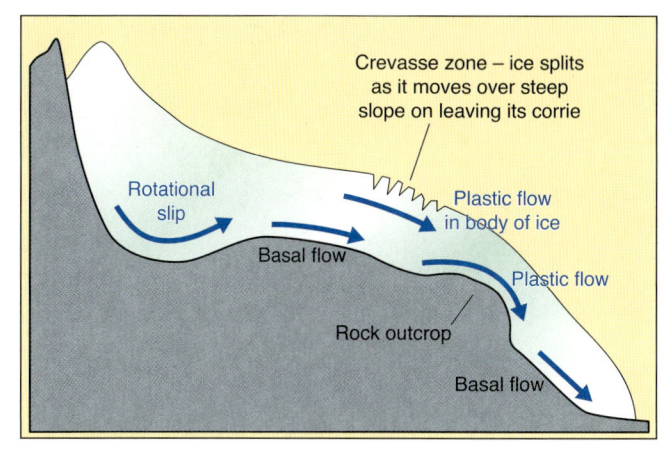

Fig. 3 The movement of glaciers

Fig. 4 Deep crevasse in ice

9.3 Types of glaciers

There are four types of glaciers.

1. **Corrie/cirque glacier**

   These are small glaciers that form in armchair-shaped hollows high up in mountainous areas.

2. **Valley glacier**

   These are larger glaciers that fill mountain valleys, e.g. the Alps.

3. **Piedmont glacier**

   These form when several valley glaciers join together on lowland areas, e.g. Iceland.

4. **Ice sheets/caps**

   These are huge masses of ice covering large continents, e.g. Antarctica and Greenland.

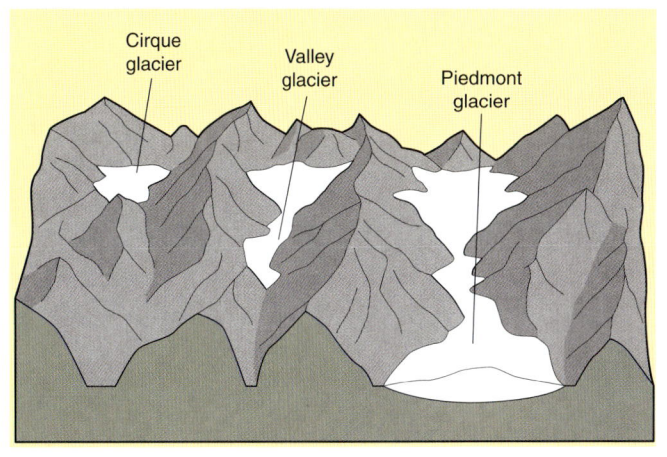

Fig. 5 Different types of glaciers

145

9.4 Glacial processes

What is a process?

A process is anything that happens to change the earth's surface. There are three glacial processes.

1. Erosion
2. Transportation
3. Deposition

weblink
Glaciers erode bedrock

In mountain regions glacial erosion is more common. On lowlands, however, glacial and fluvioglacial deposition is more common as melting is more likely to take place here because it is warmer. Transportation of rock particles can happen in both the uplands and lowlands.

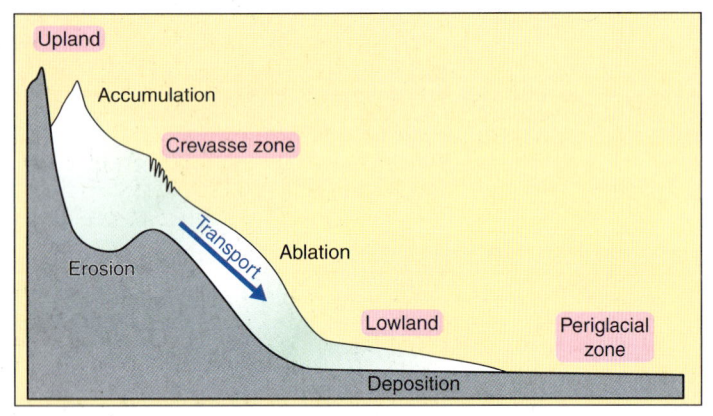

Fig. 6 Diagram and photograph showing accumulation, ablation and periglacial zones of a glacier in Alaska. The broken red line in the photograph shows where snow build-up (accumulation) gives way to melting (ablation). Above the red line fresh snow is whiter. Below the red line the melting ice is greyer in appearance.

Processes of glacial erosion

Plucking

The weight of the ice puts huge pressure on the base and sides of a valley. This causes the base and sides of the ice to melt, creating a thin film of meltwater for the ice to slide over (**basal flow**). This meltwater seeps into cracks and crevices in the rock. When it refreezes it expands, crumbling the rock and sticking to it. Later when the ice moves it drags or plucks the rock fragments away. Plucking works in the same way as when you take an ice cube tray from the freezer and your fingers stick to it.

Abrasion

The plucked rock fragments stuck in the glacier act like sandpaper as the ice moves along. They scrape away the landscape (**abrasion**) as the ice moves, creating deep scratches called **striations** or **striae**. Striae may help to indicate the direction of ice movement.

Processes of glacial transport

The rock fragments plucked and abraded by the ice are carried along with it. This material is called **moraine**.

Moraine carried along while stuck to the bottom of the ice is called **ground moraine**. Moraine that finds its way into the ice through crevasses is called **englacial moraine**.

Rocks from the valley walls that are broken up by frost shattering (freeze-thaw action) and fall onto the sides of the glacier are called **lateral moraine**.

Fig. 7 Glacial striae, County Kerry

Fig. 8 A valley glacier, Mer de Glace, France

Processes of glacial deposition

All material deposited by ice as it melts is called **drift**. There are two types of drift.

GLACIAL DRIFT
- Till: this is unlayered (unsorted); boulder clay dropped by melting ice.
- Fluvioglacial drift: this is layered (sorted) sand and gravel deposited by meltwater.

Fig. 9 below shows the various zones involved in glacial environments. Different processes are dominant in each.

Zone of erosion
Plucking
Abrasion
Freeze-thaw

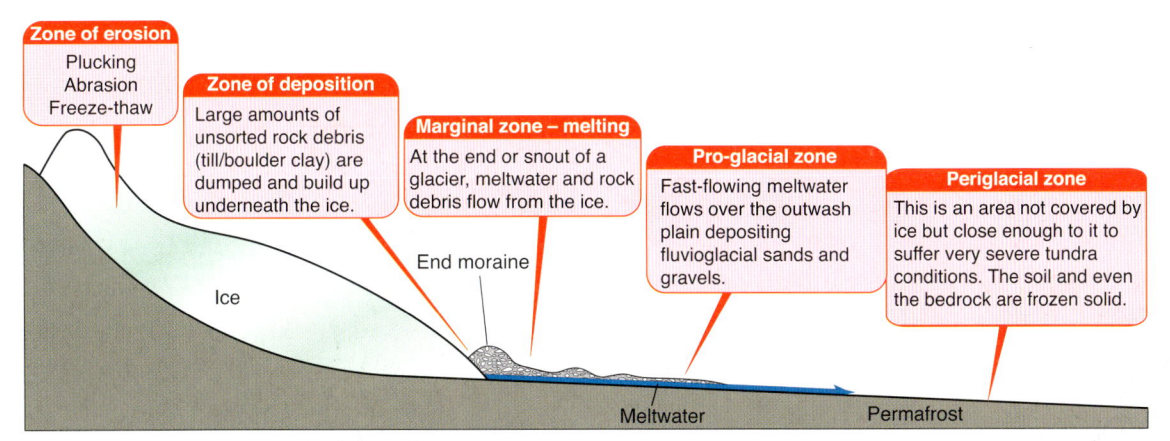

Zone of deposition
Large amounts of unsorted rock debris (till/boulder clay) are dumped and build up underneath the ice.

Marginal zone – melting
At the end or snout of a glacier, meltwater and rock debris flow from the ice.

Pro-glacial zone
Fast-flowing meltwater flows over the outwash plain depositing fluvioglacial sands and gravels.

Periglacial zone
This is an area not covered by ice but close enough to it to suffer very severe tundra conditions. The soil and even the bedrock are frozen solid.

Ice — End moraine — Meltwater — Permafrost

Fig. 9 Diagram to show glacial environments

9.5 Glacial landforms

Landforms made by glacial erosion

There are many landforms created by glacial erosion. They are listed below.

	Landform	Example
1.	Corrie/cirque	Devil's Punchbowl, County Kerry
2.	Arête	Between Upper and Lower Lough Bray, County Wicklow
3.	Pyramidal peak	Carrauntuohil and Brandon Mountains, County Kerry
4.	U-shaped valley	Gap of Dunloe, County Kerry
5.	Ribbon lake	Mount Brandon, County Kerry
6.	Truncated spurs	Glencree, County Wicklow
7.	Hanging valley	Glendalough, County Wicklow
8.	Fiord	Killary Harbour, County Mayo/Galway

Exam Note: You need to name, explain and apply the glacial processes involved in your explanation of landform formation.

Fig. 10 Glacial landscape in Switzerland

Fig. 11 The Matterhorn, Switzerland

Fig. 12 Glendalough, County Wicklow

Corrie, arête, pyramidal peak

These are landforms of upland glacial erosion.
Main processes: freeze-thaw, nivation, rotational slip, plucking, abrasion.
Examples: Corrie – The Devil's Punchbowl, County Kerry
Arête – Mount Brandon, County Kerry
Pyramidal peak – Carrauntuohil Mountain, County Kerry

A **corrie** or **cirque** is an armchair-shaped hollow high up in the mountains. Corries are the birthplace of all glaciers. If two corries form back to back, a knife-edged ridge called an **arête** is formed between the two corries. Freeze-thaw action makes the arête sharp and jagged.

Where a number of corries form around a high mountain, continued erosion of their back walls creates a **pyramidal peak**, e.g. the Matterhorn in Switzerland.

CHAPTER 9: GLACIAL PROCESSES, PATTERNS AND LANDFORMS

IN DEPTH: Corrie

- At the beginning of the ice age, snow started to build up in hollows on the mountain tops in the sheltered north and northeast facing slopes.
- Freeze-thaw action occurred on the rocks above the snow-filled hollows. This created scree which then fell onto the snow or was washed under it by summer meltwater.
- Over time, the rock fragments were mixed into the ice. Continued build-up of snow squashed it to form **firn** and **blue glacier ice**. This ice deepened and widened the hollow by plucking and abrasion. The process of creating a hollow like this is called **nivation** or **snow patch erosion**. The weight of the ice eventually becomes so great that it slides by **rotational slip** and pulls away from the back wall of the hollow. However, some ice remains attached to the back wall, creating a deep crevasse called a **bergschrund**. The hollow is now called a corrie.
- When the ice age was over the corrie filled with water, creating a lake called a **tarn**.

All IN DEPTH sections contain material you need to know if you are studying this chapter in detail.

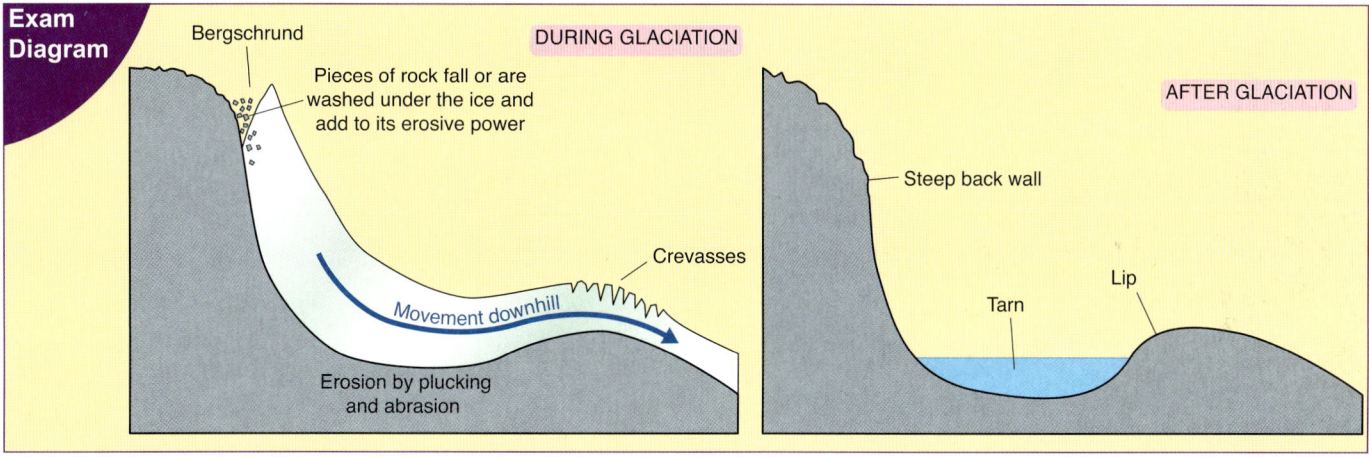

Exam Diagram

DURING GLACIATION
- Bergschrund
- Pieces of rock fall or are washed under the ice and add to its erosive power
- Crevasses
- Movement downhill
- Erosion by plucking and abrasion

AFTER GLACIATION
- Steep back wall
- Tarn
- Lip

Fig. 13 How a corrie is formed

Fig. 14 As the ice moves out of the corrie, its surface is stretched and this causes the ice to split into crevasses on the ice surface (like splitting a chocolate-covered caramel bar).

149

CORE UNIT: PATTERNS AND PROCESSES IN THE PHYSICAL ENVIRONMENT

Fig. 15 Corrie glaciers, Chugach Mountains, Alaska

Fig. 16 The largest corrie in Ireland is Coumshingaun in the Comeragh Mountains. Its back wall is 700 m deep. The helicopter flying on the left-hand side of the photograph is dwarfed by it.

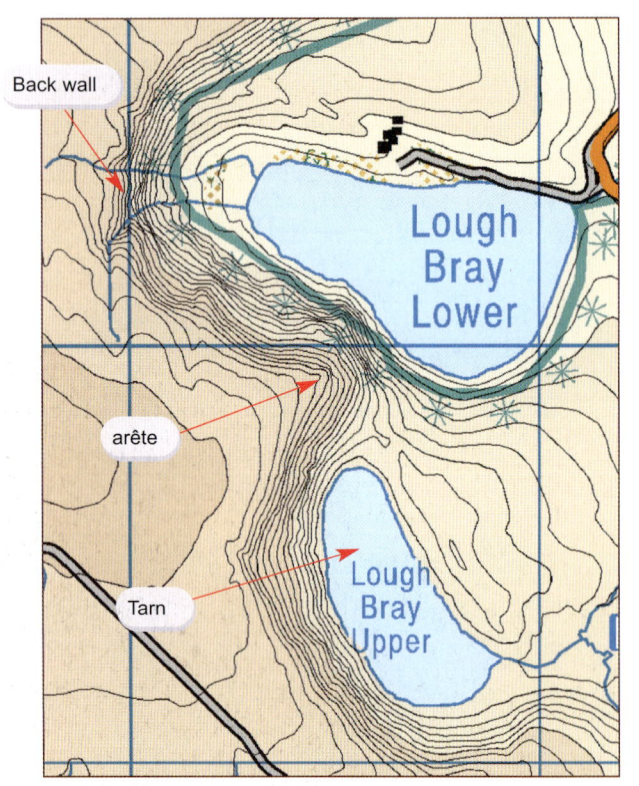

Fig. 17 Corries, arêtes and tarns at Upper and Lower Lough Bray, County Wicklow

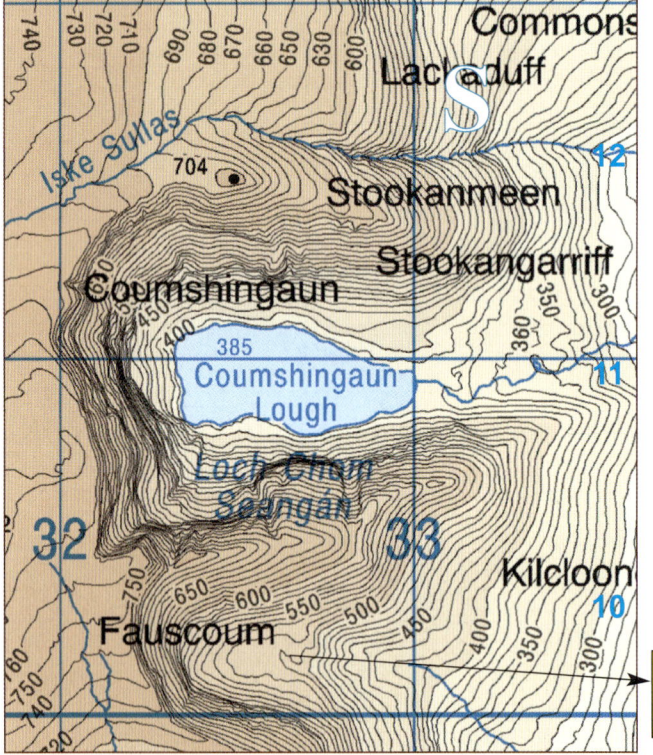

Fig. 18 Coumshingaun area showing corries, arêtes and tarns

CHAPTER 9: GLACIAL PROCESSES, PATTERNS AND LANDFORMS

U-shaped valleys, truncated spurs, hanging valleys, fiords and ribbon lakes

These are landforms of glacial erosion.

Main processes: deepening and widening of existing river valleys by plucking, abrasion, freeze-thaw action.

Example: Glendalough, County Wicklow

When corrie glaciers move downhill, they travel into existing V-shaped river valleys. They widen and deepen these valleys to create wide, flat-floored U-shaped valleys.

IN DEPTH: U-shaped valleys and associated landforms

- The movement of ice causes friction which heats and melts the bottom layer of the ice. This thin layer of meltwater seeps into rock layers, refreezes and sticks to pieces of bedrock. When the ice moves it plucks out loose rock fragments. This ice, now armed with sharp angular rock fragments, **abrades** the valley, widening and deepening it.
- The moving ice cuts straight through the valley wearing away everything in its path. It erodes the bases of interlocking spurs, cutting them off and leaving truncated spurs. These are visible as steep jagged cliffs along the sides of the U-shaped valley.
- Well-developed U-shaped valleys are also called glacial troughs and have distinct characteristics of lateral and vertical erosion – steep headwalls, truncated spurs, hanging valleys and ribbon lakes.

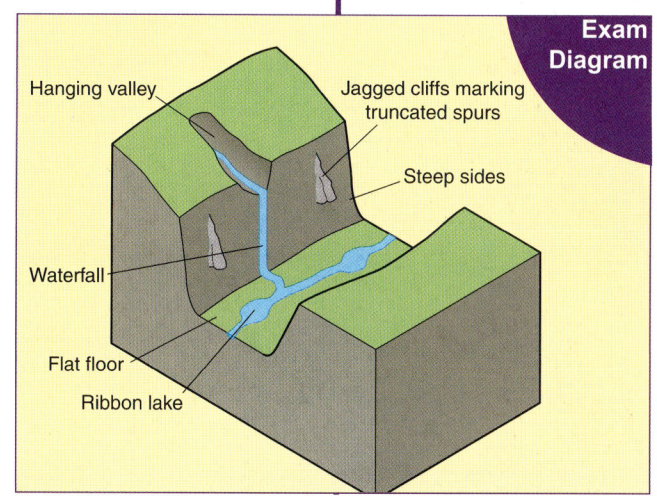

Fig. 19 A U-shaped/glaciated valley

Fig. 20 U-shaped valley, also called a glacial trough, at Glendalough, County Wicklow

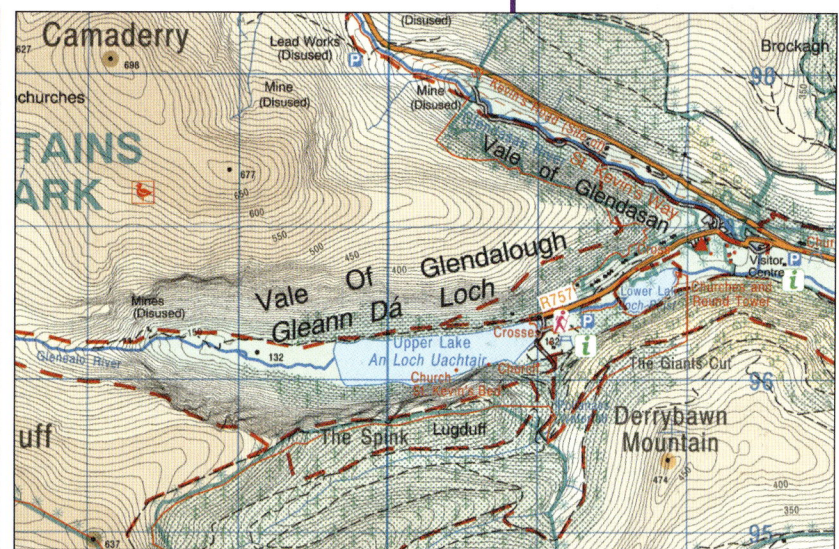

Fig. 21 U-shaped valley, a hanging valley and ribbon lakes

151

CORE UNIT: PATTERNS AND PROCESSES IN THE PHYSICAL ENVIRONMENT

- **Hanging valleys** are the valleys of former river tributaries which were glaciated.
- Tributary glaciers were smaller so they contained less ice than the main valley glacier, and therefore they did not erode as deeply into their valley. When the ice age ended they were left hanging above the main valley. Hanging valleys are often marked by a waterfall, e.g. Pollanass above Glendalough.
- **Fiords** form when a glacial trough is flooded by rising sea levels after an ice age, e.g. Killary Harbour on the Galway/Mayo border and Sogne Fiord in Norway.
Fiords are deepest at the landward end. At their mouth there is often an underwater lip which can be a hazard to ships and submarines.

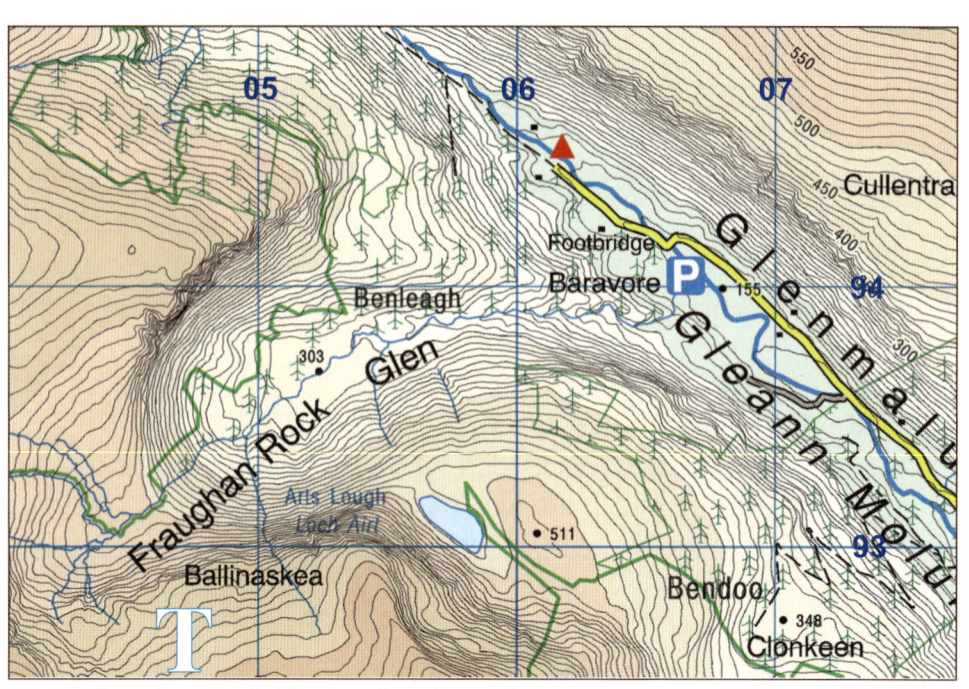

Fig. 22 Fraughan Rock Glen is a hanging valley

Activity

Find the spot heights in Fraughan Rock Glen and at Baravore using Fig. 22. Work out the difference in height between the hanging valley floor and the floor of Glenmalure Valley.

weblink
U-shape valley formation

Fig. 23 Photo of Killary Harbour – an Irish fiord

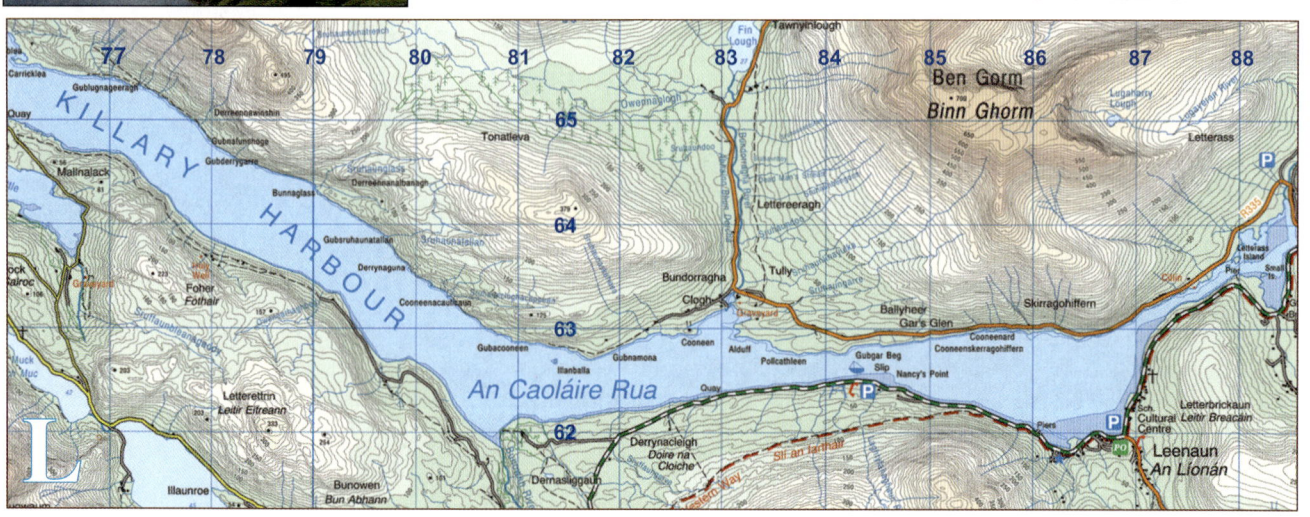

Fig. 24 Map showing Killary Harbour – an Irish fiord

CHAPTER 9: GLACIAL PROCESSES, PATTERNS AND LANDFORMS

- **Ribbon lakes** formed where soft rocks occurred on the valley floor. These were more easily eroded by plucking and abrasion. The hollows created are known as **basins**. After the ice age, the basins filled with water and were joined by a stream to form a chain of small lakes called ribbon lakes or **paternoster lakes**. These are seen in Glendalough, County Wicklow and Glenbeigh, County Kerry.

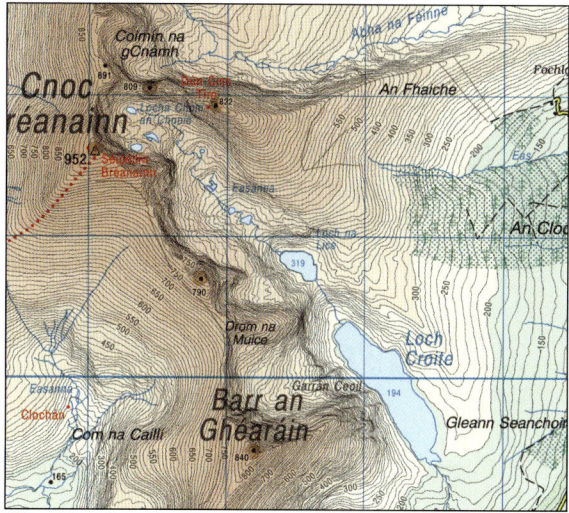

Fig. 25 Map showing ribbon lakes in County Kerry

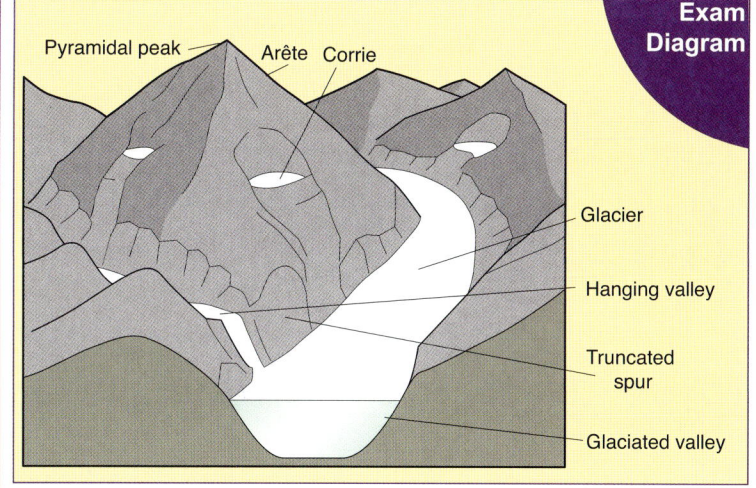

Fig. 26 Glaciated landforms in an upland region

Fig. 27 Ribbon lakes, Mount Brandon, County Kerry

Landforms made by glacial deposition

When a glacier melts (**ablation**) it deposits its load. Any material dropped by ice is called **drift**. This drift can be large amounts of unlayered (unsorted) rock debris (**till** or **boulder clay**), which ranges in size from large boulders to clay, sand and dust grains.

Drift can also be made up of sediments dropped by glacial **meltwater**. These are called **fluvioglacial deposits**. They formed as meltwater and rock debris flowed from the front (**snout**) of the glacier. Fluvioglacial deposits are layered (**sorted**) and shaped to make distinctive landforms which are called fluvioglacial landforms. These are dealt with in more detail later in the chapter.

	Landform	Example
1.	Boulder clay plain	The Central Plain
2.	Moraine	Glendasan Valley, County Wicklow
3.	Drumlin	Strangford Lough, County Down to Clew Bay, County Mayo
4.	Erratic	Scottish granite on the east coast of Ireland

153

CORE UNIT: PATTERNS AND PROCESSES IN THE PHYSICAL ENVIRONMENT

Boulder clay plains

This is a landform of glacial deposition.
Main processes: plucking, melting, transportation, deposition.
Example: The Golden Vale, Munster.

> **IN DEPTH: Boulder clay plains**
>
> - Boulder clay, or glacial till, is an **unsorted/unlayered** ground moraine which was deposited across the landscape by the retreating melting glaciers.
> - Boulder clay is a mixture of soil and rocks. Most people think of ice as white and clean but in fact it is often covered with rock and full of broken pieces of rock. Sometimes you can hardly see the ice at all. This debris falls out as the ice melts.
> - As the ice rapidly melted, boulder clay up to 30 m deep was deposited across the Irish landscape, providing a deep, well-drained and fertile soil in certain regions. Similar deposits are found in Europe, e.g. the North European Plain.

Fig. 28 Cliff in West Clare made of boulder clay

Moraine

This is a landform of glacial deposition.
Main processes: mass movement from valley sides, transport, melting, deposition.
Example: Glendasan Valley, County Wicklow.

Rocky material carried on, in or under the ice is called a **moraine**. When the ice melts this material is deposited on the land and forms ridges of stone and boulder clay which, depending on their location in the valley, have different names (see Fig. 30).

Fig. 29 Moraines being carried by glaciers in the Swiss Alps

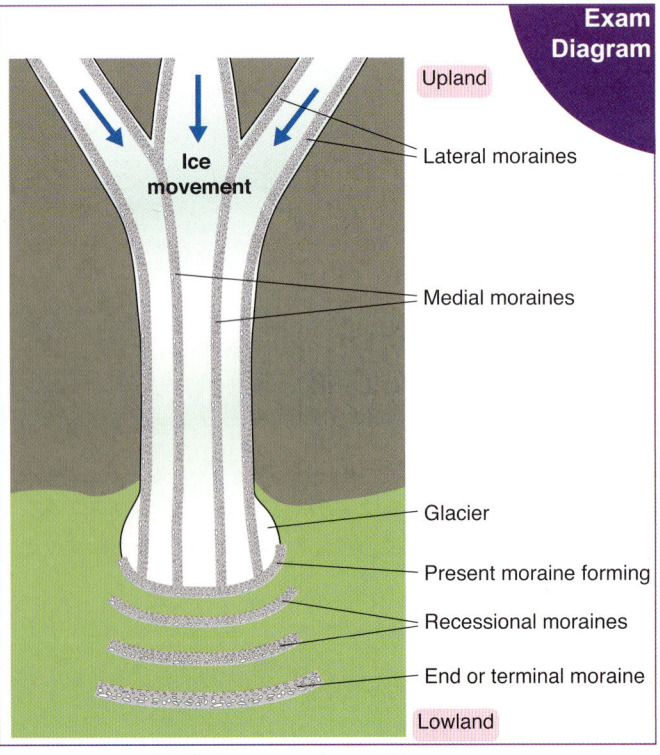

Fig. 30 The different types of moraine

154

CHAPTER 9: GLACIAL PROCESSES, PATTERNS AND LANDFORMS

IN DEPTH: Moraines

- Freeze-thaw action on the mountainsides above the ice formed scree which fell onto the top and sides of the glacier. This scree added to the already plucked rock material and was held close to the valley side by the ice. Once the glacier melted, the scree fell to the ground at the valley sides, blanketing it in a gently sloping ridge of unsorted stones and boulders called **lateral moraine**. **Englacial** and **ground moraine** as well as **medial moraine** are carried to the snout of the glacier and deposited there as **end moraines**. Meltwater streams flow through and out of this end moraine. The very large South Ireland end moraine sweeps across Ireland in a crescent shape from South Wicklow to the Shannon estuary.
- **Medial moraine** is a ridge of debris formed where two lateral moraines meet at the junction of two glaciers. Large glaciers may have many medial moraines visible as darker-looking stripes on their surface. The moraine is carried further down the valley by the main glacier until it is deposited at the front (snout) of the glacier.
- As the ice glacier retreats, it stops now and again and deposits smaller ridges of debris at the front. These are **recessional moraines**.
- **End (terminal) moraine** is a crescent-shaped ridge of debris, which marks the furthest point reached by the ice.

Fig. 31 Moraine deposited by ice in the French Alps

Drumlins

These are landforms of glacial deposition.
Main processes: plucking, melting, friction, deposition.
Example: County Monaghan.

Drumlins are small, oval-shaped hills made from boulder clay ('drum' meaning small hill). They range in size from 25 to 100 metres high, 0.5 km wide and 1 km long. One end is steep (known as the **stoss side**) and faces the direction of ice movement, the other end has a gentler slope (the **lee side**). In Ireland the drumlin belt runs from Strangford Lough, County Down to Clew Bay, County Mayo.

IN DEPTH: Drumlins

- Drumlins are formed beneath the ice when an ice sheet is heavily laden with boulder clay and is melting but still able to move forward. Friction between the ground and the ice causes the load to be deposited. As the ice moves forward it moulds the deposited material into distinctive egg-shaped mounds.
- Some drumlins have a large boulder at their centre and are called **rock drumlins**. Rock drumlins form where a large boulder gets in the way of the ice, causing deposition around it. Drumlins tend to occur in large groups called **swarms** and the resulting landscape is often called a **basket of eggs landscape**.

CORE UNIT: PATTERNS AND PROCESSES IN THE PHYSICAL ENVIRONMENT

Fig. 32 A drumlin near Monaghan

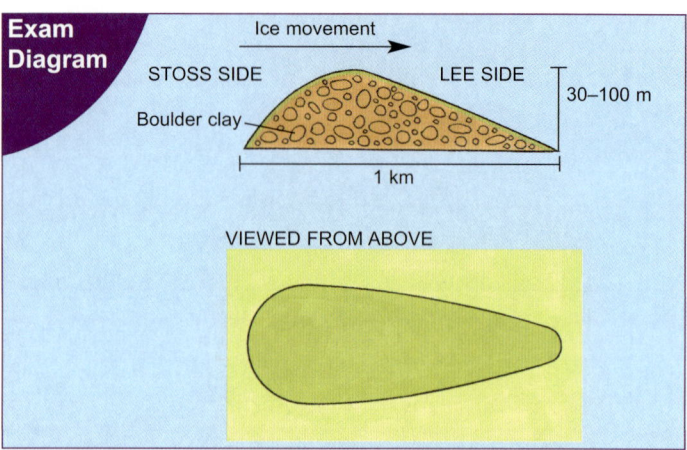

Fig. 33 A drumlin

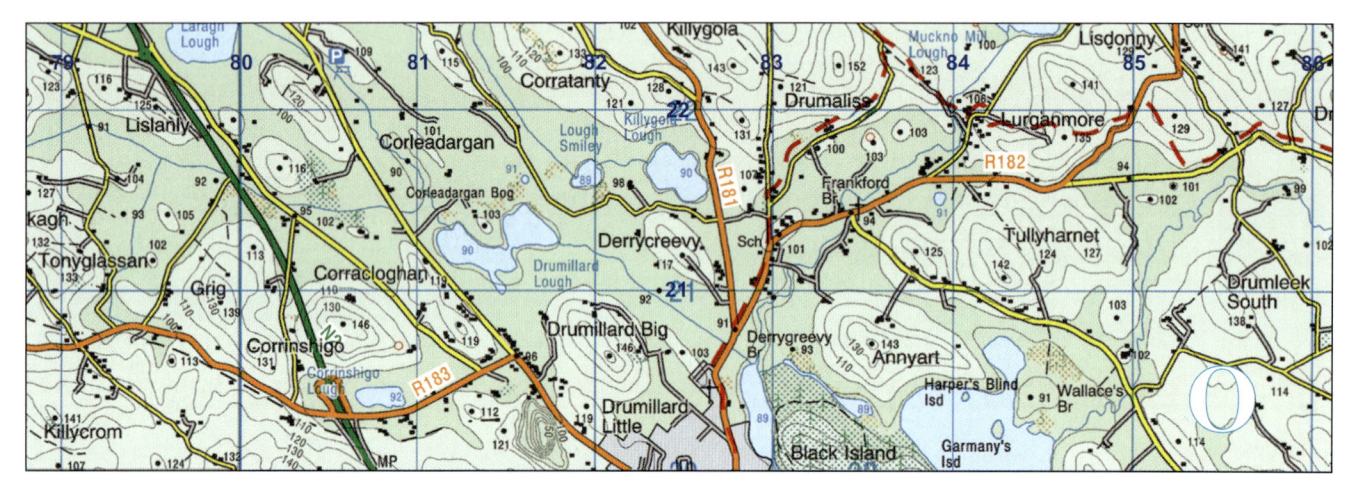

Fig. 34 Map to show drumlins, County Monaghan. Note placenames on this extract.

Activity

Look at the OS map in Fig. 34 and answer the questions.
1. What is the direction of ice movement shown by the drumlins?
2. Choose five drumlins and work out their average height.

Erratics

These are landforms of glacial deposition.
Main processes: plucking, transportation, melting, deposition.
Example: The Burren, County Clare.

Erratics are large boulders that have been picked up by the ice in one area, then transported long distances before being deposited in an area which may have a completely different rock type. Many are left perched on a hillside, e.g. near Lough Duff, Black Valley, Killarney. Many are found on the Burren. Erratics of Scottish origin can also be found across Ireland.

Fig. 35 An erratic, County Clare

CHAPTER 9: GLACIAL PROCESSES, PATTERNS AND LANDFORMS

Landforms made by fluvioglacial deposition

Landforms made by meltwater flowing under and out of glaciers are known as fluvioglacial landforms. These are all depositional landforms.

	Landform	Example
1.	Outwash plain	The Curragh, County Kildare
2.	Esker	Esker Riada, Clonmacnoise, County Offaly

Outwash plains

These are landforms of fluvioglacial deposition.
Main processes: melting, transportation, sorting, deposition.
Example: The Curragh, County Kildare.

Outwash plains are large areas of sand and gravel which have been deposited across the landscape by glacial meltwater flowing from the snout of the melting glacier.

Fig. 36 Outwash plain in Alaska. The Curragh in County Kildare once looked like this.

> **IN DEPTH: Outwash plains**
>
> - Sand, gravel and clay were washed through the end (terminal) moraine. The heaviest gravels were deposited closest to the retreating glacier, leading to the formation of an outwash plain, while finer materials were carried further away and deposited as loess/limon, creating fertile, easily cultivated farmland, e.g. the Paris Basin. The outwash plain is thickest close to the terminal moraine. In Ireland the Curragh is underlain by sands and gravels so it is very well drained and ideal for sheep rearing and horse racing but not good for arable farming, unless well fertilised.
> - Sometimes small hollows develop on the outwash plain where a large block of ice was buried in the outwashed sands and gravels. When it melted, the top collapsed so that hollows are left which often contain lakes. These are called **kettle holes**. The remaining conical-shaped sand gravels either side of the kettle hole form mounds called **kames**, e.g. Curracloe, County Wexford.

Eskers

These are landforms of fluvioglacial deposition.
Main processes: melting, transportation, sorting, deposition.
Example: The Esker Riada.

Eskers are long winding ridges of stratified (layered) sands and gravels created by rivers of meltwater flowing beneath melting ice sheets.

CORE UNIT: PATTERNS AND PROCESSES IN THE PHYSICAL ENVIRONMENT

IN DEPTH: Eskers

- When the ice was melting rapidly, streams of meltwater flowed under the ice, making tunnels at the base of the ice. The meltwater carried large quanities of sand and gravels, which were deposited on the floor of the tunnels. This deposition usually happened when the stream lost energy as it left the tunnel. The heaviest load was dropped first with the lighter sediment deposited on top. Over time, many layers of deposits built up.
- When the ice age was over, these deposits were revealed as snake-like ridges of sorted sands and gravels, winding across the landscape and running across hills and valleys. These esker ridges are usually between 20–30 m high and are very different in composition to the surrounding landscape.
- Over time, weathering and mass movement reduced the height of eskers making them perfect for routeways. The ancient route, An tSlighe Mhór, was constructed on esker deposits extending from Galway to Dublin known as the Esker Riada. Today, part of the Dublin–Galway rail line runs upon the Esker Riada.

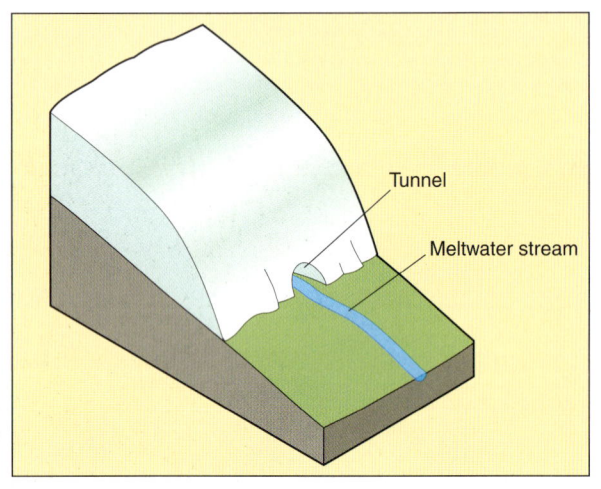

Fig. 37 Esker formation: Meltwater streams deposit sand and gravel under the ice as they flow. Over time, a winding ridge of sand and gravel is exposed as the ice retreats.

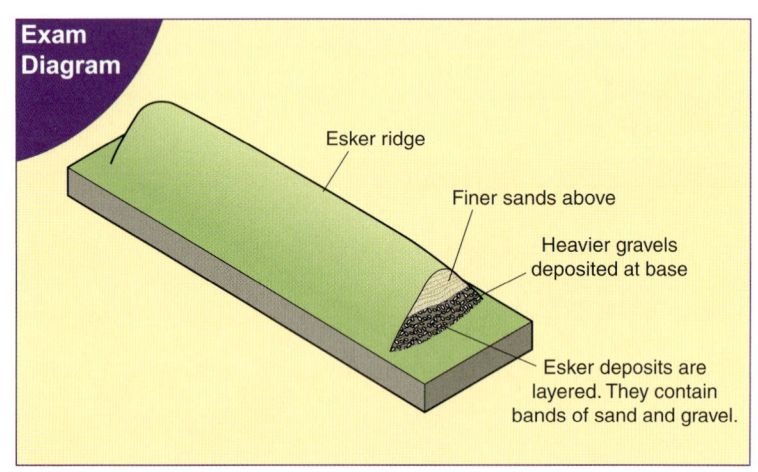

Fig. 38 Enlarged diagram showing how eskers are formed from layers of sand and gravel.

Fig. 39 An esker deposited by the ice in Iceland

Fig. 40 The Kilcormac Esker, County Offaly

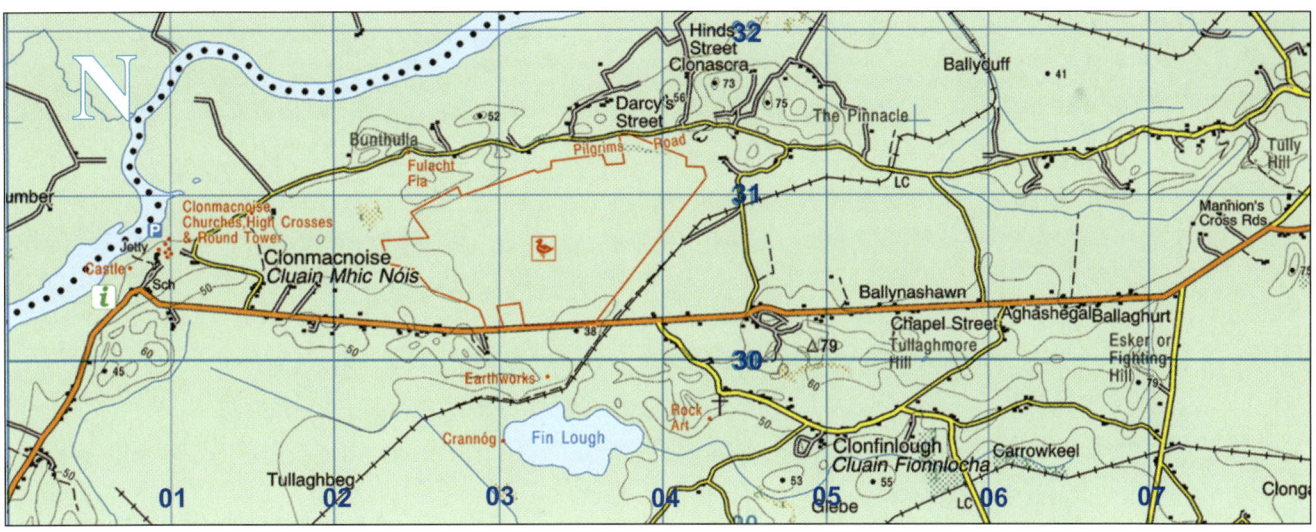

CHAPTER 9: GLACIAL PROCESSES, PATTERNS AND LANDFORMS

Fig. 41 Map of eskers around Clonmacnoise, County Offaly. Note how the roads and settlements (modern and ancient) are located on or near the eskers. The roads in particular follow the esker routes. This area is part of the 'Shannon Callows' floodplain area which is flooded each winter. Eskers have provided dry point settlements for over one thousand years in this area.

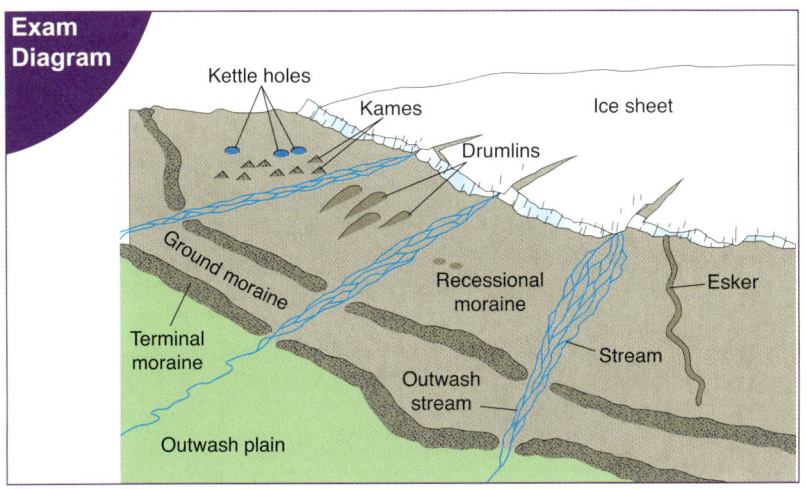

Fig. 42 Landforms of glacial deposition

Fig. 43 Outwash plains, eskers and moraines in Iceland. Note the road on stilts in the centreground of the image.

9.6 The glaciation of Ireland

Europe has had four major ice ages. The last two of these reached Ireland. The first to cover Ireland is called the **Munsterian Ice Age,** which began about 175,000 years ago and lasted for 75,000 years. It was followed by an interglacial which lasted 30,000 years.

The next ice age to affect Ireland is called the **Midlandian Ice Age.** It started 70,000 years ago and ended about 10,000 years ago. Ireland was at its warmest about 5,000 years ago.

The Munsterian glaciation

About 175,000 years ago thick ice sheets spread from Europe and Scotland, covering all of Ireland except for the highest peaks. These peaks stuck up above the ice sheets as **nunataks**. They were weathered by freeze-thaw action. Carrauntuohil, County Kerry is an example of a nunatak.

The Midlandian glaciation

About 70,000 years ago another ice sheet spread across Ireland. This ice sheet only reached as far south as a line from Wicklow to the Shannon estuary.

- The South Ireland end moraine marks the furthest point reached by this glacier (see Fig. 45).
- The Midlandian glacier bulldozed over the earlier Munsterian deposits, re-depositing them in the midlands.
- Eskers were deposited at that time across the midlands.
- Drumlins were deposited in the north and central lowlands.
- Till/boulder clay was deposited across the central lowlands.
- Local ice caps developed in the Wicklow, Mourne, Cork and Kerry Mountains due to the colder climatic conditions in the upland areas.

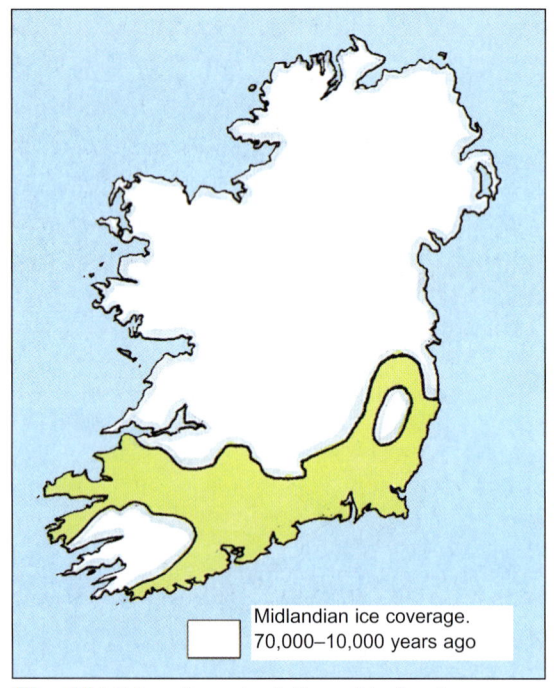

Fig. 44 Midlandian glaciation of Ireland

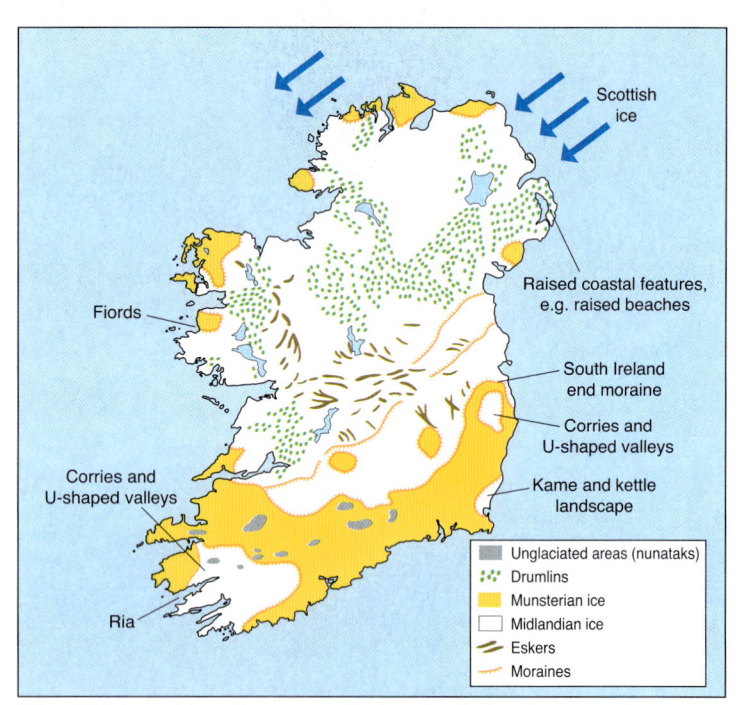

Fig. 45 Map of landforms made by glaciation in Ireland

CHAPTER 9: GLACIAL PROCESSES, PATTERNS AND LANDFORMS

Chapter Revision Questions

1. Explain how glacier ice builds up.
2. What are the main types of glacier?
3. How do glaciers move?
4. Name and describe the processes of glacial erosion.
5. (a) Name and draw **two** landforms of glacial erosion.
   (b) Describe in detail the formation of the landforms you named in part (a).
6. Name and draw **two** landforms of glacial deposition and describe in detail their formation.
7. Discuss the formation of **two** fluvioglacial landforms.
8. On the diagram below showing an alpine glaciated region, identify the arête, cirque, fiord, hanging valley, pyramidal peak, truncated spurs, and U-shaped glacial trough.

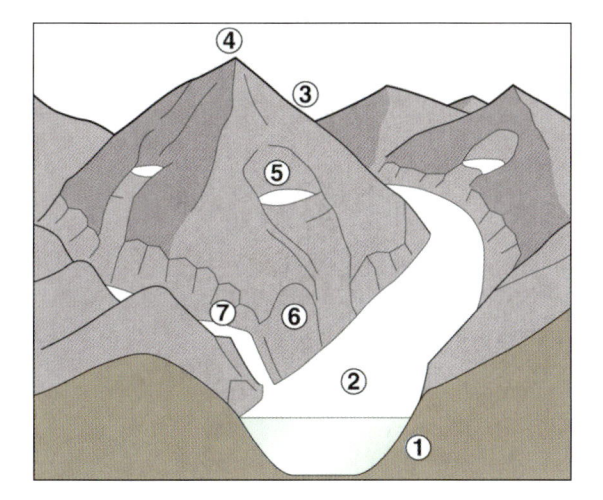

Number	Landform
1	
2	
3	
4	
5	
6	
7	

161

CORE UNIT: PATTERNS AND PROCESSES IN THE PHYSICAL ENVIRONMENT

LC Exam Questions

Higher Level students must be able to answer Ordinary and Higher Level questions.

■ OL Questions

9. Study the Ordnance Survey and photograph extracts below and answer the following questions.
   (a) Name the glacial feature marked X on the map.
       Write the correct name: _____
   (b) Name the glacial feature marked Y on the photograph.
       Write the correct name: _____
   (c) Were features X and Y formed by the process of erosion or deposition?

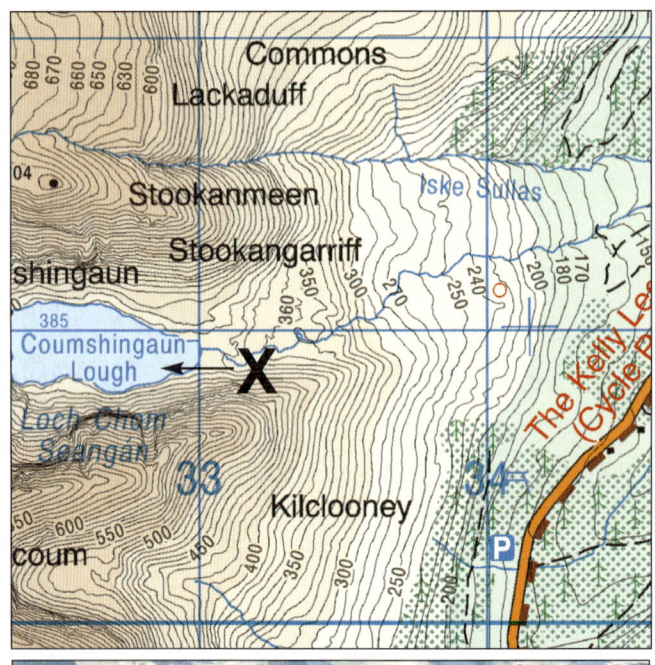

■ HL Questions

10. Examine the diagram below showing some glacial landforms.
    Answer each of the following questions.
    (i) Name each of the landforms A, B, C, D, E and F.
    (ii) Explain briefly what is meant by a fluvioglacial process.
    (iii) Name any **two** fluvioglacial landforms.

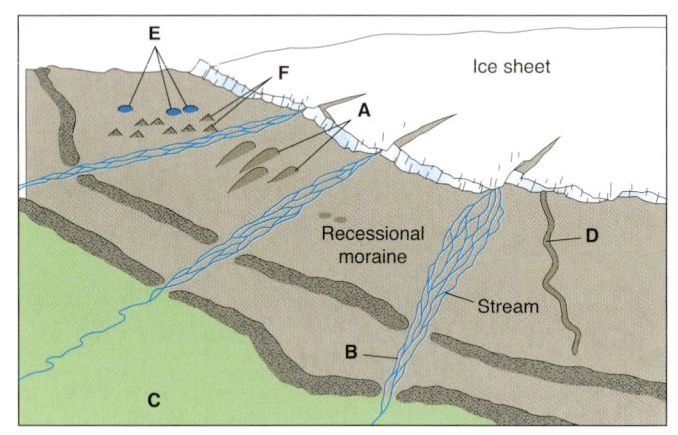

11. Explain with the aid of a labelled diagram(s) the formation of **one** landform of erosion that you have studied.

12. Explain the formation of **one** landform of erosion and **one** landform of deposition that you have studied.

13. Explain with the aid of a labelled diagram(s) the formation of **one** landform of deposition that you have studied.

CHAPTER 9: GLACIAL PROCESSES, PATTERNS AND LANDFORMS

LC Exam Questions

14. The area shown on the OS map below has been shaped by glacial processes.
    (i) Name **one** landform on the map that was formed by glacial processes and give a six-figure grid reference for its location.
    (ii) Describe and explain with the aid of diagram(s) the processes involved in the formation of this landform.

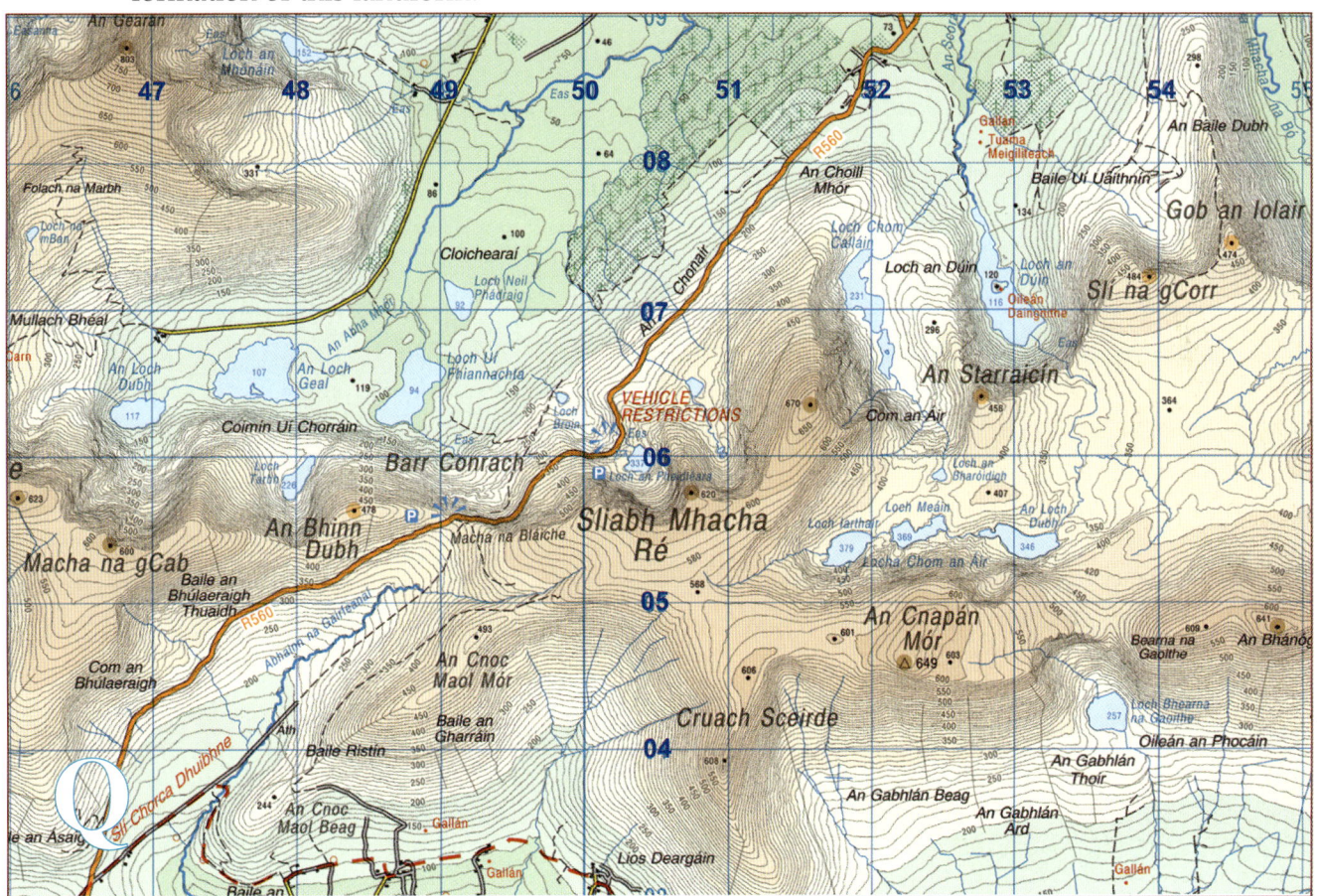

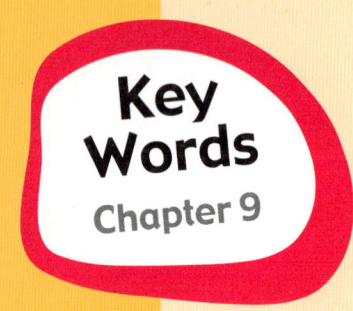

CORE UNIT: PATTERNS AND PROCESSES IN THE PHYSICAL ENVIRONMENT

Key Words Chapter 9

Key Words

You should be able to explain both verbally and in writing each of the key words listed below.

ablation
abrasion
accumulation
arête
basal flow
basins
bergschrund
cirque/corrie
crevasses
drift
drumlins
englacial moraine
erratics
eskers
fiords
firn/neve
fluvioglacial deposits
glacial troughs
ground moraine
hanging valleys
kames
kettle holes
lateral moraine

lee side
medial moraine
meltwater
Midlandian Ice Age
Munsterian Ice Age
moraine
nivation/snow patch erosion
nunataks
outwash plains
paternoster lakes
plucking
pyramidal peak
ribbon lakes
rock drumlins
rotational slip
snout
steep headwalls
stoss side
striae/striations
tarn
terminal moraine
truncated spurs
U-shaped valley

Digital Resources are available for this chapter at mentorbooks.ie/resources

CHAPTER 10

Coastal Processes, Patterns and Landforms

Learning Outcomes

At the end of this chapter you will be able to:
- Name and explain the coastal processes of erosion, transport and deposition.
- Identify coastal landforms on diagrams, maps and photographs.
- Describe the formation of coastal landforms in Ireland.
- Describe how human activities affect natural coastal processes.
- Describe some methods used to protect the coast from erosion.

Contents

10.1	Waves	166
10.2	Marine/coastal processes	169
10.3	Landforms of marine erosion	170
10.4	Landforms of marine deposition	175
10.5	Human interaction with coastal processes	181
	Case Study 1: Bull Island, County Dublin	183
	Case Study 2: Courtown Beach, County Wexford	185

Exam Note

If you are studying this chapter in detail, you must be able to explain **marine** processes and how the landforms are made. You must be able to identify them on diagrams, maps and photos. The extra material you need to know is indicated by a yellow arrow. If you are not studying this chapter in detail, then you should be able to identify the landforms on diagrams, maps and photos and briefly explain the processes that made them.

Revision Space

Chapter Revision Questions – LC Exam Questions – Key Word List 188

CORE UNIT: PATTERNS AND PROCESSES IN THE PHYSICAL ENVIRONMENT

10.1 Waves

The factors controlling the height and strength of waves are:
- Wind speed
- Wind duration
- Fetch.

The wind blowing across the surface of the sea creates waves. The ability of waves to shape the coast is influenced by the strength of the wind and the length of time it blows. If a gentle breeze blows, wavelets appear. If the breeze stops, so do the waves. Stronger winds and storms out at sea produce larger waves which may last for hours and travel long distances.

The size of waves is affected by the **fetch**, which is the distance a wave has travelled before it reaches land. Large fetches produce bigger waves because the wind has had longer to blow over the surface of the sea, forming bigger swells, e.g. the west coast of Ireland.

When waves break, water rushes up the beach. This is known as the **swash**. Some of the water will seep into the sand, the rest returns to the sea as the **backwash**.

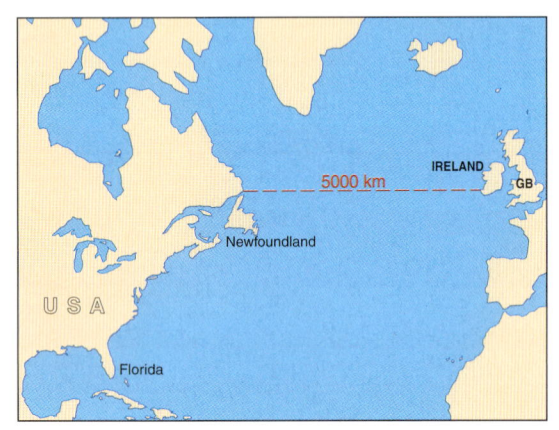

Fig. 1 The fetch on the west coast of Ireland

Fig. 2 The fetch on the east coast of Ireland

Fig. 3 Floating weather buoys measure the height and frequency of waves.

weblink
Wave motion

CHAPTER 10: COASTAL PROCESSES, PATTERNS AND LANDFORMS

Swash leaves material on the beach.

Backwash removes material from the beach.

Fig. 4 Swash and backwash

Constructive waves (spilling breakers) – building up our coastline

Some waves have a powerful swash that can carry debris up the beach but have little energy left in the backwash to drag the debris away again. As a result, **deposition** occurs. These types of waves are called constructive waves. A wide sandy beach is the best evidence of deposition by constructive waves. Constructive waves break some distance from the shore, and the surf rolls in gently up the beach. Constructive waves form gently sloping beaches.

Fig. 5 Constructive waves (spilling breakers)

167

Destructive waves (plunging breakers) – destroying our coastline

Destructive waves have great strength, large fetches and can **erode** soft coastlines very quickly. **Destructive waves** occur during storms and high tide conditions. They **plunge** powerfully against the coastline. Their backwash digs into the land removing large quantities of rock, sand and earth. They may throw large stones up on the shore creating a storm beach. Destructive waves form steeply sloping beaches. Coastlines change rapidly during storm conditions as beaches are removed and cliffs eroded.

Destructive waves normally curl over, forming a tunnel until the wave breaks.

Fig. 6 Destructive waves (plunging breakers)

DESTRUCTIVE WAVES	CONSTRUCTIVE WAVES
High frequency (more than 10 per minute)	Low frequency (under 10 per minute)
Backwash is stronger than the swash	Swash is stronger than the backwash
Removes beach material	Deposits beach material
Tall waves which drop down forcefully onto the shore	Long low waves which spill gently over the beach

Fig. 7 Differences between destructive and constructive waves

Wave refraction

Wave refraction is the bending of wave crests as they approach headlands and islands. In this way they copy the shape of the coastline. In Fig. 8 the headland is further out to sea than the bay and the water around it is shallower. At first, the waves approaching the coast are straight. Friction with the sea bed causes the part of the wave near the headland to slow down, while the rest of the wave carries on at the same speed. This difference in speed along the wave makes it curve towards the headland. This is called wave refraction. The constant curving of the waves concentrates erosion on the headlands, leading to the presence of cliffs, caves, arches and stacks.

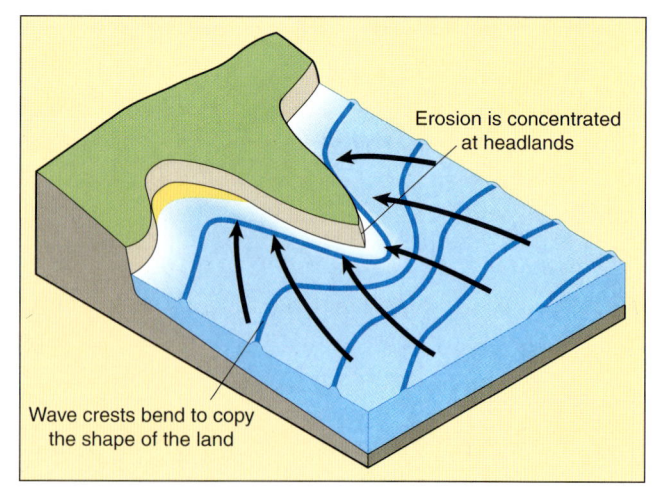

Fig. 8 Wave refraction

weblink
Animation of wave refraction

10.2 Marine/coastal processes

A process is anything that changes the landscape.
Marine processes are **erosion**, **deposition** and **transport**.
These are performed by the action of waves, tides and currents.

Processes of marine/coastal erosion
Hydraulic action
This is the crushing force of tonnes of water in each wave wearing the land away, e.g. the pressure of large Atlantic waves is nearly 10,000 kg/m^2. Hydraulic action is most effective on soft coastlines such as Louth, Dublin and Wexford.

Abrasion
This is the scraping away of the coastline as waves throw stones and sand against the coast. Abrasion is most effective at high tide and during storms.

Air compression
Air compression occurs when waves break against the coast. Air gets trapped and compressed in small cracks in rocks. When the wave moves away, the air is released. This causes expansion and compression in the rock which then shatters.

Attrition
This is when the load carried by the waves is itself worn down by its constant rolling and knocking together. This is why beach cobbles are usually well rounded. Eventually all beach stones will be worn down to sand-grain size by attrition.

Solution
Solution occurs when salts in sea water dissolve rock by chemical means. Chalk and limestone coasts are most easily eroded this way.

Fig. 9 Hydraulic action by storm waves

Fig. 10 Storm beach stones are well rounded by attrition

Processes of marine deposition
Deposition occurs when the **sea loses its energy**. Waves, tides and local currents combine to drop sand and shingle at particular locations.
 The conditions required for deposition are:
 1. Gently sloping beaches which reduce wave energy.
 2. Shelter from strong winds and currents creating calmer seas.
 3. Constructive waves allowing sand to settle on the beach.

Many bays and inlets have these conditions, allowing beaches and other depositional features to form there.

Fig. 11 Beach near Dingle, County Kerry

CORE UNIT: PATTERNS AND PROCESSES IN THE PHYSICAL ENVIRONMENT

weblink
Longshore drift

Processes of marine transport
Huge amounts of material are **carried along** our coastlines each day. Waves and currents are constantly moving sand along the coast due to a process called **longshore drift**.

Longshore drift (littoral drift)
This is the movement of material along the coast. It occurs because the coastline is irregular and waves do not break parallel to the coast (wave refraction). The swash moves sediment up the shore at an angle and the backwash pulls the sediment back out to sea at a right angle to the shore.

The result of longshore drift is that much of the sea's energy is spent moving material up and down the shore. This is why a sandy beach is the best natural protection a coastline could have from sea erosion.

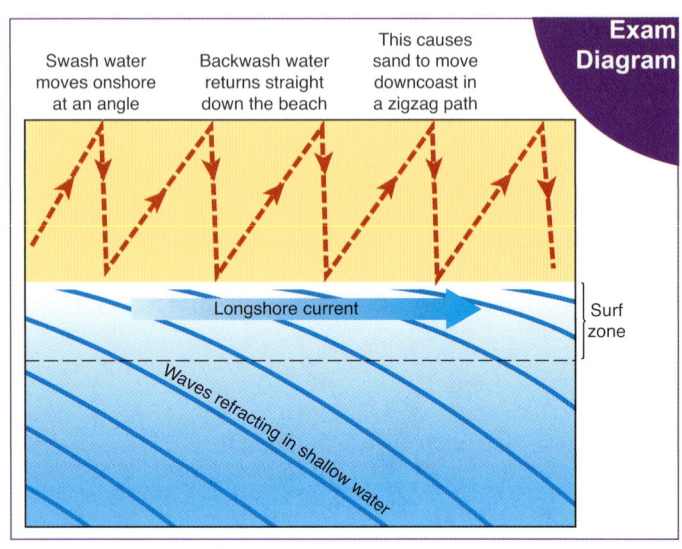

Fig. 12 Longshore drift

Breaking waves also produce currents which flow parallel to the shore. Where the waves break (surf zone) the water is turbulent and carries fine sand grains in suspension and rolls larger pebbles along the sea floor. These local currents along the shore can be very powerful and can carry swimmers along parallel to the coast quite quickly.

10.3 Landforms of marine erosion

weblink
Longshore drift

Landform	National Example
1. Cliffs and wave-cut platform	Slieve League, County Donegal
2. Bays and headlands	Howth Head and Dublin Bay
3. Caves, sea arches, sea stacks	Hook Head, County Wexford

Cliffs and wave-cut platforms
Cliffs and wave-cut platforms are landforms of marine erosion.
Main processes: abrasion, hydraulic action, air compression, solution, attrition, undercutting, collapse.
Example: Cliffs of Moher, County Clare.

Cliffs are landforms of marine erosion. They are steep slopes formed where the land meets the sea. They can form in hard and soft coastlines.

CHAPTER 10: COASTAL PROCESSES, PATTERNS AND LANDFORMS

IN DEPTH: Cliffs and wave-cut platforms

- The erosional processes of **hydraulic action, abrasion** and **air compression** combine to exploit weaknesses in a rock face. They form a notch or overhang. The notch is enlarged until the weight of the unsupported rock above is so great that it **collapses**. A steep cliff is formed.
- The fallen debris lies at the bottom of the cliff, protecting it from further erosion. Gradually the hydraulic force of the sea removes this debris depositing it on the sea bed some distance out to sea. This accumulation of debris is called a wave-built terrace.
- Over time, the repeated collapse of the rock at the cliff face causes it to retreat inland. Eventually the force of the sea is unable to erode a notch this far inland and mass movement, such as slumping, takes over as the main cause of cliff formation.
- The original base of the cliff is left as a rocky shore in front of it. This may be exposed at low tide. It is called a wave-cut platform.
- The structure of the rock plays an important part in determining the type of cliff that is formed (vertical or sloping). Rocks with layers that are horizontal (See Fig. 13) or dipping towards the sea are easily undercut and collapse frequently. Cliffs with vertical faces are formed. Cliffs made from unjointed rock such as granite are harder to erode and form more gently sloping cliffs, e.g. Slieve League in Donegal.
- Soft coastlines made of glacial till are the least resistant to the erosive power of the sea. Every tide can wash soil from the base of these cliffs and heavy rainfall may cause slumping, e.g. Killiney, County Dublin.
- Actively eroding cliffs are characterised by a lack of vegetation on their steep faces and well-developed notches or signs of recent slumps.

> All **IN DEPTH** sections contain material you need to know if you are studying this chapter in detail.

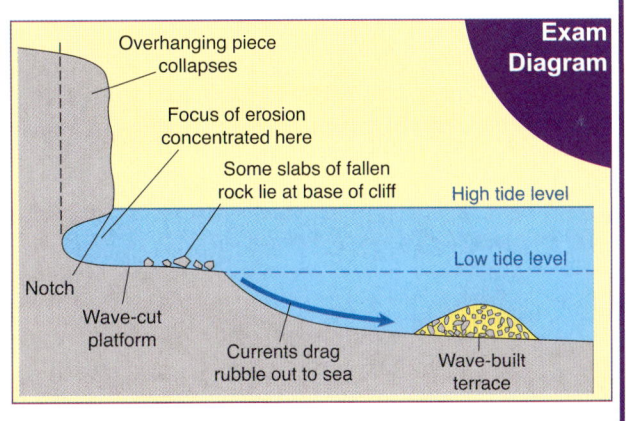

Fig. 13 Cliff formation

weblink Cliff retreat

Fig. 14 Hard coastline on Inis Mór, Aran Islands, County Galway. Note wave-cut platform and cliff.

Fig. 15 Slumping along soft coastline at Dunmore East, County Waterford

171

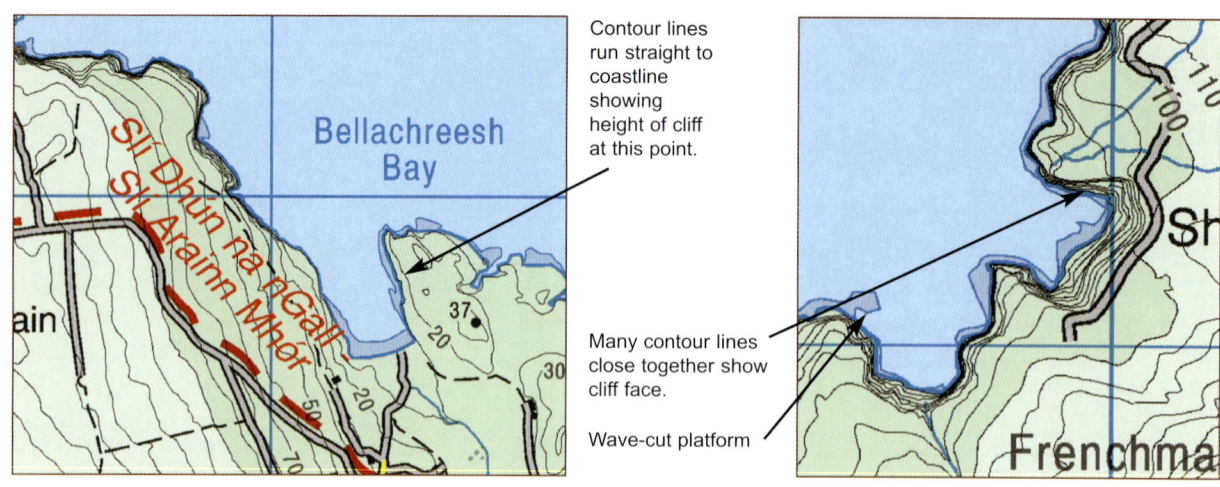

CORE UNIT: PATTERNS AND PROCESSES IN THE PHYSICAL ENVIRONMENT

Fig. 16 OS maps showing cliffs and wave-cut platforms in County Donegal

Bays and headlands

Bays and headlands are landforms of marine erosion.
Main processes: hydraulic action, abrasion, air compression.
Examples: Galway Bay and Black Head, County Clare.

Bays are large curves (indentations) in the coast, while **headlands** are areas of land that jut out into the sea. These features form when bands of soft and hard rock are found along the coastline.

> ### IN DEPTH: Bays and headlands
>
> - The processes of marine erosion such as **hydraulic action**, **air compression** and **abrasion** combine to attack the different rock types along the coast. Soft rock, e.g. limestone is eroded more quickly, creating a curve or bay in the coast. Hard rock, e.g. granite, is eroded more slowly. It stands out of the coast as a headland.
> - As waves bend around the coast, wave refraction concentrates **erosion** on the headlands.
> - Bays may contain beaches which form when constructive waves deposit rock debris due to a reduction in wave energy. As the bay is eroded further into the land, the sea has less energy and deposition continues to occur forming a **bay head beach**.

Dublin Bay formed because the soft limestone was eroded more quickly than the resistant metamorphic rocks of Bray Head and Howth Head.

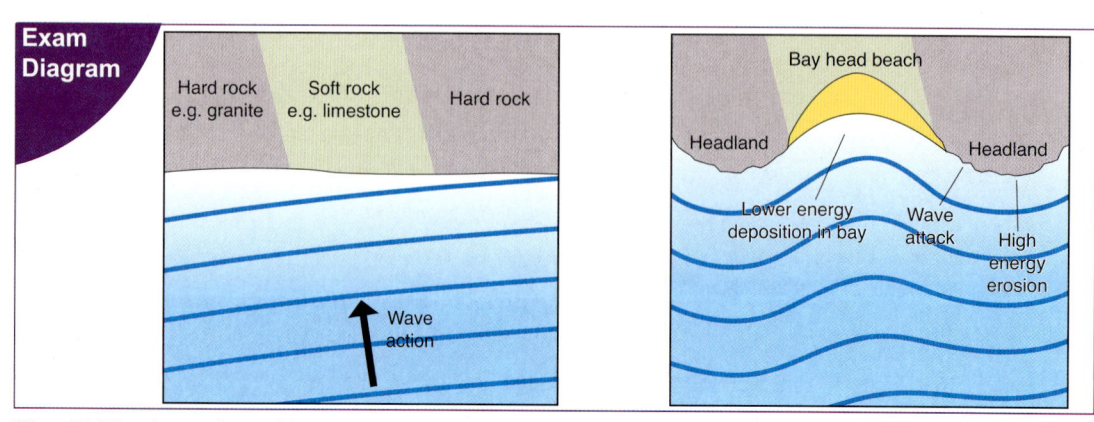

Fig. 17 The formation of bays and headlands

CHAPTER 10: COASTAL PROCESSES, PATTERNS AND LANDFORMS

Fig. 18 Bay and headland at Slea Head, County Kerry

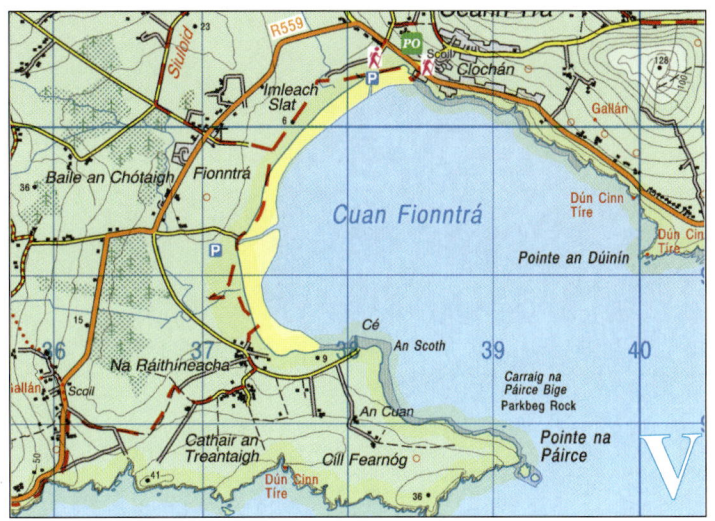

Fig. 19 Map to show bays and headlands in Ventry, County Kerry

Caves, arches, stacks and stumps

These are landforms of marine erosion.

Main processes: hydraulic action, abrasion, air compression, solution.

Examples:
1. Small **caves** are found in the cliff face at Loughshinny, North County Dublin.
2. **Arches** are found at Hook Head, County Wexford.
3. **Stacks** are found along the Clare coastline near Kilkee and also along the Sligo and Mayo coasts, e.g. Downpatrick Head.

Caves are hollows in rocky cliff faces and headlands. Large caves do not form in soft coastlines.

> ### IN DEPTH: Caves, arches and sea stacks
>
> - **Hydraulic action, abrasion** and **air compression** combine to enlarge existing joints and lines of weakness in a rock face.
> - Air compression is very effective. As the waves smash against the rock, air is compressed in the lines of weakness in the rocks and then released hundreds of times an hour. This weakens and shatters the rock, creating small hollows. Once formed, a hollow is enlarged to form a cave. Now the combined forces of marine erosion continue to deepen the cave. Solution and air compression can also cause the formation of a tunnel in the roof, known as a **blowhole**. If the roof of the long tunnel collapses, a **geo** is formed.
> - If two caves form either side of a headland, they may join up to form an arch. Over time, weaknesses in the roof of the arch are attacked by the sea and weather and the roof may collapse leaving a **sea stack**.
> - Eventually marine erosion and weathering will wear the stacks down until they are **stumps** barely visible above the water. It is then they are most dangerous to boats.
>
> Fig. 20 Sea arch, Mizen Head, County Cork

173

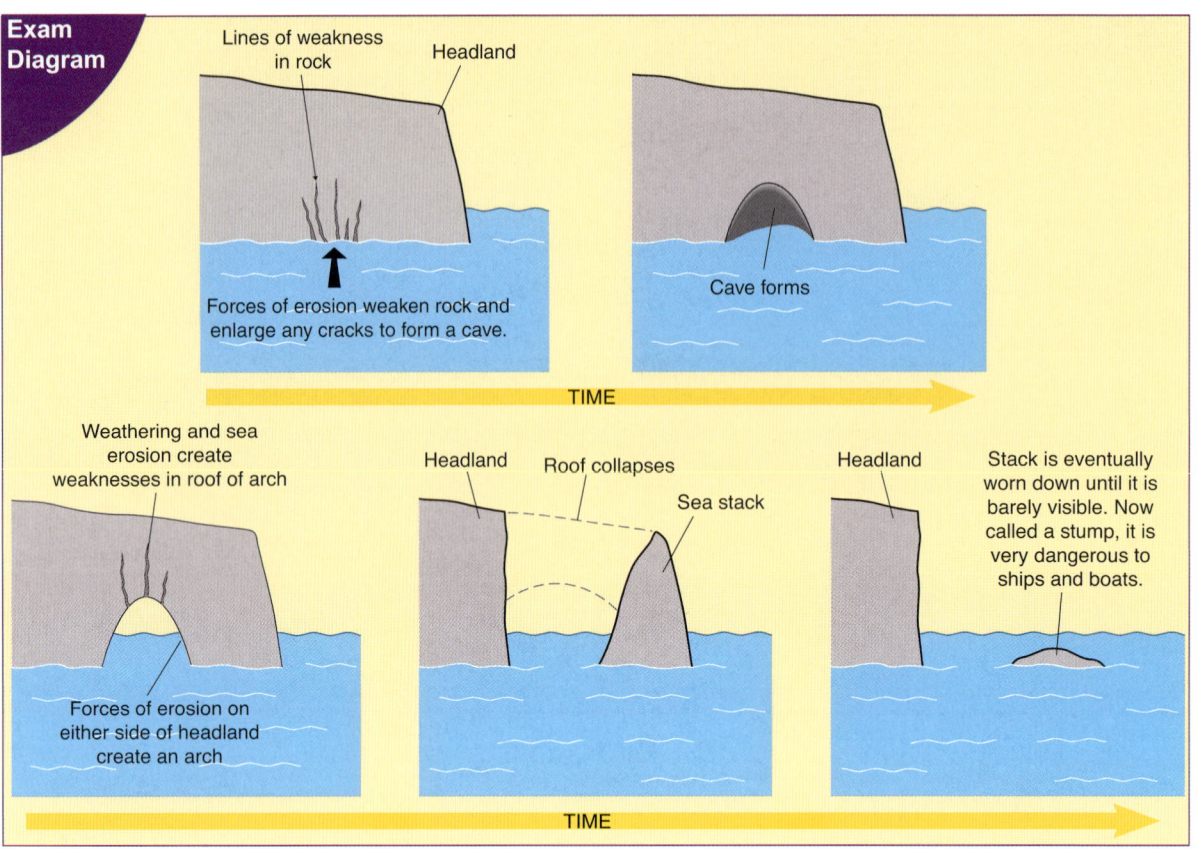

CORE UNIT: PATTERNS AND PROCESSES IN THE PHYSICAL ENVIRONMENT

Exam Diagram

- Lines of weakness in rock
- Headland
- Forces of erosion weaken rock and enlarge any cracks to form a cave.
- Cave forms

TIME →

- Weathering and sea erosion create weaknesses in roof of arch
- Forces of erosion on either side of headland create an arch
- Headland
- Roof collapses
- Sea stack
- Headland
- Stack is eventually worn down until it is barely visible. Now called a stump, it is very dangerous to ships and boats.

TIME →

Fig. 21 The formation of caves, arches, stacks and stumps

Fig. 22 Sea stack at Downpatrick Head, County Mayo

Fig. 23 Geo in Dunmore East

Fig. 24 Slieve League Cliffs in County Donegal

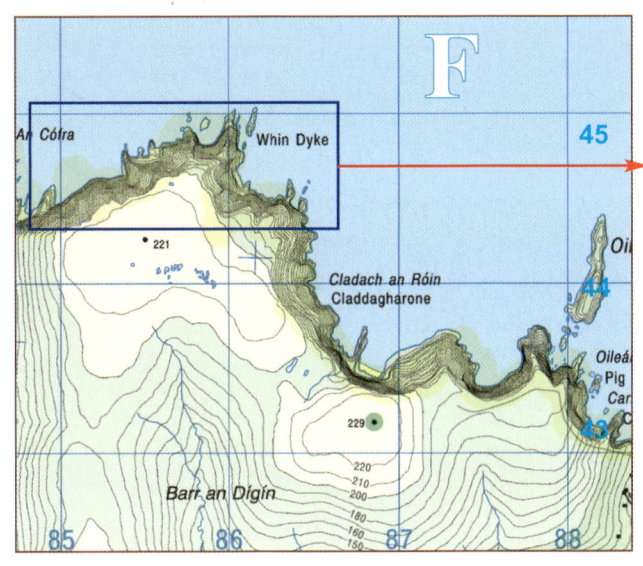

CHAPTER 10: COASTAL PROCESSES, PATTERNS AND LANDFORMS

Fig. 25 Map to show stacks and stumps along the Sligo coast

Fig. 26 Close-up of Fig. 25

10.4 Landforms of marine deposition

Landform	National Example
1. Beach	Tramore, County Waterford
2. Sand spit	Inch Strand, County Kerry
3. Sand bar and lagoon	Lady's Island, County Wexford
4. Tombolo	Sutton tombolo, County Dublin

Fig. 27 A beach with marram grass and sand dunes

Beaches

Beaches are landforms of marine deposition.
Main processes: constructive waves, longshore drift, deposition.
Example: Tramore, County Waterford.

Constructive waves and longshore drift leave large deposits of mud, sand, shingle and larger stones as beaches on our coast.
For a beach to form there must be:
1. A sheltered area to trap sediment.
2. Longshore drift to transport material to the beach.
3. Constructive waves to deposit beach material between the high and low tide marks.

Many bays provide these conditions and the beaches that form there are known as bay head beaches.

weblink
Beach drift

175

CORE UNIT: PATTERNS AND PROCESSES IN THE PHYSICAL ENVIRONMENT

IN DEPTH: Beaches

- Beaches may be divided into two zones, the **backshore** and the **foreshore**.
- Constructive waves have a powerful swash which drags sediment (**beach fabric**) up the shore. The wave slows down as it travels up the shore and some of the water seeps (**percolates**) into the sand. The backwash is weak and unable to drag larger pebbles back down to the sea. However, it can carry finer particles of sand and mud. Over time constructive waves **sort**/arrange the beach deposits. Heavier stones are left high up on the backshore, while finer sand and mud is left closer to the low tide mark on the foreshore. Large stones are only carried by storm waves and are deposited at the top of the beach as **storm beaches**.
- On a typical beach some or all of the following landforms may be found.

    Berms: These are long steps or terraces which form on shingle beaches in summer when constructive waves push beach sediment into long low ridges. Berms mark the junction between the backshore and the foreshore.

    Cusps: Crescent-shaped hollows formed where shingle changes to sand. Cusps form as a result of complex wave actions which sort heavier material into crescent-shaped patterns. Cusps generally occur on pebble beaches. They form on beaches where the wind blows mainly at an angle to the beach.

    Runnels and ridges: Runnels are broad depressions in the sand of the foreshore, ridges are gentle rises in it. If you have ever walked out to sea in shallow water and it gets deeper for a while then shallower, you have walked across a runnel and ridge. They are formed by the action of constructive waves.

- Longer stretches of beach tend to lie on the east coast of Ireland while on the west coast most beaches are found in small bays. This is because the west coast of Ireland is exposed to the full force of the destructive Atlantic waves, so sheltered bays and inlets are the only calm places in which beaches can form.

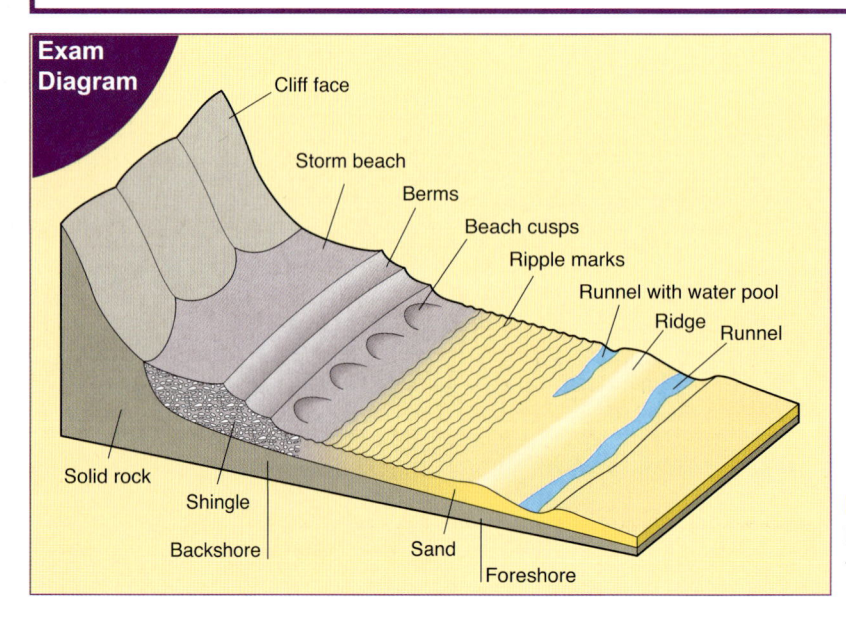

Exam Diagram

Fig. 28 Some landforms that may be found on a beach

CHAPTER 10: COASTAL PROCESSES, PATTERNS AND LANDFORMS

Fig. 29 The photograph shows some well-developed cusps on a pebble beach.

Fig. 30 Beaches in a sheltered bay in County Donegal

Sand spits

Sand spits are landforms of marine deposition.
Main processes: longshore drift, constructive waves.
Example: Inch Strand, County Kerry.

They are long deposits of sand attached to the land at one end.
Sand spits are created when the process of longshore drift is interrupted in some way either by a change in the shape of the coast or by human activity such as building a sea wall. They are commonly found attached to headlands.

IN DEPTH: Sand spits

- Where the coast changes direction longshore drift is unable to move material further along the coast and the material is deposited at this point. Longshore drift continues to pile sand up here. Eventually a long ridge of sand extends out to sea and may be exposed at low tide.
- Over time the spit builds up, becoming visible at high tide. Vegetation may grow, its roots stabilising the sand. Wind action may create sand dunes on the spit. Most spits have wide sandy beaches and dunes. Behind the dunes on the landward side a salt marsh may develop.
- Wave action and local currents often make the end of the spit curve, e.g. Inch Strand, County Kerry. When a sand spit grows across a bay it seals it off from the sea. This enclosed water area is called a **lagoon**, e.g. Lady's Island Lake, County Wexford.

Fig. 31 Map showing bays, headlands and beaches between Rush and Skerries, County Dublin

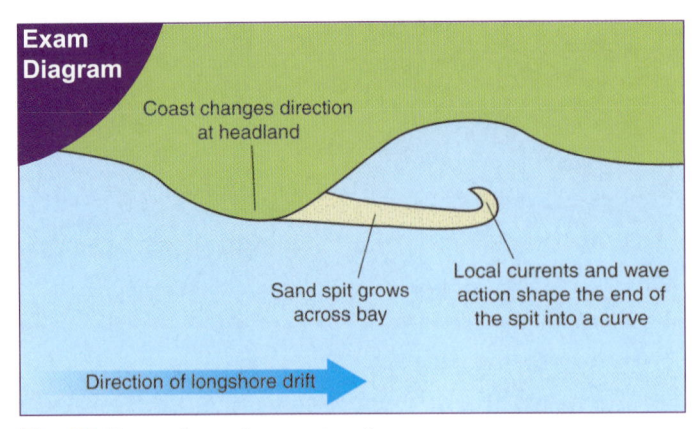

CORE UNIT: PATTERNS AND PROCESSES IN THE PHYSICAL ENVIRONMENT

Fig. 32 Formation of a sand spit

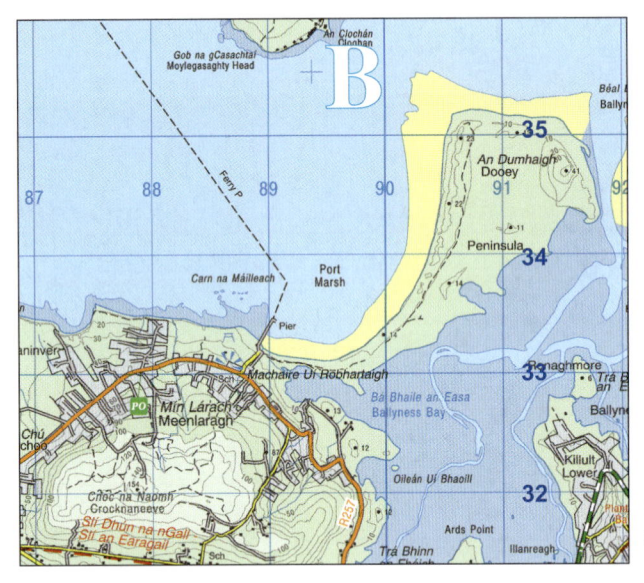

Fig. 33 Map showing a sand spit at Dooey, County Donegal

Fig. 34 Inch Beach sand spit, County Kerry

Tombolo

A tombolo is a landform of marine deposition.
Main Processes: longshore drift, wave refraction, deposition.
Examples: Sutton, County Dublin and Castlegregory, County Kerry.

A **tombolo** is a sandbar or sandspit that connects an island to the mainland. Tombolos are common around the west coast of Ireland and are made of shingle, sand and stone.

178

CHAPTER 10: COASTAL PROCESSES, PATTERNS AND LANDFORMS

IN DEPTH: Tombolos

- Tombolos are formed in two ways by the action of **wave refraction** and **longshore drift**.
  1. As waves approach the shallow water near an island they slow down and begin to wrap around (wave refraction) the island. The wave patterns caused by the island trigger longshore drift currents on each side of the island. These longshore drift currents then collide in the sheltered area between the island and the mainland. This causes deposition to occur leading to the formation of a ridge of sand or shingle. Over time the ridge connects the island to the mainland and a tombolo has formed (Fig. 35).
  2. In some places an island is located in the path of the prevailing longshore drift current. Longshore drift produces a sand spit where the coastline changes direction. The sand spit may grow along the coast until it reaches an island forming a tombolo (Fig. 36).
- Tombolo deposits are often layered with coarser sediments at the base and finer sands at the top of the tombolo. Tombolos are easily eroded by storms and destructive waves. They are often reinforced to provide access to islands for tourists and the local population who may live on the island.

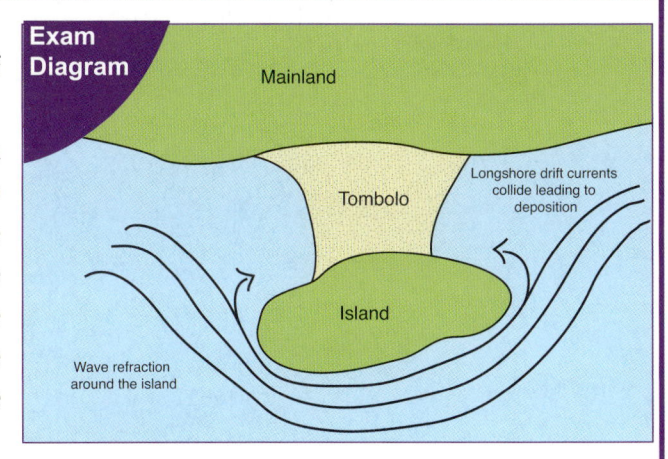

Fig. 35 The formation of a tombolo (a)

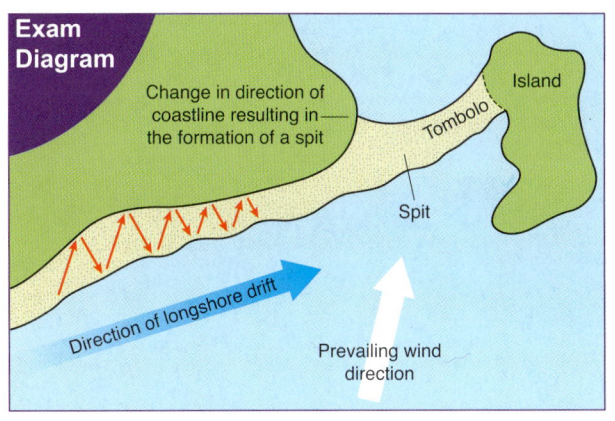

Fig 36 The formation of a tombolo (b)

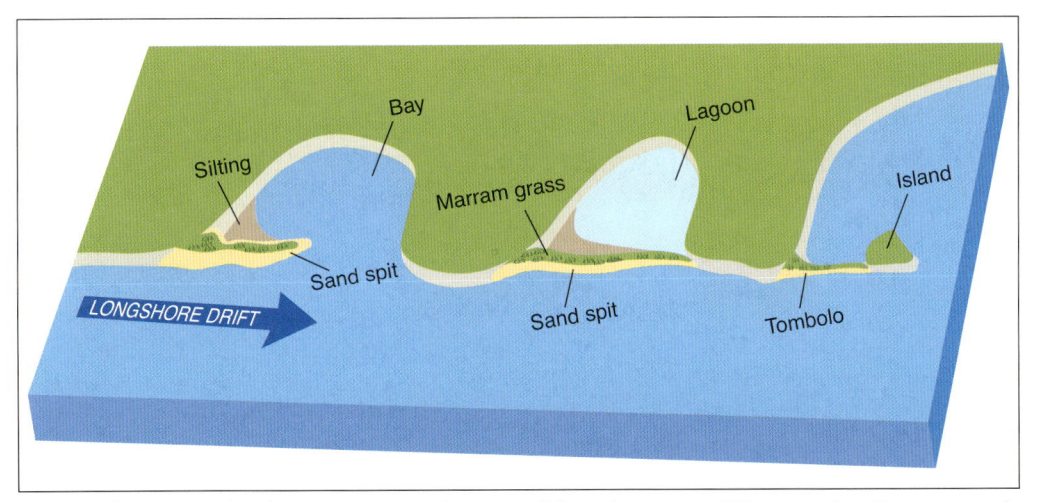

Fig. 37 Some sand spits grow across bays and form lagoons. Other sand spits grow and connect islands to the mainland forming a tombolo.

weblink
Spit and tombolo formation

179

CORE UNIT: PATTERNS AND PROCESSES IN THE PHYSICAL ENVIRONMENT

Fig. 38 Map of North County Dublin coast

Activity

Look at the map of the North Dublin coastline in Fig. 38.
Copy the table and then complete it.

Landform	Letter	Grid Reference	Formed by erosion or deposition
Cliff			
Tombolo			
Beach			
Sea stack			
Wave-cut Platform			
Headland			

10.5 Human interaction with coastal processes

Exam Note: You must study human interaction with river processes OR coastal processes OR mass movement processes

Coastal protection methods

In order to protect the coastline many methods of coastal management are used. These often affect the natural processes of erosion, transport and deposition.

Methods used to protect the coast fall into one of two groups: soft methods or hard methods.

Soft methods encourage deposition

Soft methods are designed to encourage beaches and dunes to form or get bigger. They may trap sediment moving along the coast or deflect waves to re
direct the transport of sediment in order to keep harbours free of sediment.

Soft methods usually work to strengthen the natural processes already at work in the sea, for example beach and sand-dune formation and longshore drift. Beaches are the best natural defence against the sea.

The following soft methods are used to encourage deposition:

1. **Fences** in **sand dunes** encourage build-up of wind-blown sand in dunes. Fences also prevent trampling of **marram grass**, which helps to stabilise the dune.
2. **Beach mats** are placed in front of dunes to trap sand and encourage plant growth.
3. **Beach nourishment** means that sand is pumped onto a beach to build it up.
4. **Groynes** are wooden or concrete walls which are build out at sea to trap the sand carried by longshore drift.

Fig. 39 Human activities affect coastal processes.

Fig. 40 Sand fences and marram grass encourage deposition.

181

CORE UNIT: PATTERNS AND PROCESSES IN THE PHYSICAL ENVIRONMENT

Fig. 41 Groynes at Rosslare Strand, County Wexford. Work out the direction of longshore drift in this photo.

Fig. 42 Map of Rosslare Strand to show groynes built along a sand spit. Note the beaches forming at the groynes protecting the sand spit.

Hard methods prevent erosion

These usually work to resist the force of the sea. They are carefully engineered structures designed to protect the coast from destructive storm waves and general wave action.

The following structures are built to do this:

1. **Sea walls** are built to prevent erosion of valuable land on the sea front, e.g. Tramore sea wall.

2. **Rock armour** are 1–2 tonne boulders placed in front of the coastline or at an existing sea wall. They absorb the energy of the waves, e.g. Courtown, County Wexford.

3. **Revetments** are sloping banks built to absorb the energy of the sea, e.g. Balagan Point, County Louth.

4. **Breakwaters** are concrete walls built some distance offshore to reduce the force of the waves before they hit the coast.

5. **Gabions** are wire mesh cages filled with large stones placed at the base of cliffs to absorb the energy of the waves, e.g. Newcastle Beach, County Wicklow.

Fig. 43 Tetrapods and rock armour in Spain

CHAPTER 10: COASTAL PROCESSES, PATTERNS AND LANDFORMS

Fig. 44 Rock armour and groynes protect this beach. Groynes are very effective methods for widening a beach and protecting the coast.

Fig. 45 Sea wall at Lahinch, County Clare

Bull Island, County Dublin

CHAPTER 10 Case Study 1

In Dublin Bay humans have changed the natural processes of coastal transportation, erosion and deposition.

Changing erosion processes in Dublin Bay

Before the 18th century, the natural process of longshore drift carried sand and silt southwards across Dublin Bay. The bay had two major sandbanks: the North Bull and the South Bull. These sandbanks prevented access to Dublin Port. The word 'bull' is adapted from the word 'ball' which in the 18th century meant 'sandbank'.

Dredging was carried out but ships frequently ran aground on the sandbanks causing expensive losses of cargo and many people were drowned.

In 1801 Captain William Bligh surveyed Dublin Bay and recommended the building of two sea walls, the North and South Bull Wall. Constructed between 1818 and 1824, the two walls changed the pattern of sea currents and deposition in Dublin Bay and helped maintain a clear channel into the port.

Fig. 46 Map of Bull Island

183

The Bull Walls acted like a funnel, speeding up the flow of water in the River Liffey as it flowed into the sea. They also increased the speed of the tidal flow in and out of the harbour. The increased hydraulic action of the river and tidal currents successfully kept the port clear of sand.

Changing transport and deposition processes in Dublin Bay

However, the North Bull Wall blocked the movement of sediment by longshore drift. As a result sand was deposited against the North Bull Wall. This deposition resulted in the formation of sand dunes and a salt marsh up against the North Bull Wall. Over time this deposition formed a sand spit called the North Bull Island.

The North Bull Island is a low-lying, dune-covered sand spit running parallel to the coast between Clontarf and Sutton in the northern half of Dublin Bay.

The island is approximately 200 years old and extends five kilometres in length. It is about one kilometre wide. It has a well developed dune system which runs the length of the island.

On the seaward side is Dollymount Strand, on the leeward side is a lagoon and salt marsh. At low tide the bed of the lagoon is exposed as mudflats which provide vital winter feeding grounds for migratory wildfowl such as Brent Geese from the Canadian Tundra and Iceland. North Bull Island is still growing but storms erode the seaward edge. The main human pressure on the island is erosion of the sand dunes due to the activities of thousands of visitors on summer days.

HUMAN IMPACT ON COASTAL DEPOSITION PROCESSES IN DUBLIN BAY	
Before the Bull Walls were built	**After the Bull Walls were built**
Deposition occurred in the sheltered mouth of the River Liffey.	Deposition occurred beside the North Bull wall forming Bull Island.
Sand bars shifted frequently and endangered shipping.	Both of the Bull walls increased the speed of tidal flow of water, keeping the mouth of the River Liffey clear of sediment and preventing sand bar formation.
Dublin harbour was only 1.8 m deep.	The harbour is now 6 -12 m deep.

Fig. 47 Bull Island, Dublin, looking south across Sutton tombolo

CHAPTER 10: COASTAL PROCESSES, PATTERNS AND LANDFORMS

Courtown Beach, County Wexford

CHAPTER 10 Case Study 2

Courtown Beach is a good example of how human activities have protected the coast from natural erosion processes.

1. In County Wexford erosion rates are some of the highest in the country, up to two metres per year in places. Severe erosion of more than one metre per year affects 13 km of Wexford coast.

2. Courtown is a major tourist centre in the county. The tourist industry in the Gorey/Courtown area has been built up around the Blue Flag beach at Courtown.

3. Coastal erosion of the beach at Courtown has been a major problem. Action has had to be taken to protect the beach. In addition, the dune and backshore area is an area of scientific interest. Any further dune erosion will lead to the loss of significant areas of tourist and amenity land as well as environmental damage to the adjacent woodland area.

Fig. 48 Location map of Courtown

Fig. 49 The result of severe coastal erosion along the Wexford coast

185

Soft coastal protection methods

1. Soft methods work with nature rather than resist it. Wexford County Council used a variety of soft engineering techniques including dune reclamation, sand fencing and marram grass planting in an attempt to trap sand and slow the erosion of the beach and dunes.

2. Winter storm waves overwhelmed many of their attempts to protect the shore. The council then had to use hard rock banks (revetments) and rock armour in order to prevent the immediate threat of further coastal erosion. Soft engineering techniques may be used on the dunes north of the Ounavarra river mouth where erosion rates are lower and there is less pressure on the beach and backshore area.

Fig. 50 Coastal defence at Courtown

3. Several alternative beach protection methods have been considered but not constructed:
   1. Beach nourishment
   2. Groynes
   3. Offshore breakwaters.

No method on its own would be enough to cure the problem. Wexford County Council has considered a number of options to provide the most suitable method of protecting this valuable stretch of coastline.

Some of the options that were identified by initial surveys of the coast at Courtown are described below.

Beach nourishment

This is when sand is added to the beach to replace that removed by longshore drift. Sand is pumped onto the beaches from sites under the sea off the coast. However, a beach nourishment scheme would be affected by the process of longshore drift. The rate of loss of beach material would be such that the maintenance cost would be too high.

Groynes

1. These walls are built at right angles to the shoreline and placed in a line stretching up and down the beach. They trap sediment carried by longshore drift.
2. A system of groynes could be used to stabilise the problem. However, during severe storms at Courtown, sediment would be carried out to sea. Either a regular renourishing programme or the use of specially shaped groynes would be required. However, any groyne system makes access difficult along the beach, and it is therefore unlikely to be acceptable on such an important recreational beach. Groynes have been used successfully further down the coast at Rosslare Strand.

Offshore breakwaters

1. Breakwaters are concrete walls placed some distance offshore. Tidal conditions at Courtown make the use of offshore breakwaters to control sediment movement an attractive option. The breakwater would slow the rate of longshore drift and allow the beach to grow.
2. As well as controlling the longshore drift, offshore breakwaters have the advantage of reducing the energy of waves reaching the beach during storms, thus reducing erosion.

> Archaeologists have found evidence of many villages that existed along the Wexford coast. They are underwater today.

So what is happening at Courtown?

During recent winter storms, damage was done to existing rock armour north of the harbour entrance at Courtown. Wexford County Council had to reinforce the coastline with 50,000 tonnes of fresh rock armour. Larger stones are being placed in front of the shore and revetment banks are being upgraded to prevent the sea overtopping the banks and eroding the land behind it.

Fig. 51 Working on coastal defence at Courtown

CORE UNIT: PATTERNS AND PROCESSES IN THE PHYSICAL ENVIRONMENT

Chapter Revision Questions

1. Explain the terms fetch, swash and backwash.

2. Explain the characteristics of constructive and destructive waves.

3. Name and explain **three** processes of marine erosion.

4. What conditions are necessary for coastal erosion to take place?

5. Explain the process of wave refraction. Draw a labelled diagram to show this.

6. With the aid of a diagram explain the process of longshore drift.

7. Match the processes A–E with the landforms 1–5.

Process	Landform
A. Air compression	1. Cave
B. Hydraulic action	2. Beach
C. Deposition	3. Sand spit
D. Longshore drift	4. Rounded beach pebbles
E. Attrition	5. Cliff

Letter	Number
A.	
B.	
C.	
D.	
E.	

8. Describe, giving examples and referring to the processes involved, the formation of the following landforms of marine erosion: cliff, cave, sea stack, arch.

9. Describe, giving examples and referring to the processes involved, the formation of the following landforms of marine deposition: beach, tombolo, sand spit.

10. What is the difference between hard and soft coastal protection methods? Name two examples of each.

11. How and why have humans affected the processes of erosion, transport and deposition in Dublin Bay?

12. How and why have humans affected coastal processes at Courtown, County Wexford?

Chapter 10: Coastal Processes, Patterns and Landforms

LC Exam Questions

Higher Level students must be able to answer Ordinary and Higher Level questions.

■ OL Questions

13. (i) Examine the photographs below of coastal landforms and correctly match each of the letters on the photograph with one of the named landforms in the table below.

Landform	Letter
1. Sea arch	
2. Blowhole	
3. Cliff	
4. Beach	

(ii) Which of the landforms named above was formed by the process of deposition?

14. Study the map extract and photograph that follow and answer the questions.
    (i) The feature marked X on the map joins Omey Island to the mainland.
        Was it formed by deposition or erosion?
    (ii) Name the feature marked Y on the photograph.
    (iii) Was it formed by deposition or erosion?

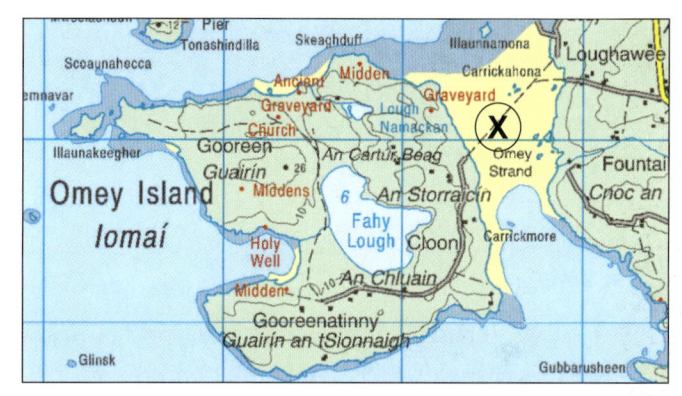

15. Select any **one** of the following surface processes:
    (a) Sea/marine action
    (b) River action
    (c) Glacial action
    (d) Mass movement.

    Explain the formation of any **two** Irish landforms caused by your selected process with the aid of diagrams.

16. Describe and explain how humans attempt to control **one** of the following surface processes:
    • River processes
    • Coastal processes
    • Mass movement.

189

CORE UNIT: PATTERNS AND PROCESSES IN THE PHYSICAL ENVIRONMENT

LC Exam Questions

■ **HL Questions**

17. (a) Identify **one** erosional and **one** depositional landform evident in the photograph to the right.
    (b) Describe and explain the process at work in the formation of any **one** of these landforms.

18. Explain with the aid of a labelled diagram(s) the formation of **one** landform of erosion that you have studied.

19. Explain the formation of **one** landform of erosion and **one** landform of deposition that you have studied.

20. Examine, with reference to example(s) that you have studied, how human activities have impacted on either river, coastal or mass movement processes.

21. The area of Ventry Harbour shown on the Ordnance Survey map below has been shaped by coastal processes.
    (i) Name **one** landform on the map that was formed by coastal processes and give a six-figure grid reference for its location.
    (ii) Describe and explain with the aid of diagram(s) the processes involved in the formation of this landform.

190

CHAPTER 10: COASTAL PROCESSES, PATTERNS AND LANDFORMS

Key Words

You should be able to explain both verbally and in writing each of the key words listed below.

Key Words Chapter 10

- abrasion
- air compression
- arch
- attrition
- backshore
- backwash
- bay
- bay head beach
- beach
- beach fabric
- beach mats
- beach nourishment
- berms
- blowhole
- breakwater
- cave
- cliff
- constructive wave
- cusp
- destructive wave
- fetch
- foreshore
- gabion
- geo
- groyne
- headland
- hydraulic action
- lagoon
- longshore drift
- notch
- marram grass
- revetments
- rock armour
- runnel and ridge
- sand dune
- sand fences
- sand spit
- sea stack
- sea stump
- sea wall
- slumping
- solution
- storm beach
- swash
- tombolo
- wave-built terrace
- wave-cut platform
- wave refraction

Digital Resources are available for this chapter at mentorbooks.ie/resources

CHAPTER 11

Mass Movement Processes, Patterns and Landforms

Learning Outcomes

At the end of this chapter you will be able to:
- Explain what mass movement is.
- Name and explain the factors that affect mass movement processes.
- Describe how mass movements are classified.
- Describe examples of each type of mass movement.
- Use case studies to show the impact of mass movement on people.
- Use case studies to show how people cause and control mass movement.

Contents

11.1	What is mass movement?	193
11.2	Factors affecting mass movement	193
11.3	Classifying mass movement	194
	Case Study 1: Lahar in Colombia, South America	197
	Case Study 2: The Derrybrien bog burst, County Galway	198
11.4	Human influence on mass movement	202
	Case Study 3: The impact of overcropping and deforestation in China	202

Exam Note

If you are studying this chapter in detail, you must be able to explain **mass movement** processes and how the landforms are made. You must be able to identify them on diagrams, maps and photos. The extra material you need to know is indicated by a yellow arrow. If you are not studying this chapter in detail, then you should be able to identify the landforms on diagrams, maps and photos and briefly explain the processes that made them.

Revision Space

Chapter Revision Questions – LC Exam Questions – Key Word List 203

CHAPTER 11: MASS MOVEMENT PROCESSES, PATTERNS AND LANDFORMS

11.1 What is mass movement?

Mass movement is the movement of material downhill under the influence of **gravity**.

The action of weathering (mechanical and chemical) and erosion processes form soil and scree which lie on the surface of the earth. This loose material is called **regolith**.

For mass movement to occur a slope must be present, whether gentle or steep. Some mass movement is so slow that it cannot be seen happening, while other types of mass movement are very fast and devastating.

Mass movements are often triggered by something. These triggers may be natural or man-made.

Fig. 1 Excavators clear a road after a landslide in Vietnam.

Natural triggers
1. Torrential rains
2. Heavy snow
3. Earthquakes and volcanoes

Human triggers
1. Building road cuttings across hillsides
2. Placing waste material on unstable slopes
3. Quarry blasting
4. Deforestation
5. Skiing in soft snow

Fig. 2 Road building on hillsides can trigger mass movement.

11.2 Factors affecting mass movement

Five factors encourage mass movement to happen.
1. Gravity
2. Slope
3. Water
4. Vegetation
5. Human activities

weblink
Mass movement

1. Gravity

Gravity helps stick the regolith (soil) to a slope or move it downhill. The speed of movement is proportional to the weight of the regolith to be moved and the steepness of the slope. Heavy particles on a steep slope will move more quickly.

2. Slope

Steep slopes cause fast movements such as avalanches and **landslides**.

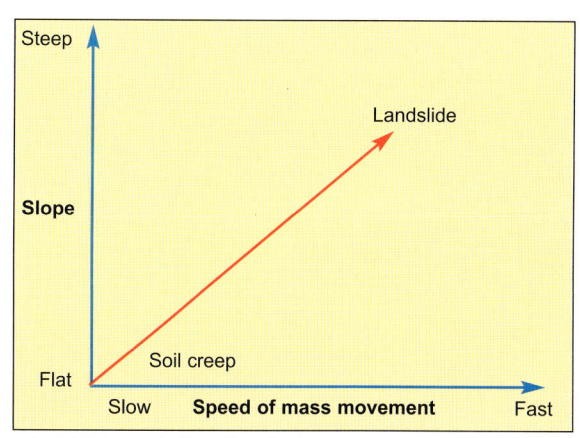

Fig. 3 The relationship between steepness of slope and the speed of mass movement

193

3. Water

Water is needed to stick soil grains together. However, too much water adds weight and helps the regolith slip downhill. When the regolith is saturated it slides easily over the ground.

4. Vegetation

The absence of vegetation increases the risk of mass movement on hills. Roots lock soil particles together, absorb water and shield the ground from rain. This prevents slippage and reduces the chance of mass movement occurring.

5. Human activities

People can increase the risk of mass movement happening by:

(a) undercutting hillsides for road and railway construction.
(b) building on unsafe areas such as landfills.
(c) building structures on slopes.
(d) building up mining waste heaps too high so that they become unstable.

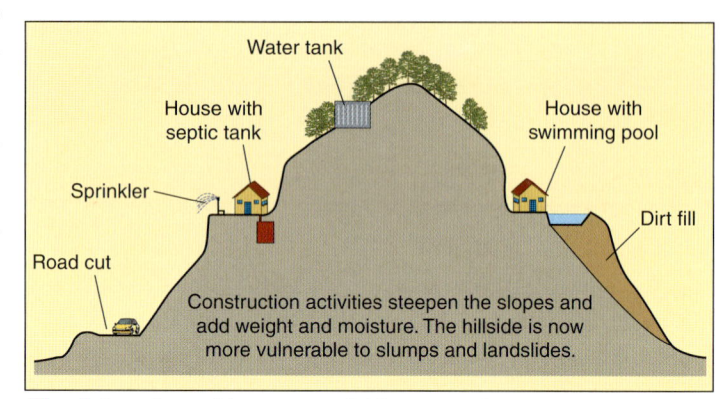

Fig. 4 A variety of human activities can trigger mass movement.

11.3 Classifying mass movement

Mass movement can be classified according to its:

1. Speed (fast, slow)
2. Water content (wet, dry).

TYPE OF MASS MOVEMENT	EXAMPLES
1. Slow	Soil creep and solifluction
2. Fast and wet	Mudflows, lahars, bog bursts, landslides and slumps
3. Fast and dry	Rock falls, avalanches

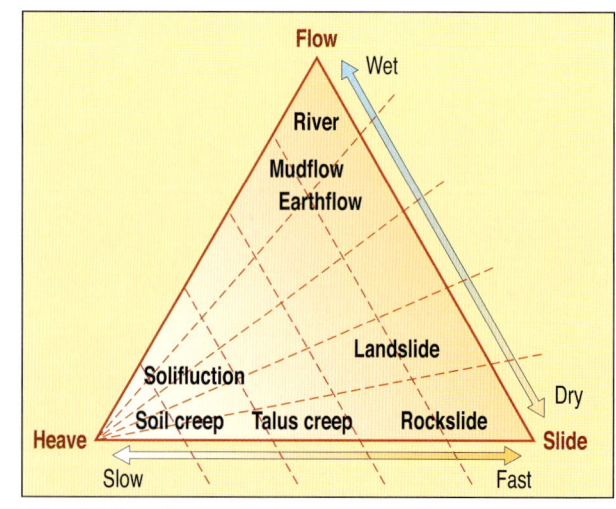

Fig. 5 The diagram above summarises the various types of mass movement. From this, we can see that a mudflow is a wet and fast type of mass movement. A rockslide is a fast, dry type of mass movement.

CHAPTER 11: MASS MOVEMENT PROCESSES, PATTERNS AND LANDFORMS

Slow mass movements

Soil creep

Main processes: freeze-thaw action, wetting, drying.

This is a very slow but continuous movement of soil downhill. It is common on grassy slopes in Ireland. **Soil creep** occurs so slowly you cannot see it happening, but it leaves tell-tale evidence behind.

Evidence of soil creep

Proof that soil creep is happening is quite widespread across Ireland. Such evidence includes:

1. Tilted telegraph poles and fences
2. Soil bulging against the upslope side of a wall on a hill causing the walls to burst
3. Terracettes (small steps) in grassy slopes
4. Cracks in roads parallel to the slope
5. Tree trunks that have curved as they try to grow straight up but their roots are moving downhill.

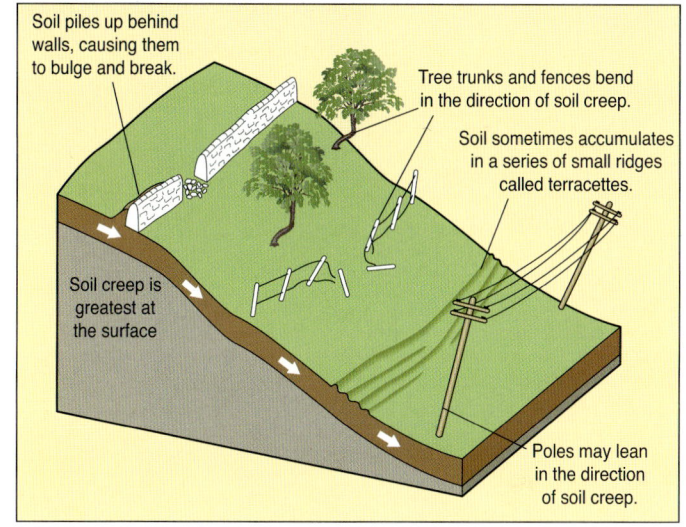

Fig. 6 Evidence of soil creep

IN DEPTH: Soil creep

Soil creep occurs due to the combination of two processes.

1. **Alternating wet and dry periods**
2. **Freeze-thaw action**

- During rainy weather soil grains expand (hydration) and are pushed up and downhill, away from each other. As the soil grains dry out during dry weather they shrink (dehydrate) and as they move closer to each other they roll slowly downhill. Repeated wetting and drying causes the gradual movement of soil downhill. Soil piles up against walls or forms **terracettes** and may cause fences and poles to tilt.
- During colder weather frost can cause the upward and downhill movement of soil grains as the ice expands. When the soil thaws, the soil grains move slowly further downhill.

All **IN DEPTH** sections contain material you need to know if you are studying this chapter in detail.

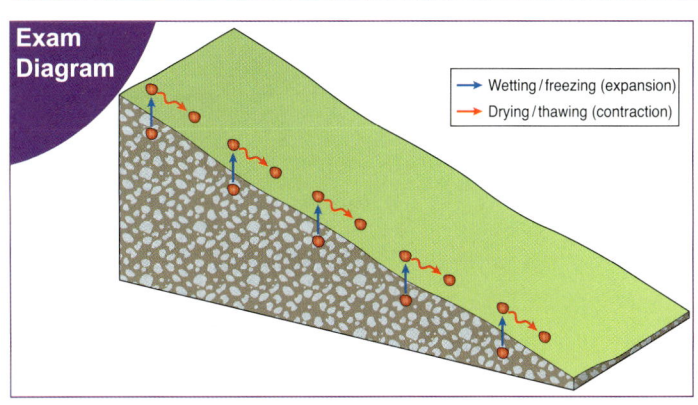

Fig. 7 How soil creep occurs

Fig. 8 Terracettes are small steps in grassy slopes.

195

CORE UNIT: PATTERNS AND PROCESSES IN THE PHYSICAL ENVIRONMENT

Fig. 9 Terracettes and curved tree trunks are evidence of soil creep.

Solifluction

Main processes: summer melting of permafrost, sliding.
Example: Upland areas in northern Canada.

Solifluction is a slow, wet form of mass movement. It produces landforms called solifluction lobes. Solifluction has probably not occurred in Ireland since the last ice age. It is common today in regions close to ice sheets (**periglacial areas**) such as Iceland, Canada and the Tundra areas of the world.

> The deepest permafrost in the world is found in Siberia. The ground is frozen to a depth of more than 300 m.

IN DEPTH: Solifluction

Solifluction occurs in areas where there is permafrost. The ground is frozen to a depth of several metres below the surface. During the summer the top metre or so may thaw out. The permafrost below prevents meltwater seeping down and so the topmost layer is a soggy mix of tundra vegetation and water. If this mix occurs on a slope it flows slowly downhill a bit like honey off a spoon and leaves behind curved bulges of soil called solifluction lobes.

Fig. 10 Solifluction lobes in Siberia, a landform created by mass movement

Fast and wet mass movements

Fast and wet mass movements 'flow' downhill like liquids but once they stop moving they quickly become completely solid, making the recovery of buried people nearly impossible. All wet mass movements contain a lot of water and are often triggered by heavy rain.

Mudflows

Main processes: heavy rain, flooding, sliding.
Example: Larne, County Antrim.

Mudflows are the most dangerous mass movements. They are slurries of mud, loose rock and water. They quickly gather speed and volume as they flow downhill. As they move, air, water and earth are mixed together and become an unstoppable river of debris. Mudflows can move over many kilometres destroying everything in their path. They occur on slopes with gradients greater than 25°, e.g. Southern Italy.

> weblink
> Mudflows in Austria

CHAPTER 11: MASS MOVEMENT PROCESSES, PATTERNS AND LANDFORMS

Lahars

Main processes: volcanic eruption, snow melt/heavy rain, flooding.
Example: Mount St Helens, USA.

Lahars occur when volcanic ash mixes with large amounts of water, making a volcanic mudflow. The water can come from torrential rain during an eruption or from snow melted from the top of an erupting volcano.

IN DEPTH: Lahars

- Lahars follow the landscape (**topography**) closely. Valleys become well-known paths of repeated lahar events. Lahars have the density of wet concrete and can travel at speeds of 40–100 km/h. Some have been recorded as reaching 300 km/h, e.g. the Mount Pinatubo eruption in the Philippines in 1991.
- When Mount Pinatubo erupted again in 1995 lahars did massive damage to farmland and roadways. The lahars left deposits which were up to four metres thick in places.

Lahar in Colombia, South America

CHAPTER 11 Case Study 1

1. This most damaging lahar occurred in 1985 on the Colombian volcano, Nevado del Ruiz. This volcano had created several devastating lahars in the past and it was a disaster waiting to happen. The town of Armero had been built on top of older lahar deposits that had flowed down the valley in 1845.

2. When the volcano erupted again in 1985 the heat of the lava melted the snow and ice on top of the mountain. The combination of ash, rock, meltwater and torrential rain caused several lahars that travelled up to 50 km/h down the slopes of the volcano. These lahars moved into the valleys and joined together to form larger flows, one of which was 30 m high and travelled at 80 km/h. This lahar hit the town of Armero, burying it under 8 m of mud and killing 23,000 of the 24,000 people in the town. The lahar hit at midnight when many of the residents were asleep – they had no chance to escape.

Fig. 11 Location map of the Nevado del Ruiz volcano and the town of Armero in Colombia

197

CORE UNIT: PATTERNS AND PROCESSES IN THE PHYSICAL ENVIRONMENT

3. The most tragic thing is that with proper planning this disaster would never have happened. Today the paths of lahars are mapped and predicted around many of the world's active volcanoes and (in developed countries at least) strict planning laws prevent settlement in lahar risk areas.

Fig. 12 The Armero Lahar of 1985

CHAPTER 11
Case Study 2

The Derrybrien bog flow/bog burst, County Galway

1. In October 2003 a bog flow (bog burst) occurred near the village of Derrybrien, County Galway. A combination of human activity and heavy rainfall triggered the burst.

2. This bog flow began within the site of a large wind farm development. The development area covers most of the summit of one of the main peaks in the Slieve Aughty Mountains. The area is covered by blanket bog to a depth of between 2.5 to 5.5 m.

3. While digging the foundations for the wind turbines, waste peat was piled up in unstable areas of the site. Bog drainage ditches were also blocked by these waste piles, allowing water to build up and adding to the weight of the bog on the hillside.

4. At first a large mass of bog moved downhill for a distance of 2.5 km. Two weeks later during heavy rain, the bog then travelled more than 20 km along the Derrywee River and entered a major fishing lough, killing more than 100,000 fish. Drinking water was polluted for weeks and had to be supplied by tanker to residents in the area. Roads were severely blocked restricting travel.

5. Many people used the event to protest against wind farms in general, but in fact poor site management and not wind farms themselves were to blame for the bog flow.

Fig. 13 The Derrybrien bog flow in County Galway

CHAPTER 11: MASS MOVEMENT PROCESSES, PATTERNS AND LANDFORMS

Slumps and landslides

Main processes: a trigger, gravity.
Example: South-east Brazil.

Slumps occur when rock or sediment suddenly moves downhill along well-defined surfaces which may be flat or curved. The common term for them is **landslide**. Landslides occur on steeper slopes and often move a larger amount of regolith.

IN DEPTH: Slumps and landslides

- Slumps are very common in Ireland especially along soft coastlines made of glacial till. When a slab of earth slips along a curved surface and rotates back on itself as it slides downslope, it is called a **rotational slump**. Water helps the slump or landslide to occur by reducing the sticking ability (**friction**) of the soil particles.
- Coastal areas are often at risk from rotational slumps as the sea undercuts the base of such cliffs.
- Some coastal rail links have been damaged in this way, e.g. Dublin to Greystones.
- Rotational slumps may be seen along the Louth coastline north of Clogher Head. Every winter slumps occur on soft coastlines around Ireland.

Fig. 14 A slump on the Louth coastline

Fig. 15 A rotational slump

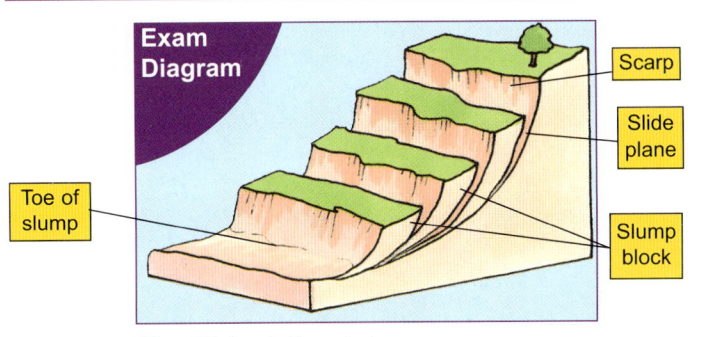

Fig. 16 Landslide at Greystones, County Wicklow

weblink
Landslides and their causes

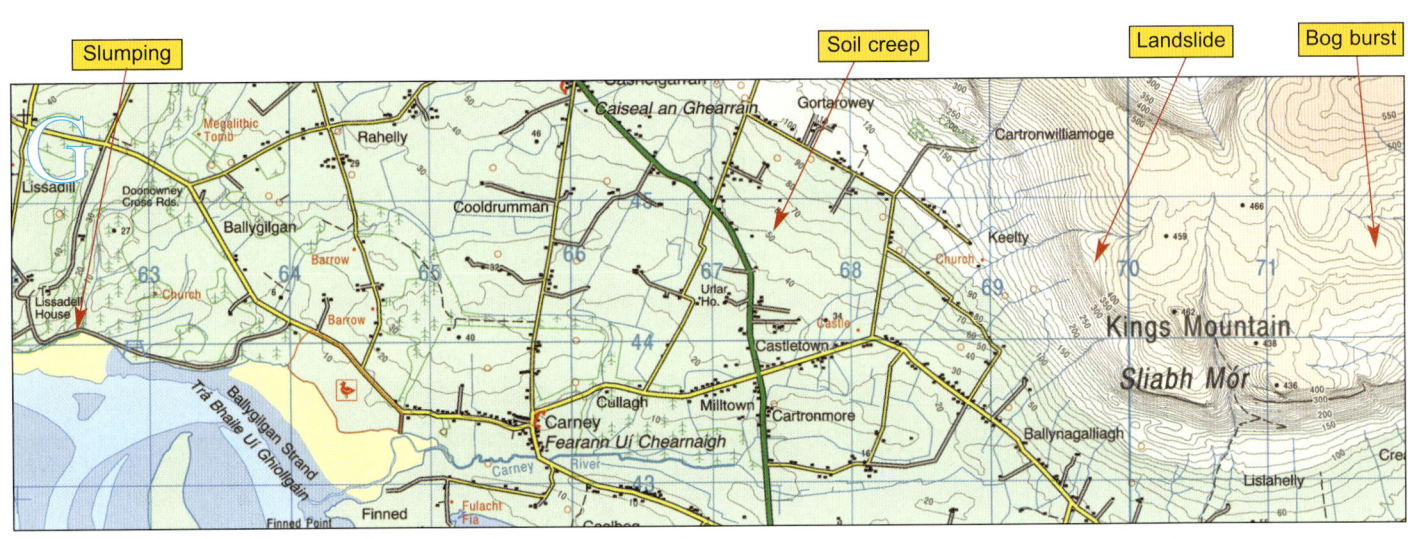

Fig. 17 Location for potential mass movement

Fast and dry mass movements

Avalanches

Main processes: gravity, weight of snow, a trigger.
Example: Swiss Alps.

Avalanches are considered to be dry mass movements because the frozen snowflakes act as dry particles. Avalanches occur when huge masses of snow and ice fall down mountainsides at great speed (up to 300 km/h). The study of avalanches is critical in the Alps where millions of skiers use the slopes each year.

IN DEPTH: Avalanches

weblink
Avalanches – further information

- Snow on a mountain builds up in layers. These layers stick to each other with varying degrees of strength. An avalanche occurs when the weight of fresh snow causes the layers of snow underneath to slide over each other. On an avalanche-prone slope a very small additional load, such as the weight of a single skier, can trigger an avalanche. Huge slabs of snow slide down the mountain at speeds of up to 300 km/h.
- Certain weather conditions can increase the risk of avalanches occurring. Fresh snow and wind create the greatest avalanche danger.
- Victims of avalanches are mostly skiers, snowboarders and mountaineers. The Swiss Federal Institute for Snow and Avalanche Research says that most avalanches are triggered by sporting activities on the mountain slopes. On average 26 people are killed by avalanches – the white death – in Switzerland every winter.

Fig. 18 Rescuers search for avalanche victims in snow. It is important that people stay on official ski runs. Off-piste skiing can lead to avalanches.

Fig. 19 Avalanche in the Caucasus Mountains

CHAPTER 11: MASS MOVEMENT PROCESSES, PATTERNS AND LANDFORMS

Rock falls

Main processes: weathering, a trigger, gravity.
Example: The Conor Pass, County Kerry.

In mountainous areas where bare rock is exposed to weathering, earthquakes and repeated frost action may trigger **rock falls**. Blocks of rock fall from steep slopes. Individual blocks may fall away from (or slide down) well-developed bedding planes or joints. The falling pieces bounce and roll downhill. Over time the debris from rock falls can build up into **scree (talus)** slopes. Active scree slopes are characterised by angular stones and an absence of vegetation.

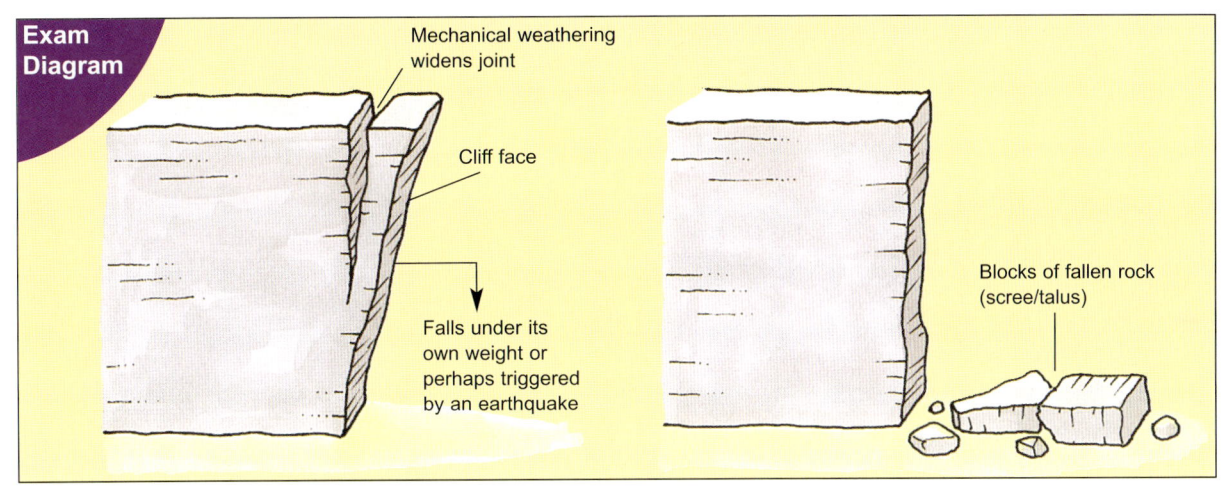

Exam Diagram

- Mechanical weathering widens joint
- Cliff face
- Falls under its own weight or perhaps triggered by an earthquake
- Blocks of fallen rock (scree/talus)

Fig. 20 A rock fall from a vertical joint

Fig. 21 Scree slope and rock fall in Glendalough, County Wicklow

Fig. 22 A warning sign on the Dorset Coast, England

Fig. 23 A rock fall in Cheddar Gorge, England

CORE UNIT: PATTERNS AND PROCESSES IN THE PHYSICAL ENVIRONMENT

11.4 Human influence on mass movement

Human activities can lead to an increase in mass movement. Landslides and soil erosion are more frequent as a result of overgrazing, overcropping and deforestation. Sometimes mass movement may be triggered by man, e.g. avalanches.

1. **Overgrazing** occurs when too many animals are allowed to graze an area of land. This damages soil structure and plants.
2. **Overcropping** occurs when land is continuously farmed in an unsustainable way.
   This reduces soil nutrients and destroys the structure of the soil, making it less fertile and easy to erode.
3. **Deforestation** occurs when large areas of forest are cut leaving a bare landscape. Forests provide natural protection for soil from rain and wind and so prevent mass movement.

CHAPTER 11 Case Study 3

The impact of overcropping and deforestation in China

Human activities which trigger mass movement.

1. Overcropping occurs when land is continuously farmed. It is not left fallow or refertilised properly. This causes the removal of nutrients from the soil. It also destroys the structure of the soil, making it loose, dry and infertile. Mass movement and erosion agents can then easily remove this soil. Deforestation is the cutting down of forests for timber and to clear land for farming.

2. Overcropping and deforestation causing soil erosion is a major problem in parts of China, which has lost more topsoil than any other region on the planet. Over 4 million hectares of cropland has been lost to soil erosion.

3. Overcropping happened for the following reasons:
   (a) Rapid population growth has also increased the demand placed on China's farmland.
   (b) The demand for higher yields to feed the growing population continues and increases the use of artificial fertilisers and pesticides. Too much of these reduce the health of the soil, pollute the region's rivers with toxic agricultural run-off and make the region more vulnerable to floods, further soil erosion and landslides.

4. The amount of farmland is reduced. Towns and cities have spread into the surrounding countryside. For example, in just 33 years an area of cropland the size of all the cropland in France, Germany and the Netherlands was converted to urban use. The remaining farmland was even more intensively cultivated, leading to overcropping.

5. This remaining farmland is being so overused that it cannot recover its lost nutrients, and it is now loose and dusty. Soil on even the gentlest of slopes moves downhill by mass movement, some barely noticeable, others as landslides. These remove vast quantities of topsoil so that bare, vacant scars are left where once there was fertile soil.

6. Forested land on hills is increasingly used as farm land. The land is cleared for farming but the exposed soil is eroding. The clearance of the tree cover removed the tree roots which had originally kept the soil anchored to the ground and protected it from strong winds and heavy rain.

> The population of China is expected to increase by at least three hundred million people by 2020.

CHAPTER 11: MASS MOVEMENT PROCESSES, PATTERNS AND LANDFORMS

Chapter Revision Questions

1. Name the **five** factors that affect mass movement. Briefly explain the effect each factor has.

2. What are the **three** types of mass movement? Name two examples of each type.

3. (a) With the aid of a diagram explain how soil creep occurs. Describe the evidence that may be visible in the landscape if soil creep has happened.

   (b) What is solifluction? Where does it occur? Describe the signs left in the landscape by the solifluction process.

4. Explain the following terms with reference to examples you have studied: mudflow, lahar, bog flow, soil creep.

5. Explain with the aid of a diagram how a rotational slump occurs.

6. Explain the term avalanche. How are avalanches triggered? What weather conditions increase the possibility of an avalanche?

7. Using examples you have studied, discuss how human activities can influence mass movement.

8. (a) Match each of the images below with the correct term:
   - Scree
   - Terracettes
   - Avalanche

   (b) State whether each image is as a result of mass movement or weathering.

A   B   C

CORE UNIT: PATTERNS AND PROCESSES IN THE PHYSICAL ENVIRONMENT

LC Exam Questions

Higher Level students must be able to answer Ordinary and Higher Level questions.

■ OL Questions

9. Examine this diagram of mass movement.

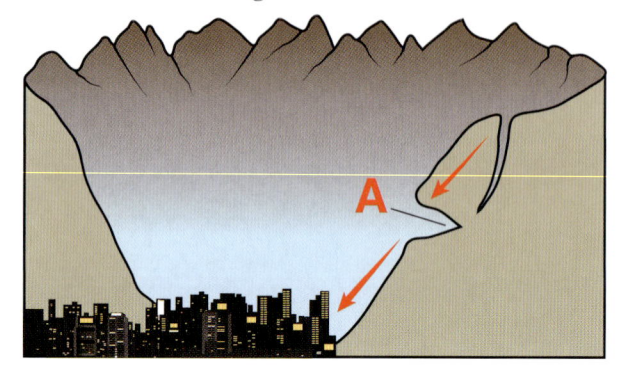

   (a) What type of mass movement could occur here?
   (b) What human activity at the area marked A could trigger a mass movement?

10. Explain briefly what is meant by mass movement.
11. Describe and explain any **two** processes of mass movement.

■ HL Questions

12. Describe and explain how humans attempt to control one of the following surface processes:
    • River processes
    • Coastal processes
    • Mass movement.
13. Describe and explain **two** mass movement processes that you have studied.
14. (a) Identify an area on the OS map below which has very steep slopes and give a six-figure grid reference for its location.
    (b) Describe and explain one mass movement process which might operate in an area such as this.

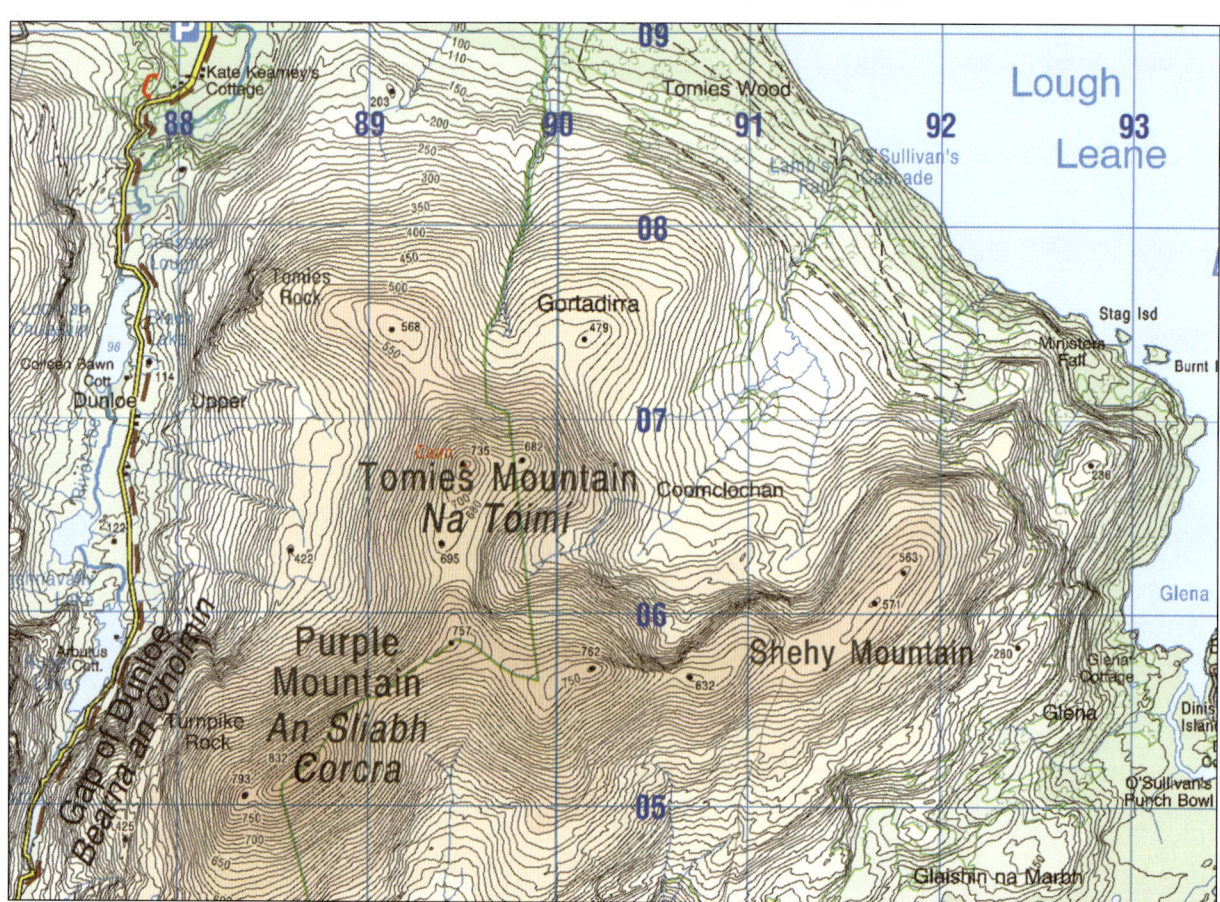

Key Words

You should be able to explain both verbally and in writing each of the key words listed below.

- avalanches
- deforestation
- lahars
- landslides
- mass movement
- mudflows
- overcropping
- overgrazing
- permafrost
- regolith
- rock falls
- rotational slumps
- scree/talus
- slumps
- soil creep
- solifluction
- solifluction lobes
- terracettes

Digital Resources are available for this chapter at mentorbooks.ie/resources

CHAPTER 12

Isostacy and Eustacy

Higher Level

Key Theme

Isostatic and eustatic processes involve adjustments to the balance between land and sea. This balance may change over time.

Learning Outcomes

At the end of this chapter you will be able to:
- Explain the terms isostacy and eustacy.
- Explain how changing sea/land levels affect river processes.
- Discuss the ancient development of Irish rivers.
- Understand the cycle of erosion and the formation of peneplains.

Contents

12.1	Introduction: The balance between land and sea	207
12.2	Isostatic and eustatic processes	207
12.3	River rejuvenation: Isostacy's influence on rivers	208
12.4	The ancient development of Irish rivers	210
	Case Study: Superimposition and river capture on the River Suir	212
12.5	Cycle of erosion and peneplains	213

Revision Space

Chapter Revision Questions – LC Exam Questions – Key Word List 214

CHAPTER 12: ISOSTACY AND EUSTACY

Higher Level

12.1 Introduction: The balance between land and sea

Over time a balance happens between the uplift and wearing down (**denudation**) of the earth's crust by weathering and erosion processes. Sometimes this balance is upset; uplift may happen faster than denudation for example. When this happens, sea levels change. These changes occur in two ways, **isostacy** and **eustacy**. In response unique river landforms occur. These unusual landforms are caused by changes in the level of the land and sea relative to each other.

12.2 Isostatic and eustatic processes

Isostatic changes

Isostacy is the process whereby the **land rises or falls** relative to sea level. The earth's solid crust floats on the more liquid mantle below in the same way that a ship floats on water. The weight of huge ice sheets on the land can cause the earth's crust to **push** into the mantle, in a similar way to when a ship is heavily loaded. When the ice is removed, the crust slowly returns to its original level, thus raising the land out of the sea. Similarly, when unloading a ship, it will float higher in the water.

Only the area of land affected by this ice may be raised from the sea so that sea level changes are local not global in extent. These local changes in sea level are called **isostatic sea level changes**.

Isostatic sea level changes may also happen when tectonic plates collide and cause uplift of land in certain areas, e.g. fold and block mountains.

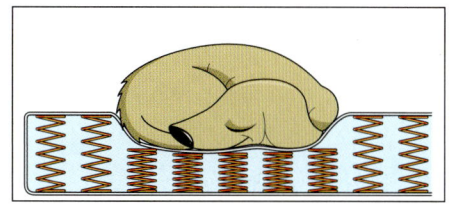

Fig. 1 What will happen to the springs when the dog gets up?

Eustatic changes

Eustacy is the process whereby **sea level rises or falls** relative to the land.

During an Ice Age the sea level drops because rain and river water is locked away in ice sheets on land and does not reach the sea. This lowers sea levels across the world. When the ice melts, large volumes of meltwater flow into the sea and cause global rises in sea levels. Such global changes in sea levels are called **eustatic sea level changes**.

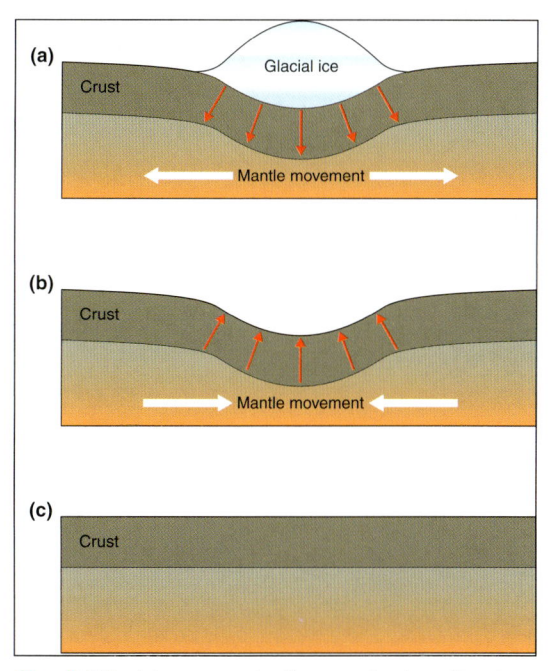

Fig. 2 What happens to the crust when the ice melts?

207

CORE UNIT: PATTERNS AND PROCESSES IN THE PHYSICAL ENVIRONMENT

Higher Level

12.3 River rejuvenation: Isostacy's influence on rivers

When a river's base level of erosion either rises or falls, **rejuvenation** happens. Rejuvenation means 'to make young again'. For a river this means it will begin to flow faster with renewed energy to reach sea level (known as a river's **base level**) even though it has flowed through its entire course.

Causes of rejuvenation

1. Isostacy: This is when land rises out of the sea due to tectonic activity raising the crust (called **isostatic uplift**). Isostatic uplift also occurs when a great weight is removed from the land (e.g. melting of an ice cap). The land gradually rises in response to the removal of the weight.
2. When water is locked away as ice, it causes a **lowering** of the sea level across the world.

Impact on a river's landforms

For a river to be rejuvenated, there has to have been a **drop** in the sea level (isostacy and eustacy). The **river's mouth** is now higher above sea level and the river has further to travel to reach the sea. This steeper gradient to the new base level gives the river extra energy and enables the river to renew or rejuvenate the process of **vertical erosion**. Erosional processes start to make a new **long profile** for the river.

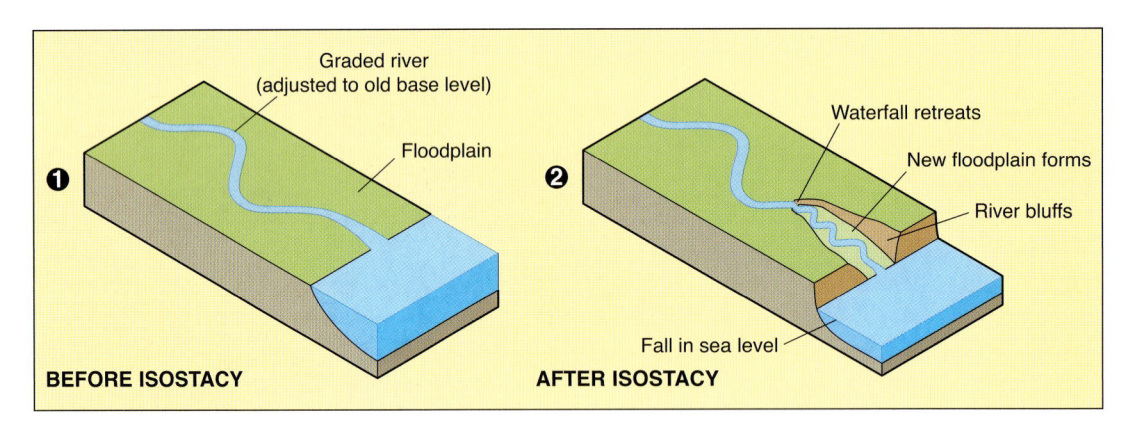

Fig. 3 The development of a rejuvenated river

Landforms of rejuvenation

1. **Knickpoints**
2. **River terraces**
3. **Incised/entrenched meanders**

These distinctive landforms show that rejuvenation has occurred and that there has been a fluvial adjustment to the new base level.

Chapter 12: Isostacy and eustacy

Higher Level

1. Knickpoints

Knickpoints are small waterfalls and rapids that mark the point of rejuvenation on a river's course after the land has risen out of the sea due to isostatic uplift.
Example: The River Barrow

Vertical erosion begins again. The river tries to erode down to a new base level. Erosion starts at the river mouth and works its way back upstream by **headward erosion**, cutting a new long profile. The point at which this newly eroded profile meets the old profile is marked by a waterfall or rapids, and is called a **knickpoint**. This is a definite break of a slope where the old profile meets the new river profile.

If rejuvenation has occurred more than once, the river may have several knickpoints, each one marking the renewed energy of the river as it begins to cut a new long profile into its old profile.

Some Irish rivers have several knickpoints, indicating several changes in sea level, e.g. the Shannon, Barrow, Nore and Suir rivers. Most knickpoints in Ireland today can be found in the mature and old stages of the river at 150–200 m above sea level showing that the sea once reached this level in the past.

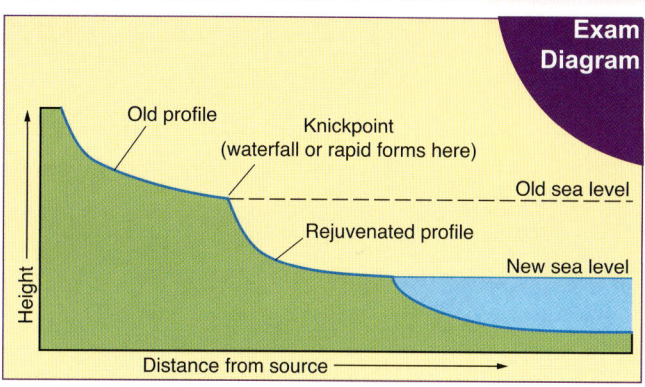

Fig. 4 Profile of a rejuvenated river

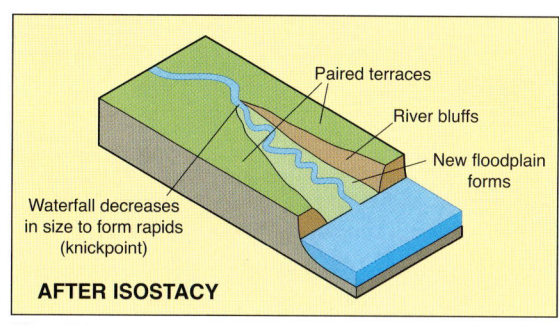

Fig. 5 The development of knickpoints and paired terraces after isostacy

2. River terraces

River terraces are flat stepped areas on each side of a river valley representing former floodplains.
Example: River Barrow

As a result of rejuvenation, **vertical erosion** by the river is **renewed** and the river cuts a new and narrower channel for itself. This leaves the former floodplain well above the present-day river level. Over time the river develops a new floodplain at a lower level within the older floodplain.

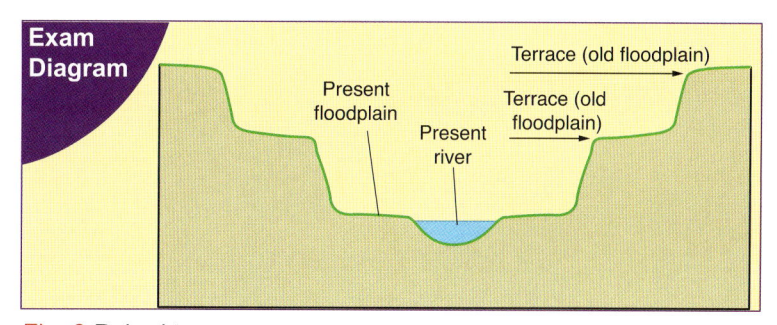

Fig. 6 Paired terraces

The new valley is gradually widened by lateral erosion. The remnants of the former floodplain are left as steps (**terraces**) high above either side of the rejuvenated river. These are called **paired river terraces**. If rejuvenation were to happen again, another set of terraces would be left, giving the river valley a **stepped** appearance (stepped terraces). Each set of terraces is often matched with corresponding knickpoints in the long profile.

CORE UNIT: PATTERNS AND PROCESSES IN THE PHYSICAL ENVIRONMENT

Higher Level

3. Incised/entrenched meanders

These are steep-sided meanders in the mature and old age stage of a river. **Example:** River Nore

As the rejuvenated river has renewed energy, it erodes vertically deep into the existing river valley. It engraves its meandering pattern into the bedrock below. The meander sides are steep and narrow and are called **incised meanders**.

This feature is well developed along the River Nore, south of Thomastown in County Kilkenny and along the River Barrow, north of New Ross, County Wexford.

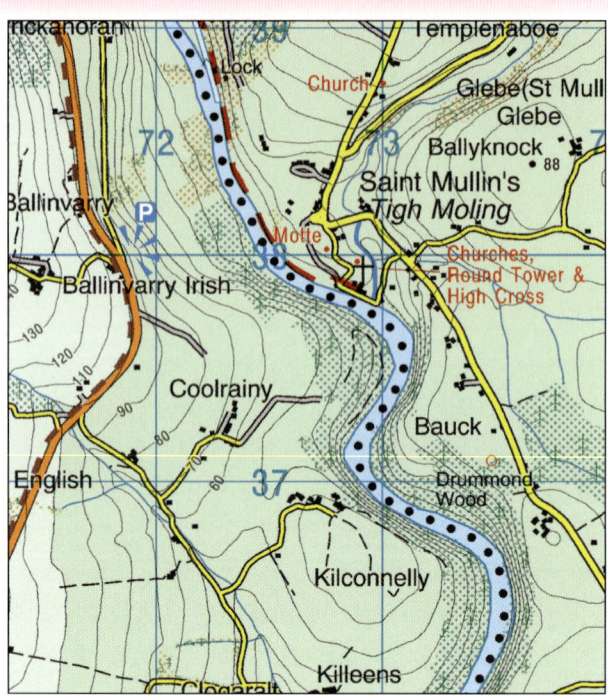

Fig. 7 Incised meanders on the River Barrow. Note the contour lines showing steep valley sides at each meander.

Fig. 8 Rejuvenated river in Colorado, USA. Note paired terraces, incised meanders and knickpoint.

12.4 The ancient development of Irish rivers

Superimposition

Superimposition occurs when a river imprints/stamps its course into older rocks beneath it. About 135 million years ago Ireland was covered by a warm, shallow sea. Chalk deposits were laid down at this time. They covered the older, folded sandstone and granite rocks below.

Later, much of Ireland was uplifted out of the sea exposing the sea bed which was then weathered and eroded. The rivers that formed at this time were the earliest ancestors of the rivers we see today.

CHAPTER 12: ISOSTACY AND EUSTACY

Higher Level

The Rivers Barrow, Slaney and Nore, as well as the south-flowing parts of the Rivers Suir, Blackwater, Lee and Bandon, all flowed south across the chalk landscape because the land they flowed over tilted towards the south. These rivers are called **consequent streams** because their flow is a result (consequence) of the slope of the land.

When these rivers had cut down through the chalk layer, they then began to erode the older rocks underneath. These older rocks were made of folded sedimentary sandstone rocks.

The rivers were able to vertically erode into the landscape which was much older than the rivers themselves. The rivers cut across the ridges (anticlines) in the folded rocks below. They imprinted (**superimposed**) their drainage patterns on the older rocks below.

This is seen on the River Barrow which has cut down into the Leinster granite at Graiguenamanagh, County Kilkenny. The deep north–south gorges of the River Lee and River Blackwater were caused by their **superimposition** upon east–west trending anticlines.

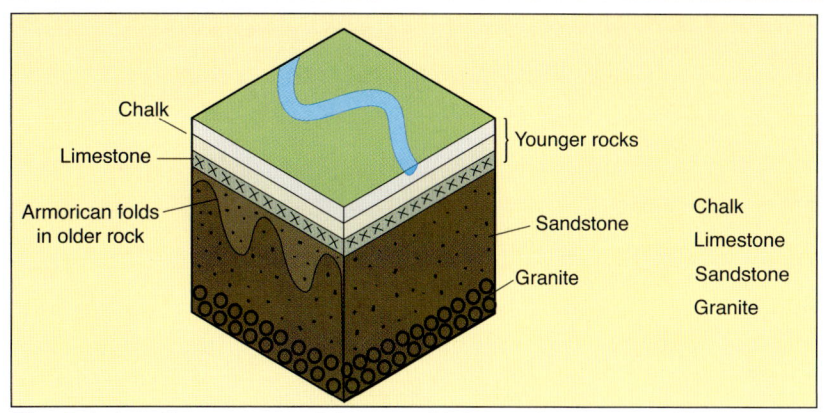

Fig. 9 A river flows over rock layers which are then removed by erosion.

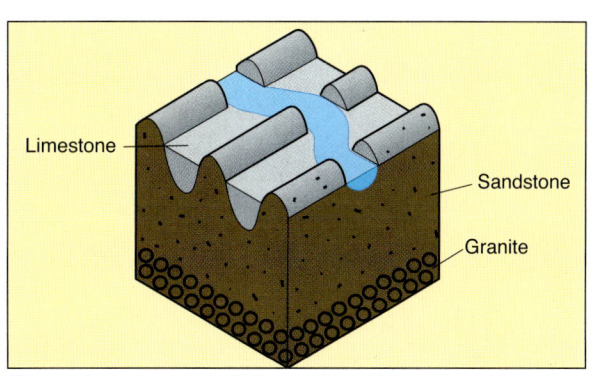

Fig. 10 **Important Information:** The river is now flowing over older rocks that have been exposed by erosion and weathering. The existing stream pattern has been superimposed on the newly exposed landscape.

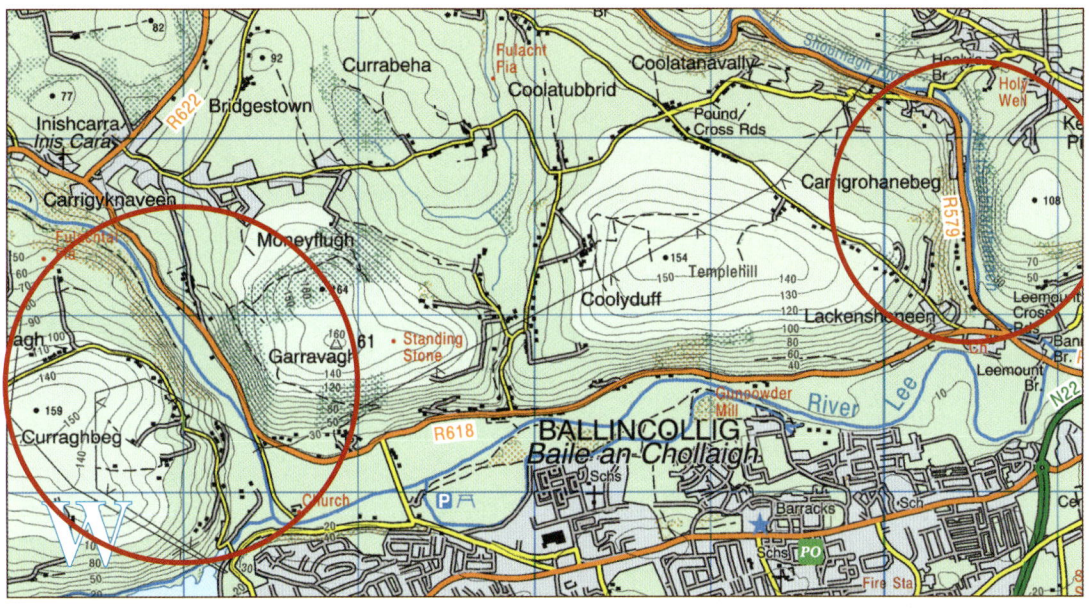

Fig. 11 The Shournagh River and the Inniscarra Gorge in Cork show how rivers have cut across a ridge of sandstone. They have superimposed themselves on an older landscape.

weblink
Landscapes - European Rivers

211

CORE UNIT: PATTERNS AND PROCESSES IN THE PHYSICAL ENVIRONMENT

Higher Level

CHAPTER 12 Case Study

Superimposition and river capture on the River Suir

An unusual drainage pattern can be seen in the rivers in Munster. This pattern can be explained by looking at the processes of **superimposition** and **river capture** – a part of the ancient development of Irish rivers. The River Suir shows unusual bends in its course. It flows south for a distance and then suddenly turns to flow east towards the sea. This happens because of the following events in the development of its drainage pattern.

1. In the past the main south-flowing (**consequent**) Rivers Suir and Barrow cut downwards and both superimposed themselves into folded rocks that had an east-west trend. The River Suir entered the sea at Youghal.
2. A young east-flowing (**subsequent**) tributary of the River Barrow flowed in an east-west trending valley. The River Barrow entered the sea at Waterford.
3. By a process of **headward erosion** the tributary of the River Barrow met up with the south-flowing River Suir and captured its water, diverting its course. This created a sudden right-angled bend in the River Suir near Clonmel.
4. The point of capture is called an **elbow of capture**.
5. In the past, the River Suir entered the sea at Youghal. Today, due to river capture it has a longer course and reaches the sea at Waterford.
6. The empty part of the valley south of the elbow of capture is known as a **windgap**.
7. South of the elbow of capture, the beheaded River Suir is now much smaller than it once was, since it has lost much of its water to the subsequent stream. It is now too small for its valley. This river is known as a **misfit stream** which is the present-day River Blackwater south of Cappoquin. The Blackwater enters the sea at Youghal.

weblink Stream piracy

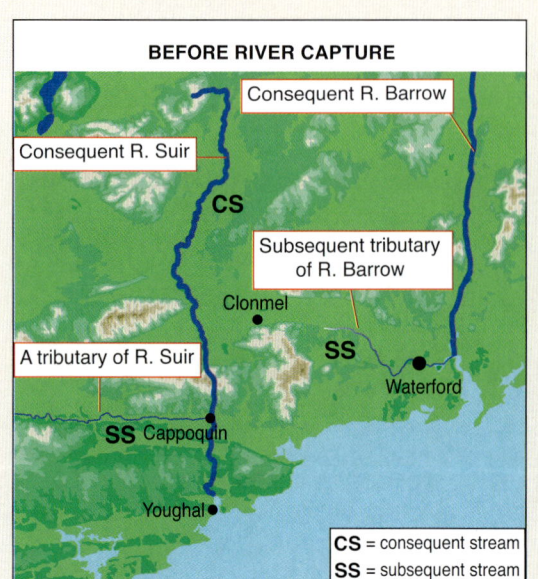

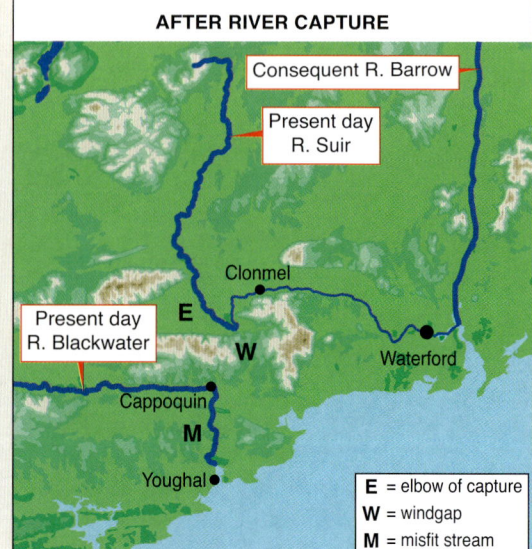

Fig. 12 Diagrams to show the course of the River Suir and River Blackwater

CHAPTER 12: ISOSTACY AND EUSTACY

Higher Level

12.5 Cycle of erosion and peneplains

The term **cycle of erosion** means the repetitive uplift of land and its wearing down (denudation) to a lower level. The processes of weathering and erosion wear away the uplifted land, eventually forming an almost flat, plateau-like surface called a **peneplain** (almost flat). The peneplain may contain low hills (residual hills) that are the remains of the once uplifted land surface. The cycle of uplift and peneplain formation may happen several times to a landscape due to plate movement.

Peneplain surfaces occur in Munster where Armorican folding formed mountains which have been worn down by weathering and erosion. From the Comeragh Mountains to the sea in Cork, a series of smooth upland surfaces (peneplains) occur that were possibly formed by wave action when the sea was much higher than it is today.

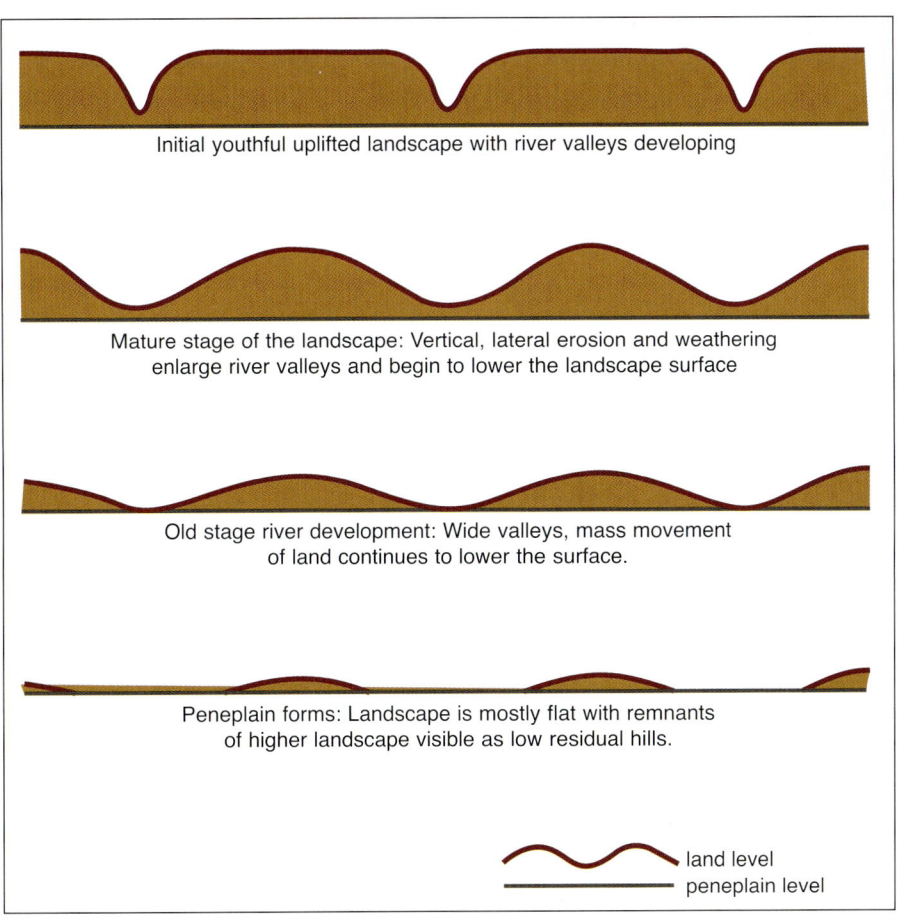

Fig. 13 Development of a peneplain

213

CORE UNIT: PATTERNS AND PROCESSES IN THE PHYSICAL ENVIRONMENT

Chapter Revision Questions

1. Explain the terms isostatic sea level changes and eustatic sea level changes.
2. Explain the term base level of erosion.
3. Explain the term river rejuvenation.
4. Explain **two** causes of river rejuvenation.
5. Name and explain **two** landforms made by river rejuvenation.
6. Draw labelled diagrams to show a knickpoint and paired terraces.
7. Explain how knickpoints are formed.
8. Explain the terms superimposition and river capture.
9. Explain the terms windgap and elbow of capture.

LC Exam Questions

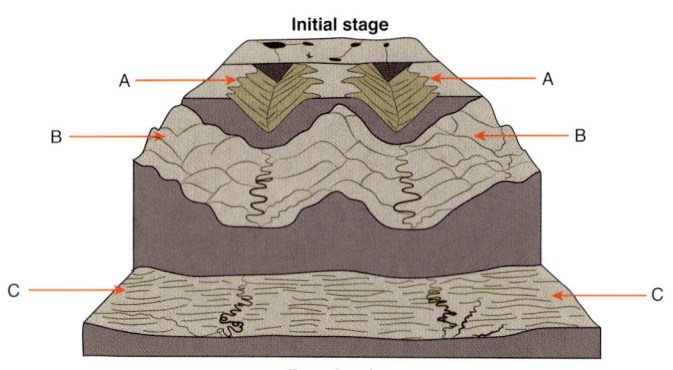

10. Examine the diagram above which shows the stages in the cyclical development of a fluvial landscape and answer each of the following questions.
    (i) Name each of the stages **A**, **B** and **C**.
    (ii) Name **one** fluvial landform from each of the stages **A**, **B** and **C**.
    (iii) Explain briefly what is meant by peneplain.
    (iv) Explain briefly what is meant by base level.

11. Explain the term isostacy.
12. With the aid of a diagram, explain the process of river capture. How has it affected the course of a named Munster river you have studied?
13. Isostatic processes involve adjustments to the balance between land and sea. Discuss how these processes have shaped the Irish landscape over time.
14. Explain how rivers adjust to a change in base level, with reference to example(s) that you have studied.

Key Words

You should be able to explain both verbally and in writing each of the key words listed below.

base level
consequent stream
cycle of erosion
elbow of capture
eustacy
eustatic sea level changes
headward erosion
incised/entrenched meander
isostacy
isostatic sea level changes
isostatic uplift
knickpoint
misfit stream
paired river terraces
peneplain
rejuvenation
river capture
river terrace
subsequent stream
superimposed
superimposition
terraces
windgap

Digital Resources are available for this chapter at mentorbooks.ie/resources

CHAPTER 13

OS Maps and Aerial Photos

Key Theme

Map and aerial photograph interpretation are key geographical skills which can be applied to a wide variety of geographical topics.

Learning Outcomes

At the end of this chapter you will be able to:
- Use a variety of skills to read and interpret information provided in OS maps and aerial photographs.

Contents

13.1	OS map-reading skills	217
13.2	Map interpretation	232
13.3	Aerial photo skills	239
13.4	Aerial photo interpretation	241

Revision Space

Chapter Revision Questions – LC Exam Questions – Key Word List 250

CHAPTER 13: OS MAPS AND AERIAL PHOTOGRAPHS

13.1 OS map-reading skills

A map represents a scaled-down plan of parts of the earth's surface. In this chapter you will learn the following map-reading skills:

1. Scale
2. Legend
3. Direction
4. Co-ordinate systems
5. Height
6. Slope
7. Area
8. Distance
9. Cross sections
10. Sketch maps
11. Calculating gradients **(HL)**

1. Scale

What is 'scale'?
Map scale is the relationship between a unit of length on a map and its corresponding length over the ground.

There are three different ways of describing scale on a map.
1. **Statement of scale:** The statement of scale is written below the scale bar on the legend on the map. On the scale bar in Fig. 1, the statement of scale is 2 centimetres to 1 kilometre.
2. **Linear** or **graphical scale:** Linear scales allow you to convert map distance to actual distance on the ground. You will use this scale bar later in the chapter.
3. **Representative fraction (RF):** A representative fraction indicates how many units on the earth's surface are equal to one unit on the map. On the scale bar in Fig. 1, the RF is 1:50,000.

RFs may be shown as an actual fraction (e.g. $\frac{1}{25,000}$) but are more usually written as a mathematical proportion with a colon (i.e. 1:25,000).
   So 1:50,000 means that for every 1 unit measured on the map there are 50,000 units on the ground. For example, if 1 centimetre on the map = 50,000 centimetres on the ground, then 1 centimetre = 500 metres (50,000 cm) and 2 centimetres = 1 kilometre (100,000 cm).

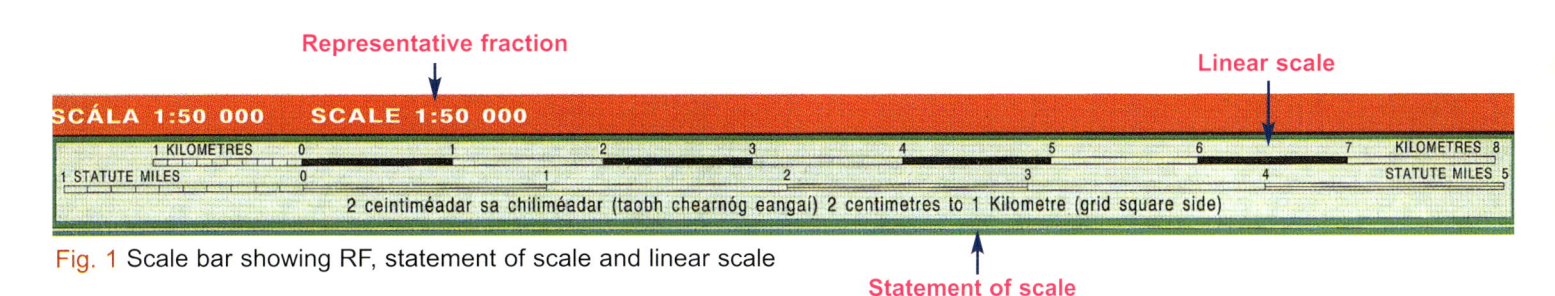

Fig. 1 Scale bar showing RF, statement of scale and linear scale

217

CORE UNIT: GEOGRAPHICAL INVESTIGATION AND SKILLS

> **Activity**
>
> Look at Figs. 2, 3 and 4.
> 1. For **each** give the RF and the statement of scale.
> 2. Rank the maps in order of scale – largest scale first.
> 3. Which map shows most detail? Write one reason for your answer.
> 4. Which map shows least detail? Write one reason for your answer.

Maps of different scales are used to show different levels of detail. When you zoom in on a map or photograph, your view of the map gradually changes from **small scale** to **large scale**. This changes the amount of detail we see.

(a) Small-scale maps

These maps show large areas with little detail, e.g. a map of the whole world could be at the scale of 1:100,000,000. The representative fraction (RF) of $\frac{1}{100,000,000}$ is very small.

A world map shows the names of countries and some larger capital cities, but it does not include minor cities, towns or villages.

A weather map on the TV news is also a small-scale map – it shows a large area in little detail, e.g. Europe.

Fig. 2 This is a small-scale map of the world.

218

CHAPTER 13: OS Maps and Aerial Photographs

(b) Large-scale maps

These maps show small areas in greater detail, e.g. town plans (1:1,000). The RF of $\frac{1}{1,000}$ is a larger fraction than the $\frac{1}{50,000}$ maps with which you are familiar.

These maps may show street names, rivers, mountains, hills and all major historical sites.

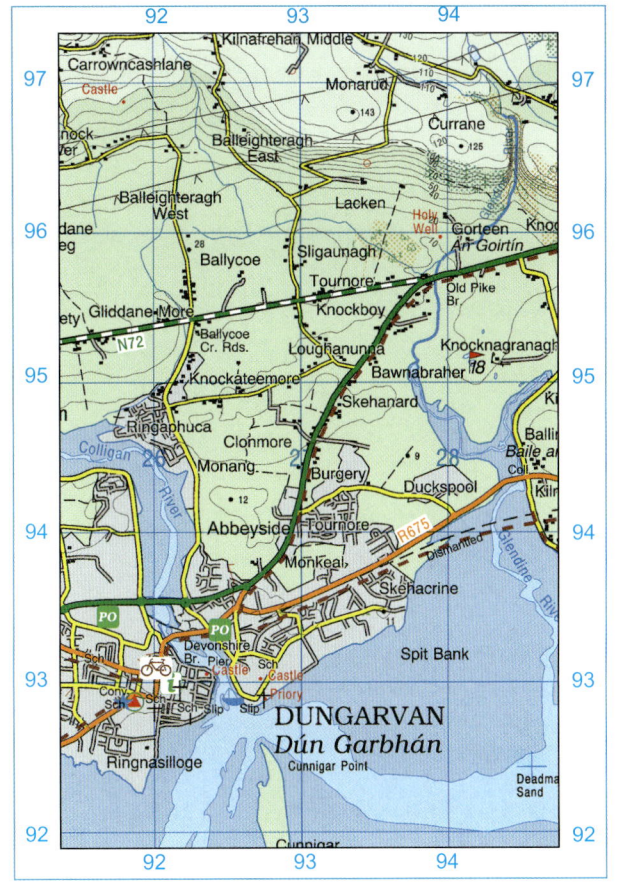

Scale: 1 to 50,000

Fig. 3 This is an OS map extract of Dungarvan in County Waterford at a scale of 1:50,000.
1 centimetre represents 500 metres ($\frac{1}{2}$ a kilometre).

Scale: 1 to 1,000

Fig. 4 This is an urban town plan of Dundalk at a scale of 1:1,000. In this map 1 cm represents 10 metres. This map shows a small area in large detail.

219

CORE UNIT: GEOGRAPHICAL INVESTIGATION AND SKILLS

2. Legend

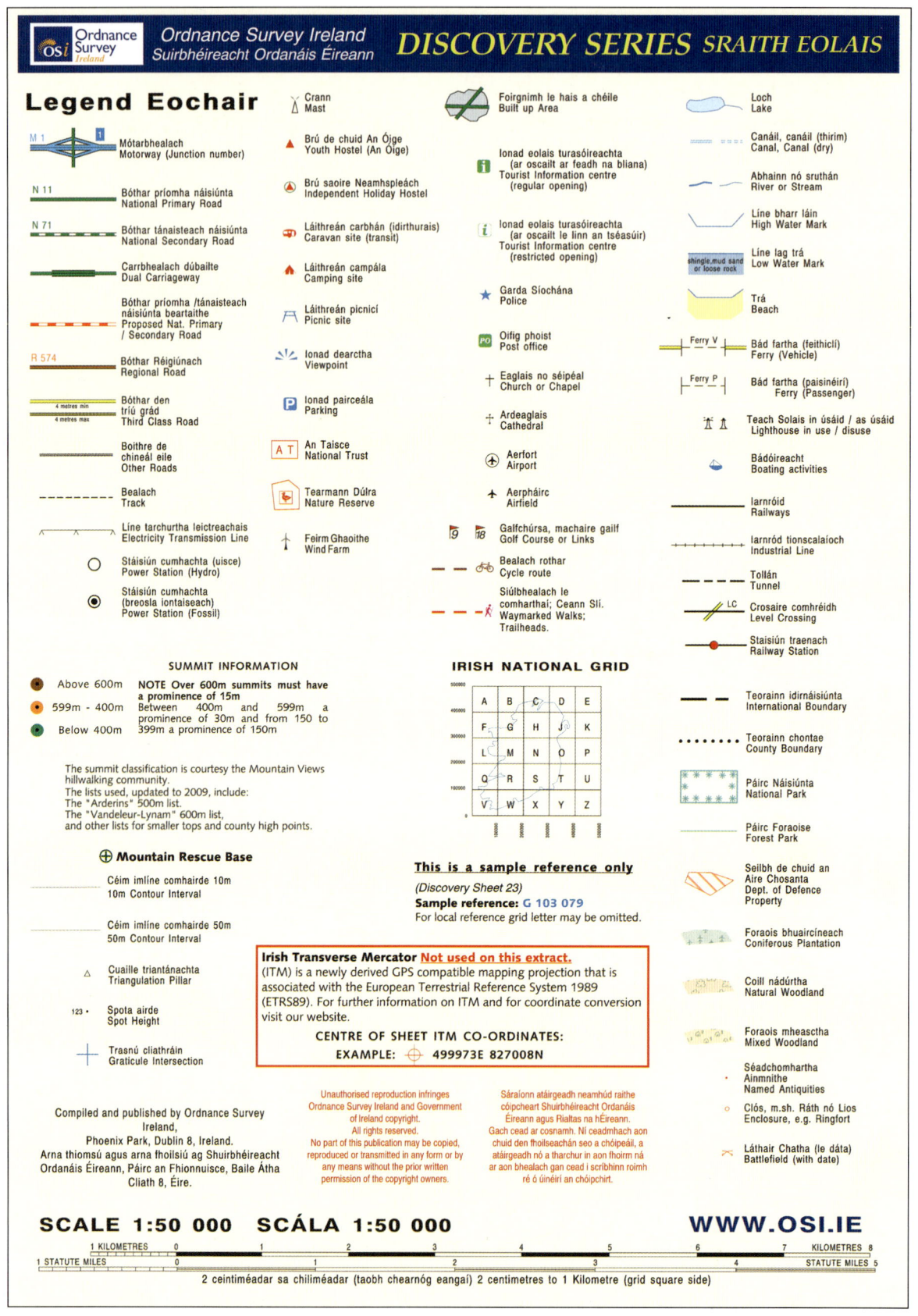

Fig. 5 The symbols that appear on OS maps are explained on a page called a legend or a key. In order to read OS maps correctly, it is important to be familiar with items on this legend.

3. Direction

Compass directions are used to give directions on maps.

When you hold the map so that the writing on it is the correct way up, the top of the map is pointing north. In the Leaving Cert Exam, an arrow with an N marked on it is often used to show north on the OS map.

You should learn the directions of the compass on Fig. 6.

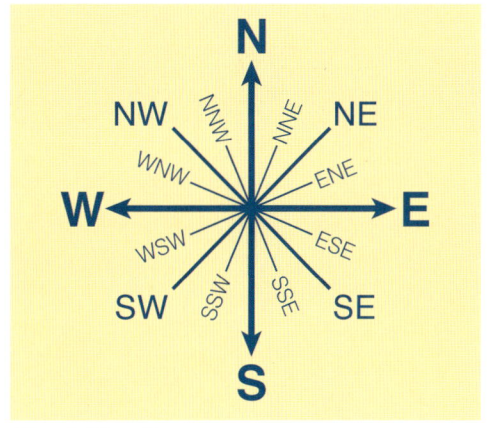

Fig. 6 Directions on a compass

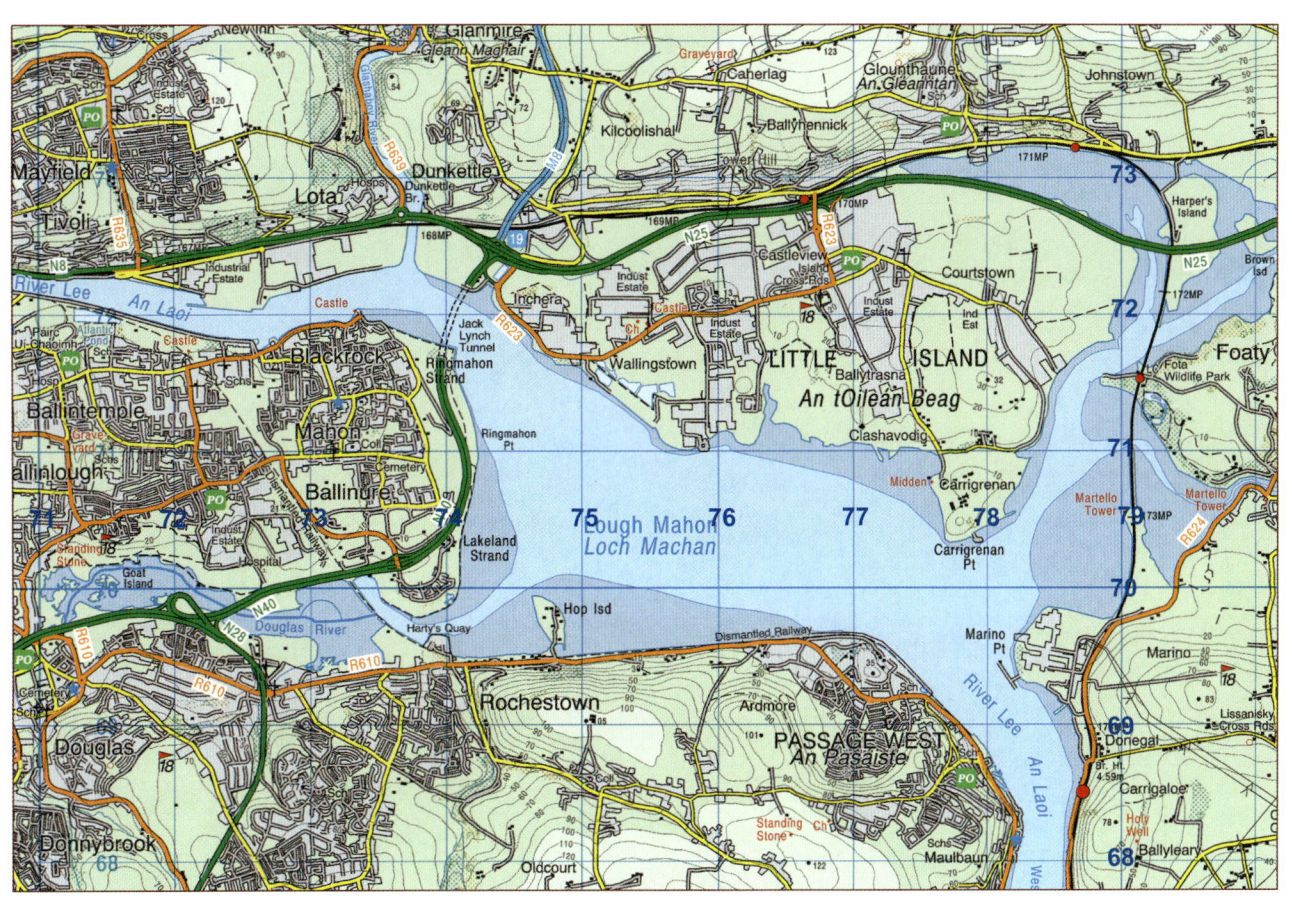

Fig. 7 OS map extract of Cork city

Activity

Map Skills Exercise
1. In which direction is the post office at Passage West from Little Island?
2. State the direction from the railway station at Fota Wildlife Park to Blackrock.
3. Which direction is the journey from the Jack Lynch Tunnel to the railway station near Carrigaloe?
4. State the direction of the journey to the post office on Little Island from Rochestown.
5. In which direction is the journey from the golf course at Douglas to the post office at Passage West?

221

CORE UNIT: GEOGRAPHICAL INVESTIGATION AND SKILLS

4. Co-ordinate systems: latitude, longitude, Ireland's National Grid and grid references

Latitude and longitude

Lines of latitude and longitude provide a global scale location.
Lines of latitude are drawn horizontally across the globe and are numbered every 10 degrees north or south of the equator. They are also known as **parallels**.

Lines of longitude are drawn vertically from pole to pole and are numbered every 15 degrees east or west from the **Prime Meridian** (0°). The Prime Meridian passes through Greenwich in London.

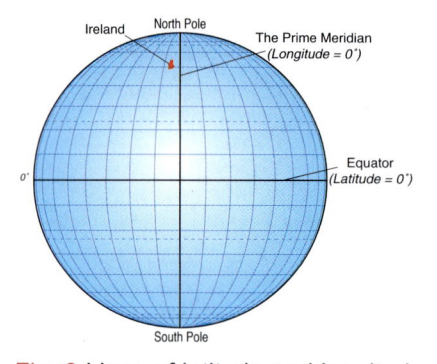

Fig. 8 Lines of latitude and longitude

The National Grid

The National Grid locates places in Ireland.
It divides the country into 25 squares or **sub-zones**. Each square is labelled with a letter from the alphabet, A to Z (no letter I). Each letter represents an area in the country. Identify the sub-zone in which you live.

Each sub-zone is divided into 100 equal parts numbered 00 to 99. Each part is marked by vertical lines called **eastings** and horizontal lines called **northings**. These are the blue lines you see on your OS map extract.

Each easting and northing line has a number. By using these co-ordinates or **grid references**, you can find the exact location of any place in Ireland.

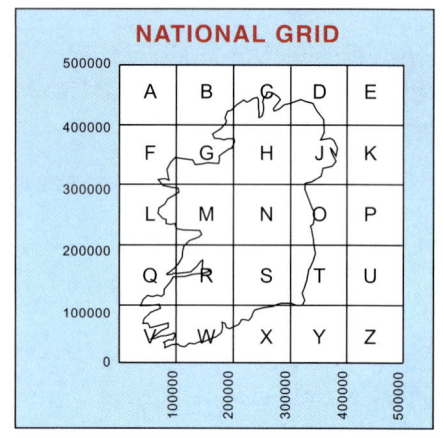

Fig. 9 The National Grid of Ireland

Grid references

To give an exact location on the National Grid, we use grid references. This involves 'finding **LEN**'.

- **L** = Identify the sub-zone **L**etter.
- **E** = Read the **E**asting co-ordinate (vertical lines). Count them eastwards.
- **N** = Read the **N**orthing co-ordinate (horizontal lines). Count them northwards.

There are two types of grid references depending on the detail needed:
1. four-figure grid references.
2. six-figure grid references.

Always read eastings first! Walk along the corridor (easting) and then go up the stairs (northing).

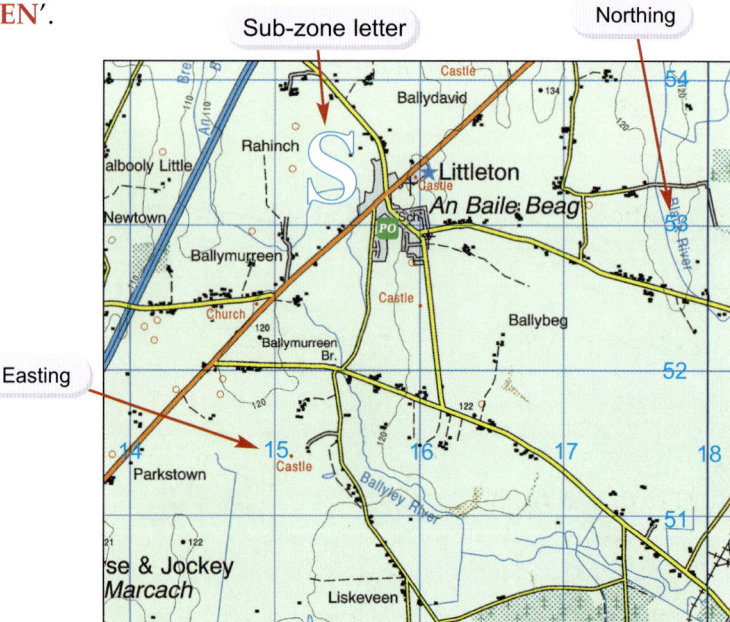

Fig. 10 Sub-zone letter, eastings, northings

222

CHAPTER 13: OS MAPS AND AERIAL PHOTOGRAPHS

1. Four-figure grid references

This **gives a less detailed location** for large areas or features which are quite easy to see on the map, e.g. a lake, a forest, a large town.

> On Fig. 11:
> The location of Lough Dan is sub-zone = O
> Easting co-ordinate = 15
> Northing co-ordinate = 03
> Therefore, the location of the lake of Lough Dan is O 15 03.

Activity

Map Skills Exercise (A)
1. What is located at O 14 05?
2. Locate the following as four-figure grid references.
   (a) Kanturk Mountain.
   (b) Scarr Summit.
   (c) The village of Laragh at the intersection of all of the valleys.

2. Six-figure grid references

This type of grid reference gives a more exact location.

It can locate specific landforms, sites or services on the map, e.g. an oxbow lake, ringfort or post office.

The same basic method is used to get this grid reference as is used to get a four-figure reference but an extra two numbers are added. These numbers are the further division in tenths of the distance between any two eastings or northings.

> On Fig. 11:
> The post office at Laragh is located at sub-zone = T
> Easting = 140
> Northing = 966
> Therefore, the post office at Laragh is T140 966.

Activity

Map Skills Exercise (B)
1. What is located at T 163 987?
2. What is located at T 147 982?
3. Give a six-figure grid reference for the car park to the west of Laragh.
4. Give a six-figure grid reference for the top of Paddock Hill north of Laragh.

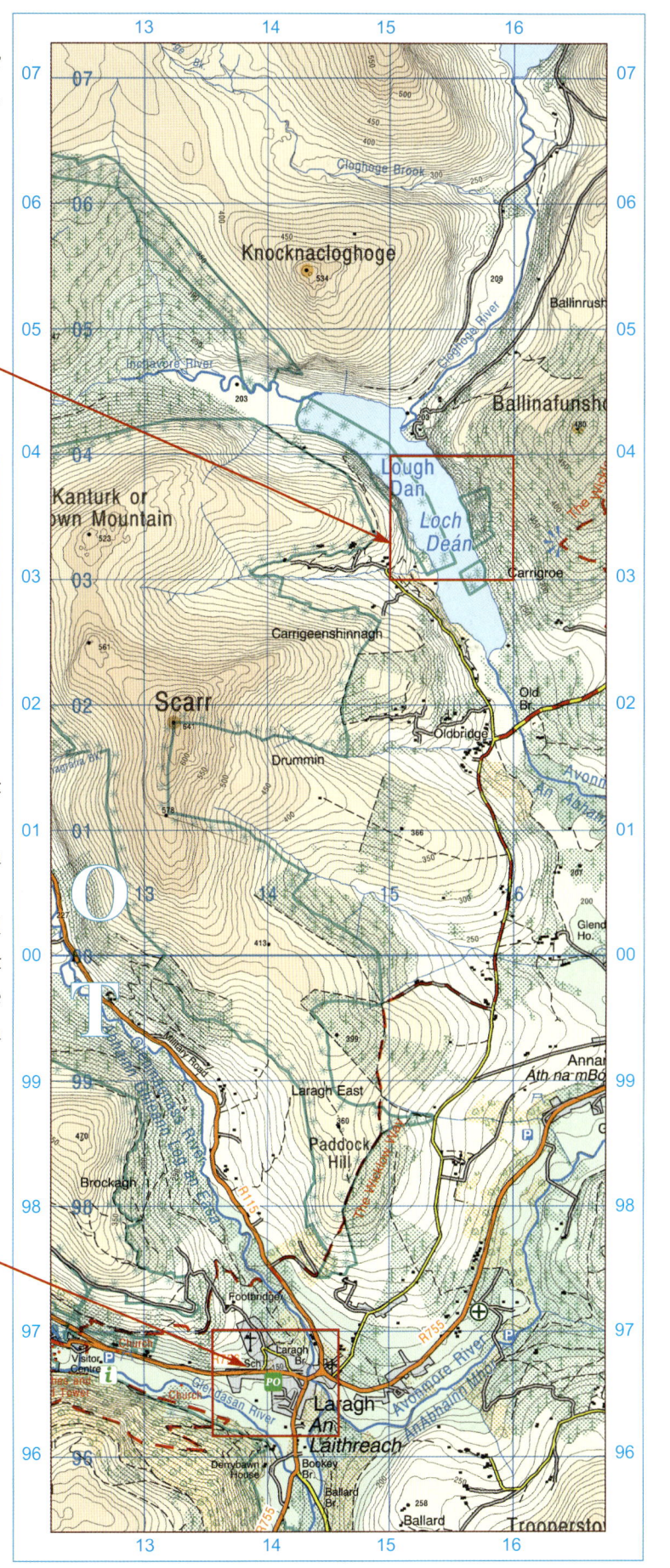

Fig. 11 OS map, County Wicklow

223

CORE UNIT: GEOGRAPHICAL INVESTIGATION AND SKILLS

5. Height

Heights above sea level in Ireland are measured in metres above mean sea level at Malin Head in County Donegal. This headland is used as the base line location because a headland can be an open area of sea and thus gives a more accurate sea-level reading. This base level is called **Ordnance Datum (OD)**.

Height can be shown on maps in the following ways:

(a) Colour layering
(b) Contour lines
(c) Spot heights
(d) Trigonometrical station / triangulation station.

Height (m)

- Above 600m
- 599m – 400m
- Below 400m

Name	Symbol
Contour line	—— 150 ——
Spot height	240 •
Triangulation pillar	△ 240

Fig. 12 Colour layering and symbols showing height on OS maps

(a) Colour layering

Colour is used to show height on OS maps. These colours give an immediate view of the lowland and highland parts of the map. See Fig. 12.

(b) Contour lines

These are lines which join all points of the same height above sea level (or OD).

As well as height, they also show the shape and slope of the land. Contour lines placed close together indicate steep land.

(c) Spot heights

Spot heights show the height of particular points. They are drawn as a black spot with a number beside it representing its height in metres.

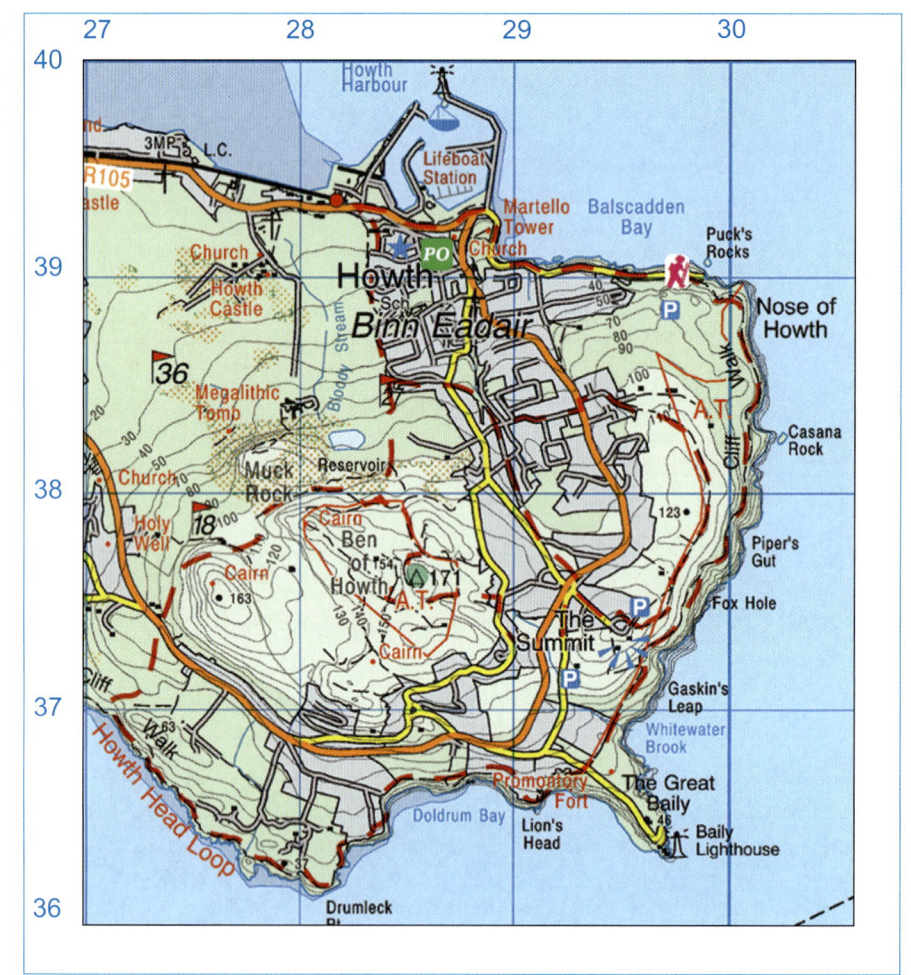

Fig. 13 Different ways of showing height on an OS map

Activity

Look at Fig. 13.
Name and locate an example of each method used to show height on this OS map.

CHAPTER 13: OS MAPS AND AERIAL PHOTOGRAPHS

(d) Trigonometrical/triangulation pillars

These fulfil the same role as spot heights except they are marked as open triangles on the map with the height written beside them. They are located on specific places which were important to surveyors in the past. The surveyors built a pillar to hold surveying equipment at the point marked. These stations usually show the highest peaks in a mountain range and have had further importance to communication systems in the country as TV, radio and phone masts are often constructed close to these points.

Fig. 14 Triangulation station

6. Slope

Contour lines can be used to work out the shape and slope of the land, e.g. they show the shapes of river, marine and glacial landforms such as V-shaped valleys, cliffs and corries and gentle, even and steep slopes.

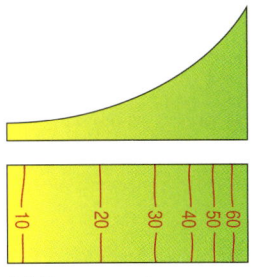

(a) **Concave slope**

(a) **Concave slopes** have a steep upper section (contour lines close together) and a gentle lower section (contour lines widely spaced).

(b) **Convex slopes** have a gentle upper section (widely spaced contours) and a steep lower section (contour lines are closely packed together).

(b) **Convex slope**

(c) **Even/graded/uniform slope**

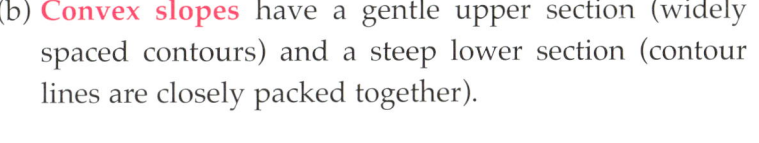

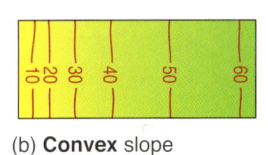

(c) **Even, graded or uniform slopes** have contours that are evenly spaced.

(d) **Stepped slopes** have contours that show a combination of flat and steep sections. **Steep slopes** have contours that are close together.

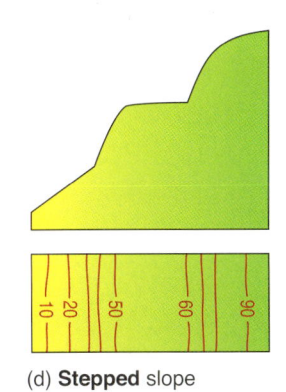

(d) **Stepped slope**

225

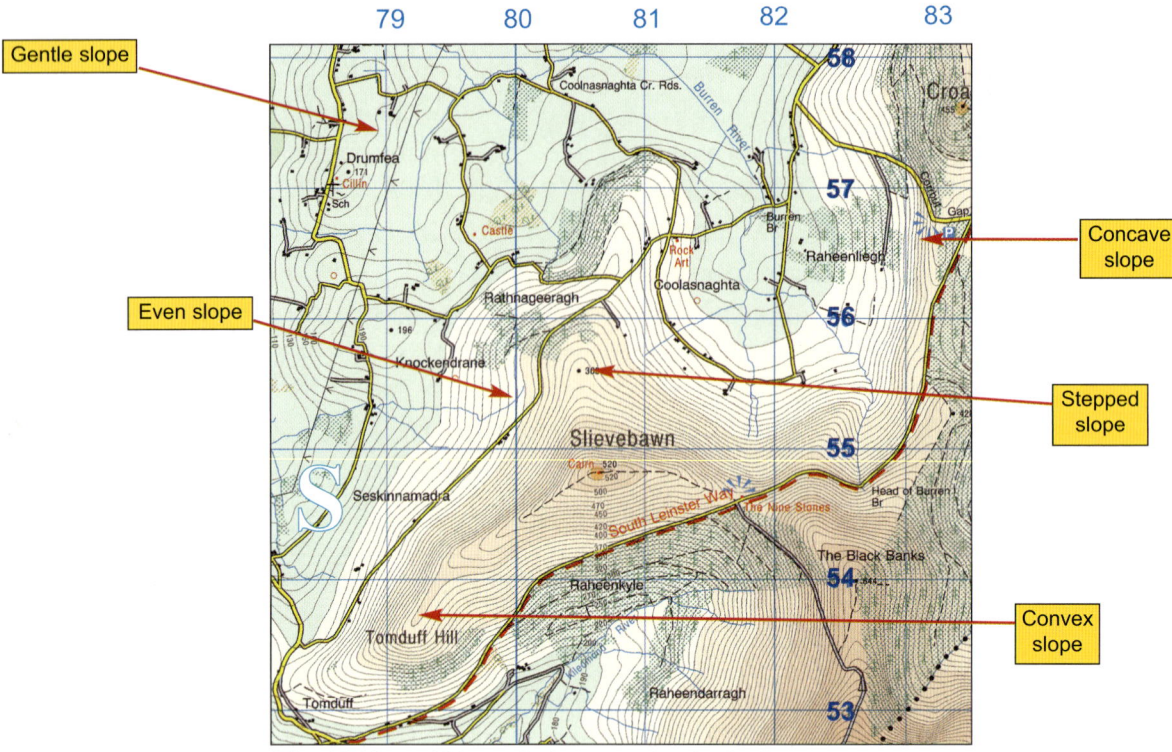

CORE UNIT: GEOGRAPHICAL INVESTIGATION AND SKILLS

Fig. 15 Map of Mount Leinster region in Carlow

7. Area

Remember: Each grid square is equal to 1 km².

To calculate the area of a rectangular region:
1. Count the number of full grid squares across the top of the map.
2. Count the number of full grid squares up the side of the map.
3. Multiply the two figures. That is the area in square kilometres.

In Fig. 16, the area of the whole map is 4 × 4 grid squares = 16 km².

To calculate the area of an irregularly-shaped region:
(e.g. forest park, a lake, mountain ranges, coastal area):
1. Count and place a tick in each complete grid square within the region.
2. Any square more than half covered by the item you are looking at is counted as one full square.
3. Add the two together. That is the approximate area in square kilometres.

The area of map covered by land on the Ventry map is 8 km².

Fig. 16 OS map of Ventry Harbour

Activity

What area of the map in Fig. 16 is covered by the sea?

226

8. Distance

There are two ways to calculate the distance between two places on a map.
1. **Straight line method.**
2. **Curved line method.**

1. To measure straight line distance (as the crow flies) between two points:

(a) Place the edge of a piece of paper on the two points on the map.
(b) With a pencil make a mark on the paper's edge where it touches the two points.
(c) Place the marked paper edge along the linear scale bar and read the distance.
(d) Using the linear scale bar, count the number of full kilometres to the right of the 0 km mark.
(e) Place any remaining measurement to the left of the 0 mark to get the tenths of the kilometre for an exact distance.

Short cut: If the map is 1:50,000 in scale, use a ruler to measure the distance between the 2 points in centimetres and divide by 2. This will give the answer in kilometres.

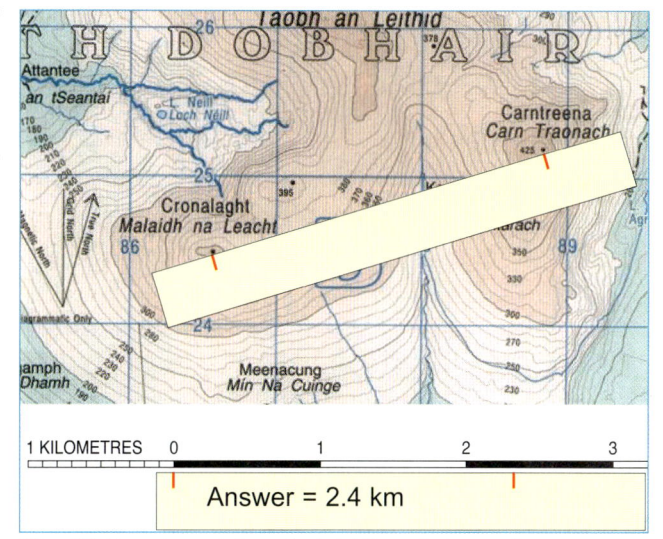

Fig. 17 How to get the straight line distance from Cronalaght to Carntreena in County Donegal

2. To measure curved line distance between two points:

This usually involves measuring roads, railways, rivers or coastlines.
In order to measure a curved line distance, break the distance into a series of small straight sections which you will mark on the edge of a strip of paper.

(a) Find your starting and finishing points on the map.
(b) Place the edge of a strip of paper on the starting point on your map. Mark the paper at this point. Line up the edge of the paper with the road or rail line to be measured.
(c) Make another mark on the paper and map where the road line moves away from (or under) the paper.
(d) Keeping the marks you made on the map and paper together, turn the paper to meet the road underneath and mark the next section of straight line.
(e) Repeat the procedure until you reach the end of the distance to be measured.
(f) Find the distance by measuring it along the linear scale bar.

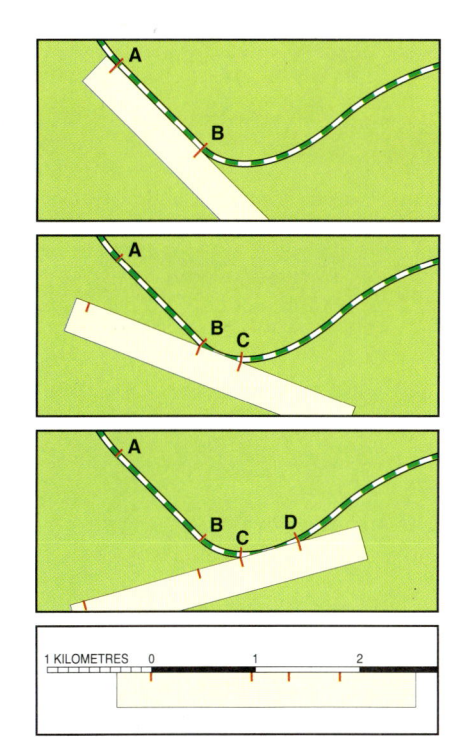

Fig. 18 How to get the curved line distance between two points

CORE UNIT: GEOGRAPHICAL INVESTIGATION AND SKILLS

Fig. 19 OS map of Sligo used to calculate distance

Activity

Using the map and scale bar above, answer the following questions:
1. Calculate the straight line distance in kilometres between the following places:
   (a) The railway station at G 687 361 and the camp site at G631 401.
   (b) The railway station in Sligo and the youth hostel at G 685 365.
   (c) The parking place in Rosses Point village and the parking place at Yeats' Grave.
2. Calculate the distance in kilometres:
   (a) Along the R291 from Rosses Point to the junction with the N4/N15 at G692 367.
   (b) Along the rail line from the railway station south to where it leaves the map.

9. Cross sections

A cross section is a side view of the landscape. It also shows whether one place can be seen from another (**inter-visible**) or if there is a mountain in between.

To draw a cross section, you will need graph paper, a pencil and a strip of paper.
1. Place the edge of the strip of paper along the line of the section to be drawn (**A–B**).
2. Mark the beginning and end of the section. If contours are tightly spaced, mark every 50 m.
3. Mark all the contours on the edge of the paper, noting the heights of each point.
4. On a sheet of graph paper, draw a base line the same length as the section you have just drawn (X-axis). Transfer all the markings and heights from your paper onto the base line.
5. Choose a vertical scale: In Fig. 21 the scale used is 2 cm = 100 m.
6. Draw a vertical line (Y-axis) at the left-hand edge of the base line and mark the vertical scale along this line. (2 cm = 100 m)
7. Using the heights marked on the base line, mark with a point each height using the vertical scale.
8. Join all the points.
9. Write the vertical scale you have selected (e.g. 2 cm = 100 m) and the horizontal scale (taken from the OS map) which is usually 1:50,000.
10. Write the title on your cross section.

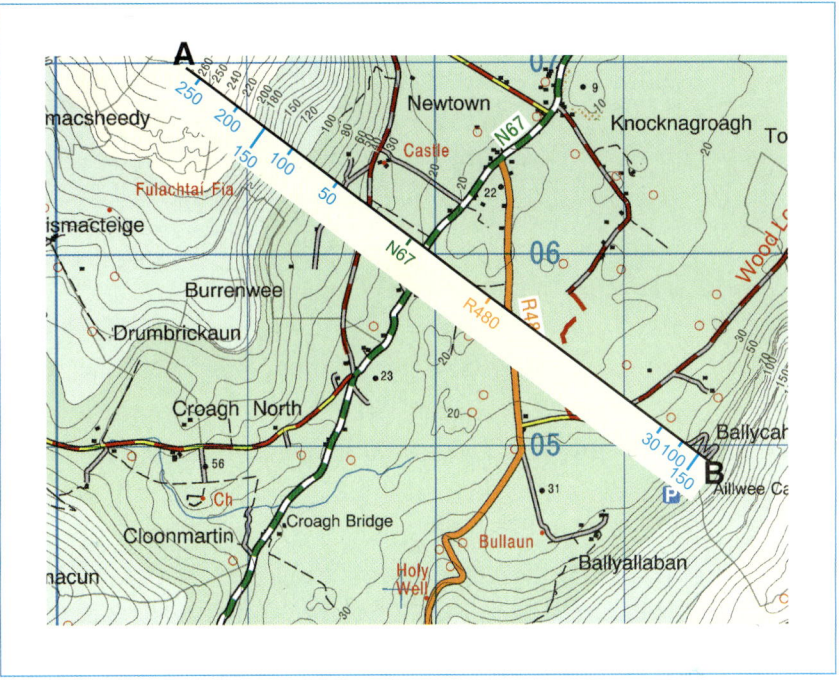

Fig. 20 Cross section

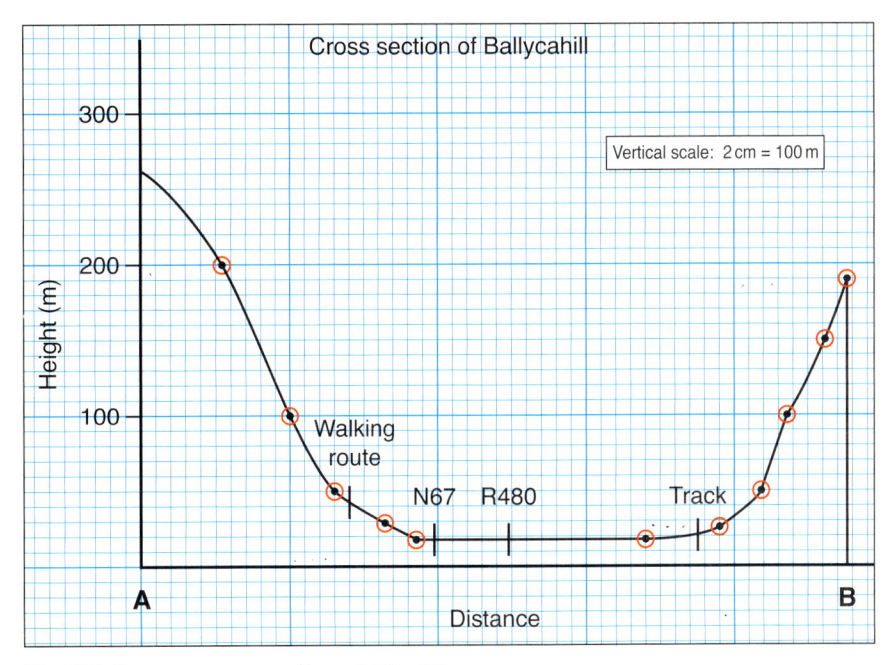

Fig. 21 Drawn cross section of Fig. 20

CORE UNIT: GEOGRAPHICAL INVESTIGATION AND SKILLS

10. Sketch maps

How to draw a sketch map to **half scale**.

1. Measure the map across the top with a ruler and divide your answer by two. This is the width in centimetres of the top and bottom of your frame.
2. Measure up the side of the map and divide your answer by two. This is the height in centimetres of the left and right sides of your frame.
3. Using **graph paper** and a ruler, draw the frame of your sketch in the **same shape** as the OS map.
4. Using a light pencil, divide the map and sketch into three evenly-spaced rows and three evenly-spaced columns. Use these rows and columns to draw the items in the correct position and in proportion.
5. Put a **title** and **sub-zone** letter on your sketch.
6. Mark the coastline and major lakes if shown.
7. Mark and label only what you have been asked to draw in the question.
8. Use a **key** to explain your colour code, labels and symbols if used.
9. Draw a **north arrow** and state the **scale**. If the scale of the map is 1:50,000, then half scale is 1:100,000 or 1 cm = 1 km.
10. Roads, rivers and rail lines should be represented by drawing a single line and then colour coded accordingly. (See Figs. 22 and 23.)

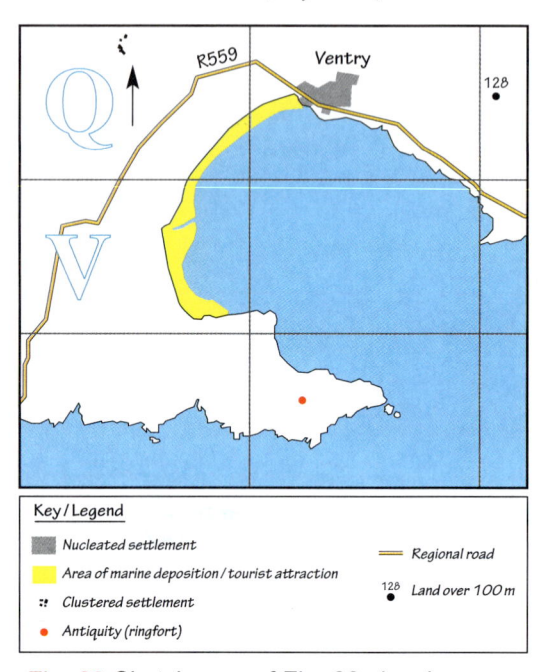

Fig. 23 Sketch map of Fig. 22 showing required symbols

Fig. 22 OS map of Ventry Harbour

CHAPTER 13: OS MAPS AND AERIAL PHOTOGRAPHS

11. Calculating gradients *Higher Level*

Gradient is a measure of the steepness of a hill or slope. Gradient can be expressed as a ratio and also as a percentage.

The average gradient of a slope is calculated from the contour lines on a map between two points.

How to calculate a gradient

To find the average gradient of a slope, the vertical distance (**rise**) as well as the horizontal distance (**run**) between two points on a slope has to be worked out. See Fig 24 below. The gradient is calculated by using the following formula:

Average Gradient = Rise ÷ Run

It is then possible to multiply this ratio by 100 to express the gradient as a percentage. See Fig. 25 on the next page.

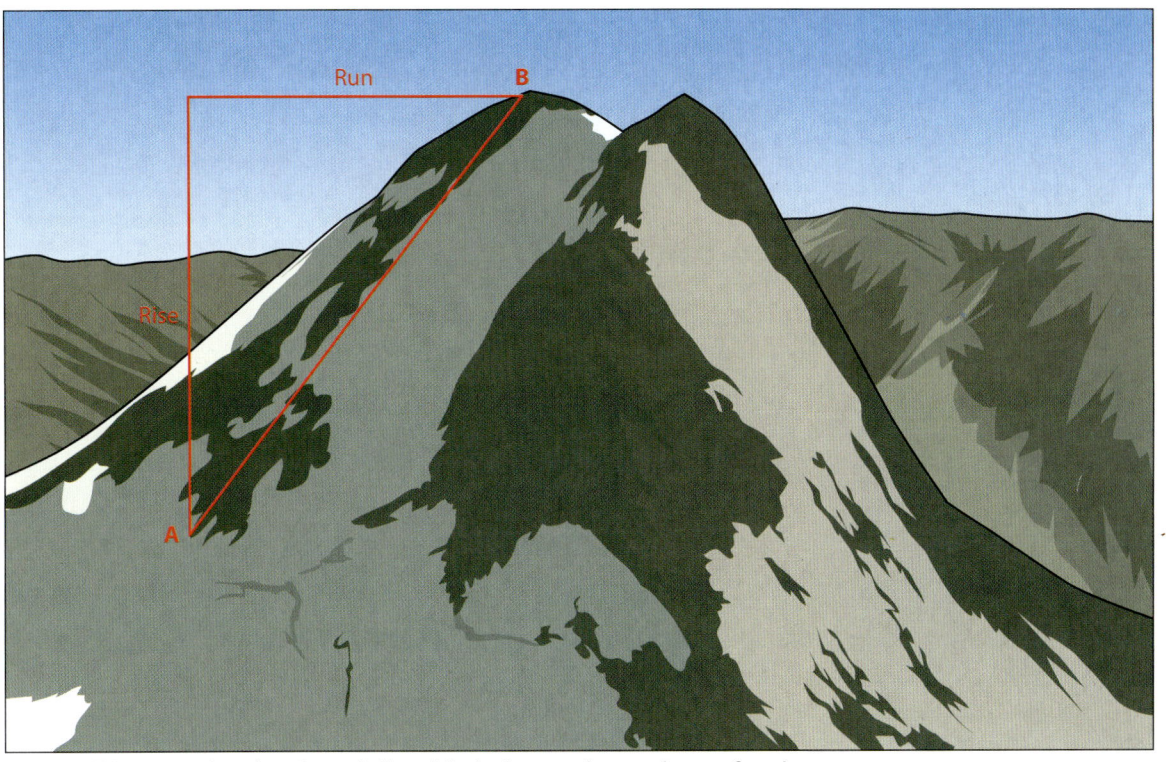

Fig. 24 Diagram showing the relationship between rise and run of a slope

231

The example below shows how to calculate the average gradient of the slope X – Y.

> **Calculating the gradient of a slope – Example**
>
> **We want to calculate the gradient of the slope along the red line X-Y.**
> From the contour lines we can work out that the 'Rise' is 275 m or 0.27 km as we climbed from 366 m to 641 m along the line. By measuring the straight line distance along the line as shown earlier on page 227, we can work out the length of the line or 'Run'. In this case it is 2.5 km.
>
> Using the formula **Rise divided by Run** the average gradient is 0.27/2.5 = 0.11. Multiplying by 100 gives the gradient as a percentage 11%.
>
> Often the gradient is stated as a representative fraction. This can be done by dividing the **Rise** into itself and into the **Run**.
>
> Using the above calculation, Rise/Run = 0.27/2.5 we can divide top and bottom by 0.27 to give the gradient in the form 1: 9.3. (0.27/0.27 = 1 and 2.5/0.27 = 9.3).
>
> This means that for every 1 m climbed we travel along 9.3 m.
>
> Fig. 25 Calculating the gradient of a slope

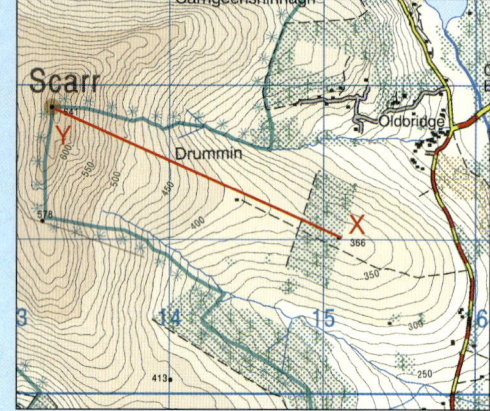

13.2 Map interpretation

Map interpretation involves a description and explanation of the patterns and shapes shown using symbols. Using any OS map as an example, you can see evidence of physical processes, human settlement and/or transport infrastructure, (see Legend, page 220).

Symbol recognition involves recognising symbols that represent historical sites, functions, land uses, communications/transport, infrastructure and other features.

Pattern recognition involves identification of landforms (see Chapters 8–11) and description of site and situation of settlement.

Symbol recognition

Many features are shown on an OS map using symbols. These symbols are explained on a page called a legend or key. All maps contain legends.

Using OS maps and their legends, you can describe:

1. **Relief and landscape features**
2. **Antiquities**
3. **Settlement patterns**
4. **Land use and function.**

CHAPTER 13: OS MAPS AND AERIAL PHOTOGRAPHS

1. Relief and landscape features

The map below shows a variety of coastal, glacial and fluvial landforms.

Labels on map: Bay, Plateau, Hill, Cliff, V-shaped valley, Col (small dip between two hills), Dendritic drainage pattern, Ridge and watershed, Meander, Confluence, Concave slope, Floor of glaciated valley, Ribbon lakes, Arête, Corrie and tarn, Waterfall, Convex slope, Even slope, Trellis drainage pattern, Floodplain, Mudflat, Beach, Tombolo, Estuary, Sand spit, Headland, Floodplain

Fig. 26 Relief and landscape features commonly found on OS maps

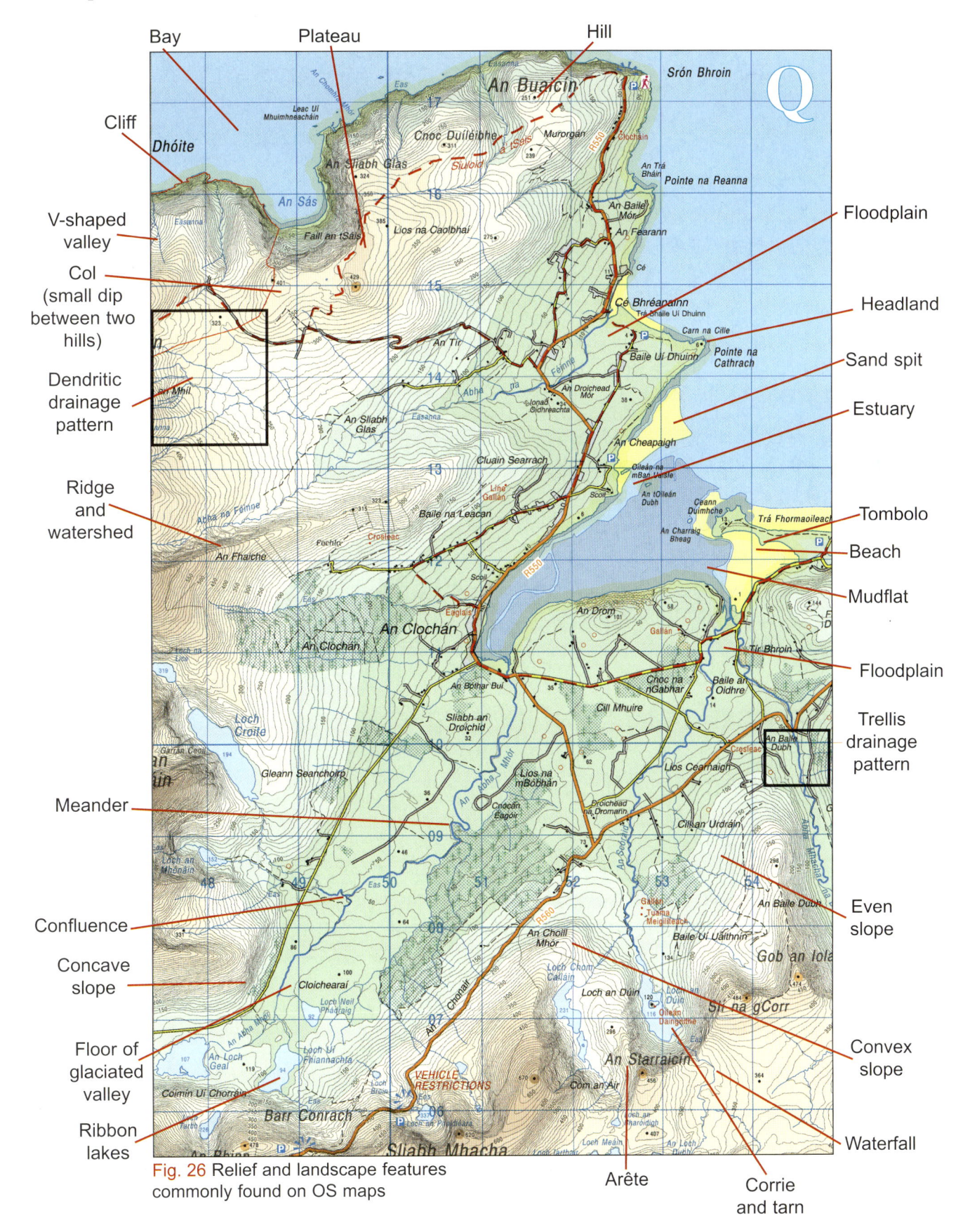

233

CORE UNIT: GEOGRAPHICAL INVESTIGATION AND SKILLS

2. Antiquities

These are represented by a red dot and red writing on an OS map. They represent different times in the history of settlement of the area and show where people lived in the past and what features of the landscape attracted them to settle there, e.g. defence, water supply, fertile land.

Fig. 27 Crannóg In Lough Key, Co. Roscommon

Historic ages and their map evidence

Stone Age: 4000BC to 2400BC
Megalithic tombs, stone circles, cairns, rock art, middens.

Bronze Age: 2400BC to 600BC
Standing stones, dolmens, Fulacht Fia, barrows (burial mound), stone rows, copper mines and wedge tombs.

Iron Age: 600BC – 600AD
Crannóg, hillfort, ring fort, stone forts, promontory fort, Ogham stone, souterrain, togher.

Early Christian era: 6th – 11th century
High cross, holy well, monastic site, round tower, graveyard, cross-inscribed stone, place names beginning with Cill or Kil/Kill.

Norman/Medieval: 12th – 13th century
Castle, keep, motte and bailey, moat, walls, tower house, abbey, gate, place names with a prefix, e.g. Baile, Bally.

Plantation: 16th – 18th century
Fortified houses, demesne, towns with landlord's name, e.g. Charleville, Randalstown.

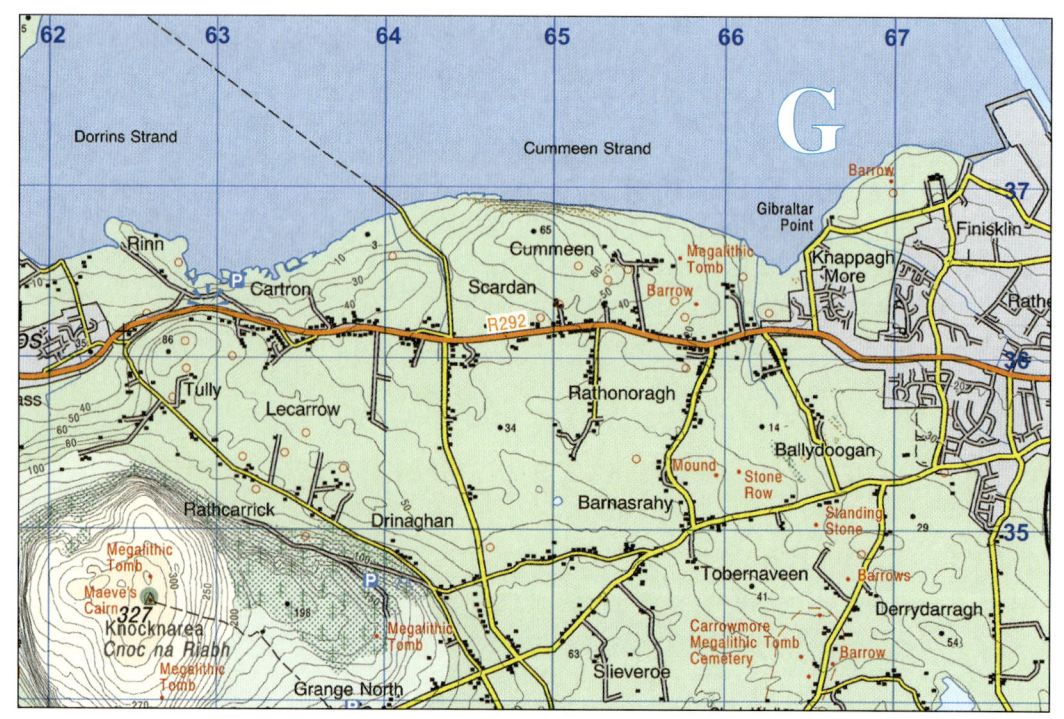

Fig. 28 OS map of Sligo showing ancient settlements

3. Settlement patterns (rural)

Individual buildings/houses in rural areas are represented on OS maps as **small black squares**.

Settlements can be one of these four patterns:
(a) Linear/Ribbon
(b) Clustered/Nucleated
(c) Dispersed/Scattered
(d) Absence of settlement.

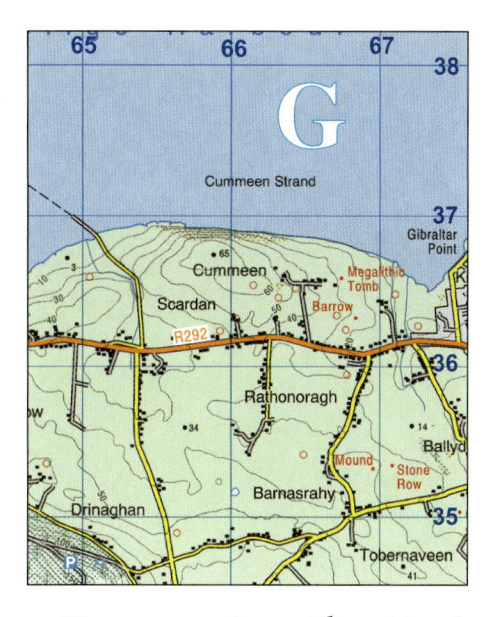

Fig. 29 Linear settlements

(a) Linear/ribbon

This is the most common pattern seen in rural areas. Houses run along either side of roads. **Linear settlement** develops because services such as electricity, water and sewage are installed and supplied more cheaply along roadsides.

Many houses are built on sites made available by farmers as they sell off sections of their land. These sites with road frontage are more valuable.

(b) Clustered/Nucleated

In the case of **clustered settlement** patterns in rural areas, houses are close to each other. This pattern may occur because people in the past settled around a water source – a spring or well – or in an easily-defended site (e.g. castle).

In the 18th century, people tended to cluster close to landlord estates (demesnes) because they also worked on the estate. Over time, many grew in size to become villages and towns, e.g. Adare, County Limerick.

As the size of the clustered settlement grows, the pattern is relabelled as 'nucleated', because a definite centre, usually due to a market function, developed, i.e. an urban area. In these built-up urban areas it is impossible to show every building. Therefore, **nucleated settlements** are shaded grey on the map.

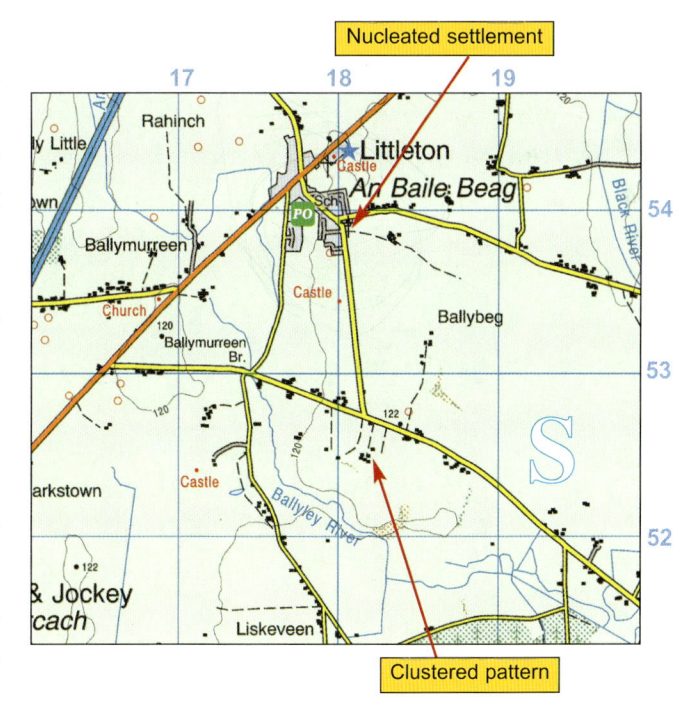

Fig. 30 Clustered and nucleated settlement in a rural area of County Tipperary

(c) Dispersed/Scattered

In this case many houses/buildings are scattered across the map.

Relief, aspect, altitude, access to a water supply and soil quality are the greatest influences on this pattern. There are often isolated houses on large farms in lowland areas with fertile soils. In upland areas **dispersed settlement** occurs due to relief, aspect and poor soil quality.

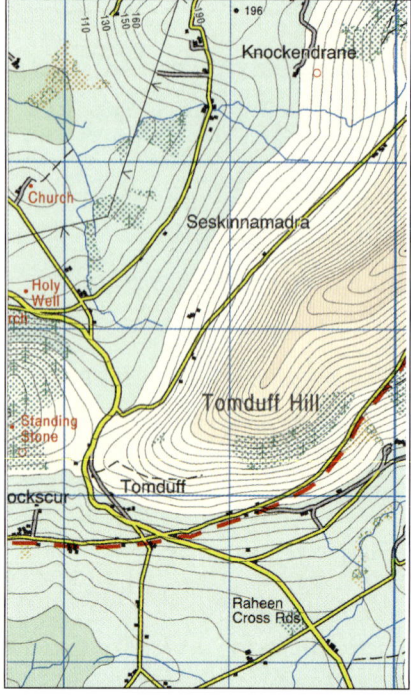

Fig. 31 OS map of Mount Leinster region in County Carlow

(d) Absence of settlement

The most common reasons for absence of settlement in an area are annual flooding on a river floodplain; areas of poor drainage; northerly aspect; steep high ground; good agricultural land where there are many large fields; forested areas and coastal areas with erosional landforms.

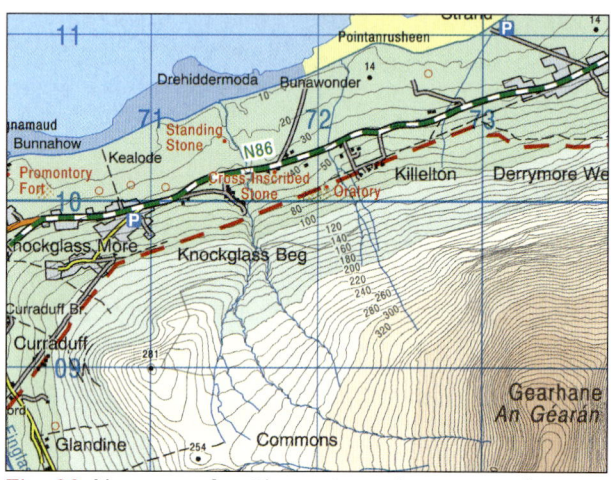

Fig. 32 Absence of settlement on steep ground

In summary, all of these settlement patterns and antiquities reflect aspects of the physical, social, economic and historical environment.

In the past, water supply was one of the most important locational factors for settlement. In some cases, the settlement may have become depopulated at a later date due to emigration or an ageing workforce, e.g. the deserted village of Achill Island.

The quality of the land is also an important factor – people prefer to live in fertile areas where they can grow crops and raise livestock. However, due to historical factors such as the Plantations (16th century) and the Famine (1845–48), often the most unproductive land was settled by the native Irish as the best land was used for planter estates.

Modern settlement is less influenced by physical factors and more influenced by social and economic factors such as transport routes.

4. Land use and function

A variety of land use and functions can be identified by their symbols on OS maps.

Land use means what is actually **built/found** on a piece of land, e.g. a school or farm.
Function means what **service** the building/land provides, e.g. education, agriculture.

Use the table below to improve your skills at recognising land use and functions on OS maps.

OS Map Symbol	Land use	Function (Ricepots)
 • Abbey • Priory • Church	Cathedral – modern Church – modern Abbey – historic Priory – historic Church – historic	Religious
	Racecourse Golf course Boating activities	Recreation
Demesne 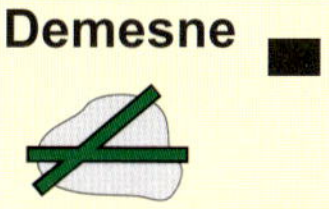	Estate house Houses Built-up area	Residential
Ind. Est. 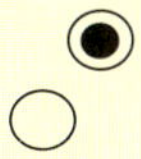	Power station (thermal) Power station (HEP) Industrial estate	Industry (secondary economic activities)
Sch Coll	School College, University	Education
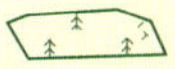	Fishing port Farm land Forest (coniferous)	Economic activities (primary)
 A T	Quayside Shipping channel National Parks	Port Open spaces
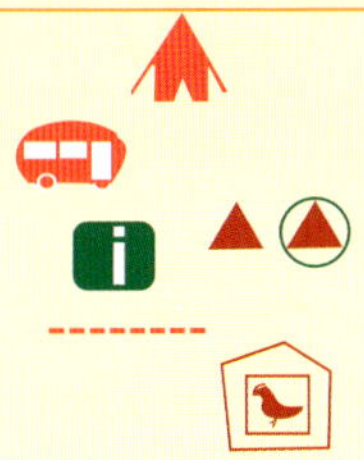	Camping site Caravan site Hostels Marina, slipway Tourist information office Walking path Nature reserve	Tourism
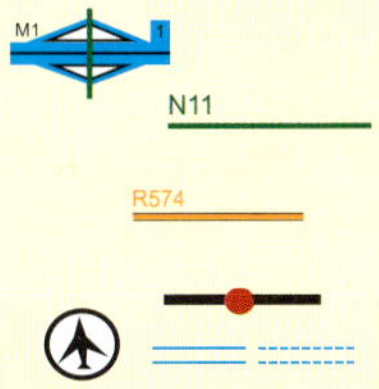	Motorway National Primary route Regional road Railway Station Airport Canal	Transport (historic transport land use)
Fire St Hosp 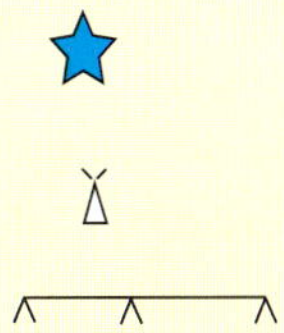	Garda station Fire station Communications mast Hospital Electricity transmission line (pylon)	Services

Fig. 33 OS map symbols, land uses and functions

237

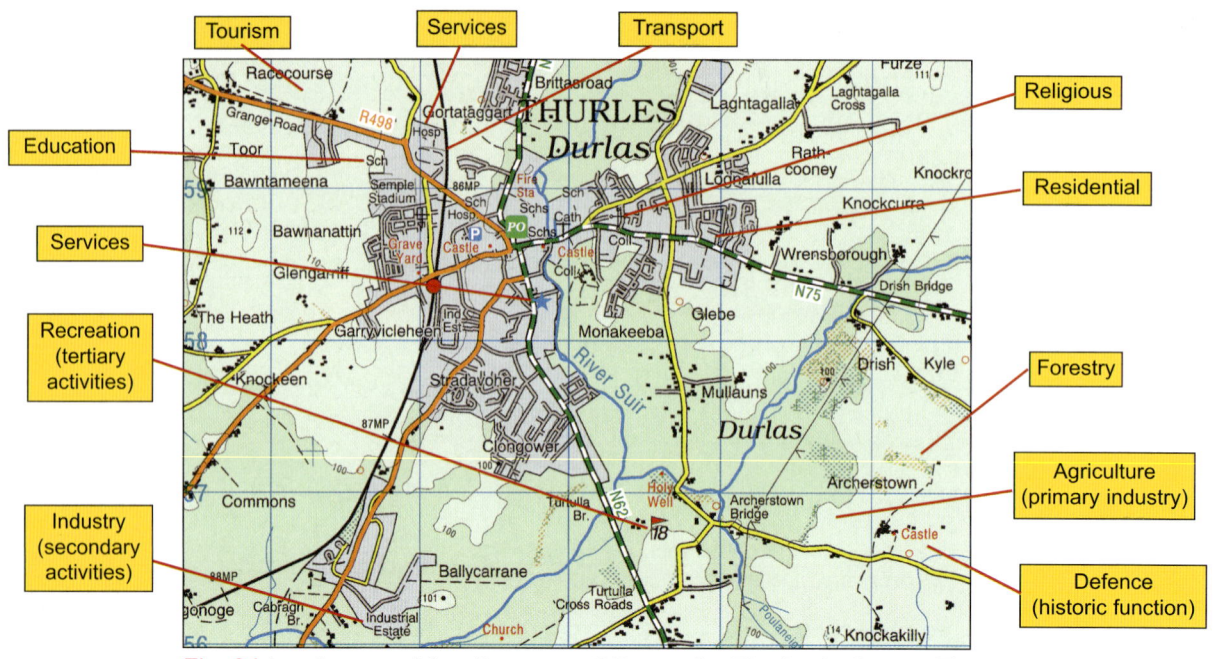

CORE UNIT: GEOGRAPHICAL INVESTIGATION AND SKILLS

Fig. 34 Land use and function on an OS map for Thurles in County Tipperary

Functions change over time

Transport networks develop and change. This can often be seen on an OS map. The table summarises the types of transport and when they were in use in the past.

SUMMARY OF TRANSPORT USES	
Canals	1700s-1800s for transport of goods and people. Modern use is for tourism and recreation.
Railways	1800s – present
Roads	1600s – present
Airports	1950s – present
Shipping	Viking times – present ports

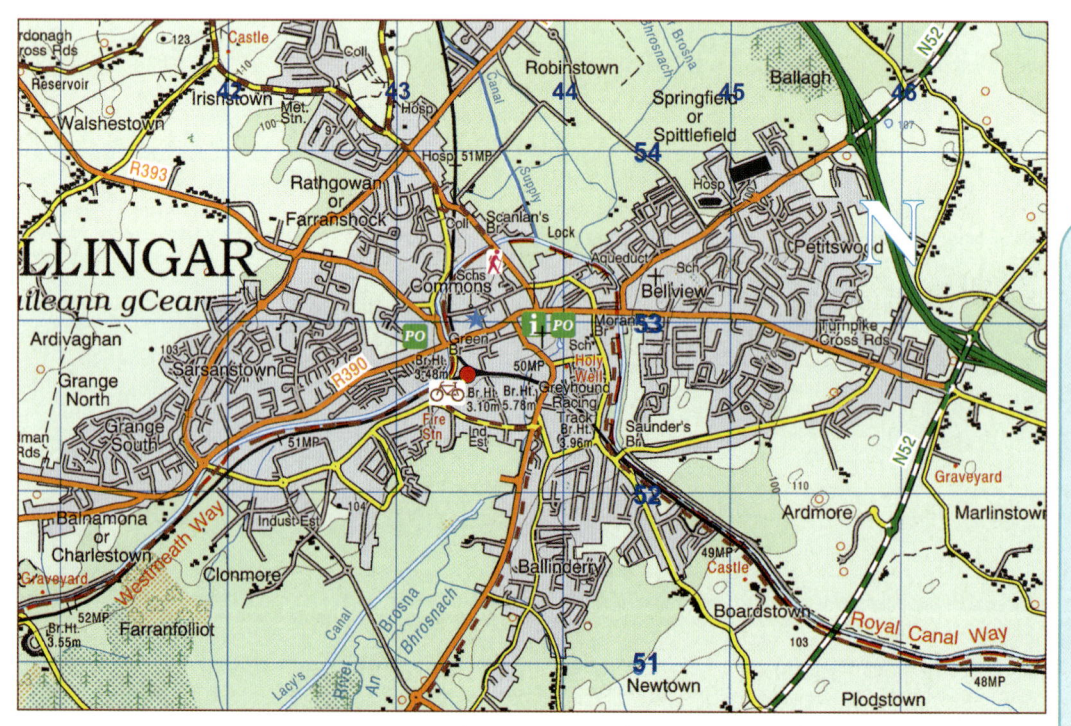

Fig. 35 OS map of Mullingar showing different modes of transport

Activity

Look at Fig. 35.
1. Identify the different types of transport in Mullingar.
2. What evidence is there that the transport network has developed over time?
3. In your answer, name each type of transport, give the grid reference of its location and state its time of development in the past.

CHAPTER 13: OS MAPS AND AERIAL PHOTOGRAPHS

13.3 Aerial photo skills

Aerial photographs taken at different altitudes and angles can give us more up-to-date information than even the most recent of OS maps. Using maps and photos together helps us to build a better picture of an area.

Aerial photographs are taken from an aeroplane or helicopter. They show the present, but can also indicate features from the past that are invisible from the ground, e.g. ancient crop marks, overgrown/demolished ancient settlements.

Aerial photos can be of two types: **vertical** and **oblique**.
- **A vertical photograph** is taken when the camera points directly down over the subject matter of the photograph. The scale on this type of photo is the same across the image (i.e. true to scale). **Use compass points to find the location.**
- **An oblique photograph** is taken when the camera is pointing at an angle to the ground. It gives a side view of objects so they have depth, making them easier to identify. Oblique photographs can be **low oblique** (no horizon visible) or **high oblique** (horizon is visible). **Use left, right, foreground, centreground and background notation to find location.**

Fig. 36 Example of high oblique photo – Ballymun, Dublin

Fig. 37 Example of low oblique photo – Waterford City

239

CORE UNIT: GEOGRAPHICAL INVESTIGATION AND SKILLS

Finding location on aerial photos

Location on vertical photos

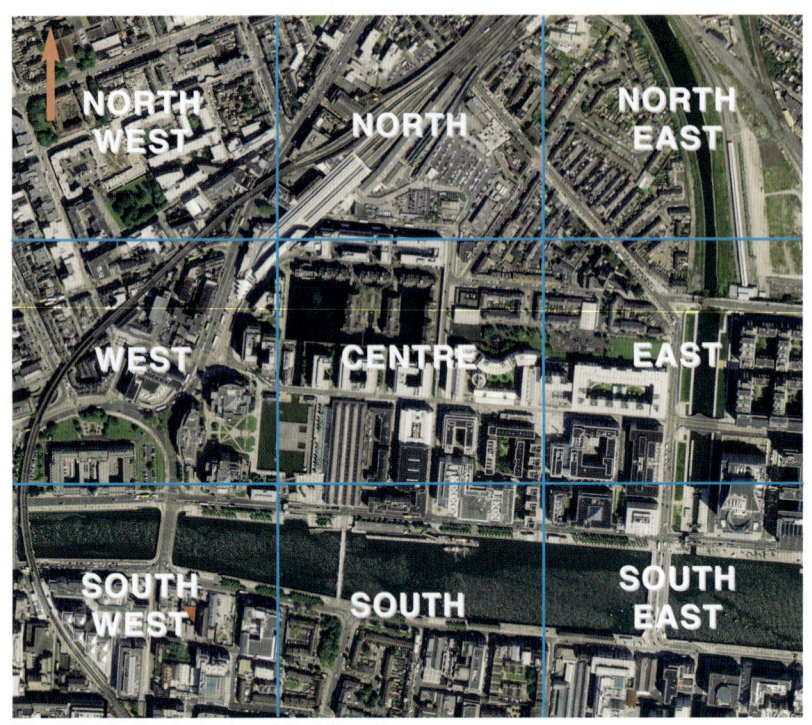

Fig. 38 Vertical photo of Dublin city

Activity

Look at Fig. 38.

Complete this exercise in your copybook.

1. A narrow pedestrian footbridge is located in the _____ of the photo.
2. A carpark is located in the _____ of photo.
3. A railway bridge is located in the _____ of the photo.
4. A residential area is located in the _____ the photo.

Look at Fig. 39.
Locate: (a) The caravan park.
(b) The lake.
(c) The forest.

Location on oblique photos

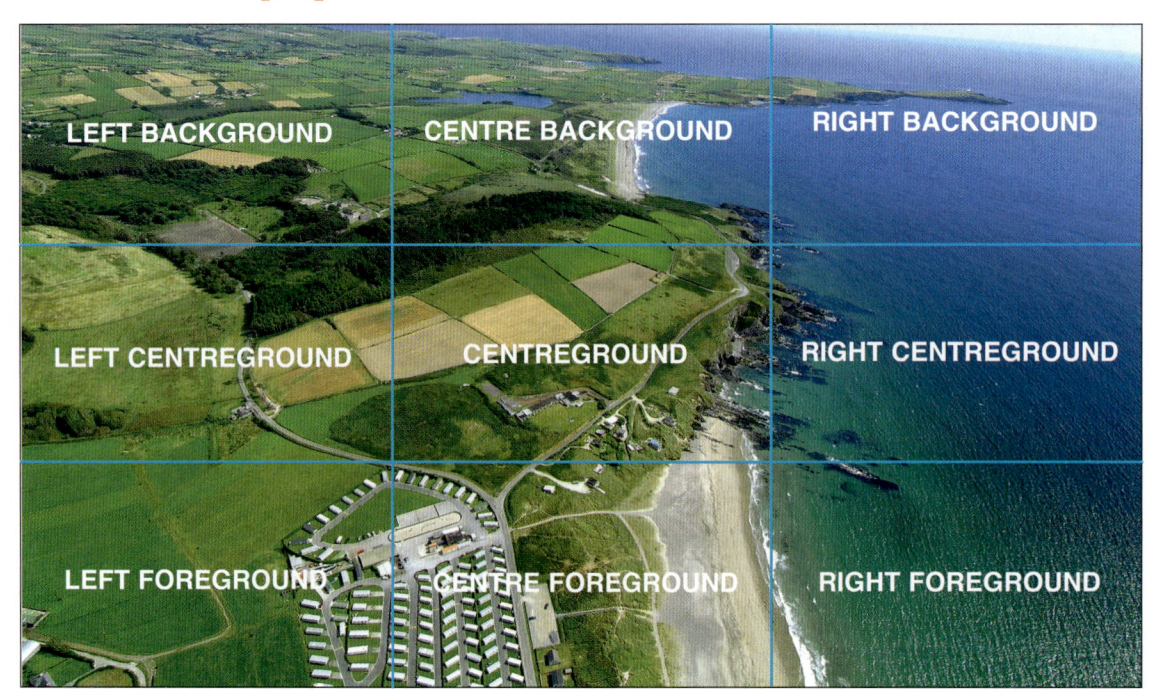

Fig. 39 Oblique photo of the south coast of County Cork

Chapter 13: OS Maps and Aerial Photographs

Working out direction using a map and photo

To find out which way the camera was pointing when the picture was taken, use the following method:

1. Identify two major landmarks. For example, in Figs. 40 and 41 below, a lake and a meandering river are visible.
2. Draw a line joining the landmarks on the photo.
3. Draw a line joining the same two landmarks on the OS map.
4. By comparing the direction of the line on both the map and the photo, it should be possible to calculate the direction in which the camera was pointing.

Now work out the direction the camera was pointing at in the map and photo below.

Fig. 40 View from the head of the Glendalough valley above the upper lake

Fig. 41 Map of Glendalough, County Wicklow

13.4 Aerial photo interpretation

Using aerial photos you can see and describe land use and function, street pattern, house types, traffic management, historic developments and time of year.

Land use

From a photo, you can see rural landscapes and identify details such as what type of farming is carried out on the land. In a town, land use refers to what is built in an urban area, e.g. church, railway station.

Irregular and smaller fields under grass imply pasture and livestock farming. The field colour, size and shape also indicate the agriculture type, e.g. green grass means pastoral farming, glasshouses indicate market gardening. In towns photos show many land uses, e.g. roads, schools.

The table on the next page shows main land uses and examples of buildings that might be visible on aerial photos.

Function

The term function refers to the services the land use provides, e.g. transport.

The function of some buildings will be easy to identify due to buildings and structures nearby, e.g. a large building with basketball courts, tennis courts and large playing fields around it usually depicts an education or recreation function.

Each function you identify must be supported with clear evidence from the photo based on the buildings and land uses you can see.

FUNCTION (RICEPOTS)	PHOTO EVIDENCE OF LAND USE
Religious	Church, graveyard, abbey, convent, cathedral, round tower
Residential	Housing estates, playgrounds, apartments, terraced/detached housing
Recreation	Pitches, parks, river/coastal walks, playgrounds, golf courses, racetracks, beach, leisure centre, marina
Industrial (secondary economic activities)	Industrial estates, factories, warehouses, chimney stack, mill, power lines
Commercial	Shops, terraced multi-coloured buildings with large ground floor windows, car parks, shopping centres, petrol stations, market square, mart, CBD (Central Business District)
Education	Schools, colleges, playgrounds, pitches, tennis courts, car parks
Economic activities (Primary: farming, fishing, forestry, mining)	Fields (crops, grazing land), glasshouses, quarry, forest, port, trawlers, dock side, quay
Port	Harbour, ships, boats, yachts, docks/quayside, container parks, cranes
Power generation	Large building with pylons and overhead cables, chimney stacks, dams and reservoirs, wind farms
Open spaces	Greenfield and derelict sites, car parks, parks
Transport (tertiary economic activity)	Roads, car parks, bridges, railway lines, railway station, port, canal, canal locks, river, airport
Tourism (tertiary economic activity)	Physical and man-made attractions, beaches, forestry, river, mountains, golf course, horse riding, boating, caravans, camping site, interpretative centres.
Services (tertiary economic activity)	Garda station, radio mast, hospital, banks, court house, jail, offices
Defence (in the past)	Castle, town walls, fortified house, town wall gates

CHAPTER 13: OS MAPS AND AERIAL PHOTOGRAPHS

Fig. 42 Aerial photo of Athlone

Activity

Identify and locate four land uses and four urban functions visible in this photo.

Town street layout

Town layout or settlement shape can be clearly shown by drawing a simple sketch of a photo of the area. If used with a town plan, streets on the photo can also be named. Older settlements tend to have narrow, winding streets and are quite random with little planning. Modern settlements and housing developments/estates show clear order in their planning and design.

The main street of Irish country towns is usually easy to identify due to the common use of bright multi-coloured paint on the walls. Large front windows indicate shopfronts. There may also be more traffic on this road or the road may be pedestrianised.

CORE UNIT: GEOGRAPHICAL INVESTIGATION AND SKILLS

Fig. 43 Aerial photo of town street layout – Killarney

Activity

Draw a sketch map half the length and half the breadth of this photo of Killarney. On it, mark and identify the following:
- The street plan
- Residential land use
- Woodland
- Commercial land use

244

CHAPTER 13: OS MAPS AND AERIAL PHOTOGRAPHS

House types

You should be able to identify one or more of the following house types from a photo:

1. Detached
2. Semi-detached
3. Bungalow
4. Terraced
5. Apartments.

Fig. 44 High density apartments

Traffic management and congestion

TRAFFIC CONGESTION BLACK SPOTS

Junctions
Schools
Shopping centre exits
Narrow streets
Streets with parking
Churches
Traffic lights

Fig. 45 Traffic management in Limerick

METHODS USED TO SOLVE TRAFFIC CONGESTION	HOW THESE METHODS WORK
Roundabouts	Increase traffic flow at junctions.
Yellow boxes	No entry unless exit free. Reduce congestion.
Double yellow lines	No parking. Keep roads clear for traffic.
Off-street parking	Keep roads clear for traffic.
Car parks	Keep roads clear for traffic.
Park and ride centres	Reduce number of commuter cars.
One-way streets	Reduce congestion on narrow streets.
Bus lanes	Reduce bus journey times.
Pedestrian streets	Reduce accident/congestion in shopping streets.
Bypasses	Reduce 'through traffic' in city centre.
Traffic lights	Control traffic at junctions used by pedestrians.

Historic development

The historic development of a town can also be seen from a photograph. The table below shows some structures, their age and past functions.

TIME	BUILDING	FUNCTION/USE
6th century: Early Christian	Church ruin	Religious services
12th–13th century: Norman	Castle, priory	Defence, religion
16th–18th century: Plantation	Market square	Trade
19th century–21st century	Mills, canals Shopping centre School	Industry, transport Business Education

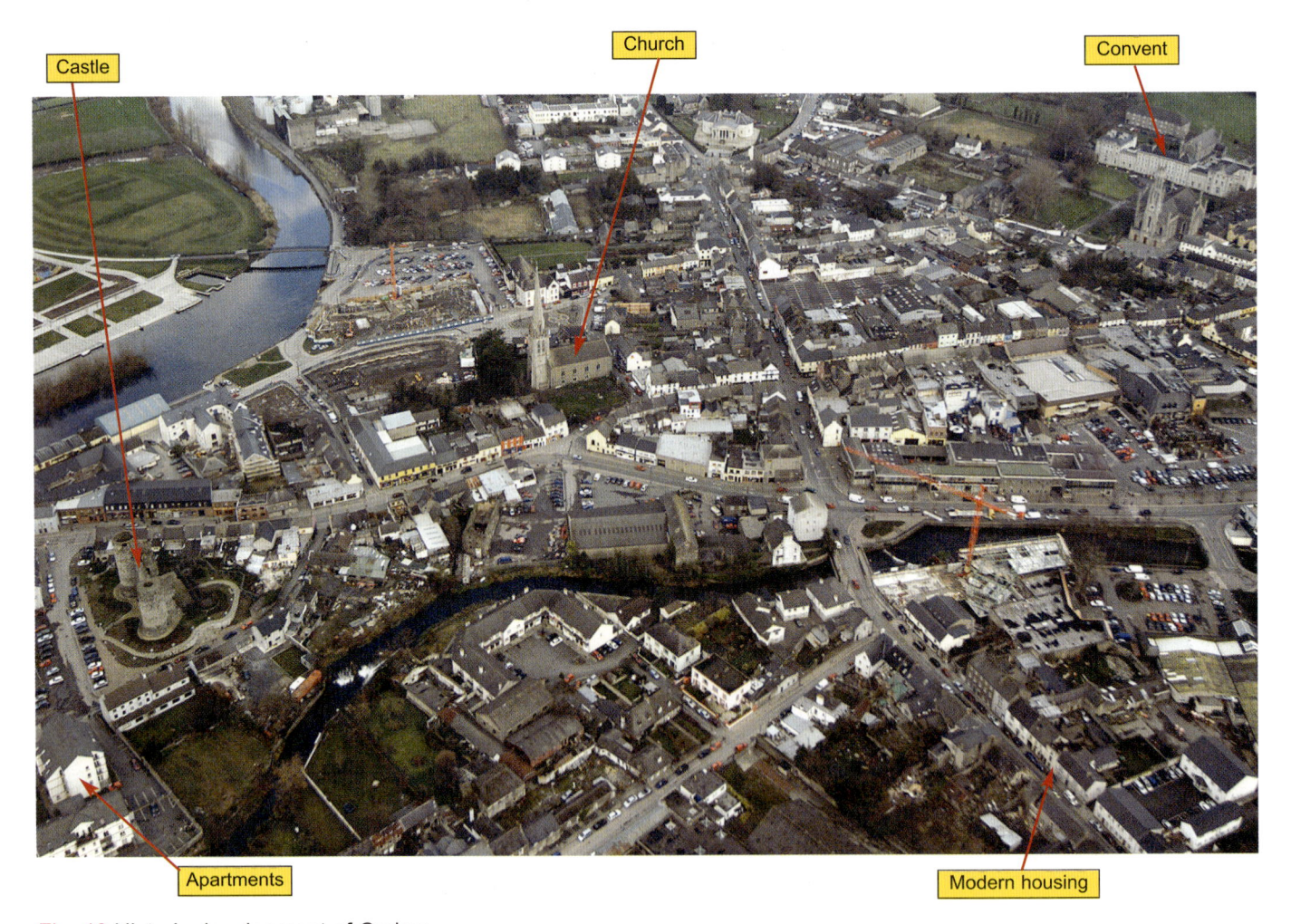

Fig. 46 Historic development of Carlow

Using photos to place new developments in an area

In the Leaving Certificate exam, you may be asked to choose a suitable site for a new development by carefully examining a photograph. All new developments need space but some need more than others. Consider the following when making your decision:

1. Are **greenfield** or **brownfield sites** available? Greenfield sites are usually found on the edge of towns. They are larger and cheaper to buy and redevelop. They are usually farmland that has been rezoned for another use. Brownfield sites already have some buildings on them and are found in towns. These cost more to buy and redevelop and do not have as much space but are often in profitable, accessible locations in towns.
2. Traffic – consider parking / access / deliveries / lorries / cars.
3. Noise – consider the noise levels from people or machinery / traffic / day and night noise levels.
4. Pollution – consider the effects of pollution in the air, water, noise, light (lights disturb people at night).
5. Is there a workforce, market and transport infrastructure close by?

NEW DEVELOPMENTS	POSSIBLE LOCATION
Swimming pool	Close to town, near schools, housing estates.
Computer factory	Greenfield site outside towns with good transport links.
Leisure centre	Close to town/in town.
School	Near residential areas and away from busy roads.
Shopping centre	Large brownfield site in town or on edge of town on large greenfield site.
Industrial estate	Edge of town away from residential areas, good transport links.
Multi-storey car park	Brownfield site in town.
Hospital	Close to town, near housing, room for car park and easily accessible.

Drawing sketch maps of aerial photos

1. Use graph paper.
2. Draw a frame half the width and half the height of the photo you are given. It should be the same **shape** as the photograph, i.e. landscape, portrait.
3. Divide the sketch into three equally spaced columns and three equally spaced rows.
4. Sketch in the items that are listed in the question you are answering. For example, if the question mentions a church, make sure you include the church in your sketch.
5. Draw the **outline** of areas of land use. For example, if there is a housing estate in the photograph, do not draw each house in the estate. In the example below, the residential land use is represented by coloured shapes and these shapes are explained in the key.

6. Use **block** colour neatly.
7. The items you draw in your sketch should be in the **same position and have the same relative sizes on the sketch as in the photo**. For example, if an area of forestry is in the left background of the photo, it should be in the left background of your sketch. If it covers a small area on the photo, it should cover a small area on your sketch. This is why the grid is drawn on the sketch – to help you position and size items correctly.
8. Use a key to explain any symbol or colours in your sketch. Make sure you give a title to your sketch.

Fig. 47 Aerial photo of Drogheda

Fig. 48 Sketch map of aerial photo. Note how the land uses are shown by block shading.

CHAPTER 13: OS MAPS AND AERIAL PHOTOGRAPHS

Uses of maps and photos

PHOTOS CAN SHOW: ✓

Actual buildings, their relative sizes and positioning

Derelict sites available for redevelopment

Relative ages of buildings

Areas of traffic congestion/traffic management

A small area in great detail

Land use

Street patterns

Time of year

PHOTOS CANNOT SHOW: ✗

Large areas except from a great height which then loses image detail

Slopes clearly

Accurate scale – in the case of oblique photos. Oblique photos make near objects look bigger than they really are

Building functions clearly – in the case of vertical photos

The names of important buildings

Exact locations

MAPS CAN SHOW: ✓

Large areas

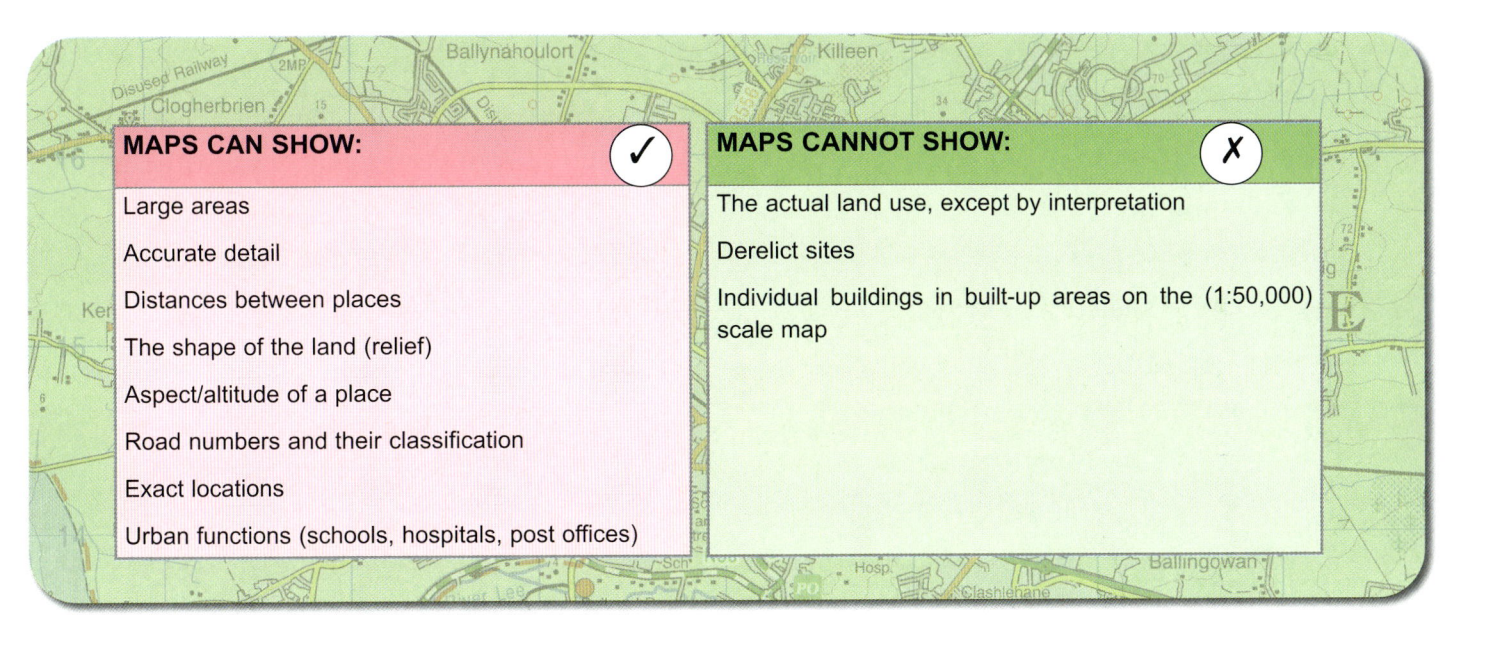

Accurate detail

Distances between places

The shape of the land (relief)

Aspect/altitude of a place

Road numbers and their classification

Exact locations

Urban functions (schools, hospitals, post offices)

MAPS CANNOT SHOW: ✗

The actual land use, except by interpretation

Derelict sites

Individual buildings in built-up areas on the (1:50,000) scale map

249

CORE UNIT: GEOGRAPHICAL INVESTIGATION AND SKILLS

Chapter Revision Questions

OS Map Skills Questions (based on OS map page 251)
1. State the scale of the map on page 251.
2. Calculate the area of land south of northing 15.
3. Calculate the straight line distance between the railway station at Blennerville and the 9-hole golf course at Kerries.
4. Calculate the distance in kilometres of the disused railway line.
5. Describe, with reference to the map, **three** land uses and their functions visible on this map.
6. Give six-figure grid references for **three** different antiquities shown on the map.
7. State the direction travelled from:
    (i) Blennerville to the Tralee Institute of Technology.
    (ii) Tralee Institute of Technology to Parkboy.
    (iii) Parkboy to the sewage treatment plant.
8. Draw a sketch map of the OS map extract. Mark and identify the following:
    (i) the third class road network
    (ii) the village of Blennerville
    (iii) any two post offices
    (iv) an area of coastal deposition
    (v) the highest point on the map
    (vi) the railway lines
    (vii) an area of mixed woodland
    (viii) an electricity transmission line.

Aerial Photo Skills Questions
9. Using the aerial photo on page 253, choose a suitable location for the development of a new leisure centre. Give **two** detailed reasons for your answer.

CHAPTER 13: OS MAPS AND AERIAL PHOTOGRAPHS

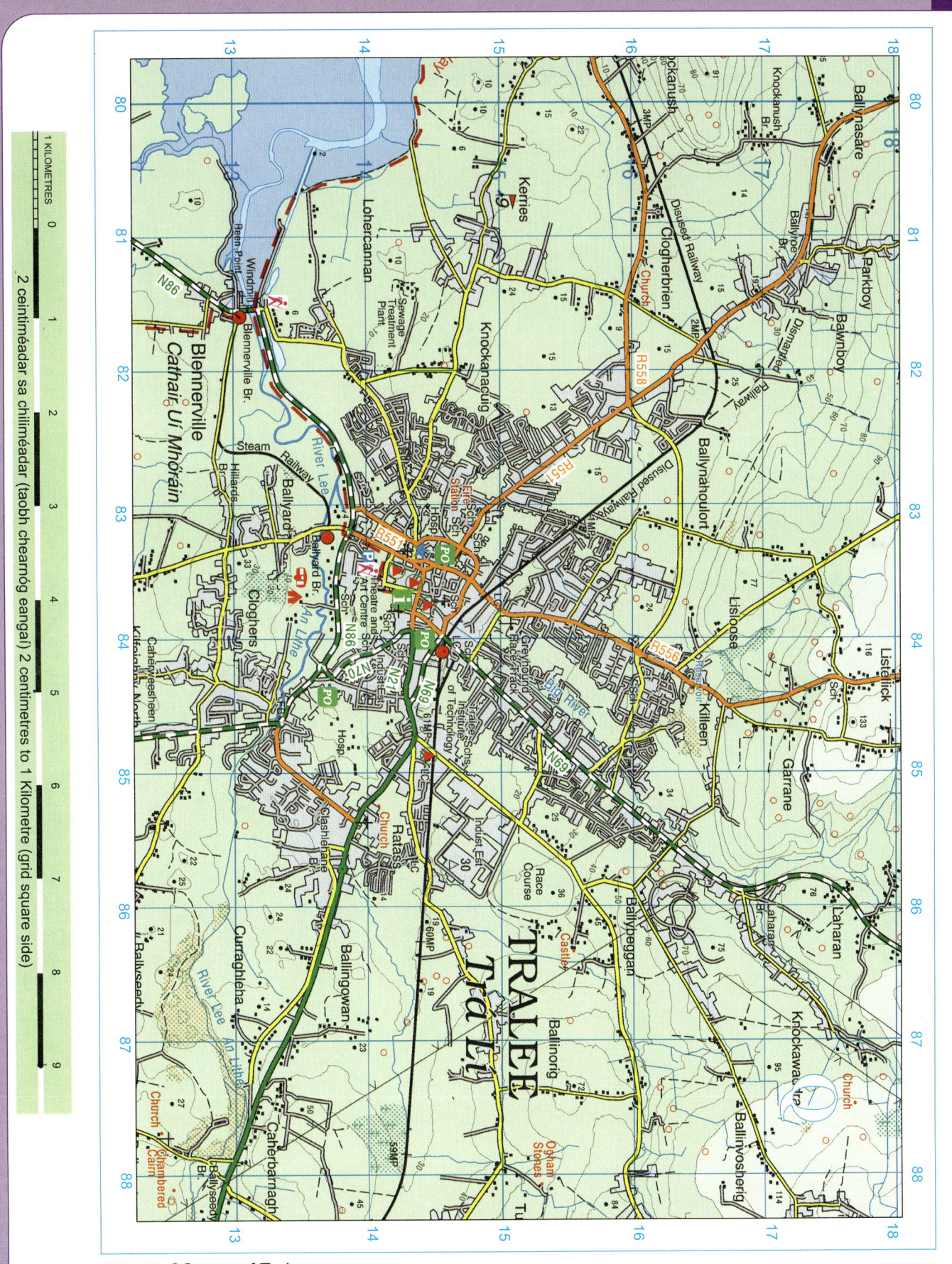

Fig. 49 OS map of Tralee

251

CORE UNIT: GEOGRAPHICAL INVESTIGATION AND SKILLS

LC Exam Questions

Using the OS map on page 251 and the aerial photo of Tralee on page 253, answer the following questions.

Aerial Photos Questions

10. Draw a sketch map half the width and half the height of the photo on page 253. Mark and identify the following:
    (a) A residential area
    (b) An area of recreation
    (c) An area of agricultural land use
    (d) An area of industrial land use.
11. Using the correct notation, locate the following:
    (a) The sports ground
    (b) The railway station
    (c) An area of housing
    (d) An area of farmland.
12. What time of year was this photograph of Tralee taken?
13. State the type of photo (low oblique/high oblique/vertical).
14. Name, describe and locate **three** different land uses visible in this photograph.
15. Name, describe and locate **three** different functions of the town of Tralee.
16. Describe the variety of residential land use visible in this photograph.

OS Map Questions

17. Draw a sketch map to half scale of the OS map of Tralee on page 251. Mark and identify the following:
    (a) The built-up area of Tralee
    (b) The railway lines
    (c) The N21
    (d) A golf course
    (e) Any two antiquities from different eras
    (f) A spot height over 100 metres.
18. Using map evidence, identify and describe three functions of Tralee.

CHAPTER 13: OS MAPS AND AERIAL PHOTOGRAPHS

Fig. 50 Aerial photo of Tralee

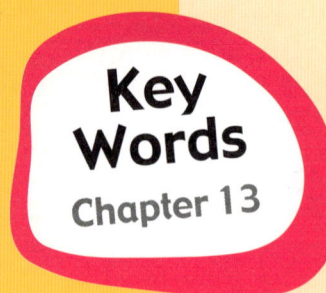

CORE UNIT: GEOGRAPHICAL INVESTIGATION AND SKILLS

Key Words — Chapter 13

Key Words

You should be able to explain both verbally and in writing each of the key words listed below.

- clustered settlement
- concave slope
- convex slope
- dispersed settlement
- easting
- even/graded/uniform slopes
- greenfield/brownfield site
- grid reference
- high oblique photograph
- intervisible
- land function
- land use
- large-scale map
- linear/graphical scale
- linear settlement
- low oblique photograph
- northing
- nucleated settlement
- oblique photograph
- representative fraction (RF)
- small-scale map
- statement of scale
- steep slopes
- stepped/compound slope
- sub-zones
- vertical photographs

Digital Resources are available for this chapter at mentorbooks.ie/resources

CHAPTER 14

Weather Maps, Satellite Images and Graphical Skills

Key Theme

Interpretation of weather maps and satellite images is a key geographical skill. Graphing skills can be applied to a wide variety of geographical topics.

Learning Outcomes

At the end of this chapter you will be able to:
- Identify, explain and interpret symbols on weather maps and charts.
- Read and interpret a variety of charts and tables showing statistical data.
- Draw a variety of graphs to Leaving Certificate Exam standard.
- Use satellite images to examine large areas of the earth's surface.

Contents

14.1	Introduction	256
14.2	Weather maps and charts	256
14.3	Representing statistical data on graphs and charts	260
14.4	Drawing graphs for the Leaving Certificate Exam	267
14.5	Satellite images	270

Revision Space

LC Exam Questions – Key Word List 271

14.1 Introduction

Our world is increasingly represented by maps, satellite photos, graphs and tables of statistics. Today, mobile phones and some cars have global positioning systems **(GPS)** as standard. Emergency teams use satellite maps to pinpoint search areas. Zoomed-in, clear images of our homes and landscapes can be taken from satellites hundreds of kilometres above the ground. Information from census data, maps, statistics, satellites, aerial photos and other sources can be combined to develop Geographical Information Systems (GIS). The data is combined in a series of overlapping layers from which patterns, changes and developments in the physical and human environment can be seen.

> **weblink**
> Explaining GIS

14.2 Weather maps and charts

Weather map symbol	Name	Weather conditions
	Cold front	Big, towering cumulus and cumulonimbus clouds form. Produces quite heavy rain, often in sudden showers which soon pass. Winds tend to be quite strong and gusty along cold fronts. Feeling cool.
	Warm front	Clouds change from high cirrus to low, thick stratus cloud as front approaches. Weather is overcast and grey. Air pressure drops. Feeling warmer.
	Warm sector (The zone between a warm and cold front.)	Heavy stratus cloud covering the sky. Drizzle and rain lasting several hours. Misty, mild, damp weather.
	Occluded front	Thick stratus clouds, overcast grey skies with showery rain.
H	High pressure (**anticyclone**)	In summer, warm, dry, cloudless sunny skies. Very calm winds. In winter, cold but sunny weather, clear skies, calm winds.
L	Low pressure (**depression**)	Changeable weather depending on what type of front is passing over at the time. Usually cloudy, wet and windy.

Fig. 1 Weather maps and charts

Isolines

An *isoline* is a line on any map that shows where something is the same, e.g. contour lines. The isolines seen on weather maps are listed below.

Name	Description	Unit
Isotherm	Joins places with equal temperature	Degrees Celsius, °C
Isobars	Join places with equal air pressure	Millibars (mb)/hectopascals (hPa)
Isohel	Joins places with equal amounts of sunshine	Hours
Isotach	Joins places with equal windspeed	Km/h, m/s
Isohyet	Joins places with equal precipitation	mm

CHAPTER 14: WEATHER MAPS, SATELLITE IMAGES AND GRAPHICAL SKILLS

DEPRESSION

Fig. 2 Synoptic chart of depression

ANTICYCLONE

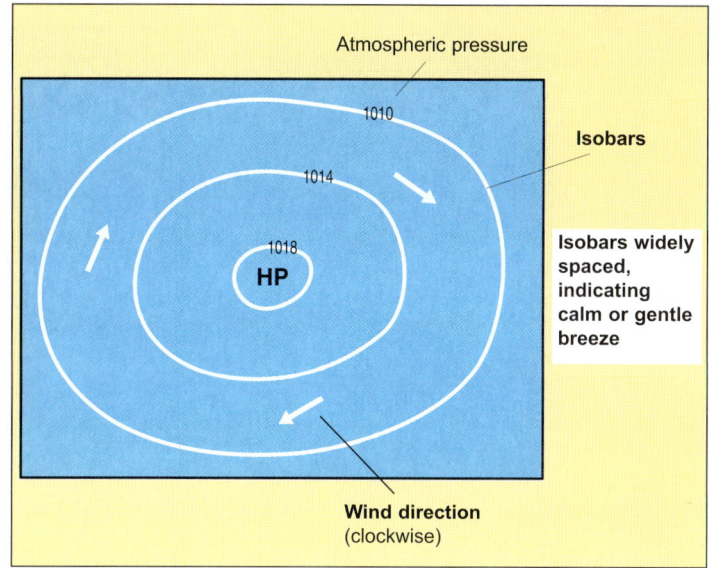

Fig. 3 Synoptic chart of anticyclone

LP = Low pressure
HP = High pressure
996 = Air pressure in hectopascals or millibars

Fig. 4 Cloud cover for the low (depression) shown in Fig. 5

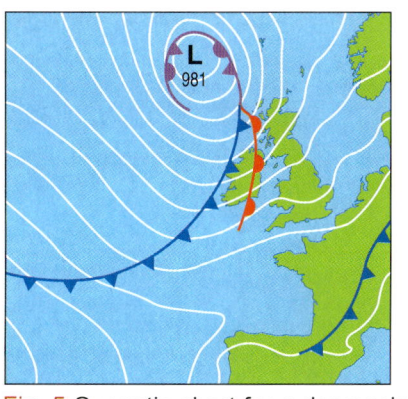

Fig. 5 Synoptic chart for a depression (low)

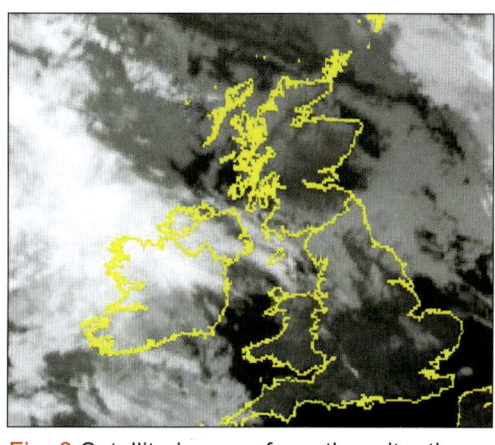

Fig. 6 Satellite image of weather situation in Fig. 5

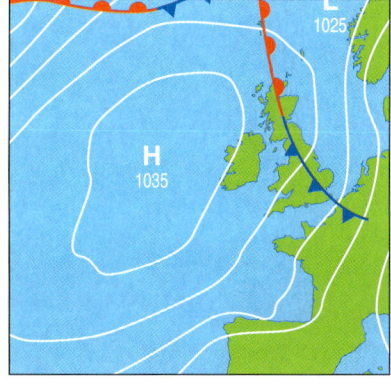

Fig. 7 Synoptic chart for the anticyclone (high) shown in Fig. 8

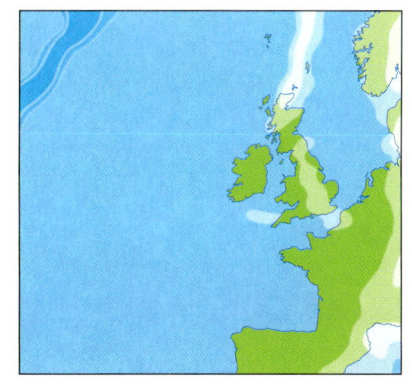

Fig. 8 Cloud cover for the anticyclone (high) shown in Fig. 7

weblink
Cold fronts: compare and contrast

257

CORE UNIT: GEOGRAPHICAL INVESTIGATION AND SKILLS

SUMMARY OF WEATHER MAPS

EXPLANATION OF SYMBOLS

- ↰31 = Wind direction and wind speed in km/h
- 0 = Temperatures in degrees Celsius
- ☀ = Fair weather
- ⛅ = Cloudy with bright spells
- 🌧 = Rain
- 🌦 = Showers

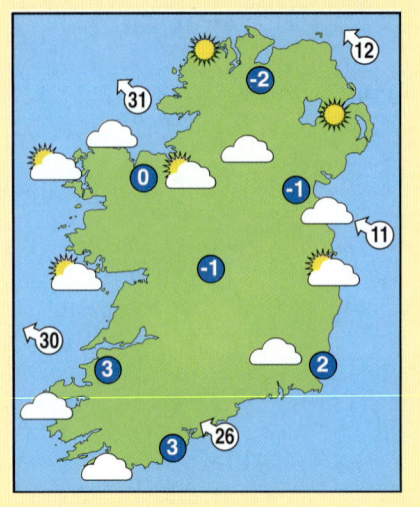

Weather in brief
Mainly dry but cold tonight.
Widespread ground frost.
Low of +3 to -2 degrees.

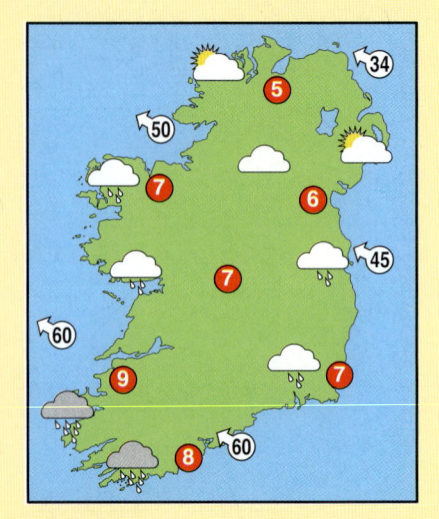

Tomorrow
Rain spreading countrywide from the south-west.
High of 5 to 9 degrees.
Dry at first. Wet and windy later.

Fig. 9 Summary of weather maps

Exam Note

REMEMBER!
Don't forget to state the unit of measurement with your answers, e.g. wind speed in km/h, temperatures in degrees Celsius, °C.

Skills Exercise 1

1. Examine the weather and cloud maps A to D and answer the questions that follow.

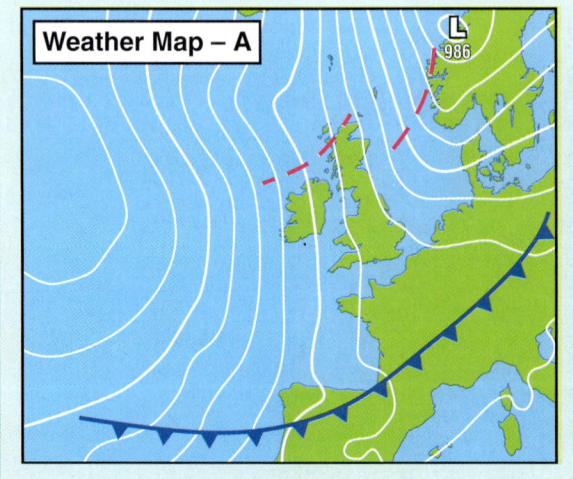

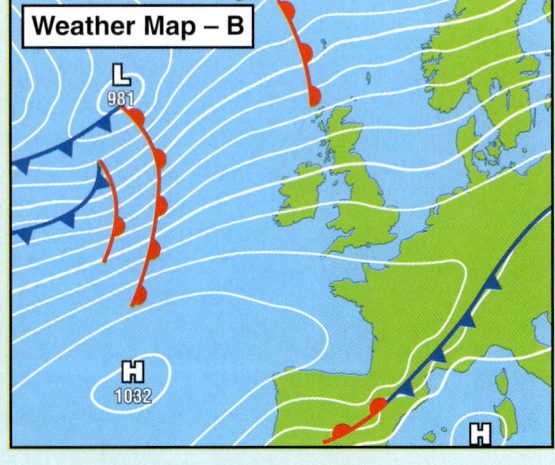

Weather Map – A

Weather Map – B

weblink
Met Éireann

CHAPTER 14: WEATHER MAPS, SATELLITE IMAGES AND GRAPHICAL SKILLS

Weather Map – C

Weather Map – D

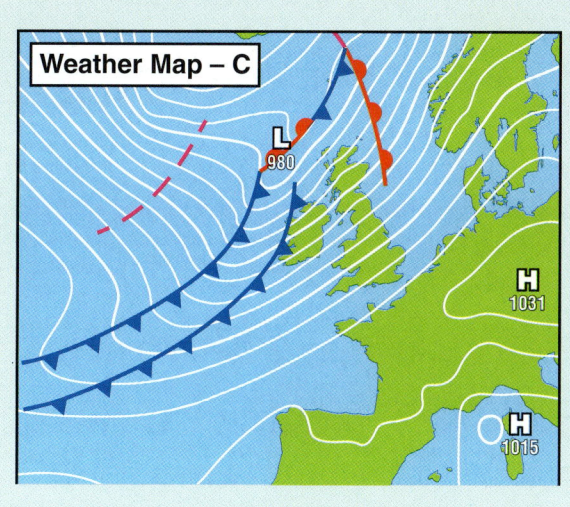

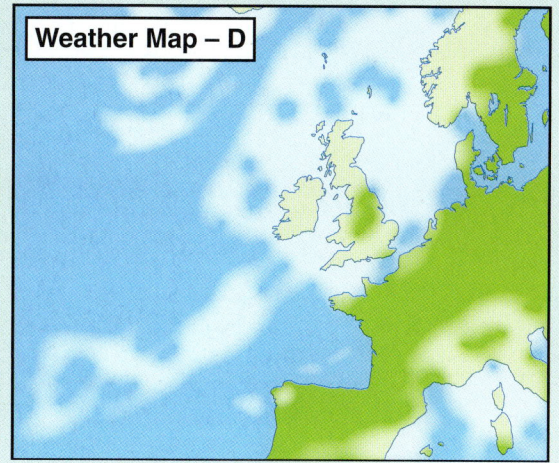

(a) Categorise the type of weather front over Central Europe in Weather Map A.
(b) State the barometric pressure of the anticyclone in Weather Map B.
(c) Is Ireland experiencing strong or light wind conditions in Weather Map C?
(d) Which of the Weather Maps A, B or C is represented by Cloud Map D?

2. **The Atlantic Weather Chart below shows a weather situation in June.**

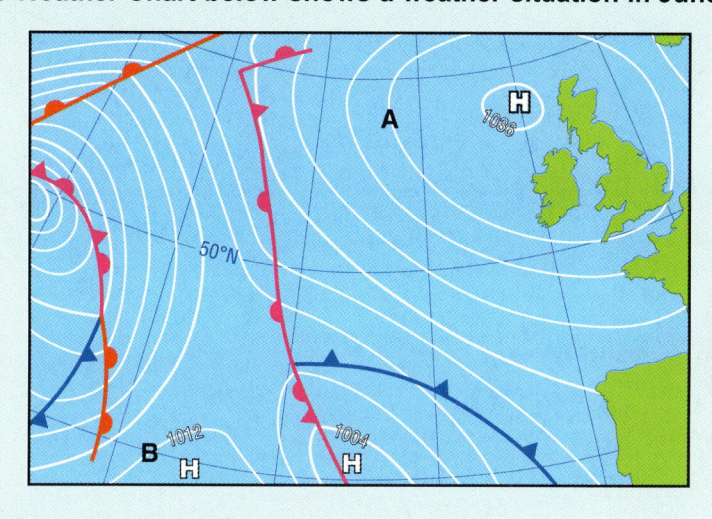

Exam Note

REMEMBER!
Always quote the units of measurement when stating weather conditions, e.g. 1012 mb.

Examine the chart and answer the questions that follow.

(i)   Is Ireland under the influence of a depression or an anticyclone?
(ii) Name the type of line at A on the map.
(iii) What is the barometric pressure at B on the map?
(iv) Which of the descriptions below best describes weather conditions over Ireland?
      Tick the correct box.
      Continuous light or heavy rain   ❏
      Showers with strong winds   ❏
      Calm dry weather with warm temperature   ❏

259

14.3 Representing statistical data on graphs and charts

Statistical data can be represented in many ways. This section contains a variety of charts and graphs that could be used in the Geographical Investigation. You may also be asked to draw, read and interpret them in an exam.

1. Pie charts

Pie charts show the proportions of parts to the whole. In Fig. 10, the pie chart emphasises the proportion of bedload stone shapes at different sites along the river.

Pie charts are used to emphasise important elements.

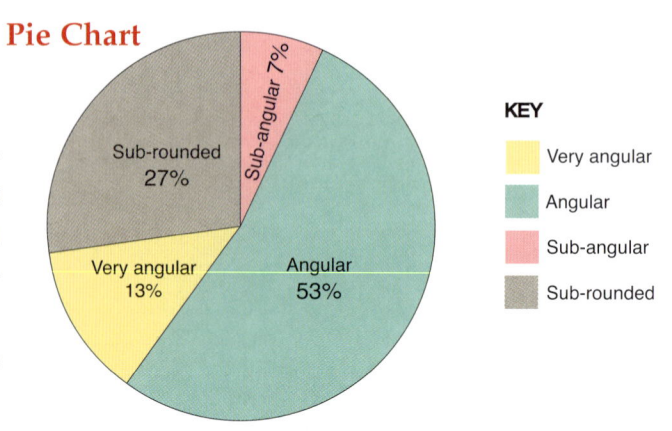

Pie Chart

Sub-angular 7%
Sub-rounded 27%
Very angular 13%
Angular 53%

KEY
- Very angular
- Angular
- Sub-angular
- Sub-rounded

Fig. 10 **A pie chart** representing stone shapes in a sample

2. Bar charts/graphs

Bar graphs can be drawn horizontally or vertically. This type of graph is very useful when comparing two or more similar items. Data can also be grouped.

In the example below, the bar graph shows the percentage of retired people living with a severe illness, an illness or in need of frequent hospital care.

(a) Vertical bar chart

	% with a severe illness	% with an illness	% in need of frequent hospital care
65-69	44.9	30.7	8.1
70-74	46.6	28.3	10.5
75-79	57.7	57.7	16.9
80+	73.6	57.6	34.9

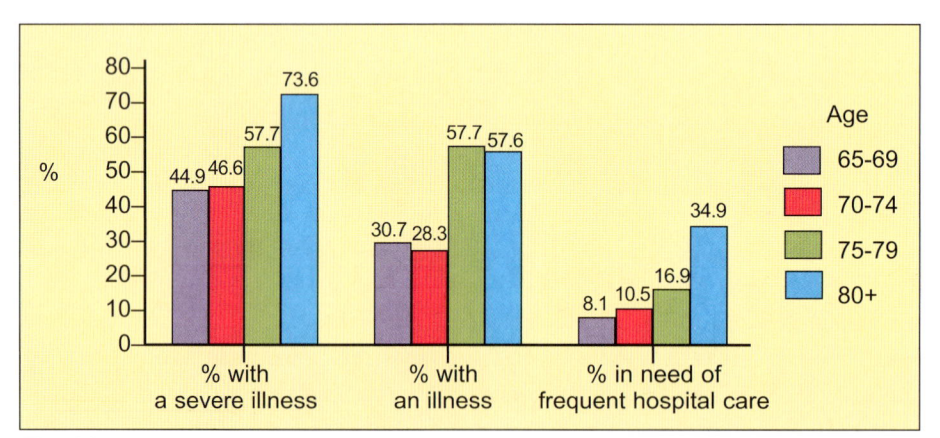

Fig. 11 **A vertical bar graph** showing the percentage of retired people in the USA with an illness and their age

> **Skills Exercise 2**
>
> **Examine Fig. 11.**
> (a) State the percentage of people who are 80+ years old (i) with a severe illness (ii) in need of frequent hospital care.
> (b) State the age group with the lowest percentage of people (i) with an illness (ii) a severe illness.

CHAPTER 14: WEATHER MAPS, SATELLITE IMAGES AND GRAPHICAL SKILLS

(b) Horizontal bar chart

In the example below, the horizontal bar charts shows how many years of life are lost to AIDS in each of the 20 countries listed and the percentage of adults with AIDS in each of these countries.

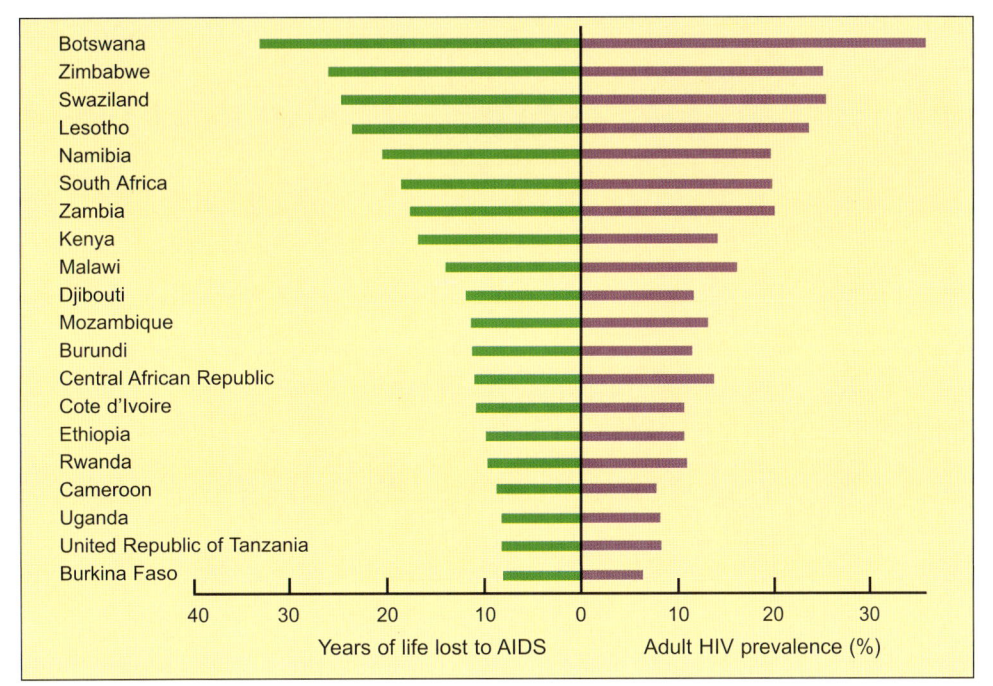

Fig. 12 A **horizontal bar chart** showing years of life lost to AIDS and the percentage of adults living with AIDS in 20 countries

Skills Exercise 3

Examine Fig. 12.
(a) State the percentage of adult HIV prevalence in Zambia.
(b) State the years of life lost to AIDS in Botswana and Rwanda.
(c) Which country has the highest number of years of life lost to AIDS?
(d) What is the percentage difference between Burkina Faso and Botswana in years of life lost to AIDS?

(c) Stacked bar chart

Stacked bar charts show more than one set of information in each bar.

The bar chart below shows sources of air pollution in Victoria, Australia and percentage rates of how heavily these sources are polluting the air.

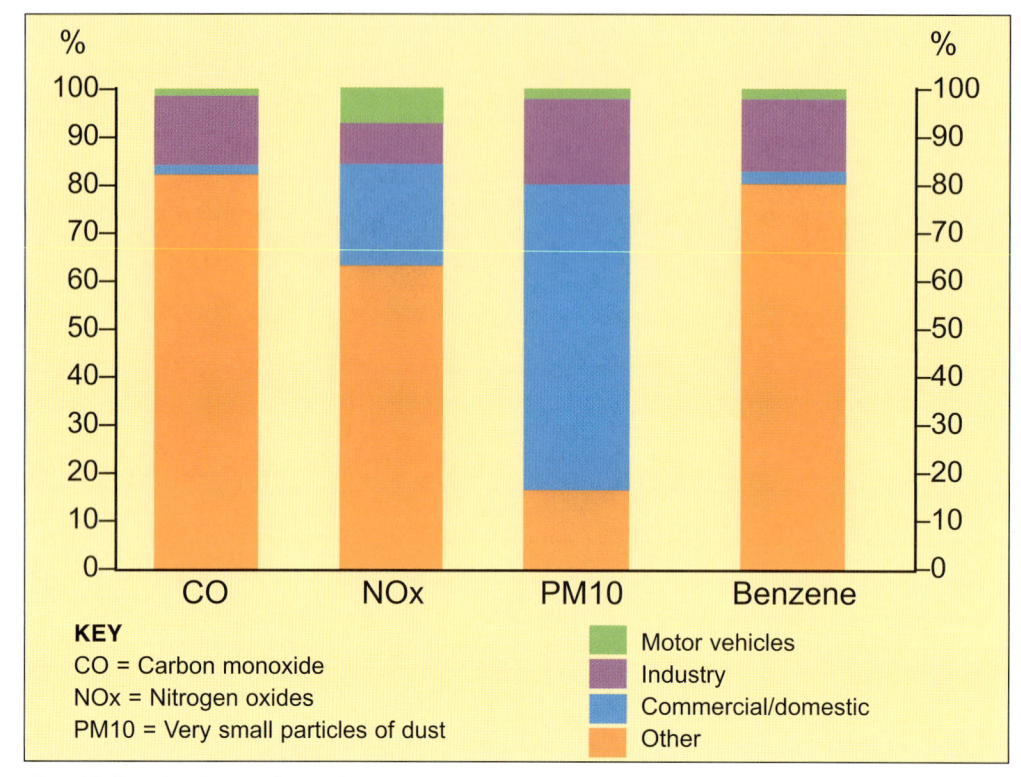

KEY
CO = Carbon monoxide
NOx = Nitrogen oxides
PM10 = Very small particles of dust

- Motor vehicles
- Industry
- Commercial/domestic
- Other

Fig. 13 **Stacked bar chart** showing air pollution sources in Victoria, Australia

Skills Exercise 4

Examine Fig. 13.
(a) What percentage of CO air pollution is due to (i) industry and (ii) other sources?
(b) What percentage of PM10 pollution is due to commerical/domestic sources?
(c) What percentage of Benzene pollution is due to motor vehicles?

3. Trend graphs

Trend graphs show trends in a set of data **over time**, e.g. population growth, birth and death rates and river discharge. They can also show the relationship between two variables. This trend graph shows how much fuel the US used from 1980 to 2004 and how much fuel it is likely to use from 2004 to 2030.

Trend graph

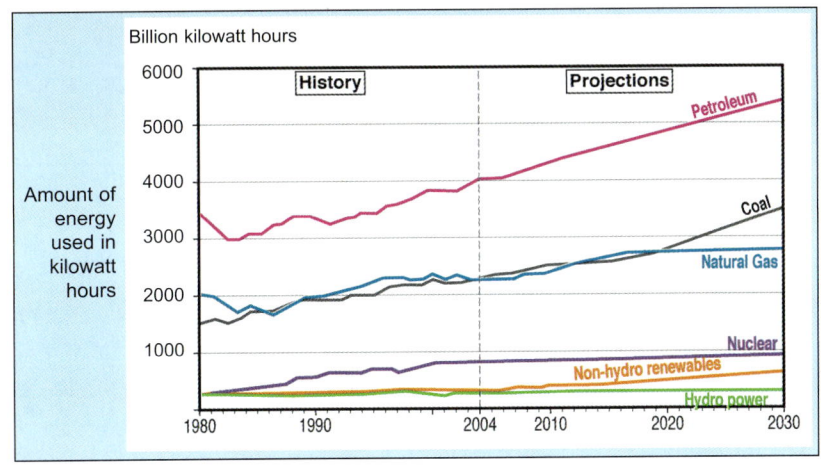

Fig. 14 **Trend graph** showing US energy consumption in kilowatts, 1980 – 2030

Skills Exercise 5

Examine Fig. 14.
(a) What is the projected amount of energy use provided by petroleum in 2022?
(b) What was the actual amount of energy use provided by coal in 1994?

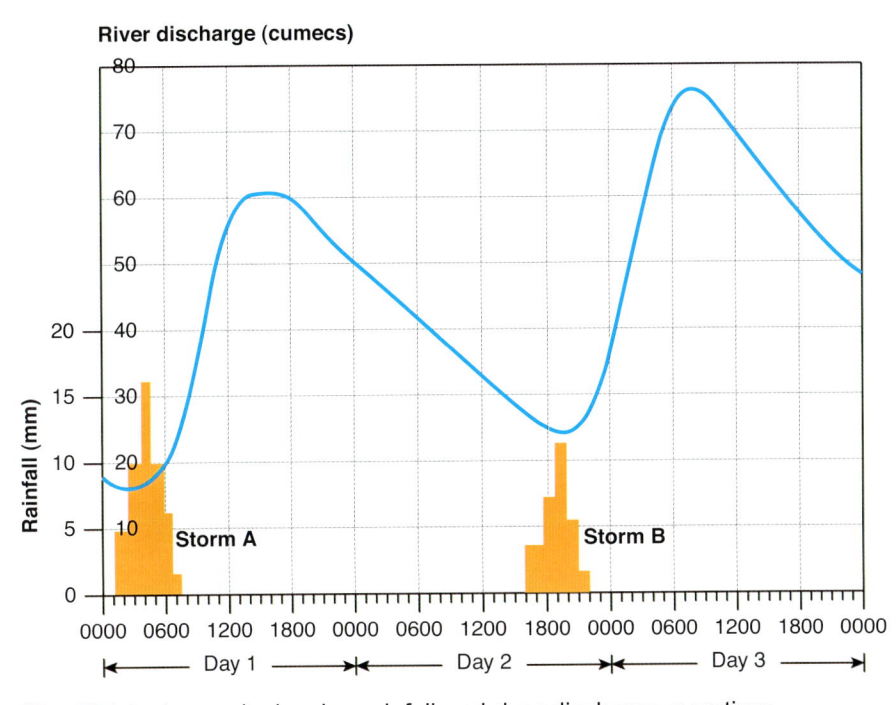

Fig. 15 A hydrograph showing rainfall and river discharge over time

Skills Exercise 6

Examine Fig. 15.
(a) What was the maximum river discharge?
(b) What was the maximum rainfall in Storm A?
(c) At what time on Day 1 did the river discharge reach 50 cumecs?
(d) Explain one reason why the discharge during Storm B is greater than that for Storm A.

263

CORE UNIT: GEOGRAPHICAL INVESTIGATION AND SKILLS

4. Triangle graphs

This type of graph is often used in relation to employment structures, soil structures, water contents and mass movements. Fig. 16 is a triangular graph showing the employment structure in three countries – A, B and C.

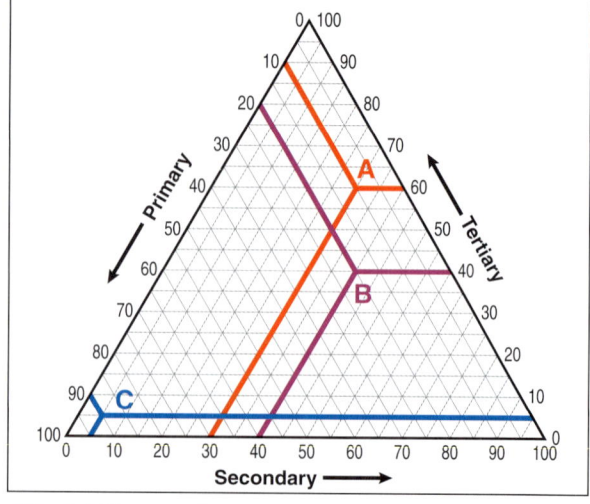

Fig. 16 The employment structure of country A is 10% primary, 30% secondary and 60% tertiary.

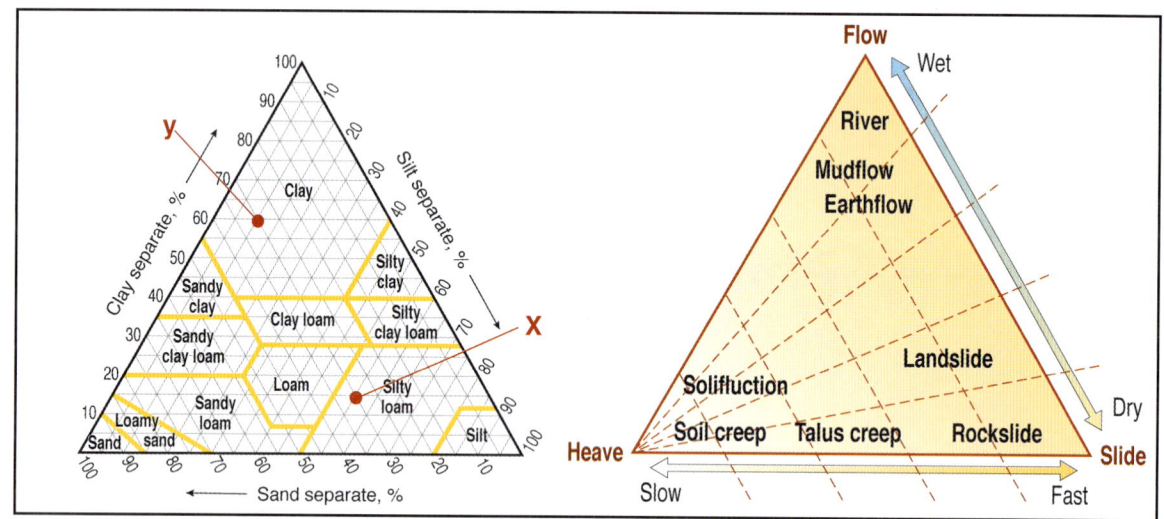

Fig. 17 A triangle graph showing soil composition

Fig. 18 A triangle graph showing mass movement classification

In Fig. 17 the soil marked X has 30% sand, 55% silt and 15% clay. This makes it a silty loam. In Fig. 18, a mudflow is a fast, wet, flowing type of mass movement.

Skills Exercise 7

Examine Fig. 17.

(a) What is the composition of the soil marked Y?
(b) What is the name of the soil with the following composition: 15% silt, 70% sand, 15% clay?

CHAPTER 14: WEATHER MAPS, SATELLITE IMAGES AND GRAPHICAL SKILLS

5. Climographs

Climographs combine bar graphs and trend graphs to show two different sets of data on one chart. Sometimes each side has a different scale, e.g. in Fig. 19 temperature is shown in degrees Celsius on the left-hand scale and rainfall is shown in millimetres on the right-hand side. The bars indicate the level of rainfall and the lines indicate temperature.

Climographs

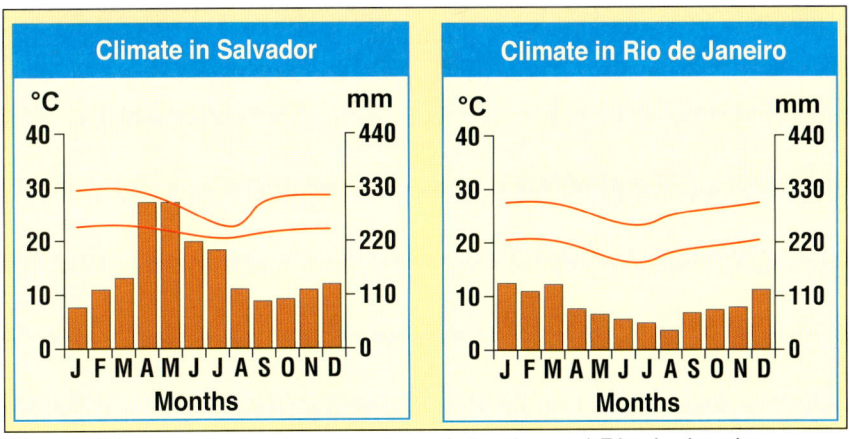

Fig. 19 Climograph showing climate in Salvador and Rio de Janeiro

Skills Exercise 8

Examine Fig. 19.
(a) What is the average temperature in Salvador in February?
(b) What is the average rainfall in millimetres in Rio de Janeiro in January?

Exam Note

REMEMBER!
Always quote the units of measurement when stating weather conditions, e.g. 1012 mb.

6. Radar charts

Radar charts compare the values of a number of sets of data.

In Fig. 20 we see the direction from which the wind is blowing and the percentage frequency of wind direction.

Skills Exercise 9

Examine Fig. 20.
For Dublin Airport:
– State the percentage of time for which the winds were westerly.
For Rosslare:
– State the most common wind direction. For what percentage of time did this wind blow?
For Valentia Observatory:
– State the percentage of time for which winds were: (i) southerly (ii) easterly.

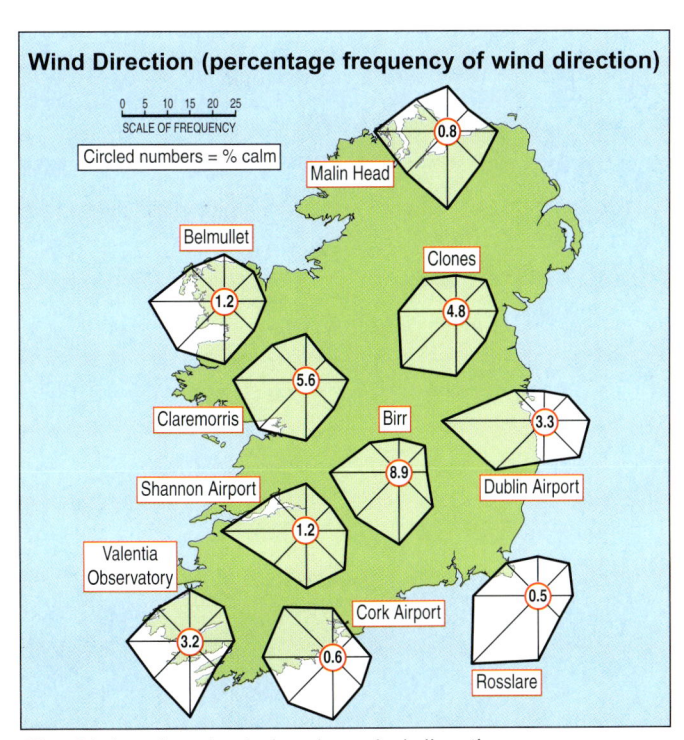

Fig. 20 A radar chart showing wind direction

265

CORE UNIT: GEOGRAPHICAL INVESTIGATION AND SKILLS

7. Wind roses

Wind roses are used to present wind speed data and wind direction data that have been collected over time, so that the dominant wind pattern for a particular area can be determined.

Wind roses are also useful as they project a large quantity of data onto one graphical plot.

The length of each 'arm' is proportional to the amount of time for which that wind speed was observed from that direction. The different colours on each arm indicate the wind speed.

Wind rose

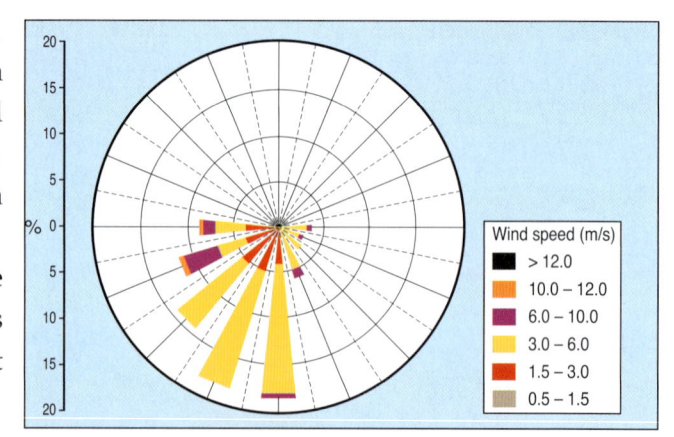

Fig. 21 A wind rose showing wind direction and speed

Skills Exercise 10

Examine Fig. 21.
Calculate the percentage of days with wind speeds between 3–6 metres per second (mps) from the south-west.

8. Choropleths

Choropleths are maps on which information is presented using a colour-coded system.

Choropleths

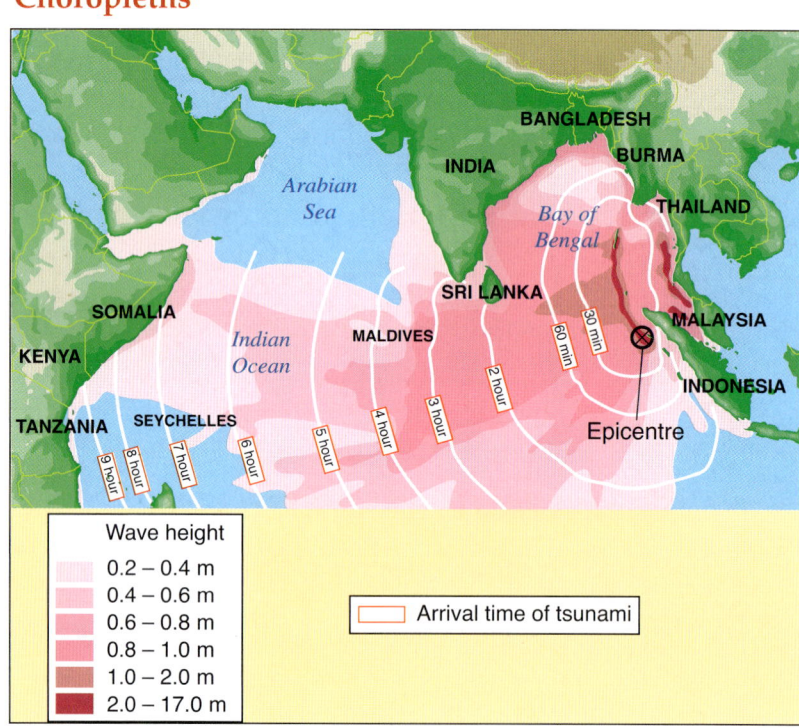

Fig. 22 The area affected by the tsunami that hit South-East Asia, December 2004

Skills Exercise 11

Examine Fig. 22.
(a) How many hours after the earthquake did the tsunami reach:
   (i) Sri Lanka? (ii) Somalia?
(b) What is the height of the wave at these two locations?
(c) What is the height of the wave at the epicentre?

CHAPTER 14: WEATHER MAPS, SATELLITE IMAGES AND GRAPHICAL SKILLS

Skills Exercise 12

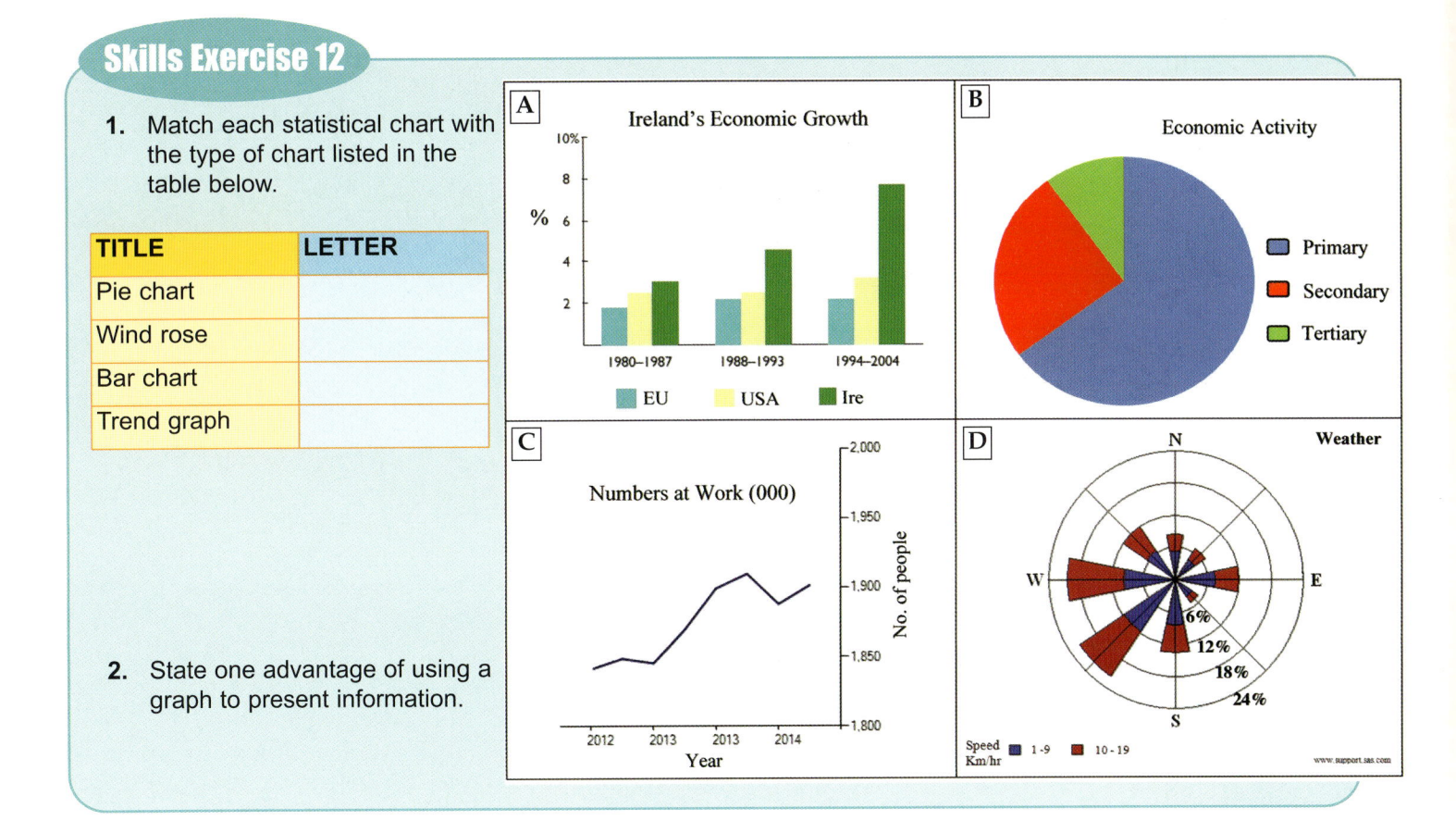

1. Match each statistical chart with the type of chart listed in the table below.

TITLE	LETTER
Pie chart	
Wind rose	
Bar chart	
Trend graph	

A Ireland's Economic Growth

B Economic Activity

C Numbers at Work (000)

D Weather

2. State one advantage of using a graph to present information.

14.4 Drawing graphs for the Leaving Certificate Exam

To draw a graph representing data from a table, follow the guidelines given below. These guidelines are based on the Leaving Certificate marking scheme.

1. Always use **graph paper**. There are marks awarded for the use of graph paper. Ask the exam supervisor for this paper.
2. Always put a **title** on your graph. The title can be copied from the title on the data table given in the question.
3. If drawing a bar or trend graph, make sure the x and y **axes** of your graph are drawn with a ruler and **labelled**. Ensure that the **scale** is carefully shown. If drawing a pie chart, use a compass to draw the circle and carefully mark the centre.
4. **Accurately** show the information from the data table using bars/points/sectors.
5. Ensure that the bars are evenly spaced and that each bar is the same width.
6. There are often marks available for overall **presentation**. Neatness gets you marks. Use colour wisely. Do not scribble with biro to colour a bar or pie sector.

Which graph to use?

1. Trend graphs show **changes over time**.
2. Bar charts/graphs and pie charts show **comparisons** or **single sets of data**.
3. When in doubt, draw a bar chart.

267

CORE UNIT: GEOGRAPHICAL INVESTIGATION AND SKILLS

Q.

Drawing a trend graph

Atmospheric CO_2 – Ireland

The table below refers to the amount of CO_2 in the atmosphere in Ireland.

Year	1980	1985	1990	2000	2002
Metric tonnes per capita	7.7	7.5	8.7	11.2	10.9

Use graph paper to draw a graph that shows the data in the table above.

(30 marks)

Leaving Certificate Paper, OL

Marking Scheme – Drawing a graph for 30 marks

Title or chart named	2 marks
Graph paper used	2 marks
Vertical axis labelled	3 marks
Horizontal axis labelled	3 marks
5 items at 4 marks each	20 marks

A.

TREND GRAPH TO SHOW ATMOSPHERIC CO_2 IN IRELAND 1980–2002

- Title 2 marks
- Graph paper used 2 marks
- Vertical axis labelled 3 marks
- 5 points plotted correctly 4 marks each
- Horizontal axis labelled 3 marks

(Vertical axis: METRIC TONNES PER CAPITA, 1–12; Horizontal axis: YEAR, 1980–2010)

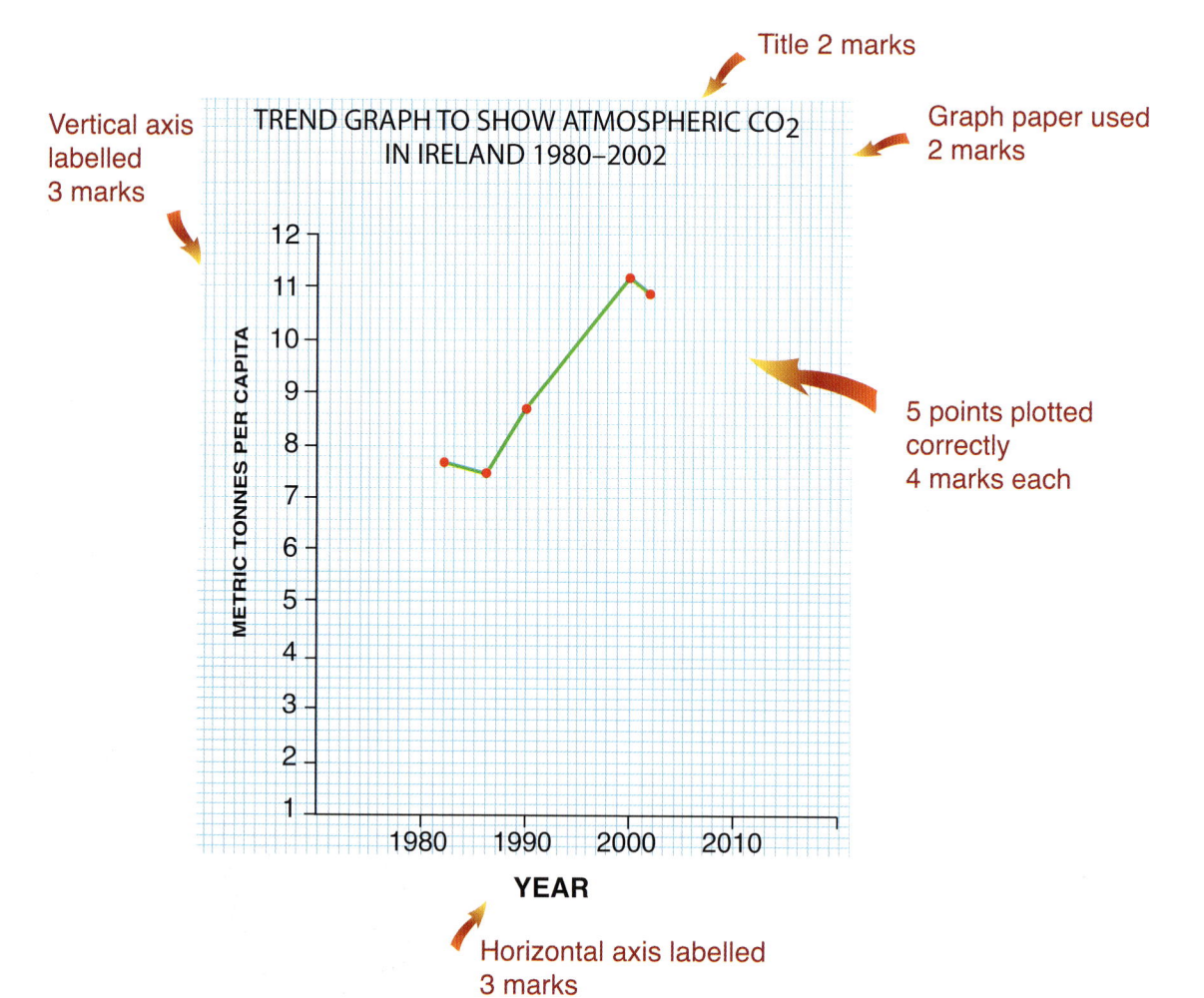

268

CHAPTER 14: WEATHER MAPS, SATELLITE IMAGES AND GRAPHICAL SKILLS

Q. Drawing a bar graph

Employment Structure

Examine the table below, showing the percentage of people in employment in various economic sectors in Ireland (1984–2004).

	YEAR	
SECTOR	1984	2004
Primary	24%	6%
Secondary	31%	28%
Tertiary	45%	66%

Using graph paper, draw a graph suitable to illustrate this data.

(20 marks) Leaving Certificate Paper, HL

Marking Scheme – Drawing a graph for 20 marks

Title or chart named	2 marks
Use of graph paper	2 marks
Scaled axis	2 marks
6 bars/points plotted (at 2 marks each)	12 marks
Overall presentation (neatness and key)	2 marks

Accept bar chart / histogram / trend graph / scatter graph / pie chart etc.

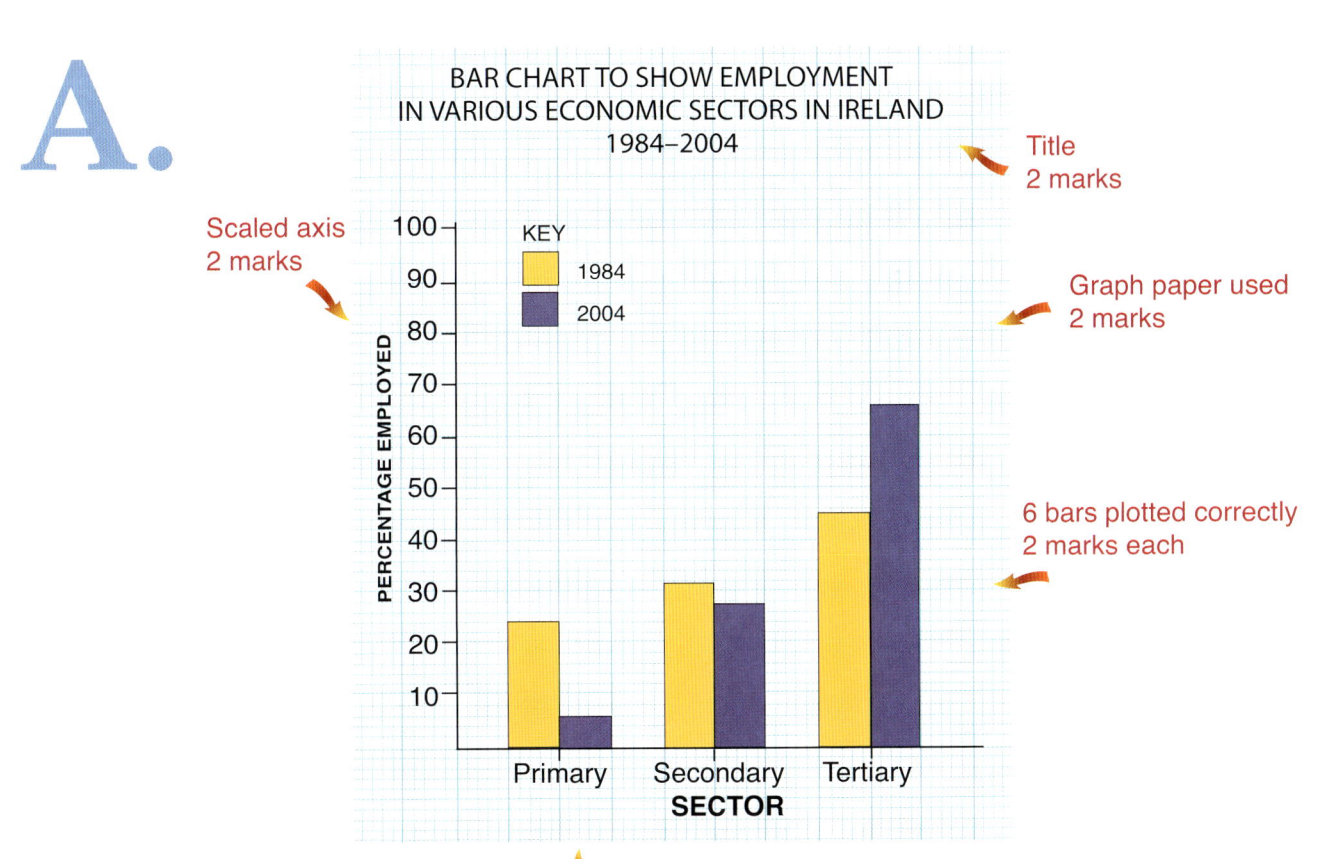

A.

BAR CHART TO SHOW EMPLOYMENT IN VARIOUS ECONOMIC SECTORS IN IRELAND 1984–2004

Title – 2 marks

Scaled axis – 2 marks

KEY: 1984 (yellow), 2004 (blue)

PERCENTAGE EMPLOYED (y-axis: 0–100)
SECTOR (x-axis: Primary, Secondary, Tertiary)

Graph paper used – 2 marks

6 bars plotted correctly – 2 marks each

Overall presentation – 2 marks

269

CORE UNIT: GEOGRAPHICAL INVESTIGATION AND SKILLS

14.5 Satellite images

Satellite photos are used in many situations. Disaster areas, urban growth, hurricanes, ground cover, deforestation, sea surface temperatures, wave heights, volcanic activity, forest fires and the greening of the planet at springtime can all be seen by satellites. In the Leaving Certificate exam you will be expected to identify landforms and events on satellite images.

weblink
Satellite images

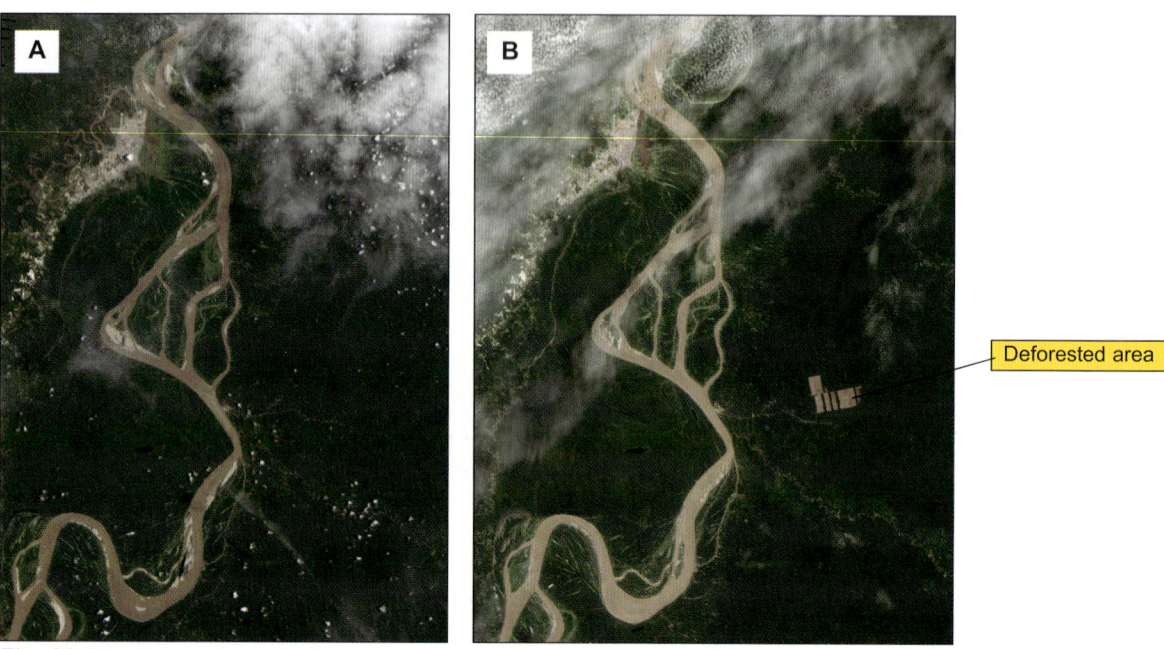

Fig. 23 Satellite images showing untouched forest in Peru in Photo A and the start of deforestation in Photo B

Fig. 24 Flooding on the Mississippi River, USA

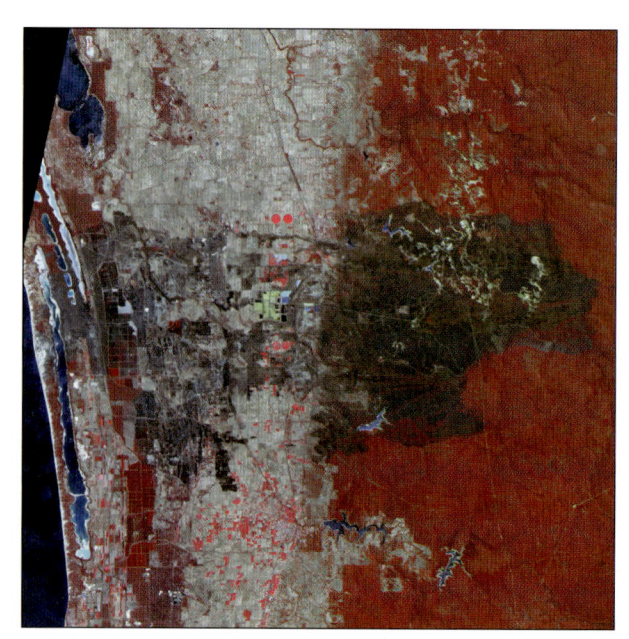

Fig. 25 A fire burn scar in Western Australia

CHAPTER 14: WEATHER MAPS, SATELLITE IMAGES AND GRAPHICAL SKILLS

Chapter Revision Questions are covered within Chapter 14

LC Exam Questions

1. Examine the population graphic below for the Republic of Ireland (State) and Cork-South Central and answer the questions.
   (i) In which age group is the greatest overall percentage of population in the State?
   (ii) What is the total percentage of the population in the 35-39 age group in Cork South-Central?
   (iii) What percentage of Cork South-Central's population is over 65 years?
   (iv) What is the difference in population in the 20-24 age group between Cork South-Central and the State?

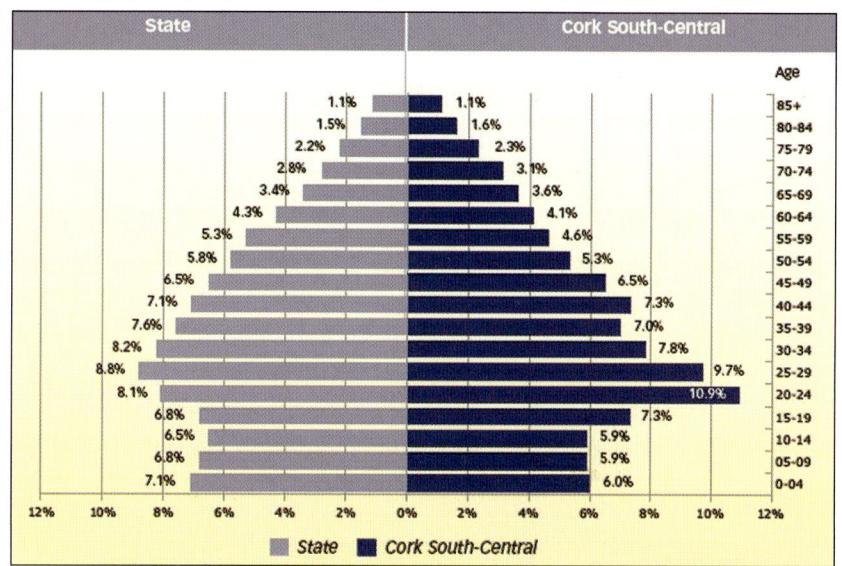

2. Examine the weather charts below and answer each of the following questions.
   (i) Match each weather chart with the element of weather that it represents, by writing the correct letter in each case, in the table below.

Elements of Weather	Letter
Temperature	
Rainfall	
Cloud	
Pressure	

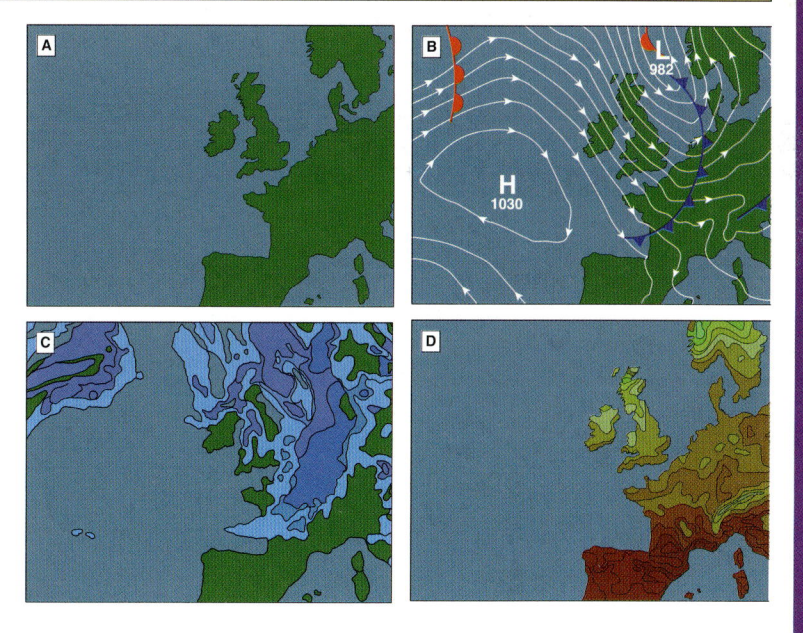

   (ii) Indicate whether the statement below is true or false, by ticking the correct box.
   'Isobars are lines joining places of equal pressure on a weather chart.'
   True ❏
   False ❏

271

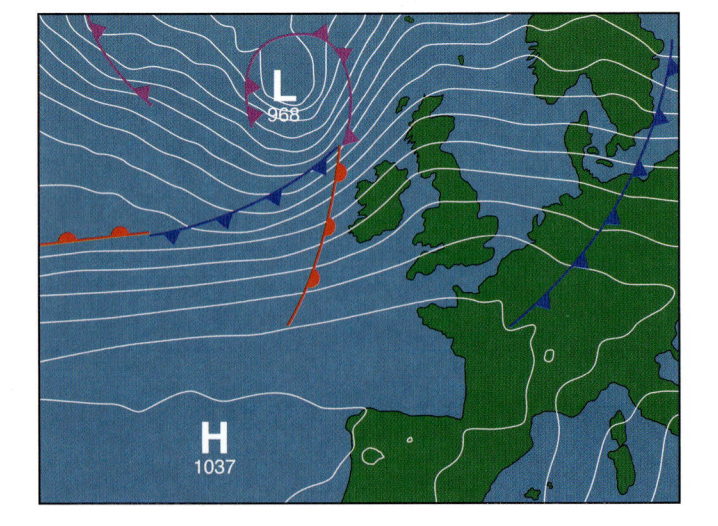

CORE UNIT: GEOGRAPHICAL INVESTIGATION AND SKILLS

LC Exam Questions

3. Examine the wind rose to the right and answer each of the following questions.
   (i) What percentage of wind blowing from the south west was at a speed of between 1–9 km/h?
   (ii) What percentage of wind blew from the north west?
   (iii) From what direction did the wind blow most frequently?
   (iv) From what direction did the wind blow least frequently?

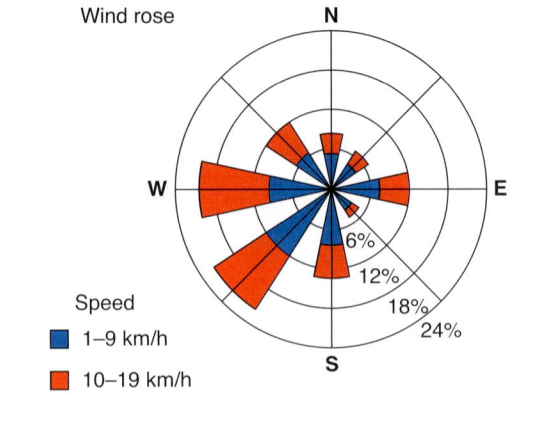

4. Examine the table to the right which shows Daily Irish Speakers in Gaeltacht Areas in 2006 and 2011 and answer the following questions.
   (i) What was the percentage change in Daily Irish Speakers in All Gaeltacht Areas between 2006 and 2011?
   (ii) Calculate X, the decrease in the total number of Daily Irish Speakers in the Meath County Gaeltacht area between 2006 and 2011.
   (iii) How many Gaeltacht areas had an increase in the number of Daily Irish Speakers between 2006 and 2011?
   (iv) Explain briefly one reason why the percentage of Daily Irish Speakers in the Mayo County Gaeltacht area fell by 8.5% between 2006 and 2011.

Gaeltacht Area	2006	2011	Change in Daily Irish Speakers	
	Persons	Persons	Total	Percentage
Cork County	867	982	115	13.3
Donegal County	6,956	7,047	91	1.3
Galway City	571	636	65	11.4
Galway County	9,654	10,085	431	4.5
Kerry County	2,394	2,501	107	4.5
Mayo County	1,281	1,172	-109	-8.5
Meath County	336	314	X	-6.5
Waterford County	456	438	-18	-3.9
All Gaeltacht Areas	22,515	23,175	660	2.9

5. Examine the Irish weather chart to the right. State whether each of the following statements is true or false by ticking the correct box.
   (i) The weather over the Iberian Peninsula is very calm.
      True ❏   False ❏
   (ii) There is a cold front over central and northern Europe.
      True ❏   False ❏
   (iii) There is an anticyclone affecting Ireland and Great Britain.
      True ❏   False ❏
   (iv) Winds are light over Ireland.
      True ❏   False ❏

CHAPTER 14: WEATHER MAPS, SATELLITE PHOTOS AND GRAPHICAL SKILLS

LC Exam Questions

6. Examine the weather chart to the right and indicate whether each of the following statements is true or false, by ticking the correct box.
   (i) The pressure over the south-west coast of Ireland is 1022 hPa.
   True ☐ False ☐
   (ii) There is a warm front located on the south coast of England.
   True ☐ False ☐
   (iii) Ireland is under the influence of a north-easterly airflow.
   True ☐ False ☐
   (iv) Winds over Ireland are strong to gale force.
   True ☐ False ☐

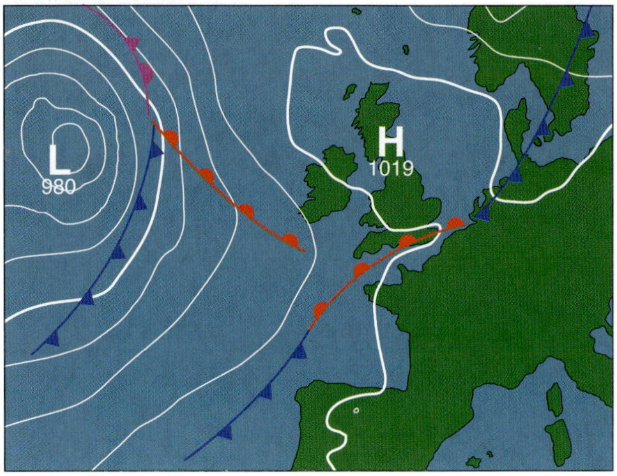

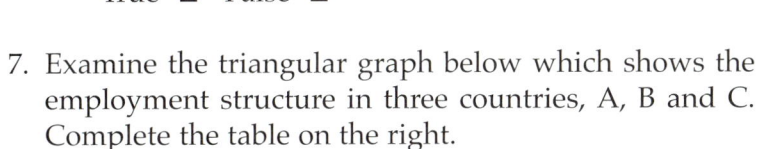

7. Examine the triangular graph below which shows the employment structure in three countries, A, B and C. Complete the table on the right.

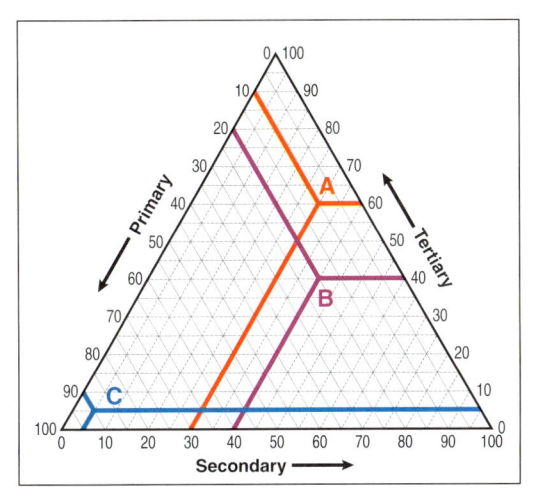

EMPLOYMENT STRUCTURE	COUNTRY
Primary 20%, Secondary 40%, Tertiary 40%	
Primary 90%, Secondary 5%, Tertiary 5%	
Primary 10%, Secondary 30%, Tertiary 60%	
Which country would appear to have the most developed economy?	

8. Examine the pie chart which shows the consumption of renewable energy in the European Union (EU) in 2011 and answer each of the following questions.
   (i) What was the percentage of hydro power consumed?
   (ii) Calculate X, the percentage of solar energy consumed.
   (iii) Calculate B, the percentage of biomass generated from wood and wood waste.
   (iv) Explain briefly what is meant by geothermal energy.

273

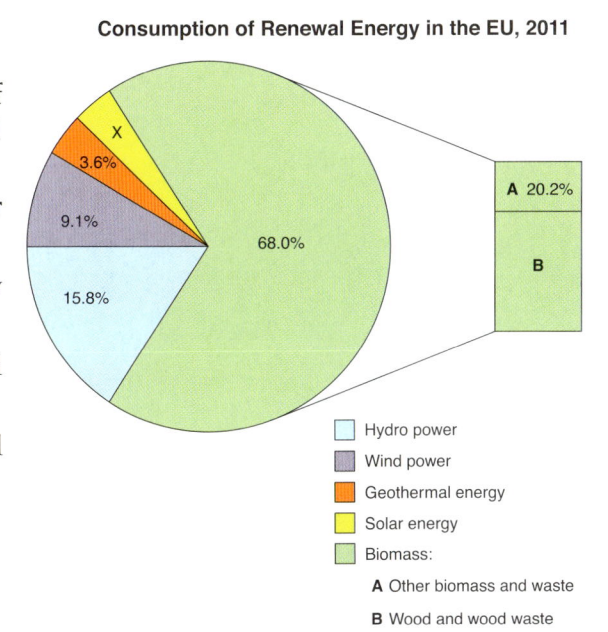

CORE UNIT: GEOGRAPHICAL INVESTIGATION AND SKILLS

LC Exam Questions

9. Match **each** weather map symbol in Column A with its description in Column B.

Column A	Column B
A	Warm Front = 1
B	Isobars = 2
C	Anticyclone = 3
D	Cold Front = 4

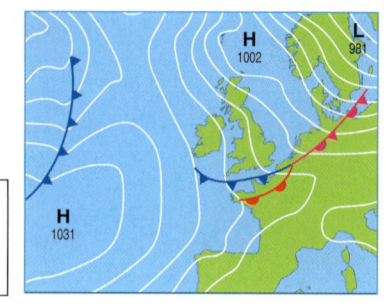

   ___ = A   ___ = B
   ___ = C   ___ = D

10. Examine the table to the right, showing selected unemployment statistics for 2014.
    Using graph paper, draw a graph suitable to illustrate these data.

Country	Unemployment rate (% of adult population)
Austria	4.9%
Estonia	9.3%
France	10.9%
Latvia	11.5%
Poland	9.9%
Spain	25.8%

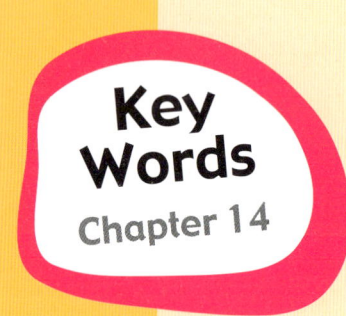

Key Words Chapter 14

Key Words

You should be able to explain both verbally and in writing each of the key words listed below.

anticyclone
depression
isobar
isohel
isohyet
isoline
isotach
isotherm

Digital Resources are available for this chapter at mentorbooks.ie/resources

CHAPTER 15

Physical, Administrative and Cultural Regions

Key Theme

A region is an area of the earth's surface that is distinctive in some way. Regions can be identified by one or more human and/or natural characteristics, e.g. cultural or landscape. Boundaries of regions can change over time. These changes affect cultural groups. The study of regions illustrates the geographical complexity of the interaction between economic, cultural and physical processes.

Learning Outcomes

At the end of this chapter you will be able to:
- Define the term region.
- Identify the groups into which regions can be classified.
- Explain how climate and landscape can be used to define a region.
- Define the term administrative region and explain how central and local government is organised in Ireland and France.
- Define the term cultural region and discuss the characteristics of language and religious regions in Ireland, Europe and in Islamic regions.
- Discuss how language regions in Ireland have changed over time.
- Discuss changes to political boundaries and their impact on cultural groups in Poland.

Contents

15.1	The concept of a region	276
15.2	Climatic regions	277
15.3	Administrative regions	282
	Case Study 1: Functions of local and central government agencies in Ireland	282
	Case Study 2: Functions of local and central government agencies in France	284
15.4	Cultural regions	285
	Case Study 3: Gaeltacht regions in Ireland	285
	Case Study 4: Language regions in Belgium	289
	Case Study 5: Religious regions in Northern Ireland	292
	Case Study 6: Islamic regions	293
15.5	The complexity of cultural regions – Boundary changes	295
	Case Study 7: Boundary changes in Poland	295

Revision Space

Chapter Revision Questions – LC Exam Questions – Key Word List 297

15.1 The concept of a region

A **region** is an area with a characteristic (or characteristics) that sets it apart from other areas, making it distinctive or unique in some way, e.g. the Sahara desert in Africa or the 'sunny south east' of Ireland. A region can be identified on the basis of a variety of characteristics such as its landscape, climate, economic development, language, religion or government.

People may move between regions bringing their way of life with them and introducing it to the people of their adopted region.

Types of regions

There are five types of regions, as show in the table below.

TYPES OF REGIONS		
Regions		**Examples**
1. Physical regions	Climate	Cool temperate – Ireland Mediterranean – Mezzogiorno, Italy
	Geomorphic (landscape)	Upland – Munster Ridge and Valley province Lowland – Paris Basin; North European Plain Rock type – the Burren, County Clare
2. Administrative regions	Local authorities	Dublin City Council, district councils French *départements*
	EU administrative regions	Ireland's Southern region Northern and Western (N&W) region
3. Cultural regions	Language	Ireland – Gaeltacht; Belgium – Flanders, Wallonia Basque region of Northern Spain
	Religion	Northern Ireland; Islamic World
4. Nodal/urban/city regions		Dublin Paris
5. Socio-economic regions	Core regions (wealthy)	Urban – Paris; Dublin; Randstaad Industrial – Milan; Turin; Genoa; Ruhr Agricultural – Paris Basin; North Italian Plain
	Peripheral/less developed regions Regions of industrial decline	N&W region, Mezzogiorno; Northern Norway Sambre Meuse Valley, Belgium North coast of Spain; Drogheda

It is important to remember that **physical** and **human factors** influence the development/underdevelopment of most regions. These determine the region's uniqueness and progress. The symbols shown in the table below are used throughout the regional section of this book to indicate when a physical or human factor is being discussed.

FACTORS AFFECTING REGIONS	
Physical Factors	**Human Factors**
Climate Relief Drainage Soils Resources	Population Transport Government/EU policy History Market

CHAPTER 15: PHYSICAL, ADMINISTRATIVE AND CULTURAL REGIONS

15.2 Climatic regions

1. Climatic regions

Climatic regions are areas of the world that experience a particular climate. Climatic regions tend to be large in size, covering entire countries and sections of the globe. For example, the Tundra climate encircles the earth north of the Arctic Circle. It is found in all countries that have land in this zone. So Canada, Greenland, Northern Norway, Northern Sweden, Northern Finland and Russia are united in one climatic region – the Tundra climatic region.

Climate is an important physical factor that influences the distribution and type of natural vegetation, population density and animal species found in a region. For example, we tend to associate camels, cacti and nomadic tribes with deserts.

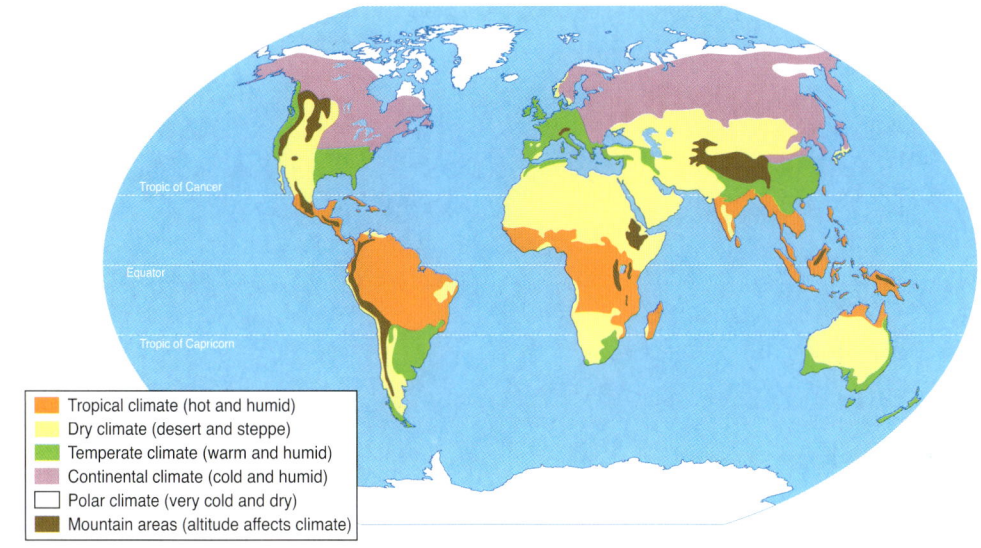

Tropical climate (hot and humid)
Dry climate (desert and steppe)
Temperate climate (warm and humid)
Continental climate (cold and humid)
Polar climate (very cold and dry)
Mountain areas (altitude affects climate)

Fig. 1 The world's main climatic zones

Climates on earth can be divided into hot, temperate and cold climates. Within these three divisions, there are further subdivisions.

Hot Climates	Temperate Climates	Cold Climates
Equatorial Savanna Monsoon Desert	Cool temperate oceanic Warm temperate oceanic (Mediterranean) Cool temperate continental	Tundra (sub-arctic) Boreal (coniferous forest)

Cool temperate oceanic climate – North-west Europe: Ireland

Ireland and north-west Europe have a cool temperate oceanic climate.

This type of climate is found on the western sides of continents between latitudes 40° to 55° north and south of the equator. Therefore, Ireland has mild winters (average 6°C in January) and moderately warm summers (average 15°C in July). Rainfall is frequent throughout the year (1,500 mm), with more rainfall in winter.

Ireland's climate is influenced by several factors, including latitude, the sea, south-westerly winds and the movement of frontal depressions.

(a) The influence of latitude on Ireland's climate

Ireland is located between 51.5° and 55.5° north of the equator. This influences the amount of sunshine and the temperatures that we experience throughout the year. Ireland's climate is moderate because of its latitude between the equator and North Pole.

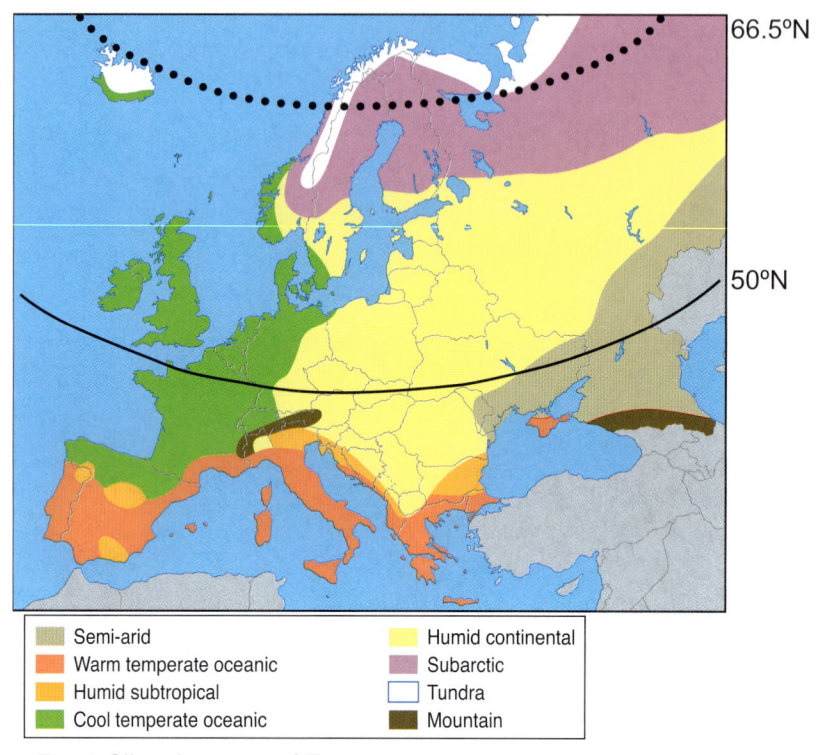

Fig. 2 Climatic zones of Europe

(b) The influence of the sea on Ireland's climate

The sea warms and dampens the prevailing south-westerly winds and keeps the coast free of ice in winter.

The sea acts as an enormous storage heater. The sea warms up slowly in spring and summer and holds this heat until the winter. Throughout the winter, the sea gradually loses the warmth it picked up earlier in the year. This keeps our land temperatures in winter much higher than they should be, given our latitude. Without the influence of the sea, average winter temperatures in Ireland could be 10°C colder. The warm ocean current – the **North Atlantic Drift** – keeps the water warm and prevents it from freezing, as well as being a source of heat for the south-westerly winds.

In summer, the land heats quickly and the sea is relatively cold. Sea breezes blowing onshore in the afternoons keep summer temperatures down.

In the central part of Ireland, away from the sea's influence, temperatures are slightly more extreme, with average summer temperatures of 16°C and in winter of 2.5°C, (see Fig. 4 on page 279).

(c) The influence of frontal depressions on Ireland's climate

Cold (**polar**) and warm (**tropical**) air masses meet over the Atlantic Ocean forming the **polar front**. Movement of the polar front creates disturbances in the atmosphere called **depressions** or lows.

These depressions move across the Atlantic Ocean from west to east. Ireland lies in the path of these depressions causing our weather to change from day to day. The rainfall created in these depressions is called **frontal rain**. This is the most common type of rain, occurring throughout the year, (see Chapter 14, page 256).

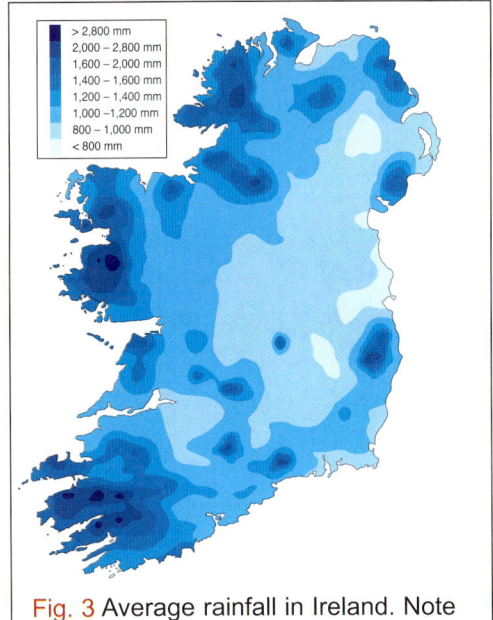

Fig. 3 Average rainfall in Ireland. Note the high rainfall levels over the upland areas

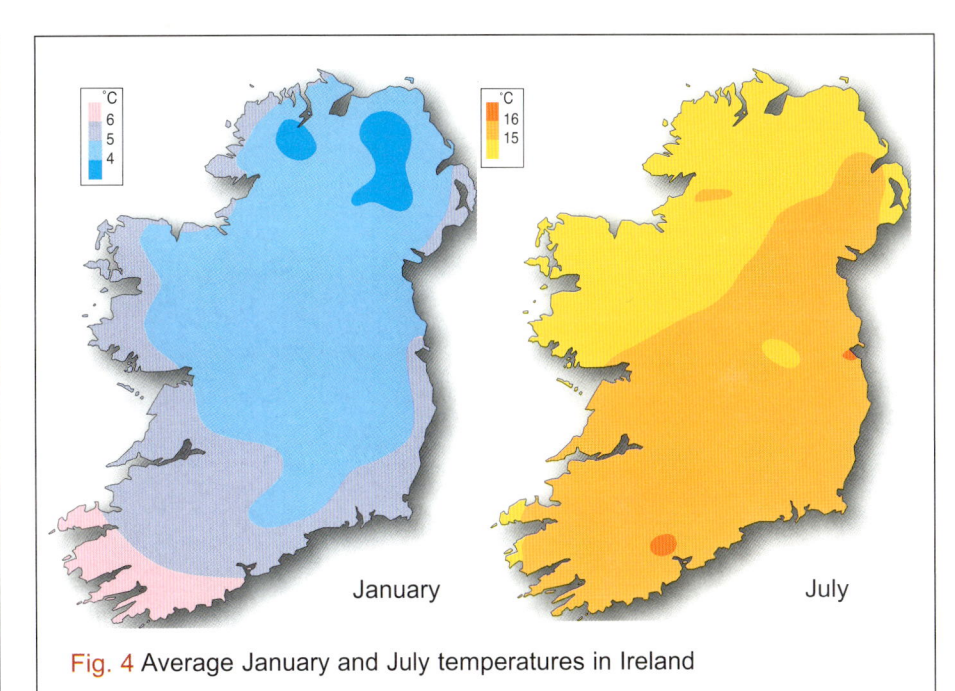

Fig. 4 Average January and July temperatures in Ireland

(d) The influence of south-westerly winds on Ireland's climate

The prevailing south-westerly winds blow across several thousand kilometres of the Atlantic Ocean before reaching Ireland. This influences Ireland's temperatures and precipitation levels.

This prevailing wind picks up water vapour by evaporation on its journey across the ocean. When the moist air reaches land, it is forced to rise above the mountains along the west coast, causing **relief rainfall**. This is why precipitation in some parts of the west of Ireland is more than treble (2,800 mm) that of the eastern part of the country (800 mm), (see Fig. 3 above).

Fig. 5 Relief rain over mountains in Kerry. Note leeward side and windward side.

2. Geomorphic regions (landscape)

Geomorphic regions have unique landscapes based on their rock type, structure and relief, e.g. the Karst landscape of the Burren in County Clare.

You have already studied a geomorphic karst region in Chapter 7. The final geomorphic region you will study is the North European Plain.

The North European Plain

The **North European Plain** is a lowland region covering more than half of Europe. It includes Poland; northern Germany; southern Scandinavia; Belgium; the Netherlands; northern and western France; and the Romanian, Bulgarian and Hungarian plains. Several physical factors combine to make the North European Plain one of the most densely populated areas of Europe. This region is particularly important to your study of the Paris Basin core region in Chapter 20.

Soils

During the last ice age, continental ice sheets covered parts of this region. Wherever the glaciers stopped, they deposited great quantities of moraine and boulder clay. The meltwater also deposited sands and gravels.

Strong winds blew across these deposits and lifted fine sands and silts, redepositing them across the southern edge of the plain as **limon**, or **loess**. Limon makes a very fertile, stoneless soil. As a result, it is heavily cultivated, e.g. the Paris Basin.

Climate

The climate of the North European Plain:
- Generally mild and moist, adding to the agricultural prosperity of the region.
- Rainfall is evenly distributed throughout the year.
- Temperatures are moderate.

Drainage

Large rivers such as the Seine, the Rhine, the Elbe and the Loire flow across the region in a north-westerly direction, providing fertile alluvium, natural communications and trade routes.

Relief and resources

The lowland landscape (**topography**) has allowed intensive commerical agriculture and the development of one of the world's most efficient transportation networks. Major roads, railways, rivers and canals stretch across the plain linking major cities such as Paris and Berlin.

The plain is at the heart of European industrial power. Coal and iron ore deposits lie beneath the glacial sediments in Germany, Poland, France and Belgium. The rivers, soils, climate and abundance of mineral/metal resources helped the region become highly industrialised, attractive for settlement and one of the most densely-populated areas in Europe, e.g. the Paris Basin.

weblink
Geomorphic regions in Europe

CHAPTER 15: PHYSICAL, ADMINISTRATIVE AND CULTURAL REGIONS

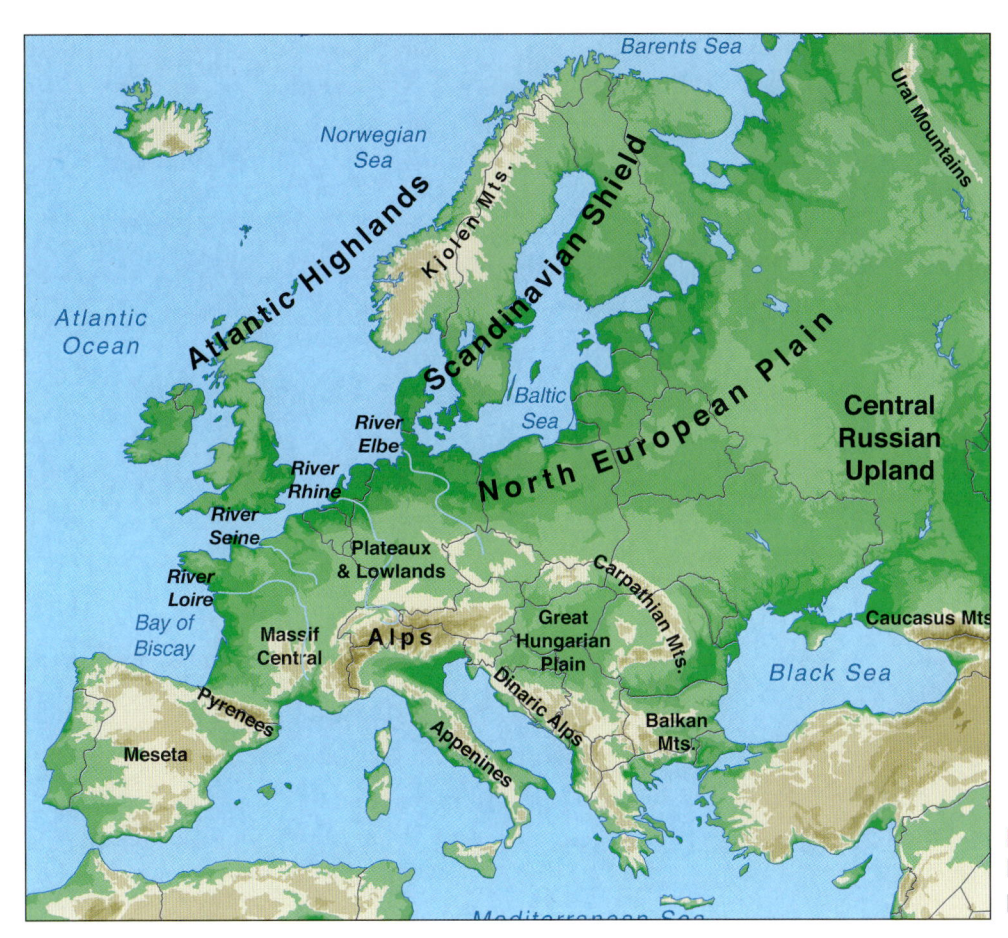

Fig. 6 The location of the North European Plain and other physical regions of Europe

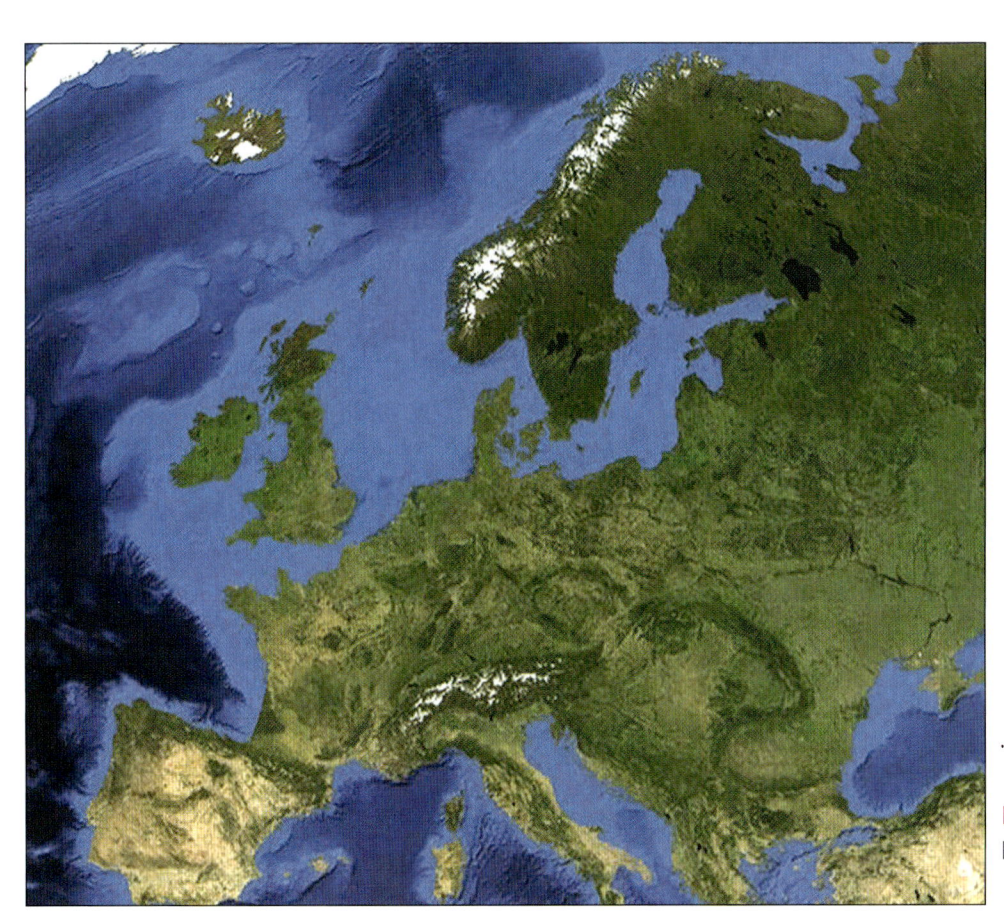

Fig. 7 Satellite photo showing the physical landscape of Europe

281

CORE UNIT: REGIONAL GEOGRAPHY

15.3 Administrative regions

Administrative regions are areas controlled by local or central government agencies. Local agencies are town councils and county councils. Central agencies are government departments.

We will examine two case studies – Ireland and France.

CHAPTER 15

Case Study 1

Functions of local and central government in Ireland

(a) At local level

Local government deals with motor taxation, housing, water supply, road construction and repair and maintaining public parks, swimming pools and other public leisure facilities such as libraries. The ability of the local government to carry out its functions depends upon the levels of financial support provided by the central government. The introduction of the Local Property Tax in 2013 provided local government with an extra source of funding. Local and regional government structures were revised in 2014.

Local government occurs at three levels:

1. **County/city level:** There are 26 County Councils, three City Councils (Dublin, Cork and Galway), two City and County Councils (Limerick City and County Council, and Waterford City and County Council).
2. **Municipal district level:** Each council administrative area, apart from the three Dublin county councils and the three city councils, has a system of districts based on electoral areas. Each council has at least two municipal districts. There are 95 municipal districts across Ireland.
3. **Regional assembly level:** The membership of a regional assembly consists of members of the local authorities within the region. In January 2015 three Regional Assemblies were established to replace the former Border Midlands West and Southern and Eastern Regional assemblies.

THE RESPONSIBILITIES OF LOCAL AND CENTRAL GOVERNMENT AGENCIES	
Local government	**Central government**
1. Fire brigade services, school warden 2. Parking 3. Motor taxation and road repair 4. Planning and provision of housing 5. The maintenance of recreational facilities, e.g. public parks, swimming pools and other public leisure facilities such as libraries 6. Environmental protection, water supply and sewerage, litter management 7. Heritage issues 8. Health and education, e.g. clinics and Education and Training Boards (ETBs) 9. Elections	The provision of larger, more expensive national services, such as: 1. School buildings 2. Roads 3. Hospitals 4. Courts.

CHAPTER 15: PHYSICAL, ADMINISTRATIVE AND CULTURAL REGIONS

Funding for services

(b) At regional level

The EU divides Europe up into many administrative regions in order to allocate funds for projects such as road building and farm improvement. Today Ireland is divided into three **regional assemblies**. Each assembly receives different amounts of EU funding.

- The **Northern and Western Regional Assembly (N&W)**
- The **Southern Regional Assembly**
- The **Eastern and Midland Regional Assembly**

These three regional assemblies replaced the former regional assemblies of the Border Midlands West (BMW) and Southern and Eastern (S&E) assemblies.

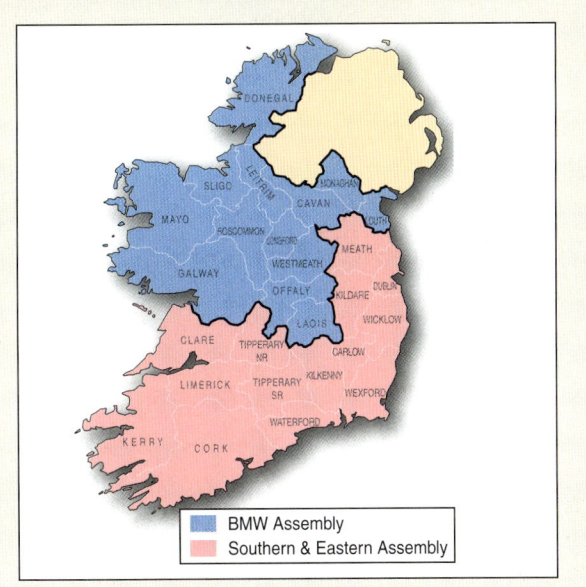

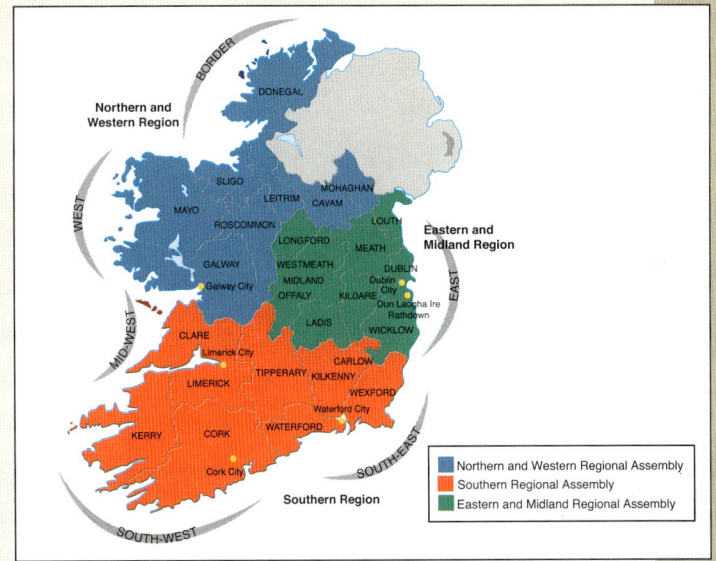

Fig. 8 Ireland's regional assemblies before 2015

Fig. 9 Ireland's regional assemblies today

Functions of regional assemblies:

- To manage and monitor the European Regional Development Fund (ERDF) regional programmes.
- To promote the co-ordination of public services in the region.
- To monitor and make proposals in relation to the general impact of EU funding.
- To make public bodies aware of the regional implications of their policies and plans.

Funding for services

The source of funding for the services listed in the table on the bottom of page 282 provided by local and central government, includes:

1. Local Property Tax
2. Rates on commercial and industrial buildings.
3. Income from goods and services (housing rents, planning fees).
4. Exchequer grants from the central government.
5. Internal capital receipts (sale of houses, land).
6. Borrowing.

CORE UNIT: REGIONAL GEOGRAPHY

CHAPTER 15
Case Study 2

Functions of local and central government in France

Like Ireland, France also has a three-level (tier) local government administration system. The three levels are the *commune*, the *département* and the *région*. Each level is a distinct legal body, responsible for funding and providing the same types of local services and projects as in Ireland.

Communes

Formed in 1789, they are the oldest form of local authority in France. They are responsible for water supply, lighting, park maintenance and primary school buildings. They are similar in size to small Irish towns, villages and parishes with an elected mayor and assembly. Most *communes* have less than 1,000 people. Central government is urging smaller communes to merge together to increase efficiency.

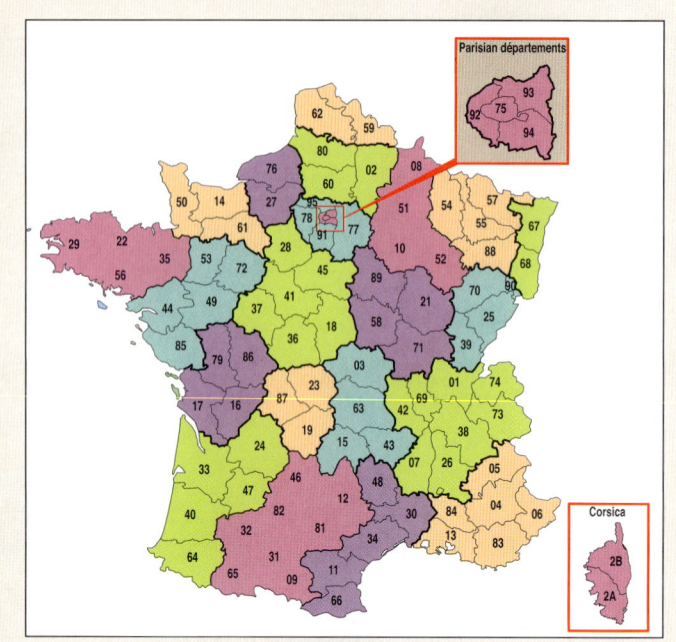

Fig. 10 *Départements* in France

Départements

Formed in 1790, they are responsible for planning, public housing, car tax, secondary schools and colleges, roads, health and social services. There are 101 *départements* – 96 in France (including Corsica) and 5 overseas. All have a similar size and shape. Similar to Irish counties, each *département* is identified by a two-digit number which is used on car number plates and postcodes.

Régions

These were formed in 1982 to decentralise government services and decision making. They are responsible for regional planning and economic development as well as funding schools and colleges across the region. Each *région* has a unique cultural identity, e.g. Brittany. They are similar to Irish provinces. In 2016 France reduced the number of regions to save on administrative costs. Today there are 18 regions – 13 in France and 5 overseas.

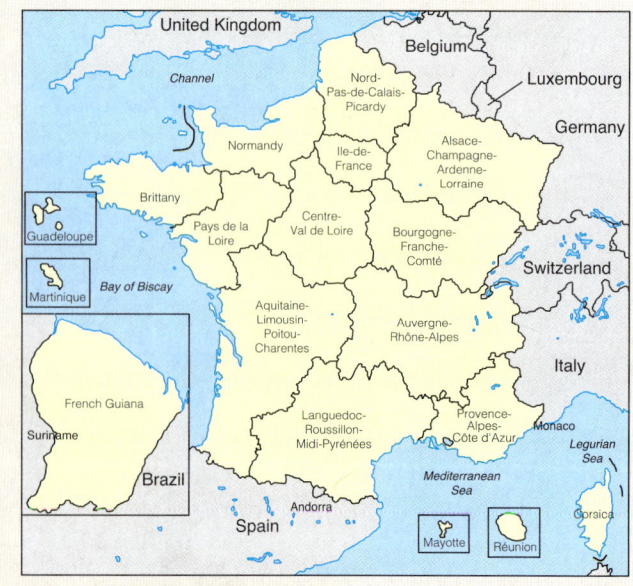

weblink France

Fig. 11 *Régions* in France

284

CHAPTER 15: PHYSICAL, ADMINISTRATIVE AND CULTURAL REGIONS

15.4 Cultural regions

Cultural regions are areas where people share a specific language, religion and/or way of life.

Language

Language is an essential part of a country's tradition and culture. In many countries, there is an official state language; however, people may also speak a local version of it (a **dialect**) or a completely different language to the official national language.

Below are two case studies on cultural regions associated with language.

Gaeltacht regions in Ireland

CHAPTER 15 Case Study 3

The Gaeltacht is a group of regions in Ireland where Irish is spoken as the first language in the community and at home. It is a cultural region based on its language. Other cultural activities associated with the Irish language include *sean nós* singing, set dancing, *céilís* and storytelling.

Fig. 12 Road sign in the Gaeltacht region of County Donegal

Location of Gaeltacht areas

- Irish-speaking communities are mainly found on the western and south-western coasts of Ireland, covering large areas of Counties Donegal, Mayo, Galway, Cork and Kerry. The Gaeltacht is a rural region with a population of about 91,862 of which about 60% of the residents are fluent in Irish and use the language in the community and at home. Donegal is the largest Gaeltacht area in Ireland. An Daingean (Dingle) in County Kerry is the largest Gaeltacht town. Smaller Gaeltacht areas are found in Counties Meath and Waterford.

Fig. 13 Live music, played on traditional Irish instruments like the bódhran, is a cultural activity in Gaeltacht areas.

The Formation of Gaeltacht Areas

- Following independence from Britain in 1922 only about 18% of people spoke Irish on a daily basis. In 1925 the Free State government set up the **Commission for Irish Speaking Districts** (*Coimisiún na Gaeltacht*). In 1926 it established the boundaries for the Gaeltacht based on the numbers of people speaking the language. The Gaeltacht was categorised into *Fíor* (true) Gaeltacht regions (over 80% speaking Irish) and *Breac* (partial) Gaeltacht regions (25%–79% speaking Irish).

- Today the Department of Arts, Heritage, Gaeltacht and the Islands has responsibility for promoting the cultural, social and economic wealth of the Gaeltacht region. It provides government funding to develop the Gaeltacht economy. ***Údarás na Gaeltachta*** was established to improve the economic, social and cultural development of the Gaeltacht.

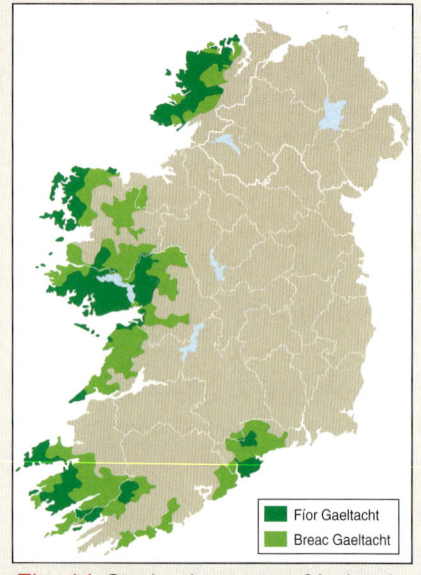

Fig. 14 Gaeltacht areas of Ireland in 1926

Factors affecting the Gaeltacht region

Several physical and human factors have combined to make the Gaeltacht a unique cultural region based on its language. These factors include relief, soils, history, infrastructure, services, population, government and EU support.

Physical factors

- Mountainous relief
- Remoteness
- High rainfall
- Poor soils

The Gaeltacht regions are the most remote, scenic and rural parts of the country. They generally have mountainous relief, high rainfall and poor peatland soils. The infertile, acidic, peatland soils covering much of the Gaeltacht area leads to limited farm incomes. The harsh remote physical landscape has limited economic development. These factors have led to out-migration of Irish speakers.

Human factors

- The Plantations
- The Famine
- Government and EU support

Ireland's history has also affected the Gaeltacht regions.

1. Plantations

Irish was the first language spoken by the majority of the population until the time of the Plantations in the 16th century. During the Plantations many Irish farmers

CHAPTER 15: PHYSICAL, ADMINISTRATIVE AND CULTURAL REGIONS

were forced by British landlords to leave their land and move to the more remote and less fertile lands of the western counties ('to Hell or to Connacht'). This led to the survival of the language in the Gaeltacht regions we see today in Donegal, Kerry and Mayo.

2. **During the Great Famine** (1845-1848), the high death rate and mass emigration led to a dramatic reduction in numbers of Irish speakers in the country. By the end of the famine only 1.5 million people spoke Irish in the country and these were mainly concentrated in Munster and Connacht. Economic, political and business life was conducted through English and the Irish language continued to be associated with poverty. National schools taught through English with the result that many people had little or no understanding of the language.

Fig. 15 Donegal, a Gaeltacht region

These factors have led to out-migration of younger people, leaving older Irish speakers in isolated communities. This has had two effects: firstly the number of Irish speakers is declining and secondly the role of *Údarás na Gaeltachta* in attracting industry to the region is made even more challenging.

3. **Government support for Irish language regions**

In the 21st century the main threat to the survival of the language in Gaeltacht regions is in-migration of non-Irish speakers and the influence of English-speaking media such as satellite TV and the internet.

- Encouraging Irish speakers to remain in the Gaeltacht is important to the survival of the Gaeltacht as a cultural region. The government recognises this by providing extra financial support to Gaeltacht families. These include grants paid to families in the Gaeltacht who can satisfy the Department that Irish is their usual spoken language, a grant paid to qualified families in the Gaeltacht to accommodate learners of Irish while they attend recognised Irish colleges and grants paid to qualified applicants in the Gaeltacht to build new houses and to improve existing houses.

- A 20-year national strategy (2010-2030) has been implemented by the government with the aim of increasing to 250,000 the number of people using Irish on a daily basis outside of the education system.

weblink
Support for Irish language in decline

TG4 and Raidió na Gaeltachta
Use Irish in their TV and radio programmes

Údarás na Gaeltachta
Promotes the economic and social development of Gaeltacht areas

The GAA
Promotes the use of Irish in all their sporting and social activities

Support for the Irish language today

Gaelscoileanna
Support the development of Irish-speaking schools

Foras na Gaeilge
Promotes the use of Irish across Ireland

The Irish Language Act
A law ensuring the provision of public services and documents through Irish, e.g. driving licences

Boundary changes to the Irish Gaeltacht

1. Since 1926 the numbers of people speaking Irish in the Gaeltacht region as their everyday language has decreased.

2. The size of the 1926 Gaeltacht was considerably reduced in 1956 following economic emigration and a review of Gaeltacht boundaries. Figs. 16 and 17 (1926 and today) clearly show the dramatic changes in the Gaeltacht boundaries.
   - The inclusion of Clochán-Bréanann in County Kerry in 1974.
   - The inclusion of a part of West Muskerry in County Cork.
   - The creation of a new Gaeltacht area (Baile Ghib and Rath Chairn) in County Meath in 1935.
   - The inclusion of Baile Ghib and Rath Chairn into the Gaeltacht regions in 1967.

3. Today sections of the 1926 Breac Gaeltacht (25% to 79% fluent speakers) have completely disappeared. Fíor Gaeltacht areas (over 80% fluent speakers) are also shrinking and survive only in isolated, mainly coastal communities.

4. Any future reduction in the area of present Gaeltacht regions could have an economic impact on the people living there. They are currently in receipt of grants payable to Irish speakers. They may lose these grants if their homes are no longer located inside any Gaeltacht boundaries.

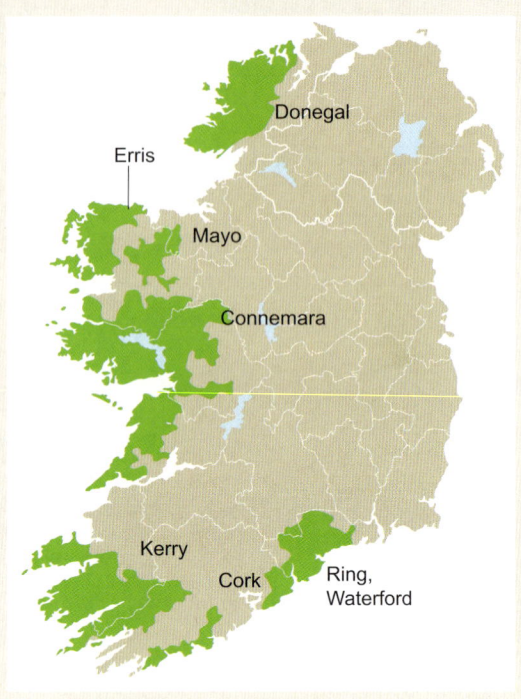

Fig. 16 Gaeltacht areas of Ireland in 1926

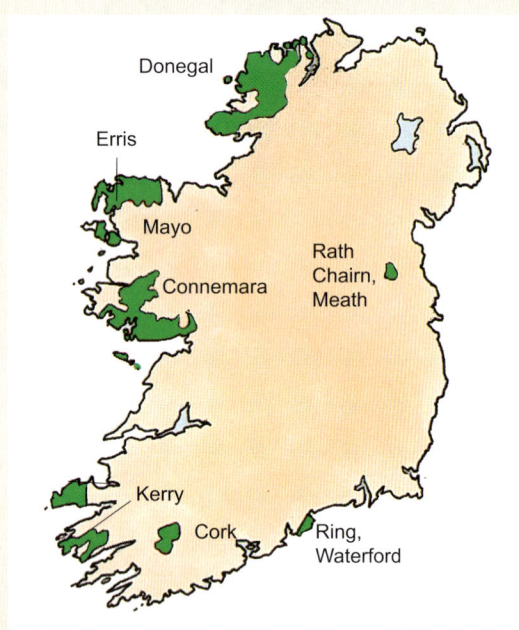

Fig. 17 Gaeltacht areas in Ireland today

CHAPTER 15: PHYSICAL, ADMINISTRATIVE & CULTURAL REGIONS

Language regions in Belgium

CHAPTER 15 Case Study 4

1. Belgium (population of 10.6 million people) is a country divided by language. The division of the population based on language has led to political, social and economic division of the country. It is such an extreme division that an official language line stretches across the country separating Dutch-speaking **Flanders** in the north from French-speaking **Wallonia** in the south. The people in each region rarely mix.

2. Southern Belgium is known as Wallonia. It is a French-speaking region. The main cities are Namur, Liège and Charleroi. Wallonia was once a wealthy industrial region based on its coal resources but since the 1960s it has undergone economic decline and has a high unemployment rate (11.8%). The people are Catholic and progressive in their outlook.

3. In northern Belgium or Flanders people speak Flemish – a variation of Dutch. Sixty per cent of the Belgian population is Flemish. The main cities are Antwerp and Ghent. The capital city, Brussels, is officially bilingual but most people there speak French. In northern Belgium people are also Catholic but are more republican and conservative in their outlook. Flanders had an economy mainly based on agriculture with little industry but since the 1960s Flanders has undergone economic growth and accounts for 87% of Belgian GDP.

Fig. 18 The Belgian linguistic divide

Factors leading to the division of Belgium

Physical factors – Location, resources

1. Flanders' economy was based on its fertile farmland. Because of this, the Walloons thought Flanders was poor and economically underdeveloped. The more urban and industrialised French-speaking Walloons had a sense of superiority over the Flemish.

2. Flanders has access to the North Sea and Atlantic Ocean via the port of Antwerp. This has been a major advantage in attracting modern industrial development to the region. This gives economic strength to the continuing Flemish desire for independence.

3. In the past Wallonia's wealth was based on coal reserves in the Sambre-Meuse Valley. This coal led to the development of iron and steelworks that provided employment and wealth for the region up to the 1960s. This provided economic power to Wallonia over Flanders.

4. Wallonia is closer to the industrial regions of France and Germany. This provided an important market for its coal and was a source of wealth during the Industrial Revolution. When the coal ran out in the 1960s, the region lost its wealth and became an unemployment blackspot with social problems as a result. The social and economic fortunes of the Walloons have been reversed.

weblink
Belgium - divided

CORE UNIT: REGIONAL GEOGRAPHY

Human factors – History, government

1. Before the French Revolution, Belgium was a region governed by the Netherlands that contained large numbers of French speakers (Walloons).

2. When the French Revolution occurred, the Walloons began to seek Belgian independence from the Netherlands but they brought the regions of Flanders with them. Belgium became an independent state in 1830 and French became the national language.

Fig. 19 The National Belgian Parliament in Brussels

3. An official language line separating Flanders and Wallonia was established in 1917, (see Fig. 18). Since then both Wallonia and Flanders have their own governments. A third region, the East Cantons, is German-speaking.

4. The Walloons controlled the economic and industrial life in Belgium between 1830 and 1940 causing resentment amongst the Flemish. The mainly agricultural Flemish people felt like second-class citizens in their own country even though they were in the majority. By 1930, laws were enacted that made Flemish the language of government, education, road signage and the courts in Flanders. Brussels became bilingual.

5. In 1980 the constitution was revised to form federal governments in Flanders, Wallonia and Brussels. Each region now has social and political autonomy (self-government) from each other but representatives from each region are elected to the Belgian national government. The regions control 40% of all public spending and are responsible for roads, urban projects, health services, the environment and education.

Effects of language division in Belgium

1. This language division in Belgium has many effects on the daily life of the population. The people in each region rarely mix. Each region has its own schools which follow different subject curricula. There is no national University of Belgium. Each region has its own shops, transport networks, soccer teams, TV stars and radio stations. Government press conferences and publications are in both languages. Walloons who wish to buy property in Flanders are required to take a language exam to show they can speak Flemish.

Fig. 20 Brussels, capital city of Belgium

Before they take office, politicians have to pass a language exam to show they can speak both languages.

2. In primary schools Flemish- and French-speaking children are educated separately, often in the same buildings. Public libraries must have equal numbers of Dutch and French books. Political meetings in Flanders must be in Dutch even if all those present are French speakers.

3. The Brussels region faces difficult challenges because of the language differences. Brussels is in Flanders, but is mainly French-speaking. It is the centre of the EU government. People from Wallonia have moved to Brussels for work. In the eyes of the conservative Flemish, many towns around Brussels are being 'colonised' by French speakers. Should Flanders seek independence, it would want Brussels to be its capital city. The cultural differences between the Walloons and Flemish people are threatening the continued existence of the Belgian nation.

Religion

Religion can make regions unique. Religion shapes group identity and can act as a unifying force or as a source of social conflict, strongly dividing people.

This world map (Fig. 21) showing distinct religions is very generalised as it is difficult to show minority groups on a small-scale map.

Political expansion, conquest, colonisation and missionary work were responsible for the distribution of religions worldwide.

Today, migration and population growth contribute to the expansion of religions.

On pages 292 – 294 you will read two case studies on cultural regions associated with religion.

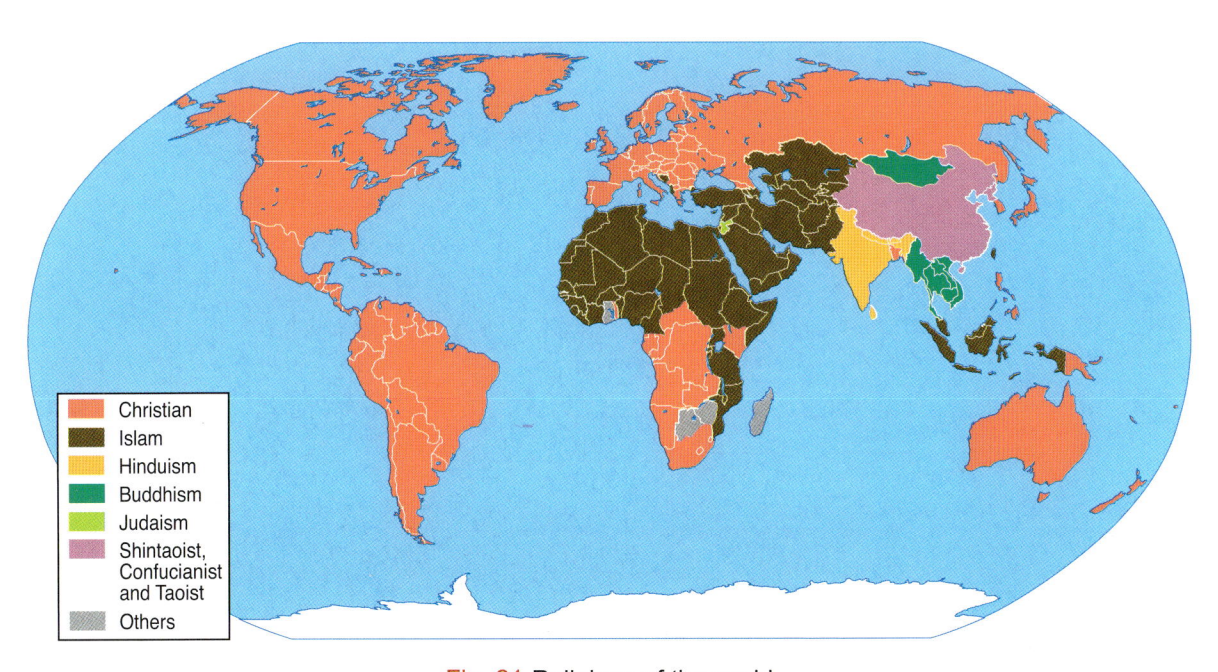

Fig. 21 Religions of the world

CORE UNIT: REGIONAL GEOGRAPHY

CHAPTER 15
Case Study 5

🚹 Religious regions in Northern Ireland

Northern Ireland can be seen as a separate region based on the distribution of the Protestant and Catholic religions.

1. The **plantation** of the Northern Irish counties during the 16th and 17th centuries is a human factor that led to the concentration of Protestants in Northern Ireland. These settlers (planters) came from Scotland and England.

2. The planters' religion was a unifying cultural force which separated them from the native Irish Catholic inhabitants. Over time, the Protestant religion became associated with the political struggle to remain part of the United Kingdom as expressed today in unionism and loyalism. In turn, Catholicism became associated with the struggle to re-unify Ireland as expressed today in republicanism and nationalism. Gradually, several counties in Northern Ireland developed majority Protestant populations.

3. Today, areas with a strong Protestant **tradition** tend to be urbanised areas such as north Armagh, north Down, Antrim and north Derry. In most of these areas, up to three-quarters of the population claim a Protestant identity. In some areas, e.g. Tyrone and Fermanagh, there is a Catholic majority.

4. In Belfast and other large urban areas, there are distinct zones in which either Protestants or Catholics live. In Catholic areas, e.g. west Belfast, these zones are often marked by kerbstones painted green, white and orange as well as wall murals of the tricolour or scenes of Irish history, e.g. the Easter Lily, the 1916 Rising.

5. In Protestant areas, e.g. east Belfast, the kerbstones may be painted red, white and blue and murals of the Queen or William of Orange are painted on the walls. In Belfast, the Peace Line – a physical division built across roads and between housing areas – separates these areas to minimise sectarian violence.

6. Sport is another aspect of everyday life which can reveal a link with either Catholicism or Protestantism in Northern Ireland. Catholics tend to support GAA, Glasgow Celtic F.C., Cliftonville and the Republic of Ireland soccer team, while Protestants tend to support Glasgow Rangers F.C., Linfield and the Northern Ireland soccer team.

7. **Integration** is slowly improving in schools, but it is still an issue in areas where children are sent to schools reflecting their religion. In certain areas, children are conscious of wearing football jerseys as it implies their **religious identity**, which could lead to hostility.

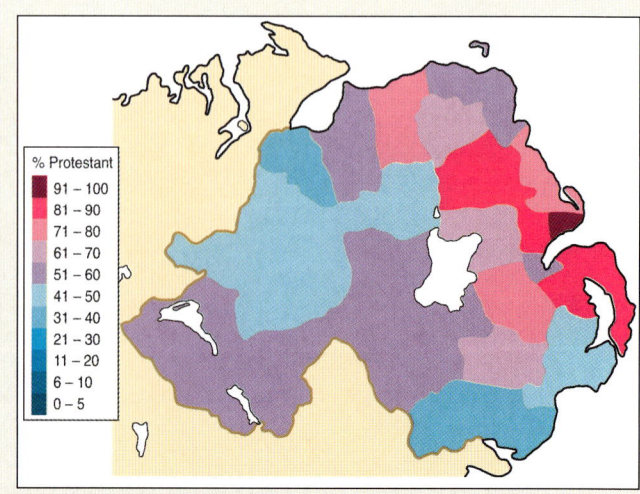

Fig. 22 Distribution of the Protestant religion in Northern Ireland

CHAPTER 15: PHYSICAL, ADMINISTRATIVE AND CULTURAL REGIONS

Islamic regions

CHAPTER 15 Case Study 6

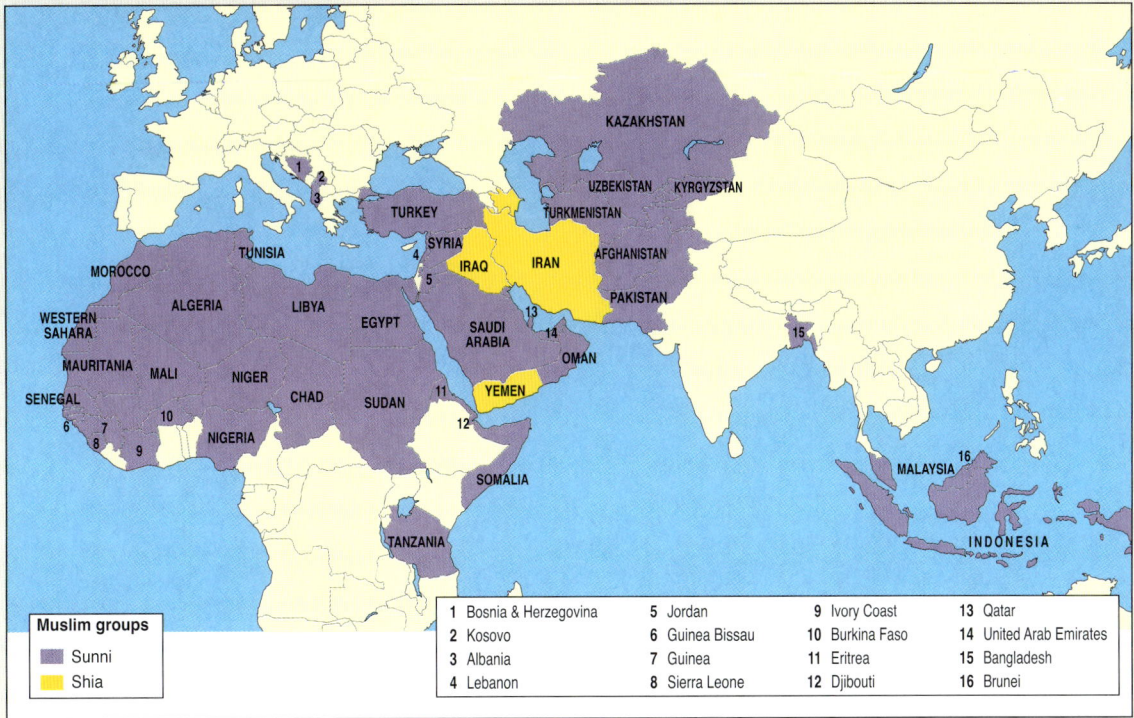

Fig. 23 The Islamic religion is divided into Shia and Sunni religious regions.

1. A large cultural region based on the religion of Islam is distributed across the Middle East, North Africa and Indonesia. In 570 AD, the prophet Mohammed founded the Islamic religion in what is now Saudi Arabia. Followers of Islam are called Muslims. More than 21% (over 1.7 billion) of the world's population is Muslim.

2. Within 100 years of the death of Mohammed, the Muslim Empire stretched across Central Asia, east to India and west to Spain. Muslim armies conquered vast areas of land. They drew up treaties with these conquered people which gave local religions the status of 'protected minorities'. However, many of the conquered people quickly converted to Islam.

3. Muslim merchants and travellers introduced Islam into the Indian sub-continent, especially present-day Pakistan and Bangladesh. Islam spread further east into Malaysia, Indonesia and the Philippines.

4. During the Middle Ages, there were regular conflicts between Christians and Muslims. These Crusades were organised by Christian leaders to regain conquered territories but the only real success was in Spain which today is a Christian country.

5. Followers of Islam are divided into two groups called Sunni Muslims and Shia Muslims. The origin of these groups dates back to just after Mohammed's death when the question of leadership and religious control led to a division between the followers of Mohammed.

6. The majority of Muslims are Sunni Muslim. Shia Muslims are more common in Iran, Southern Iraq, Libya and Pakistan, although many countries have both groups.

7. All Muslims follow the teachings written in the Qur'an (Koran). The Qur'an contains the basic beliefs (The Five Articles of Faith) of Islam and strict guidelines for Muslim daily life (The Five Pillars of Faith).

8. All Muslims attach great importance to the idea of belonging to the family of Islam. Religion is central to everyday life in Muslim communities. A typical day involves worshipping in a mosque and praying five times a day whilst facing in the direction of Mecca. Mecca, a city in Saudi Arabia, is regarded by Muslims as the holiest city in the world.

9. Muslim customs differ among countries and local traditions, e.g. in Saudi Arabia women are obliged to remain completely covered by wearing a burka, while in other countries, women must keep only their hair covered with a scarf when outside the family. Arranged marriages are also quite common in Muslim countries.

10. Muslims are not allowed to drink alcohol or gamble. When entertaining, men and women tend to socialise in different parts of a building. Certain foods are forbidden to Muslims, e.g. pork.

Fig. 24 The Masjid al-Haram is the largest mosque in the world. It is in Saudi Arabia.

CHAPTER 15: PHYSICAL, ADMINISTRATIVE AND CULTURAL REGIONS

15.5 The complexity of cultural regions – Boundary changes

Boundaries and the size of regions may change over time. Many changes have been made to large-scale political boundaries, e.g. the partition of India to create Pakistan, the division of Yugoslavia into separate states and the division of Sudan into North and South Sudan.

On a smaller scale, changes to political constituencies in Northern Ireland during the 1920s had an impact on the political power of Catholics. On a similar smaller scale, changes to Gaeltacht boundaries (see pages 285–288) affect funding in that region.

Changes to political boundaries, whether at national or at constituency level, can have an impact on the cultural groups living in the affected regions.

Boundary changes in Poland

CHAPTER 15 Case Study 7

Poland is an example of a country that has undergone many changes to its political boundaries. These border changes have had a considerable impact on the ethnic composition of its population.

Before the Second World War

- Poland was a much bigger country before the Second World War than it is today (see Fig. 25). Until the end of the 1930s, Poland had a variety of ethnic groups such as Catholic Poles, Jews, Armenians, Germans, Dutch, Ukrainians and Orthodox Christians.
- Its borders were east of its present location.

During the Second World War

- In 1939, Poland was invaded by Nazi Germany. The Nazis killed about 3.5 million Polish Jews and more than one million Polish Catholics. The country, devastated by war, had its population reduced from 35 million to 23 million.

Fig. 25 Pre-Second World War Polish borders marked in orange. Red shows modern borders of Poland and its neighbours.

295

CORE UNIT: REGIONAL GEOGRAPHY

After the Second World War

- New boundaries were designed for Central Europe by Stalin, Churchill and Roosevelt (the leaders of Russia, Britain and the United States) at the Yalta conference. Poland became a Communist state under Russian influence.
- Poland lost a third of its pre-Second World War land area, which was taken over by the Soviet Union.

Fig. 26 Poland today

- The Allied Powers (i.e. Russia, Britain and the USA) gave Poland a large part of eastern Germany.

Impact of boundary changes

1. The Second World War dramatically reduced Poland's former ethnic diversity. Massive migrations of Polish refugees occurred as they left Soviet- and German-owned lands. Many Germans left and moved west.

2. Hundreds of thousands of Ukrainians were forced to leave Poland to settle in the Soviet Union. Most of the Jews who survived the Holocaust emigrated to Israel or to the USA.

3. As a result of this mass migration, today Poland has a very small population of ethnic minorities – roughly 5% in total. This figure is made up of Germans (who live mostly in south-west Poland), Belarussians (who live in eastern Poland) and Ukrainians.

Fig. 27 Downtown Warsaw, the capital city of Poland, has been modernised in recent years.

Chapter Revision Questions

1. What is a region?
2. Name five different types of regions. Give an example of each.
3. Use the world map and table on page 277 to name and locate an example of (a) a hot climate; (b) a temperate climate, (c) a cold climate.
4. What climatic region do the following countries have in common – North Canada, Greenland, North Finland?
5. Name Ireland's climate and give a general description of it referring to prevailing winds, rainfall and temperature in your answer.
6. Describe and explain how latitude, ocean currents and prevailing winds influence Ireland's climate.
7. Why is it wetter in the west of Ireland than in the east?
8. Name two air masses which meet close to Ireland and state what effect the polar front has on Ireland's climate.
9. Explain the term geomorphic region. Name two examples and describe one of them.
10. Match each of the region types in Column A with its description in Column B.

Column A	Column B
A Geomorphic regions	1. Local councils/corporations/constituency boundaries/county divisions
B Cultural regions	2. Less-developed regions/core regions/peripheral regions
C Administrative regions	3. Regions based on distinctive landscapes and rock type
D Socio-economic regions	4. Regions that are associated with language and religion

A	B	C	D

11. What are administrative regions?
12. How do local government and central government agencies differ in their administrative responsibilities?
13. Briefly describe the three levels of administration in Ireland.
14. Name two of the services provided by each level of administration in Ireland. How are the services funded?

15. Draw an outline map of Ireland. On your map, mark and label the Northern and Western regional assembly area, the East and Midlands regional assembly area and the Southern regional assembly area.
16. Briefly describe each of the following terms: *commune*, *département*, *région*.
17. (i) Draw a sketch map to show the location of Gaeltacht regions in Ireland.
    (ii) Describe two challenges facing Gaeltacht regions.
    (iii) Explain two human factors causing the decline of the Gaeltacht.
    (iv) How does the Irish government support Gaeltacht regions?
    (v) Explain the terms Breac Gaeltacht and Fíor Gaeltacht.
18. Name two languages spoken in Belgium. Draw a sketch map to show the linguistic cultural divide in Belgium.
19. How has the economic importance of Flanders and Wallonia changed over time?
20. How has the Belgian government recognised the importance of the two cultures in Belgium?
21. State three everyday effects of the language divide on the people of Belgium.
22. What event in Irish history brought the Protestant religion to Northern Ireland?
23. Which areas of Northern Ireland are most closely associated with the Protestant religion?
24. How is religious identity shown on both sides of the religious divide in Northern Ireland?
25. What regions of the world are associated with Islam?
26. Name the two major divisions within the Islamic faith.
27. Name three Muslim customs.

CHAPTER 15: PHYSICAL, ADMINISTRATIVE AND CULTURAL REGIONS

LC Exam Questions

Higher Level students must be able to answer Ordinary and Higher Level questions.

OL Questions

28. Match the description of a region with the example of a region by writing the correct letter in each case in the table below.

A	A city in a core region.	1. The Alps
B	A less developed economic region.	2. Paris
C	A region defined by language and culture.	3. Mediterranean
D	A region defined by climate factors such as temperature and rainfall.	4. The South of Italy/Mezzogiorno
E	A region defined by physical factors such as relief.	5. The Basque Region of Spain

A	B	C	D	E

29. The culture of a region is often defined by religion, language, music, dance and games. Describe and explain the importance of culture in any region that you have studied.

HL Questions

30. 'A region is an area which may be identified by one or more characteristics.' Briefly explain this statement, using a sketch map to illustrate an example or examples.
31. Examine, with reference to examples that you have studied, how the physical landscape can be used to define regions.
32. Describe and explain the importance of culture in defining any area you have studied.

33. Match each map to a type of region it represents by writing the correct letter in the table below.

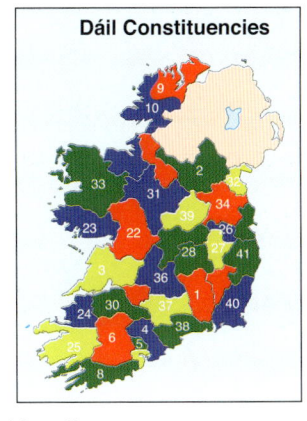

Map A — Gaeltacht Areas
Map B — Greater Dublin Area
Map C — Dáil Constituencies
Map D — Towns of over 40,000

Region Type	Letter
Urban region	
Cultural region	
Core region	
Political region	

299

CORE UNIT: REGIONAL GEOGRAPHY

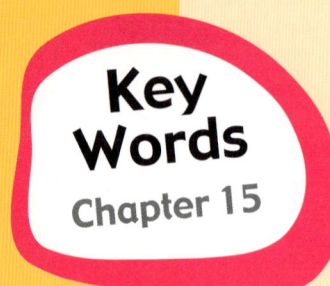

Key Words — Chapter 15

Key Words

You should be able to explain both verbally and in writing each of the key words listed below.

administrative region
breac/partial gaeltacht
climatic regions
commune
cultural region
département
depressions
fíor/true gaeltacht
Flanders
frontal rain
geomorphic regions
human factors
limon/loess
nodal/urban/city regions
North Atlantic Drift
North European plain
physical factors
physical region
plantation
polar
polar front
socio-economic regions
region
région
regional assemblies
relief rainfall
tropical
topography
Wallonia

Digital Resources are available for this chapter at mentorbooks.ie/resources

CHAPTER 16

Socio-Economic Regions

Key Theme

A region is an area of the earth's surface that is distinctive in some way. Regions can be identified by one or more human and/or natural characteristics, e.g. socio-economic regions.

Learning Outcomes

At the end of this chapter you will be able to:
- Define the term socio-economic region.
- Discuss the characteristics of each type of socio-economic region and name an Irish and European example of each type.
- Discuss the cause and impact of industrial decline in an Irish and European region.
- Discuss the importance of EU funding to socio-economic regions.

Contents

16.1	Socio-economic regions	302
16.2	Regions of industrial decline	304
	Case Study 1: Drogheda, County Louth	305
	Case Study 2: The Sambre-Meuse Valley, Belgium	308
16.3	EU funding for socio-economic regions	310

Revision Space

Chapter Revision Questions – LC Exam Questions – Key Word List 313

CORE UNIT: REGIONAL GEOGRAPHY

16.1 Socio-economic regions

Socio-economic regions are regions that have unique social and/or economic characteristics. They may be important urban industrial and service centres or they may lack industrial development and be centres of low population with few services. Some socio-economic regions are problem areas because they have high unemployment levels. This may be due to declining industrial development or the presence of conditions that do not attract modern industry.

We will study three types of Irish and European socio-economic regions.

(i) Core regions	Ireland – The Greater Dublin Area Europe – The Paris Basin
(ii) Peripheral/ Less developed regions	Ireland – The Northern and Western Region Europe – Mezzogiorno, Italy
(iii) Regions of industrial decline	Ireland – Drogheda: Decline due to business competition Europe – Sambre–Meuse Valley (Belgium): Decline due to depletion of resources

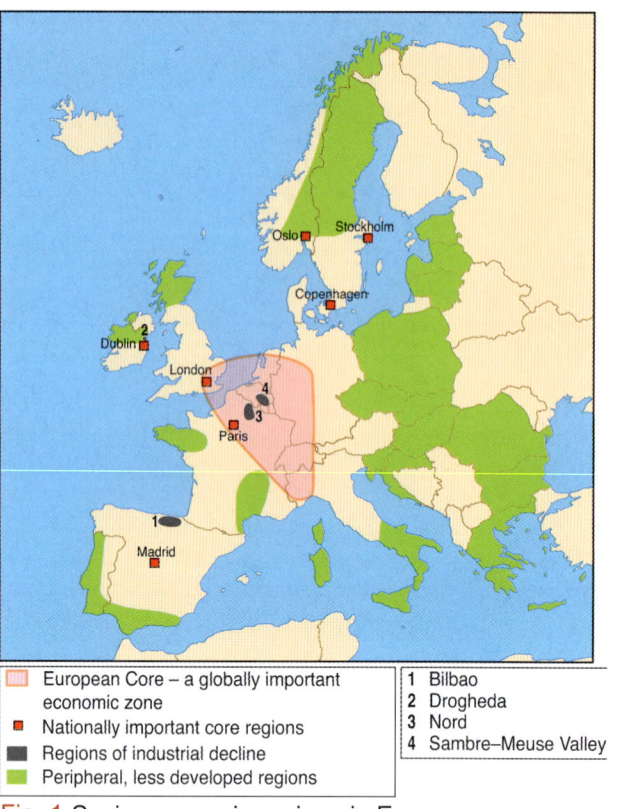

Legend:
- European Core – a globally important economic zone
- Nationally important core regions
- Regions of industrial decline
- Peripheral, less developed regions

1 Bilbao
2 Drogheda
3 Nord
4 Sambre–Meuse Valley

Fig. 1 Socio-economic regions in Europe

Physical and **human** factors influence the development of regions. These factors may hinder or advance the development of a region.

FACTORS AFFECTING SOCIO-ECONOMIC REGIONS	
Physical Factors	Human Factors
Climate Relief Drainage Soils Resources	Population Transport Government/EU policy History

(i) Core regions

Core regions are generally accessible wealthy areas. They have physical and human factors that attract settlement and industry, e.g. the Greater Dublin Area and the Paris Basin.

Core regions are:
- likely to possess many natural resources such as coal or fertile land.
- usually regions with a climate that supports intensive agriculture.
- often lowland areas easily accessible by road, rail, canal, river and sea.
- highly urbanised.
- centres of business, services, government administration and decision making.
- regions where incomes are higher. Within the European Union, incomes in core regions are 10% higher than the EU average.
- regions with high population densities.

- centres of further education, research and development.
- regions where migration is common.
- home to many multinational companies (MNCs).

(ii) Peripheral/less developed regions

Peripheral/less developed regions are poorer socio-economic regions. They have physical and human factors that discourage settlement and economic activity.

Peripheral/less developed regions:
- are often remote, inaccessible mountainous areas.
- have few resources.
- have poor soils.
- have poor transport infrastructure and higher transport costs that reduce their ability to compete successfully in the marketplace.
- suffer from out-migration and therefore have low population densities.
- have lower incomes than core regions. Within the EU, incomes in peripheral regions are 10% lower than the EU average.
- are not favoured as industrial locations and so have higher unemployment rates.
- are more dependent on primary activities, e.g. farming, forestry and fishing.
- use government incentives to encourage businesses to locate in these areas. Such industries tend to be branch plants of multinational companies.
- are areas where tourism is very important and is often based on outdoor activities such as golf, fishing, walking and water sports.
- have fewer health and higher educational facilities.

An example of a peripheral region in Europe is the **Mezzogiorno** (southern Italy). In Ireland, the **N&W (Northern and Western)** region is considered to be a peripheral region.

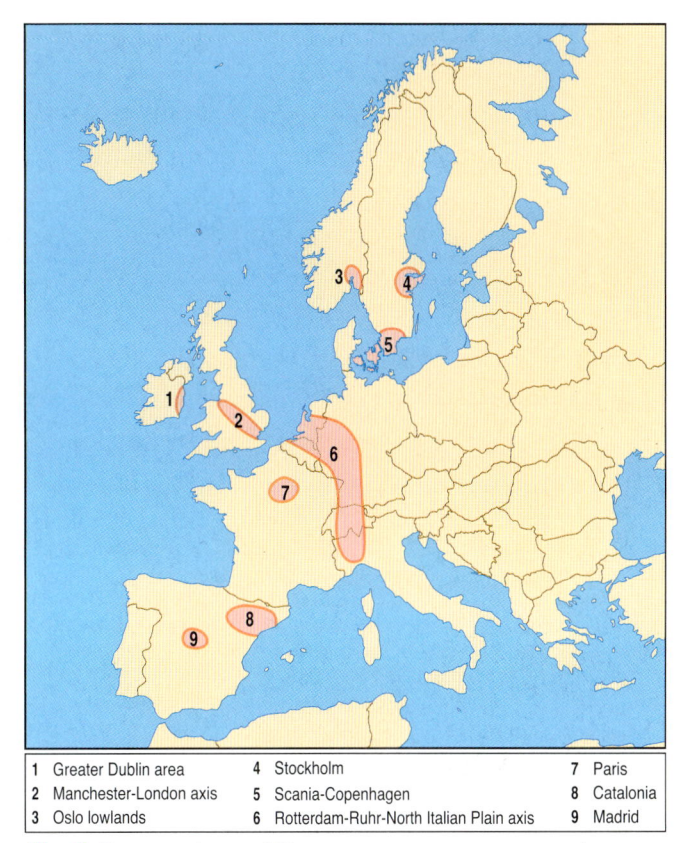

1	Greater Dublin area	4	Stockholm	7	Paris
2	Manchester-London axis	5	Scania-Copenhagen	8	Catalonia
3	Oslo lowlands	6	Rotterdam-Ruhr-North Italian Plain axis	9	Madrid

Fig. 2 Core regions of Europe

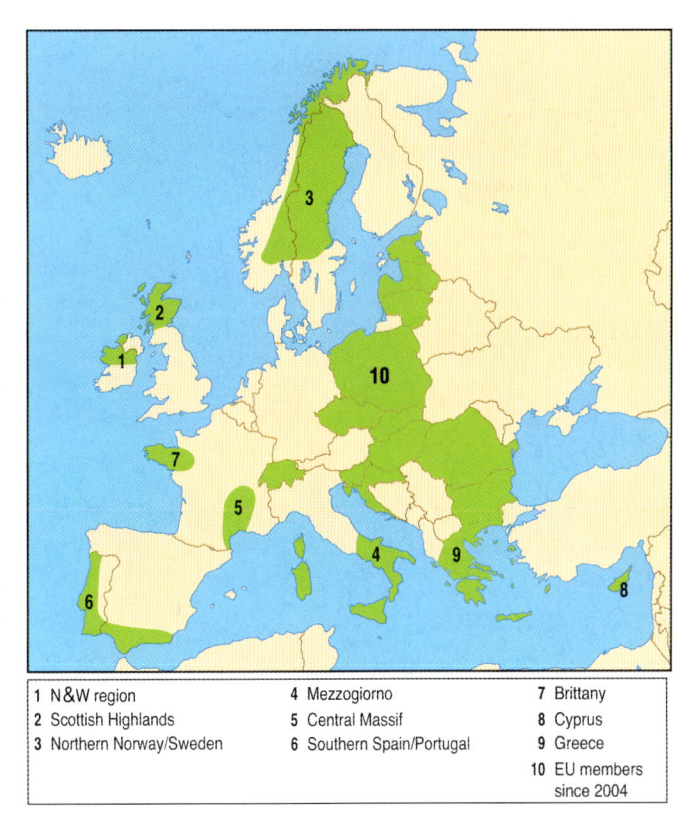

1	N&W region	4	Mezzogiorno	7	Brittany
2	Scottish Highlands	5	Central Massif	8	Cyprus
3	Northern Norway/Sweden	6	Southern Spain/Portugal	9	Greece
				10	EU members since 2004

Fig. 3 Peripheral regions of Europe

CORE UNIT: REGIONAL GEOGRAPHY

16.2 Regions of industrial decline

In several areas of the world, industrial regions which were once major economic centres have declined in importance and currently face many problems.

Regions of industrial decline are characterised by high unemployment, derelict buildings, urban decay and out-migration.

Causes of industrial decline

There are two main reasons for industrial decline in a region.
(a) Depletion of natural resources.
(b) Competition from other regions with cheaper business costs.

(a) Depletion of resources

In Europe, the industrial region of the **Sambre-Meuse Valley** in Belgium and **Bilbao** in the Basque region of northern Spain both declined in importance because local coal and iron ore deposits were depleted. These centres were very important industrial areas up until the mid-20th century. When the resources were used up, industries closed and these regions became centres of high unemployment, social deprivation and derelict landscapes.

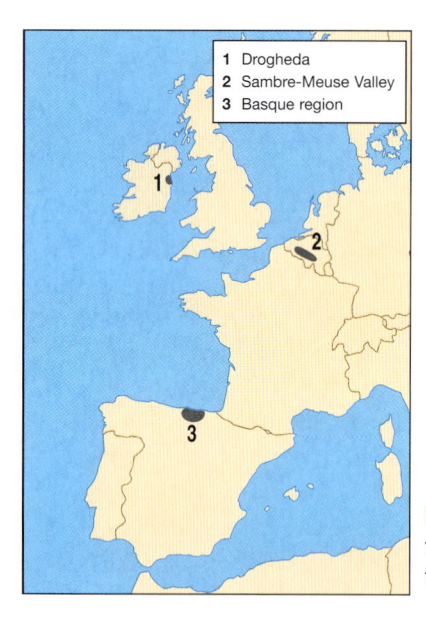

Fig. 4 Location of Drogheda, the Sambre-Meuse Valley and the Basque region

(b) Competition

Ireland never experienced an industrial revolution and therefore, lacked the large-scale industrialisation found in Europe, although several Irish counties, towns and cities had important industrial functions, e.g. **Drogheda** and **Cork** city. In the 1970s, after Ireland joined the European Economic Community (now called the EU), some Irish manufacturing companies closed because of the availability of lower-priced products from European manufacturers. High unemployment rates and emigration occurred. The town of Drogheda, once a bigger port than Dublin, is an example of an urban region that declined in industrial strength. Today, it is becoming a dormitory town for Dublin and a retail centre.

CHAPTER 16: SOCIO-ECONOMIC REGIONS

Drogheda, County Louth

CHAPTER 16
Case Study 1

Human factors such as international competition and economic recession caused a major decline in the industrial base in Drogheda in the mid-1970s.

The town has a long, proud, industrial history based on its port function close to the mouth of the River Boyne. Until the mid-1980s, Drogheda had a wide variety of industries.

Early industrial strength

1. In the 1500s, most of Drogheda's trade was with Liverpool. Yarn and linen were major exports and Drogheda Port was more important than Dublin Port at that time. By the 18th century, it was the fourth largest town in Ireland after Dublin, Cork and Waterford. It exported grain and linen. In the early 1800s, the Drogheda Steam Packet Company was founded and the Drogheda railway viaduct was built.
2. Drogheda was famous for its textile industry. Raw cotton from Dublin, Glasgow and Liverpool was brought to Drogheda where it was spun and bleached in the textile factories. At its peak, there were up to 20,000 hand weavers in Drogheda and the surrounding area.
3. Four linen mills existed in the town. Each employed over 700 people. By 1972, one of these mills – the Greenhills Mill – was famous worldwide for its sheets and towels which were exported to Japan, America, China and Europe.
4. As well as textiles, Drogheda had a thriving ironworks and shipbuilding company, which built engines for the Brazilian railway and vats for the Guinness brewery in Dublin.
5. Other industries in the town included the Donaghy & Son Boot Factory (which made over 8,000 pairs of boots a week), the Drogheda Gas Company and the Drogheda Fertiliser Company. The Drogheda Oil and Cake Mills produced ingredients for biscuits, margarine and soap, accounting for almost 15% of the export revenue from Drogheda Port.
6. Before the 20th-century decline in industry, over 50% of the population was employed in manufacturing.

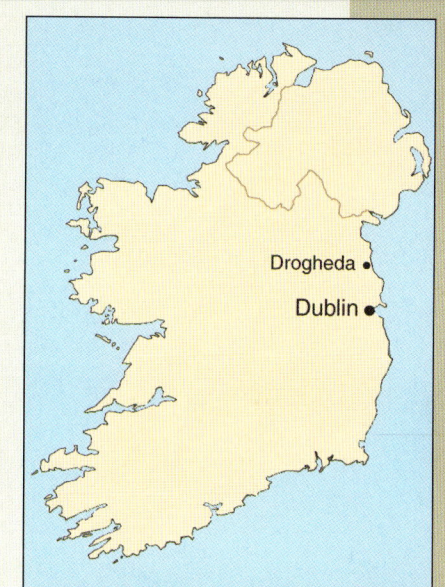

Fig. 5 Location map of Drogheda

The 1970s – a time of decline for Drogheda

1. The 1970s were a time of economic depression throughout the world. Ireland's economy faced many problems and all areas of the country were affected, including Drogheda. In addition, after Ireland joined the European Economic Community (EEC) in 1973, Drogheda's industries found it increasingly difficult to compete with similar products being manufactured within and outside the EEC.
2. This competition contributed to the closure of these traditional industries by the 1980s. Drogheda became an unemployment blackspot with unemployment rates as high as 30% in certain areas. This decline was not confined to Drogheda. Across Europe, the traditional industries of iron, steel and textiles declined in many countries, e.g. the Sambre-Meuse Valley in Belgium.

CORE UNIT: REGIONAL GEOGRAPHY

Industry in Drogheda today

1. Drogheda has not yet regained the reputation it once had as a manufacturing town. However, 31% of its workers are employed in manufacturing compared to 19% in the rest of Ireland.
2. There are several modern industries. Becton Dickinson produces medical equipment and Premier Periclase makes magnesia for the ceramics industry. Several small-scale light engineering businesses operate around the town. These companies were attracted by the educated workforce, transport, access to a large market and EU membership. Many foreign firms outside the EU used Ireland's EU membership as an entry point to the large EU market.
3. Coca Cola has located its global business services hub in Drogheda providing financial and other services to the company's offices throughout the world.

Fig. 6 Housing and retail development in Drogheda

Plans to overcome the challenge of industrial decline

Plans have been put in place to overcome industrial decline and promote Drogheda as a modern business and retail centre.

1. **The Business Park**

   The Industrial Development Authority (IDA) has built a Business and Technology Park close to the M1 Motorway. This factor, combined with a good supply of labour, an educated workforce (e.g. close proximity of DIFE – Drogheda Institute of Further Education) and easy access to Dublin and Belfast, helps to make Drogheda an ideal location for investment by multinational companies.

2. **The River Boyne**

   The Boyne has an important role in the redevelopment of Drogheda. The derelict buildings of the old oil and cake mills have been redeveloped and turned into a new shopping centre. New apartments have been built beside the Boyne and a new bridge has been placed over the river. Green areas beside the river have been cultivated and redeveloped for recreation (e.g. walking paths have been placed alongside the river). Tourist attractions in the area include the site of the Battle of the Boyne and Brú na Bóinne (Newgrange).

3. **Retail centre**

   Drogheda became a retail centre with the opening of the M1 retail park in 2005. Large shopping centres (Scotch Hall and Laurence Centres), a new hotel and conference centre also opened. These provide the services and employment needed in this rapidly growing satellite town.

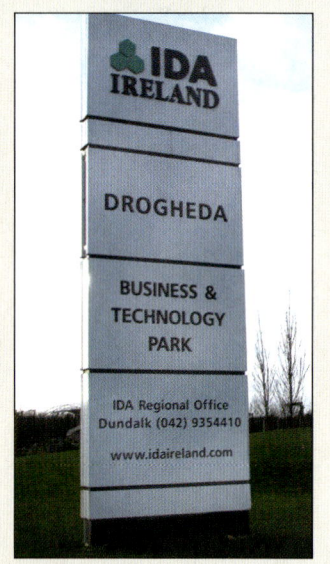

Fig. 7 Drogheda is now promoted as a business and retail centre.

CHAPTER 16: SOCIO-ECONOMIC REGIONS

Modern advantages favouring Drogheda as an industrial location
1. **Road Links:** Drogheda is located on the M1 motorway linking Dublin and Belfast.
2. **Rail:** Drogheda is on the Dublin/Belfast rail line. Freight services including container and refrigerated transport and heavy haulage facilities are available in the area.
3. **Air:** Dublin Airport is 30 minutes from Drogheda by motorway. The airport provides connections to all major European and North American centres.
4. **Seaports:** Drogheda has its own port which has been expanded and modernised and is now able to handle containerised shipping.

Labour force – Young, educated and skilled
1. The population of Drogheda has experienced a rapid growth and is now over 30,000 people. Many people have moved to Drogheda to take advantage of its easy access to the facilities of Dublin city while benefiting from much lower housing costs.
2. Drogheda is within commuting distance of Dublin; consequently, there is a growing pool of highly skilled workers based in the town and travelling to work in Dublin and Dundalk. Many of these would prefer employment opportunities in the town.

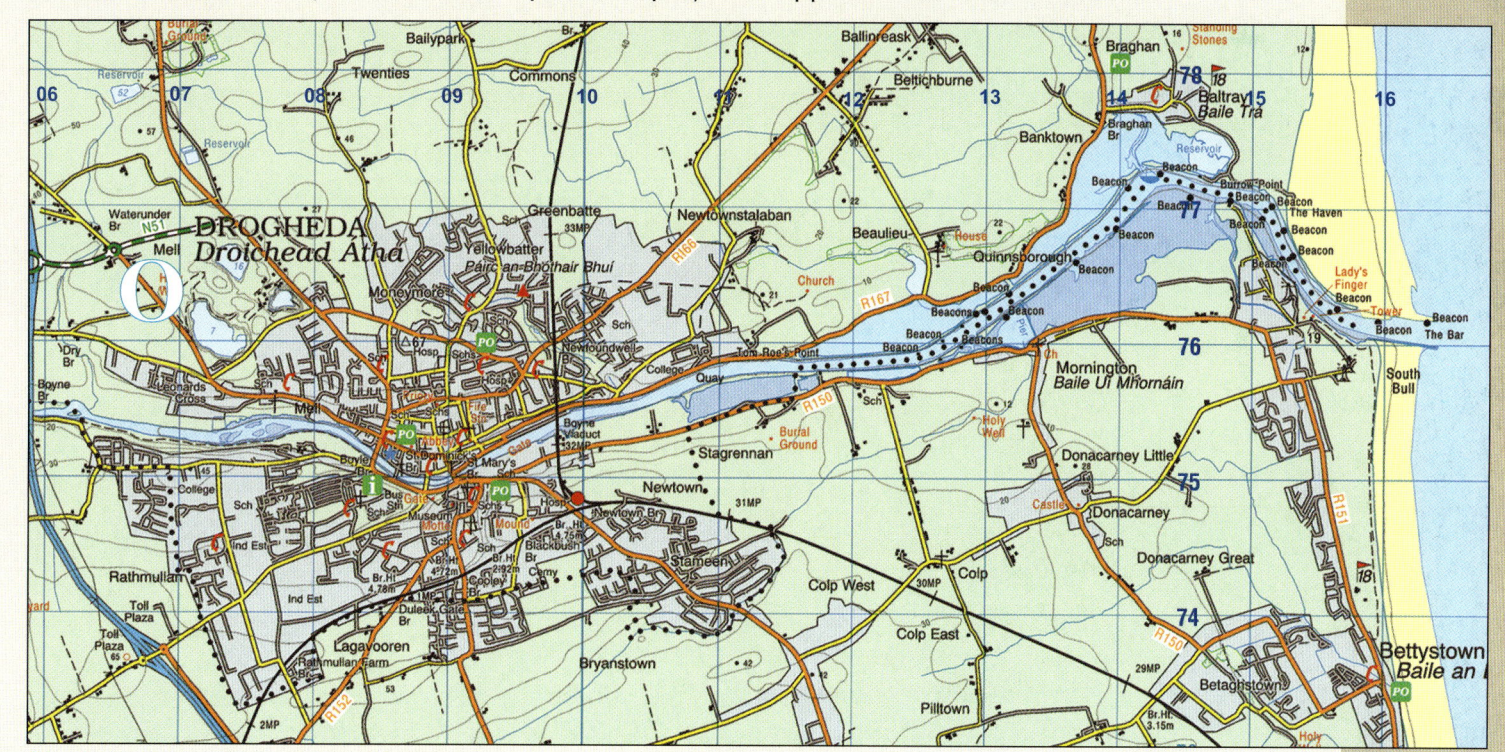

Fig. 8 OS Map extract of Drogheda

Activity

Study Fig. 8 and answer the questions.
1. Name and explain two possible impacts of the motorway route on people and business in the Drogheda region. Refer to the map in your answer.
2. Suggest a suitable location for the development of a new retail park. Explain three reasons for your decision.
3. Name and explain two reasons for the location of the industrial estates in the southwest of the town.

307

CORE UNIT: REGIONAL GEOGRAPHY

CHAPTER 16
Case Study 2

The Sambre-Meuse Valley, Belgium

Early industrial strength

1. In the late 1880s the Sambre-Meuse river valley in Wallonia, southern Belgium was the industrial core region of the country. Industry was based on coal mining and the traditional heavy industries of iron and steel, engineering and chemicals. The success of the industrialisation was due to large deposits of coal, iron ore, lead and zinc that were exposed by the river as it cut its valley into the land.
2. The main coalfields were Borinage, Charleroi and Liège. At its peak, over 120 mines employing more than 120,000 people produced roughly 30 million tonnes of coal each year.

The 1960s: time of decline for the Sambre-Meuse region

3. Over time the coal seams were exhausted and coal production declined steadily from an output of over 30 million tonnes in 1955 to just over 2 million tonnes in 1988. Any remaining seams were deep and badly fractured creating higher production costs.
4. Added to this was competition from cheaper imports of coal from America and Poland. In addition, the cleaner and cheaper resources of energy, oil and gas were replacing coal very quickly.
5. By the mid-1960s the European Coal and Steel Community (ECSC), of which Belgium was a founding member, stated that only efficient coalfields in member states should remain open. This led to the collapse of coal mining in the Sambre-Meuse region. By the end of the 1960s the region had become a problem region of industrial decline. Over 50,000 jobs were lost between 1960 and 1973. The last mine closed in 1992. Flanders quickly replaced Wallonia as the economic core of Belgium.

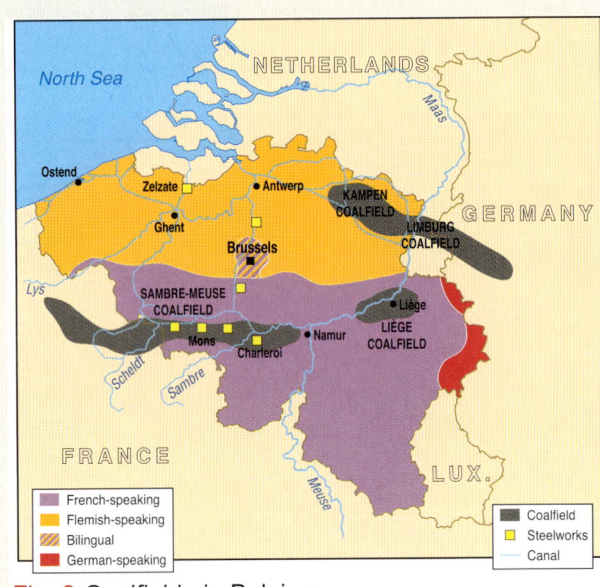

Fig. 9 Coalfields in Belgium

Problems of industrial decline

Across Wallonia the traditional industries of engineering and chemicals that depended on coal as a raw material also declined.

- They could not compete with the modern petro-chemical industries and integrated steelworks located near the coast at Zelzate in Flanders.
- These new factories were offered cheap greenfield sites, lower labour costs, room to expand and non-unionised labour.

CHAPTER 16: SOCIO-ECONOMIC REGIONS

Fig. 10 Industrial landscape in Charleroi, Belgium

- The new factories were linked by canal to the North Sea ports of Antwerp and Terneuzen through which American and Polish coal and iron ore from Sweden and West Africa were imported.
- From the 1960s Wallonia rapidly experienced high unemployment (over 20%) and had a significantly lower GDP per capita than Flanders. Unemployment forced the migration of many Wallonian workers from the region, seeking work in the capital city of Brussels and in the newly-emerging modern industries in Flanders.
- The outdated factories, poor infrastructure, derelict buildings and unsightly spoil heaps were not an attractive environment for new investment.
- The area experienced industrial decline.
- Liège survived the worst effects of the decline in coal mining as it produced more specialised goods, e.g. crystal glass, and so **industrial inertia** prevented their closure. It also had a variety of industries not related to coal, e.g. aeronautical engineering.

Plans to overcome the challenge of industrial decline in the Sambre-Meuse region

1. Government and EU support is necessary for the renewal of the region. The EU is important to the continued development of the Sambre-Meuse region through ERDF and ESF structural funding (see page 311). The Sambre-Meuse region receives €1.04 billion in funding from the EU as its GDP is less than 75% of the EU average (see Depletion of Resources, page 304).

To renew Wallonia and the Sambre-Meuse Valley, the following schemes are being implemented:

- **Investment**

    Offering low-interest loans, grants and tax incentives to private and foreign industry to encourage investment in the region. This has created over 4,000 new jobs in the region.

- **Education**

    Twenty-five per cent of ERDF funds is used to set up worker retraining schemes, improve transport links to the region and clean up the derelict environment.

CORE UNIT: REGIONAL GEOGRAPHY

- **New and modern industry**

  Building new intergrated steelworks and engineering at Liège and Charleroi using coal from the Kampen coalfield in Flanders and iron ore imported through Antwerp, Europe's second largest port. Building industrial estates to encourage modern chemical industries to the region. These chemical industries produce ammonia, fertilisers and a variety of plastics, paints, soaps, cosmetics, detergents and pesticides.

- **Communication**

  Providing improved river, canal and motorway links between Liège, Charleroi, Rotterdam, Ostend, Brussels and Cologne. The upgrading of Charleroi airport improved international access to the region, encouraging more industrial development.

- **Environment**

  Cleaning up the scarred, run-down coalmining landscape of Charleroi with many environmental improvement schemes. This makes the area an attractive place in which to live and work. In fact, 43% of ERDF investment is used for environmental renewal.

weblink
Tourism in Charleroi

Fig. 11 EU funding is used for docklands rejuvenation in Charleroi, Belgium.

16.3 EU funding for socio-economic regions

Each of the socio-economic regions you will study has various physical and human factors specific to them which influence their development. EU funding policies are a very important human factor influencing the development of member states. The main EU policies and funding which affect all EU member states are outlined below and on page 311.

All socio-economic regions receive funding from local and central government. However, as well as domestic government support, funding from the EU is made available to all member states. Various **structural** and **cohesion funds** are allocated by the EU as part of its regional policy to tackle the economic and social imbalances between states and within states. These funds are used for development of infrastructure, telecommunications, education and human resources. They are also used to support jobs in primary economic activities.

EU structural and cohesion funds

All EU regions are eligible for funding under the various **structural funds** and poorer regions receive extra funding and support through cohesion funds.

Structural funds

Four EU structural funds help reduce regional imbalance in all states.

1. The **European Regional Development Fund (ERDF)** supports the modernisation of industry and also invests in infrastructure, e.g. roads, airports and environmental protection.
2. **The European Social Fund (ESF)** assists job creation schemes and schemes to help disadvantaged people enter the workforce. The New Era awards for students to access further education is funded by the ESF.
3. **The European Agricultural Guidance and Guarantee Fund (EAGGF – Guidance Section)** helps the farming sector in all regions. Money is distributed to all EU farming regions through the Common Agricultural Policy (CAP).
4. **The European Fisheries Fund (EFF)** is used to support the fisheries industry.

Cohesion funds

Cohesion funds are extra funding for the least-developed new and existing member states who have a Gross National Income (GNI) of less than 90% of the EU average, e.g. part of the Mezzogiorno, Italy; Bilbao, Spain; Sambre-Meuse, Belgium.

The Common Agricultural Policy and Common Fisheries Policy

The **Common Agricultural Policy (CAP)** is a system of subsidies and support programmes for agriculture funded by EU structural funds. CAP combines direct payments to farmers together with price and market supports. Farmers can apply for several payment schemes.

1. **Basic Payment Scheme** (direct payment): To receive payments farmers must follow a variety of rules on the environment, public health, animal health, plant health, animal welfare and land maintenance.

Fig. 12 Farmers can apply for an additional CAP payment if their land is classified as being in a Less Favoured Area. Examples of a less favoured area include farms where there is mountainous terrain.

CORE UNIT: REGIONAL GEOGRAPHY

2. **Agri-Environment Options Scheme (AEOS)**: This rewards farmers for following environmentally-friendly farming practices.
3. Farmers in lands that are classified as **Less Favoured Areas** can apply for a further CAP payment.

The CAP helps reduce Europe's reliance on imported food but had led to over-production and the creation of 'mountains' and 'lakes' of surplus food and drink. Due to these problems the CAP has been reformed.

The **Common Fisheries Policy (CFP)** is the EU's system for the management of fisheries and aquaculture (fish farming). It sets rules governing the size of fleets, the size of fish catches and how and where fishermen can operate. It also ensures fishermen get a fair price for their catch. It is also responsible for research into fish stocks, regulating conservation of fish stocks, development of ports and fish processing plants as well as safety. Preventing illegal fishing is also an important part of fishery protection.

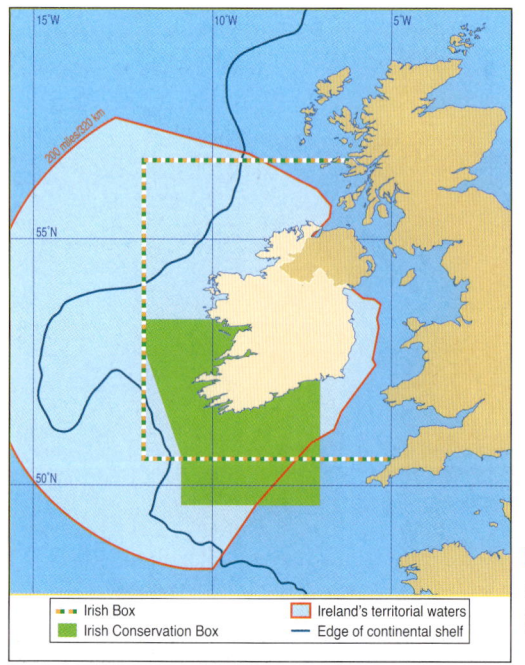

Fig. 13 The Common Fisheries Policy sets rules governing the management of fisheries and aquaculture in all EU member states.

Fig. 14 Each year fish stocks are analysed to help the EU Council decide the total allowable catches (TAC) and quotas for each fishing species.

Fig. 15 The Irish Conservation Box – the time spent in this area is limited for all vessels to protect the growth of young fish.

312

Chapter Revision Questions

Socio-economic regions

1. Name and briefly explain the **three** types of socio-economic regions. Give an example of each.
2. What is a core region?
3. Explain **three** characteristics of core regions.
4. Name **one** Irish and **three** European core regions.
5. What is a peripheral/less developed region?
6. Explain **three** characteristics of peripheral/less developed regions.
7. Name **three** European and **one** Irish peripheral region.
8. Explain the following term: region of industrial decline.
9. Explain **two** characteristics of regions of industrial decline.
10. Name **two** European and **one** Irish region of industrial decline.
11. What industries were associated with Drogheda in the past?
12. What led to the modern decline of industrial activity in Drogheda?
13. What advantages does Drogheda offer to attract industrial development today?
14. Explain why the Sambre-Meuse Valley went into industrial decline. What is being done to overcome the problems faced by the region?
15. What industries were associated with the Sambre-Meuse Valley in Belgium in the past?
16. Name and describe **one** economic challenge facing a European region you have studied.
17. Explain the terms structural fund and cohesion fund and describe their uses.
18. Explain how the CAP and the CFP affect Ireland's farmers and fishermen.

CORE UNIT: REGIONAL GEOGRAPHY

LC Exam Questions

Higher Level students must be able to answer Ordinary and Higher Level questions.

■ OL Questions

19. % of Economic Activity (Primary, Secondary and Tertiary) in Region A and Region B

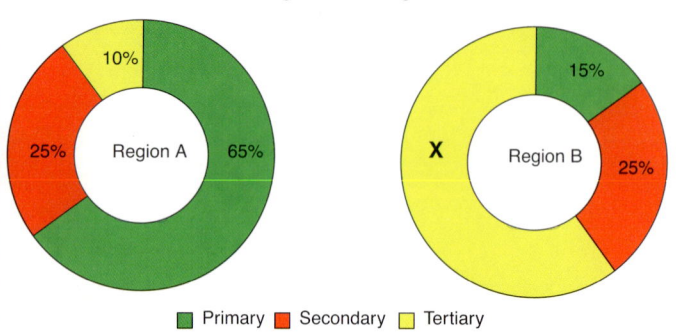

Region A: Primary 65%, Secondary 25%, Tertiary 10%
Region B: Primary 15%, Secondary 25%, Tertiary X

■ Primary ■ Secondary ■ Tertiary

Examine the charts above and answer each of the following questions.

(i) Calculate **X**, the percentage of tertiary economic activity in Region B.

(ii) Is Region B a Core or a Peripheral region?

(iii) Name an example of a Core region and an example of a Peripheral region.

(iv) Briefly describe **one** characteristic of a Core region.

(v) Briefly describe **one** characteristic of a Peripheral region.

20. 'Some regions have experienced economic decline.' Discuss the causes of economic decline with reference to an example you have studied.

21. Describe and explain **two** problems faced by any region that you have studied.

■ HL Questions

22. Look at the map of Europe. Match the number on the map with a letter given for different types of regions in the list below.

Letter	Description	No.	Example
A	A core economic region		
B	A peripheral region		
C	A cultural region		
D	A climatic region		

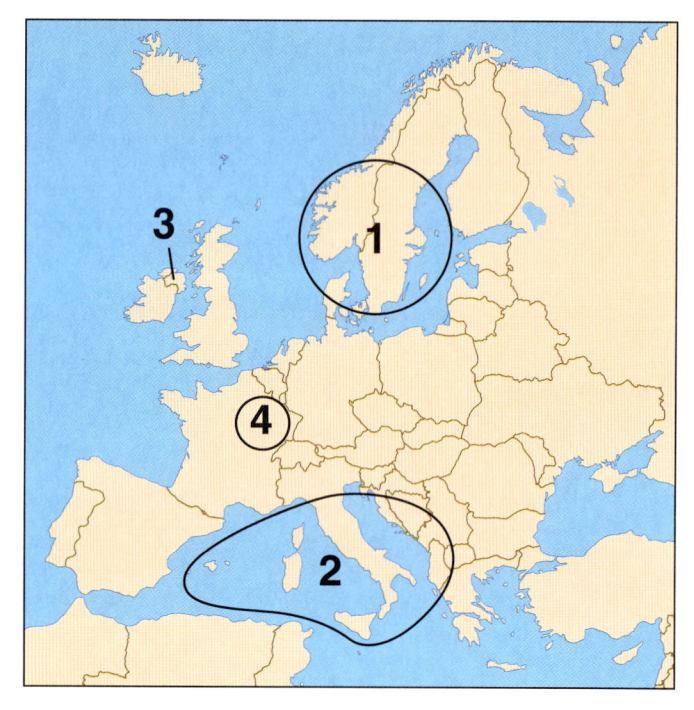

23. Examine the causes and impacts of industrial decline with reference to any region(s) that you have studied.

24. 'Economic activity in core regions differs from those in peripheral regions.' Examine this statement with reference to examples that you have studied.

25. Examine the causes and impacts of industrial decline with reference to any region(s) that you have studied.

CHAPTER 16: SOCIO-ECONOMIC REGIONS

Key Words

You should be able to explain both verbally and in writing each of the key words listed below.

cohesion funds
Common Agricultural Policy (CAP)
Common Fisheries Policy
core regions
European Regional Development Fund (ERDF)
industrial inertia
peripheral/less developed regions
regions of industrial decline
socio-economic regions
structural funds

Key Words Chapter 16

Digital Resources are available for this chapter at mentorbooks.ie/resources

CHAPTER 17

An Irish Peripheral Region

Key Theme

The study of regions shows how economic, human and physical processes interact in a particular way. This can be demonstrated by examining contrasting Irish regions.

Learning Outcomes

At the end of this chapter you will be able to:
- Describe the Northern and Western (N&W) region as a peripheral/less developed socio-economic region.
- Name and describe the physical and human characteristics of the N&W region.
- Describe primary, secondary and tertiary activities in the N&W region.
- Describe the population characteristics of the N&W region.
- Outline some government plans to reduce regional inequality in Ireland.

Contents

17.1	The N&W region – physical and human characteristics, economic activities and human processes	317
	Case Study: The Medical Technology Industry in the N&W region	326
17.2	Government policies to develop Ireland's regions	331

Revision Space

Chapter Revision Questions – LC Exam Questions – Key Word List 334

CHAPTER 17: AN IRISH PERIPHERAL REGION

17.1 The N&W region – physical and human characteristics, economic activities and human processes

In this chapter we will look at the Northern and Western (N&W) region – a peripheral/less developed socio-economic region.

A peripheral/less developed region in Ireland

The N&W region is made up of 8 counties. It has 1.1 million people and occupies one third of the land area of the state.

The northern region and the western region have several factors in common.
1. They are rural areas with low population densities (30 people per km^2).
2. There is a high dependence on primary activities.
3. Short and long-term unemployment are above the national average.
4. The transport infrastructure is underdeveloped.
5. There are low employment levels in services.
6. A high proportion of people are classified as rural poor.
7. Industrial development is based on multinational company branch plants.
8. There are high levels of out-migration.

The N&W is a **peripheral region** but it has good economic potential. It has an unspoilt environment, very little congestion and many areas of outstanding natural beauty, particularly its mountains and coastline.

The N&W region holds 18.3% of the population. However, unemployment rates remain high, particularly along the western coast. Various physical and human factors influence the development of the N&W region.

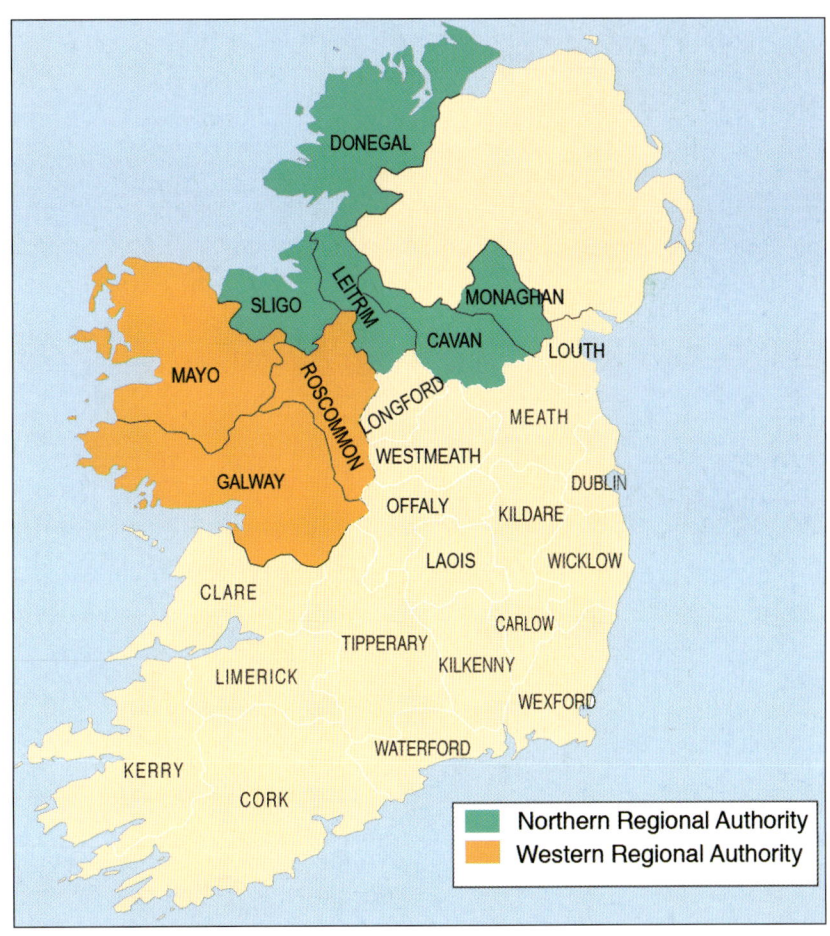

Fig. 1 The N&W region

317

CORE UNIT: REGIONAL GEOGRAPHY

Physical characteristics/factors influencing the development of the N&W region

1. Climate

- Like the rest of Ireland, the N&W has a cool, temperate, oceanic climate (see page 277).
- The higher relief creates cooler wetter conditions than in the Greater Dublin Area (GDA), especially in the western part of the N&W region where average annual rainfall in some mountainous areas can at times exceed 2,500 mm.
- Average July temperatures are 14°C (Belmullet) and average January temperatures are 5.7°C (Belmullet). Frost is more prominent in inland regions. Average annual rainfall varies from 928 mm in Clones to 1,150 mm in Belmullet. These variations are due to the influence of relief and distance from the sea.

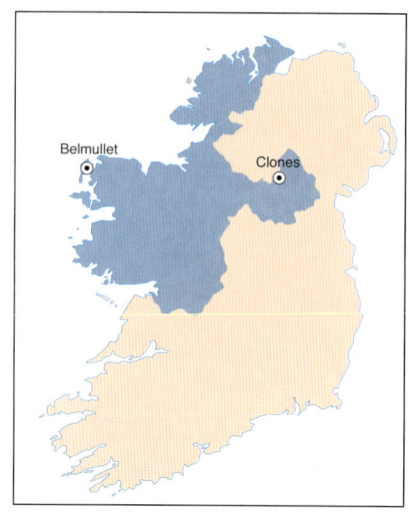

Fig. 2 Location of Clones and Belmullet weather stations in the N&W region

2. Relief and drainage

- The region has a varied relief of mountains, lakes and lowlands, which are challenges to the region's social and economic development.
- The mountains in the north-west contain acidic metamorphic and igneous rock formed during the Caledonian mountain building period 400 million years ago.
- Lowlands are found around Lough Mask in County Galway, the edges of Lough Swilly in County Donegal and south of Connemara. Much of the lowlands are unsuitable for agriculture because they are poorly drained, e.g. Roscommon, Leitrim.
- The coastline is made of headlands and sheltered bays (indented), due to erosion by powerful Atlantic Ocean waves. Clew Bay formed as a result of rising sea levels after the last Ice Age. Killala Bay in County Mayo is a ria. Killary Harbour on the border of Galway and Mayo is an important sheltered fiord.

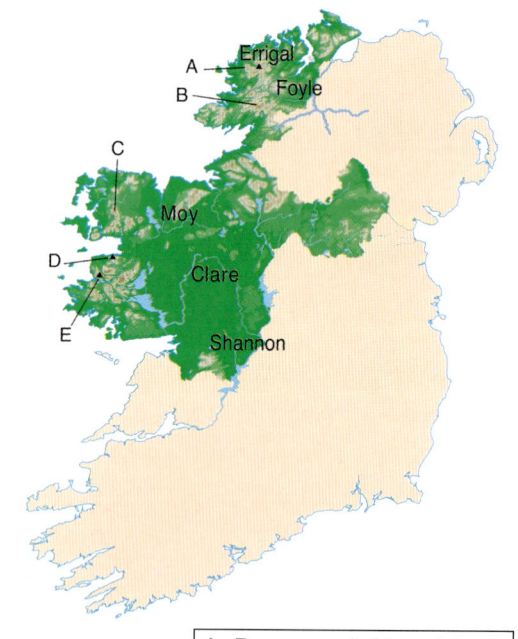

A: Derryveagh Mountains
B: Bluestack Mountains
C: Nephin Beg Range
D: Croagh Patrick
E: Mweelrea

Fig. 3 N&W – Rivers, mountains and lakes

318

3. Soils
- Soils in the N&W region are varied and generally of poor quality, e.g. peat and waterlogged/gley soils, compared to the GDA.
- Heavy rainfall has led to leaching of soils and the formation of podzol soils, which have a hard pan and are poorly drained.
- County Monaghan in the Northern region has boulder clay soils and a drumlin landscape with several large lakes, e.g. Lough Erne.
- In Connemara, glacial erosion has removed the soil cover, leaving a landscape of lakes and shallow peat soil.
- In East Galway, the limestone parent rock has led to the formation of shallow soils.
- The drainage basin of the River Shannon around Portumna has fertile alluvial soils but is often flooded and as a result has a unique **callow** landscape of flooded meadows.
- Fluvioglacial deposition has left several **eskers** running across the landscape which provide well-drained dry areas (the **Esker Riada**).

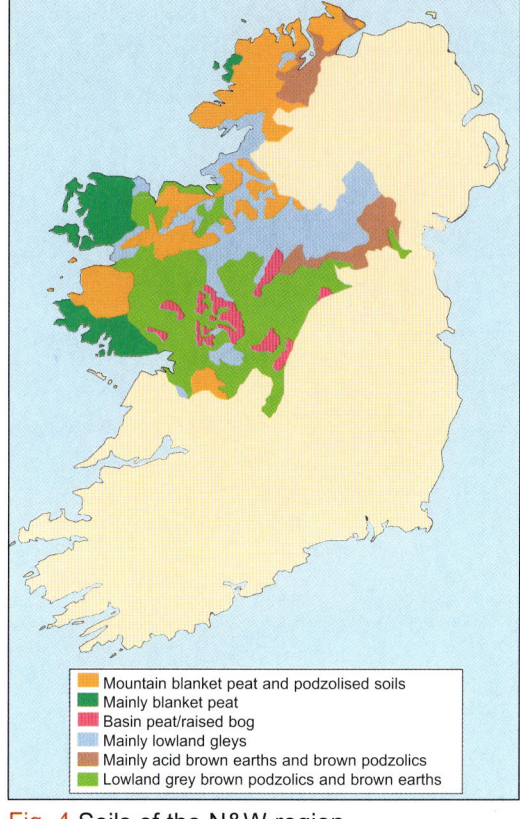

Fig. 4 Soils of the N&W region

Human processes/factors influencing the development of the N&W Region

Physical factors also interact with several human (socio-economic) factors affecting the N&W region. These factors combine to influence the primary, secondary and tertiary activities that occur in this region. Three main human factors that affect the N&W region are: **population, transport infrastructure** and **government/EU policies**.

1. Population characteristics of the N&W region

Uneven population distribution

Population distribution is uneven across the N&W region with the largest numbers concentrated near and around large lowland towns, e.g. Sligo, Letterkenny. The Western region has the largest urban centre, i.e. Galway City. The N&W region is not as urbanised as the Greater Dublin Area (GDA) – only 41% is urbanised compared to 63% of the national average.

Population density

The N&W area has 18.3% of the national population and a lower than average population density (30 people per km² compared to 66 per km² nationally). The highest density is in Galway city.

Leitrim has the lowest population density in Ireland with just 18 people per km². In general the low population density is due to the mountainous relief, poor soils and the impact of out-migration of young people from the region. There is a high elderly dependence ratio due to out-migration of young people. The majority of farmers are over 55 years of age.

CORE UNIT: REGIONAL GEOGRAPHY

Well-educated workforce

The region has a well-educated workforce but there is out-migration of young workers from rural areas. Galway is the largest urban centre due to the availability of workers, education, markets, better transport and job opportunities. Services are concentrated in urban areas. Other large towns have grown, e.g. Castlebar and Sligo, due to rural-to-urban migration. Only 13% of graduates from the N&W region find work close to their homes. Therefore, many have been forced to migrate. This brain-drain is due to the lack of suitable job opportunities for the educated workforce.

> People below the age of 15 and over 65 are classed as **dependents**.

Fig. 5 The poor soils and mountainous relief of the N&W have contributed to a low population density.

Standard of living

Within the N&W region, parts of the larger urban areas of Galway and Sligo show symptoms of extreme disadvantage. These disadvantages are in unemployment and the provision of health and other social services.

Remote rural areas such as Connemara and the Donegal Gaeltacht areas, Inishowen, Leitrim, West Mayo and parts of Roscommon and Cavan show signs of **rural deprivation**. These signs are low educational and skill levels, unprofitable farm holdings, unemployment and high dependency rates. Therefore, these areas have traditionally been a region of out-migration, leaving older and younger **dependents** at home.

Fig. 6 Road and rail links to the N&W region have improved but transport infrastructure is still underdeveloped.

2. Transport infrastructure

Transport infrastructure in the N&W region is underdeveloped. This hinders the development of industry in the region and also adds to the costs faced by farmers transporting their produce to markets and farms. The government aims to provide better road and rail links to the region and motorway links are now complete between Galway, Dublin and Sligo.

These improvements will aid economic development in the N&W region by reducing transport costs and improving access to local, national and international markets.

CHAPTER 17: AN IRISH PERIPHERAL REGION

3. Government/EU policy

Several government agencies direct EU and government funds to all regions of Ireland to help economic and social development. CAP, CFP (see Chapter 16, pages 311-312) and government funds are especially important to the N&W region as much of its employment is based directly or indirectly on the primary sector.

The National Development Plan (NDP) was a series of government plans aimed at reducing the imbalance between the regions of Ireland. During the 2008–2015 economic recession, the NDP was restructured. It was replaced by the **Capital Investment Plan (CIP)** 2016–2021. Some of the most important departments and their CIP funding to the N&W region are outlined below.

(a) The **Department of Agriculture, Fisheries and Food** allocates CAP, CFP and a range of government payments to farmers and fishermen in the N&W region.

　　This department offers training, afforestation grants and woodland/forest environment protection schemes. This is important as farmers add to their incomes by converting their land to forest.

　　Fishing is funded by BIM (Bord Iascaigh Mhara) through the CFP, which is responsible for developing the Irish sea fishing and aquaculture industries. The CFP is especially important for funding and supporting infrastructure development at Killybegs port in County Donegal.

(b) The **Industrial Development Authority (IDA)** is responsible for the attraction and development of **foreign direct investment** in Ireland (**FDI**). This is very important to all of Ireland but especially for the N&W region. Grants and tax incentives are offered to attract investment, e.g. low corporation tax, ready-to-go industrial sites. SOLAS, the successor to FÁS, and Local Enterprise Offices (LEOs) are important in providing training and support for Irish workers. LEOs and Enterprise Ireland are also involved in making Ireland a desirable location for industry.

(c) **Údarás na Gaeltachta** funds the economic and social development of the Gaeltacht regions.

Fig. 7 Connemara in County Galway is classified as a Less Favoured Area.

Fig. 8 The Department of Agriculture, Fisheries and Food allocates CAP and CFP payments to fishermen and farmers in the N&W region.

Fig. 9 Social and economic development of Gaeltacht regions, e.g. Irish language courses, are funded by Údarás na Gaeltachta.

CORE UNIT: REGIONAL GEOGRAPHY

Primary activities in the N&W region

Agriculture

- The wet climate, high land and generally poor soils, e.g. podzols, are an obstacle to the development of successful agriculture in the N&W region. As a result, much of the land in the region is classified by the EU as disadvantaged for farming. This is important for acquiring EU funds to support farmers. However, there are fertile alluvial soils along the Shannon and Corrib Basins, but these are often prone to flooding.
- Pastoral farming is common. Sheep are grazed in the upland areas and cattle are reared on lime-rich soils found on lower ground. Boulder clay in the Northern region is also used for pasture and cattle.
- Poultry production and mushroom production are found in Monaghan as they are not hugely dependent on ground quality.
- The wet, cloudier climate and steep relief mean that few cereals can be grown.
- Farm incomes are lower in this region than in the GDA. In order to make a living, 50% of farmers in the region have an 'off-farm' job.
- Farmers are generally older, e.g. over 55 years of age.
- Farms in the N&W region are smaller and more fragmented (scattered about the countryside) than the national average (37.1 hectares) thereby increasing production costs. The smallest farms are found in Counties Mayo and Monaghan, where the average size of a farm is 21.8 hectares.
- CAP funding is important to the N&W region to help farmers overcome these challenges.

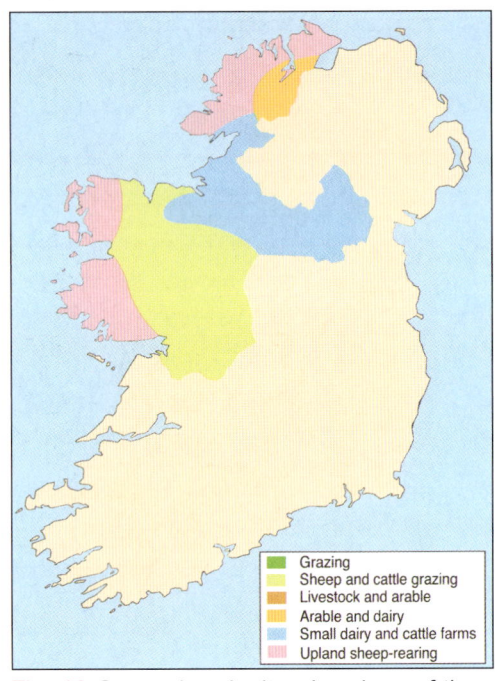

Fig. 10 General agricultural regions of the N&W region

- Grazing
- Sheep and cattle grazing
- Livestock and arable
- Arable and dairy
- Small dairy and cattle farms
- Upland sheep-rearing

Fig. 11 Pastoral farming in the upland areas of the N&W region

Fig. 12 Few cereals are grown in the west of Ireland due to the thin infertile soils and cloudier weather.

Forestry

- Galway, Mayo, Donegal and Leitrim have most forest cover due to the high percentage of marginal land (mountainous with poor soils). Twelve per cent of Donegal is forested.
- The mild, wet, Irish climate encourages rapid growth of coniferous trees such as Sitka Spruce and Scots Pine.
- Many farmers in the N&W region are part-time, adding to their farm income with another job – often forestry – to make a living, e.g. almost 14% of farmers in Donegal also have some forestry. By turning to forestry, farmers make more profitable use of their land. Afforestation of poor farmland raises farm incomes.

Fig. 13 N&W farmers often supplement their income by taking another job in forestry.

Fishing and aquaculture

The fishing and aquaculture (fish farming) sector is a key source of income in the N&W region.

Physical factors affecting fishing and aquaculture

The soils, relief and climate of the region have combined to make agriculture difficult. As a result, many people have turned to fishing. The west coast of the N&W region has a number of natural advantages for the fishing industry:

1. It is close to the rich fishing grounds of the North Atlantic.
2. It is influenced by the **North Atlantic Drift** ocean current which brings warm water and a variety of fish.
3. The sea is shallow and rich in plankton due to the wide, gently sloping **continental shelf**.
4. The **indented** coast provides natural, sheltered, pollution-free harbours suitable for aquaculture.

CORE UNIT: REGIONAL GEOGRAPHY

Human factors affecting fishing and aquaculture

The N&W region has many small coastal and island communities where there are few other employment opportunities. This is due to geographic and economic factors, such as distance from centres of economic activity, low population density and poor agricultural land.

Within the region, Donegal is the most dependent on fishing. Killybegs in Donegal is the chief fishing port in Ireland. The value and tonnage of fish landed in Killybegs is greater than any other fishing port in the country. Fishing and related activities are estimated to be worth over €50 million to the local economy each year.

Donegal has the highest number of employees in the seafood processing sector. This is 10% of all fisheries jobs in Ireland, most of which are based at Killybegs.

Aquaculture (salmon and shellfish) is an increasingly important economic activity in regions, e.g. Clew Bay and Killary Harbour in Mayo. Sea trout are farmed in Clew Bay and at Inver Bay in Donegal. Killary Harbour is a major mussel cultivator.

The importance of fishing to the N&W region is clear from the fact that roughly 60% of funding from Bord Iascaigh Mhara (BIM) for training in aquaculture, processing and catching is being spent in this region.

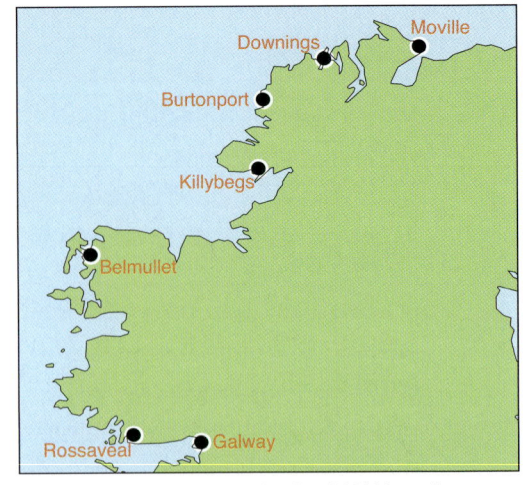

Fig. 14 Fishing ports in the N&W region

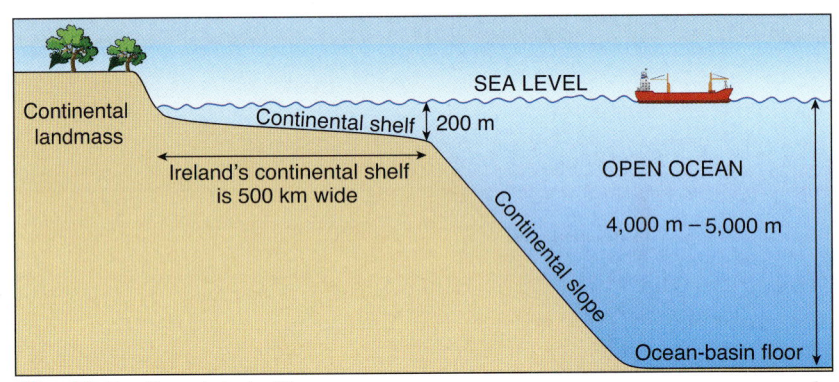

Fig. 15 Continental shelf

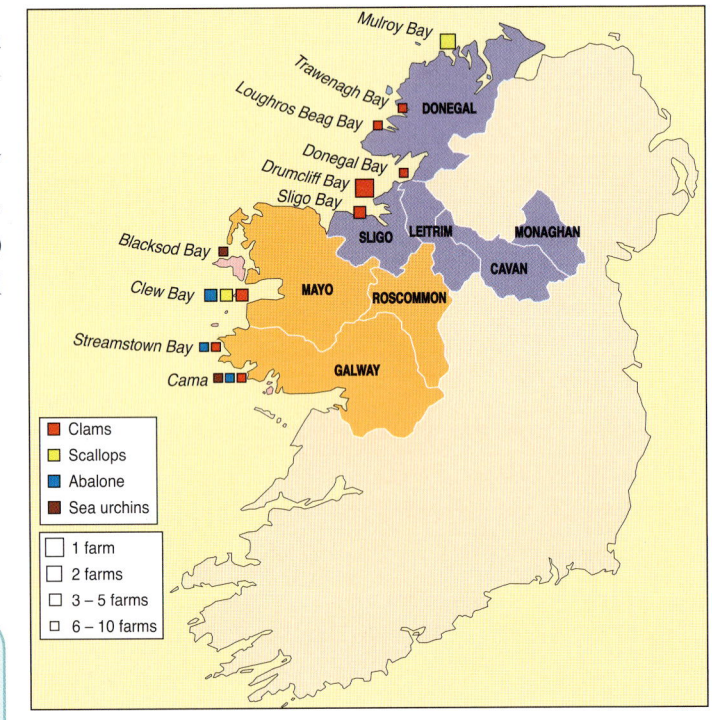

Fig. 16 Shellfish cultivation in the N&W region

Activity

Examine Fig. 16.
1. How many scallop farms are found at the following locations:
   (i) Clew Bay (ii) Mulroy Bay?
2. How many clam farms are found in Drumcliff Bay?

☀ Mineral resources

Natural gas is located in the Corrib gas field, 70 km west of Belmullet. The gas is located 3,000 metres below the seabed under 355 metres of water. The gas field will produce gas for about 20 years, supplying 60% of Ireland's natural gas needs. This is important as Ireland's other gas field off Kinsale is nearing the end of its life. A 150 km pipeline from Mayo to Galway delivers gas from the Corrib gas field into the national network.

Peat is found in the upland blanket bogs of the N&W region, e.g. the Derryveagh Mountains in County Donegal. Before Kinsale Natural Gas came on stream in 1979, turf was Ireland's most important energy resource.

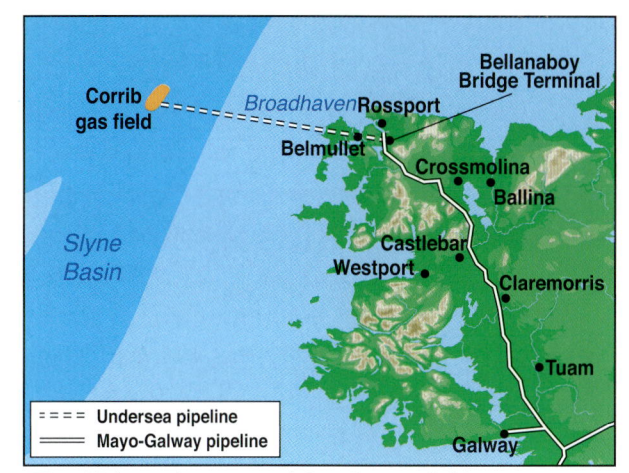

Fig. 17 Location map of Corrib gas field

weblink
Map of pipeline

Secondary activities in the N&W region

Like many peripheral locations, the N&W region is not, in general, a favourable location for manufacturing.

REASONS FOR THE UNDERDEVELOPMENT OF MANUFACTURING IN THE N&W REGION

1. Poorly developed transport infrastructure (few motorway links/less developed).
2. Low population density.
3. Peripheral location (raising transport costs).
4. Lack of power supplies capable of supporting energy intensive/energy hungry industry.
5. Small urban population (small labour pool and market).

Reliance on a few industries such as food processing, timber processing and textiles is typical of the region. The N&W lacks variety (**diversity**) in its manufacturing base. The percentage of the labour force employed in unskilled occupations is higher in the N&W than the national average and the percentage employed in professional occupations is lower.

Despite these problems the N&W is able to attract industry to the region for the reasons outlined below.

- A young, educated and skilled workforce
- Access to a large EU market of over 508 million people
- Lack of congestion
- High quality environment
- Work of IDA, Local Enterprise Offices and Enterprise Ireland
- Government and EU policies
- Scope for development of industries based on local resources, e.g. forestry.

The main centres of industry are Galway, Castlebar, Letterkenny and Sligo.

CORE UNIT: REGIONAL GEOGRAPHY

The Irish government recognises the importance of attracting industry to the N&W region and therefore, offers grant assistance and tax incentives through the IDA to new industries. For example, the Gaeltacht region in County Donegal attracts the maximum level of grant assistance, averaging up to €14,000 per job. Attracting multinational companies is vital as Foreign Direct Investment (FDI) is important to all regions in Ireland, and especially to the N&W region. The international airports at Shannon and Knock offer access to markets for raw materials and finished products.

Galway is the only urban centre with a variety of modern **knowledge-based industry** such as electronics, e.g. Hewlett Packard, Ingersoll Rand and Boston Scientific. This is due to the location of University College Galway and GMIT which provide a skilled graduate labour force. There is also a large urban market and the presence of serviced industrial estates for investors. The direct transport network to the Dublin market on the east coast by air, rail, road or sea attracts industry. These fast transport links to Dublin Port and Dublin Airport reduce costs for industries.

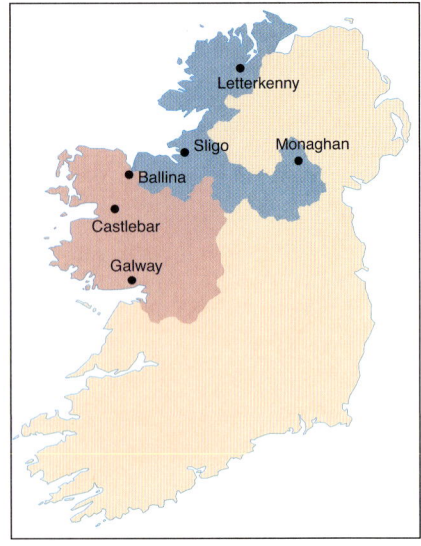

Fig. 18 Manufacturing centres in the N&W region

CHAPTER 17
Case Study

The Medical Technology Industry in the N&W region

Ireland holds a cluster of medical technology (MedTech) industries. These companies manufacture specialist medical equipment used in hospitals across the world. Nine of the top ten global companies have a manufacturing base in Ireland, e.g. Becton Dickinson and Medtronic. Ireland employs per capita the highest number of medical technology personnel in Europe.

Many medical technology manufacturing and support companies have located in the N&W region of Ireland. Several human factors encourage medical technology industries to locate in this region:

- **The labour force is young and educated.** The N&W region has a population of 1.1 million people. Forty per cent of the population is under 25 years of age. Half of the school leavers in the region go on to third-level education. This provides an educated and skilled workforce for employers.

- **The National Standards Authority of Ireland (NSAI) is globally recognised.** Once the NSAI approves a product for sale, a company can automatically receive EU-wide approval. This helps non-EU medical technology companies to rapidly gain access to the entire European market.

- The N&W region contains **centres of excellence** in bioengineering, laser applications, tool making and information technology. These service and supply companies provide the expertise needed to support the medical technology industry.

- Ireland offers a **low corporation tax of 12.5%** on all trading activities. This low rate combined with a range of other tax advantages, such as research and development tax credits and patent royalty tax exemptions, means that locating in Ireland offers a financial advantage to medical technology companies.

CHAPTER 17: AN IRISH PERIPHERAL REGION

Merit Medical, Galway

Merit Medical Systems, Inc. (MMSI) is an example of a medical technology industry that has chosen to locate in the N&W region. It produces disposable medical devices used in hospitals worldwide. It employs 1,700 people with facilities in Galway, Utah, Texas, Virginia and the Netherlands.

1. The products made include guide wires which are used to place medical devices into blood arteries and catheter devices to deliver fluids into veins and drain wounds, as well as various syringe equipment. Merit is the market leader in these products. It supplies 40%-50% of the world market.

2. The Irish branch – Merit Medical Ireland Limited – was set up in Galway in 1994 and currently employs 380 people at this facility.

3. The main inputs for the Galway factory are platinum, steel and plastic. Platinum is imported from South African mines through the UK by air and road. Plastics are imported from Salt Lake City, USA, by ship to Dublin and Galway. Steel is imported by ship and road from the UK. Products are manufactured in Galway and sent by container truck to Dublin, then by ship, air and road to the main markets in the EU, Eastern Europe and China.

4. The manufacturing plant was located in Galway for several reasons:
   - Ireland has a skilled, educated workforce. NUI Galway provides skilled graduates.
   - Ireland's location provides access to EU and Asian markets for the American company.
   - A suitable site was available.

5. While some foreign-owned Irish companies have relocated to low-cost eastern European locations, Merit Medical Ireland has stayed and expanded its Irish operations because:
   - The total 'delivered cost' of Merit's Irish-made products is still lower than if they located elsewhere.
   - The industry is highly regulated and therefore, setting up another factory in a new location is costly and time-consuming.
   - The response time between receiving orders and delivering the product is quicker in Ireland than elsewhere.
   - Ireland, and the N&W region in particular, has a supply of highly skilled and trained personnel. These would be hard to find and costly to train in a new location.

weblink
Working at Merit Medical

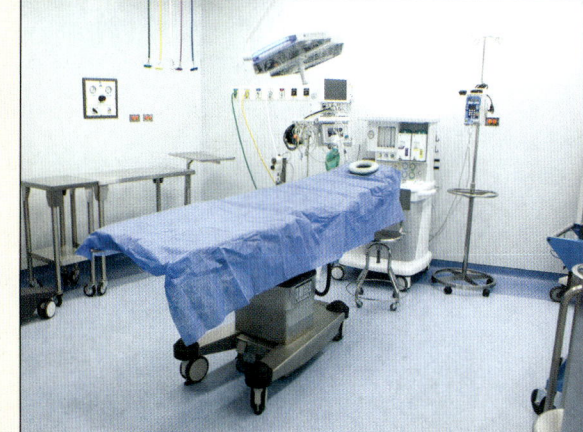

Fig. 19 Merit Medical devices are used in hospital surgeries

CORE UNIT: REGIONAL GEOGRAPHY

Tertiary activities in the N&W

Transport

Transport and communications in the N&W region are affected by physical and human factors such as the mountainous relief and low population density. Such factors hinder economic development in the region by making commuting difficult and transportation of goods expensive and time consuming.

The routes are often steep, winding and narrow due to having to travel over mountainous land and around lakes and bays. Many roads in remote upland areas of Mayo and Donegal are of poor quality and not suitable for heavy trucks, preventing economic development in these areas. Rail links are absent north of Sligo and direct routes between some urban centres in the N&W region are not well developed.

The low population density means that transport infrastructure is best developed along routes connecting the major urban centres/gateway towns of Galway, Sligo and Letterkenny.

Public transport is underdeveloped with just 4% of the population using it to get to work compared to 11% nationally.

International airports are accessible at Shannon and Knock. Smaller airports are located at Sligo and Donegal.

An efficient transport infrastructure is essential to the continued economic development of the N&W region. The National Development Plan (NDP) of the past and the current Capital Investment Plan (CIP) have improved some transport facilities through the **Transport 21** programme. This scheme aims to develop an **Atlantic Corridor** of motorway and high quality dual carriageway linking gateway towns of Waterford to Letterkenny via Cork, Limerick, Galway and Sligo.

Fig. 20 Part of the Atlantic Corridor in County Sligo

Communications

The peripheral location of the N&W region has led to the creation of many jobs based on teleservices.

With high-speed internet access business can occur without the need for roads. Teleservice businesses such as recruitment agencies, call centres, ticket sales and tour operators depend on fast broadband services. There are several call centres in operation in the N&W region. Some companies provide technical support for call centres such as FCS in Galway.

weblink
- Companies located in Letterkenny.
- Pramerica: A CEO explains why the region attracts companies.

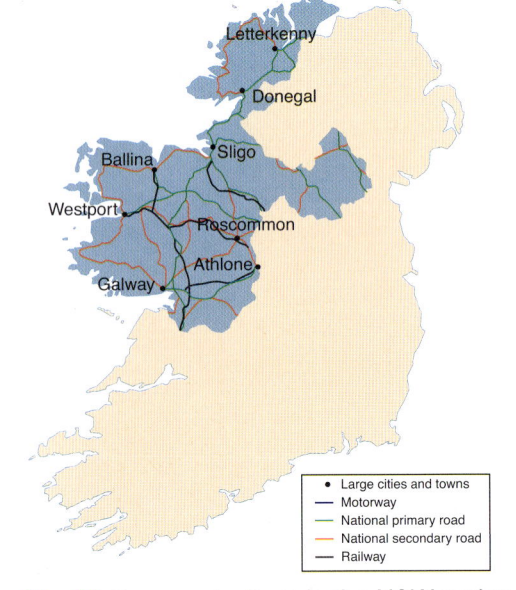

Fig. 21 Communications in the N&W region

CHAPTER 17: AN IRISH PERIPHERAL REGION

🏖️⛳ Tourism

Tourism in Ireland is an important tertiary industry. It generates over 200,000 jobs and close to €6 billion annually in revenue. Tourism provides over 4% of taxes paid to the government.

In the N&W region tourism is a tertiary economic activity dependent on the physical landscape. The scenic coasts, mountains, rivers and lakes attract both domestic and international tourists. Despite the scenic landscape, tourism in the N&W region in general has not grown as much as that in the GDA for a number of human and physical reasons.

1. Dublin Airport is the main entry point to Ireland. The majority of tourists stay in the GDA region rather than heading to the peripheral N&W region.
2. Ireland is now regarded as an expensive location to visit and this, combined with economic recession, has reduced tourist numbers.
3. Transatlantic aircraft are no longer required to stop at Shannon Airport, a crucial hub for west coast tourism. This has reduced the number of tourists travelling on to the N&W region.
4. Transport and car hire are expensive in Ireland which discourages people travelling to the N&W region.
5. Rail infrastructure in the N&W region is underdeveloped. This prevents people travelling easily to the region from their arrival point in Dublin Airport or Shannon and ferry ports.

The majority of visitors come from Britain. The number of international tourists to the region fell dramatically due to worldwide economic recession from 2008 to 2015, but it is recovering.

Donegal, Galway and Sligo are the most popular destinations in the N&W region with overseas visitors contributing over €85 million (as an **invisible export**) to the economy.

Fig. 22 Cruising on the River Shannon is a popular tourist activity

329

CORE UNIT: REGIONAL GEOGRAPHY

Tourism is very seasonal (May to August) in the N&W region. This region has a wide variety of natural and man-made attractions for tourists. It markets itself as a destination for tourists interested in outdoor activities and heritage.

Attractions in the N&W include:
- Sea cliffs at Slieve League: 125,000 visitors each year.
- Glenveagh National park: 117,000 visitors each year.
- Ben Bulben and Derryveagh mountains which are used for outdoor pursuits, horse riding and hill walking.
- The islands of Tory and Gola and many other rivers and lakes offer fishing and water sports, e.g. Ballina.
- Cruising on Lough Erne canal and River Shannon.

Fig. 23 Glenveagh National Park, County Donegal

Donegal's Gaeltacht region is attractive to tourists due to its history, culture and heritage. Donegal promotes its Irish culture with many traditional music and dance festivals held throughout the county each summer.

To counteract its peripheral location, Tourism Ireland actively promotes the fact that access to the N&W region is improving. It does this by offering fly/drive package holidays through Sligo, Galway, Knock and Donegal airports.

The most recent tourist attractions in the N&W region have been developed by Discover Ireland and local operators. Three major tourist routes have been developed: The Wild Atlantic Way, The Great Western Greenway and The Blue Way.

Fig. 24 The Wild Atlantic Way routes shown in red have been developed by Discover Ireland and local operators.

CHAPTER 17: AN IRISH PERIPHERAL REGION

17.2 Government policies to develop Ireland's regions

Several development plans have been introduced by the government in order to reduce the imbalance in wealth and economic growth between the N&W region and the South and East region in Ireland. These plans are financed by the government and/or EU funds. Funding is adjusted depending on whether the economy is in a growth phase or in recession. We will examine four of these plans.

1. National Development Plan (NDP)

There have been many NDPs over recent years. Their aim has been to create **balanced regional development** throughout Ireland in a way that is economically, socially and environmentally sustainable.

All NDPs have aimed to:
 (a) Maintain employment levels in Ireland and improve its competitiveness amongst other countries.
 (b) Provide world-class economic and social infrastructure in transport, housing, health, education and environmental services.
 (c) Create a culturally integrated society.
 (d) Support science and enterprise.
 (e) Invest in education, skills and training.

Ninety per cent of the NDP's funding was provided by the Central Exchequer, i.e. through taxes.

The first NDP identified five cities as engines of regional and national growth. These are Dublin, Cork, Limerick, Galway and Waterford. Each NDP was put into action by the NSS (National Spatial Strategy). Since 2015 the NDP has been replaced by the Capital Investment Plan (CIP).

2. National Spatial Strategy (NSS) (2002–2020)

The NSS was developed to help implement the aims of the NDP.

The NSS identified certain cities and towns in Ireland as **gateways** and **hubs** based on population and services. These gateways and hubs were developed to prevent Dublin becoming the primary focus of the Irish economy. This allowed people living in other regions the opportunity to work and live in their local area. In turn, it was hoped that rural areas around the gateway and hub centres would also develop.

The aim was that by spreading work opportunities throughout the country to gateway and hub towns, Dublin's growth would be managed and people living outside the GDA would be able to avail of the same services as those living within it.

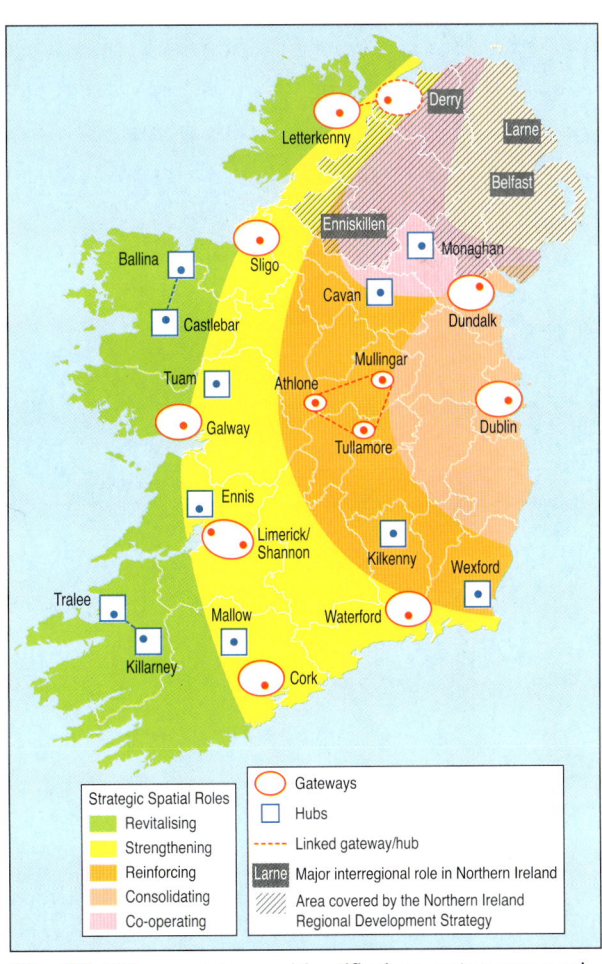

Fig. 25 Cities and towns identified as gateways and hubs

CORE UNIT: REGIONAL GEOGRAPHY

3. The Capital Investment Plan

Following on from the NDP and NSS, the Capital Investment Plan (CIP) aims to encourage regional development in the following areas:

- Housing
- Transport/Tourism
- Education
- Health
- Business
- Environment/Climate.

Over the life of the plan, €27 billion will be invested in these areas.

Fig. 26 Galway city has been identified as an engine of regional and national growth.

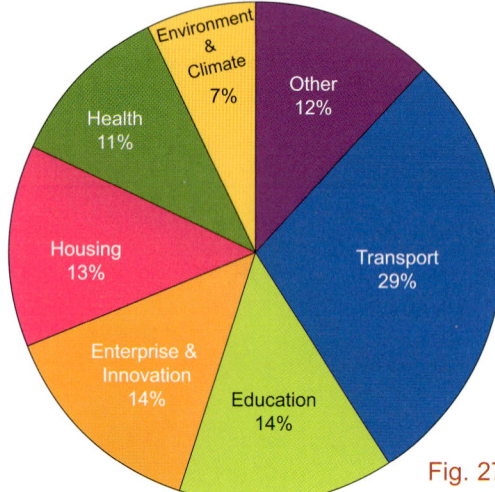

Fig. 27 Division of funding under the Capital Investment Plan

4. Transport 21 (2005 – 2015)

Transport 21 was the name given to the development of the transport system in Ireland in the 21st century. The investment covered improvements in national roads, public transport and regional airports.

Transport 21 aimed to:
1. Increase accessibility to and from all regions.
2. Ensure the sustainability of transport services, e.g. rail schemes.
3. Expand the capacity of the transport infrastructure, e.g. local expansion.
4. Increase people's use of public transport, e.g. QBC (Quality Bus Corridors).
5. Improve the quality of the transport infrastructure, e.g. upgrading the M50 and Atlantic Corridor.

Since 2016 the Capital Investment Plan invests 29% of its funding in transport.

Fig. 28 Investment in public transport is a priority under the CIP.

weblink
All about the CIP

HOW THE NDP DEVELOPED THE N&W

1. Development based on the N&W's natural resources and its tourism industry.
2. Improved access to the region as a result of the Transport 21 project.
3. Efforts to attract industries based on technology, where travel is 'electronic' and not physical, as a result of investment in electricity and broadband infrastructure.
4. Emphasis on improving services in order to keep people living and working in the region as a result of investment in health and education services.
5. Improved electricity supplies to attract more industry as a result of investment in the national electricity grid.
6. Investment in gateways, hubs, towns and rural areas.

HOW THE NSS DEVELOPED THE N&W (2002–2020)

1. Targeted investment in gateways and hubs in order to increase their appeal as places to locate industry and places to live.
2. Emphasis on locating industries in these gateways and hubs and other areas within the N&W region in order to create jobs.
3. Monitored zoning of land to ensure there is a good balance of industrial, commerical, residential and recreational land.
4. Development of an efficient and coordinated transport system.
5. Improved cultural, sporting and recreational facilities within gateways and hubs.

HOW TRANSPORT 21 DEVELOPED THE N&W (2005–2015)

1. Improved rail and road network in the region (as mentioned in NDP aims).
2. Construction of the Atlantic Corridor linking Letterkenny, Sligo, Galway, Limerick, Cork and Waterford. Roads along this route are being improved.
3. Significant investment in city and nationwide bus services.
4. Improved Western rail corridor linking Galway to Limerick

HOW THE CIP DEVELOPS THE N&W (2016–2021)

Money is being invested to improve development in:

1. Housing
2. Transport/Tourism
3. Education
4. Health
5. Business
6. Environment/Climate

Chapter Revision Questions

1. Using your atlas, draw an outline map of Ireland and mark the following: All the counties which make up the N&W; Rivers Foyle, Moy, Shannon, Erne and Corrib; the Twelve Bens, Derryveagh, and Nephin Beg Mountains; Donegal Bay, Clew Bay and Galway Bay; Letterkenny and Galway City.
2. How many counties are in the N&W region? List them.
3. Name and explain **four** characteristics that make the N&W a peripheral region.
4. Name **two** mountains and **two** rivers in the N&W region.
5. Pick **two** areas within the N&W region and describe their soils and agriculture.
6. Discuss other primary economic activities, besides farming, which provide employment in the N&W region.
7. What natural and man-made factors contribute to the success of fishing in the N&W region?
8. Name **three** industrial areas in the N&W region and describe the main reasons for the general underdevelopment of manufacturing in the region.
9. Describe the importance of the tertiary sector as a source of employment in the N&W region.
10. (i) What is the National Development Plan (NDP)?
    (ii) How did the NDP aim to help the N&W region?
11. (i) What is the National Spatial Strategy (NSS)?
    (ii) How does the NSS aim to help the N&W region?
12. (i) What is Transport 21?
    (ii) How did it aim to help the N&W region?
13. What is the Capital Investment Plan (CIP) and how does it help regional development in Ireland?
14. What steps are being taken by the N&W to attract industry to the region?
15. Examine **one** challenge facing the N&W region in the future. Discuss **one** way in which this challenge might be reduced.

Chapter 17: An Irish Peripheral Region

LC Exam Questions

Higher Level students must be able to answer Ordinary and Higher Level questions.

■ OL Questions

16. Draw a sketch map of Ireland. On it, show and name each of the following:
    - One region studied by you
    - One named town or city in this region
    - One named river in this region
    - One named area of relief (upland or lowland) in this region.

17. The figures below show the tourist regions of Ireland visited by domestic tourists.

A. IRELAND – DOMESTIC HOLIDAYS	%
Dublin	13.9
Midlands-East	12.5
South-East	15.9
South-West	20.4
Shannon	11.3
West	17.9
North-West	8.1

    Use graph paper to draw a graph that shows the data in the table above.

18. Name **one** Irish region that you have studied and answer each of the following questions.
    (i) Name **two** tourist attractions in this region.
    (ii) Explain the positive impacts of tourism in this region.
    (iii) Explain the negative impacts of tourism in this region.

19. Name **one** Irish region that you have studied and answer each of the following questions.
    (i) Name **two** types of agriculture practised in this region.
    (ii) Explain the advantages that this region has for the development of agriculture.
    (iii) Describe the challenges faced by agriculture in this region.

20. Describe the importance of any **two** of the activities below in an Irish region that you have studied.
    - Tourism
    - Transport
    - Manufacturing.

■ HL Questions

21. Examine the development of primary activities in any **one** Irish region you have studied.

22. Examine the factors that influence the development of secondary economic activity in an Irish region that you have studied.

23. Account for the development of transport or tourism in an Irish region that you have studied.

CORE UNIT: REGIONAL GEOGRAPHY

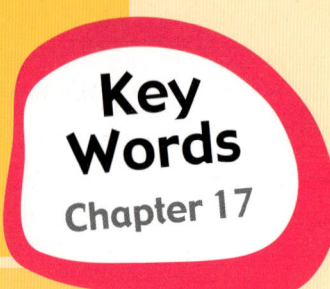

Key Words / Chapter 17

Key Words

You should be able to explain both verbally and in writing each of the key words listed below.

Atlantic Corridor
Capital Investment Plan (CIP)
dependents
Foreign Direct Investment (FDI)
gateway
hub
knowledge-based industry
National Development Plan (NDP)
National Spatial Strategy (NSS)
Northern and Western (N&W) region
peripheral region
rural deprivation
Transport 21

Digital Resources are available for this chapter at mentorbooks.ie/resources

CHAPTER 18

An Irish Core Region and an Irish City Region

Key Theme

The study of regions shows how economic, human and physical processes interact in a particular way. This can be demonstrated by examining contrasting Irish regions. The boundaries and extent of city regions may change over time.

Learning Outcomes

At the end of this chapter you will be able to:
- Describe the Greater Dublin Area (GDA) as a core region.
- Name and describe the physical and human characteristics of the GDA.
- Describe primary, secondary and tertiary activities in the GDA.
- Describe the population characteristics of the GDA.
- Describe the growth of the Dublin city region and explain how this growth is being planned and controlled.

Contents

18.1	The Greater Dublin Area (GDA) – Physical and human factors, economic activities and human processes	338
	Case Study 1: Largo Foods, Ashbourne, County Meath	344
18.2	Government policies to develop the GDA region	351
18.3	City/nodal/urban regions	352
	Case Study 2: The Dublin city region	354

Revision Space

Chapter Revision Questions – LC Exam Questions – Key Word List 359

CORE UNIT: REGIONAL GEOGRAPHY

18.1 The Greater Dublin Area (GDA) – Physical and human factors, economic activities and human processes

A core economic region in Ireland

The **Greater Dublin Area (GDA)** includes Counties Dublin, Kildare, Meath and Wicklow. It is part of the Eastern and Midland Regional Assembly. The GDA is a core economic region because:

1. The region has natural resources such as fertile brown earth soils and well-drained lowlands, leading to the development of profitable commercial agriculture. Its coastline provides sheltered harbours for the fishing industry and tourism.
2. It is a route focus/nodal point for Ireland's road, rail, air and river transport networks. The region contains an international airport and Dublin Port.
3. Dublin city is the financial and administrative capital, as well as a major service centre providing national, governmental, health and educational services. It is also the country's biggest tourist destination.
4. It has a high population density and is an area of in-migration. It has 39% of the population (1.8 million) in just 12% of Ireland's land area. It is expected to grow by 401,000 people by 2031.
5. Industry is attracted to this region because of its accessibility, resources and wealthy, educated population. In particular, Dublin city has become one of the world leaders in software development.

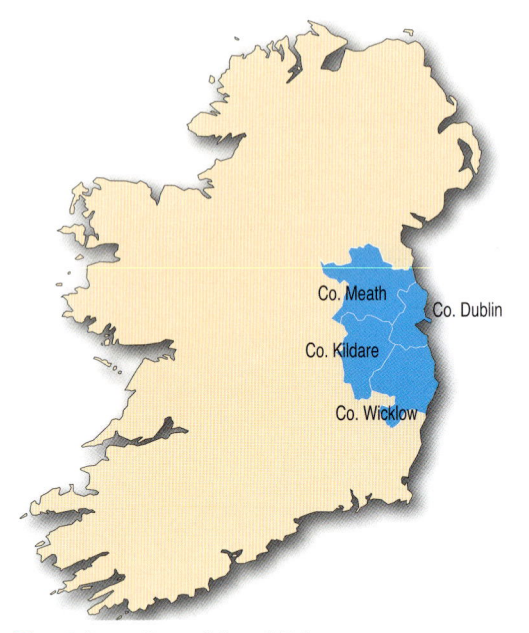

Fig. 1 Location of the GDA

REASONS FOR THE IMPORTANCE OF THE GDA IN THE ECONOMY

1. 80% of state-sponsored bodies are located in the GDA.
2. 70% of major public and private companies are located within the GDA.
3. All financial institutions have their headquarters in the GDA (financial capital).
4. Dublin city is the capital city of Ireland (administrative capital).

All of the above are interdependent, making the region a major location in Ireland for inward investment.

Physical factors influencing the development of the GDA

Climate, relief, soils and drainage are physical factors that affect the socio-economic development of the GDA.

Climate (cool temperate oceanic)	Relief and drainage	Soils
Rainfall 750 mm per year	Coastline is varied. Bays of limestone and headlands of metamorphic rock e.g. Bray Head	Fertile brown earth soils cover large area
Drier than the west due to rain shadow effect	Kildare and Meath are lowlands	Boulder clay on coastline
Wicklow mountains wetter due to relief rainfall	Wicklow mountains are barrier to development	Sandy loam soils in North County Dublin
Average temp. 5°C Jan, 15°C July		Infertile blanket peat in Wicklow

Fig. 2 Light, sandy soils favour horticulture in north County Dublin.

Human factors influencing development of the GDA

Population, transport and government policies are human factors that affect the socio-economic development of the GDA.

Population	Transport infrastructure	EU/Government Policy
Dublin has high population density (1,128 per km^2) and a large market of 1.8 million people	M50 provides connection to all regions of country and Dublin International airport. A major attraction for business	IDA and Enterprise Ireland attract FDI, develop business parks and promote Dublin as a location for industry and services
Wicklow, Meath, Kildare have lower densities due to presence of farmland and mountains	Luas and DART increase accessibility for commuters	The Department of Agriculture, Fisheries and Food makes CAP payments to farmers
Educated, skilled labour force	Port tunnel provides direct access to Dublin port	The CFP is used to develop Howth harbour
Multilingual due to high migrant population	Congestion is still a problem in city	Forestry is promoted by Coillte

Fig. 3 DART and commuter trains provide transport for the wider Dublin region.

Fig. 4 Commuters in Dublin city can use the Luas light rail system.

CORE UNIT: REGIONAL GEOGRAPHY

Primary economic activities in the GDA

Physical factors affecting agriculture in the GDA

The GDA has a profitable farming industry due to its physical and human factors.

Factor	Influence	Produce
Climate (mild maritime)	Provides 9-month growing season with soil temperatures above 6°C for most of year Rainfall 500 – 750 mm	Beef fattening on excellent grassland Vegetables are grown outside, lowering costs Wheat, barley do well in drier areas
Soils (fertile, brown earth, loam, boulder clays and well-drained sands and gravels)	Fertile, well-drained soils are productive and easily worked by machine Infertile peat soils in Wicklow Mountains	Cereals in Meath Greenhouse horticulture in North County Dublin Cattle fattening in all areas - 3,800 cattle farms Bloodstock reared in Kildare on gravel soils Sheep farms in Wicklow
Relief (low-lying in Kildare/Meath/Dublin, upland in Wicklow)	Allows use of machinery and intensive farming methods Uplands prevent use of intensive farming methods Wheat, barley, vegetables	Arable farming on lowlands Forestry on poorest land Sheep rearing on uplands

> Human and physical processes combine to produce a profitable commercial agriculture sector, making the GDA a core economic region.

Human factors affecting agriculture in the GDA

Factor	Influence
Large urban market	1.8 million people in the GDA provide a demand for high-quality, fresh produce
Transport	Excellent links of motorways and national roads reduce costs and travel time Farmers grow fresh perishable goods for the nearby market, e.g. market gardens in North Dublin
Government policy	CAP funding from EU promotes training and education of young farmers

Forestry

The area under forestry in Dublin, Meath and Kildare is much lower than in Wicklow (1,583 hectares in Meath compared to 28,102 hectares in Wicklow). This is because the lowland counties have more fertile soils and the land is used for commercial agriculture. The Wicklow Mountains have thin acidic soils, wetter climate and steeper ground. Therefore, forestry is a more productive use of this land than farming. However, overall few farmers in the GDA turn to forestry as an alternative to farming – which is in contrast to the experience of farmers in the N&W region.

Fishing

Howth is the third largest fishing port in Ireland, after Killybegs and Dunmore East. Dublin city is also ranked third in the number of people employed in fish processing after Killybegs and Cork.

Dublin Bay prawns account for 40% of the value of shellfish exports from Ireland. France, Spain and Britain are the main markets.

Fig. 5 The GDA's fishing industry is based at Howth.

Mineral resources

Ireland has three underground lead and zinc mines in production. Since 1960 we have had a string of important lead and zinc metal discoveries, ranking Ireland **first** in the world in terms of **zinc** discovered per square kilometre. The known deposits contain some 14 million tonnes (mt) of zinc metal, approximately 1.5% of the world zinc found to date. Ireland is **second** in the world for **lead** discovered per square kilometre. The largest of Ireland's lead and zinc mines, with more than 70 mt of ore in the ground, is in the GDA region at Tara Mines, Navan, County Meath. It produces over 2.7 mt of lead and zinc concentrate each year. This is also the largest lead and zinc mine in Europe and employs over 600 people.

Secondary activities in the GDA

As with all core economic regions, the GDA has many physical and human advantages (factors) which have encouraged the location of industry. Many of these advantages are concentrated in Dublin city.

Physical advantages for industry include:
1. It is on the east coast of Ireland close to the UK and European markets of over 508 million people.
2. Dublin Bay is a naturally sheltered harbour and has been a port location since Viking times. Dublin Port is the country's main international port.
3. The hinterland of Dublin is fertile farmland, which provides a variety of raw materials for the food processing industries in the region.

CORE UNIT: REGIONAL GEOGRAPHY

Human advantages for industry include:

4. Dublin city is the focus of Ireland's transport network. It is well connected to all parts of the country by road and rail. It also has international connections by air and sea through Dublin Airport and Dublin Port.
5. The region has a high population density and a young population (43% are under 25 years of age), which provides a labour force and market.
6. Dublin is a national education centre making it an attractive location for knowledge-based industries such as software development.
7. Dublin is a service centre, providing support services for manufacturing, such as marketing and technical support.
8. People are generally wealthier in the GDA than elsewhere in Ireland, making the region an attractive market for producers of high-value luxury goods.

As in all core economic regions, there is a variety of manufacturing in the GDA offering more job opportunities in modern and traditional industries, e.g. brewing, food processing, printing, clothing and electronics. The Dublin region accounts for over 90,000 jobs in manufacturing.

weblink
Ireland inspires

INDUSTRIES IN THE GREATER DUBLIN AREA	
Knowledge-based	Microsoft, IBM, Intel
Food processing	Cadbury's, Jacobs-Fruitfield, Largo Foods
Printing and publishing	Independent Newspapers
Metal fabrication and engineering	Small factories across the region, e.g. Wavin in Balbriggan, Wire Ropes Ltd in Wicklow

Unlike the N&W region where manufacturing is concentrated in a few urban centres, in the GDA it is widely dispersed. For example, Intel is located in Leixlip, County Kildare and Oriflame is located in Bray, County Wicklow. However, the influence of transport is seen in the movement of industry away from its traditional location in the Dublin docklands to suburban industrial estates and business parks close to the M50 motorway and Dublin Airport.

Focus on the food processing industry in the Greater Dublin Area

There are several physical and human factors that have encouraged the development of the food processing industry within the GDA. Well-known food producers are Cadburys (Coolock, Dublin), Tayto (Largo Foods in County Meath), Brennan's Bread (Walkinstown, Dublin), and Jacobs – Fruitfield (Tallaght, Dublin).

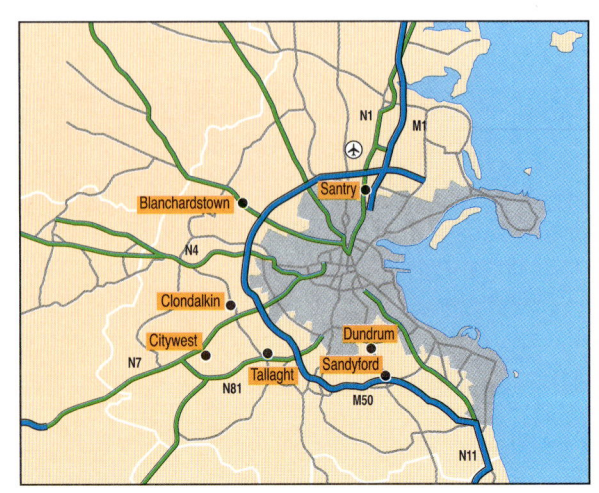

Fig. 6 Business parks and industrial estates in Dublin

Physical factors supporting the food processing industry in the GDA

- **Climate:** The region has a drier and warmer variation of the cool temperate oceanic climate and has very few frosty days. The average annual soil temperature is 10.9°C. The average rainfall is 545 mm. These moderate conditions mean that temperatures are high enough to support year-round growth of grass. The region is not too wet, cold or cloudy to prevent wheat and vegetable crop production.
- **Soils:** The region has a variety of fertile soils such as brown earths, loam and sandy soils. These soils allow a variety of crops to be grown across the region such as potatoes, barley, wheat and vegetables. These provide raw material for the processed food factories such as Green Isle vegetables and Brennan's Bread companies.
- **Relief:** The GDA has low-lying gently rolling land in Counties Kildare, Meath and north County Dublin. This enables the use of machinery. Farms in these areas are some of the largest and most *capital intensive* in the country. In Kildare, for example, the average farm size is above the national average at 49.2 hectares.

These physical factors mean that there is enough agricultural produce to supply the food processing factories in the GDA throughout the year.

Human factors supporting the food processing industry in the GDA

- **Government policy:** Farmers and processors are encouraged to use new technology, develop new products and find new food markets under a new government programme called *Food Harvest 2020*. The programme aims to increase agri-food production and the value of Irish food production exports to €12 billion by 2020.
- **Market:** The GDA has a population of over 1.8 million and is a wealthy core region in Ireland. As such it provides a local market for producers who locate their factories in the region to reduce transport costs.
- **Labour force:** The same population that provides the market also provides an educated workforce for companies looking for skilled and unskilled labour. This is an important factor affecting the location of the food processing companies in the region.
- **Transport infrastructure:** The variety and efficiency of the transport network reduces travel costs and fuel consumption for producers and is an important influence on factory location. The GDA has a well developed transport network including Dublin Airport, motorways (e.g. M50, M1, M7) and railways. Dublin Port is the main port for container freight into and out of the country.

weblink
Enterprise Ireland

Fig. 7 People provide a market and labour force for the food processing industry.

CORE UNIT: REGIONAL GEOGRAPHY

CHAPTER 18
Case Study 1

Largo Foods, Ashbourne, County Meath

Largo Foods is an Irish company established in 1983. It is the leading manufacturer and distributor of snack foods (crisps, snacks, peanuts and popcorn) in Ireland. The brands produced include Tayto, King, Hunky Dory, Perri and Sam Spudz. Largo Foods has production facilities in Ashbourne, County Meath, and employs 550 people in this Ashbourne plant. The company turnover is over €100 million. It produces about 15,000 tonnes of snack food products each year.

Location

Ashbourne is located 20 km north of Dublin on the N2 route-way. The company's founder Raymond Coyle was a local potato grower in Meath who supplied manufacturers of snack food brands, e.g. Tayto, King Crisps and Sam Spudz. He gradually expanded his business and now his company, Largo Foods, owns the brands he once supplied. He located his food processing business in his native area.

Markets

As well as supplying products to the Irish market, 20% of its business market is located in the UK. The products are shipped from Dublin Port to the UK via Holyhead.

Production and packaging

The production process is highly automated with modern robotic machines cooking and packaging the snack foods. Packaging, manufacturing and food ingredients are important costs and the company aims to control them carefully. Seventy per cent of crisp packet material is produced in three plants in northern Italy; the rest is made in Ireland. Cardboard boxes used to transport the finished product are manufactured in Ireland.

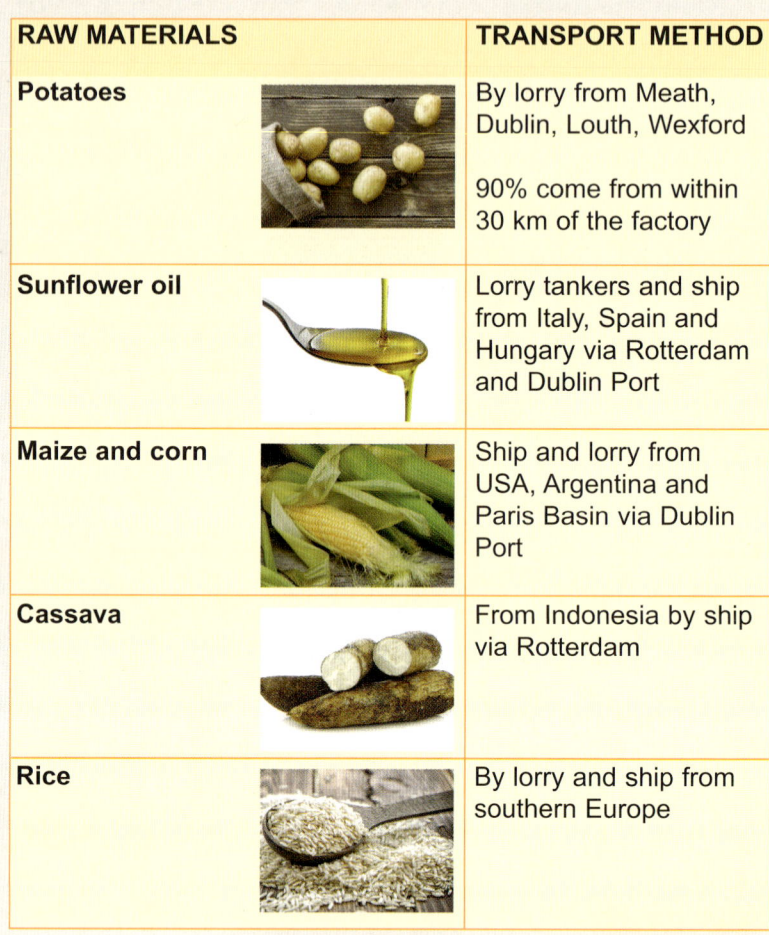

RAW MATERIALS	TRANSPORT METHOD
Potatoes	By lorry from Meath, Dublin, Louth, Wexford 90% come from within 30 km of the factory
Sunflower oil	Lorry tankers and ship from Italy, Spain and Hungary via Rotterdam and Dublin Port
Maize and corn	Ship and lorry from USA, Argentina and Paris Basin via Dublin Port
Cassava	From Indonesia by ship via Rotterdam
Rice	By lorry and ship from southern Europe

weblink
Largo Foods

Fig. 8 Largo Foods produces crisps, snacks, peanuts and popcorn.

Tertiary activities in the GDA

Most services are located in Dublin city. Twenty-one per cent of the workforce in Dublin is employed in public and professional services (finance, health care, education and legal work), reflecting the greater demand for these services in this region.

1. Transport and communications

Transport

- The GDA is the transportation centre of Ireland. Roads, air transport, railway and inland waterway systems are focused on Dublin (**nodal point**). Transport and communications-related work account for 9% of employment in the GDA.
- Due to the high population, the transportation network in the GDA is overcrowded and congestion is a problem. However, the Dublin Port Tunnel has reduced heavy traffic on city centre streets and the DART and Luas lines have been extended. The M50 upgrade and introduction of barrier-free tolling has reduced journey times along this key route around Dublin. Inter-city train links have been improved.
- Major investment in rail, road and air links has occurred under the Transport 21 project. For example, Terminal 2 at Dublin Airport caters for over 15 million passengers per year. Within the city, Quality Bus Corridors (QBCs) have enabled faster bus journeys and the Dublin Bike Scheme has been a success with over one million trips recorded, reducing the need for car transport in the city centre. Motorway links to Belfast (M1), Galway (M6) and Cork (M8) make Dublin even more accessible; shorter journey times benefit both commuters and businesses.

Communications

- The GDA is also the communications capital of Ireland. The Information, Communications and Technology (ICT) sector is leading Ireland's **smart economy** with 7 of the world's top 10 ICT companies located in the GDA, e.g. Intel.
- Many companies have their European headquarters in the region. These companies rely on fast broadband services to run their global distribution, sales and financial service networks. For example in 2016 Oracle announced that they intend to expand their workforce by 450 people in East Point Business Park.
- Telesales is a growth sector in the GDA partly as a result of its broadband facilities. Hertz has located its European call centre in Swords, County Dublin. Google has two centres in Dublin.

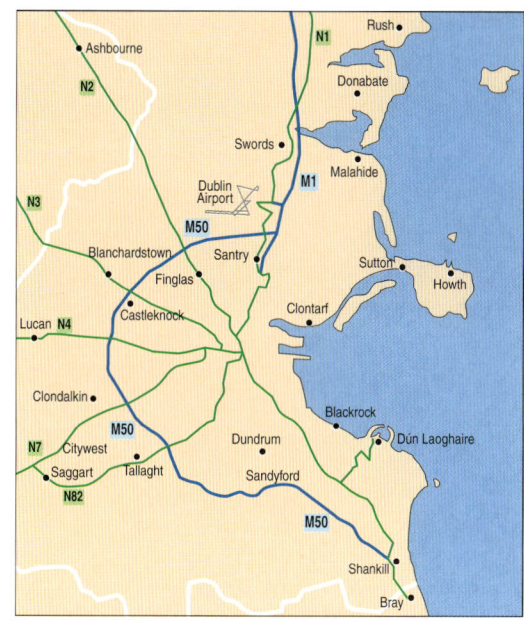

Fig. 9 National roads network in the GDA

Fig. 10 Dublin Port Tunnel

Fig. 11 Google offices in Dublin

CORE UNIT: REGIONAL GEOGRAPHY

- The City West business campus is the location for Ireland's National Digital Park. This park is a centre for e-commerce and technology companies which need high-speed digital communications.

weblink
Top 10 places to see in Dublin

2. Tourism

- The tourism and hospitality sector provides up to 200,000 jobs. Tourism generates more than €4 billion annually for the Irish economy. Every 55 tourists supports one tourism job.
- Over 7.6 million overseas visitors come to the Republic of Ireland every year. Two in every five Euros spent in Ireland by overseas visitors are spent in the Dublin region. Thirty-three per cent of tourists to the Dublin region are from mainland Europe, 25% are from the UK.
- The GDA is easily accessible through Dublin Airport with over 79 airlines operating over 450 flights per day. Ferry passengers use Dublin Port.

Fig. 12 The General Post Office (GPO) in Dublin is a historic tourist attraction.

The GDA region boasts a wealth of culture and activity holidays, e.g. Ireland's Ancient East, Destination Dublin 2020. Unlike the seasonal nature of tourism in the N&W region, tourism in the GDA is a more 'year round' industry.

Tourism attractions in Dublin

Being the capital, Dublin is a vibrant city attracting tourists all year round. It is Europe's fourth most visited capital city. Over 5.5 million tourists visit Dublin city annually, generating over €1.5 billion for the local economy.

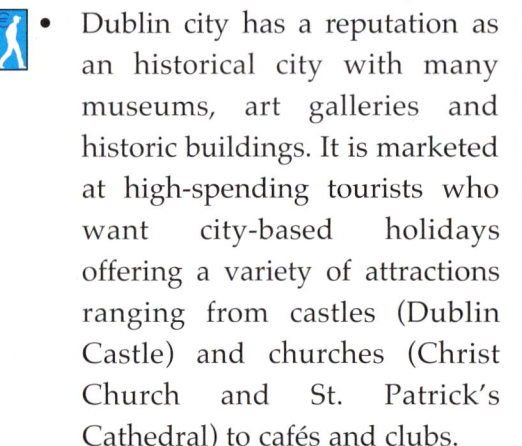

- Dublin city has a reputation as an historical city with many museums, art galleries and historic buildings. It is marketed at high-spending tourists who want city-based holidays offering a variety of attractions ranging from castles (Dublin Castle) and churches (Christ Church and St. Patrick's Cathedral) to cafés and clubs.

Fig. 13 The Ha'Penny Bridge, Dublin city

CHAPTER 18: AN IRISH CORE REGION AND AN IRISH CITY REGION

- The capital is promoted as a short-stay destination for weekend city breaks, independent of the weather, and has many repeat visitors. The attractions of modern Dublin include theatres (Abbey, Gaiety), shops (Stephen's Green, Dundrum Town Centre), restaurants, and fashionable bars and music venues (the 3 Arena).
- Dublin city is compact and easy to get around on foot or by road, rail, river taxi and tram. The Dublin 'rent-a-bike' scheme has been a huge success with over one million trips recorded. The annual Dublin Horse Show in the RDS, rugby and international soccer games in Lansdowne Road's Aviva stadium, GAA at Croke Park and concerts in the 3 Arena and other venues attract national and international visitors.

Fig. 14 Dublin attracts major sporting events

Tourism attractions outside Dublin

The rolling landscapes of **County Wicklow**, the 'Garden of Ireland', has 83 kilometres of mountain walkways (e.g. the Wicklow Way), with scenic and historic attractions such as Glendalough and Powerscourt Waterfall, as well as many blue flag beaches, e.g. Brittas Bay.

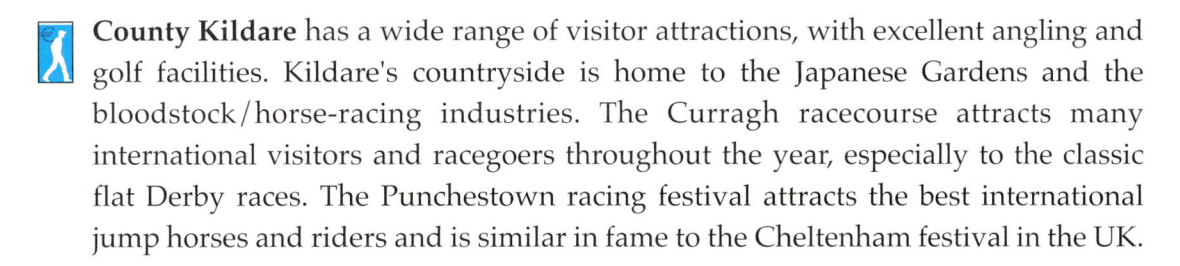

County Kildare has a wide range of visitor attractions, with excellent angling and golf facilities. Kildare's countryside is home to the Japanese Gardens and the bloodstock/horse-racing industries. The Curragh racecourse attracts many international visitors and racegoers throughout the year, especially to the classic flat Derby races. The Punchestown racing festival attracts the best international jump horses and riders and is similar in fame to the Cheltenham festival in the UK.

County Meath is Ireland's Heritage Capital. It is rich in history with castle ruins (Trim Castle), ancient stone circles and early Christian churches. It is the location for the world heritage site at Brú na Bóinne (Newgrange), which dates back to 3200 BC. The county is also host to the Irish Grand National horse race at Fairyhouse.

weblink
Tourism – facts and figures

Fig. 15 The GDA has many tourist attractions, e.g. Powerscourt in County Wicklow and Brú na Bóinne (Newgrange) in County Meath.

IT services

The GDA has a variety of internet service providers who provide employment, not just in software development, but in finance, sales, supply chain management and human resources.

The international high-tech services sector is developing rapidly and Ireland provides such services globally over the internet. The GDA is now the location for the European headquarters of multinational companies such as Google, Facebook, Yahoo, LinkedIn and eBay.

Within the GDA, Dublin is becoming the information technology capital of Europe.

Fig. 16 There is a young educated workforce in the GDA required by knowledge-based services, such as Yahoo.

If you are studying *Economic Activities* 2nd Edition (Unit 4), you could study Financial services in the GDA. See Chapter 2, pages 27-29.

Reasons for location of IT services companies in Ireland/GDA:

- A **young educated workforce:** Overall 44% of the population has a third level qualification. This attracts **knowledge-based industries** to the region.
- Dublin has **office space to rent**. The average office floor rent is €600 per m². In London it is €1,800 per m².
- **Government support** for industry and research & development (R&D): An attractive tax system, e.g. corporation tax is just 12.5% paid on profits compared to 41% in Japan, also helps to entice companies to locate here. Ireland also offers a 25% tax credit on R&D development costs.
- **Industry-focused college courses:** Such courses are available in world-class universities and institutes of technology throughout Ireland. They ensure a continued supply of qualified graduates and the availability of ongoing management training.
- The work of the **IDA (Industrial Development Authority)** and Enterprise Ireland in attracting **FDI** and the government policy to build a smart economy.

- The massive **'server farms'** of web service providers require expensive air conditioning which is cheaper to provide in the **mild Irish climate**.

IT service companies in GDA

The following IT services companies have all located in the GDA. Between them they employ almost 5,000 people.

- **Google** employs over 2,000 people. Based in Dublin's East Point Business Park and Barrow Street, many of the Dublin-based teams are engaged in supporting other Google offices across more than 25 countries in the Europe Mid East Asia (EMEA) region. Working in areas like finance, payroll, legal and HR, they also provide Google Maps and Google Local services as well as consumer products such as Gmail Calendar and advertising products such as AdSense.
- **eBay** employs more than 1,600 people at its Blanchardstown, County Dublin site together with PayPal, its online payment system. It employs people in customer service and personal account management.
- **LinkedIn** is a social networking service for business people with over one million new users per month. It has set up its international headquarters in Dublin. The jobs include a variety of business and technology roles, including positions in sales, marketing, finance and customer service. The company manages its international business from Dublin, working with teams in London and the Netherlands.
- **IBM** employs 200 people at its first-ever IBM Smarter Cities Technology Campus, located in Mulhuddart, west Dublin. It aims to revolutionise how cities provide services such as water and transport in the future. IBM employs over 3,000 people in Ireland mainly in Dublin at its Technology Campus.
- **Hertz** employs almost 1,000 people at its European Shared Services Centre in Swords, County Dublin. The Swords offices provide centralised finance and customer support services to its European vehicle rental operations.

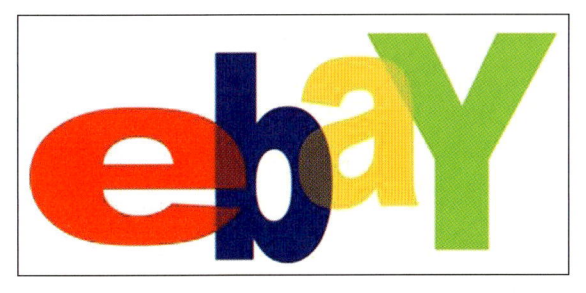

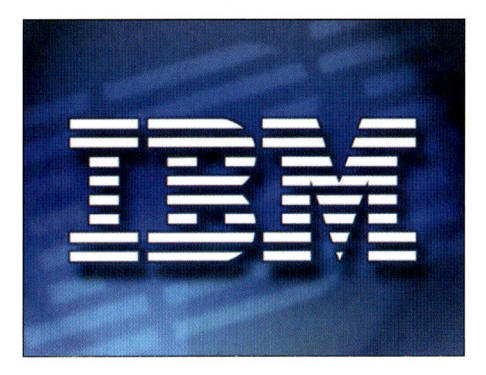

Fig. 17 Dublin is the chosen location for the international headquarters of well-known IT services companies.

CORE UNIT: REGIONAL GEOGRAPHY

Human processes in the GDA

Population density, distribution, and culture

The population of the GDA is just over 1.8 million people and is expected to grow to over 2.1 million by 2031 when it will hold 42% of the State's population.

The number of people aged 45-64 in Wicklow, Kildare and Meath is expected to double by 2021. At the same time, the number of older people (65 years or more) will increase by 133%. The area has a high proportion of young people (0-14 years) and this is expected to increase by 26% by 2021.

There is a surplus of females in the region (20,000) which reflects the greater number of female workers in tertiary activities, especially in health and education.

Going on current trends, it is predicted that births will exceed deaths by 197,000 by 2021, and by 2031 the Dublin region will have its lowest total dependency ratio. These are important statistics for the allocation of government investment in provision of facilities for childcare, schools, hospitals and services for the elderly.

The greatest density of population is in Dublin city and its suburbs. Outside of the city, the population is well distributed across the Mid-East region, chiefly in towns located close to major road networks linking the commuter zone to the city centre, e.g. Navan, Kildare.

The city is the main centre for in-migration, both national rural-to-urban migration and international immigration. This is because of the availability of jobs and services in the Dublin region.

The city is a multicultural city with over 15% of its population being foreign nationals. The Dublin region holds more non-Irish people than any other region in Ireland. For example, 67% of Ireland's Chinese population live in the GDA.

Many languages are spoken and many religions are practised in the region. This reflects several phases of migration into Dublin from the 1940s to the more recent migrations due to EU expansion and international conflict. Religions include Islam, Buddhism, Hindu, Evangelical Christianity and Judaism.

weblink
Census results statistics

Fig. 18 There is a greater mix of cultures in Irish schools.

18.2 Government policies to develop the GDA region

As is the case for the N&W, the four government plans (**NDP**, **NSS**, **CIP** and **Transport 21**) have also affected the growth and development of the GDA as outlined below. (See Chapter 17, pages 331–333 for more detail on the four plans.)

HOW THE NDP DEVELOPED THE GDA

1. Addressed traffic congestion and urban sprawl.
2. Maintained Dublin as a national gateway serving the whole country.
3. Increased jobs.
4. Developed tourism and promoted social inclusion.
5. Maintained a viable rural economy.
6. Continued the development of transport links to the rest of the country.

HOW THE NSS DEVELOPED THE GDA

1. Improved the competitiveness of the GDA so that it continues to perform on an international level as a driver for national development.
2. Monitored the growth of the Dublin city region (metropolitan area, i.e. city and suburbs).
3. Aimed to manage Dublin as a gateway so that other areas had the opportunity to develop.
4. Managed the location of industry and zoning of land.
5. Aimed to integrate transport.
6. Developed the hinterlands of County Dublin, Meath, Kildare and Wicklow by concentrating on the urban centres at Balbriggan, Navan, Naas, Newbridge, Kilcullen and Wicklow towns.

HOW THE CIP IS DEVELOPING THE GDA (2016–2021)

The Capital Investment Plan is investing €27 billion to improve the following areas of Ireland's social and economic development:

1. Housing
2. Health
3. Education
4. Transport/Tourism
5. Business
6. Environment/Climate

18.3 City/nodal/urban regions

A **city** is a unique region. All cities serve their immediate surrounding areas (hinterlands) but city regions also include an area/zone of influence which may stretch beyond the immediate hinterland.

Cities develop because of the interaction of several factors such as defence, transport, water supply, food production, trade and industry. City regions continue to grow because they offer many advantages to people and businesses. Most city regions have:

1. High standards of living.
2. Better health services than rural areas.
3. A variety of recreational facilities.
4. A skilled workforce.
5. A wealthy market for trade and industry.

For these reasons, city regions are areas of in-migration and are some of the fastest-growing regions in the world. Most city regions have well-defined zones of different land uses, e.g. **residential, industrial** and the **Central Business District (CBD)**. The majority of Europeans live in urban areas. There are over 25 cities in Europe with a population of more than one million.

In some countries (e.g. Ireland and France), the capital cities are more than twice as big as the next largest city in the country. These are termed primate cities. Dublin, for example, is more than six times larger than Cork.

Fig. 19 The Dublin city region and its hinterland.

CHAPTER 18: AN IRISH CORE REGION AND AN IRISH CITY REGION

Fig. 20 Our world is becoming increasingly urbanised.

- In most urban areas, there is a **zone of transition** where buildings are in disrepair and awaiting redevelopment. There is great competition for space in urban areas. Intensive use of land has led to the construction of high-rise buildings in many cities.
- City regions are important because they provide job opportunities and a wide range of services and goods to the people of the city and its hinterland. They also influence the social and economic development of areas beyond the city. The term nodal point applies to any region that is the focus of route-ways. All towns and cities are nodal points. They are often **administrative** and **financial capitals**.
- The zone of influence of city regions spreads beyond the city limits. Dublin is a city region whose zone of influence spreads well beyond the city to Gorey, Athlone, Ashbourne, Drogheda and beyond. Paris has a population of 12 million with a commuter belt averaging a 45-km radius from the CBD. Dublin has a commuter zone of 90 km for just over 1.8 million people.

When groups of cities grow into each other, huge urban areas known as **conurbations** are formed. These regions are **polycentric**, containing several city areas that are of similar importance. Examples of conurbations include Manchester and Birmingham in the UK. The Randstad in the Netherlands has a radius of 50 km and a population of 6 million people. It was formed by the merging of over six large towns and cities. New York City is a metropolitan area which has a population of over 20 million people and covers a conurbation with a radius of 64 km.

City regions are also spreading into the surrounding countryside. This **urban sprawl** eats up valuable farm and recreational land and adds to commuter traffic problems. Controlling the future growth of city regions is important in every country.

CORE UNIT: REGIONAL GEOGRAPHY

CHAPTER 18
Case Study 2

The Dublin city region

The **Dublin city region** is divided into four administrative counties: Dubin city council; Fingal county council; South Dublin county council and Dún Laoghaire-Rathdown county council. Its population is just 1.3 million. This region is not a fixed zone and it now influences much of the eastern coast of Ireland (See Fig. 21).

The population of Dublin and the three surrounding counties (Meath, Kildare and Wicklow) is more than 1.8 million. It is estimated that the Dublin city region will have 42% (2.2 million people) of the national population by 2031.

> The rapid economic growth of Dublin sets it apart from other regions in Ireland in several ways. Its problems are typical of many core economic regions in Europe.

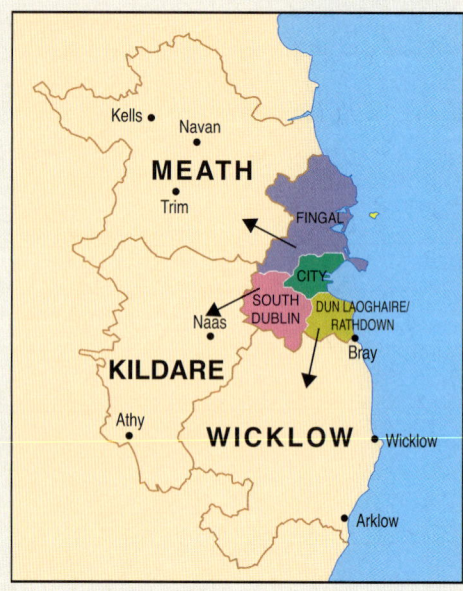

Fig. 21 The Dublin city region

Reasons for the growth of Dublin

Several physical and human factors have combined to promote the growth of the Dublin city region.

Physical factors encouraging the growth of Dublin

1. The land to the north and west of the city is low-lying, gently rolling, fertile farmland with boulder clays and brown earth soils. The mild climate promotes crop growth. These factors produce a variety of high-value crops such as vegetables and wheat. These crops are the basis of profitable farming and raw materials for the food-processing industries, which in turn provide employment.

2. Dublin is located at the mouth of the River Liffey. This has led to the development of a major port that is an important centre of economic growth and transport for the region.

Human factors encouraging the growth of Dublin

1. Dublin is the **capital city** and centre of government administration, financial services and manufacturing. This attracts people to work in the civil service, financial institutions and many other businesses in the region.

2. The performance of this region is important for the economic success of Ireland as a whole. The average economic output per person is 108% higher in this region than the state average.

3. Dublin is the centre of the national transport network (route focus). Road and rail routes are focused on the city and this further promotes economic development in the city region.

4. Dublin has the state's largest **port** with roll-on, roll-off (ro/ro) facilities, and the largest airport, Dublin Airport, handling over 191 million passengers per year.

CHAPTER 18: AN IRISH CORE REGION AND AN IRISH CITY REGION

The effects of the growth of the Dublin city region

1. **Urban sprawl** is the rapid growth of an urban area into the surrounding countryside. Urban sprawl is common around rapidly growing urban areas.

    Dublin's earliest rural to urban expansion affected the traditional dormitory towns of Greystones, Malahide and Maynooth changing them from small villages to commuter towns because of their rail links. Such was the growth of Dublin since the 1960s that new towns had to be built to accommodate the rising population. Three **new towns** were built in Tallaght, Lucan-Clondalkin and Blanchardstown. In 2006 another new town, Adamstown, 16 kilometres south west of Dublin city centre, was built. It provides 10,000 houses and facilities such as schools, shops and public transport. The town will eventually hold over 20,000 people.

    Fig. 22 Urban sprawl leads to the loss of farmland.

    Despite these new towns, the Dublin city region is still spreading into neighbouring towns and counties, e.g. Mullingar, Portlaoise, Gorey, Arklow and Navan all have large commuter populations.

2. **Increased demand for water:** On average each person in the Dublin city region uses 150 litres of water per day. Such is the increase in demand for water in the city region (over 800 million litres per day will be required by 2031) that plans to pump water from the River Shannon are being developed.

3. **Loss of valuable agricultural land:** Greenfield areas are built upon causing a reduction in available land for agriculture. It becomes difficult for farmers to expand their farms as they cannot afford to buy neighbouring land if it is zoned for housing. This leads to an increase in demand for imported food.

4. **Loss of wildlife habitats – hedgerows and wetlands:** Hedgerows provide essential living space for many species of animals, plants and insects. As land is built upon with houses and roads, this habitat is lost and the biodiversity of the area is reduced.

5. **Traffic congestion:** Dublin is the sixth most congested city in Europe. Traffic congestion is worse in Dublin than any other city in Ireland. This is due to both the high levels of car ownership created during the economic boom years of 1990 to 2007 and the availability of so many jobs in secondary and tertiary businesses in this core socio-economic region. Traffic congestion increases air pollution. Businesses lose money due to increased fuel costs and journey times. The need for careful traffic management is, therefore, clear and an important part of the CIP.

CORE UNIT: REGIONAL GEOGRAPHY

Several factors account for the high levels of congestion in the Dublin city region

1. **Commuter traffic:** Urban sprawl in the Dublin city region means many workers travel into the city from towns up to 90 km away. This adds to congestion at peak times. Average vehicle speed in the city is close to just 8 km/h on the busiest routes.

2. **Lack of public transport:** While new transport developments have occurred – e.g. the Luas and Dublin Port Tunnel, quality bus corridors, cycle schemes and an increase of over 12% in the number of buses – people still find cars more convenient for transport. Dublin does not have the integrated public transport facilities that a city of its size and population needs to tempt people away from using the car. The provision of a metro/underground rail system would reduce congestion in the future.

3. **Historic street plan:** Like many cities, Dublin's streets were built to accommodate horse and carriages and not 40-tonne trucks. Many of the narrow and winding streets (e.g. South King Street) are not wide enough for modern traffic and this has contributed to congestion. This has led to the ban on 5-axle lorries in the city centre, which has improved traffic flow.

Fig. 23 Air pollution levels rise due to traffic congestion.

Managing the growth of Dublin – a challenge for the future

To manage the growth of Dublin and reduce urban sprawl, the following changes were made:

1. Changes to Dublin council structures

Changes have been made to the administration of the city. The reason for these changes are:

(a) The Barrington report of 1991 showed that Ireland was at the bottom of the league table when it came to allocating powers and responsibilities to local government. This indicated that the central government was still too closely involved in making decisions that a local council could easily decide.

(b) The population and area of Dublin city was increasing to such an extent that it was becoming difficult for one county council to administer. For example, there was only one motor taxation office to deal with all licence and motor tax requests despite the fact that the number of car owners in the Dublin city region had increased dramatically.

(c) Decision-making structures were slow and this delayed the provision of services, e.g. council and affordable housing.

When the Local Government (Dublin) Act (1993) was passed in the Dáil, it enabled the formation of four new councils to manage the region.

(a) **Dublin City Council**
(b) **Dún Laoghaire-Rathdown County Council**
(c) **Fingal County Council**
(d) **South Dublin County Council**

weblink
Irish Regions Office

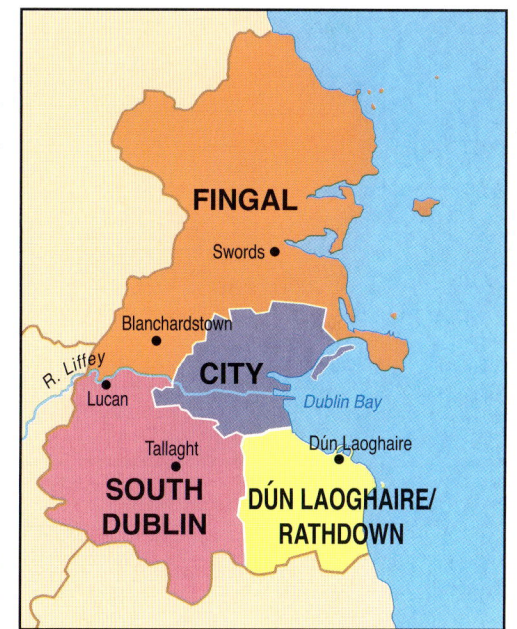

Fig. 24 The county councils formed to accommodate the increase in population of the Dublin city area

2. Make more efficient use of existing land

If Dublin continues to spread physically into the surrounding counties, it will use up valuable agricultural land and lead to more traffic congestion. In order to control the physical spread of Dublin, the city planners have to make careful plans to use existing (**brownfield**) land more wisely. This is achieved by identifying unused and derelict sites in the city and preparing them for new development. Existing buildings can also be used more efficiently, e.g. apartments over shops.

weblink
Dublin City and County Councils

CORE UNIT: REGIONAL GEOGRAPHY

The National Spatial Strategy (NSS)

A policy to control the growth of Dublin

The **NSS** aimed to balance the growth and development of Dublin by tackling growth in the metropolitan area (i.e. the city and its suburbs) and the hinterland (i.e. surrounding area) in the following ways.

In the metropolitan area:

1. Compiling a list of all derelict, vacant and underused land in the city to allow redevelopment for housing or other more efficient land use. This ensures that no land is wasted inside the city area.
2. Ensuring the best use of existing housing. Shops often have unused apartment space above them. 'Living over the Shop' schemes were set up to encourage more people to live in the city rather than building on new ground in the suburbs.
3. Some suburbs have large houses occupied by older people. Building smaller houses for older people within these areas would make more family-size houses available.
4. There are many old, inefficiently used warehouses in Dublin. These could be redeveloped and used more efficiently for newer businesses, e.g. the Docklands.

In the hinterland:

1. Develop existing towns such as Naas, Kildare, Navan, Drogheda and Arklow to draw people into jobs outside the city.
2. Develop an efficient public transport network to provide easy access between these towns and the city. This should reduce traffic congestion.

Future growth of Dublin is now managed by the **Dublin City Development Plan**, 2016-2022. This plan will manage:

- Land use zoning
- Housing
- Retailing
- Traffic flow
- Environment
- Urban development and regeneration.

Fig. 25 Derelict buildings in Dublin could be redeveloped and used for new businesses/housing.

Chapter Revision Questions

1. What factors make the GDA a core economic region?
2. Name the counties which make up the GDA.
3. Describe the climate and relief of the GDA.
4. Write an account of the soil types and agricultural production within the GDA.
5. List and explain **five** factors which make Dublin an attractive location for industry.
6. Name and locate the different types of manufacturing to be found within the GDA.
7. Discuss tertiary activities which provide employment within the GDA.
8. (i) Outline the importance of a good transport system to a core region.
   (ii) Explain how Transport 21 aims to improve Ireland's transport system.
9. Examine **one** challenge facing the GDA in the future. Discuss **one** way in which this challenge may be reduced.
10. Describe the manufacturing industries in the GDA and N&W regions.
11. 'The scale of tertiary activity is greater in the GDA than in the N&W'. Describe **three** pieces of evidence to show that this statement is true.
12. Discuss the tourism industry in the GDA region. In your answer, focus on a tourist destination and its attractions.
13. What is a city region?
14. Name **one** Irish and **one** other European city region.
15. Why are city regions important?
16. Explain the terms (i) CBD (ii) primate city.
17. What are conurbations? Name **two**.
18. What are the advantages of city regions?
19. Name **two** problems found in city regions.
20. What factors lead to the development of cities?
21. Why do city regions attract in-migration of workers and business?
22. What is the Dublin city region and what is its population?

CORE UNIT: REGIONAL GEOGRAPHY

LC Exam Questions

Higher Level students must be able to answer Ordinary and Higher Level questions.

■ OL Questions

23. Draw a sketch map of Ireland. On it, show and name each of the following:
    - One region studied by you
    - One named town or city in this region
    - One named river in this region
    - One named area of relief (upland or lowland) in this region.

24. Examine the development of **two** contrasting economic regions in Ireland.

25. Discuss how any **two** of the following factors influence the development of manufacturing industry in an Irish region that you have studied:
    - Availability of transport networks
    - Access to raw materials
    - Markets
    - Government and European Union policies

26. (i) Name any **one** urban area in Ireland which you have studied.
    (ii) Explain **one** reason for the growth of that urban area.
    (iii) Describe **one** problem this growth has caused within that urban area.

27. Explain how any **two** of the following influence the development of agriculture in an Irish region that you have studied:
    - Climate
    - Relief and soils
    - Markets

28. Name **one** Irish region that you have studied and answer each of the following questions:
    (i) Name **two** tourist attractions in that region
    (ii) Explain the positive impacts of tourism in this region.
    (iii) Explain the negative impacts of tourism in this region.

■ HL Questions

29. Account for the development of agriculture in an Irish region that you have studied, with reference to any **two** of the following factors:
    - Relief
    - Climate
    - Markets.

30. Examine the factors that influence the development of secondary economic activity in an Irish region that you have studied.

31. Discuss the factors that influence the development of one tertiary economic activity in an Irish region that you have studied.

32. Regions can be defined by many factors including:
    - economic
    - human
    - physical.

    Explain how any **one** of the above factors has defined an Irish region you have studied.

33. Account for the development of transport or tourism in an Irish region that you have studied.

34. Examine the development of **one** urban area in any Irish region studied by you.

35. Account for the distribution of population throughout an Irish region that you have studied.

36. 'Economic activity in core regions differs from activity in peripheral regions.'

    Examine this statement with reference to examples you have studied.

Key Words

You should be able to explain both verbally and in writing each of the key words listed below.

brownfield
capital intensive
core economic regions
conurbations
Dublin City Development Plan
Dublin City Region
GDA
hinterland
knowledge-based industries
new towns
nodal point
polycentric
primate cities
urban sprawl

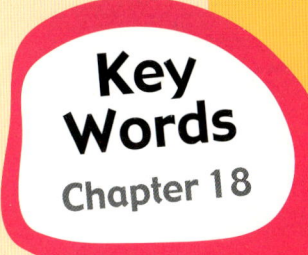

Digital Resources are available for this chapter at mentorbooks.ie/resources

CHAPTER 19

A European Peripheral Region

Key Theme

The study of regions shows how economic, human and physical processes interact in a particular way. This can be demonstrated by examining two contrasting European regions.

Learning Outcomes

At the end of this chapter you will be able to:
- Describe the Mezzogiorno as a peripheral/less developed region.
- Name and describe the human and physical characteristics of the Mezzogiorno region.
- Describe primary, secondary and tertiary activities in the Mezzogiorno region.
- Describe the population characteristics of the Mezzogiorno region.

Contents

19.1	The Mezzogiorno – Physical and human factors/characteristics	363
19.2	Economic activities and human processes in the Mezzogiorno	366
	Case Study: The Metapontino region – A success story	370
19.3	Human processes in the Mezzogiorno	376

Revision Space

Chapter Revision Questions – LC Exam Questions – Key Word List 378

CHAPTER 19: A EUROPEAN PERIPHERAL REGION

19.1 The Mezzogiorno – Physical and human factors/characteristics

A peripheral/less developed region in the Mediterranean

In Italy, the south or **Mezzogiorno** region is a less developed/peripheral region. It makes up 40% of Italy's land area and has 35% of its population (21 million), but it is one of the poorest regions in Italy. The Mezzogiorno is made up of the regions of Abruzzi, Campania, Molise, Puglia, Basilicata, Calabria, Lazio and the islands of Sicily and Sardinia, (see Figs. 1 and 2).

Unemployment rates are high (20% in some regions) and the area has traditionally suffered from out-migration. It is also one of the least developed regions in the EU with GDP at less than 75% of the EU average. Billions of euros have been spent on the region through a government scheme called the *Cassa per il Mezzogiorno* (see page 368) and through EU funding.

The Mezzogiorno faces several problems and challenges, including mountainous relief, drought, illegal immigration, organised crime, corruption, high unemployment, low incomes and poor technical skills compared to the north.

Fig. 1 The regional divisions of Italy

Physical factors/characteristics – climate, relief, drainage and soils

The Mezzogiorno has positive and negative physical characteristics that influence its socio-economic development.

Climate	Relief	Soils and drainage
Mediterranean	85% of land is mountainous (over 400 m)	Poor thin soils on mountains. Soil erosion is a problem triggered by summer storms and earthquakes
Hot (29°C) summers, drought due to influence of Azores High Pressure belt and dry NE trade winds	Apennine Mountains extend north-south along the Italian Peninsula. Granite hills in Calabria (toe of Italy) and limestone plateaux elsewhere	Fertile alluvium deposited on flood plain of River Volturno and along Adriatic coast
Mild (11°C) moist (500 mm) winters due to influence of Atlantic depressions	Lowland areas in Puglia and around Naples are intensively farmed	Fertile volcanic soils in Sicily and Campania
Frost is rare	Coastal lowlands have poorly drained marshlands and mudflats	Terra Rossa soils developed on limestone used for vines
Irrigation in summer required	Volcanic mountains (Vesuvius, Etna, Stromboli) formed by collision of African and Eurasian tectonic plates	Few rivers on limestone areas. The south of the region has short fast-flowing rivers, e.g. River Agri and River Bradano

363

CORE UNIT: REGIONAL GEOGRAPHY

Fig. 2 Regions of the Mezzogiorno

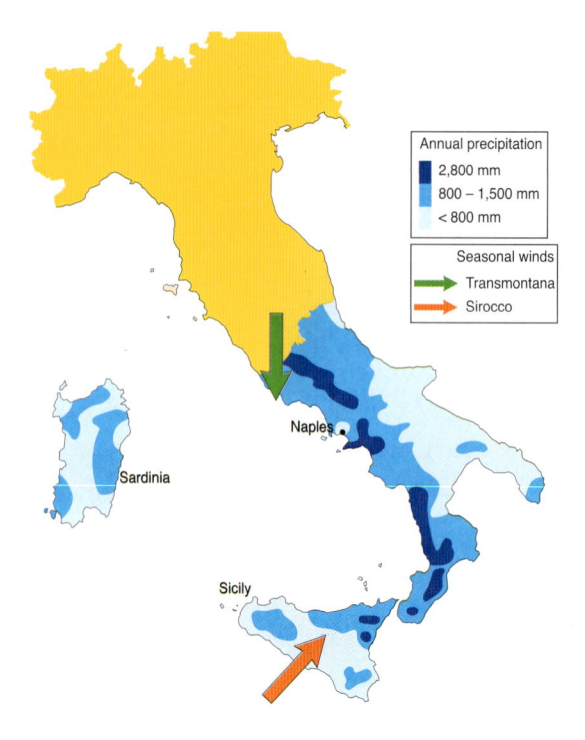

Fig. 3 Annual precipitation and seasonal winds in Naples and Sicily

Activity

Look at the graphs below.
For Naples, state the maximum daily temperature and rainfall in June. For Sicily, state the maximum daily temperature and rainfall in June.

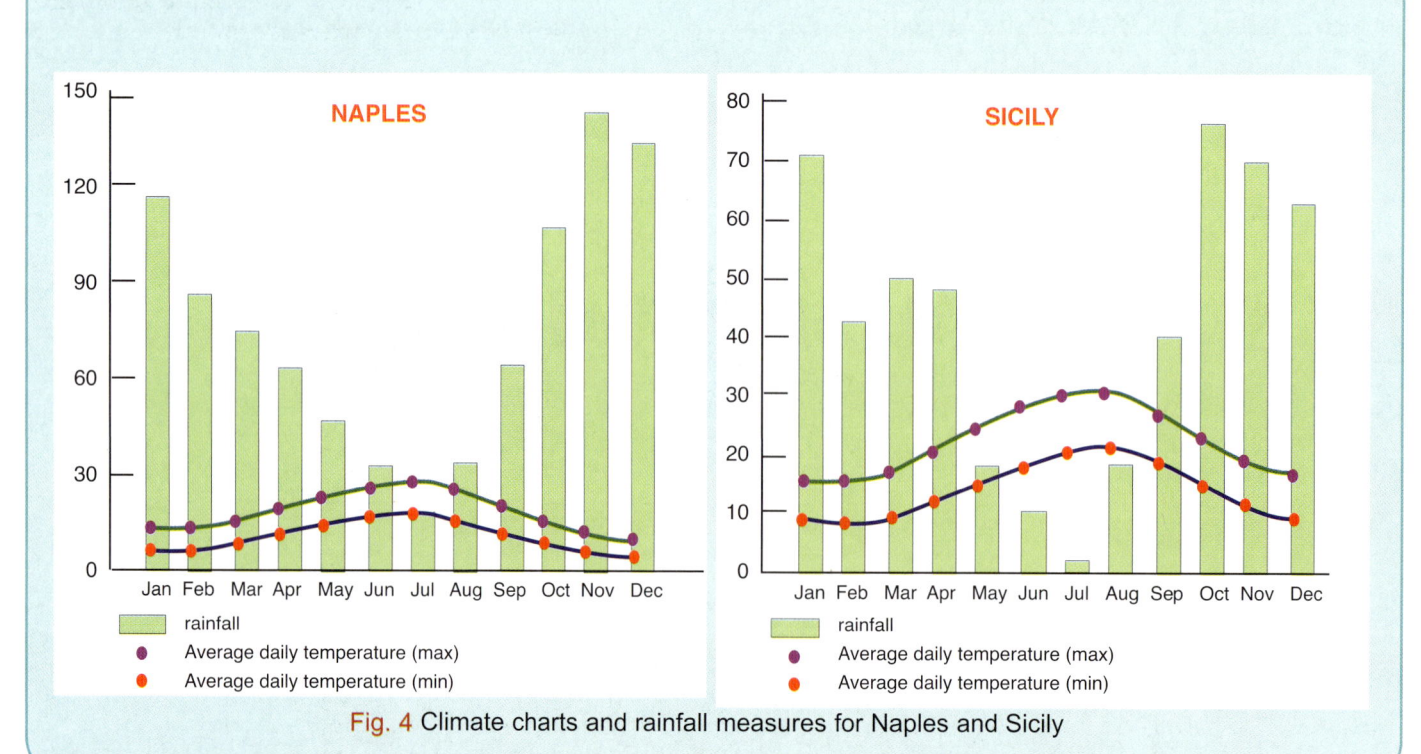

Fig. 4 Climate charts and rainfall measures for Naples and Sicily

CHAPTER 19: A EUROPEAN PERIPHERAL REGION

Fig. 5 Satellite map of Mezzogiorno

Fig. 6 Relief and drainage of Mezzogiorno

Fig. 7 'Rock houses' dug into the rock by ancient inhabitants of Matera in Southern Italy.

Fig. 8 A limestone plateau in Calabria

Fig. 9 Steep infertile slopes make farming difficult in the Mezzogiorno.

365

CORE UNIT: REGIONAL GEOGRAPHY

👤 Human factors

The **physical** factors interact with several **human** factors affecting the development of the Mezzogiorno region.

Four main human factors affect the Mezzogiorno region. They are: (i) the historic system of land ownership, (ii) population, (iii) transport and communications and (iv) government and EU policies. These human factors have created challenges to the development of the region. You will read about these in detail later in this chapter.

As with Ireland, funding and support schemes provided by the Italian government and the EU have all played a part in trying to overcome the problems faced by the Mezzogiorno region. Such was the level of poverty and decline in the Mezzogiorno that in 1950 the government set up the *Cassa per il Mezzogiorno* (South Italian Development Fund) in an effort to reduce the economic imbalance between the north and south. Its aims were to stimulate the economic and social development of the region. It focused on agricultural, then industrial and infrastructural reform.

The EU allocates structural and cohesion funds to the region e.g. CAP, CFP. The Mezzogiorno has a GDP below 75% of the EU average. Therefore, it receives more cohesion funding.

HUMAN CHARACTERISTICS OF THE MEZZOGIORNO REGION	
Land ownership system	System of absentee landlords and poor tenant farmers prevented development of agriculture, (see page 367).
Population	New industries were unwilling to locate there due to elderly, uneducated population.
Transport infrastructure	Needed massive investment by government to overcome physical isolation of the region, (see page 375).
Government policy	In the 1950s the government started a massive investment programme called the *Cassa* scheme to improve farming, industry, tourism and transport, (see page 368). The region qualifies for extra EU structural funds.

19.2 Economic activities and human processes in the Mezzogiorno

Primary activities in the Mezzogiorno

☀ Agriculture

1. The **Mediterranean climate** provides warmth and sunshine, which promotes the early ripening of salad crops, olives, citrus fruits and vines. These are high-value crops sold throughout northern Europe. Several crop harvests are possible each season.

   Winter salads, vegetables and citrus fruits are grown in market gardens around the large industrial areas of Bari, Brindisi and Taranto and around Naples.

Fig. 10 Agriculture is an important source of employment in the Mezzogiorno despite the poor relief.

CHAPTER 19: A EUROPEAN PERIPHERAL REGION

2. The Mediterranean climate and soil is perfect for growing olives. The olive tree is found only in the Mediterranean countries of Europe, Africa and the Middle East. It is a very drought-resistant tree but cannot tolerate frost or very wet conditions. Olive production continues to increase, making Italy the largest producer of olive oil in the world.
3. Sheep and goats graze the higher mountains; vines/grapes are grown on lower slopes.
4. Further south the aridity and poor soils mean farming is limited to olive growing, sheep-rearing and wine production (*viticulture/viniculture*).

Like all peripheral regions, agricultural development in the Mezzogiorno faces several challenges.

CHALLENGES FACING THE DEVELOPMENT OF AGRICULTURE IN THE MEZZOGIORNO

1. Droughts affect the region in summer.
2. The region has underdeveloped water supplies.
3. Mountainous land unsuitable for farming.
4. Local markets with limited buying power due to widespread poverty in the region.
5. Underdeveloped transport network – the region is very isolated.
6. High transport costs due to long distances to EU markets.
7. Poorly-educated population.
8. Out-migration of young workers to the cities.
9. Underdeveloped farms due to ageing farmers unwilling/unable to use new technology.
10. Unfair land ownership system.

Despite the poor soils and mountainous terrain, agriculture is an important source of employment in the region.

Problems created by the land ownership system in the past

- Absentee landlords owned vast land estates known as *latifundia* and rented small plots of land called *minifundia* to tenant farmers. Landless labourers called *braccianti* worked the land. They were very poor.
- The *latifundia* estates were underdeveloped as 75% of tenant farmers had no security on the land they farmed. Therefore, some tenants put little effort into improving soils or output as they might easily be evicted the following rental year.
- In some areas even fertile soils remained underdeveloped because of lack of interest. Therefore, the *latifundia* estates of the Mezzogiorno gave low yields yet took up huge areas of land (*extensive farming*). Sheep and goats were reared on these estates and low-quality wines were produced for local markets.

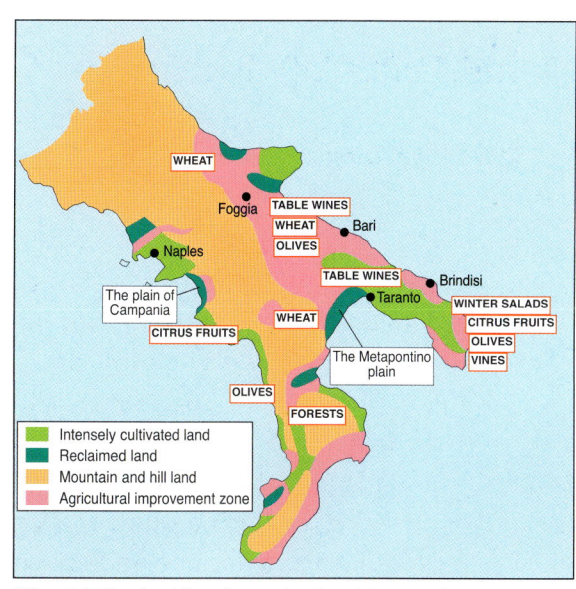

Fig. 11 Typical land use in the Mezzogiorno

367

- Seventy per cent of the *minifundia* were smaller than three hectares in size. Such small farms resulted in overcropped and overgrazed land. This meant that the soils were easily eroded and quickly became useless.

Solving the agricultural problems of the Mezzogiorno

1. The government *Cassa* scheme was important because it tackled some of the biggest socio-economic challenges facing the Mezzogiorno. It broke up the *latifundia* and *minifundia* estates. This land was then redistributed to the former tenant farmers and to the *braccianti*. Farms averaged 5 to 50 hectares. These land ownership reforms increased the amount of land available for cultivation and helped the general development of the economy.
2. Investment in technology and mechanisation helped the economy to move away from **subsistence farming** to profitable **commercial farming**.
3. **Reclamation schemes** took place at the marshes of the **Metapontino area**. Irrigation schemes were put in place using water from local rivers and wells.
4. Farmers were trained to farm their land more efficiently and to grow wheat and other high value **cash crops** such as peaches, strawberries and flowers. Productivity increased tenfold. Meanwhile, construction of the motorway known as the **Autostrada del Sole** helped farmers to get their produce quickly to market.
5. New villages and towns were built on the reclaimed coastal lowlands. **Co-operatives** were set up to purchase produce in bulk for and from the farmers, raising their incomes.

Fig. 12 Tenant farmers now own their land, increasing production.

Problems with the *Cassa* scheme: agriculture

1. Unfortunately, increased mechanisation did not provide many new jobs. There are still about 200,000 landless seasonally-employed day labourers/*braccianti*.
2. Some of the farms are still too small (less than five hectares) to make economically viable farms.
3. In Sicily, the Mafia, which today is still influential, has hindered government efforts to implement reforms. Sicily continues to have extremely low per capita incomes and high unemployment levels. It still has many workers in the hidden economy.
4. Only 10% of the region was actually affected by land reform.
5. Overgrazing and drought are serious problems facing the area, as they lead to soil erosion, especially at times of flash flooding caused by irregular rainstorms.

Farming in the Mezzogiorno today

- Reforms brought about by the *Cassa* scheme, EU structural funds and the CAP have made farms much more productive.
- There has been a change from low-value crops to high-value produce such as vegetables and citrus fruits in the coastal lowlands.
- Incomes are higher than in the past.
- Fertilisers, reclamation and irrigation schemes have allowed farmland become more productive.
- There has been an increase in the irrigated cultivation of vegetables and salad crops, especially along the southern and eastern coasts.
- Wheat is now grown in the large reclaimed marsh area of the Metapontino.
- The most intensive commercial farming occurs on the coastal lowlands.

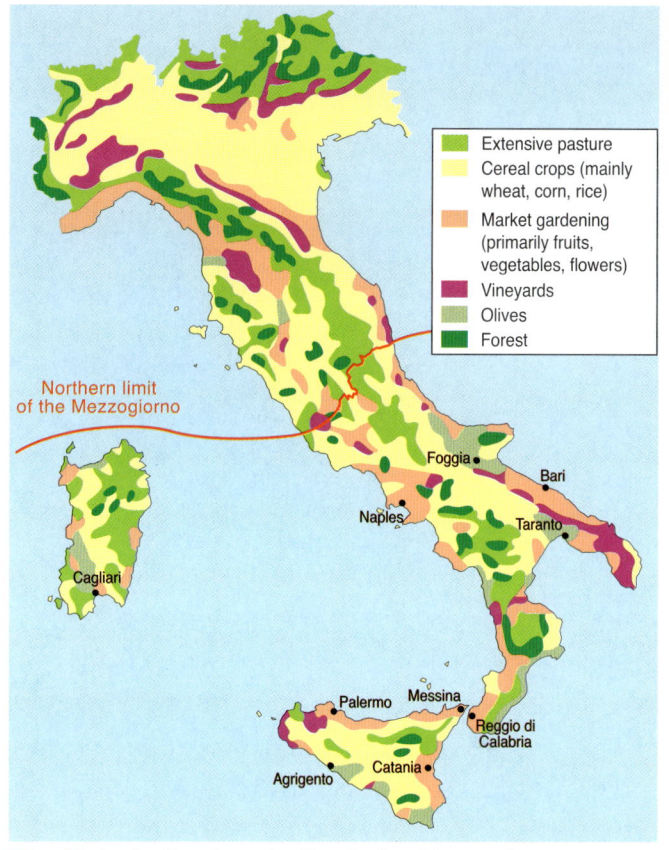

Fig. 13 Agricultural production in the Mezzogiorno

Forestry in the Mezzogiorno

- The climate does not allow the growth of dense stands of trees.
- The natural woodland of the region is mixed deciduous and evergreen hardwoods of cork oak, cypress, maritime pine and olive trees. These trees can tolerate the high temperatures and drought conditions. They also grow well in very poor, thin soils requiring few nutrients. In the higher hills, beechwood, pine and silver fir trees grow. In Calabria chestnut trees are harvested.
- In areas where forests have been cleared, soil erosion has increased and all that grows is grass scrub called *maquis* and flowery plants known as *garrigue*. Commercial forestry is not an important activity because of continuous deforestation.

Fig. 14 Olive trees grow well in the poor, thin soils of the Mezzogiorno

CORE UNIT: REGIONAL GEOGRAPHY

CHAPTER 19
Case Study

The Metapontino region – A success story

This region is a coastal area beside the Ionian Sea. It has been transformed from a poor, unproductive region to one of the most profitable agricultural areas in the Mezzogiorno.

1. Before the reforms of the *Cassa* scheme, it produced wheat and olives. Its coastal plain was poorly-drained marsh infested by insects that carried malaria.

2. Under the *Cassa* scheme, the marshes were drained, making fertile soil. The rivers were harnessed for irrigation and land was redistributed amongst over 5,000 families. Farm sizes are now on average six hectares.

3. As a result, the region now produces high-value cash crops of vines/grapes, citrus fruits, flowers and salad crops. Transport links have been improved and farmers are now 10 times more productive than in the past.

Fig. 15 Map of the Metapontino region

Fishing

- The Mediterranean is not as rich a fishing ground as the large open waters of the Atlantic coasts of Northern Spain. The chief varieties fished are anchovy, tuna and sardines. Much of the catch is sold to the ever-growing tourist population in the resorts along the coast. Remaining fish is processed (fish meal), frozen or canned. Most coastal towns have small fishing ports. The fishing industry is facing problems.

- The Mediterranean sea has a high salinity (saltiness) and is quite polluted which affects nutrient and oxygen levels and also limits the growth of plankton.

- Italy has a narrow continental shelf, hindering plankton growth. Increasing pollution is further damaging breeding grounds. The Adriatic coast of Italy suffers regular summer algae blooms due to the high concentration of nitrates from sewage in the water.

Fig. 16 A fishing town in the Mezzogiorno

CHAPTER 19: A EUROPEAN PERIPHERAL REGION

Mineral and energy production in the Mezzogiorno

The Mezzogiorno region is limited in mineral wealth.
1. There is natural gas at Basilicata, Molise, Sicily and Calabria. Oil, sulfur and potash has been found near Siracusa in Sicily. There are no coal deposits.
2. The permeable nature of the rock and the regular occurrence of summer drought has limited the region's potential for large-scale hydroelectric power.
3. The bulk of electricity produced in the Mezzogiorno is generated in thermal power stations using imported oil and local reserves of natural gas.

Secondary activities in the Mezzogiorno

Like many peripheral regions, wide-scale industrialisation never really occurred in the Mezzogiorno. It was by-passed by the industrial revolution due to physical and human factors. Today it is still underdeveloped. It attracts just 1% of Italian foreign direct investment (FDI).

Industry before 1950

Before 1950, the Mezzogiorno was unattractive for industry because it had:
1. A lack of resources.
2. A poor transport infrastructure due to the mountainous landscape.
3. A peripheral location – remote from large markets.
4. An unskilled and uneducated workforce.
5. A poor local market with little money available for investment.
6. An underdeveloped agricultural sector.
7. A high rate of emigration.

weblink
Industry in the Mezzogiorno

The *Cassa* scheme and industry

From 1965, the *Cassa* scheme promoted industry and tourism in the region. The scheme received funding of €2.3 billion between 1965 and 1970 to promote industrial location in the south by:
1. Providing finance to small and medium-sized industries; funding education and training schemes.
2. Giving grants and tax incentives to companies who relocated to the Mezzogiorno in an attempt to attract industry and others to decentralise operations from the north.
3. The selection of **growth centres** for investment in industrial development (see Fig. 17).
4. Offering cheaper land and greenfield sites for development and improving transport infrastructure.

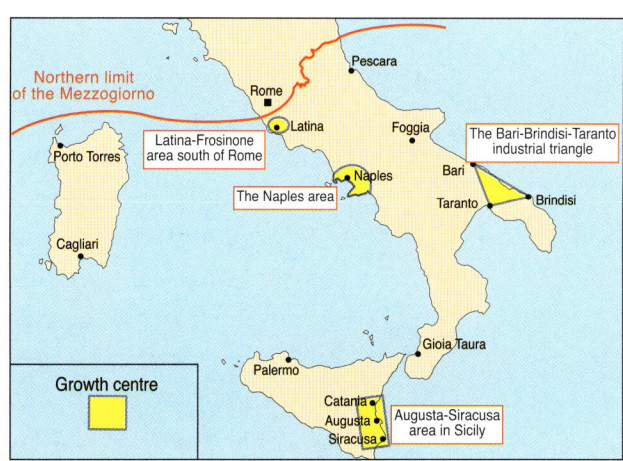

Fig. 17 Map of growth centres in the Mezzogiorno

371

5. Developing the natural gas deposits in Naples, Sicily and Calabria.
6. Enacting laws whereby 60% of all investment by public and semi-state enterprises must take place in the region.

The four industrial centres selected by the *Cassa* for investment are still important growth centres today. These four centres were selected on the basis of their market, resources, energy supply, labour force, ports and infrastructure.

1. **The Bari-Brindisi-Taranto industrial triangle**
   Steelworks, petrochemicals, electronics and engineering. This is the most successful growth centre.

2. **The Naples area**
   Chemicals, oil refining, car manufacturing, shipbuilding.

3. **The Latina-Frosinone area south of Rome**
   Engineering, car manufacturing, oil refining, chemicals and steel.

4. **The Augusta-Siracusa area in Sicily**
   Oil refining, petrochemicals and engineering.

Fig. 18 Naples was selected as one of four industrial growth centres.

Problems with the *Cassa* scheme: industry
Despite all of these initiatives, the *Cassa* has had limited success and the Mezzogiorno still remains poor. The reasons are:
1. Most factories were **capital intensive**, i.e. they provided little employment because machinery, not people, did most of the work. Some became known as 'cathedrals in the sun'.
2. Many factory workers were still involved in farming and took time off on a regular basis to undertake farm-work, lowering industrial productivity. Also, workers were not properly trained. As a result, many found the change to regular hours and factory work difficult to adjust to and absenteeism became a huge problem.
3. The larger industries failed to attract other industries to the region. There was no **multiplier effect** as planned.
4. There is a **brain-drain** of young educated people. This reduces the labour force.
5. Town planning and industrial developments were not integrated, i.e. new towns were built far away from industrial developments leading to severe traffic congestion. There is still no bridge connecting Sicily to the mainland, discouraging investment there.
6. Organised crime and corruption is a major problem. It bleeds healthy firms of cash they need to invest in their business. Naples and Calabria are the areas worst affected by this problem.

CHAPTER 19: A EUROPEAN PERIPHERAL REGION

Industry today

The region continues to be economically disadvantaged compared to the north of Italy. The *Cassa* scheme tried to encourage social and economic development using a combination of grants, subsidies, loans and tax incentives designed to attract investment and jobs. The scheme created over 300,000 jobs in new industries but more than 2 million jobs were lost in agriculture.

The recent promotion of food processing factories has been more successful as they can link with local food production areas.

As you can see from Fig. 19, the industries that developed in these growth centres were the capital-intensive heavy industries of oil refining, petrochemicals and chemicals. These industries used local supplies of gas and imported oil. Steelworks and shipbuilding were established at coastal locations offering deep-water port facilities. Electronics and engineering companies chose to locate in areas with an educated workforce and a large market such as Naples.

Many of Italy's engineering, steel and chemicals factories are run by state-owned companies, some of which are the largest in Europe. The most successful heavy industry is the state-owned steelmaker Finsider, which opened steelworks in Taranto in the Apulia region in 1964. Taranto was chosen because it offered a deep-water port, good infrastructure, a local skilled workforce and proximity to an energy source. Most of the steel manufactured here leaves the Mezzogiorno region as not enough steel-using industries have been built here to use up this supply. EU structural funds have been used to address some problems. Between 1989 and 1993, more than €13 billion was invested in roads and education by the EU in the region. Today Apulia is the fastest growing region in the Mezzogiorno.

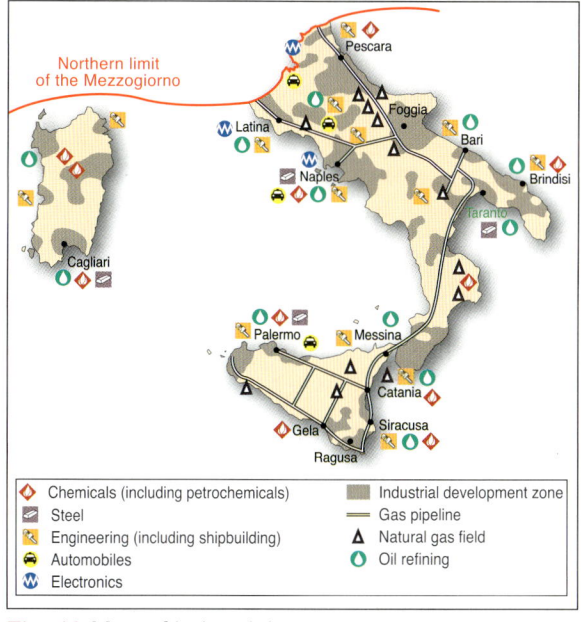

Fig. 19 Map of industrial centres

Tertiary activities in the Mezzogiorno
Tourism

Peripheral regions such as the Mezzogiorno are often dependent on tourism, based on the landscape and climate. The Mezzogiorno also has many historical and cultural attractions.

Tourism is growing but it is doing so at a slow pace and further investment in infrastructure and facilities is needed if the area is to compete with the north. Tourism is most successful along the coast but has yet had little impact inland.

Fig. 20 Procida, an island near Naples

CORE UNIT: REGIONAL GEOGRAPHY

Tourist attractions in the Mezzogiorno

1. The Mediterranean climate is hot, dry and sunny. Temperatures average 29°C in summer, attracting beach and city tourists. In winter, temperatures rarely fall below 11°C, although the mountain peaks are covered in snow, attracting skiers. This means that tourism can occur all year round, rather than only in summer.

2. The variety of unspoilt, natural and beautiful landscapes – such as the Bay of Naples, the Amalfi coast, sandy beaches and snow-peaked mountains, volcanoes such as Vesuvius and Stromboli – attract tourists throughout the year.

3. Tourists who like to visit ancient ruins can visit the historical cities of Pompeii and Naples. The art and architecture found in cities throughout the region is also of great interest.

4. The relaxed and family-oriented culture of Italians offers a child-friendly and stress-free holiday to tourists. Restaurants welcome children at all times.

5. The Adriatic coast of the Puglia region has a strong Greek and Roman influence, fine beaches and interesting historical sites.

6. Sicily is becoming increasingly popular as a tourist destination. It has been quite successful at promoting its history, beaches and festivals.

The *Cassa* scheme and tourism

The *Cassa* scheme recognised the many attractions of this **invisible export**. The Mezzogiorno has great potential as a tourist destination. Therefore, 15% of the *Cassa*'s funding was for tourism development.

The *Cassa* scheme developed more than 25 regions for tourism by providing grants to upgrade and build accommodation and provide facilities. It improved accessibility by building a motorway and an airport at Reggio in Calabria. It also improved ferry connections to Sicily and Sardinia. Along with EU structural funding these measures all helped to reduce the region's isolation. However, airport facilities at Reggio are still poor and traffic congestion is a major problem.

Fig. 21 Ancient ruins in Pompeii, an important tourist attraction

CHAPTER 19: A EUROPEAN PERIPHERAL REGION

Transport and communications

Transport and communications are key areas for improvement as these have been a human factor discouraging economic development in the region. Several regions in the Mezzogiorno qualify for extra EU funding because their GDP is less than 75% of the EU average. These regions are Campania, Puglia, Calabria and Sicily. Several physical and human factors affect transport and development.

- The main transport problem in the Mezzogiorno is the mountainous landscape of narrow winding roads that are snow-covered in winter or blocked by landslides triggered by heavy rain or earthquakes. The mountain roads cannot cater for the large trucks needed to carry goods in sufficient quantities to markets. Other problems include the need for costly bridges across valleys and tunnels through high mountains. The large distance from the wealthy, urban, northern Italian markets of Milan and Turin means long journey times and therefore high transport costs. Even within the Mezzogiorno, journey times are slow. It takes over 4 hours to go by train from Bari to Naples – a distance of just 250 kilometres. High speed rail does not exist south of Naples.
- Most of the transport infrastructure in southern Italy was rebuilt after the destruction caused by the Second World War.
- The ports of Naples, Taranto and Augusta are economically important export and import hubs for oil, gas and industrial goods. Italy is an important nation for container shipping in the Mediterranean. Today the port of Gioia Tauro in Calabria is the busiest container port in the Mediterranean.

> The EU ERDF Structural funding for Italy has concentrated on improving transport and communications infrastructure. Of the €32.2 billion EU structural funds being invested in Italy between 2014–2020, 70% will go to the development of the Mezzogiorno region.

Fig. 22 Roads in the Mezzogiorno often require the construction of tunnels through mountains and bridges across valleys due to the region's relief.

Fig. 23 Taranto Port, Puglia

375

The *Cassa* scheme and infrastructure development

Within the *Cassa* scheme, the **Vanoni Plan** was proposed. It was a massive investment in road infrastructure. A major motorway project, the *Autostrada del Sole*, was constructed connecting Milan to Naples. At 754 km, it is the longest Italian motorway and is considered the 'spinal cord' of the country's road network. It was designed to reduce transport times and costs for businesses and to encourage further economic development in the Mezzogiorno.

19.3 Human processes in the Mezzogiorno

Population density and distribution

The Mezzogiorno contains about 21 million people, with 65% living in rural areas. The average population density is 40 per km². The distribution of population in the Mezzogiorno region of Italy is uneven. Physical and human factors affect the population distribution in this region.

Physical factors affecting population distribution in the Mezzogiorno region of Italy

Soils and relief (landscape) affect where people can live. The Campania region around Naples and Mt. Vesuvius has the highest population density (400/km²) due to the low-lying land covered with fertile volcanic and alluvial soils. The lowest population density is in Basilicata (<99/km²), a remote upland region with poor soils.

In the past, the narrow coastal plains were uncomfortable, humid, mosquito-infested marshlands. People avoided these lowland areas even though they had fertile alluvial soils, preferring to live in small hilltop villages that were also easy to defend. Therefore, today, the rural population is distributed across a network of small- to medium-sized villages in upland areas.

The Apennine Mountains stretch north to south through the Mezzogiorno. These Alpine fold mountains contain limestone and have few rivers. The Apennines have low population density because the land is very steep, 45% is mountainous (over 400 m) and soil erosion is a problem. The mountains prevent profitable farming and are a barrier to communications; in Abruzzo, snow covers the high mountain passes in winter.

Human factors affecting population distribution in the Mezzogiorno

The Mezzogiorno is a poor peripheral economic region. It attracts just 1% of Italy's Foreign Direct Investment; organised crime starves healthy firms of money they might otherwise spend on investment so there is a lack of well-paid factory work. With unemployment at 25%, out-migration is a problem. Educated people leave to find work in the north of Italy. Over 4 million people left the region between 1950 and 1970. These were mostly from rural areas, thus lowering the population density.

CHAPTER 19: A EUROPEAN PERIPHERAL REGION

From 1950, the *Cassa per il Mezzogiorno* scheme funded agricultural and industrial development. This affected the distribution of population because drainage of marshes, irrigation and reclamation of coastal lowlands made these areas suitable for farming and settlement. People were encouraged to relocate from their upland villages to farms on the coastal plains. This lowered the population density in the uplands and increased densities on the lowlands.

The *Cassa* scheme developed heavy industry at the growth centres in Bari, Brindisi and Taranto as well as Naples and Palermo. This attracted people to live in these coastal port towns. The towns provided jobs in heavy industry such as oil refining and steel manufacture. Population density increased in the towns, e.g. Palermo in Sicily.

Investment in tourism under the *Cassa* scheme attracted people to work in the scenic coastal areas such as Sorrento. Airports and rail services were improved, providing employment in these sectors.

As well as having internal rural to urban migration, the Mezzogiorno is an entry point for international migrants. During the 1990s thousands of Albanian refugees fled from conflict in the former Yugoslavia to Apulia in eastern Italy. This led to a rapid rise in population density there. Since 2014, the population density in Sicily has been rising rapidly due to the arrival of African migrants and Syrian refugees. They travel by boat from Libya and arrive in Sicily daily, straining housing and medical services. By 2016, Italy had already received more than 150,000 migrants and refugees. These people try to reach Italy because it is part of the EU **Schengen Area**. This is the group of 26 EU countries which has removed border controls and allows free movement of people and goods.

Once migrants arrive in a Schengen Area country, they can travel to their preferred country in which to settle or seek asylum. In Italy, the main countries of origin of asylum seekers arriving there are Nigeria and Mali.

> **weblink**
> What is the Schengen Area?

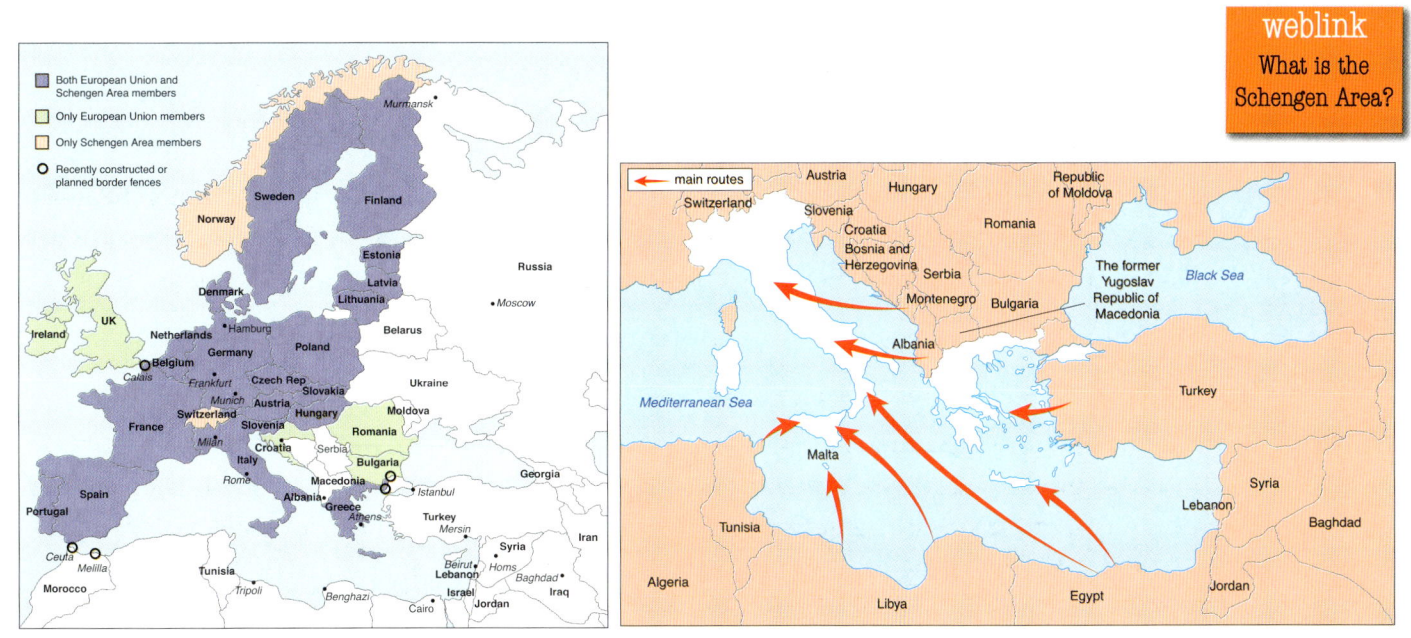

Fig. 24 Schengen Area countries

Fig. 25 Sea routes into Italy

377

CORE UNIT: REGIONAL GEOGRAPHY

Chapter Revision Questions

1. Using your atlas, draw a map of Italy. Locate and mark the following: two mountain ranges; two rivers; the neighbouring countries of Albania, Croatia, Serbia and Switzerland; the three regions of Italy. Focusing on the Mezzogiorno region, locate and mark six towns; three seas; Sicily, Sardinia and Corsica.

2. Using figure A to help you, describe the main characteristics of a Mediterranean climate.

3. Look at the climograph below and to the right. Answer the following questions:
   (a) In the Mezzogiorno, which month is the wettest month?
   (b) Which is the coldest month?
   (c) Calculate the annual range of temperature.

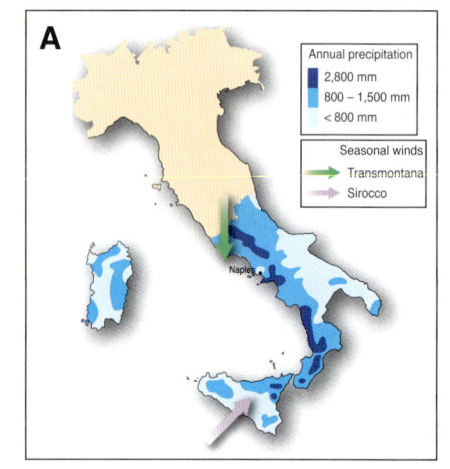

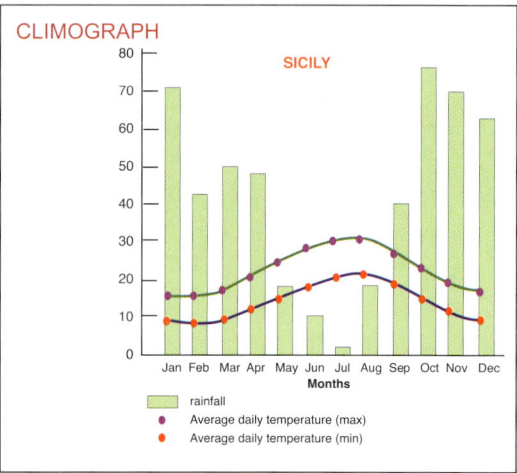

4. Name any **three** physical and **four** human (socio-economic) factors that influence the development of the Mezzogiorno region. Which ones hinder its development?

5. How do farmers in the Mezzogiorno deal with problems of drought and poor land?

6. Outline the advantages and disadvantages for the development of agriculture in the Mezzogiorno.

7. Explain the following terms: irrigation, *latifundia*, *Cassa per il Mezzogiorno*.

8. How has the *Cassa* scheme improved agriculture in the Mezzogiorno?

9. (i) Discuss the disadvantages of the Mezzogiorno for the location of industry.
   (ii) Describe efforts made by the *Cassa* to encourage industrial development in the region.

10. List the **four** regions selected as growth centres for development in the Mezzogiorno. Give **two** examples of industry established at each region. Explain why they set up in these regions.
11. Name and describe **four** advantages the Mezzogiorno has for the creation of a successful tourist industry.
12. Write a brief account of the role played by the *Cassa* to promote tourism.
13. Describe/outline the tourist attractions in the Mezzogiorno.
14. Explain the importance of the EU to the Mezzogiorno.
15. Describe the population characteristics of the Mezzogiorno.
16. Describe the cause and impact of migration into the Mezzogiorno region.
17. Describe/account for the distribution of population in the Mezzogiorno region.

LC Exam Questions

Higher Level students must be able to answer Ordinary and Higher Level questions.

■ OL Questions

18. Explain the importance of **one** of the primary industries listed below to the economy of any European region studied by you.
    - Agriculture
    - Forestry
    - Fishing
    - Mining/Energy.
19. Describe any **two** problems facing agriculture or manufacturing industry in a European region – not Ireland – of your choice.
20. Name a European region (not in Ireland), that you have studied and answer each of the following questions.
    (i) Name **two** tourist attractions in this region.
    (ii) Explain the reasons why tourists are attracted to this region.
    (iii) Describe **one** problem associated with tourism in this region.
21. Name a European region (not in Ireland) that you have studied and explain any **two** of the following:
    - The importance of transport to this region
    - The reasons why tourists are attracted to this region
    - The type of farming practised in this region
    - The reasons for the development of industry in this region.

CORE UNIT: REGIONAL GEOGRAPHY

LC Exam Questions

■ HL Questions

22. Draw an outline map of a European region (not in Ireland) that you have studied. On it, correctly show and name the following:
    - A named feature of relief in the region
    - A named river in the region
    - Two named urban centres in the region.

23. Account for the development of agriculture in a European region (not in Ireland) that you have studied, with reference to any **two** of the factors listed below:
    - Relief
    - Markets
    - Climate.

24. Describe and explain any **two** factors that influence the development of secondary economic activities in a European region (not in Ireland) that you have studied.

25. Examine the factors that influence the development of **one** tertiary economic activity in a European region (not in Ireland) that you have studied.

26. Account for the distribution of population throughout a European region (not in Ireland) that you have studied.

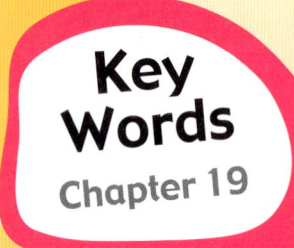

Key Words Chapter 19

Key Words

You should be able to explain both verbally and in writing each of the key words listed below.

Autostrada del Sole
braccianti
brain drain
capital intensive
cash crops
Cassa per il Mezzogiorno
commercial farming
co-operatives
extensive farming
garrigue
growth centres

latifundia
maquis
Mediterranean climate
Metapontino area
Mezzogiorno
minifundia
reclamation schemes
Schengen Area
subsistence farming
Vanoni plan
viniculture/viticulture

Digital Resources are available for this chapter at mentorbooks.ie/resources

CHAPTER 20

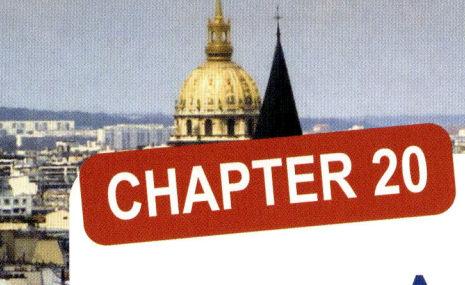

A European Core and City Region

Key Theme

The study of regions shows how economic, human and physical processes interact in a particular way. This can be demonstrated by examining two contrasting European regions. The boundaries and extent of city regions may change over time.

Learning Outcomes

At the end of this chapter you will be able to:
- Describe the Paris Basin as a core region.
- Name and describe the human and physical characteristics of the Paris Basin.
- Describe primary, secondary and tertiary activities in the Paris Basin.
- Describe the population characteristics of the Paris Basin.
- Describe the growth of the Paris city region.
- Explain how the growth of the Paris city region is being planned and controlled.

Contents

20.1	The Paris Basin – Physical and human characteristics, economic activities and human processes	382
20.2	The Paris city region	393

Revision Space

Chapter Revision Questions – LC Exam Questions – Key Word List 396

CORE UNIT: REGIONAL GEOGRAPHY

20.1 The Paris Basin – Physical and human characteristics, economic activities and human processes

A core economic region in Europe

The Paris Basin is a wealthy core socio-economic region because it has many natural and human advantages for settlement and industrial location, e.g. relief, climate, soils, accessibility and a population of 22 million people (one third of the total French population).

The Paris Basin is low-lying and has a variety of fertile soils which have developed on the different rock types in the area. Each soil is associated with a particular type of agriculture, e.g. the clay soils of the Brie region support grasslands and dairy farming.

KEY
Two urban centres:
■ Paris
• Lille
Two physical features:
River Seine
La Falaise (chalk scarps)
- - TGV route

Fig. 1 The Paris Basin – location within France

The Paris Basin is the largest manufacturing centre in France. The transport network of this region is well developed. Paris is the capital city and also the centre of government in France. The Paris Basin is a centre of in-migration and is culturally mixed.

Physical characteristics of the Paris Basin

The Paris Basin has positive physical factors leading to its development as a socio-economic core region. These are **climate**, **relief**, **soils** and **drainage**.

CLIMATE	RELIEF	SOILS	DRAINAGE
In **west of region**, **maritime climate** has cool summers (16°C) and mild (5°C) winters Rain throughout the year, average 800 mm per year Influenced by sea	Low-lying with upland ridges (scarps) in the east Highest ridge is Falaise de France	**Limon** soil in centre of region is extremely fertile; main cereal-growing region	River Seine and tributaries (Oise, Yonne, Marne) flow north-west across the centre of the region
In **east of region**, **continental climate**, hot (19°C) and cold (2°C) winters. Not influenced by sea Summer convectional rain average 700 mm per year	Relief caused by huge Armorican syncline/ downfold in underlying sedimentary rock layers Edges of rock layers are seen at the scarps	Sand and gravel soils in south of Paris Basin Well-drained infertile soils on chalk scarps in east	River Loire flows west across the southern part of the region
Central Paris Basin has **transitional climate** between the two climates described above	Layers of chalk, limestone and clay covered by sands and gravels produce distinct farming zones called *pays*	Clay soils in Brie region Fertile alluvial soils deposited by Rivers Seine, Somme and Loire	River Somme flows west across the north of the region

CHAPTER 20: A EUROPEAN CORE AND CITY REGION

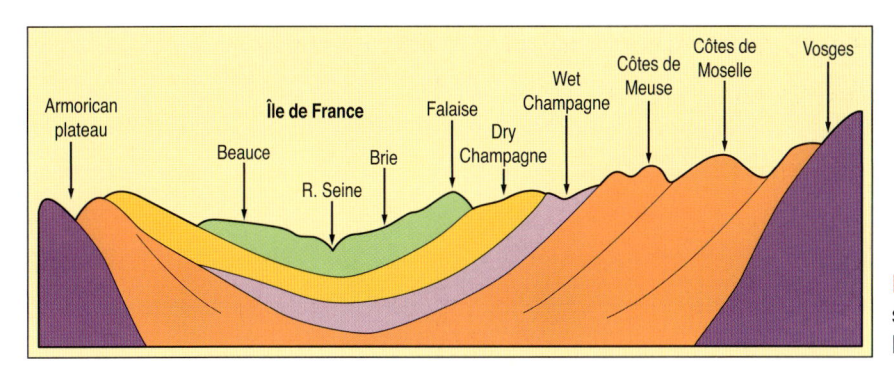

Fig. 2 Rock structure of the Paris Basin

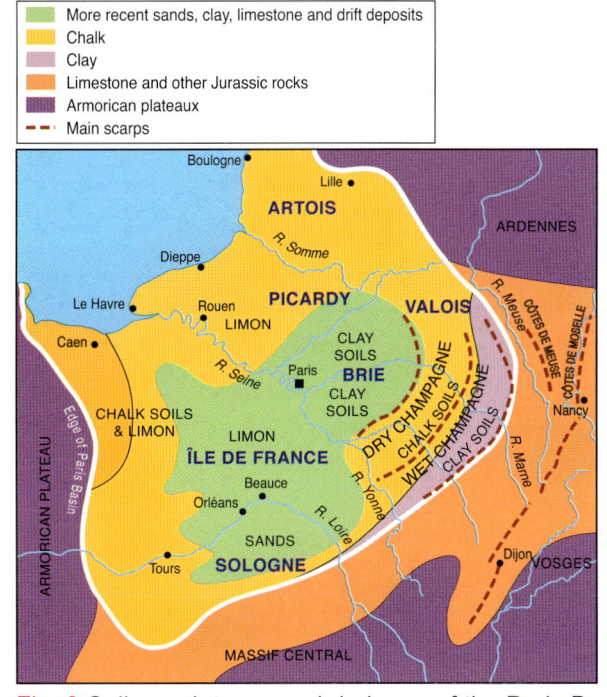

Fig. 3 Soils, rock types and drainage of the Paris Basin

🏌 Human factors/characteristics of the Paris Basin

Three main human factors affect the Paris Basin region. They are: **population dynamics**, **transport infrastructure** and **government/EU policies**.

POPULATION DYNAMICS	TRANSPORT INFRASTRUCTURE	GOVERNMENT/EU POLICY
Paris Basin holds one-third population of France (22 million)	Well-developed network of road, rail and canal systems	*Schéma Directeur* is plan used to control growth of Paris city
Contains both an educated, skilled labour force and an unskilled labour force	Located in centre of EU, fast connections to all EU cities make Paris Basin an attractive location for industry.	French government has designated certain areas of Paris Basin as **competitive clusters** to encourage economic development.
Wealthy local market and large EU market nearby	Two hours to London by train, one hour to Brussels and six hours to Frankfurt by road	Because France is so wealthy (6th largest GDP in world) the EU gives less CAP and Structural Fund support to the region than to other EU countries

383

CORE UNIT: REGIONAL GEOGRAPHY

Primary activities in the Paris Basin

Primary activities in the region have been influenced by physical and human factors, e.g. fertile soils, mild climate, low-lying relief, educated farmers and proximity to a rich urban market. These factors have led to profitable commercial intensive farming in the Paris Basin.

Agriculture

The Paris Basin has historically been an important producer of agricultural products for the following reasons:

- Close to the River Seine, alluvial soils favour **intensive commercial farming**. The fertile limon soil and the climate (maritime/continental) have allowed the production of wheat, barley and maize cereal crops throughout the region.
- Spring and early summer rainfall help crop growth and the long hours of summer sunshine are ideal for ripening crops.
- The low-lying relief allows for large (over 400 hectares), mechanised and highly productive farms.
- The consumer market for farm produce is very big. Almost 22 million people live within the Paris Basin so farmers have easy access to a rich local market, reducing their transport costs.

Fig. 4 Cereal growing in the Paris Basin

CHAPTER 20: A EUROPEAN CORE AND CITY REGION

A number of distinctive farming regions called **pays** have developed based mainly on the soil and rock types of the region.

1. **Artois** and **Picardy**

   This is a low-lying, flat, limon-covered *pays* which specialises in cereal production, e.g. barley and wheat. On the coast, the climate is wetter due to the influence of the sea which makes soils heavier. As a result, dairy farming is common.

2. **Brie**

   In this *pays*, clay soils occur. This soil produces good pasture land. Farmers here are dairy producers, famous for cheese (Brie cheese) and butter. Being so close to the urban area of Paris, they also supply fresh milk to the city.

3. **The Île de France**

   This is a low-lying, flat region covered with fertile limon soil. Most farms are very large (over 400 hectares), highly mechanised, capital intensive, and produce wheat. Yields are the highest in France. It is known as the 'bread basket of France'.

4. **The Champagne regions**

   These regions have clay-covered valleys between chalk ridges (**scarps**). The chalk ridges of the dry Champagne *pays* are infertile, well-drained soils but because they have a southerly aspect they are suitable for vines. It is here around the town of Reims that the famous champagne wine is produced. These are some of the most northerly vineyards in Europe and as a result the wines from here have a unique taste. The production of wine is a specialist type of farming called **viticulture/viniculture**.

   In the low-lying clay-covered wet Champagne *pays*, soils are better suited to pasture with dairying and beef cattle.

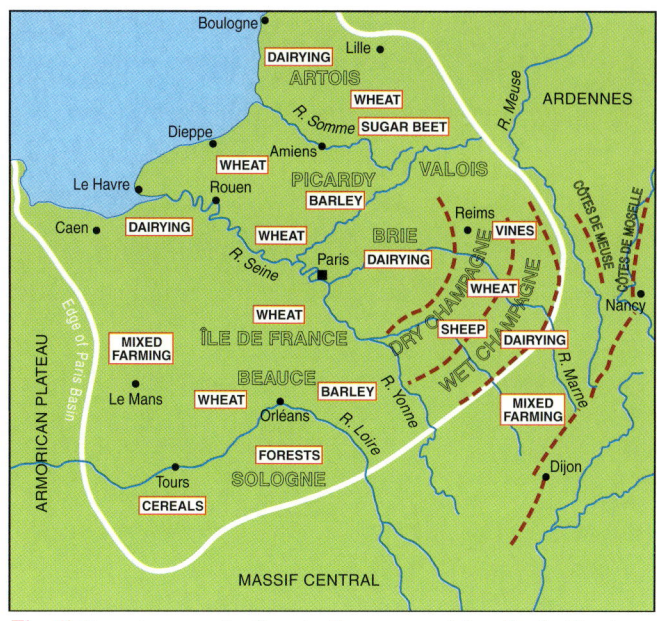

Fig. 5 Farming production in the *pays* of the Paris Basin

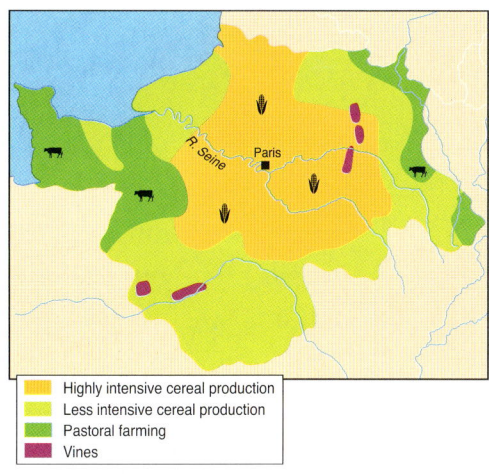

Fig. 6 Agriculture in the Paris Basin

Fig. 7 The chalk soils of the dry Champagne *pays* is suitable for vines.

385

Energy production in the Paris Basin

Energy consumption in the Paris Basin is high. Oil and gas are imported through the port of Le Havre where oil refining and petrochemical production form the basis of the economy.

Oil and natural gas

France has small oil reserves estimated at about 150 to 160 million barrels. They are located in the Paris Basin and in the Aquitaine region to the south.

France is the third greatest oil-consuming country in Europe after Germany and Russia and tenth greatest in the world. It has to import 95% of its oil needs. As the Paris Basin does not contain any gas reserves, gas is brought to the region by pipeline from gas wells in the Aquitaine Basin and from the Netherlands.

Coal

Small reserves of coal existed in the north of the region Nord Pas de Calais, but in 2004 coal production was phased out completely. France now imports its coal needs.

Nuclear energy

France depends heavily on nuclear power for its electricity supply. It imports uranium from Niger in Africa. Seventy-five per cent of French electricity is generated by nuclear power and its nuclear-generating capacity has increased by about ten per cent over the past decade. France sells €3 billion worth of nuclear energy to other EU countries every year through its state-owned electricity company, EDF. Ten of its fifty-eight power stations are located in and around the Paris Basin.

Fig. 8 France relies heavily on nuclear energy for its electricity supply.

CHAPTER 20: A EUROPEAN CORE AND CITY REGION

Secondary activities in the Paris Basin

Paris has more manufacturing industries than any other region in France. It is the economic centre of the country and a major industrial centre. It contains over 20% of the French workforce, and its factories produce a wide variety of goods.

Paris is known for such luxury products as expensive jewellery (Cartier), perfume (Yves Saint Laurent) and high-fashion (Chanel) clothing.

Car manufacturers such as Citroën have assembly plants in the city suburbs.

The Central Business District (CBD) is on the north side of the river, where busy offices, small factories and fashionable shops are found. Specialist educational and academic printing and publishing activities are located close to the universities in the city, e.g. the world-famous Sorbonne university.

Fig. 9 Paris is famous for its high fashion industry.

Heavy steel manufacturing (rail, steel and oil refining) is located further out from the city, along the river, close to the Canal St Denis. Food processing is a major industry in the region producing cheese (Brie), wine, bread and vegetables.

The Paris Basin is attractive to industry for the following human and physical reasons:

1. Access/communications

The River Seine runs through Paris for 13 km and its tributaries (e.g. Oise, Yonne, Marne) provide a natural transport network across the region. It has large international ports at Paris, Rouen and Le Havre. These ports enable raw materials and finished products to be transported easily. The low-lying relief enabled the development of the rail and road networks which are focused on Paris – a **nodal point**.

The road network and TGV rail network is focused on Paris city making Paris very accessible and attractive to industry. This allows the manufacturing industry to easily distribute products and receive raw materials. The transportation network includes a metro and several airports as well as a direct rail link via the Channel Tunnel to London. The region is well serviced by air as it has three international airports. Canals have been developed to provide access to the city. The canals have historically been used by heavy industry.

Fig. 10 The Eurostar travels to destinations in Britain, Germany, Holland, Belgium and Switzerland as well as destinations within France.

CORE UNIT: REGIONAL GEOGRAPHY

> **weblink**
> Paris Basin – secondary activities

2. Agricultural raw materials

There is a variety of agricultural products grown on the fertile soils, e.g. cereals, vines (wine), cattle (cheese, beef and milk), aromatic plants and seeds (lavender). These provide raw materials for the spin-off food processing and cosmetics industries.

3. Population

The Paris Basin contains 22 million people who provide a skilled and educated labour force. The population of Paris city is over 12 million people. One third of the Parisian population is made up of people aged between 20 and 39 years and one quarter of the population has management skills. Many of these people are wealthy and also provide a market for manufactured luxury goods. This attracts industry to the area.

4. Government policy

- The government has encouraged industrial development in the Paris Basin by naming eight **competitive clusters** in the region. These clusters bring industry, business and research together and aim to increase production in many new and existing industries. An example of one such cluster is **Cosmetic Valley**, a large area to the west of Paris. Covering six French *départements* in three regions (all within a one-hour drive from Paris city), it includes 800 companies and six universities, accounting for 70,000 jobs and a turnover of €25 billion (including chemistry, packaging, and testing dedicated to the cosmetic and perfumery industry).
- Cosmetic Valley is a centre for many businesses in the cosmetics industry from growing aromatic plants, creating and formulating products, manufacturing perfumes and cosmetics, control, testing and analysis laboratories, advertising and design and packaging.

Fig. 11 The Cosmetic Valley within the Paris Basin covers six *départements* in three *régions*.

CHAPTER 20: A EUROPEAN CORE AND CITY REGION

Tertiary activities in the Paris Basin

The Paris Basin is known for its tourism and transport services which are focused on the city of Paris. The city is a nodal point and is easily accessible to all by air, road and rail links.

Tourism

Some 76 million people visit France each year. Of these the Paris Basin receives 45 million tourists annually. Paris is the world's most visited city. It attracts nearly 30 million tourists annually and tourism accounts for just over 25% of employment in the city region. There is a wide variety of natural and man-made tourist attractions in the Paris Basin. Tourists are attracted by the history, culture, scenery and fashion of the capital city – Paris – and its surrounding region. Tourism is worth 7% of France's GDP.

Most tourists come from Britain, America, Germany, Italy and Japan.

Fig. 12 A view of the Eiffel Tower, Paris

Factors encouraging tourism in the Paris Basin:

1. **The city is easily accessible.**
   The city and region is easily accessible by air, rail and road.

   It has three international airports (Charles de Gaulle, Orly and Paris Beauvais).

   Travelling around the region is very easy via the metro, suburban and intercity rail services and the high-speed TGV. There is also a high-speed land link to the UK via the Channel Tunnel. These transport methods make the city an important tourist destination for both domestic as well as overseas visitors.

Fig. 13 The glass pyramid at the entrance to the Louvre Museum

2. **There is a range of accommodation and tourist attractions.**
   Paris offers a wide range of accommodation catering for every category and age group of visitor, from the most luxurious to basic hotels, along with self-catering apartments and hostels.

389

CORE UNIT: REGIONAL GEOGRAPHY

Attractions in Paris city
- The Disneyland Resort theme park is a short direct train journey from Paris city. It averages more than 12 million visitors each year. It is open all year round, offering a holiday for every age group.
- The city of Paris has many famous and unusual buildings, museums, theatres and galleries, e.g. Notre Dame Cathedral, the Louvre museum, the Eiffel Tower. The Louvre attracts 5 million visitors each year and the Eiffel Tower attracts 5.5 million tourists. It is the most valuable monument in Europe, worth €435 billion to the French economy. This is nearly one-fifth of the entire French GDP.
- Paris is also one of the fashion capitals of the world. Chanel, Christian Dior and Yves Saint Laurent are manufactured in the region and sold in the exclusive fashion houses along the Boulevard Haussmann and the Champs Élysées.

Fig. 14 Disneyland Resort, Paris, is near Marne-la-Vallée – one of the 'new' towns.

Attractions in the Paris Basin region
- The beaches of Normandy, which preserve the battle sites of the Second World War, attract many thousands of people who wish to remember those who died in the war and others who are interested in military history.
- Versailles, a city outside Paris renowned for its royal chateau, is an important attraction for history, art and architecture enthusiasts. As with other attractions in this region it is linked by an excellent train route.

Fig. 15 Normandy Beach

Fig. 16 Gardens at the Versailles Palace

Communications and transport in the Paris Basin

Like all core economic regions Paris has an excellent integrated transport infrastructure. The development of its transport network has been helped by the flat, low-lying or gently undulating landscape (topography) as well as the River Seine and its tributaries.

Paris has been building its transportation system for centuries and is continuously improving it under a long-term masterplan called the *Schéma Directeur*, (see page 394). Under this plan a large proportion of the growing Parisian population (over 1.5 million) was to be located in 5 new towns built about 25 km from the city. Providing transport infrastructure for this population affected the location and type of transport services that were built, e.g. rail, metro and road systems.

As in Ireland the French transport network radiates out from its capital city. As a result the Paris Basin is highly accessible because it is a route focus/nodal point.

Paris is a central hub of the national intercity rail network. Six major railway stations are connected to three networks: (i) The **TGV** serving four high-speed rail lines, (ii) the normal-speed Corail trains and (iii) the suburban rail lines (Transilien).

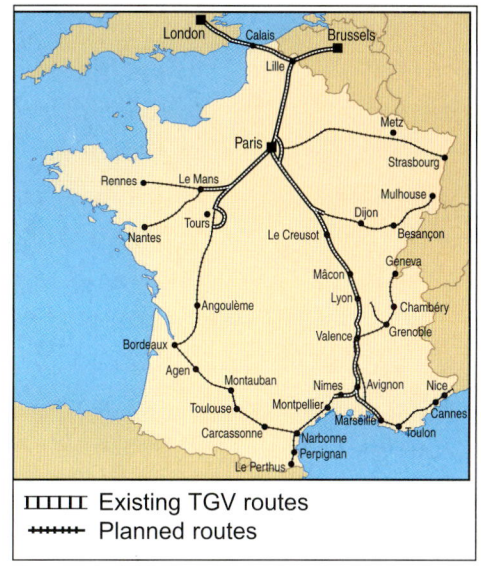

Fig. 17 TGV map of Paris and France

The most important transportation system in Paris is the metro. Over 4.2 million people travel by metro in Paris city each day, greatly reducing traffic congestion in the city. Many other commuters who live further out in the Paris Basin, e.g. Rouen, use the TGV (high-speed trains).

Ninety per cent of the electrical energy used by metro, trains and tram transport is produced by nuclear and hydroelectric power plants. As a result pollution levels in Paris are lower than the EU average despite all the traffic.

Paris is served by two major airports: Orly Airport, which is south of Paris, and the Paris-Charles de Gaulle Airport, near Roissy-en-France, which is one of the busiest in the world. It is the hub for the national airline, Air France. A smaller airport at Beauvais Tille, 70 km north of the city of Paris, is used by charter and low-cost airlines.

Paris is the focus of the French road network and is surrounded by three motorways: the Périphérique and two other motorways serving the inner and outer suburbs.

Fig. 18 A metro station in Paris

CORE UNIT: REGIONAL GEOGRAPHY

Like Dublin, Paris also has a bike-sharing system called *Vélib* (free bike). More than 20,000 public bicycles are available at 1,450 parking stations, and they can be rented for short and medium distances. As in Dublin this has proved to be very successful.

Due to the high population, traffic congestion is still a problem in the city. Reducing the number of cars is a priority. Bus lanes have been introduced but have not significantly reduced congestion as Parisians prefer to use their cars instead of the bus. The recent introduction of the electric car rental scheme, Autolib, allows Parisians to use public transport to access the city and then rent a car for short periods of time with free parking. This scheme helps to reduce the volume of traffic in the city and region.

The recent construction of offices and residential buildings at La Défense, a major business district to the west of Paris, has been successful in reducing congestion. The high rise and compact nature of this international business centre has reduced congestion as it is completely pedestrianised and is well served by public transport.

Fig. 19 Traffic in Paris city centre

Fig. 20 La Défense - an important business centre in Paris

Human processes in the Paris Basin

Population density, distribution and culture

Paris is a wealthy, core region, administrative capital and centre of financial services. It is one of the world's leading business and cultural centres. The majority of the residents are educated with a high standard of living, providing a market and labour force for the agricultural, industrial and service sectors. There is generally low unemployment.

One third of the population of France live in the Paris Basin (22 million people out of a population of 66 million). Outside of Paris city the population is well distributed throughout the region.

The greatest density is found in Paris city centre where the population density is over 20,000 per km². Approximately 10 million people live in suburbs beyond the 'Periphérique' ring road. The remainder of the population live in the commuter zone up to 45 km from Paris, made accessible by the efficient metro and SNCF trains.

Paris, as with all socio-economic core regions, has been the main area for in-migration. National and international migration is common. Paris offers better job opportunities and has over 30% of the country's economically active age group of 19 to 64-year-olds. Like the rest of France, Paris has an **ageing population** and depends on migrants to fill jobs and increase the population because migrant families traditionally have a higher birth rate. The natural increase is 110,000 per year.

International migration has led to a diverse range of cultures in the region, most especially in the city itself. This cultural melting pot had its origins chiefly in post-war France. After the Second World War, government schemes were set up to attract people to move to France to rebuild the country. Many migrants came from Europe and China but the majority came from former French colonies, especially from North and West Africa. Stricter immigration laws were passed in the 1980s making it more difficult for people from other countries to settle in France. These laws slowed down the rate of immigration considerably. Net migration rate is now just 1.09 per 1,000.

Today over 8% of the population of the city was born in another country. A large immigrant population of over 1.3 million people live in Paris. The majority of non-nationals work in low-paid jobs, especially in the services sector. Most live in the poorer suburbs in high-rise buildings, e.g. La Courneuve. Many of these poor suburbs lack basic services and this has led to social unrest and violence, e.g. race riots in 2005, as well as calls for strict citizenship regulations.

Discrimination, racism, unequal job opportunities and increasing isolation is felt by many migrant groups. Despite the affluence of most of the city, many migrants live in poverty. Some shanty town-style dwellings even exist along parts of the city transport routes, e.g. along the RER rail route to Charles de Gaulle airport. Economic recession since 2008 has seen the rate of in-migration decline although Paris still attracts many thousands of migrants each year.

> Paris and its suburbs is the largest **melting pot** in France with an immigrant population of some 1.3 million people.

20.2 The Paris city region

The sprawling city of Paris and its suburbs are home to over 12 million people. It is the fifth largest city in the EU. Paris dominates all aspects of French economic and social life. It is a **primate city**. The next largest city is Marseilles. Paris is the centre of decision making, employment and cultural activities in France. It contains 20% of the national workforce. The boundary of Paris city is changing over time as the population expands due to in-migration.

This growth of Paris has slowed the development of other towns and cities in the region as people and businesses prefer to be in or close to Paris.

Therefore, urban planners have had to encourage the growth of the surrounding towns and control the growth of Paris. Dublin city planners are facing a similar challenge.

Fig. 21 High density and high intensity land use in Paris

CORE UNIT: REGIONAL GEOGRAPHY

Reasons for the growth of Paris:

1. It is a bridging point across the River Seine.
2. It is in the centre of the fertile floodplain of the River Seine and limon-covered Paris Basin.
3. It is the focus of road and rail routes in France.
4. It is the capital city.
5. It is the focus of industrial development.
6. It has a long tradition in craftmaking and the textiles industry.
7. It is a centre of in-migration.

Government policy to control the growth of Paris

The *Schéma Directeur*

In the late 1950s and early 1960s, Paris city suffered from overcrowding; traffic congestion; air, water, noise and visual pollution; inner-city decay and urban sprawl.

To overcome these problems, city planners in 1965 published a major plan called the *Schéma Directeur* to accommodate the expected population growth to 14 million by the 21st century. This plan is constantly updated.

Its aims are:

1. To control the rate of growth of the city.
2. To expand the metropolitan area to take in the entire Paris Basin, including cities which, although situated almost 200 km from Paris, are only an hour away by high-speed train.
3. To improve housing conditions in socially disadvantaged areas, reducing social unrest.
4. To improve and enlarge land available for recreational space.
5. To improve the transport system.
6. To develop employment in the city and the suburbs.
7. To protect the natural environment.

Fig. 22 Planning the growth of towns around Paris

Fig. 23 The *Schéma Directeur* aims to improve run-down housing in Paris.

CHAPTER 20: A EUROPEAN CORE AND CITY REGION

The *Schéma Directeur's* new-town policy

The *Schéma Directeur* planners chose a policy that encouraged the growth of towns around Paris. As in Dublin, a **new-town policy** was started north and south of the River Seine.

These growth centres saw five new towns being built, which grew quite quickly, e.g La Défense (business and shopping centre) and Marne-la-Vallée (near Disneyland Resort, Paris).

The most successful is St. Quentin-en-Yvelines, 30 km south-west of Paris with a population of more than 150,000 and 40,000 new jobs. The area around Disneyland Resort, Paris at Marne-la-Vallée has also succeeded in accommodating the decentralisation of Paris.

Overall urban renewal/regeneration, industry, housing and trade have improved and are being carefully monitored to stop urban sprawl and environmental pollution in the Paris region and hinterland.

Since it began the *Schéma* has been revised regularly to adapt to the changing needs of modern society. The most recent plan provides planning directives for the region up to 2030.

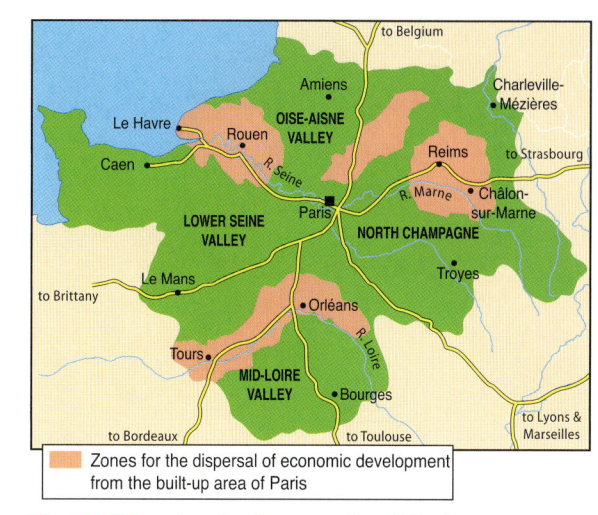

weblink
French national statistics

Fig. 24 Planning for the growth of Paris

Fig. 25 Social and affordable housing in Paris

Fig. 26 The suburb of La Défense

Fig. 27 The business and shopping area of La Défense

Chapter Revision Questions

1. Using your atlas draw a map of France. Locate and mark in the following: the Pyrenees; the French Alps; neighbouring countries of Belgium and Spain; the Rivers Seine, Rhône, Saône and Loire; the Paris Basin region; Paris, Lyons, Tours, Lille, Marseilles, La Harve and Calais.

2. Briefly describe and draw the rock structure and soils of the Paris Basin.

3. Describe and account for the differences in climate across the Paris Basin.

4. Draw a sketch map of the Paris Basin. Mark in and label the different soils and farming regions/*pays*.

5. Pick any **two** farming areas (*pays*) in the Paris Basin and briefly describe the soil type, rock type and farm produce.

6. What forms of energy are used in the Paris Basin? Briefly discuss the source of these energy resources.

7. List **three** reasons why the Paris Basin is attractive to industry.

8. Name and describe **three** attractions the Paris region offers tourists.

9. Explain in detail why Paris is a core socio-economic region.

10. What factors have led to the growth of the Paris city region?

11. What is the *Schéma Directeur*? Why was it needed?

12. What are the aims of the *Schéma Directeur*?

13. Name **three** new towns built around the edge of Paris.

14. Discuss the operation of planning strategies to control urban growth in a city you have studied.

CHAPTER 20: A EUROPEAN CORE AND CITY REGION

LC Exam Questions

Higher Level students must be able to answer Ordinary and Higher Level questions.

■ OL Questions

15. Draw a sketch map of a European region (not in Ireland) that you have studied. On it, show and name each of the following:
    - Two named towns or cities
    - One named river
    - One named area of relief (upland or lowland).

16. Name a European region (not in Ireland) that you have studied and explain any **two** of the following:
    - The importance of transport to this region
    - The reasons why tourists are attracted to this region
    - The type of farming practised in this region
    - The reasons for the development of industry in this region.

17. Explain how any **two** of the following influence the development of agriculture in a European region (not in Ireland) that you have studied:
    - Relief and Soils
    - Climate
    - Markets.

18. Name **one** urban area in a European region (not in Ireland) that you have studied. Explain **two** reasons for the growth of this urban area.

■ HL Questions

19. Examine the development of primary activities in one non-Irish European region of your choice.

20. Describe and explain any **two** factors that influence the development of secondary economic activities in a European region (not in Ireland) that you have studied.

21. Examine the factors that influence the development of **one** tertiary economic activity in a European region (not in Ireland) that you have studied.

22. Examine how any **two** of the factors listed below have influenced the development of one urban area in a European region (not in Ireland) that you have studied:
    - Transport
    - Location
    - Primary economic activity.

23. 'The boundaries of city regions have changed over time.' Discuss this statement with reference to one example you have studied.

24. Account for the distribution of population throughout a European region (not in Ireland) that you have studied.

CORE UNIT: REGIONAL GEOGRAPHY

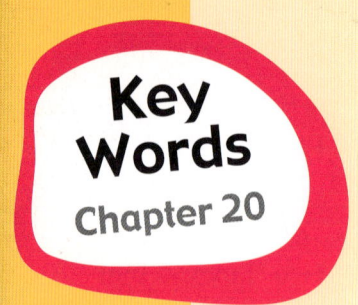

Key Words — Chapter 20

Key Words

You should be able to explain both verbally and in writing each of the key words listed below.

ageing population
Artois
Brie
Champagne regions
competitive clusters
continental climate
Cosmetic Valley
Île de France
intensive commercial farming
limon
maritime climate
metro
pays
primate city
route focus/nodal point
scarps
Schéma Directeur
topography
transitional climate
viticulture/viniculture

Digital Resources are available for this chapter at mentorbooks.ie/resources

CHAPTER 21

Brazil – A Contintental Region

Key Theme

The study of regions shows how economic, human and physical processes interact in a particular area.

Learning Outcomes

At the end of this chapter you will be able to:
- Describe the physical characteristics of Brazil.
- Describe the primary, secondary and tertiary activities of Brazil.
- Describe the differences between urban and rural Brazil.
- Describe Brazil's population characteristics and its culture.
- Give a brief account of different cultures within Brazil.

Contents

21.1	Physical characteristics and economic activities	400
	Case Study 1: Car manufacturing in Brazil	410
21.2	Population dynamics: Density, distribution and culture	415
	Case Study 2: The Amerindian tribes	421
21.3	City region in Brazil	422
	Case Study 3: Urban growth of São Paulo	423

Revision Space

Chapter Revision Questions – LC Exam Questions – Key Word List 425

399

CORE UNIT: REGIONAL GEOGRAPHY

21.1 Physical characteristics and economic activities

Background information

- Brazil is famous for its football, carnivals and Amazonian rainforests. It is the fifth-largest country in the world after China, India, USA and Indonesia. Brazil is a country of young people; almost two thirds of its people are under 30 years of age. Its population is about 204 million.
- Brazil is a country of inequality. Its wealth is very unevenly distributed – 60% of its population live in poverty. A United Nations Development Programme (UNDP) report stated that the richest 10% of Brazilians are 85 times wealthier than the poorest 10%. Over 40 million Brazilians live on less than €1 per day.
- South America was colonised by Portuguese and Spanish explorers. The official language of Brazil is Portuguese.
- Like the US, Brazil is divided into states. It has 26 states and one federal district where the capital city of Brasilia is situated. The central government is located in Brasilia. Each state has its own government. Within each state there are town councils that deal with decisions at local level.

At its widest, Brazil is 4,319 km wide – almost the distance from London to New York.

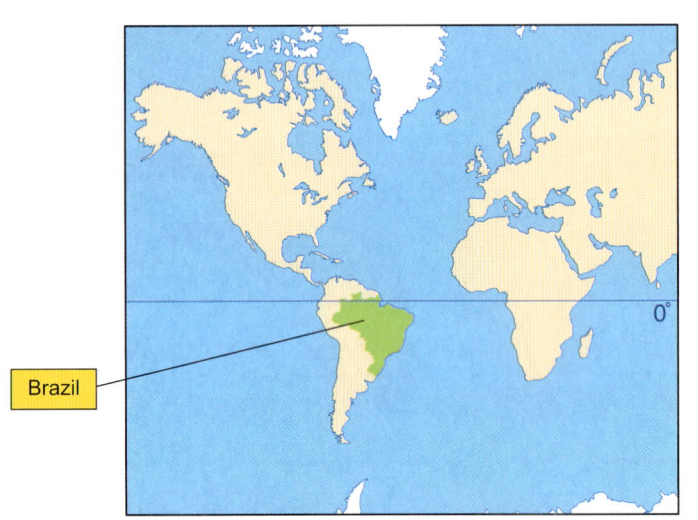

Fig. 1 Location of Brazil in the world

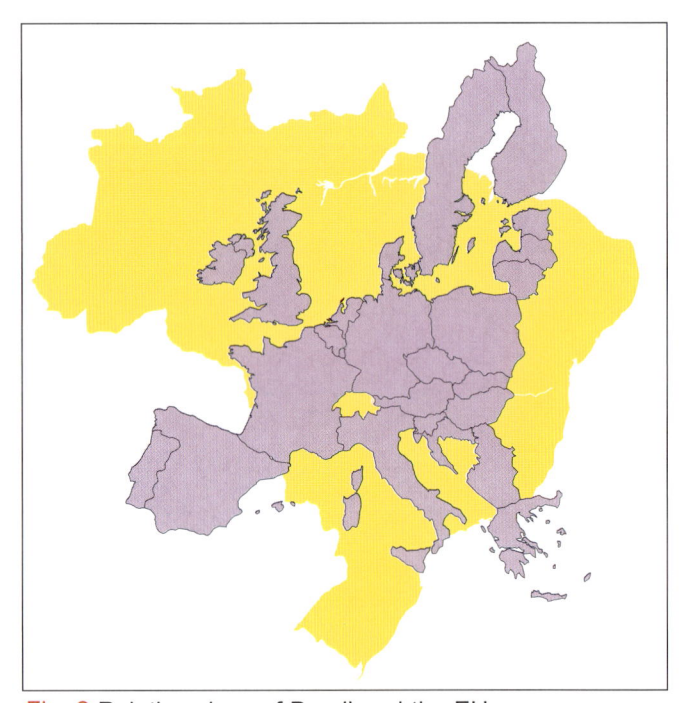

Fig. 2 Relative sizes of Brazil and the EU

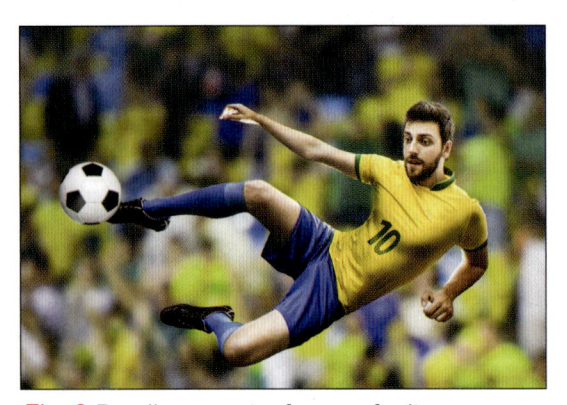

Fig. 3 Brazil, a country famous for its soccer

CHAPTER 21: BRAZIL – A CONTINENTAL REGION

Physical characteristics of Brazil

Brazil is such a big country that there are many variations in its physical landscape.

Climate	**Tropical climate** covers most of Brazil
	Sunny, warm and humid all year
	Rainfall varies from 1,500 mm to 2,000 mm per year
	Relief rain in Brazilian highlands
	Dry season occurs in west-central Brazil.
	Temperatures vary from 23°C to 30°C due to influence of the highlands
	Atlantic breezes moderate temperatures along coast
	Equatorial climate occurs in Amazon lowlands
	Hot (32°C) and humid (90%) all year
	Convectional rainfall each day (> 2,000 mm)
	No seasons
	Semi-arid climate in north-east Brazil
	Caused by complex pattern of four different air masses
	Severe droughts and high temperatures (38°C)
	Annual rainfall 278 mm
Relief and drainage	**Lowlands:** Found along the Amazon River Basin located in central and northern regions of Brazil
	Uplands: Found at the Brazilian highlands which cover 60% of the country. They are located in the south-east of Brazil. Guiana highlands are in north Brazil.

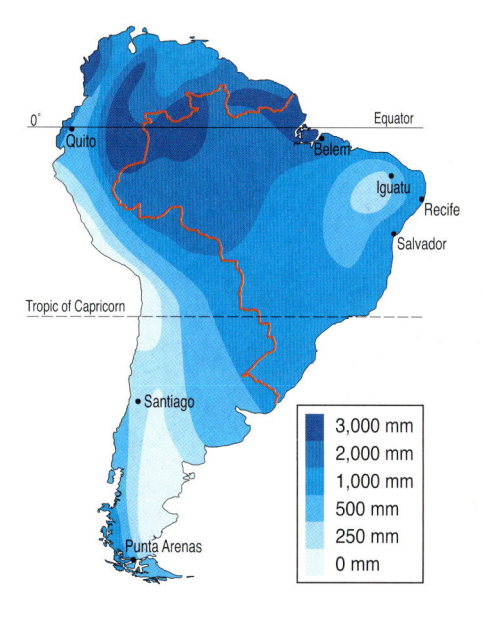

Fig. 4 A tropical climate covers most of Brazil.

Fig. 5 Relief regions of Brazil
- Brazilian plateau/highlands
- Central plains and Amazon lowlands
- Guiana highlands

Fig. 6 Drainage of Brazil

Fig. 7 Rainfall in Brazil

When in flood, the Amazon river system covers an area twice the size of Ireland to a depth of 10 m.

The distance between the equator and the Tropic of Capricorn is about 3,000 km.

401

CORE UNIT: REGIONAL GEOGRAPHY

Soils	**Terra rossa soil:** Dark, humus rich, red, fertile. Located in São Paulo state Used for coffee growing Fertile alluvial soils found in **Amazon Basin** **Latosol** formed under lowland tropical rainforest which becomes infertile laterite due to deforestation
Natural vegetation	**Tropical rainforest** covers 60% of country Most of forest is protected but illegal deforestation is occurring 90% of forest on the densely populated south-east coast has been cleared **Savanna/cerrado** found in central Brazil on uplands It is grassland containing trees and shrubs The region has a dry season from November to January and trees conserve water by having thick bark Intensive soya and corn farming threaten the plants of the Savanna **Thorny scrub/caatinga** Found in north-east Brazil, this vegetation is stunted thorny trees called the White Forest due to the pale colour of the trees. This region has extremely hot soil temperatures of 60°C so plants adapt by having roots that grow upwards to capture moisture.

Fig. 8 Tropical rainforest in Brazil

Fig. 9 A satellite image of Brazil

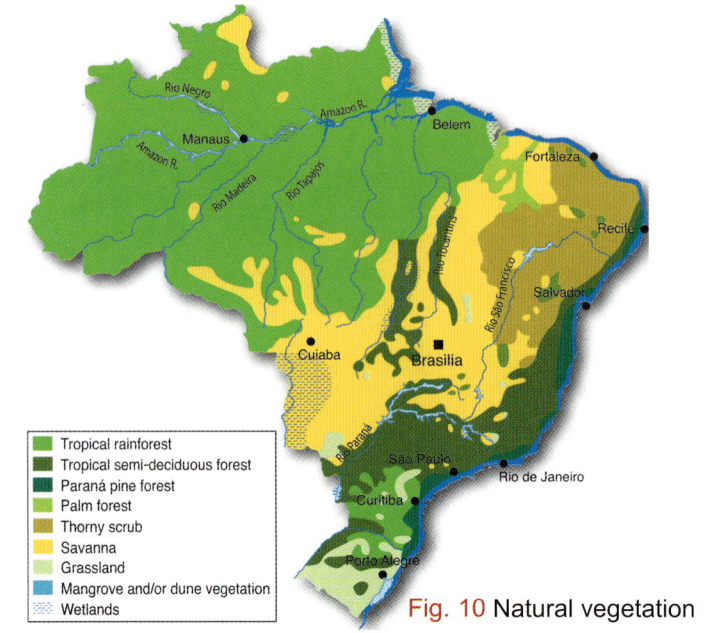

Fig. 10 Natural vegetation

402

CHAPTER 21: BRAZIL – A CONTINENTAL REGION

Primary activities in Brazil

Brazil has many resources. It is a major producer of agricultural, mineral and timber products. Its rank in the production and export of some primary products is shown in the table below. Physical and human factors influence the development of primary activities.

1st	It is the world leader for the production and export of **coffee, beef, sugar** and **oranges**.
2nd	It is ranked second in the world for the production of **soya beans**.
3rd	It is ranked third in the world for the production of **poultry**.
6th	It is ranked sixth in the world for **pork** and **milk** production.

Agriculture

Areas along the coast and in the Brazilian highlands are productive due to the climate, relief, drainage and soils. In the north-east of Brazil, poor soils and dry climate hinder farming. The cooler uplands are suitable for growing coffee beans. The tropical climate which covers most of the country encourages the growing of sugar-cane.

Agriculture and agribusiness is worth about 25% of Brazil's GDP; farmland occupies over 60 million hectares. The EU buys roughly 42% of Brazil's agricultural exports of coffee, cattle, sugar cane, crops and wood.

Brazilian farmers are encouraged to use modern techniques and the government invests millions in research and development of new farming methods and crops. In some areas sophisticated crop rotation is now being used involving a six-year cycle of corn, eucalyptus, soya and pasture to preserve soil fertility and keep yields high. This also reduces farmers' dependence on any one crop.

Cash crops
Cash crops are grown with the sole purpose of being sold to pay off international loans/debts.

Crop production

About 7% of the farmland in Brazil is arable. Corn, soya and sugar cane are the main crops. Brazil and Argentina account for half of the global production of **soya beans**. To improve production, Brazilian scientists have developed soya plants that can grow in the hot conditions of the savanna regions of Brazil. These areas were once difficult to farm because of the climate and acidic soils. Soya is an important cash crop for Brazil. Soya farms are highly mechanised and employ only one person for every 400 acres. An area approximately the size of Britain is under soya bean farms.

In the 1980s Brazil was in economic crisis so its government managed to bring the debt and economy under control using a series of **Structural Adjustment Programmes (SAPs)** introduced by the World Bank and IMF. SAPs encouraged the production and export of cash crops such as soya as a means of paying off Brazil's debt.

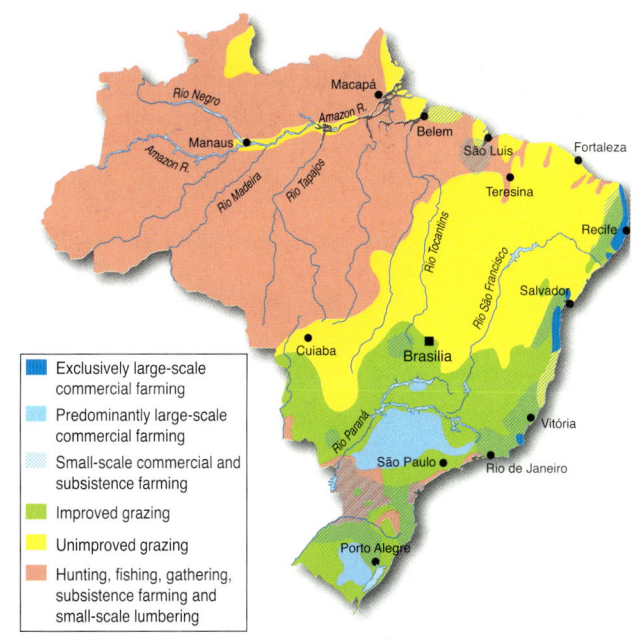

Fig. 11 Agricultural land use in Brazil

Core Unit: Regional Geography

The high soya bean production is partly due to the need for non-genetically modified soya in Europe and the demands for safe animal food by European farmers following BSE scares. However, soya bean production is linked to increased deforestation in the Amazon as land is cleared for soya plantations.

The tropical climate over much of Brazil means that wheat production is only successful in the southern states where temperatures are cooler. Because of this, Brazil imports a significant amount of wheat, e.g. 6.5 million tonnes in 2016.

Fig. 12 Harvesting soya beans in Brazil

Sugar cane production employs over 900,000 people. Fifty per cent of the sugar cane is used to produce a biofuel called **ethanol** which is used as an alternative to petrol. Ninety per cent of the sugar cane is grown in south-central Brazil, where the tropical climate encourages its growth.

Coffee production

- Brazil is the world's largest and most powerful producer of coffee. It grows one third of the world's supply of coffee beans. Per capita consumption of coffee is 4.2 kg per year.
- The coffee industry provides an income for more than 10 million people. Production in 2015 was worth over €8 billion to the economy.
- Production of instant coffee is controlled by several multinational companies, e.g. Nestlé, Kraft and Douwe Egbert. It is a labour-intensive industry as the delicate coffee plants require constant attention and the drying process is only partly automated in many regions.
- The major coffee-producing areas (see Fig. 13) are found along the south-east coast with Minas Gerais growing 46% of all Brazilian coffee. A wide variety of coffee beans are grown with the Arabica bean the most common. Like the wine-producing regions of France, each coffee-growing region in Brazil grows coffee beans with a distinctive flavour reflecting variations in soil, relief and rock type.

Fig. 13 Coffee-producing areas of Brazil

The influence of physical factors (soils, relief and climate) on the coffee industry in Brazil is very important as coffee plants require specific growing conditions. Brazil has all the conditions necessary for coffee plants to grow strongly.

Growing conditions required for coffee plants

1. A tropical climate with temperatures ranging from 15°C to 24°C.
2. Absence of frost.
3. Deep well-drained soils.
4. Humid conditions with plenty of rain (1,500 mm – 2,000 mm per year).
5. High altitude (over 700 m to reduce pest attack).

weblink Coffee prices

The rainfall, humidity and temperature conditions associated with the tropical climate encourage coffee growth. Coffee trees flower between September and November. Humidity is needed during this period to ensure coffee buds will develop properly. The buds turn into beans that growers will start harvesting in June. Any frost or dry conditions during the budding season can seriously damage the annual crop.

Large parts of Brazil have deep well-drained terra rossa soils and the Brazilian highlands provide the correct altitude for plants.

Fig. 14 Drying coffee beans in the sun is slow and labour intensive.

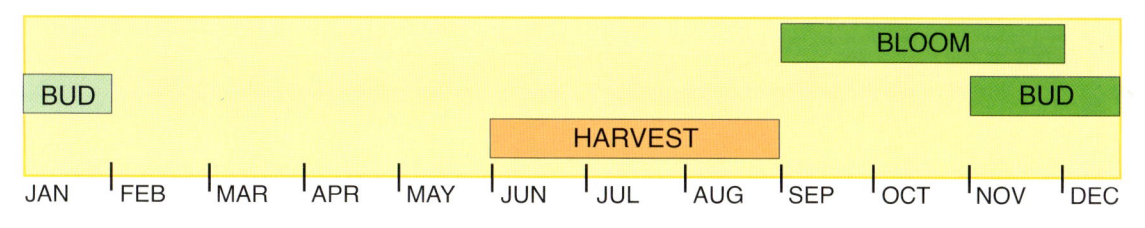

Fig. 15 Coffee crop calendar for Brazil

Cattle production

One thousand hectares and six hundred cows are needed to make a reasonable living. Meadows and pastures occupy about 19% of the country. Cattle production takes up the largest amount of farmland, causing forest clearance. Deforestation for beef production is controversial and has led to demands by environmentally-conscious consumers to have beef produced on land that has not been taken from rainforests.

	SEVEN QUICK FACTS ON CATTLE PRODUCTION IN BRAZIL
1.	Brazil has over 208 million cattle – more than one for each person in the country.
2.	Over 35 million cattle are slaughtered each year.
3.	Brazilians consume on average 38 kg of beef per person each year. Brazil is ranked third in beef consumption, behind Argentina and Australia.
4.	Brazil has one of the world's largest commercial cattle herds.
5.	Ten per cent of beef is exported and this figure is increasing.
6.	Brazil is the world's largest exporter of beef.
7.	Cattle production provides over 360,000 direct jobs. The labourers are mostly descended from migrants who came to Brazil from other parts of the world, especially Europe and Africa.

Forestry

- Forestry is an important economic activity in Brazil. If the rainforest of Brazil was a country, it would be the size of the ninth largest country in the world. The main trees harvested are tropical hardwoods, e.g. teak, mahogany. These are high-value hardwoods where a single tree may be worth €15,000.
- More than 85% of timber production from natural forests comes from the Amazon region, where over 3,000 logging companies are in operation.
- Just under 2% of the total forest cover is commercially planted forest of mainly pine and eucalyptus trees. These forests are concentrated in the south of the country where they are used in the cellulose and paper industry. The value of exported timber from Brazil is worth roughly €3 billion per year, with 33% of these exports going to EU member states. Other major markets include the USA and China. Within Brazil, the state of São Paulo is the largest consumer of timber products.
- In Amazonia legal timber is produced from native forest areas or from managed forests. However, it is estimated that as much as 80% of the total timber production in the Amazon is from illegally cleared forest.
- Recent reforms are aimed at improving this situation. New regulations on forest management have been driven by global concern over deforestation in the Amazon. However, it is difficult to enforce these reforms and much of the forest is still illegally burned and cleared by cattle ranchers and soya growers.

Fig. 16 Cattle ranching is one of several causes of deforestation in Brazil. Can you name two other causes?

Fig. 17 Aerial view of deforestation in the Amazon

Mining

- Brazil has deposits of minerals such as diamonds, iron ore, copper, gold, oil, bauxite, zinc, tin, nickel, platinum and uranium. Many of these are exported in their raw state.
- Brazil has 1.8% of world reserves of copper. The only producer of copper concentrate in Brazil is located in the state of Bahia, producing almost a quarter of a million tonnes of copper concentrate.
- Scrap copper is also processed along with almost half a million tonnes of copper imported from Chile and Peru.
- Copper is exported to Argentina (33%) and the United States (28%). This is worth over €84 million.

Fig. 18 Mining in Minas Gerais State, Brazil

Oil

- In 2007 two large oil and gas fields were discovered 250 km off the coast of Rio de Janerio. They are the Tupi field and the huge Sugar Loaf field.
- The Sugar Loaf field is the fourth largest oil field in the world, equivalent to 40% of all oil ever discovered in Brazil. It is a deep water field.
- These two fields make Brazil the tenth largest producer of oil in the world.
- The country now has reserves of over 700 million barrels and is one of the biggest oil suppliers in South America.
- These will reduce the country's reliance on imported crude oil and improve the country's balance of payments. Brazil currently produces around 80 million barrels of crude oil each year, of which 26 million barrels are exported. When the price of oil is €35 a barrel, then Brazil's oil exports earn almost €1 billion a year.

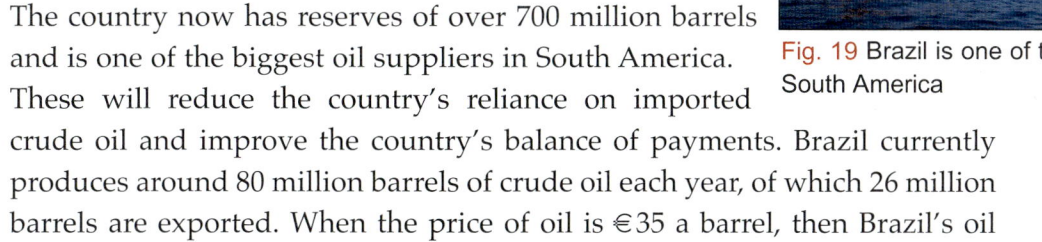

Fig. 19 Brazil is one of the biggest oil suppliers in South America

Secondary activities in Brazil

Brazil is a **Newly Industrialised Country** (**NIC**). This means that its economy is undergoing rapid industrialisation, increased **foreign direct investment (FDI)** and increased global trade. Today, Brazil is part of the **BRIC trading bloc** of Brazil, Russia, India and China. Manufacturing is a growth industry in Brazil. The percentage employed in the manufacturing industry in Brazil is increasing by almost 3% per year, especially in the south-eastern state of São Paulo.

The main industrial products ranked by the value of sales are diesel oil, processed iron ore and cars. The south-east region produces over €384 billion worth of manufactured products each year, 60.7% of total sales. Other manufactured products include machinery, processed food, electronic equipment and textiles. Brazil is also the world's third largest producer of commercial aircraft.

Modern manufacturing in Brazil is the result of human factors, mainly government policies, that have combined with its physical factors such as resources, soils and climate.

CORE UNIT: REGIONAL GEOGRAPHY

Location of industry in Brazil

The industrialised economic hub of Brazil is found along the south-east coast around the cities of Rio de Janeiro, São Paulo and Belo Horizonte. Many multinational companies have located their head offices in these cities. These cities each contain a labour force, ports and raw materials and they provide a large market. The most successful manufacturing industries are cars, steel, petrochemicals, engineering and cement. Just over 40% of the country's population (79 million) is concentrated in the south-east of Brazil. The area is rich in minerals and its manufacturing industries are the most advanced in the country.

Fig. 20 São Paulo is an important business centre.

Physical factors affecting location of manufacturing in Brazil

Most manufacturing is located in the south-eastern states of Brazil because of a combination of physical factors listed below.

1. **Raw materials** such as limestone and iron ore are found nearby in the Minas Gerais region. In addition, most ironworks and steelworks are here.
2. **Oil and gas fields** have been discovered and exploited offshore from Rio de Janeiro.
3. The south-east coastline has many **sheltered deep water harbours** which are now used for the import and export of raw materials and finished goods by ship.
4. Brazil has huge supplies of **cheap hydroelectric power (HEP)**, 90% of which is produced in the Amazon Basin. Nearly €69 billion has been spent on several hundred power projects, most under the *Avança Brasil* scheme (see page 409). This has encouraged the location of energy intensive steel industries close to their raw materials in the south east.

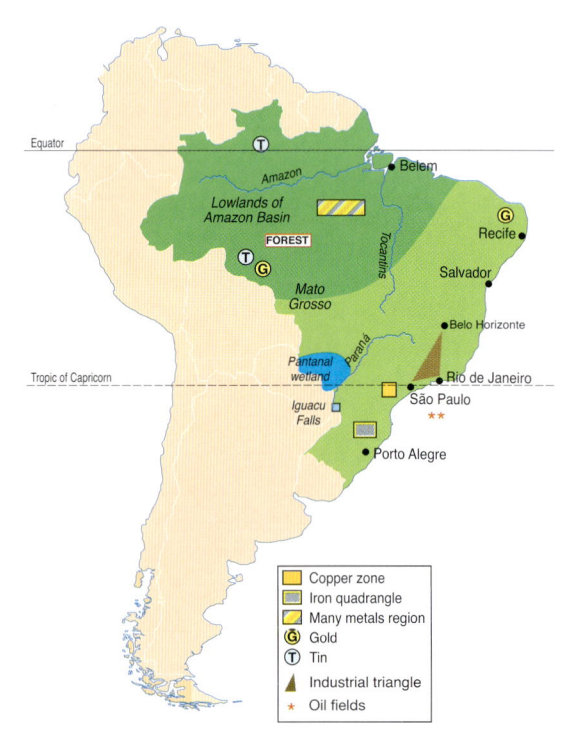

Fig. 21 The location of raw materials and natural resources in Brazil.

408

Human factors leading to the development of industry in Brazil

Government policy

Government policy has been responsible for the rapid growth of this Newly Industrialised Country (NIC). Industrial development grew rapidly after the Second World War when shortages of imported goods forced Brazil to consider making its own. A huge industrial investment programme for self-sufficiency, the **Import Substitution Industrialisation scheme (ISI)**, was established using World Bank loans. Many large multinational companies, e.g. Shell and Ford Motors, set up factories in the country.

As well as being self-sufficient, the government also wanted to protect its manufacturers from outside competition. **Tariffs** and **bans** were placed on imported products. This made foreign goods too expensive to buy and there was little trade with other countries.

Several government policies/programmes have been implemented since the 1970s to further develop Brazil's economy and open up manufacturing industries to the world. These are:

(i) The **National Ethanol Programme**
(ii) The formation of **Mercosur**
(iii) *Avança Brasil* **(Advance Brazil)**

These have had a major impact on manufacturing in Brazil and have supported the economy.

(i) The National Ethanol Programme

In the 1970s economic problems began to appear due to Brazil's dependence on imported oil. When the **oil crisis** of 1973 triggered a huge rise in worldwide oil prices, Brazil could not afford to pay for the oil it needed to import. In order to reduce oil imports a government scheme called the **National Ethanol Programme** was launched. Under this scheme cars using fossil fuels were replaced with cars that used ethanol (a **biofuel**) produced from sugar cane. Brazilian car manufacturers developed cars that could run on a mix of ethanol and petrol or on ethanol alone. This reduced petroleum imports.

(ii) Formation of Mercosur

In 1991 the Southern Common market, Mercosur, was established. This allowed free trade between South American countries and provided a large market for Brazilian manufactured goods. Trade then began to increase with other South American countries. Soon after, the government introduced a new currency called the *Real* (pronounced *ray-al*) to encourage economic growth.

(iii) *Avança Brasil* (Advance Brazil)

The Brazilian government has a plan called *Avança Brasil* 2000–2020 (Advance Brazil). This plan, costing €38 billion, is designed to encourage economic growth. It plans to cover much of the Amazon rainforest with 10,000 km of highways, hydroelectric dams, power lines, mines, gas and oilfields, canals, ports, logging concessions and other industrial developments.

weblink
News from Brazil

CORE UNIT: REGIONAL GEOGRAPHY

CHAPTER 21
Case Study 1

Car manufacturing in Brazil

1. Car manufacturing is a growth industry in Brazil. In 2016 car sales increased by 14% and over 3 million new cars were sold. Brazil has the fifth largest car market in the world. There are 13 domestic Brazilian car manufacturers as well as North American and European multinational companies such as Ford Motors, Volkswagen, Fiat and General Motors to supply demand. The car manufacturing industry is located in the south-east of Brazil in the cities of São Paulo, Rio de Janeiro, Belo Horizonte, Curitiba and Porto Alegre.

2. The Brazilian car manufacturing industry employs over 130,000 people. Brazilian car engineers are world leaders in the design of small cars. Wealthy business entrepreneurs see the car industry as a profitable opportunity.

3. The majority of cars in Brazil run on flex fuel (E85), a combination of petrol and ethanol. The manufacture of electric cars is not a profitable business because (a) Brazil has its own oil reserves and (b) its sugar plantations which provide the raw material for ethanol have a strong political lobby. Diesel fuel is not commonly used in passenger cars in Brazil, although buses and trucks rely on this fuel.

Fig. 22 Cars are important to Brazil's prosperity.

Advantages that Brazil has for car manufacturing

1. There is a pool of skilled and cheap labour.

2. The Brazilian government has encouraged car manufacturing by removing taxes on new cars. In a country where the cost of running a car is 37% higher than elsewhere in South America, this measure has been successful in encouraging sales. Local and regional governments support the development of manufacturing plants by paying up to 50% of their set-up costs. This attracts foreign multinational companies.

3. There is plenty of electricity for the factories from gas, nuclear and hydroelectric power stations.

4. It has low levels of car ownership (1 car for every 6.5 people) compared to North America (1 car per 2 people). This means the potential new car sales market in this NIC is much larger than in other countries where car ownership is more common. As Brazil develops, its population is getting wealthier and more people have spare income that they can use to buy a car.

5. Due to the **multiplier effect**, there are many component factories in the cities that make parts like tyres, brake pads and material for car seats. This reduces production costs.
6. The south-eastern states are close to the ports of Rio de Janeiro and Santos for exporting cars to other countries.

> The **multiplier effect** refers to how an increase in one economic activity (e.g. car manufacturing) can cause an increase in other related economic activities (e.g. tyre manufacturing).

Such is the attraction of south-east Brazil for car manufacturing that General Motors has invested €22 billion in its Brazilian plants and Ford Motors is investing €2.75 billion creating 1,000 new jobs in the industry. Fiat has already invested €2.1 billion in its existing huge factory in Betim near Belo Horizonte, making it Fiat's largest global assembly plant.

Despite increases in car ownership, Brazil's transportation infrastructure across its 26 states is one of the worst in the world. The Brazilian government intends to spend over €13.6 billion on improving the road infrastructure plus roughly the same amount on public transportation (rail, metro and bus). These factors will encourage continued growth in the manufacture of passenger cars and trucks.

Fig. 23 Location of car manufacturing plants in south-east Brazil

Fig. 24 Car assembly line

Tertiary activities in Brazil

Service industries are a growth sector in Brazil due to improvements in tourism, transport, healthcare and education. The services sector employs the majority of workers in Brazil.

Transport in Brazil

The transport infrastructure in Brazil is underdeveloped and the scale of improvements required is an economic burden on the country. The quality of transport facilities is uneven. Cities generally have better services than rural areas.

Physical factors such as the size of the country, extensive areas of forest and wetland and the isolation of urban areas from each other make the provision of an efficient transport network costly and difficult.

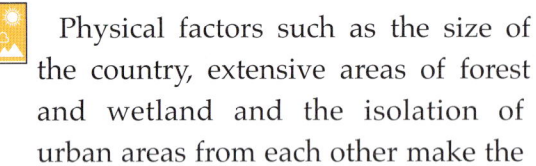

Fig. 25 Road is the main transport method in Brazil.

Human factors such as government policy have led to improvements in infrastructure. The government plans to improve transport services by privatising rail lines, modernising ports, introducing toll roads and decentralising road maintenance to local governments.

Roads

- Road is the main method of transport in Brazil.
- Road costs are huge due to large distances and poor road surfaces that cause increased maintenance and fuel costs. Only 10% of Brazil's road network is paved, and even these are poorly maintained.
- The best roads are the privately-operated main toll roads, e.g. the main São Paulo-Rio de Janeiro motorway.
- The government aims to invest one per cent of GDP in transport infrastructure. The **Trans Amazon Highway** is a major road project that is opening up the Amazon Basin to further development. Over 10,000 km of roads across the interior to neighbouring countries in the west are under construction.

Rail

- Railways remain underused and account for only 25% of total freight movement. Only the lines operated by iron ore exporters are used to their full capacity.
- The country's 30,000-km rail network has grown by 20% since it was privatised and upgraded in the late 1990s but the most efficient rail routes are limited to a few well-developed tourist routes. A high-speed (350 km/h) bullet train connecting São Paulo and Rio de Janeiro is planned but has faced many setbacks and delays. It aims to carry 18 million passengers per year.
- Most cities have metros and São Paulo has one of the most advanced public transport systems in the world.

Water

- Brazil's great potential for river transport remains largely unexploited. Waterways currently account for only 13% of haulage traffic, even though Brazil has a 48,000-km network of navigable rivers.
- Ports such as the one at Santos near São Paulo, which handles around one quarter of the country's foreign trade, have undergone some modernisation over the past 15 years.
- Ports remain congested and expensive, especially at harvest times when trucks laden with grain arrive for loading. This raises transport costs.

Fig. 26 The port of Santos, Brazil

Air

The country's main international airports are in São Paulo, Brasilia and Rio de Janeiro. These are also congested. Congestion is an important issue that has been reduced in order to cope with increased traffic during the World Cup (2014) and the Olympic Games (2016).

Tourism in Brazil

Tourism is a growth industry in Brazil. It is becoming an important part of the Brazilian economy by providing jobs. More than eight million people are employed in tourism and two million of these are directly employed in the sector. Tourism income is worth €60 billion per year to the economy and tourism accounts for 7.1% of Brazilian economic activity. It is an important **invisible export**.

Overall domestic tourists account for 11% of tourism-related spending in Brazil. Most domestic tourists are from São Paulo. They account for 27.8% of domestic tourism expenditure. This reflects the higher income levels of people in São Paulo which is an economic core region of Brazil.

weblink
Brazil – tourist information

Tourism attractions in Brazil

Brazil has natural and man-made attractions.

- **Rio de Janeiro has many iconic sights:** the Pão de Açúcar (Sugar Loaf Mountain), with its cable car; the Corcovado, with its statue of Jesus Christ the Redeemer; Copacabana and Ipanema Beach with their mosaic sidewalks.
- **Ecotourism** is developed in the Amazon Valley cities such as Belém and Manaus, the Iguaçu Falls in the south and the wetlands of the Pantanal located in the western central region.
- Brazil is famous for its **carnival**, which usually takes place in February. The carnivals in Rio de Janeiro, Salvador and Olinda are the most famous.
- **São Paulo** is also a major city destination attracting 1.7 million foreign tourists throughout the year.

CORE UNIT: REGIONAL GEOGRAPHY

Fig. 27 Tourist attractions in Brazil include the cable car at Pão de Açúcar, Rio de Janeiro and the Iguaçu Falls.

One million extra tourists visited Brazil during the 2014 World Cup although only 600,000 were expected.

Despite being such a large country with so many attractions, international tourism to Brazil is underdeveloped. Only about 6 million tourists visit Brazil each year. This is a tiny amount compared to Spain's 52 million tourists per year. Foreign tourists are economically important, spending €2.2 billion a year in the country. Its reputation as a tourist destination was boosted by hosting international sporting events such as the World Cup (2014) and the Olympic Games in 2016. Brazil aims to attract 14.1 million visitors by 2024.

Reasons for the underdevelopment of Brazilian tourism

1. **Crime:** Brazil is seen as a dangerous destination due to illegal drug business, kidnappings and crime – all of which have been widely covered by the international media.
2. **Misleading advertising:** During the 1970s and 1980s the Brazilian government's international tourism brochures showed scantily-clad women by the beach or dancing during carnival. This promoted illegal sex tourism and discouraged families and older travellers from visiting the country.
3. **Lack of tourism infrastructure:** The poor road and rail network combined with badly-trained workers in the catering industry has discouraged all but the hardiest tourists, e.g. backpackers, who don't mind tough conditions.

Promoting tourism in Brazil

The Brazilian government launched its *Plano Aquarela* 2020 (**Plan Watercolour 2020**). This international campaign aims to double the number of foreign visitors by 2020. The plan promotes five tourism sectors: **sun and beach holidays; ecotourism; sports; culture and business**; and **event holidays**. Hosting major sporting events such as the 2014 World Cup and the 2016 Olympic Games was part of its strategy to promote tourism in Brazil. Such events have led to improved road and rail infrastructure under the *Avança Brasil* scheme and an increase in well-trained staff in hotels, restaurants and the main tourist destinations.

CHAPTER 21: BRAZIL – A CONTINENTAL REGION

21.2 Population dynamics: Density, distribution and culture

Population characteristics

Brazil is the largest country in South America. It has a population of about 204 million people and is the fifth most populous country in the world. Brazil's fertility rate is 1.7 births per female which is lower than that of the USA. Its death rate is 6.35 per 1,000. Brazil is a young country with 62% of its population under 29 years of age.

The population increased rapidly between 1940 and 1970 as Brazil passed through Stage 2 and into Stage 3 of the **Population Cycle**. This population increase was due to a decline in the mortality rate because of better nutrition and healthcare. In the 1940s the annual population growth rate was 2.4%, rising to 3% in the 1950s.

Since the 1970s population growth has decreased significantly. This was due to a drop in birth rates caused by improved wealth, healthcare and literacy as economic modernisation and urbanisation occurred. From 1960 to today, life expectancy throughout Brazil rose from 51 years to 78.6 years for women and 71.3 for men. In the past many people were lucky to live to 44 years.

Changes in the shape of the population pyramids in Fig. 28 below show this effect. Today the population growth rate is only 1.2% per year. This is just slightly faster than the world average.

Activity

Describe three changes in the shape of the population pyramids below between 1975 and 2050. State one reason for each of the changes you see.

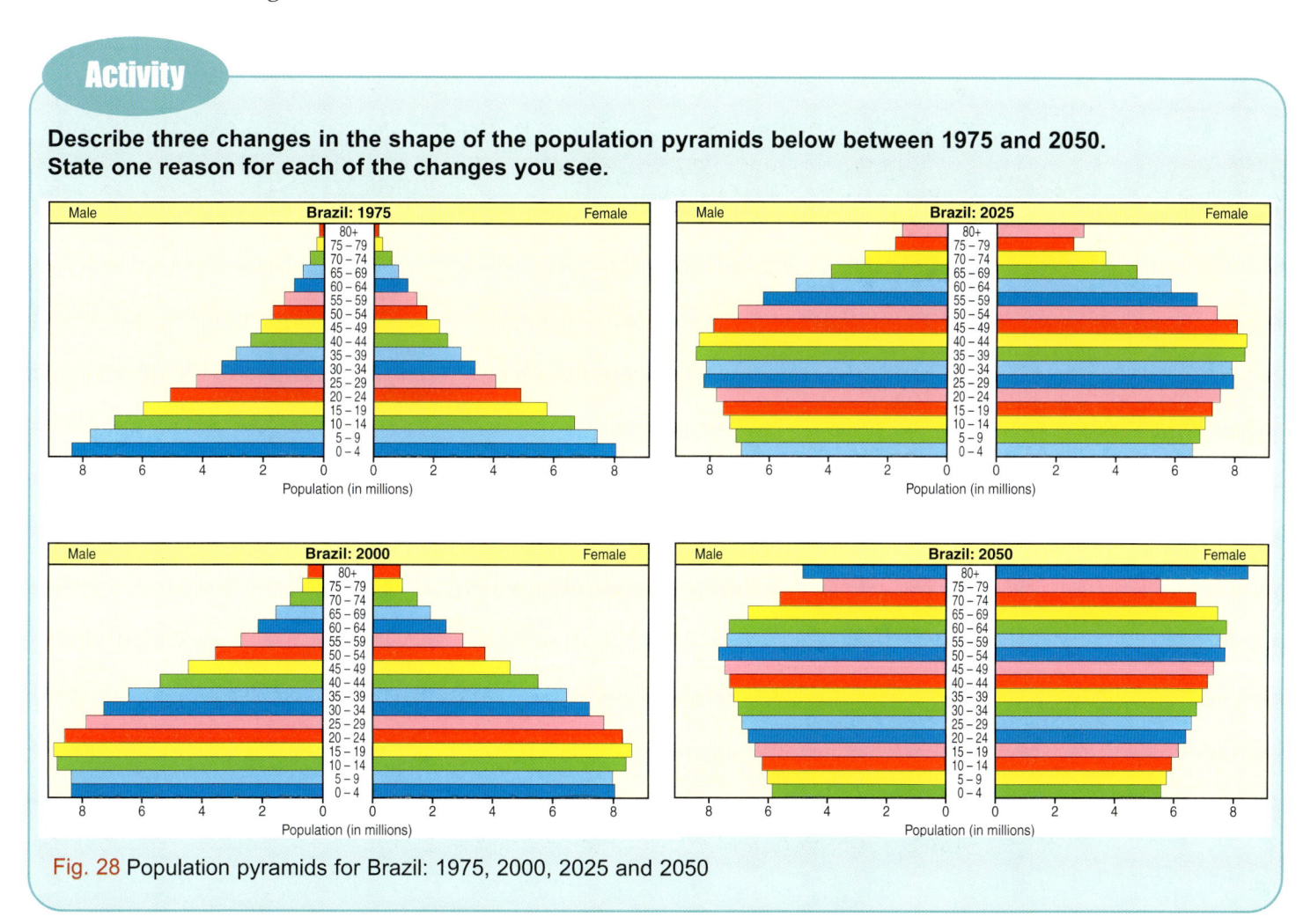

Fig. 28 Population pyramids for Brazil: 1975, 2000, 2025 and 2050

415

CORE UNIT: REGIONAL GEOGRAPHY

Population density and distribution

Brazil's low average population density of 22.3 people per km² is due to the country's large size. Patterns of internal migration have had a major impact on the distribution of the population. In Brazil, 67% of the population live on or near the Atlantic coast of the south-eastern and north-eastern states, as these were the areas which were first colonised. They are accessible, cooler and more urbanised.

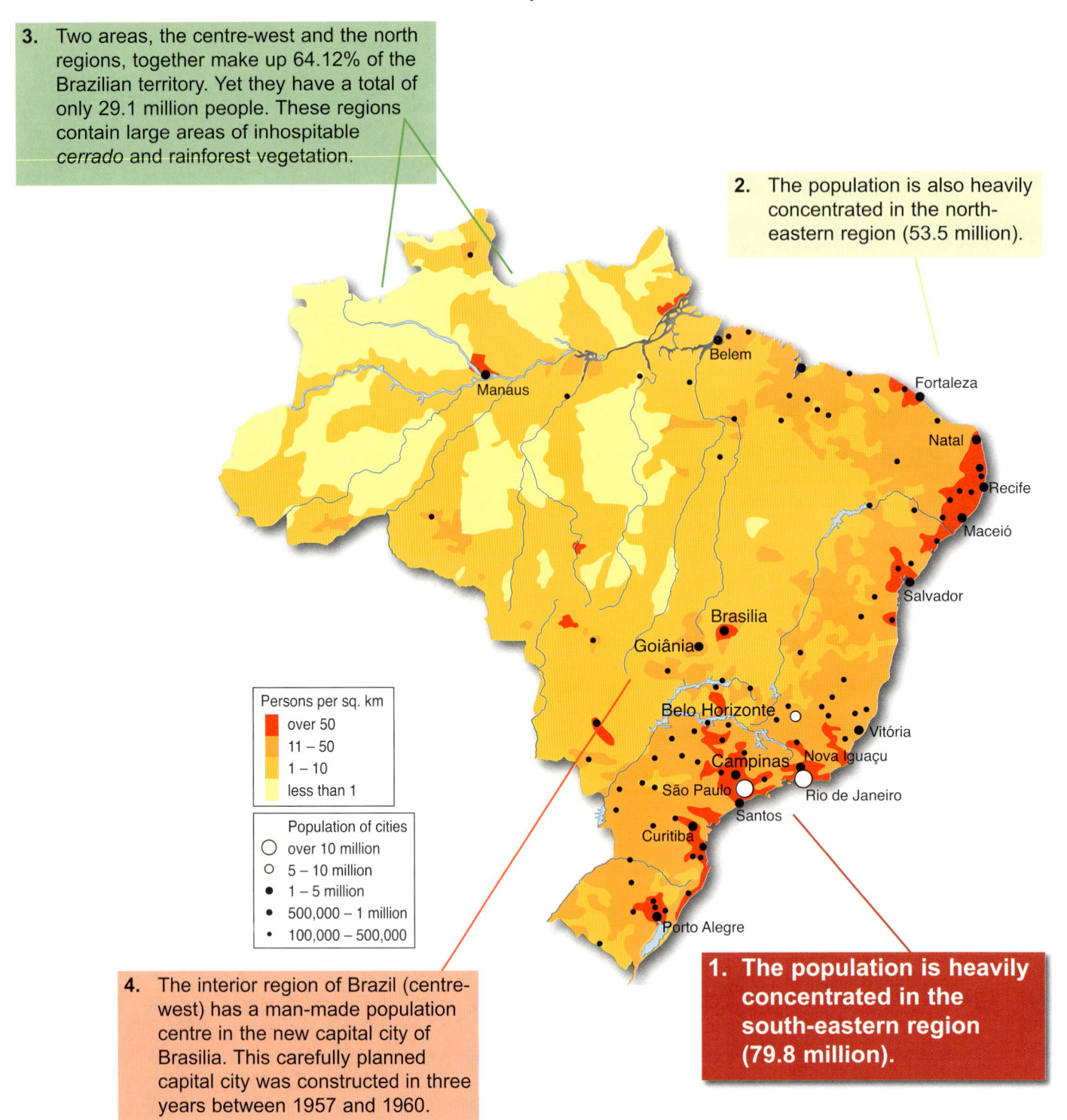

3. Two areas, the centre-west and the north regions, together make up 64.12% of the Brazilian territory. Yet they have a total of only 29.1 million people. These regions contain large areas of inhospitable *cerrado* and rainforest vegetation.

2. The population is also heavily concentrated in the north-eastern region (53.5 million).

Persons per sq. km
- over 50
- 11 – 50
- 1 – 10
- less than 1

Population of cities
- over 10 million
- 5 – 10 million
- 1 – 5 million
- 500,000 – 1 million
- 100,000 – 500,000

4. The interior region of Brazil (centre-west) has a man-made population centre in the new capital city of Brasilia. This carefully planned capital city was constructed in three years between 1957 and 1960.

1. The population is heavily concentrated in the south-eastern region (79.8 million).

Fig. 29 Population density in Brazil

Migration in Brazil

The population density and distribution is a direct result of internal and international migration. As much as 40% of its population has migrated at some point in their lives. The huge scale of **rural to urban migration** has caused rapid urban growth and led to the existence of shanty towns called *favelas* in most major cities. Government sponsored **urban–rural resettlement programmes** have also led to new settlements in the Brazilian interior.

Impact of international migration

International migration to Brazil was due to **colonialism** by the Portuguese who first colonised Brazil in the 15th century. Over the next 400 years the Portuguese settlers established a plantation system of agriculture, producing sugar cane and coffee. They used imported slave labour. These slaves were forced migrants taken from west Africa to the city of Salvador in north-east Brazil which was the largest slave port in the world at the time. African slave descendents now form an important part of Brazil's population and culture in the north-east region.

European migrant plantation owners exported coffee, gold, sugar and timber using slave labour. The coffee trade caused rapid economic growth in the state of Minas Gerais and attracted many more international migrants from Germany and Italy. These European migrants became very wealthy business people who then influenced the political system in the country. A social system of rich, powerful, colonial landowners/politicians and a poor powerless working society developed.

Tensions caused by this extremely unequal society eventually led to important social and economic changes in Brazil over the last 200 years. Examples of such change include:
1. Declaring independence from Portugal in 1882.
2. The abolition of slavery in 1888.
3. The construction of a new capital city, Brasilia, in the 1960s in order to reduce the influence of the former colonial capital, Rio de Janeiro, and to develop the Amazon region.

> **weblink**
> Brazil - news on economy

The impact of internal migration on population distribution

The towns established by Portuguese settlers, e.g. Rio de Janeiro and São Paulo, are today rapidly growing **mega-cities**. These cities have grown due to unique migration patterns within Brazil and population growth.

1. **Voluntary rural to urban migration**
   - Farmers are amongst the poorest people in Brazil. Almost 43% of the nation's poorest people are found in the agricultural sector. Small farmers, especially those from the north-east, who scarcely make a living from the land, see moving to the cities as a way to escape their desperate poverty. Therefore, there is continued migration of farmers from the land to the cities.

- North-east Brazil is one of the poorest regions in the country with 32% of all poor Brazilians concentrated in this one area. Much of the region is dry *cerrado* – vegetation that is hard to cultivate. People in this region have migrated from the countryside to the main city of Belem but the majority of poor rural dwellers move to the richer south-eastern cities of Salvador, Rio and São Paulo. There they find unskilled work in manufacturing or services and live in *favela* settlements.
- The south-east of Brazil is an economic core region. Per capita GDP in the south-east is 300% greater than that of the north-east. There are more opportunities for skilled and unskilled workers. The movement of millions of rural and urban poor from all areas of Brazil to the cities of Rio de Janeiro and São Paulo in the south-east has led to rapid urban growth and the development of *favelas* in these cities.

2. Organised urban to rural migration

- For many decades the Brazilian government encouraged the settlement of the interior of Brazil, focusing on the new capital city of Brasilia. It was intended to be a gateway to the riches of the Brazilian interior. These government-sponsored settlement programmes encouraged hundreds of thousands of poor urban families to move from the city slums to farmland in central Brazil.
- Land was sold cheaply (a few euros per hectare) or even given away free. Other poor workers moved to the interior because construction workers were required to build Brasilia. These workers lived in temporary camps about 30 km away on the outskirts of the newly developing city. Upon completion of Brasilia it was presumed these workers would return to their home area but this never occurred. Many continued to live in the camps which quickly became *favelas*. The people in them are called the 'anti-Brasilias'.
- Urban to rural migration has had an impact on the population distribution in Brazil. In some regions, such as the southern state of Bahia, 28% of people in the region are there because of the government settlement programme. However, these people soon found they had swapped one type of poverty for another as once the forest was cleared for farming, the latosol soil quickly became infertile and unproductive.

Fig. 30 Brasilia was built to encourage development and settlement in the Amazon region.

Cultural regions in Brazil

Brazil is a racially mixed country but also a remarkably integrated society. Its population shows the results of large-scale historic and modern immigrations and integrations. Any divisions between people tend to be socio-economic rather than racial.

Fig. 31 Brazil has a mix of population groups.

Ethnic groups

Most Brazilians descend from five population groups:

1. Native Americans (Amerindians) living mainly in the north-west border regions and remote parts of the Amazon Basin, e.g. the Yanomami. Before colonisation there were an estimated six million **Amerindians**. Today only a few hundred thousand pure-blooded Amerindians remain.
2. The Portuguese, whose ancestors colonised Brazil in the 1500s, are found mostly in the south-eastern regions.
3. Black Africans, whose ancestors were brought over to Brazil as slaves, are concentrated in the north-east around Salvador.
4. European immigrants who came to Brazil in the 1800s and in the first half of the 20th century from various parts of western, central and eastern Europe.
5. The Japanese who first came to Brazil from the early 1900s to the 1940s. Most live in São Paulo State or the south of the country. (In fact Brazil contains the largest number of people of Japanese ancestry outside of Japan.)

Considerable intermarriage between these groups has taken place creating a multi-racial society.

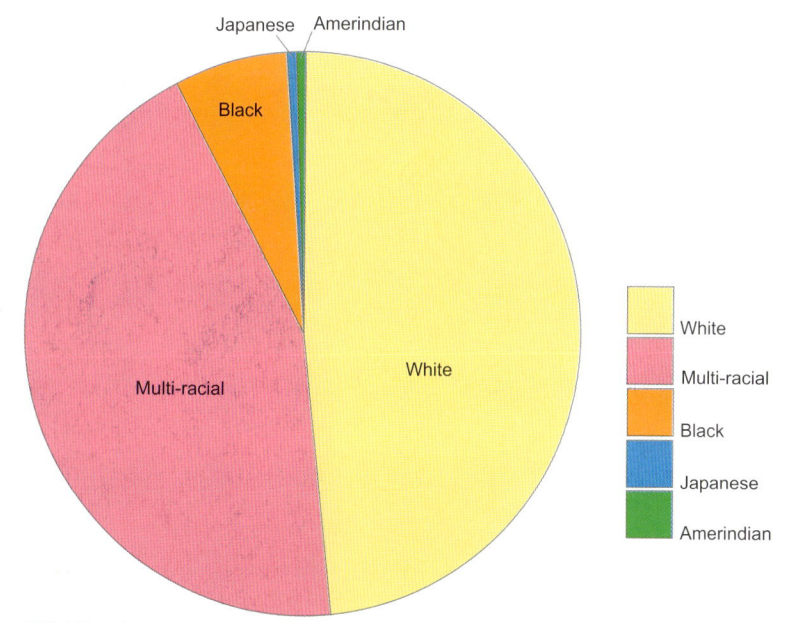

Fig. 32 Pie chart showing the breakdown of population in terms of origin

CORE UNIT: REGIONAL GEOGRAPHY

Language, religion and festivals

An important unifying factor in Brazil is the Portuguese language which has been adopted by all Brazilians. It is the official and most widely spoken language in the country. Brazilian Portuguese is strongly influenced by Amerindian and other immigrant languages. Spanish is also spoken in the border areas and in schools. Other languages include German, Italian, Japanese, English and Amerindian languages.

There are 163 different indigenous languages. In the east and north-east regions of Brazil, most native Indian languages have been lost due to prejudice and official policy. This is a similar situation to the fate of the Irish language during the Plantations. Today, according to the Brazilian constitution, teaching in indigenous Amerindian areas must be bilingual in order to maintain the cultural identity of the native peoples.

The presence of Roman Catholicism is another unifying force. Brazil has the largest Roman Catholic population in the world. More than 73.8% of the population is Roman Catholic. There is also a significant Protestant minority and a number of African religions. In Salvador, for example, the African Candomblé religion is common reflecting the African origin of its inhabitants.

Two religious festivals are important in Brazilian culture. The **Mardi Gras** carnival at the beginning of Lent takes place throughout the country. In Salvador, a mid-August festival takes place called the *Boa Morte* (Good Death) festival. This festival combines elements of Catholicism (the Feast of the Assumption of the Virgin Mary) and the Candomblé worship of female spirits.

Fig. 33 Brazilian children learn Portuguese and Spanish in school.

Fig. 34 Mardi Gras is an important festival for Brazilians.

The Amerindian tribes – A cultural group in Brazil

It is estimated that there are 206 **indigenous/native** tribes in Brazil amounting to 896,000 people. Sixty per cent of all Amerindian tribes are concentrated in the Amazon Basin. They make up small communities that are the remains of once larger native (indigenous) populations. There are still very few Amerindians living in such a large area of land, a fact used against them by those who think that they are standing in the way of development.

Brazil is believed to have the largest number of un-contacted people in the world. Today the National Indian Foundation reports the existence of 67 different un-contacted tribes. Before colonisation by Portuguese settlers there were over six million Amerindians. Since then their numbers have decreased dramatically due to disease, slavery and massacre, invasion of their territory, deportation and government assimilation schemes.

The best known Amazonian Indians are the Yanomami. The Yanomami depend on the forest for their livelihood. They practice a method of farming called **shifting cultivation** which involves the use of slash and burn to clear a small area of the forest in which to live. They are quite nomadic, frequently moving to avoid overusing the land. They grow bananas, gather fruit, hunt animals and fish.

Recognition of their native Amerindian lands is necessary for the survival of the Amazonian Indians but it does not protect them from continuous threat and conflict. Miners, mineral prospectors, loggers and landowners continue their legal and illegal onslaught into interior lands to exploit valuable rainforest resources ranging from wood to gold, copper to diamonds.

However, in the large areas which they occupy, the Amerindians have preserved an amazing culture in terms of biodiversity and knowledge that has an unknown market value. Brazilian indigenous people have made enormous contributions to the world's medicine with their knowledge of medicinal plants.

Fig. 35 Amazonian river settlement

Fig. 36 Mining is a cause of deforestation in Brazil.

Fig. 37 Amazonian Indians

weblink
The lost tribes of the Amazon

21.3 City region in Brazil

The cities and towns of Brazil have the greatest population density. Almost 80% of Brazilians live in urban areas. Cities are growing quickly for several reasons: People have large families, life expectancy is rising (since 1960 life expectancy has risen steadily; today it is 73 years for men and 78 years for women), and rural to urban migration is causing urban growth. The greatest density of population is in São Paulo, Rio de Janeiro and Salvador.

The gap between the rich and poor in Brazil is clearly seen in the cities. Many cities have squatter settlements known as *favelas*. These areas of irregular and poor-quality housing are often crowded onto hillsides and as a result, *favelas* suffer from frequent landslides during heavy rain. Most *favelas* are inaccessible to traffic due to their narrow streets. The explosion in *favela* growth dates from the 1940s when the government's industrialisation programme attracted hundreds of thousands of migrants into the cities. It is estimated that there are more than 3,500 *favelas* in Brazil. Most of these are found in three cities: Rio de Janeiro, São Paulo and Recife.

In recent decades *favelas* have been troubled by drug-related crime and gang warfare. Police have little or no control in many *favelas*. These problems have led to government schemes to renew the *favelas*.

> **weblink**
> Rio de Janeiro – video
> Favela violence – news clip

Fig. 38 There are few services inside a *favela*.

Fig. 39 A *favela* in Rio de Janeiro

CHAPTER 21: BRAZIL – A CONTINENTAL REGION

Urban growth of São Paulo

Case Study 3

São Paulo began as a missionary centre on fertile land beside the River Tietê.

Today, São Paulo is the largest city in South America with a population of over 17 million. It is a densely populated (7,216 people per km²) **agglomeration** – a city made up of smaller urban centres. São Paulo is made up of 39 urban areas that have grown and merged to make one huge city. The city is over 80 km wide and 40 km long.

There are jobs and better health and education services available in the city; these act as pull factors attracting migrants. São Paulo is now the most ethnically diverse city in the country.

1. São Paulo is the business centre of South America. Its wealth was originally based on the coffee industry. It rapidly industrialised in the 20th century and today it is a global services centre. Its huge market is a magnet for multinational corporations. Economic growth has increased employment and wages.

Fig. 40 In São Paulo *favelas* exist side-by-side with the gleaming skyscrapers of the business district.

2. People move to São Paulo's *favelas* to escape the poverty-stricken interior of the country or the drought-ridden north-east of Brazil where unreliable rains and government policies have left many people struggling to cope on poor land (push factors). Over 20% of people in São Paulo are from the north-east of Brazil.

3. Because of rural to urban migration São Paulo has the greatest number of *favela* residents of any city in Brazil. The largest *favela* settlement in the city is Heliópolis.

4. There are many urban problems in São Paulo. These include:
   - **Traffic congestion**
   - **Air and water pollution**
   - **Growth of *favelas* and overcrowding**
   - **Lack of formal housing**
   - **Lack of basic water, sewerage and electricity supplies in favelas.**

The most serious of these urban problems in São Paulo are traffic congestion, the growth of *favelas* and the resulting air and water pollution.

Traffic causes 90% of São Paulo's air pollution, leading to respiratory problems in residents. São Paulo's pollution levels are worsened by poor infrastructure design, old polluting vehicles and petrol prices that are among the lowest in the world (encouraging car ownership). Government initiatives to reduce traffic and congestion in São Paulo include an orbital motorway to reduce city traffic by 20%, additional metro lines and improvements to the rail system. These are designed to encourage people to use public transport and to remove cars from the densely populated city centre areas.

In 2015 a major ring road was completed. This 'Mario Corvas Beltway' takes heavy traffic bound for the port of Santos away from the city centre.

Fig. 41 *Favelas* are notorious fire hazards – flames spread quickly due to cramped conditions and the use of poor building materials to construct the makeshift houses.

5. **Pollution:** The local government introduced an air pollution control programme, whereby motorists are required to leave their vehicles at home one day a week. This system has reduced the volume of cars in the city and cut daily emissions of carbon monoxide by at least 550 tonnes. However, rich motorists get around this by owning more than one car. The super rich use helicopters to get around; São Paulo has the highest use of commuter helicopters in the world. Most tall buildings in the central business district have helipads.

6. ***Favelas*:** São Paulo has tackled the *favela* problem in two ways. Up until the 1990s the government response was complete neglect. When ignoring the problem did not resolve it, the local government evicted people, demolished the *favelas* and constructed buildings on the newly vacant land. Meanwhile, the displaced residents were given modest relocation payments and encouraged to move 'somewhere farther out', usually onto low-lying or poor quality public land. This approach only moved the *favelas* further out to the suburbs.

Since the 1990s the local government introduced a slum demolition-and-redevelopment programme nicknamed **Cingapura** (the Portuguese pronunciation of Singapore). Under Cingapura, the municipality of São Paulo cleared out all the *favelas* built beside rivers, railway lines and highways. They then built footpaths and brightly painted multi-storey housing blocks, each with its own gated entryway. These apartments have running water, sewerage and electricity.

But these high-rises are unpopular with residents who prefer to renovate their informally built homes in the *favelas*. So the local government now improves their existing homes. The streets are paved and street lighting is installed. This combines an improved sense of community with better housing and social services.

CHAPTER 21: BRAZIL – A CONTINENTAL REGION

Chapter Revision Questions

1. Using an atlas and/or maps from this textbook, draw an outline map of Brazil. On it mark the following: One named neighbouring country; the cities of Curitiba, Recife, Rio de Janeiro, Salvador, São Paulo, Brasilia and Belo Horizonte; the Brazilian highlands; the Amazon and Tocantins rivers, the states of Bahia and Minas Gerais; the equator and the Atlantic Ocean; the Trans Amazon Highway.
2. Name **one** lowland and **one** upland region in Brazil.
3. On an outline map of Brazil mark and label the River Amazon, River Parana, River Tocantins and River São Francisco.
4. Describe the **three** main climatic zones of Brazil.
5. Name and describe **three** soils found in Brazil.
6. Describe **three** types of natural vegetation found in Brazil.
7. List the physical and human factors influencing the development of Brazil.
8. Describe agriculture in Brazil under the headings: Crops, Cattle and Forestry.
9. (i) What natural advantages does Brazil have for coffee production?
   (ii) Where are the main coffee producing regions?
   (iii) How important to the Brazilian economy is coffee production?
10. Describe mining and oil production in Brazil.
11. Brazil is an important manufacturing nation. Outline the development of manufacturing in Brazil since the Second World War.
12. Why is most manufacturing located in the south-east of Brazil?
13. Describe the socio-economic factors affecting car manufacturing in Brazil.
14. Describe transport services in Brazil under the headings: Roads, Rail, River, Air and Port Services, Problems, Government influence.
15. Describe tourism in Brazil under the headings: Physical attractions, Human attractions, Disadvantages, Economic importance, Government influences.
16. What effect did colonialism have on the population of Brazil?
17. What effect has internal migration had on the population distribution of Brazil?
18. What is the birth rate, death rate and life expectancy in Brazil?
19. What is the population density in Brazil? Describe the distribution of population.
20. Name, locate and account for the presence of three different cultural groups in Brazil.
21. Describe **two** reasons for the growth of São Paulo.
22. Describe **two** problems caused by the growth of São Paulo and how they are being reduced.

CORE UNIT: REGIONAL GEOGRAPHY

LC Exam Questions

Higher Level students must be able to answer Ordinary and Higher Level questions.

■ OL Questions

23. Name a continental/sub-continental region (not in Europe), that you have studied and answer each of the following questions.
    (i) Name **one** primary economic activity that contributes to the economy of this region.
    (ii) Explain the advantages that this region has for the development of the primary economic activity named in part (i) above.
    (iii) Describe **one** problem faced by this primary economic activity in this region.

24. Describe the development of the manufacturing industry in any one continental/sub-continental region (not in Europe) that you have studied. Clearly state the name of the region in your answer.

25. Describe the influence which either climate or the physical landscape has on the development of tourism in any non-European continental or sub-continental region which you have studied.

26. Name a continental/sub-continental region (not in Europe) that you have studied and explain any **two** of the following with regard to this region:
    • The type of farming practised in the region
    • The reasons for the development of industry in the region
    • The reasons why tourists are attracted to the region.

27. Describe and explain the reasons for the growth of any urban area in a continental/sub-continental region (not in Europe), that you have studied.

■ HL Questions

28. Draw an outline map of a non-European/sub-continental region you have studied. Mark and identify on it:
    – a major city
    – a named physical region
    – a named river
    – the location of a named resource.

29. Describe how any **two** of the following have influenced human activities in a continental/sub-continental region you have studied:
    – climate
    – soil
    – relief
    – drainage.

30. Examine **two** factors that have influenced primary activities in a non-European region you have studied.

31. Describe and explain any **two** factors that influence the development of manufacturing in a non-European continental/sub-continental region that you have studied.

32. Account for the development of **one** tertiary economic activity in any one continental/sub-continental region that you have studied.

33. Describe and explain the growth of **one** major urban area in a continental/sub-continental region that you have studied.

34. Describe and explain the importance of culture in defining regions in a continental/sub-continental region that you have studied.

35. Account for the growth and distribution of population in a continental/sub-continental region (not in Europe) that you have studied.

CHAPTER 21: BRAZIL – A CONTINENTAL REGION

Key Words

You should be able to explain both verbally and in writing each of the key words listed below.

agglomeration
Amazon Basin
Avança Brasil
Amerindians
biofuel
BRIC trading bloc
cash crop
colonialism
equatorial climate
favela
Import Substitution Industrialisation Scheme (ISI)
indigenous/native people
latosol
National Ethanol Programme
Newly Industrialised Country (NIC)
mega city
Mercosur
Plan Watercolour 2020
rural to urban migration
terra rossa soil
thorny scrub/*caatinga*
Trans Amazonian highway
tropical climate
tropical rainforest
savanna/*cerrado*
semi-arid climate
Structural Adjustment Programme (SAP)

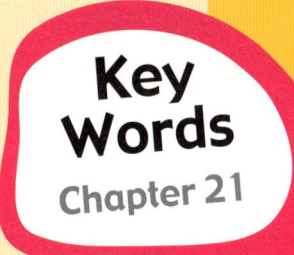

Digital Resources are available for this chapter at mentorbooks.ie/resources

CHAPTER 22

The Complexity of Regions

(a) The growth and impact of the European Union
(b) The interaction between the Republic of Ireland and Northern Ireland

Key Theme

The boundaries and the extent of regions may change over time. The study of regions illustrates the geographical complexity of the interaction between economic, cultural and physical processes.

Learning Outcomes

At the end of this chapter you will be able to:
- Outline the key events in the growth of the European Union (EU).
- Identify the current EU member states.
- Discuss the advantages and disadvantages of EU enlargement.
- Discuss the social, political and economic impact of EU expansion.
- Discuss the economic, political and cultural links between the Republic of Ireland and Northern Ireland.

Contents

22.1	European Union development and expansion	429
22.2	Economic and social impacts of EU expansion	432
	Case Study 1: The impact of EU enlargement on Ireland's economy, society and culture	433
	Case Study 2: Turkey's application to join the EU	435
22.3	Economic, political and cultural interaction between the Republic of Ireland and Northern Ireland	437

Revision Space

Chapter Revision Questions – LC Exam Questions – Key Word List 441

CHAPTER 22: THE COMPLEXITY OF REGIONS

22.1 European Union development and expansion

The Beginnings of the European Union

The building of a united Europe was one of the greatest undertakings of the 20th century. Its aim was to end the old hostilities that led to the two world wars and to create more prosperity through co-operation among all Europeans.

In 1950, the French Foreign Minister, Robert Schuman, announced his plan which was the first step towards the modern EU.

Schuman wanted to encourage social and economic co-operation among countries that produced coal and steel. In 1951, six countries signed a treaty creating the **ECSC – The European Coal and Steel Community**. It was the first common market uniting the coal and steel industries of Belgium, France, West Germany, Italy, Luxembourg and the Netherlands.

Since 1951 there have been a further seven phases of development and expansion of the ECSC. Today it is called the **European Union (EU)** and has 28 member countries. These developments have included important treaties that all members have agreed to implement. Ireland has had several referenda to approve such treaties, e.g. the Lisbon Treaty of 2009. Each member state has to make changes to their national laws in order to develop common laws shared by all EU member states, e.g. Common Agricultural Policy (CAP). These changes are called **sovereignty** changes. (Sovereignty is the right of a country to make laws for itself that are independent of any other organisation's laws, including the EU.)

The growth of the EU is outlined in the maps on this page and page 430. A timeline provided on page 431 briefly summarises the development of the EU.

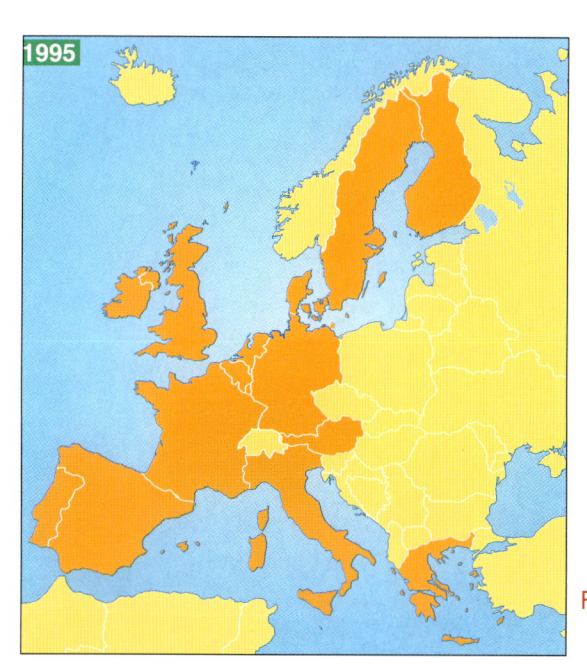

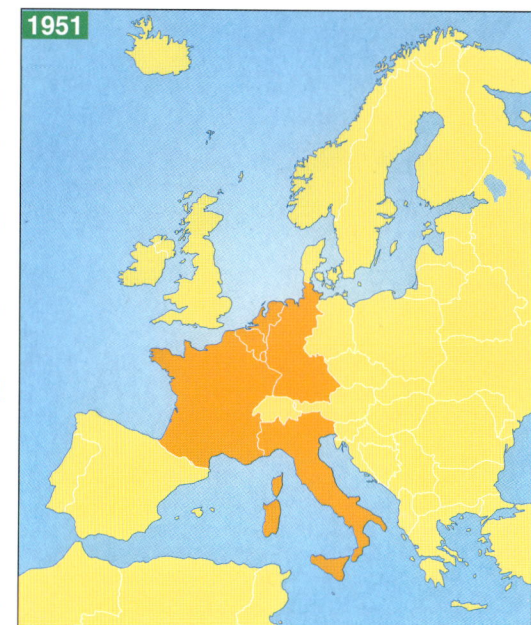

Fig. 1 The six members of the European Coal and Steel Community (ECSC), 1951

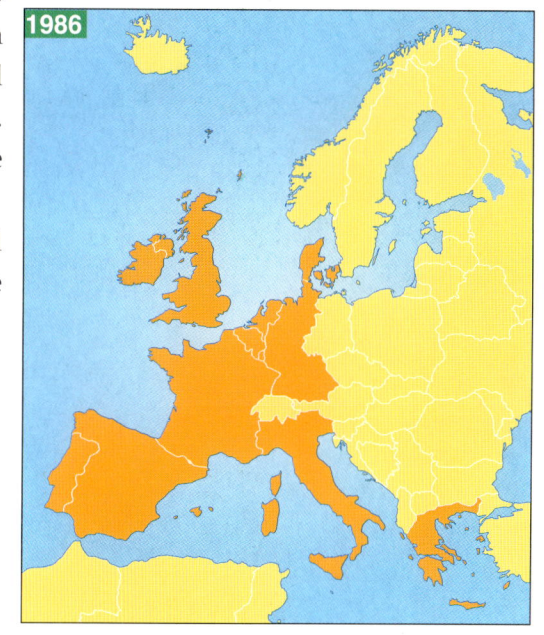

Fig. 2 The 12 members of the European Community (EC) in 1986

Fig. 3 The 15 members of the European Union (EU) in 1995

429

Core Unit: Regional Geography

Eurozone: Some EU members use the Euro currency. It is the official currency of these countries. These are called Eurozone countries.

Keep up-to-date with new Eurozone countries by checking Eurostat online.

Accession is the application process for new EU members.

The **Schengen Agreement** was signed by EU members – except the UK and Ireland. It allows the free movement of people and goods between EU countries.

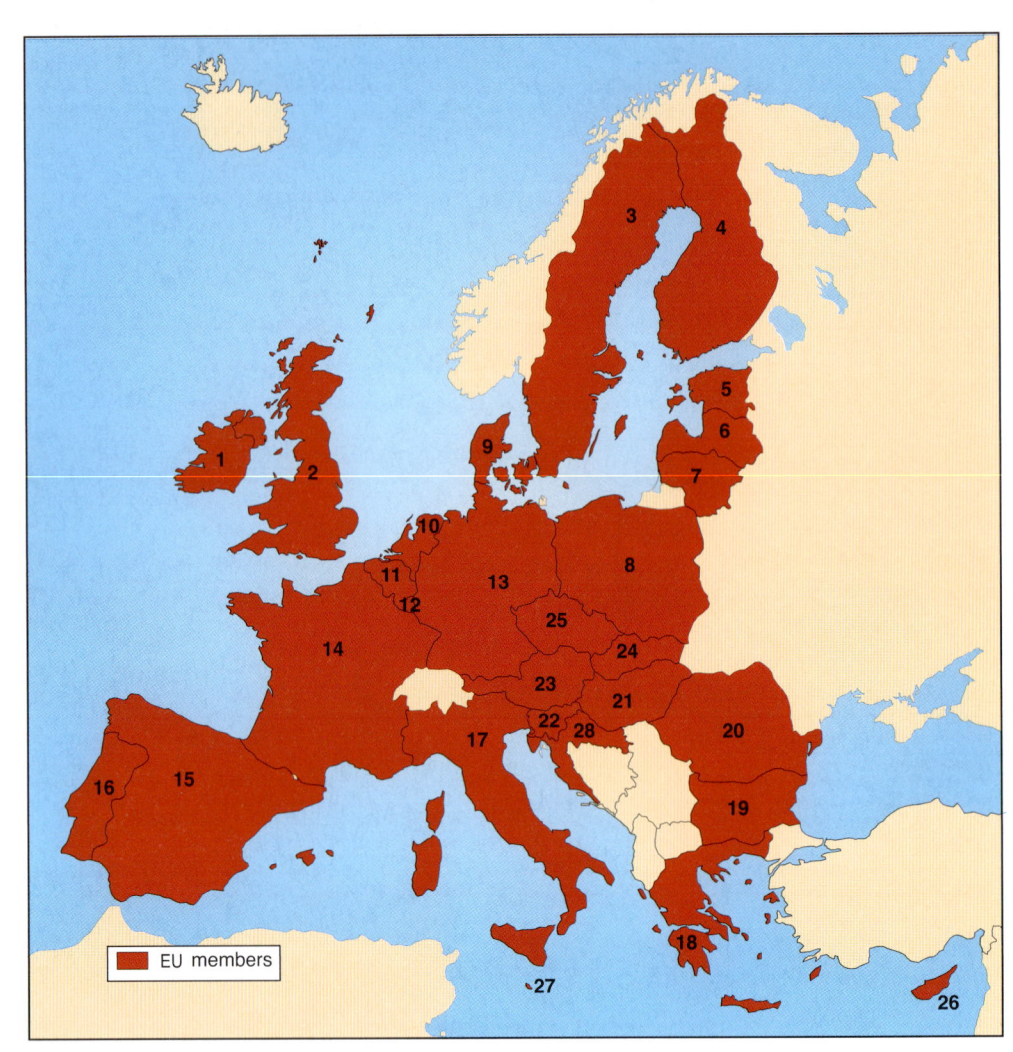

Fig. 4 The 28 members of the European Union

1. Ireland	8. Poland	15. Spain	22. Slovenia
2. Britain	9. Denmark	16. Portugal	23. Austria
3. Sweden	10. Netherlands	17. Italy	24. Slovakia
4. Finland	11. Belgium	18. Greece	25. Czech Republic
5. Estonia	12. Luxembourg	19. Bulgaria	26. Cyprus
6. Latvia	13. Germany	20. Romania	27. Malta
7. Lithuania	14. France	21. Hungary	28. Croatia

weblink History of the EU

TIMELINE SUMMARY OF THE DEVELOPMENT OF THE EU, 1951–2015

1951	The European Coal and Steel Community (ECSC) is established. Its members are **Belgium**, **France**, **Italy**, **Luxembourg**, **West Germany** and the **Netherlands**.
1957	The Treaties of Rome are signed by all members of the ECSC. The first treaty is an agreement to allow free trade between members of the ECSC and renames the ECSC as the European Economic Community (EEC). The second treaty is known as the Treaty of the European Atomic Energy Community (Euratom) and it aims to develop and grow nuclear industries in EEC member states.
1965	The EEC is renamed as the European Community (EC). The European Parliament, the European Commission, the European Court of Justice and the Council of Ministers are created.
1973	**Ireland**, the **UK** and **Denmark** join the EC.
1979	European Monetary System (EMS) established.
1981	**Greece** joins the EC.
1986	**Spain** and **Portugal** join the EC.
1987	The Single European Act (SEA) is passed.
1987	Turkey applies to join the EC.
1989	The Berlin Wall collapses and communism comes to an end.
1990	West Germany and East Germany reunify and the Schengen Agreement comes into operation.
1992	The Maastricht Treaty is signed.
1993	The Maastricht Treaty comes into effect. The EC is renamed the European Union (EU).
1995	**Austria**, **Finland** and **Sweden** join the EU.
1997	The Amsterdam Treaty is signed, allowing the EU to reform its institutions in order to allow more countries to join.
1999	The Euro is created as the new single currency in all member states, except the UK, Denmark and Sweden.
2000	The European Parliament approves the enlargement of the EU, meaning that there is now no legal obstacle to allowing more members to join. The Nice Treaty is finally agreed upon after months of tricky negotiations between member states.
2002	Euro notes and coins replace national currencies in 12 EU states: Austria, Belgium, Finland, France, Germany, Greece, Ireland, Italy, Luxembourg, Netherlands, Portugal, Spain.
2003	The Nice Treaty officially comes into operation.
2004	Ten new members join the EU: **Latvia**, **Lithuania**, **Cyprus**, **Malta**, **Estonia**, **Slovenia**, **Slovakia**, **Poland**, **Hungary** and the **Czech Republic**. These ten countries became members of the EU on May 5, 2004, during Ireland's presidency of the EU, making a 25-member EU.
2007	**Romania** and **Bulgaria** join the EU. Slovenia joins Eurozone.
2008	**Malta** and **Cyprus** join the Eurozone currency
2009	The Lisbon Treaty is signed into law. **Slovakia** joins Eurozone.
2011	**Estonia** joins the Eurozone. Talks continue regarding membership for **Croatia**, **Macedonia**, **Montenegro**, **Albania**, **Serbia**, **Bosnia-Herzegovina** and **Iceland**. Membership for Turkey still has to meet accession conditions set out by the EU.
2013	**Croatia** joins EU.
2014	**Latvia** joins Eurozone.
2015	**Lithuania** joins Eurozone.

22.2 Economic and social impacts of EU expansion

Reasons for the expansion of the EU

Due to the high standard of living in the EU member states, other countries applied to join. The largest expansion of the EU occurred between 2004 and 2013 when 13 new members joined. Various steps had to be taken to allow the EU to absorb the new applicants, e.g. the Amsterdam, Nice and Lisbon Treaties.

The issue of expansion has caused much debate among EU members. Some members strongly opposed the idea of admitting more countries, arguing that the cost of funding these poorer countries would be too high. Others were in favour of expansion, pointing out that increasing the prosperity of poorer states would ultimately benefit Europe as a whole by providing a larger market.

EU states are willing to welcome new members provided they fulfil the political criteria for accession to the EU. These are:

1. Being a democracy.
2. Having a basic rule of law, i.e. a constitution.
3. Having strong respect for human rights, including respect for and protection of minorities.
4. Agreeing to an economic and monetary union with EU members.

After many enlargements, the EU today covers most of Europe with a population of over 508 million. It will continue to allow countries to join for economic, political and social unity and to protect human rights, the environment, the economy and the people of all member states. Its future is based on strong political unity among member states.

Creating an EU of 28 member states took more than 60 years. EU enlargement presents an unprecedented challenge for unity and cohesion (achieving the same level of development) among member states. Modern issues of migration and integration of different cultures into the EU will take careful management.

Economic advantages of joining the EU

The transfer of funds from the richer core of the community, such as Germany, to the poorer peripheries, such as Ireland, benefited farming in this country and in other member states. Being members of the **Eurozone** encourages trade among EU members.

In 1974, the EU Heads of Government agreed to set up the **European Regional Development Fund** (**ERDF**) to encourage economic growth through subsidies. These subsidies are called **structural funds** and they provide important financial help to all regions of Europe.

By being an EU member, countries can trade freely without import tariffs. This encourages Foreign Direct Investment (FDI) by non-EU countries, e.g. USA.

Economic and social impacts of EU Expansion

	POSITIVE IMPACT OF EU EXPANSION	NEGATIVE IMPACT OF EU EXPANSION
Economic	1. Access to EU structural funds to improve agriculture, fishing, industry and tourism 2. Access to EU bailout funds in times of recession or banking crises 3. Large market (508 million) for business 4. Increased standard of living for EU members as investment in transport, education and health services takes effect 5. Higher incomes and investment by non-EU companies seeking access to EU market 6. The removal of border controls under the Schengen Agreement aids rapid movement of goods and people across borders.	1. Cost of enlargement – more than €25 billion is needed to develop poorer members 2. Economic inequality – newer members are poorer than older ones 3. Unemployment in poorer member states is higher, e.g. Bulgaria 12 million new jobs are needed in these countries 4. Eastern European members have less developed services and industries They need investment in modern infrastructure. This is paid for by wealthier countries.
Social/Cultural	Migration of EU nationals Social and cultural diversity	Racism and discrimination against EU migrants occurs in some countries.

The impact of EU enlargement on Ireland's economy, society and culture

CHAPTER 22 Case Study 1

The 21st-century enlargement of the EU has had several economic, social and cultural impacts on Ireland.

Economic impacts of expansion

1. EU expansion has opened up new opportunities for Irish businesses in terms of exporting goods, outsourcing labour and creating investment opportunities abroad.
2. Ireland's foreign-owned sector also benefited from the expansion of trade. Numerous foreign companies moved here, enticed by the low corporation tax rate of 12.5% and tariff-free trade with the EU. However, a number of countries have since followed Ireland's lead in offering low rates of corporation tax, e.g. Latvia now has a rate of 15%. The workers in the more advanced new member states do not differ very much from Ireland in terms of their skill levels while their labour costs are much lower.
3. Immigrants to Ireland from the other EU states have levels of education that are comparable to the native labour force in Ireland. However, they often earn less than the native labour force.

CORE UNIT: REGIONAL GEOGRAPHY

4. Migrant workers have two positive impacts on the Irish economy in terms of GNP growth. Firstly, their taxes contribute to the economy when they buy goods and services while living here. Secondly, their presence means that wage rates have grown more slowly because of the availability of labour in the economy.

5. While Ireland has largely benefited from in-migration of people from the new member states, the scale of this migration had increased the price of renting and buying accommodation, and has increased congestion on transport and other infrastructure, e.g. schools.

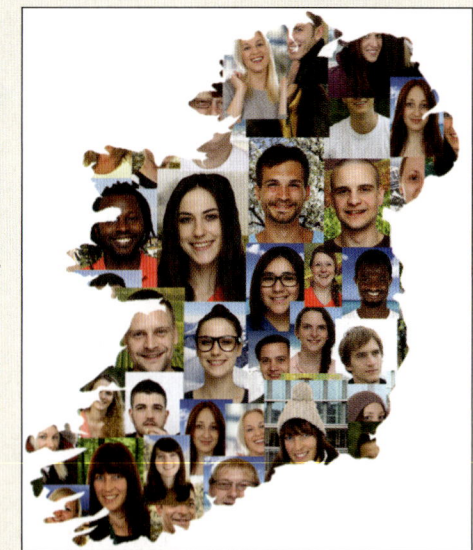

Social and cultural impacts of expansion

Migration to Ireland by EU citizens has had a lasting impact on the Irish workforce and wider society.

1. The composition of the Irish population has changed due to increasing cultural diversity. EU and other immigrants made up 12% of the Irish population in 2014. Rapid increase in this percentage is expected in the next few years.

2. Migration has increased pressure on Irish workers to become multilingual. Irish workers still have a long way to go in terms of competing with other European workers as the majority of Irish people only speak one language. Today many people in Europe speak English and another language. Irish people need to speak another major language to compete with their European counterparts.

3. The arrival of EU migrants has led to the emergence of new communities across the country, e.g. Polish.

4. Irish society is much more aware of its capacity for racism and government campaigns against racism have been implemented, e.g. 'Show Racism the Red Card'.

weblink
Central Statistics Office – up-to-date census data.

weblink
Discussion of Britain's changing relationship with the European Union is available on mentorbooks.ie/resources

Fig. 5 Campaigns against racism are more active in Ireland.

Fig. 6 Shops selling Polish food have opened in many cities and towns in Ireland.

CHAPTER 22: THE COMPLEXITY OF REGIONS

Turkey's application to join the EU

CHAPTER 22 Case Study 2

FACTS ON TURKEY
Population: 70.5 million
GDP: €740 billion
An officially secular state (this means government and religion are separate) with a Muslim population.
Strong military influence in government.
Connects the European and Asian continents and controls the entrance to the Black Sea.
Turkey's move towards EU membership is hindered by complaints that human rights and press freedom are not respected by the government and by its alleged mistreatment of the Kurdish people.

Fig. 7 Map of Turkey

The application by Turkey to join the EU has been under consideration since 1987. Its application for membership highlights three issues facing Europe in the 21st century. These can be summarised as:
1. Political issues at the European level.
2. Economic and social issues.
3. Geo-political issues (global political issues).

Political issues at the European level

1. The opposition of Austria to the opening of accession talks with Turkey revived memories that the Turks were stopped at the gates of Vienna from conquering Europe in 1683. This, like the Battle of the Boyne in Ireland, is an example of how historical political events can affect modern political decisions.
2. The French and Austrians have promised their people a vote on Turkish entry and at present there are clear majorities against Turkish membership in both countries. On the Turkish side, some nationalists are unhappy at being dictated to by the EU and would like to stop the accession process.

Fig. 8 Turkey is an officially secular state with a Muslim population.

Economic and social issues

1. If it became a member, Turkey would be the biggest member state in terms of land area. It would be much poorer than other members and would require massive transfers of wealth from the EU. The migration of poorer Turks to wealthier EU states would place an economic and social strain on those states.
2. Turkey is a democracy with a president and elected political parties. However, the army plays a much bigger role in political affairs than would be acceptable elsewhere in Western Europe. The current rule of law and respect for human rights and fundamental freedoms need to be improved.

CORE UNIT: REGIONAL GEOGRAPHY

Geo-political issues (global political issues), e.g. international migration

1. Turkey borders some of the world's most troubled hot spots, e.g. Iraq, Iran, Syria. It also has a land border with Greece which is an EU member state. The Edirne region of north-west Turkey borders Greece, (see Fig. 9 below).

   Due to conflict in Syria and Libya, millions of refugees and economic migrants have fled to EU countries. Many of these took dangerous sea routes across the Mediterranean to Italy. However, thousands more, especially those with children, took – and continue to take – the somewhat safer land routes through Turkey. More than 2.3 million Syrian refugees now live in Turkey following the start of the Syrian civil war in 2011.

   Thousands of others, who just want to pass through Turkey on their way to wealthier EU countries such as Germany, arrive daily. So far, the flow of migrants has cost the Turkish government over €7.6 billion. These figures will continue to rise.

   The EU, worried about its security and economic stability, wants Turkey to return economic migrants to their home countries or to keep them in Turkey. After decades of debating Turkey's EU application, the economic reality is forcing the EU to consider offering Turkey membership in return for help in controlling the flow of migrants.

   The EU border agency FRONTEX now has responsibility for the EU border crossing points between Turkey and EU countries.

   Fig. 9 Map showing migration land route across Turkey into Greece and Bulgaria.

2. The Americans and the British are strongly in favour of Turkey's accession to the EU. As a member of NATO, Turkey is important today in the fight against the spread of Islamic extremism.

3. The island of Cyprus has been divided between Greece and Turkey since the 1970s. Turkey refuses to recognise the Greek Cypriot government. This is another issue that needs to be resolved before Turkey can join the EU.

22.3 Economic, political and cultural interaction between the Republic of Ireland and Northern Ireland

Regions do not always have well-defined boundaries. Links between people who have something in common may reach across the political boundaries drawn by governments. These links may be sporting, political or business activities, common languages and/or religions.

An example of this is the complex relationship between the Republic of Ireland and Northern Ireland.

The Republic of Ireland and Northern Ireland
(a) Economic interaction
Trade

For many years trade between the Republic and Northern Ireland was restricted by customs and security posts at the border. This slowed down the movement of goods and people, thus damaging the growth of trade between the two regions. Since 1973, barriers that restricted trade between the two regions have been reduced.

Since the **Good Friday Agreement** in 1998, physical restrictions on the movement of people, goods and services between the two regions have eased. Border controls have been removed and people can now travel freely between the North and the Republic. This has had an important economic effect on the two regions. The value and volume of goods traded between the two countries continues to increase.

The change in the economic interaction between Northern Ireland and the Republic of Ireland is shown in Fig. 10 on the next page. We depend on the North for many useful goods and services. In turn they are an important customer for produce from the Republic. Economic connections between the two are continually being strengthened.

Over the past few years hundreds of thousands of shoppers from the Republic of Ireland have travelled across the border to shop in Northern Ireland. Many cash-strapped southern consumers found it impossible to ignore the difference in the price of goods between Northern Ireland and the Republic. The price difference was due to a favourable exchange rate, a lower VAT rate, a lower tax rate on alcohol and lower profit margins for Northern Ireland's retailers. Southern retailers in border areas experienced closures and job losses as a result of cross-border trade. However, crossing the border is not always worthwhile as changing exchange rates and increased tax rates in Northern Ireland often make buying goods there less attractive for shoppers from the Republic.

> **weblink**
> Discussion of Britain's changing relationship with the European Union is available on mentorbooks.ie/resources

CORE UNIT: REGIONAL GEOGRAPHY

Trade share (%) by sector (N-S) North-South

- 60.63%
- 6.11%
- 2.39%
- 6.70%
- 4.41%
- 2.54%
- 4.04%

Trade share (%) by sector (S-N) South-North

- 41.08%
- 3.15%
- 4.55%
- 13.17%
- 3.73%
- 5.93%
- 5.19%
- 2.14%
- 5.53%
- 5.77%
- 5.91%

Total cross-border trade by sector

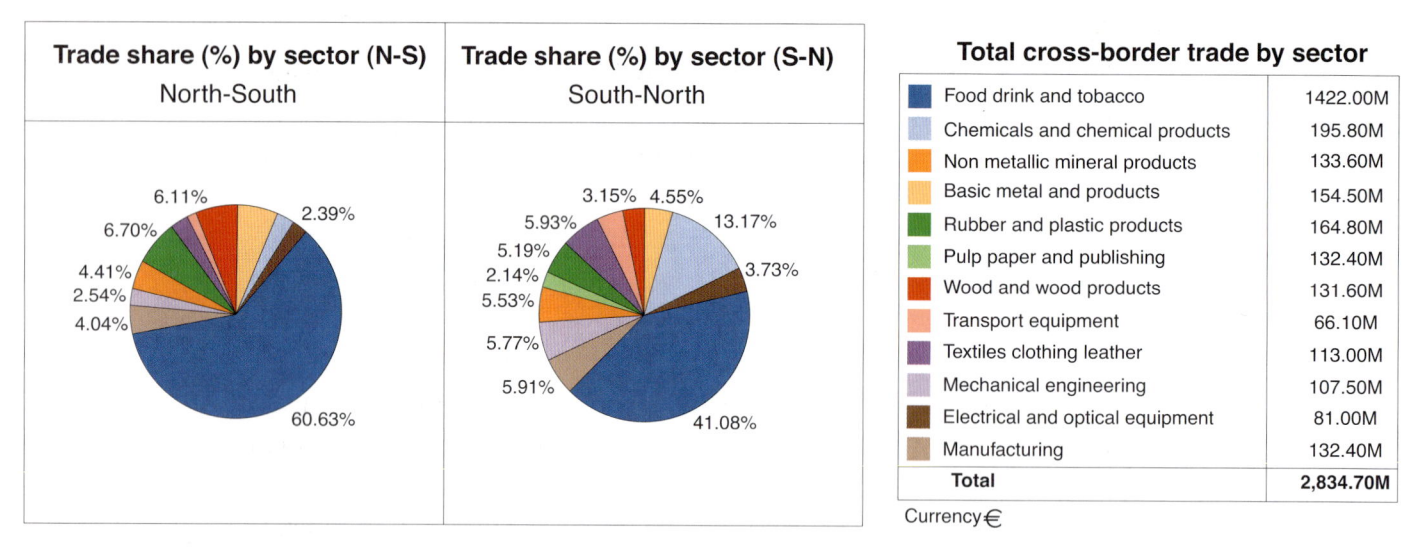

Food drink and tobacco	1422.00M
Chemicals and chemical products	195.80M
Non metallic mineral products	133.60M
Basic metal and products	154.50M
Rubber and plastic products	164.80M
Pulp paper and publishing	132.40M
Wood and wood products	131.60M
Transport equipment	66.10M
Textiles clothing leather	113.00M
Mechanical engineering	107.50M
Electrical and optical equipment	81.00M
Manufacturing	132.40M
Total	**2,834.70M**

Currency €

Fig. 10 Trade between the Republic of Ireland and Northern Ireland

weblink — Tourism statistics

Tourism

Tourism is another important economic activity that links the two regions.

In 2015 tourists from the North made 1.7 million trips to Ireland. This generated €335 million for the Irish economy.

Locations visited by Northern Ireland tourists, 2015	No. of tourists Revenue generated
Dublin	448,000 €96.4 million
East & Midlands	201,000 €35.6 million
South-East	103,000 €25.9 million
South-West	108,000 €23.9 million
Shannon	79,000 €20.4 million
West	96,000 €19.9 million
North-West	673,000 €112.2 million

Fig 11 Visitors from Northern Ireland. Numbers, revenue and locations visited.

(b) Political interaction

In the past the political relationship between the Republic of Ireland and Northern Ireland had been difficult. There were several reasons for this:

(i) Article 2 of the Irish constitution which claimed authority (**jurisdiction**) over the whole island of Ireland.

(ii) 30 years of religious (**sectarian**) conflict between Catholics and Protestants in the North prevented full political interaction between the Irish and British governments.

The **Good Friday Agreement** in 1998 brought peace and political stability to Northern Ireland and led to increased political co-operation between Northern Ireland and the Republic of Ireland. The Northern Ireland Assembly was established as part of the Good Friday Agreement in order to ensure that both communities – unionist and nationalist – participate in governing the region. It has authority to legislate on a wide range of areas and to elect the **Northern Ireland Executive** (cabinet). It sits at Parliament Buildings in Stormont in Belfast.

There are six North-South Bodies which work together on cross-border issues, looking jointly at renewing and developing roads, airports, waterways, language, trade, business, agricultural research and tourism between the Northern Ireland and the Republic.

(c) Social and cultural interaction

- Cultural links between Northern Ireland and the Republic of Ireland are varied. Some organisations and events operate on an all–Ireland basis, e.g. the Fleadh Cheoil, the GAA, Comhaltas Ceoltóirí Éireann and the Scout Association of Ireland. Boxing and rugby clubs operate across the 32 counties and both sports have a mix of unionist and nationalist members.
- There is a lack of interaction between nationalist and unionist groups within some sports. The GAA, for example, has traditionally had a strong nationalist membership. Until recently, members of the Northern Ireland security forces were excluded from membership of the GAA. In the spirit of the Good Friday Agreement, some of its rules were changed to remove the ban.
- Education is another area where cultural interaction between the two groups has been minimal. This is due to the physical separation of loyalist and nationalist communities. As a result, most schools rarely have an even mix of religions and their location can lead to difficulties if children from a nationalist background attend a mainly loyalist school or vice versa. However, the number of integrated schools in Northern Ireland is increasing.
- Other organisations and events promote co-operation and links between the North and the South, e.g. the President's Award (**Gaisce**) for developing individual skills and taking part in community work and Carshare, a cross-border initiative developed by the Northern Ireland Department for Regional Development and the Republic's Department of Transport, Tourism and Sport.

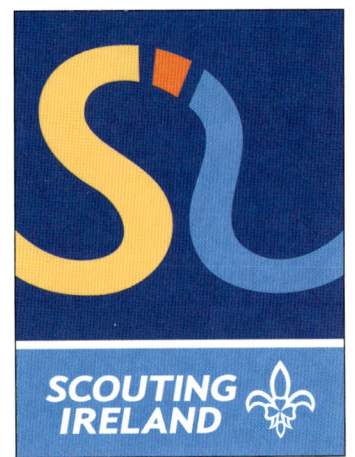

Fig. 12 Rugby clubs operate across the 32 counties.

Interreg – An EU scheme to promote social, economic and cultural development between regions

At European level a programme known as **Interreg** has been developed to foster co-operation between regions. The Republic and Northern Ireland have both benefited from participation in this scheme.

Interreg is financed by the EU's European Regional Development Fund (ERDF). More than €13 billion has been allocated to all border regions within the EU, including Ireland's border region.

Investment in local business development by Interreg has helped to expand the level of trade between North and South. Developing local industry and investment in small and medium-sized enterprises (SMEs) provides new business opportunities and creates economic strength and growth.

Northern Ireland now has a similar corporation tax to the Republic, i.e. 12.5%. This rate increases the attraction of the whole of Ireland for Foreign Direct Investment (FDI).

CHAPTER 22: THE COMPLEXITY OF REGIONS

Chapter Revision Questions

European development and expansion

1. Draw a map of the EU in your copybook. Colour-code it using the list below according to the date these countries joined.

Founding members:	colour green
1973 member(s):	colour yellow
1981 member(s):	colour red
1986 member(s):	colour blue
1995 member(s):	colour purple
2004 member(s):	colour brown
2007 member(s):	colour pink
2013 member:	colour orange

2. Look at pages 429–431 to find out what happened in each of the years listed below. Copy this timeline into your copybook and write your answer after each year. Four have been completed for you.

Year	Event in EU development
1951	
1957	
1962	
1965	
1973	
1979	
1986	
1987	Single European Act signed
1989	
1990	
1992	
1993	
1995	
1997	Amsterdam Treaty on reforming EU
1999	
2000	
2002	Euro coins in circulation
2004	
2007	
2008	
2009	
2011	
2013	
2014	
2015	

441

CORE UNIT: REGIONAL GEOGRAPHY

3. Name and describe **two** economic challenges and **two** economic advantages to the enlargement of the EU.
4. What is the likely political impact of EU enlargement on member states? Use examples in your answer.
5. Using sources of information other than your textbook, pick a country that has joined the EU since 2000. Write **three** points of information about it.
6. 'Turkey has many issues to address before becoming a member of the EU'. Discuss this statement.
7. How did the Good Friday Agreement improve social and economic relations between Northern Ireland and the Republic of Ireland?
8. Name **three** cultural links between Northern Ireland and the Republic of Ireland. Use your own knowledge where necessary.
9. Describe Interreg and how it helps to develop enterprise/business.

LC Exam Questions

Higher Level students must be able to answer Ordinary and Higher Level questions.

■ OL Questions

10. Examine this map of Europe which shows FOUR different categories of countries in Western Europe.

    Match the following countries with the correct categories:
    (a) Existing member states
    (b) New member states
    (c) Applicant state
    (d) Non-EU states

Countries	Category
Turkey	
Poland, Slovenia	
Norway, Switzerland	
Romania, Bulgaria, Croatia	

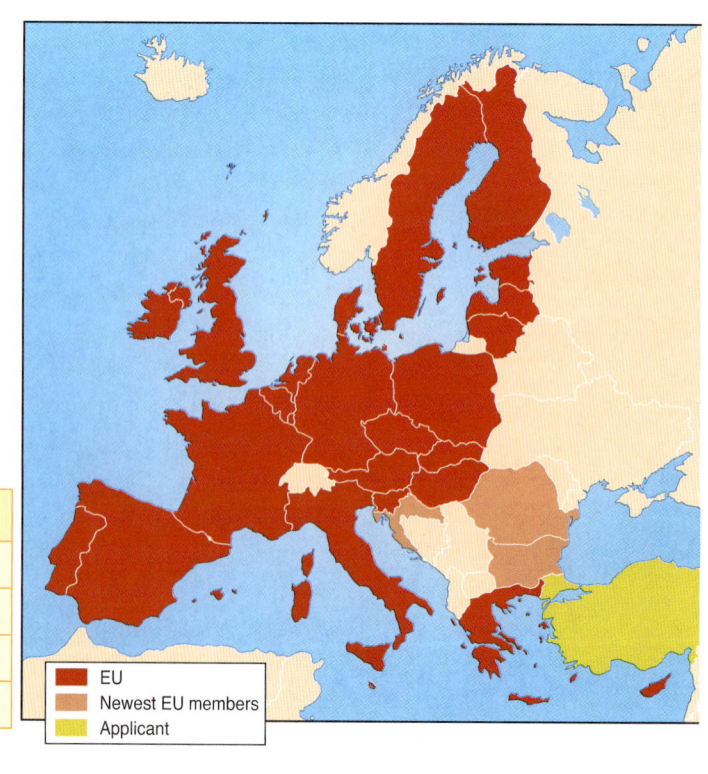

442

11. In 2004 ten new countries joined the European Union.
    (i) Name and describe **one** positive effect this had on Ireland.
    (ii) Name and describe **one** problem which this has created for Ireland.

■ HL Questions

12. Describe and explain **two** impacts on Ireland of the enlargement of the European Union.
13. Examine the economic and/or cultural impact of expansion on any **one** member state of the EU.
14. Fill in the following table, which refers to the European Union (EU).

Description	Letter	Country
Not a member of the European Union		
One of the original six members of the EU		
Joined EU in 1973		
Joined EU in 2004		

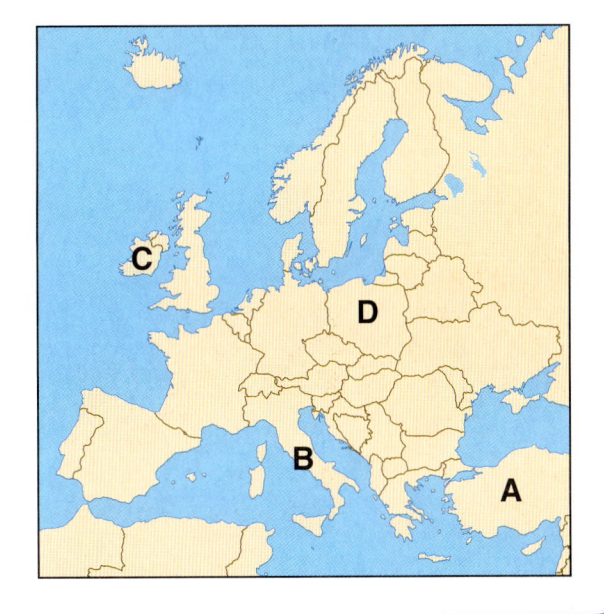

CORE UNIT: REGIONAL GEOGRAPHY

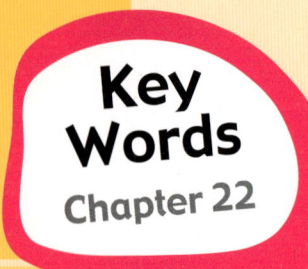

Key Words — Chapter 22

Key Words

You should be able to explain both verbally and in writing each of the key words listed below.

accession
ECSC – The European Coal and Steel Community
European Union (EU)
Eurozone
Good Friday Agreement
Interreg
Schengen Agreement
sovereignty

Digital Resources are available for this chapter at mentorbooks.ie/resources

Index

A
Ablation 144
Abrasion
    Glacial erosion 146
    Marine erosion 169
    River erosion 116
Accession 430
Accumulation
    River 69
    Glacial 144
Acid lava 42
Active volcano 41
Administrative regions
    Local government in France 284
    Local government in Ireland 282
Aerial Photographs
    Direction 241
    Finding location on 240
    Function 242
    Historic development 246
    House types 245
    Land use 249
    Oblique 239
    Sketch of 247
    Uses of 241
    Vertical 239
African Rift Valley 63
Agent of denudation 85
Agent of erosion 91
Agglomeration 423
Air compression 169
Alluvium 128
Alpine folding 59
Amazon Basin 402
Amsterdam Treaty 431
Anticline 58
Anticylone 256
Arches 173
Arête 148
Armorican folding 59
Artois 385
Ash 42
Asthenosphere 8
Asymmetrical fold 58
Atlantic Corridor 328
Attrition
    Marine erosion 169
    River erosion 116
Autostrada del Sole 368
Avalanches 200
Avança Brasil 408

B
Backshore 176
Backwash 166
Bank caving 116
Basal flow 146
Basalt 68
Base level of erosion 111
Basic lava 42
Batholiths 48
Beaches
    Bay head beach 172
    Bays 172
    Cusps 176
    Fabric 176
    Mats
    Nourishment 181
    Storm beach 176
Bedding planes 69
Bedload 116
Bergschrund 149
Berms 176
Biofuel 409
Biological weathering 85
Block mountains 62
Blowhole 173
Bottomset beds 131
Boulder clay plains 154
Braccianti 367
Brain drain 372
Brazil
    Amerindians 419
    Colonialism 417
    Cultural regions 419
    Deforestation 405
    Favelas 417
    Import Substitution Industrialisation Scheme (ISI) 409
    Migration 417
    Physical characteristics 401
    Population 415
    Primary activities 403
    Secondary activities 407
    Tertiary activities 412
Breac Gaeltacht 286
Breakwaters 182
BRIC trading bloc 407
Brie 385
Brownfield sites 247
Bull Island 183

C
Calcite cement 70
Calcium bicarbonate 98
Calcium carbonate 98
Calderas 44
Caledonian folding 59
Capital intensive 343
Capital Investment Plan (CIP) 321
Carbonation 88
Carbonic acid 88
Cash crops 368
Caverns 102
Caves 102
Cavitation 116
Chalk 70
Champagne regions 385
Chemical weathering 85
Chemically formed 69
Cirque glacier 145
Clints 100
Clustered settlement 235
Co-operatives 368
Coal 70
Coastal protection 181
Cohesion funds 310
Cold front 256
Collision 16
Column 103
Common Agricultural Policy (CAP) 311
Common Fisheries Policy (CFP) 311
Commune 284
Compacted 69
Competitive clusters 383
Concave slope 225
Conglomerates 71
Consequent streams 211
Conservative plate boundary 18
Constitution 432
Constructive (divergent) plate boundary 15
Constructive/spilling waves 167
Continental crust 9
Continental drift 11
Continental–continental plate collision 16
Conurbations 353
Convection currents 9
Convergent plate boundary 16
Convex slope 225
Core 8
Core regions 276
Corrasion 116
Corrie 145
Cosmetic Valley 388
Courtown 185
Crevasses 145
Crust 8
Crystallisation of salts 85
Cultural regions 276

D
Decentralisation 395
Deltas
    Arcuate 132
    Bird's Foot 132
    Estuarine 132
Denudation 85
Départements 284
Dependents 320
Depression 279
Destructive plate boundaries 16
Destructive/plunging waves 168
Dispersed settlement 236
Diurnal range 87
Divergent plate boundary 15
Dolerite 68
Dolines 101
Dome volcanoes 46
Dormant volcano 41
Drainage patterns
    Dendritic 112
    Radial 113
    Trellis 113
Drift 147
Drogheda 305
Drumlins 155
Dublin City Development Plan 358
Dublin City Region 354
Dykes 48

E
Earth, structure of 8
Earthquakes
    Aftershocks 27
    Depth
    Early warning system 34
    Effects of 31
    Global Seismic Network 28
    Japan earthquake, 2011 32
    Intensity 29
    Magnitude 29
    Prediction 35
    Preventing earthquake damage 35
    Shock waves 27
    Tremors 27
Easting 222

INDEX

ECSC (European Coal and Steel Community) 429
Elastic rebound 27
Elbow of capture 212
Endogenic forces 8
Enlargement 432
Epicentre 27
Equatorial climate 401
Erratics 156
Eskers 157
Estuary 110
Ethanol 404
EU (European Union) 429
Eustatic processes 207
Even slope 225
Exfoliation 85
Exogenic forces 8
Extensive farming 367
Extinct volcano 41
Extrusive volcanic landforms 44

F
Fault gouge 73
Fault lines 18
Fault scarp 61
Faulting
    Types of faulting 61
Favela 417
Fetch 166
Fíor Gaeltacht 286
Fiords 151
Firn 144
Fissure 97
Flanders 289
Floodplains 128
Fluvial processes 114
Fluvioglacial deposition 157
Focus 27
Fold mountains 59
Folding 57
Foliation 73
Foreign Direct Investment (FDI) 321
Foreset beds 131
Foreshore 176
Fossils 70
Freeze–thaw action 85
Function 237

G
Gabions 182
Gaeltacht regions in Ireland 285
Garrigue 369
Gateway 331

Geo 174
Geomorphic 280
Geosyncline 60
Geothermal energy 79
Glacial
    Abrasion 146
    Deposition 146
    Drift 147
    Erosion 146
    Landforms 148
    Plucking 151
    Processes 146
    Transport 147
    Trough 151
Glaciated valley 151
Glaciation
    Of Ireland 159
    Midlandian Ice Age 159
    Munsterian Ice Age 159
Glaciers
    Ablation 144
    Accumulation 144
    Movement of 144
    Types of 145
Gneiss 73
Gondwanaland 11
Good Friday Agreement 437
Gorges 119
Graben 61
Graded profile 111
Graded slope 225
Granite 68
Graphs
    Bar 260
    Choropleths 266
    Climographs 265
    Pie 260
    Radar charts 265
    Scatter plot
    Trend 263
    Triangle 263
    Wind rose 266
Greater Dublin Area
    Physical characteristics 338
    Population 350
    Primary activities 340
    Secondary activities 341
    Tertiary activities 345
    Transport services 345
Greenfield sites 247
Grikes 100
Growth centres 371
Groynes 181
Gypsum 71

H
Hanging valleys 151
Hawaiian Islands 20
Headlands 172
Headward erosion 209
High oblique photo 239
Hinterland 341
Horst 62
Hotspots 20
Hub 331
Hydration 88
Hydraulic action
    Marine erosion 169
    River erosion 116
Hydrolysis 88
Hypabyssal rock 68

I
Iceland 79
Igneous rock 68
Île de France 385
Incised meanders 210
Inner core 8
Inorganically formed 71
Intensive commercial farming 384
Interlocking spurs 121
Interreg 440
Islamic world 293
Island arcs 17
Isobar 256
Isohel 256
Isohyet 256
Isoline 256
Isostatic uplift 208
Isotach 256
Isotherm 256

J
Japan earthquake, 2011 32
Joints 98

K
Kames 157
Karst 97
Kettle holes 157
Knickpoints 209
Knowledge-based industries 348

L
Laccoliths 49
Lacrustine delta 130
Lagoon 177
Lahars 197
Land function 242

Land use 241
Landslides 193
Language regions
    Belgium 289
    Decline of Irish language 286
    Support for Irish language 287
Large-scale map 219
Lateral erosion 116
Latifundia 367
Latosol 402
Laurasia 11
Lava
    Acid 42
    Basic 42
    Plateaux 47
Lee side 155
Levees 129
Limb 58
Limestone
    Karst landscapes 97
    Pavement 100
    Surface landforms 99
    Underground landforms 99
Limon/loess 280
Linear scale 217
Linear settlement 235
Liquefaction 31
Lisbon Treaty 429
Lithification 69
Lithosphere 8
Littoral drift 170
Load 114
Long profile 111
Longshore drift 170
Lopoliths 49
Low oblique photo 239

M
Maastricht Treaty 431
Magnetism 13
Mantle 9
Maquis 369
Marble 72
Marine delta 130
Marine deposition
    Landforms 175
    Processes of 175
Marine erosion
    Landforms 170
    Processes of 170
Marine transport
    Processes of 170
Maritime climate 382

Index

Marram grass 181
Mass movement
    Classifying 194
    Deforestation and 202
    Derrybrien bogflow 198
    Factors affecting 193
    Human influence on 202
    Overcropping and 202
Mature stage/middle course 124
Meander scars 124
Meanders 124
Mechanically formed 69
Mechanical weathering 85
Mediterranean climate 366
Mega city 423
Meltwater 157
Mercosur 409
Merit Medical 327
Metamorphic aureole 48
Metamorphic rock 72
Metamorphism
    Dynamic 73
    Effects of 73
    Regional 73
    Thermal 72
Metapontino area 368
Metro 391
Mezzogiorno
    Cassa per il Mezzogiorno 363
    Migration
    Minifundia 367
    Physical characteristics 363
    Population 376
    Primary activities 366
    Secondary activities 371
    Tertiary activities 373
Mid-ocean ridge 15
Mid–Atlantic Ridge 16
Migrating meanders 125
Misfit stream 212
Modified Mercalli scale 29
Mohorovicic discontinuity 8
Moraine
    Englacial 147
    Ground 147
    Lateral 147
    Medial 155
    Recessional 155
    Terminal 155
Mortlakes 124
Mount St Helens 52
Mountain building 59
Mudflows 196
Mudstone 71

Munster ridge and valley province 60

N

National Development Plan (NDP) 321
National Ethanol Programme 409
National Spatial Strategy (NSS) 331
Neve 144
Newly Industrialised Country (NIC) 407
Nice Treaty 431
Nivation 149
Nodal point 345
Normal fault 61
North Atlantic Drift 278
Northern and Western region (N&W region)
    Physical characteristics 318
    Population 319
    Primary activities 322
    Secondary activities 325
    Tertiary activities 328
Northing 222
Notch 171
Nucleated settlement 235
Nunataks 160

O

Oblique photo 239
Occluded front 256
Oceanic crust 9
Oceanic–continental plate collision 17
Oceanic–oceanic plate collision 17
Old age stage/lower course 118
Old Red Sandstone 60
Onion weathering 87
Organically formed 70
Orogeny 59
OS Maps
    Ancient settlement 234
    Area 226
    Calculating gradients 231
    Cross sections 229
    Direction 221
    Distance 227
    Grid references 222
    Height 224
    Latitude and longitude 222
    Legend 220

    National grid 222
    Rise 231
    Run 231
    Scale 217
    Settlement patterns 235
    Sketch of 230
    Slope 225
Outer core 8
Outwash plains 157
Overfold 58
Overthrust fold 59
Oxbow lakes 124
Oxidation 89

P

P (primary) waves 28
Pacific Ring of Fire 17
Pangaea 11
Paris Basin
    Physical characteristics 382
    Population 392
    Primary activities 384
    Secondary activities 387
    Tertiary activities 389
Passive plate margin 9
Paternoster lakes 153
Pays 382
Peneplains 213
Permafrost 196
Permeable 71
Pervious 98
Piedmont glacier 145
Pillars 103
Plan Watercolour 414
Plantations 292
Plastic flow 91
Plate boundaries
    Conservative/transform /transverse 18
    Constructive/divergent 15
    Destructive/convergent 16
    Passive plate margin 9
    Summary of 22
Plate tectonics 10
Plateaux 47
Plates 9
Plucking 146
Plumes 18
Plunge pool 123
Plutonic landforms 48
Plutonic rock 68
Point bar 125
Polar 279
Polar front 279

Polycentric 353
Porous 71
Primate cities 352
Pumice 43
Pyramidal peak 148
Pyroclastic flow 43
Pyroclasts 43

Q

Quartzite 72

R

Reclamation schemes 368
Recumbent fold 58
Regional assemblies 282
Regions
    Administrative 282
    City 302
    Climatic 277
    Complexity of cultural regions 295
    Cultural 285
    Geomorphic 280
    Industrial decline 304
    Peripheral 303
    Socio-economic 301
Régions 284
Regolith 193
Religion 291
Representative fraction 217
Resurgent stream 102
Reverse fault 62
Revetments 182
Ribbon lakes 153
Richter scale 29
Rift valleys 63
Rivers
    Capture 212
    Cliff 125
    Course 110
    Clonmel 137
    Confluence 110
    Deposition 114
    Depth 115
    Drainage basin area 110
    Drainage patterns 112
    Energy 114
    Erosion 111
    Estuary 110
    Human interaction with 134
    Landforms 119
    Life cycle 118
    Load 114
    Mature stage landforms 124
    Mouth 110

Index

Old stage river landforms 129
Processes of river deposition 117
Processes of river erosion 116
Processes of river transport 116
R. Rhine 134
Rejuvenation 208
Saltation 117
Source 110
Splashback 123
Suspension 117
Terraces 209
Three Gorges Dam 136
Transport 116
Tributaries 110
Velocity 117
Watersheds 110
Youthful stage landforms 119
Rock armour 182
Rock cycle
    Human interaction with 76
    Tara Mines 77
Rock drumlins 155
Rock falls 201
Rotational slip 149
Rotational slumps 199
Route focus 391
Runnel and ridge 176

S
S (secondary) waves 28
Salt 71
Saltation 117
Sambre-Meuse Valley 308
San Andreas Fault 18
Sand dune 181
Sand fences 181
Sand spits 177
Sandstone 71
SAP (Structural Adjustment Programme) 403
Satellite photographs 270
Savannah 402
Scarps 385

Schéma Directeur 391
Schengen Area 377
Scree 86
Sea stacks 173
Sea walls 182
Sea-floor spreading 16
Sedimentary rock
    Chemically formed 71
    Lithification 69
    Organically formed 70
    Inorganically formed 71
Seismic 28
Seismographs 28
Seismometers 28
Semi-arid climate 401
Shale 71
Shield volcanoes 45
SIAL 9
Silica 42
Sills 48
SIMA 9
Simple fold 58
Single European Act 431
Sinkholes 101
Slate 73
Slumps 199
Small-scale maps 218
Snout 153
Soil creep 195
Solifluction 196
Solifluction lobes 196
Solution
    Marine 169
    Rivers 116
Sovereignty 429
Stacks 173
Stalactites 103
Stalagmites 103
Statement of scale 217
Stepped slope 225
Stoss side 155
Strata 69
Strato volcano 46
Striae 146
Structural funds 311
Stumps 173
Subduction 17
Subsequent streams 212
Subsistence farming 368

Sub zone 222
Superimposition 210
Surf zone 170
Surface processes, summary of 91
Surface waves 28
Suspension 117
Swallow holes 101
Symmetric fold 58
Syncline 58

T
TACs 312
Talus 86
Tara Mines 77
Tarn 149
Tear fault 62
Tectonic cycle 9
Tension 61
Tephra 42
Terra rossa soil 402
Terracettes 195
Terranes 17
Tetrapods 182
Thrust fault 62
Tombolo 178
Topography 280
Topset beds 131
Traction 117
Trans Amazon Highway 412
Transform fault 62
Transform plate boundary 15
Transverse plate boundary 15
Treaties of Rome 431
Trench 17
Tropical climate 401
Tropical rainforest 401
Truncated spurs 151
Tsunami 31
Turkey's application 435
Turloughs 102

U
U-shaped valley 151
Uniform slope 225
Urban sprawl 353

V
V-shaped valleys 119
Valley glacier 145
Vanoni Plan 376
Vent 41
Vertical erosion 115
Vertical photo 239
Viniculture 367
Viticulture 367
Volcanic bombs 43
Volcanic cones 44
Volcanic explosivity index 43
Volcanic igneous rock 68
Volcanic landforms 44
Volcanic plugs 44
Volcanoes
    Active 41
    Distribution 41
    Dome 46
    Dormant 41
    Effects of 50
    Extinct 41
    Lava plateaux 47
    Measuring methods 51
    Prediction of 51
    Products of 42
    Shield 45

W
Wallonia 289
Warm front 256
Water table 102
Waterfalls 123
Watershed 110
Wave refraction 168
Wave-built terrace 171
Wave-cut platform 171
Waves 166
Weather maps 256
Weathering 85
Wegener, Alfred 11
Windgap 212

Y
Youthful stage/upper course 119